KAPLAN ALLIED HEALTH

Allied Health Industry and Fundamentals

KAPLAN HIGHER EDUCATION

 Wolters Kluwer | Lippincott Williams & Wilkins
Health
Philadelphia · Baltimore · New York · London
Buenos Aires · Hong Kong · Sydney · Tokyo

Chapters 1–6 from *Nursing Student Success Made Incredibly Easy*.
Copyright 2005, Springhouse, Ambler, Pa.

Chapters 7–9, 14–17 from Molle EA, et al. *Comprehensive Medical Assisting*, 2nd ed.
Copyright 2005, Lippincott Williams & Wilkins, Philadelphia, Pa.
Study guide and worksheet sections for chapters 7–9, 14–17 from West-Stack C and Howe BB.
Study Guide: Comprehensive Medical Assisting, 2nd ed.
Copyright 2005, Lippincott Williams & Wilkins, Philadelphia, Pa.

Chapters 10–11 and corresponding worksheet sections from Buchholz S. *Henke's Med-Math:
Dosage Calculation, Preparation and Administration*. 5th ed.
Copyright 2006, Lippincott Williams & Wilkins, Philadelphia, Pa.
Excerpts in chapter 10 from Ansel HC. *Pharmaceutical Calculations*. 12th ed.
Copyright 2006, Lippincott Williams & Wilkins, Philadelphia, Pa.

Chapters 12–13 from Roach S. *Pharmacology for Health Professionals*.
Copyright 2005, Lippincott Williams & Wilkins, Philadelphia, Pa.
Study guide and worksheet sections for chapters 12–13 from Zorko J.
Study Guide for Pharmacology for Health Professionals.
Copyright 2005, Lippincott Williams & Wilkins, Philadelphia, Pa.

Chapter 18 from *Professional Guide to Complementary and Alternative Therapies*.
Copyright 2001, Springhouse, Ambler, Pa.

Introduction to the HIPAA Privacy Rule from Rockel K.
Stedman's Guide to the HIPAA Privacy Rule.
Copyright 2006, Lippincott Williams & Wilkins, Philadelphia, Pa.

Publisher: Julie K. Stegman
Acquisitions Editor: John Goucher
Project Manager: Matt Hauber
Production Manager: Eric Branger
Art Coordinator: Jennifer Clements
Cover Design: Armen Kojoyian
Compositor: Aptara, Inc.

KAPLAN MISSION STATEMENT

Kaplan helps individuals achieve their educational and career goals.
We build futures one success story at a time.

ABOUT KAPLAN HIGHER EDUCATION

Kaplan Higher Education offers certificate and degree programs, on campus and online, that prepare students for employment in fields including health care, business, criminal justice, fashion, design and graphic arts, information technology, and paralegal studies. At campuses in the United States and abroad, as well as via online programs through Kaplan University and Concord Law School, we offer educational opportunities that help people advance their careers and improve their lives. Each of our schools is separately accredited by one of several national or regional accrediting agencies approved by the U.S. Department of Education.

Kaplan is responsive to the needs of adult learners, many of whom juggle work, family, and other responsibilities. Our comprehensive support system provides financial aid counseling, academic advising, study skills workshops, time management guidance, and more. Our faculty is committed to ensuring that our students get the maximum value from their experience.

Kaplan, Inc., entered the postsecondary education industry in 2000, with the acquisition of Quest Education Corp., a network of 30 schools. Today, Kaplan Higher Education has become Kaplan's largest business, serving 68,000 students through more than 70 schools in 21 states and online programs in the United States and abroad. The company is market-driven, adding locations and programs in areas that will best serve local employment needs. The company's curricula include programs designed to lead to entry-level employment in many of the country's fastest growing occupations, as projected by the U.S. Department of Labor.

ACKNOWLEDGMENTS

We are pleased to present to you the *Kaplan Allied Health: Allied Health Industry and Fundamentals* module series, a compilation of materials focusing on fundamental principles that help develop proficient and sensitive medical professionals.

Designed to serve a broad audience of medical, therapeutic, pharmacy, and dental students, this guide offers interdisciplinary readings and activities for academic strategies, medical law, math, health sciences, and complementary medicine.

Primary acknowledgment must go to the many dedicated instructors who continually take on challenges of all shapes and sizes aimed at improving education. The professional literature and journals acknowledge individual contributions, but textbooks cannot adequately pay such tribute. Albert Einstein identified this problem, commenting that although "there are plenty of well-endowed (professionals) . . . it strikes me as unfair to select a few of them for recognition." We are indebted to all these unnamed people.

On a more immediate level, we would first like to thank our consulting editor and publisher, Lippincott Williams & Wilkins, for their expert and exhaustive work. We are especially grateful to Susan Katz, John Goucher, Matt Hauber, Eric Branger, Julie Stegman, Dale Gray, Dana Knighten, Leigh Wells, and Michael Marino for their enthusiasm and cooperation in making these books a reality. They have processed a formidable number of materials with dedication, attention to detail, knowledge, and editorial skill.

In addition, we thank the Kaplan Higher Education Faculty Advisory Board for providing educational guidance. They deserve grateful recognition for their indispensable help.

We gratefully acknowledge the following Faculty Advisory Board members:

Anthony Devore, Texas Careers
Denise Gemmel, Technology Education College
Bruce Gilden, Maric College, North County Campus
Mary Hitchens, Maric College
Tereas O'Mara, Professional Careers Institute
Thomas Reynolds, Texas Careers
Lisa Stephens, Professional Careers Institute

CAAHEP COMPETENCIES

Upon completion of this unit, students will be able to demonstrate mastery of the following CAAHEP competencies:

A ADMINISTRATIVE COMPETENCIES
  1 Process Insurance Claims
    a   Organize a patient's medical record
    d   File medical records

B CLINICAL COMPETENCIES
  1 Fundamental Procedures
    a   Perform handwashing
    d   Dispose of biohazardous materials
    e   Practice standard precautions
  4 Patient Care
    b   Obtain vital signs
    h   Maintain medication and immunization records

C GENERAL COMPETENCIES
  2 Legal Concepts
    a   Identify and respond to issues of confidentiality
    b   Perform within legal and ethical boundaries
    c   Establish and maintain the medical record
    d   Document appropriately
    e   Demonstrate knowledge of federal and state health care legislation and regulations
  4 Operational Functions
    b   Perform routine maintenance of administrative and clinical equipment
    d   Use methods of quality control

CONTENTS

UNIT 1

ACADEMIC STRATEGIES 1

CHAPTER 1: Your Attitude and Goals 3
CHAPTER 2: Controlling that Meandering
Mind 11
CHAPTER 3: Managing Your Time 19
CHAPTER 4: Textbook and Classroom
Strategies 29
CHAPTER 5: Tips on Test-Taking 45
CHAPTER 6: Stress? What Stress? 57

UNIT 2

MEDICAL LAW AND ETHICS 67

CHAPTER 7: Law and Ethics in the Health
Care Setting 69
CHAPTER 8: Health Records and Records
Management 89
CHAPTER 9: Quality, Privacy, and
HIPAA 105

UNIT 3

MATH FUNDAMENTALS 119

CHAPTER 10: Math Fundamentals 121
CHAPTER 11: Systems of Measure 139

UNIT 4

INTRODUCTION TO PHARMACOLOGY 151

CHAPTER 12: Principles of Pharmacology 153
CHAPTER 13: Preparing and Administering
Medications 169

UNIT 5

INFECTION CONTROL AND VITAL SIGNS 183

CHAPTER 14: Medical Asepsis and Infection
Control 185
CHAPTER 15: Surgical Instruments and
Sterilization 209
CHAPTER 16: The Clinical Laboratory 229
CHAPTER 17: Measurements and Vital
Signs 251

UNIT 6

COMPLEMENTARY AND ALTERNATIVE MEDICINE 281

CHAPTER 18: Overview of Complementary
and Alternative Medicines 283

GLOSSARY 299
INDEX 305
STUDY GUIDE 323
WORKSHEETS 373

Academic Strategies

Your Attitude and Goals

CHAPTER OBJECTIVES

In this chapter, you'll learn:

1. How a positive, responsible approach to a studying task improves learning.
2. How motivation can be intrinsic (derived from personal desire) or extrinsic (derived from physical reward).
3. Why goals are more likely to be achieved when they're personal rather than set by others.
4. Why goals should be specific and have a completion date.

ATTITUDE

Attitude is the approach you take to complete a task. It's often a reflection of how much interest you have in a task or how meaningful the task is to you. Your attitude toward learning, studying, and test taking affects the goals you set for yourself and the techniques and strategies you use to reach those goals. Attitude also strongly affects your level of success in improving your learning skills.

How Attitude Affects Studying

When you approach a difficult subject with the right attitude, you can:

- gain a clear idea of your role in learning
- establish clear learning goals
- study more efficiently
- achieve better grades and improve academic performance.

It's up to you.   Having the right attitude can be described as having a willingness and desire to learn. Here are some attributes of the "right stuff."

- The student accepts responsibility for learning rather than expecting others to teach her.
- The student participates in the learning process rather than being a passive recipient of knowledge.
- The student actively listens, asks questions, and seeks answers to those questions.
- The student takes charge of what will be learned from the course and, in effect, how well she'll do in the course.

Got it?   How do you know if you have the right attitude about studying? Find out more about your own attitude by checking the "attitude meter." (See *Attitude meter.*)

ATTITUDE METER

Each of the statements below describes someone with a positive attitude. How many of the traits do *you have?*

- You're naturally good at studying.
- You're strongly interested in learning, regardless of the topic.
- You're receptive to new information.
- You don't rely strictly on a teacher to tell you what to study.
- You have faith in yourself and your ability to learn.
- You use a support system as often as possible.
- You take care of your mind and body.
- You keep a consistently positive attitude.

Developing a Winning Attitude

A student with a winning attitude expects success, even when tackling the most complex new material. Such students have faith in their own abilities, particularly in their ability to attend classes, complete assigned readings, conduct research, and understand the material presented. Building and using support systems, taking care of yourself, and maintaining consistent focus on your goals are key to having and keeping a winning attitude.

A little help, please.   One way to build and maintain a winning attitude is to seek out and accept support from other people and resources, including:

- colleagues
- fellow students
- formal and informal discussion groups
- friends and family
- resource centers, such as libraries and media centers
- teachers and tutors.

Exercise your attitude.   Attitude is often reflected in how well a person takes care of herself. Getting enough sleep, eating properly, and exercising can help you maintain a healthy mind, body, and attitude. Looking good and feeling good are big attitude boosters.

Steady as she goes.   It's important to keep a positive attitude for the long haul rather than backsliding into complacency in the middle of a task. Developing a good attitude may take time, but it's worth the effort. A consistently positive attitude allows you to cope effectively in the face of minor setbacks.

MOTIVATION

Motivation is the thing that makes a person *want* to do something. Motivation:

- causes a person to initiate an activity. In the case of studying, the motivation may be the need for achievement, a high test score, or a good grade in the course.
- helps the person move toward a goal, closing the gap between the starting point and the final objective.
- spurs the person to persist in her attempts to reach the goal.

How Motivation Affects Studying

Motivation to improve study skills and succeed at learning may be *intrinsic* (an inborn factor that drives a person to learn) or *extrinsic* (a benefit derived from learning).

Coming from within…   Intrinsic motivation includes:

- a general desire to learn
- a sense of curiosity

- a willingness to take risks
- an innate sense of wanting to excel at something
- an inherent interest in the subject at hand.

…Or without. Extrinsic motivation includes the desire for:

- better grades or test scores
- improved self-esteem
- a sense of fulfillment
- increased competence in the subject being studied
- valuable credentials on a resume
- a better job
- an opportunity to earn a higher salary.

Toward a gold star. Think back to when you were in elementary school. At that time, the reward you received for a job well done may have been a gold star. The teacher's idea was to establish that sticker as a motivator, something you would value and strive to earn.

Adults can establish their own sources of motivation. At the start of a task, decide what your reward will be for your hard work. You may decide that the work itself is its own reward, but you may find it more inspiring to aim for something more — a pat on the back, lunch out with friends, new shoes, or a few days of rest and relaxation.

Reach for the sky. When choosing a motivator, aim high. Choose a motivator that makes the hard work worthwhile. Then be sure to collect the reward.

Don't underestimate the value of intangible rewards. You may find that reveling in a sense of satisfaction or accomplishment may be a stronger motivator than earning a more tangible reward.

Get personal. To gain insight into personal motivators, think about things you do on a regular basis and then determine the source of motivation for completing each task. For example, suppose you exercise at a gym twice per week. Why do you do that? To look and feel good? To get your dollar's worth of membership dues? To meet new people?

Identifying and understanding your particular motivating factors for non-school-related situations can help you successfully find motivating factors for school-related situations.

Long-lasting Rewards

A wide range of long-lasting rewards can be gained from developing successful study habits and improving your test-taking skills. Those rewards include:

- a deeper understanding of the subject matter
- an ability to apply improved skills to other subject areas
- enhanced self-esteem, leading to greater success in other endeavors
- improved grades and test scores
- improved socioeconomic status as a result of learning marketable skills.

SETTING GOALS

Procrastination, poor concentration, and lack of motivation take root when a student lacks clear goals. Without clearly defined goals, it's easy to become distracted. To avoid distraction, set goals for yourself.

Some goals should be easy to reach and some should be hard. Some goals should be long-term and some short-term. The more attractive the goal, the more motivated you'll be. The goal should be specific and include a time for completion. Setting a time or date for completion of the goal helps you to focus on the goal and gives you a sense of purpose.

Accomplishing a Goal

Accomplishing a goal involves creating a measurable and achievable goal, determining that the goal is something worth working toward, and devising strategies to achieve the goal.

Does it measure up? A goal should be stated in measurable terms. For example, "I want to master the double-entry system of note-taking by the end of October" is a more specific objective than "I want to improve my study skills."

We have the technology. Determine whether the goal is achievable. Is there enough time to pursue the goal and, more important, do you have the necessary skills, strengths, and resources to achieve the goal? If not, modify the goal.

Do the ends justify the means? Make certain that achieving the goal is genuinely worthwhile. The goal should have a positive impact on your life and be consistent with your basic values.

In addition, determine why the goal is worthwhile. Make sure that reaching the goal will give you a sense of accomplishment.

EXERCISE YOUR MIND
Accomplishing a short-term goal

Short-term goals can be accomplished by following a series of steps that gradually move you toward your goal. To accomplish a short-term goal:

- write the goal in measurable terms.
- set a date for completing the goal.
- check that the goal can be accomplished in the time allotted.
- identify potential problems and determine ways of preventing them.
- create a series of specific steps for achieving the goal.
- set a schedule for completing each step.

Expect the worst, achieve the best.   Anticipate potential problems in meeting your goal. Take yourself step by step through your plan for achieving the goal, and ask yourself what can go wrong at each step. Then plan ways to prevent or overcome these problems.

At the same time, devise strategies and steps for achieving the goal. What will you need to begin? What comes next? Then set a timeline for accomplishing each step. (See *Accomplishing a short-term goal.*)

Goal Structures

Students in a classroom can be greatly influenced by other people involved in accomplishing the same goal. The influence of others on your goals is called the *goal structure* of the task. The three goal structures are:

1. cooperative, in which students believe their goal is attainable only if other students reach the same goal
2. competitive, in which students believe they will reach their goal only if other students don't
3. individualistic, in which students believe their own attempt to reach a goal isn't related to other students' attempts to reach goals.

Grades and Goals

If an instructor concentrates class efforts on competitive grading, students tend to focus on performance goals rather than learning goals. Do as much as you can to focus on learning rather than focusing on getting a good grade or doing the work just to get it finished. By understanding the value of the assigned work and how the information you gain will be useful in the future, you can more readily prepare for learning and, thus, become more successful.

The power of the "A".   Focusing on learning doesn't mean, however, that you shouldn't consider grades at all. Grades are an integral part of the entire school experience and can be powerful motivators themselves. Grades also serve as checkpoints to help you evaluate your pro-gress and adjust your plan for success accordingly. Try to use the desire to earn good grades as a short-term goal without sacrificing the more important long-term goal of getting a good education.

Personal payload.   When you're forced to do something you don't really want to do, you'll be less likely to succeed because the goal isn't your own. The successful student must *want* to succeed, and learning itself should be a primary goal and its own reward.

Reaching your Goals

Approach each goal you've set for yourself consistently and with a clear sense of purpose. Reaching your goals involves setting goals continually, monitoring your progress, determining time frames for your goals, prioritizing goals, challenging yourself to reach higher goals, committing to success, revising your goals when necessary, and linking short-term goals with longer-term ones.

Getting into the goal-setting habit.   If you haven't already begun to set goals, start the habit now. If the goals you've identified so far haven't motivated you as well as you had hoped they would, review the goals and, if necessary, set new ones.

Putting pen to paper.   Keep a journal for long-term, intermediate, and short-term goals. Use to-do lists to keep track of the immediate goals that form a part of everyday life. You'll tend to commit your resources more readily to a written goal than to one you've only thought about but haven't recorded. In addition, writing the goal makes it more concrete and easier to review periodically.

List goals according to how long it will take to reach them. Typical goal categories are long-term (5 to 10 years), intermediate (3 to 5 years), short-term (6 months to 2 years), and immediate (this month, this week, or today). Prioritize your goals. Without priorities, you may spend your energy trying to achieve too many goals at once.

Challenge yourself.   Keep your goals high enough to inspire you and reasonable enough to seem always within your reach. For example, if your long-term goal is to be an allied health professional, your intermediate goal may be to finish school. You may find that your greatest challenge lies in becoming one of the top students in your class.

Commit to the actions required to achieve the goal. Understand that you may not succeed immediately. Learn from your failures and reassess your action plan.

Rewrite, revise, revisit, review.   Review your goals and revise them as necessary. At certain points, more inspiring goals may present themselves and short-term and immediate goals may require revision. It's better to change goals and strategies as circumstances change than to lose focus on your long-term goals by refusing to change short-term ones.

The domino effect.   Long-term, intermediate, short-term, and immediate goals should be linked in focus to your overriding goals. For example, reading 15 pages of course material today (your immediate goal) leads to achieving a good grade in the class (short-term goal), which leads to graduation (intermediate goal), which, in turn, leads to the opportunity to become an allied health professional (long-term goal).

Types of Goals

Long-term study goals generally relate to career goals. However, some people simply enjoy studying as a means of self-improvement. Again, if the long-term goal is truly the student's choice, then the student is self-motivated and excited about the result, prompting the student to keep on track.

Intermediate goals are usually 3 to 5 years in the future and are keys to achieving long-term goals. For example, careers that require extended education necessitate the intermediate

MEMORY JOGGER

Setting goals is an invitation to success. As with any invitation, you should **RSVP**. Make sure your goals are **r**easonable, **s**pecific, **v**erifiable, and **p**ay off in the end.

goal of acceptance into the appropriate centers for higher learning.

Hops, skips, and jumps.   The steps toward an intermediate goal are a series of *short-term goals*, usually set 6 months to 2 years in the future. Particularly when studying toward a goal (such as a certain degree), the short-term goals could be set per semester or per academic year.

The dash.   Each short-term goal can be further divided into smaller tasks, or *immediate goals*, which can be accomplished in 30 minutes to an hour on a daily basis until each study task is completed. A series of 15 to 20 small tasks might be part of the plan for completing an otherwise frustrating 20-page paper. The result is a finished essay and the chance to experience 15 to 20 successes along the way! (See *Accomplishing a long-term goal.*)

EXERCISE YOUR MIND
Accomplishing a long-term goal

Although long-term goals can be daunting to think about, keeping an eye focused on them can help you accomplish short-term goals more successfully. To accomplish a long-term goal, begin by describing where you want to be in 20 years. What do you want to be doing, and where? Write down these 20-year goals. Then ask yourself these questions:

- What will I need to accomplish in 5 years to be able to reach my 20-year goal? (Write down these goals as your 5-year goals.)
- What will I need to accomplish in 6 months to reach each 5-year goal? (Write down these goals as your 6-month goals.)
- What will I need to accomplish this week to reach my 6-month goals? (Write down these goals as your weekly goals.)

Examine the goals
Now list at least five reasons it's important for you to reach your 20-year goal. List at least three negative things that could happen if you don't reach your goal.

Oh, what to do, what to do?   When immediate goals are listed and prioritized, a daily to-do list is created. Each goal must:

- be reasonable (can be completed in 30 to 60 minutes)
- be specific
- be verifiable or measurable (can be crossed off the list when it's completed)
- have a payoff (reward) when achieved.

Treats for triumph.   Rewards give you additional reasons to reach a goal. A reward can be small or large, depending on the person and the goal. To serve as an effective motivator, a reward should be desirable. You might reward yourself with dinner at your favorite restaurant or that CD you've had your eye on for the last few weeks.

The reward should also fit the task. That means finishing a task that takes all of 30 minutes doesn't necessarily warrant a weekend shopping trip.

Peers and punishment.   In addition to rewards, other types of external motivation include peer pressure and punishment. By sharing goals with a friend, you create additional pressure to perform. Punishment, denying yourself certain privileges if you don't complete a task, rarely works as a motivator.

Missing the mark.   If you fall short of a short-term goal, you may become discouraged and miss a step toward achieving a long-term goal. Try to recoup the loss by reviewing your goals and adjusting them as appropriate. In the long run, it's more efficient to achieve the goal in the first place, even if it's a little behind schedule. (See *Evaluating a goal.*)

Staying on Task

Sometimes it's hard to get started on a project or assignment. The important thing is to take some action, even if it's not as much as you had planned. To get yourself started, break a large project down into manageable parts, and then schedule deadlines for completing each part. Gaining closure on each part, handling deadlines effectively, avoiding *burnout* (a state of exhaustion and loss of motivation), and juggling all your other responsibilities efficiently will keep you on the right path toward your goals.

From start to finish.   *Closure* is the positive feeling you get when you finish a task. One way to obtain closure is to divide a task into manageable goals, list them, and check them off the list as each one is finished. For example, to complete a reading assignment on time, divide the total assignment into smaller assignments by setting a certain number of pages as a goal to be reached each day. Every time you reach one of these small goals, you'll feel a sense of closure that will help propel you toward the next goal.

Dueling deadlines.   Several tasks might have the same deadline. Although changing from one task to another may give you a break, changing tasks too often actually wastes

EXERCISE YOUR MIND

Evaluating a goal

Evaluating a goal is a different process than creating one. Evaluation allows you to create more useful, achievable goals. Practice evaluating a goal by completing this exercise. Decide whether each of the listed goals is satisfactory or if it's lacking in some way. Use the key to denote your decision. Keep in mind that if a goal is unsatisfactory, more than one letter may apply.

Key

S — Satisfactory
M — Measurable outcomes lacking
D — Deadline lacking
O — Other people are needed to achieve the goal

Goals

1. _____ Know all assigned mathematical formulas by the end of next month.
2. _____ Appreciate art more fully as the result of visiting an art gallery.
3. _____ By Tuesday, identify the handouts to be used for the final examination.
4. _____ Become a better reader.
5. _____ Improve my anatomy and physiology grade by 1 quality point by participating in a group-study project before the end of the term.
6. _____ Complete all assigned readings by next Wednesday.
7. _____ Read my notes immediately after each class so I can make additions or corrections.
8. _____ Improve my grade in fundamentals by 10 points between the midterm examination and the final examination by joining a study group and meeting with the group 3 days per week for the rest of the marking period.

Your goals

List five of your own goals, and evaluate them.

1. _____
2. _____
3. _____
4. _____
5. _____

time. It slows your momentum on one task and necessitates that you'll have to review tasks that have been put aside when you return to them.

To avoid problems from changing tasks too often, determine how much time you have for the task. If you have only an hour, don't switch tasks; an hour isn't enough time to maintain peak efficiency.

When working on a long-term project that needs to be set aside to complete more immediate tasks, stay organized. To ease the return to the first project, make a list of questions, write notes, identify objectives, and compile references, papers, and other materials pertinent to the task. Then keep all the materials in one place, so you can reach them easily and get started more quickly.

The juggling act. Everyone has to manage a wide assortment of life activities: fitness, relationships, chores, finances, hobbies, sports, work, and others. Add academics and school activities into the mix, and the need for organization becomes clear. Set aside time each day for work as well as for play to make the most of your time.

When you face what seems like too many tasks, prioritize each task by writing the tasks on paper. Then assign each with a 1, 2, or 3, with 1 being the most important tasks and 3 being those that can wait. First, concentrate on completing the 1s, then the 2s, and lastly the 3s. Prioritizing tasks on paper helps you focus on the most important tasks and gives you a sense of accomplishment.

Believe in Yourself!

Tell yourself that you can do this: you can pass this course; you can be an allied health professional. Think about "the little engine that could" in the popular children's book. The engine kept repeating, "I think I can, I know I can." Keep telling yourself that you *can* do it. With hard work and organization, you can accomplish your goals.

You have chosen to undertake a profession with difficult subject matter. At the first sign of problems, seek help. Most faculty will give help to a struggling student who has motivation, desire, and a good attitude, and who works to accomplish goals. Asking for help is a sign of strength, not weakness.

TAKE A BREAK!

At a Crossroads

Look for key terms in the crossword puzzle below. Relax and enjoy — don't stress! (Answer key on next page.)

Across
- 5. Incentive to perform a task
- 7. Marks indicating quality of work
- 8. Due dates
- 11. State of exhaustion from overwork
- 12. To consider in detail

Down
- 1. A pledge
- 2. Focus
- 3. Objectives
- 4. An inborn motivational factor
- 6. State of mind; approach
- 9. Favorable outcome
- 10. A motivational benefit from learning

Answer Key

2

Controlling that Meandering Mind

CHAPTER OBJECTIVES

In this chapter, you'll learn:

1. How important it is to have good concentration.
2. How the brain processes through registration, short-term memory, long-term memory, and working memory.
3. Why effective study strategies include practice, spaced study, reduction of interference, associations, lists, and imagery.
4. How memory skills can be improved by using various memory enhancement strategies.

CONCENTRATION

The more focused your concentration, the more efficiently you can use your study time. To improve your concentration skills, first identify the distractions that impede concentration. Then use one or more study techniques to improve your ability to concentrate and, thus, to learn.

Distractions

Distractions that interfere with concentration can originate from internal or external sources. An *internal distraction* is something you think or feel that detracts from focusing on your studies. Hunger and emotions, such as anger or sadness, are internal sources of distraction. *External distractions* stem from something in your study environment. Loud noises, an uncomfortable chair, and poor lighting are examples of external sources of distraction.

Slow down, you talk too fast!   Sometimes, people — even your instructors — can be sources of external distraction. (See *Meandering mind.*) The instructor may speak rapidly, covering a lot of material in a short time. Conversely, the instructor may speak slowly, causing you to become bored and unable to concentrate fully.

Where's my dictionary?   The instructor may use jargon or big words without clear meanings, either of which makes

understanding the material more difficult and impedes your concentration. Regardless of the source, you need to learn how to deal with distractions and to concentrate your attention fully on the material under study.

Learning to Concentrate

To improve your concentration skills, you must *want* to learn the material. Internal motivation is the key to initiating and maintaining concentration. In addition, you need to be awake and alert, and prepared to see, hear, and learn. Being awake and alert allows you to use your class or study time more efficiently and removes the need to review the material a second time when it should have been learned the first time.

Improving your concentration during class and study sessions can help improve retention and foster better scores on tests, quizzes, and assignments.

Eyes front.   During class time, try these strategies to help you stay focused:

- Sit up front. The closer you sit to the front, the less distraction there will be between you and the instructor.
- Take a walk between classes to calm down. Walk briskly for 5 to 10 minutes to help ease tension.
- Meditate before class. Find a calm place, close your eyes, sit up straight, relax your arms and legs, and picture something simple, still, and peaceful. Breathe deeply and slowly for about 5 minutes.
- Limit caffeine intake. Caffeine is a central nervous system stimulant. Although a little caffeine can heighten awareness temporarily, too much caffeine can make you jumpy and reduce your ability to concentrate.

Study hard, study right!   Try these strategies to help improve concentration during study sessions:

- study when the time is right for you, during periods of alertness
- study in a familiar, comfortable place
- study under natural light (sunlight) or incandescent light (an ordinary light bulb) rather than fluorescent light, to lessen eye strain
- set realistic study goals for a study session
- make a specific to-do list before you start studying
- focus your study on one topic at a time
- drink water to prevent dehydration and enhance your ability to maintain focus
- vary your study activities. For instance, include in your study time reading, taking notes, and just plain thinking to keep your study process active
- take short breaks in your studying every 45 minutes to 1 hour
- remove visual distractions from the study area. These distractions can break concentration and stimulate daydreaming.

ADVICE FROM THE EXPERTS

Meandering mind

Some people seem to remember everything they hear and see, including the entire name of a person they've just met. Others find that their minds tend to wander easily and can't remember as much as they'd like. Do you have a meandering mind? To find out how well you tend to pay attention, ask yourself the questions below. The more you answer yes, the more likely it is that you have a meandering mind and could benefit from strategies to improve your concentration.

- Do you generally forget the names of people you've just met?
- Do you find yourself commonly asking people to repeat what they've just said?
- Do you tend to lose track of what's going on, as if you're snapping out of a daydream in the middle of an event?
- Do you sometimes stare blankly at a page?
- Do you sometimes feel as if you don't remember what you've just read, even though you know you read the material?

- Study in an atmosphere of *white noise,* a low-level background sound that masks outside distractions. For example, the sound of soft instrumental music can help mask the annoying sound of a clattering air conditioner.

Power napping.   If you're having trouble staying awake and alert when studying, try taking a power nap. A short nap of 5 to 15 minutes — but not longer — can rejuvenate the body and mind. Research indicates that a power nap can replenish the level of amines in the brain. Amines play a role in helping you maintain attention and remain alert and aware.

Improving Concentration

There's nothing like practice to improve your concentration. Strategies for improving concentration skills include maintaining a consistent state of mind, reading and relaxing, and *thinking globally* (within a large framework of knowledge).

Stress-free Learning and Recall

If you're relaxed during study, you're more likely to recall information. To reduce stress when you study, keep yourself rested and learn to work within a global framework.

Give your brain a break.   Ideally, you should rest right before a test and before and right after learning new material. Your brain needs time to relax, sort through information, and then store the information for later retrieval. Sleep is particularly important in this regard. During deep sleep, the brain continues to sort and store information, saving important memories and allowing unnecessary ones to be forgotten.

However, keep in mind that during sleep you can forget important information if your brain hasn't moved it out of short-term memory. Before you go to sleep at night, make a short quiz of 5 to 10 questions from the material you think you've learned. When you wake up in the morning, take the quiz to see how you do. If you've forgotten important information, study it again.

Think globally, study locally.   The brain is able to recall information more efficiently when the item being recalled exists within a larger framework of knowledge, or more global understanding. For example, a small area of a street map is easier to understand and recall when considered within the larger framework of a map of the entire city.

In applying this concept to studying, try to learn more about a topic in general before focusing on the particular assigned topic. Television programs, videos, or film documentaries can be good sources of such information, as can magazine articles written for the lay public.

For instance, if you've been assigned a topic of caring for a patient after a coronary artery bypass graft, you might start your studying by reading an article on heart surgery in *Newsweek* or *Reader's Digest.* Then, when you read about coronary artery bypass grafting in a professional textbook, you'll be able to apply the new knowledge more readily and remember key facts longer.

MEMORY

Information is stored in different ways and in different forms, which is why you can remember some things clearly and others hardly at all. Memory isn't a sense but a skill that can be developed and improved.

Early Memories

Most people can't recall the first year of their life. That's because brain structures responsible for memory don't fully develop until about age 2. In addition, children generally learn to speak after their first year of life, not before. As a result, information stored as memories during the first year of life can't be stored in words.

Some events in childhood, though, remain as clear, vivid memories long after the event has taken place in that person's history. For instance, you may clearly remember your first day in school. That's probably because going to school was a new event for you and your brain had to create a new category for it. Later on, going to school became less and less memorable.

Processing Information

How your brain processes memories determines what you remember and what you forget. The three basic stages involved in information processing are:

1. registration
2. short-term memory
3. long-term memory. (See *Making memories last.*)

Registration

In *registration,* the initial stage of information processing, information is received and may eventually be understood and selected to be remembered. The process of registration involves three phases: reception, perception, and selection.

What a lovely reception.   In *reception,* you sense something or someone but you don't yet recognize what it is or what it means.

At least, that's my perception.   In the second phase, *perception,* you recognize what you've seen and attach a meaning to it.

Be selective.   The final phase of registration involves *selection,* in which your brain selects information to be remembered. The information selected depends on a number of factors, including the:

- material at hand
- purpose for remembering

EXERCISE YOUR MIND

Making memories last

There are many ways to embed what you learn in your long-term memory. Putting these tips into your study regimen can help you retain key information.

Working alone

- Attach a strong emotion to the material.
- Rewrite the material.
- Build a working model of a physical aspect of the material being studied.
- Create a song about the material or change the words to an existing song.
- Draw a picture or create a poster using intense colors.
- Repeat and review the material within 10 minutes, 48 hours, and 7 days.
- Smear a droplet of your favorite perfume onto a reminder note to help you remember the contents of the note.
- Summarize the material in your notes.
- Try to immediately apply what you've learned to activities in your daily life.
- Use mnemonics and acronyms to organize the material.
- Write about the material in a journal.

Working with others

- Act out the material or role-play a situation related to the material being studied.
- Join a study group or other support group.
- Discuss the information with a peer to gain an additional perspective and solidify the material in your mind.
- Make a video or audiotape related to the material being studied.
- Make up and tell a story about the material.

- learner's background knowledge
- content and difficulty level of the information
- way the information is organized.

Is it useful?   A person selectively ignores or processes information depending on the usefulness of the information in meeting the person's goals. Information perceived by the learner to be useful tends to be processed. Information perceived to be less useful tends to be ignored.

Ignored information is quickly forgotten; processed information is transferred into *short-term memory* — the second stage of memory processing.

Short-term Memory

All information selected by the brain to be remembered enters short-term memory, which can last as little as 15 seconds. The brain's short-term memory can't hold much information, nor can it hold the information for long. Research indicates that short-term memory can hold five to nine chunks of information, depending on how well the information is grouped.

For example, the numbers 1, 8, 6, 0, 1, 8, 6, and 4 can be recalled by chunking the numbers into dates — 1860 and 1864. *Chunking* the information into smaller bits makes it easier to recall the information and allows more memory space for other information.

Chunking info.   When learning new information, your brain has more difficulty organizing, or chunking, the new information because it's unsure of the relationships between pieces of information. That's why learning small chunks of material at a time works better than trying to learn one large chunk all at once.

Wait, there's more.   Such factors as age, maturation, amount of practice, meaningfulness of the information, and complexity of information also affect the size of short-term memory. From short-term memory, the brain either forgets the information or moves it to long-term memory.

Long-term Memory

After you rehearse and chunk information, your brain can move it to long-term memory. Information stored in *long-term memory* is organized and stored for long periods, but its duration depends on how completely the information has been processed and how often you use it. Although many techniques can be used to aid in the transfer of information from short-term to long-term memory, the most important one is to use the information right away.

Working Memory

Researchers have developed the term *working memory* to describe how your brain stores and retrieves information from short-term and long-term memory. You can improve your *working memory* — your ability to store and recall information — through the use of four specific strategies:

1. selection
2. association
3. organization
4. rehearsal.

Selection

During *selection,* choose the information you want to remember and begin selecting ways to process the information.

Being more consciously aware of what material is important is a key first step in learning the information. When you *really* want to know someone's name, you make a conscious effort to remember it. Learning new material begins with making a conscious decision to remember it.

Association

After selecting the information you want to remember, create an *association* to the information. The associations you make between something you already know and something you're trying to learn serve as memory cues that allow you to more easily retrieve the information later.

Organization

During *organization,* memorization takes place in an ordered way. You might break a process into smaller chunks, each consisting of only a few steps. Using several smaller steps, you can push the information into long-term memory through repetition. Rewriting the steps, repeating the steps verbally, or role-playing the steps will help you remember them more efficiently and will clear your working memory for the next piece of new information to be learned. *Mnemonics* — memory aids, such as acronyms, acrostics, associations, and rhymes — can be particularly effective in organizing chunks of information.

Rehearsal

Rehearsal involves repeatedly reviewing information you've learned. Take a tip from the acting profession: One of the best ways to memorize material is to repeat it — or rehearse it — over and over for short periods of time.

Practice makes perfect. These short bursts of rehearsal are more effective than long bouts of rehearsal. For example, rather than rehearsing the steps in a process pressure repeatedly for 1 hour each day, rehearse the steps for 15 minutes four times per day. Frequency of rehearsal really pays off when you have a lot of information to remember.

Memory Retrieval

After information is processed, it may or may not remain in long-term memory. Information that doesn't remain in long-term memory is forgotten. Information may be forgotten as a result of infrequent use, depending on how interested you are in the information, what your purpose is for learning, how frequently you use the information, and how many connections with other pieces of information you've made for the memory.

Interested? In general, the more interested you are in a topic, the stronger your memory of it will be. For instance, if you know you'll be quizzed on a particular piece of information in a class, you'll be more likely to commit that information to long-term memory. Purpose, frequency of use, and

EXERCISE YOUR MIND

Searching for a lost memory

Can't remember something important? Try these strategies to search for a lost memory.

1. Say or write down everything you can remember that relates to the information you're seeking.
2. Try to recall events or information in a different order.
3. Re-create the learning environment or relive the event. Include sounds, smells, details of weather, nearby objects, other people who were present, what you said or thought at the time, and how you felt.

number of connections all play similar roles in forming long-term memories.

Now, where did I put those keys? The ability to answer questions regarding information you learned a long time ago depends on your ability to recall seldom-used information. Such information may be difficult, or even impossible, to locate in memory because it hasn't been used in a long time. (See *Searching for a lost memory.*)

Up to the challenge? To keep your long-term memory ready for challenges, plan a review session once each month. During your review, read aloud your notes from the previous month and add bookmarks to your notes so you can find the content easily later. For instance, if you drew a diagram in your notes, put a note in the margin so you can find the corresponding section of your textbook. If you missed a question on a recent test, highlight and rewrite your notes about the question so you'll know the correct answer the next time.

Spending an hour or two each month reviewing information will help keep it fresh in your mind and keep those synapses firing.

Knowing isn't always understanding. It's possible for information to be memorized without being understood. With *rote memorization,* the information can be used only in situations similar to the one in which it was learned. For instance, you may have memorized a concept in chemistry when you were in high school, but because you didn't really understand it, you may find it impossible to apply that learning in your college chemistry class. Understanding a concept, as opposed to just memorizing it, helps to solidify the concept in your long-term memory. You might explain the concept to someone else to bolster your memory even further.

Using the depth gauge.   The more deeply a topic is processed by the brain, the more solid is the long-term memory of that topic. Processing depth depends on how the learner processes the information and on a number of other factors, including the learner's:

- background knowledge
- desire for learning
- intended use of the information
- intensity of concentration
- level of interest in the topic
- overall attitude.

STUDY STRATEGIES

By using a number of study strategies, you can give yourself the greatest chance to recall information later — on tests or in the clinical setting. Using different study strategies gives the brain more pathways to use when recalling information.

Key study strategies include:

- using practice and repetition
- using spaced study
- minimizing interference and distractions
- associating familiar items with items to be remembered
- making lists
- using imagery.

Practice

In learning, practice makes permanent. Practice aids the storage of information in long-term memory. It also makes retrieval of information from long-term memory into working memory more automatic.

Rehearsal forms.   Practice methods assume many forms, depending on the amount of time spent practicing, the depth of learning that takes place as a result, and the manner in which the information is learned. Rehearsal can take three forms:

1. *Auditory* — repeating information aloud or in discussion
2. *Visual* — reading information silently over and over
3. *Semantic* — writing or diagramming information repeatedly. Pay particular attention to the concept maps and diagrams in this book and in your textbooks, as well as those given to you by your instructors. They present information in a different format, allowing you to see relationships among concepts. Drawing concept maps yourself reinforces understanding.

Can you hear me now?   In general, auditory and semantic practices yield better results because they involve active processes rather than the more passive practice of silent reading. Rewriting information while saying it aloud can double your efficiency in learning. Learning takes place more readily as a result of active practices than passive ones.

Spaced Study

Spaced study consists of alternating short study sessions with breaks. This method is also known as *distributed practice*. Study goals are set by time (for example, reading for at least 15 minutes) or task (for example, reading a minimum of three pages). After reaching these goals, the student takes a 5- to 15-minute break.

The secret to spaced study success.   Spaced study works because:

- it rewards hard work
- work is completed in manageable portions
- work is completed under a deadline of time or task, so the time spent studying is spent efficiently
- working memory has limited capacity, so breaks provide time for information to be absorbed into long-term memory
- study breaks keep the student from confusing similar details when studying complex, interrelated information
- separate study sessions are more likely to involve different content cues. The greater the number of study sessions, the greater the likelihood that the content cues overlap with material on the test, thus improving recall.

Interference Reduction

Like radio signals creating static, *interference* occurs when new information conflicts with background knowledge. When two radio signals fall close to each other on the radiowave spectrum, it can be difficult to tune in one fully because of interference from the other. A similar kind of interference occurs in long-term memory. If you have many similar experiences or memories, you may find it difficult to retrieve information about a certain experience.

For instance, if you're trying to learn a large number of new terms and two of the terms are similar, you might have difficulty remembering either or both. To avoid interference, try to relate new information to previously learned information. Think about what makes the new information different from the previously learned information.

Take a breather.   If you need to study the subjects one right after the other, take a break between the study sessions. When you return to study the second subject, try studying in a different place. Making different associations for each subject will help you and your brain organize information more efficiently.

Associations

To develop the necessary links among information and increase your ability to apply what you've learned, consider how to associate and organize information. (See *Developing associations.*) Applying knowledge to different situations is a critical aspect of learning that requires a deep understanding

EXERCISE YOUR MIND

Developing associations

Associating information you want to learn with information you already know can help you remember key pieces of information more easily. Use these questions to help you develop associations among study items.

- What, if anything, does the item remind you of?
- Does the item sound like a familiar word or rhyme with one?
- Can you link the item with a memory of a familiar location?
- Can you draw a picture to link your memory with the item?
- When you think of the item, can you visualize something familiar?
- Can you rearrange letters in the name to form an acronym?
- Can you form connections that make sense between one concept and another?

of the material. *Associations* form links between familiar items and items to be remembered. When established, the links become automatic.

Recalling a familiar item cues the recall of the other item. To be effective, associations must be personal, perhaps associating a song or smell with the item to be remembered.

Word games. Acronyms and acrostics each associate key information to an easily remembered word or phrase, thereby improving memory of the information.

Forming acronyms or acrostics can help in recalling lists of information. *Acronyms* are created from the first letter or the first few letters of each item on a list. *Roy G. Biv* is a commonly used acronym that stands for the colors of the rainbow in order (red, orange, yellow, green, blue, indigo, and violet). *HOMES* is another common acronym, this time for the names of the Great Lakes (Huron, Ontario, Michigan, Erie, and Superior). Acronyms need not be real words.

Acrostics are phrases or sentences represented on the vertical axis and are created from the first letter or first few letters of items on a list. For example, an acrostic representing the lines on the treble clef of a sheet of music is *Every Good Boy Does Fine,* which stands for the notes as they appear vertically, from the bottom up, on a treble clef: E-G-B-D-F.

Elaborate, please. Understanding how concepts can be connected with one another helps you learn by allowing for the elaboration of ideas. *Elaboration* enables you to reframe information in terms of what you already know about the topic.

You provide your own logic from your knowledge of how the new information fits with previously learned information.

Lists

Lists serve as another memory aid. The arrangement of a list depends on your goals and the course emphasis and content. Sometimes an instructor suggests organizational structures for lists by identifying types of information to remember — for example, dates, names, and places.

Lists help organize ideas by categorizing information according to some commonality. Recalling the name of the organizing concept helps you remember the details located within it. The organization of information in the list depends on having a classification system of some kind. Because items relate to one another within the system, you can rearrange and reorganize information as needed to aid recall.

Imagery

People commonly think in images rather than in words. The use of visual aids in studying can help you recall familiar and unfamiliar information. In addition, images are stored differently in the brain than are words. Imagery provides an additional way to encode information. The brain stores four kinds of memories easily:

1. patterns
2. pictures
3. rhymes
4. stories.

Link 'em up. Mental associations link concrete objects with images (for example, a picture of a tree with the word *tree*) or abstract concepts with symbols (for example, a picture of a heart with the word *love*). Mental imagery also can be used to link unrelated objects, concepts, and ideas through visualization.

Add a little color. You can use visual representations to help compress and synthesize class notes. Because visual representations of ideas are processed by a different area of the brain than are words, they provide another way to recall information.

Adding meaningful doodles, colors, or symbols to your notes allows you to organize and then visualize information to be learned. A technique called *recall mapping* can be highly useful in this regard. When you use visual representations efficiently, you'll remember more information with less effort.

IMPROVING MEMORY SKILLS

You can improve your memory skills through memory-boosting strategies, including:

- writing new information correctly
- using repetition
- using environmental cues

- understanding the information
- developing your own memorization techniques
- using vivid imagery
- having faith in yourself.

Look alive!   Being aware of everything around you is the first step in developing better recall. Be observant. Look for landmarks. Practice paying attention to the big things, and you'll become more attentive to the little ones too.

To remember information, the information must first be registered in your brain correctly. If a piece of information doesn't register, try to expose yourself to the information again. For example, if a new acquaintance's name doesn't register the first time you hear it, ask for the name again. Then repeat it to confirm it.

Now that makes sense!   Make sure you thoroughly understand what you want to remember. Information that makes sense to you and that you fully understand is easier to recall later. To boost your understanding of a topic, use several styles of learning. For instance, don't just read about a topic. Instead, read about them, watch a video, draw a picture, and talk about the topic with peers. Using various methods of learning can enhance understanding and meaning and, as a result, improve recall.

Keep your eyes on the prize.   To intensify your desire to recall information, keep a positive attitude about memory and recall. Believing that you can do something is an important step in actually doing it.

In addition, the more you keep your eyes on your overall goals, the more you can remember. The goal can serve as your incentive to remember information. The stronger the incentive, the stronger the mental connection and the longer lasting the memory.

MEMORY JOGGER

The brain easily stores patterns, pictures, rhymes, and stories. Remember these categories easily by remembering:

Patty picked a rhyming story
to remember thoughts in all their glory.

The stranger, the better!   To make images in your mind easier to recall, make them more vivid. Think of the colors as being intensely bright. Make the image bigger. Associate a strong emotion to the picture. The more unusual or absurd the mental picture, the more likely that you'll be able to recall the information associated with it.

Here are other ideas for creating vivid images:

- imagine some kind of action taking place
- form an image of an object out of proportion to the object's actual size
- exaggerate the object the way a caricature exaggerates the features of its subject
- substitute or reverse a normal role
- practice word associations using mental pictures to remember items in a list.

Keep it simple.   Probably the simplest method of remembering a piece of information is to associate the information with something familiar. You can recall one item because another item acts as a reminder. If, for example, you wanted to remember to take one of your textbooks home to do an assignment, you might place a red sticky note on your assignment book.

Repetition…repetition…repetition…   Repetition is one of the most effective recall strategies. Repetition strengthens neural pathways and, with enough use, can create nearly indelible pathways. Don't depend on repetition alone, however. Use several strategies to make sure the memory remains intact.

Variety is the spice of life.   Develop your own favorite memorization techniques, depending on the type of information that needs to be memorized. If you develop a unique memorization technique that works for you, then by all means continue to use it.

As with all techniques, though, remember that you shouldn't rely on a single technique to learn new information, no matter how well that technique has served you in the past. Using a variety of techniques will serve you best in the long run.

Remember that expanding your list of memorization techniques makes you a more flexible learner, which will allow you to learn a greater variety of material with less stress and wasted time.

3

Managing Your Time

CHAPTER OBJECTIVES

In this chapter, you'll learn:

1. How a well-organized schedule is used to maximize studying efficiency.
2. How to set priorities effectively.
3. How to avoid burnout.
4. How procrastination can be overcome by effective planning and a positive approach to projects.
5. Studying strategies and programs that improve learning skills.

SCHEDULES

The work habits of people who have achieved outstanding success invariably include a well-designed schedule. When facing several obligations at the same time, it becomes difficult to meet any of them. The purpose of scheduling isn't to feel constricted but, rather, to allow you to look ahead and free yourself from scholastic inefficiency and the anxiety that arises from not being prepared. Developing a course schedule can go a long way toward fulfilling those time management goals.

The "getting started" toolbox.   The most successful scheduling technique for most students involves short-range and long-range planning. Develop a general schedule for each term, a specific but flexible schedule for each week, and a daily to-do list. The tools you'll need to get started include:

- a long-term (semester) calendar that can be posted where you study or carried with you to class and home or dorm
- a "week-at-a-glance" calendar that includes the current semester
- colorful pens or pencils for color-coding dates and tasks
- a notepad or stack of 3″ × 5″ lined cards or sticky notes for daily to-do lists.

Alternatively, you can use an all-in-one organizer system, such as a Day Timer or Day Runner. These systems generally include short-term and long-term calendars and daily to-do lists that can be replaced as needed.

Whichever format you choose, spend time at the beginning of the term planning and writing tests and assignments on the calendar. Review at least weekly, making adjustments as necessary.

Organizing a Class Schedule

The way you organize your class schedule affects the success you achieve during the term. If you organize your class schedule well, you can manage your time more effectively. To organize your class schedule properly, spread out class periods throughout the week, schedule difficult classes when you're most alert, strive for a balance between difficult and less-difficult courses each semester, and maintain flexibility throughout the schedule.

Spread the classes around.   Some classes are scheduled on alternating days — Monday, Wednesday, and Friday, for instance. Some students may schedule all of their courses on those days, thinking that concentrating their class time and having a day or two free to study makes sense for time management. This arrangement, however, often results in being overworked and burned out on class days and then spending free days recuperating rather than studying. If possible, space your classes throughout the week.

Keep in mind that an efficient schedule fills the day as well as the week. Having sufficient time between classes gives you the opportunity to review information as soon as possible after class, which, in turn, gives you time to think through a lecture while the information is still fresh in your mind.

At sometimes you might not have the ability to choose days and times for classes. If you find yourself unable to choose your class schedule, focus on adapting to the schedule you're given. Give yourself time to study and review information within the constraints of your schedule, and always check with faculty if you have a major conflict.

Tackling the tough classes.   Your most difficult courses should be scheduled during the times you're most alert. If you prefer getting up early, schedule your most difficult course for the morning. If you do your best work after lunch, schedule your most difficult classes at that time.

If you have the option of scheduling a class on successive versus alternating days, consider the level of difficulty of the class and how interested you are in it. Difficulty level and interest in a topic affect the length of time you can concentrate on it. The more interested you are or the easier the content is for you, the longer you can sustain concentration on the topic.

Magical mix of courses.   Although some courses must be taken in sequence, most curricula are somewhat flexible. Generally, course outlines are suggestions about how to spread mandatory and elective courses over one or more terms. Taking too many difficult courses at once can be overwhelming. Taking too many uninteresting classes can lead to boredom.

To offset either situation, balance courses that you look forward to attending with those you're less interested in, and balance difficult courses with easier courses.

Oh, those commitments.   If you're like most students, you have personal commitments (such as holding a full-time or part-time job) or seasonal commitments (such as being a track athlete who trains in the spring). You may also have a hobby that dictates how much time you can devote to course work. Consider these activities and commitments when planning course work, and adjust your course schedule accordingly.

Check 'em out.   You may have the option of taking a course with two or more different instructors. If the dates and times of each course fit your schedule, you'll need to decide with which instructor you'd like to take the class. If you don't know the instructors involved, check with other students who may have insight into those instructors, or with student government associations, which commonly monitor faculty performance and make results available to students.

DAY-TO-DAY TIME MANAGEMENT

After determining your class schedule for the term, you need to turn your attention to managing your time each day. Start by setting up a calendar to record goals and major events. The purpose of such a calendar is to obtain an overview of long-term goals and commitments, which can help in planning short-term and daily activities.

Managing Your Calendar

Your calendar should include recreational as well as serious commitments. Using a calendar for the current year, mark off the months and days for the term in which you're currently enrolled. Put the calendar close to where you study so you can focus on your long-term objectives.

Use a calendar to record:

- midterm and final examination dates
- due dates for papers and other projects
- deadlines for completing each phase of lengthy projects
- test dates
- important extracurricular and recreational events
- deadlines for dropping and adding courses
- holidays, school vacations, and social commitments.

From start to finish. The beginning and end of each term are critical times for students.

Large amounts of content and course organizational material are commonly presented during the first few weeks of the term. Keep up with your readings and other work in this early period to set the pace for the term. If you start to fall behind or don't understand the content, talk with your instructor and your school's student support services. With their help in planning, you can stay on track.

The end of the term is also critical because students run out of time to bring their grades back up if they've fallen behind. Use your calendar to help spot possible distractions during these critical periods. Then plan how to eliminate the distractions or at least reduce their effects.

Is it hot in here? *Burnout* results when a student works steadily without taking a sufficient number of breaks. The causes of burnout include fatigue, boredom, and stress.

Maintaining a balance between breaks and work time — and planning for both — helps avoid burnout. A break doesn't have to be recreational; it can be a change from one task to another. For example, switching from one assignment to another assignment can relieve boredom and, thus, prevent burnout. Such planning also decreases interruptions during prime study time.

Another way to avoid burnout is to retain flexibility in your daily schedule. If you schedule commitments too tightly during the day, you won't have time to complete your goals and, as a result, may feel defeated for failing to do what you had planned.

SETTING PRIORITIES

Setting priorities is a critical task for every student. You'll need to set priorities appropriately in school and in the clinical setting as well. You'll need to set priorities for tasks, class attendance, and homework.

Tasks

A student with several tasks that have the same deadline may switch back and forth from one task to another, giving the illusion of progress. Changing tasks too often, however, wastes time because you lose momentum. For a time after the transition from one project to another, you may still be thinking about the old project when you should be concentrating on the new one. Furthermore, after returning to the first task, you have to review the material where you left off and remember what steps remained before the task could be finished.

So many tasks, so little time. You can avoid this problem by determining how much time you have available in any one period. If you have an hour or less, work on only one task; only alternate tasks if you have more than an hour. Even then, most of your attention should be focused on completing a single task (or a large portion of it), which can provide a sense of satisfaction and move you steadily toward completion of your goals.

It's rude to interrupt! If you interrupt work on a long-term project to work on another task, write a few notes about the long-term project before moving to the new task. Write down the goal of the task and a list of questions to be answered or objectives to be completed. You might jot down what steps you plan to perform next so that, when you return to the task, you can pick up where you left off right away. Also, be sure to store all materials related to the first task in the same place so you don't have to search for them when you return to the task.

Attending Class

During class, the instructor highlights the most important concepts, elaborates on information found in assigned readings, and shapes the student's understanding of the material. Instructors focus on application, analysis, and synthesis of ideas in their lectures and classroom work. Instructors use class time to present the material they think is most important for understanding the course.

To get the most out of class time, arrive on time and don't leave early. Instructors commonly use the first 5 minutes of class to make important announcements, and the last 5 minutes to summarize material or explain assignments.

Bring other assignments or readings to class in case the instructor is late or you have an unexpected break. Know the policies of your school and instructor regarding class attendance and lateness.

Risky business. Missing a class is risky. Each time you miss a class, you face the possibility that questions on the next test will relate to material covered in the class you missed.

Many students assume they can safely miss a class here and there because they pay close attention to their reading assignment. The problem with that approach is that many instructors don't use only the reading material to construct lecture notes and create classroom activities and discussions.

Instructors commonly base classroom material on their own experiences and on sources not readily available to the student, such as journal articles, educational newsletters, and other nontextbook sources of information. Even if an instructor bases her classroom activities entirely on textbook readings, you would still miss explanations of new ideas and the further development of existing content.

The body-brain split.   Here's another reason not to skip class: Learning continues outside the classroom. After class, you continue to think about the material. You may be walking home from class, showering, or doing the laundry when you come up with a question to ask or clarify in your mind a statement made in class. Just because your body is no longer located in a classroom doesn't mean your brain has finished analyzing material covered in that classroom. Give your mind a chance to help you learn; attend every class.

The bitter end.   The worst time to miss a class is at the end of the semester. Some instructors use the last few classes of the semester to review and outline the entire course or to discuss information to be covered on the final examination. Some instructors even go so far as to tell — or at least hint at — exactly what material the students should study for the final examination.

Even so, some students feel overwhelmed with studying for final examinations and end up trading class time for study time. If you schedule your study time well, you can avoid feeling the need to skip class to study. If you're truly unable to attend a class, however, ask another student if you can borrow her notes and get copies of classroom handouts for that day. That way, you'll at least be exposed to some of the material covered in class.

Doing Homework

Homework assignments typically fall into two categories: written and reading assignments. Written assignments provide an instructor with immediate feedback about how much work the student has done and how well she has understood it.

Although reading assignments don't provide immediate feedback, instructors generally consider them as important as written assignments for understanding a particular subject. Many instructors include questions on reading assignments on quizzes and tests, or ask questions in class based on assigned readings. The responses of the students help the instructor gauge the effectiveness of the assignments and whether the students have actually read the material.

Eh, what's next, Doc?   To gain the most value from homework assignments, you first need to find out what the as-

signments are for the course. Most instructors distribute a syllabus or an outline at the start of each course. These documents explain content to be covered in the course and what expectations the instructor has for the student. Some instructors also distribute reading and written homework assignments for each course. If you don't receive such an outline, approach your instructor and ask what material you should read for the next few classes. Then create your own outline, and put the assignments into your organizer so you can plan your daily and weekly schedule properly.

My dog ate my homework!   Family and other responsibilities sometimes take precedence over schoolwork. In those situations, try to balance your schedule by not overdoing it in one area at the expense of another. Postponing certain homework assignments for a short time may free up enough time to fulfill family obligations or other responsibilities. Having the support of your employer, fellow workers, and family can prove critical in this regard. However, avoid postponing homework routinely. Doing so can put you so far behind in your studies that you won't be able to catch up.

HANDLING PROCRASTINATION

Everyone procrastinates, some more so than others. In the end, procrastination results in wasted time, missed opportunities, poor performance, self-deprecation, and increased stress. Procrastinators often spend more time worrying than working.

Excuses, excuses!   People who procrastinate place low-priority tasks ahead of high-priority ones and then offer excuses for not doing the high-priority task, including:

- I'll wait until I'm in the mood
- I feel like celebrating because I finished reading one chapter
- I'll think about it tomorrow
- there's plenty of time to get it done
- I don't know where to begin
- I work best under pressure
- I have too many other things to do first.

Students may procrastinate to avoid tasks that seem boring or difficult, or they may put off working on a task because they doubt their ability to do the task in the first place. In addition, a student may wait until all available resources have been reviewed before completing a task. Regardless of the cause, procrastination needs to be identified and then overcome to succeed as a student. (See *Breaking the procrastination habit.*)

Give it a try.   When you recognize that you're procrastinating, try doing what you're thinking about postponing for just a few minutes. After you've started the task, you're likely to continue working on it.

ADVICE FROM THE EXPERTS

Breaking the procrastination habit

Procrastination habits can be hard to break but not impossible. Here are some tips for breaking your procrastination habits.

Motivators

- On one side of a sheet of paper, write your reasons for not doing something. On the other side, challenge the excuse with logic.
- Make up a list of self-motivating statements, such as "It's now or never," "No time like the present," or "Never put off until tomorrow what you can do today." Then repeat them whenever you feel like postponing a task.
- Recognize that the negative predictions you may make about a project aren't facts. Focus on the positive steps you can take toward reaching your goals, no matter how difficult those goals might be.
- Commit to completing each task. Promise yourself, a friend, or a relative that you'll get the task done. A promise to a third person can serve as a powerful motivator.

Goals and priorities

- Design clear goals, and then establish a realistic timetable to complete each one.
- Set priorities. Write down all the things that need to be done for a project in order of their importance. The greater the importance, the higher the priority.
- Break down large, complex projects into smaller, more manageable parts. For example, make an outline for a written report before composing it.
- Use your weekly schedule and daily to-do lists to keep yourself organized. Check off tasks after completion.
- Pinpoint where your delays typically start, and then focus on overcoming procrastination during those critical times.
- Write reminders to yourself about projects to be completed, and display them in conspicuous places.

Rewards

- Reward yourself. Self-reinforcement can have a powerful effect on developing a "do it now" attitude.
- Promise yourself to give up something important if you fail to meet your goal and to go someplace special if you *do* meet your goal.

Parcel it out. When you face several deadlines in the same week, it can be difficult to prioritize and get started on a task. In these cases, parcel the work, setting apart small tasks that can be accomplished quickly. Completing several small tasks provides positive reinforcement and moves you closer and closer to your goal.

Get real! Some students fail to start projects because they set impossibly high standards for themselves and are afraid they won't live up to their own expectations. Other students refuse to finish a project until they believe it's perfect, a goal they may never reach. In either case, you should weigh the consequences of handing in what you believe is a flawed project with the consequences of not handing in a project at all. Understand that a passing grade for an imperfect assignment beats a zero for not handing in an assignment at all. Use this knowledge as an impetus for getting the project completed at all costs.

Down with distractions! If a student procrastinates because she can't concentrate enough to get started on a project, she needs to remove the distractions from her study area or move to an area with fewer distractions. When undertaking a project, make sure that reference materials are nearby so that you don't interrupt your work flow to find a particular resource.

To study or not to study? Sometimes uncertainty can cause apathy and indecisiveness and, consequently, procrastination. For instance, if you aren't sure which topic you should choose for a project, you'll have a harder time making a commitment to the project and an easier time putting off getting started. To avoid procrastination caused by uncertainty, keep in mind that decisiveness is a trait of an effective leader and a successful student. Brainstorming for ideas with other students, asking your instructor for suggestions on a topic, or researching several topics that may interest you can help you decide on a topic and move you toward fulfilling your goals.

Review your goals. Lack of clear, specific goals is often a subtle cause of procrastination. If you're unsure of your goals, you'll have little reason to begin or complete a project.

Likewise, if you become very involved in working on one assignment, you may forget due dates for other commitments. Establishing long-term and short-term goals — and then periodically reviewing them — can help provide direction to the tasks you perform and keep you on track during unusually busy periods.

PREPARING TO STUDY

Effective studying doesn't just happen. It involves carefully selecting a study site, maintaining proper lighting, settling into a comfortable position, and putting yourself into the right frame of mind.

Selecting a Study Area

To find the right study area, look for a distraction-free spot where you can arrange your study materials properly. Make sure it has adequate lighting, is set at the right temperature, and is located among pleasant surroundings.

Distraction-free Site

Before you begin to study, find a calm, comfortable place to study. As you select your study site, choose an area with the fewest distractions. (See *Distraction-free study areas.*) After you find a study site you enjoy using, keep using it for subsequent study sessions. Using the same area creates familiarity and helps you begin studying as soon as you settle into the area.

Study Arrangement

Next, find the arrangement for studying you most enjoy. For most students, a desk with a comfortable, straight-backed chair makes the ideal study arrangement. You can arrange your study materials on the desk and easily reach them

---

EXERCISE YOUR MIND
Distraction-free study areas

Select two or three areas you think may be suitable to use as study areas. Then choose the area that gets the most favorable responses to these questions:

- Will I be interrupted by other people?
- Are there too many reminders of things that don't have anything to do with studying?
- Is a loud radio or television being played here?
- Does the telephone ring too often?
- Can I be here at regular intervals?
- Is the temperature comfortable or, if not, can I control the temperature?
- Can I smell cooking odors here?

MEMORY JOGGER

When you're trying to find a place to study, always remember to check out the **SALT** beforehand:

Surroundings
Arrangement
Lighting
Temperature.

---

whenever necessary. Other students feel most comfortable in a large chair or sofa, with their books and other study materials spread out on the floor at their feet.

Don't get too relaxed.   You could sit cross-legged in the middle of your bed with your study materials all around, but it's probably not a good idea. You're already familiar with your bed as a sleeping place, and you may get sleepy. Sitting under a tree with a gentle breeze blowing in a quiet place seems like a good idea, but not when the gentle breeze becomes a distraction, ruffling papers and making you constantly lose your place in your notes. Choose your study arrangement carefully, weighing the value of the comfort it provides with its ability to meet your study needs.

It's habit forming.   To help you decide which study arrangement and study area are right for you, ask yourself these questions:

- Do I have sufficient work space?
- Can I keep the work space uncluttered?
- Do I have adequate lighting?
- Am I in a position that supports my back and eliminates muscle strain?
- Are there as few distractions as possible in the area?

Whichever study arrangement you choose, stay with it. Get into the habit of assuming your study position so you can get down to the business of studying quickly, with few distractions.

Lighting

Use either natural or incandescent lighting for your study area, not fluorescent lighting. Your eyes are less likely to tire under direct light, such as that from an incandescent lamp, than under indirect light.

Direct lighting is best, keeping eye fatigue at its lowest. Keep the light from shining in your eyes by using overhead light or lighting from behind. The light should shine evenly on your work.

Temperature

Choose a study area that isn't too warm. Heat stress can decrease accuracy, speed, dexterity, and physical acuity. For most efficient studying, keep your study area cool — between 65° and 70° F (18° and 21° C).

Surroundings

Pleasant surroundings can greatly enhance study effectiveness. The sensations experienced while studying can be used later to trigger associations at test time. Pleasant surroundings also stimulate alertness. When creating the environment of your study site, focus on surrounding yourself with pleasant music, stimulating odors, and oxygen-providing plants.

Ahh, the pleasing sounds of Mozart... Minimize noise distractions while you study so you won't be disturbed. Screen your telephone calls with an answering machine. Leave the television off. You may also consider adding white noise to your environment. Instrumental music, the sound of a bubbling aquarium, and muted street sounds are examples of white noise. White noise helps cover distracting background sounds, such as the sounds of traffic or your roommate talking on the phone, and fills in periods of silence. In silence, even the sound of your own tapping pencil can be annoying.

Among the forms of white noise you can use, soothing background music is preferred. Low levels of background music can promote relaxed alertness, which stimulates learning. In addition, music induces an emotional response that can be associated with a memory and improve later recall.

...And the scent of peppermint. The two scents that most positively stimulate attention and memory are lemon and peppermint. These scents can be found in oils, candles, room fresheners, and many other products. Other scents also exert an enhancing effect on mental alertness and relaxation. (See *Scents and the mind.*)

SCENTS AND THE MIND

Certain scents have been specifically identified as influencing mental alertness and relaxation. This chart lists those scents and the ways they can affect your studying.

Scent	Effect
basil	increased mental alertness
chamomile	enhanced relaxation
cinnamon	increased mental alertness
lavender	enhanced relaxation
lemon	increased mental alertness
orange	enhanced relaxation
peppermint	increased mental alertness
rose	enhanced relaxation

Gotta get some green (plants, that is). Studying in an area where healthy plants are located can actually foster learning. Green plants remove pollutants from the air and can raise oxygen levels enough to increase productivity by as much as 10%.

Physical Comfort

Your physical comfort affects your attitude about studying. When studying, make sure you assume a comfortable posture, use an appropriate reading angle, and move around periodically to enhance study effectiveness.

Sit up, like your mom used to tell you. Read while sitting in an upright position with your back straight or bent slightly forward. Other postures — particularly lying down — impair alertness and concentration.

Get the right angle. To decrease eyestrain, hold reading material at about a 45-degree angle from the flat surface of your desk or table to give you a clear view of the whole page. Reading material should also be kept at least 15″ away from your eyes.

Get moving. Walking around periodically when studying can enhance the ability of the brain to learn new information and retain information. On average, standing increases blood flow to the brain by 5% to 15%. The greater the blood flow to the brain, the more oxygen it receives and the greater the stimulation of the neurons. So take a break about every hour to walk around, particularly if you need to ponder a point or repeat some facts to yourself. Do some stretching exercises as well to increase circulation and decrease muscle fatigue in the shoulders.

Getting Started

One of the biggest challenges to effective studying is getting started. The first step in meeting that challenge is to break down large tasks into smaller ones. Several small tasks seem more achievable than one overwhelming one, and each smaller accomplishment provides moral support to finish the other tasks.

Set the compass. By taking small steps in the direction you want to go, you may end up at your destination sooner than you thought. For instance, you may not feel like reading your assignment, but if you tell yourself that you'll read for 5 minutes, at least you'll get a little reading done. After a few minutes, tell yourself that you'll read for a few more minutes, and so on. Pretty soon, you'll have read for half an hour or maybe even an hour and be well on your way to accomplishing — if not finishing — your assignment.

Plot the course. When beginning a study session, set a course for your studying or establish a purpose for it. Ask yourself, "What do I want to get out of this session? What do I need to know from the material?" After skimming the material, decide how deeply you need to become involved with it. You may be responsible for detailed knowledge and intricate notes or you may need only a passing acquaintance with the material. Either way, plot your course before you start.

Dump those dastardly distractions.   Remove the usual distractions — the telephone, television, and talk radio. Take care of your personal distractions, such as being hungry or feeling hot. Schedule your study time so that it doesn't conflict with another activity you really want to do. Thinking about what you're missing can be a distraction in itself.

Find the right time to study, when you're feeling most efficient and receptive to information. Take a short break every hour to keep your study time energized. When concentration begins to lag, it's time for a break.

SPECIAL STUDY PROGRAMS

Since the 1940s, study programs have been popular tools for helping students improve their studying efficiency. Four of the currently popular programs are:

- SQ4R reading-study system
- PSQ5R method
- reciprocal teaching
- metalearning.

SQ4R Reading-Study System

The SQ4R reading-study system involves six steps:

1. *Survey.* Gather information necssary to formulate study goals.
2. *Question.* Formulate questions to be answered.
3. *Read.* Seek answers for the questions you raised.
4. *Reflect.* Think about what the text is trying to explain or teach you.
5. *Recite.* Ask your original questions and recite the answer to yourself. If you can't recite the answer, read the material again. Recitation can be particularly interactive when done with another person.
6. *Review.* Synthesize the reading material's meaning as a whole by determining whether you answered all your original questions and met all the goals you set forth after previewing the material. Another way to review involves answering questions posed by the author at the beginning or end of the material.

PSQ5R Method

The PSQ5R method, a system similar to the SQ4R system, involves eight steps:

1. *Purpose.* Determine your purpose for reading.
2. *Survey.* Preview the material quickly.
3. *Question.* Raise questions you think the reading should answer.
4. *Read selectively.* Read with your purpose and questions in mind.

5. *Recite.* Mentally repeat what you've learned as you go along.
6. *Reduce-record.* Write what you've learned in outline, or reduced, form.
7. *Reflect.* Mentally elaborate on what you've learned, comparing the material to previously learned material, categorizing it, or otherwise reorganizing the material.
8. *Review.* Survey your "reduced" notes (the outline) within 24 hours to enhance your knowledge of the material.

Reciprocal Teaching

In *reciprocal teaching,* the student is taught to:

- summarize the content of a passage
- ask a question about the central point
- clarify the difficult parts of the material
- predict what will come next.

Shhh…it's silent reading.   Reciprocal teaching starts when you and the instructor silently read a short passage in a book or journal. Then the instructor provides a model by summarizing, questioning, clarifying, and predicting based on the reading. You'll then read another passage, but this time you'll assume the instructor's role by summarizing, questioning, clarifying, and predicting. The instructor may prompt you by giving clues, guidance, and encouragement to help you master these strategies.

Easy on the shift.   To make reciprocal teaching effective, the shift from the instructor having control of the teaching process to you having the control must be gradual. Furthermore, the instructor must match the difficulty of the task to your own particular abilities.

Metalearning

Metalearning is a method of learning that involves asking yourself a series of questions:

- Why am I reading or listening to this?
- What's the overall content?
- What are the orientation questions?
- What's important here?
- Can I paraphrase or summarize the information?
- How can I organize the information?
- How can I draw the information?
- Can I associate the information?
- How does the information fit what I know?

Setting the stage.   In the metalearning process, state your purpose briefly. Your purpose and goals set the stage for your study session. In the case of a lecture, ask yourself what you want to get out of the class. Try to anticipate what's coming next.

Sneak preview.   Preview the material before reading or attending the lecture. For long or complicated material, translate your preview into a chapter map or outline. You may also want to write what you know about the topic and what you'd like to know or expect to learn about it. This type of warm-up starts the process of generating questions, makes you aware of what you don't know about a topic, puts you on the lookout for answers to questions, and provides a resource on which to draw later. After previewing the material, summarize the chapter in a few sentences and outline brief answers to whatever review questions may be included in the book.

Getting oriented.   Be on the lookout for orientation questions, which commonly appear on tests. An *orientation question* provides background information about a topic or concept and can take many forms, including those that ask about definitions, examples, types, relationships, or comparisons.

The purpose for identifying orientation questions is to see how many questions you can ask about the material and how many different answers you can create for each. Don't be afraid to guess at the answer. Later, when you find out the actual answer, compare it with the one you gave. If you don't find the answer to your question, try looking in a different source.

To focus or skim — that is the question.   Identify which information you should focus on, skim, or ignore. If you can't decide whether something is important, assume it is. Pay attention to your initial responses. If something surprises or confuses you, there may be a gap in your understanding of the information.

Each subject contains important terms you should know. Textbooks typically call your attention to them with italic or bold print or include the term in a glossary. Isolated facts or other details may be important — depending on your purpose for studying.

In other words… Paraphrasing a concept — putting it into your own words — can help you better understand the concept and immediately identify gaps in your learning. If you can't paraphrase a concept, you probably don't understand it well. To paraphrase effectively, use your own words and as few words as possible.

Making a connection.   Organizing information allows your brain to place pieces of information into groups or cat-

egories so you can see patterns, connections, and relationships. Try to keep the number of groups manageable — fewer than 10 — so the information doesn't become too complicated to remember.

You might also consider organizing the information visually by using a mind-mapping technique. By writing the associations you're making among pieces of information, you're making a record of your natural thought processes about the information and will be more prepared to recall it later.

A picture is worth a thousand words.   Representing information as pictures can be a great help in building understanding. Draw a picture of the information. The process of drawing the information can improve your understanding of the information and help move it into your long-term memory.

Associating new information with a song, rhyme, odor, or other environmental trigger can ease later recall. Use association and other memory-enhancing techniques to help retention and recall.

Your accumulated knowledge and understanding of the material help you decide what's important and condense new information into easier-to-manage pieces. If you already have a solid foundation of knowledge about the topic, you can more easily learn new aspects of the topic.

Engage the brain.   Raising other questions can also help engage your brain and enhance retention and later recall. Some of these questions include:

- How is this information significant?
- What does it tell us about other things?
- Is this a fact or someone's opinion?
- How can this be verified?
- Does it depend on a particular point of view?
- What if…?
- Where have I seen something like this before?
- What does that suggest about this?
- What does this remind me of?

TAKE A BREAK!

Timing is Everything

Scheduling all your activities — as well as your studies — can be quite a task! See if you can help this student schedule her activities. Remember to schedule some time for meals and some downtime so she doesn't suffer burnout!

- Meet with study group to prepare for test . . . . 2 hours
- Bake cookies for study group . . . . ½ hour
- Class . . . . 9–10:30 a.m.
- Practice tennis for match . . . . 1 hour
- Proofread paper and turn in . . . . 1 hour
- Take a bath and relax! . . . . as long as possible!
- Read 25 pages of textbook . . . . 1 hour

- Do laundry! . . . . 1½ hours
- Watch part of roommate's lacrosse game . . . . 4–6 p.m.

Tomorrow	
8 a.m.	4 p.m.
8:30 a.m.	4:30 p.m.
9 a.m.	5 p.m.
9:30 a.m.	5:30 p.m.
10 a.m.	6 p.m.
10:30 a.m.	6:30 p.m.
11 a.m.	7 p.m.
11:30 a.m.	7:30 p.m.
12 noon	8 p.m.
12:30 p.m.	8:30 p.m.
1 p.m.	9 p.m.
1:30 p.m.	9:30 p.m.
2 p.m.	10 p.m.
2:30 p.m.	10:30 p.m.
3 p.m.	11 p.m.
3:30 p.m.	11:30 p.m.

4

Textbook and Classroom Strategies

CHAPTER OBJECTIVES

In this chapter, you'll learn:

1. Why effective reading skills are critical for success in studying, and how they can be improved with the consistent application of basic reading strategies.

2. How to prepare for a lecture ahead of time and why you should review your notes after lectures.

3. Why using the principles of active reading and listening can improve comprehension.

READING SKILLS

Students receive more than 75% of their course information from printed materials. This is why solid reading skills are essential for successful studying. Effective reading skills involve strategies to improve comprehension and reading speed.

Comprehension Techniques

Reading and understanding course material provides support for lectures and classroom activities and leads to a thorough understanding of the topic under study. Improving reading comprehension involves skimming for ideas, using active reading skills, and summarizing the material.

Skimming for Ideas

The first step in reading a chapter in a textbook is to look it over without trying to read every word. *Skimming* the chapter gives you an idea of the content and shows you how the material is organized. By thinking about the structure before actually reading the material, you use your brain to organize the learning to come, which improves your ability to understand the content and recall information in the chapter.

Getting to know you.   Before reading a chapter in detail, look at the illustrations and read the captions. Then read the introductory paragraph and all the headings in the chapter. Lastly, read the chapter summary.

Use the same skimming techniques to read an entire book. First, look at the title page. Read about the author on the book jacket or on the *About the Author* page. Read the preface or other introductory material. Examine the table of contents to obtain a better idea of the book's content. Review the pages, noting emphasized words in bold or italics. Lastly, read vocabulary or glossary terms listed in the chapters or at the end of the book as appropriate.

A picture is worth a thousand words.   Review all graphs, charts, tables, and illustrations. This supplemental content is intended to expand on or clarify the material covered in the main text, so use it to your advantage.

Experience breeds familiarity.   Reading comprehension is enhanced when the reading material relates to your own background. For example, an allied health professional could most likely read faster and more readily understand a chapter about her area of expertise. Her background gives her knowledge of relevant vocabulary and an ability to more quickly understand connections among concepts. As a result, she can more easily comprehend the material.

Back to the basics.   To more easily understand material about a complex topic, try reading less advanced material on the same subject, listening to a lecture on it, or attending a seminar on a related topic.

ADVICE FROM THE EXPERTS

Improving your reading comprehension

Improving your reading comprehension doesn't have to be an impossible dream. Following these guidelines can help you more readily comprehend every reading assignment you have:

- keep your purpose for reading squarely in mind.
- if the main idea is unstated, identify the topic by looking for repetitions of key words or phrases.
- retrieve the background knowledge necessary to understand the text; use such strategies as looking up unknown words and referring to less advanced resources.
- restate the main idea through paraphrasing, summarizing, or synthesizing.

There's a pattern here.   Understanding how the text itself is organized can help you focus on the most important parts of the text. Common structural components include:

- subject development or *definition text structure,* which identifies a concept and lists its supporting details
- enumeration or *sequence text,* in which major points are listed by number or in sequence, and are commonly preceded by such clue words as *first, second, next,* and *then*
- *compare-and-contrast text,* which expresses relationships between two or more ideas (Comparisons show how ideas are similar; contrasting statements show how they're different.)
- *cause-and-effect text,* which shows how one idea or event results from another idea or event.

Using Active Reading Skills

Active reading fosters comprehension by involving more than one sense. To become a more active reader:

- read aloud
- take notes on the material you've read
- formulate some questions you'd like answered while you read
- think about the important points as outlined by the table of contents
- avoid arguing with the author when reading (you can analyze the text later)
- mark areas you'd like to read again.

While you're alert.   Read during parts of the day when you feel comfortable, alert, and unhurried. If you know you have to read 25 pages today and that you get sleepy after lunch,

---

ADVICE FROM THE EXPERTS

Power-reading symbols

Using shortcuts for labeling text can help you read faster while still understanding the text. This table shows commonly used symbols for labeling text.

Symbol	Meaning
ex	example or experiment
form	formula
MI	main idea
! or *	important information
→	results in, leads to, steps in a sequence
(1), (2), (3)	important points
circled word	process summary
?	disagree or unclear
term	important term
summ	summary
{ }	certain pieces of information relate
opin	author's opinion, rather than fact
∴	therefore

ADVICE FROM THE EXPERTS

Marking and labeling text

Marking and labeling text can help you retain knowledge about the reading you've done and make later reference easier. Remember these points when marking and labeling text:

- read a paragraph or section completely before marking anything
- mark points that answer questions you may have had before reading
- number lists, reasons, or other items that occur in a series or sequence
- identify important terms, dates, places, and names
- write main idea summaries, questions, and other comments in the margins
- put a question mark beside unclear or confusing information
- put a star or exclamation point beside information your instructor emphasizes in class, possible test questions, or what seems to be extremely important information
- write comments on the table of contents or make your own table of contents of important topics inside the front cover of the book or on the title page.

---

avoid trying to complete your reading after lunch. Instead, choose a time when you're feeling more alert. Likewise, don't try to read too much at once. If you've been reading for a long time and begin to feel your concentration slipping, take a 5-minute break.

Distraction-free zone.   Watching television, listening to music with lyrics, and engaging in numerous otherwise enjoyable activities can be distracting when trying to study. Avoid distractions by finding a quiet place to read. Sit at a desk or in a straight-backed chair bathed in natural or incandescent light. Try to avoid getting too comfortable and, as a result, becoming sleepy. Have a healthy snack and keep water handy to stave off hunger and thirst.

The handy highlighter.   If you own the book you're reading, use a highlighter to mark important ideas. (See *Power-reading symbols.*) If you don't own the book, use colored sticky notes for marking key areas. In either case, don't overdo it. Marking up too much text makes the material meaningless after a while.

Keep these highlighting tips in mind:

- when buying a used text, never choose one that has already been highlighted or otherwise marked up by another student
- if you skimmed the material before reading it, use your marks to note details that provide answers to your questions

- mark material you believe the instructor considers most important
- consider the difficulty of the language when deciding what content to mark. (See *Marking and labeling text.*) Subject depth, the number of details given, and overall vocabulary affect how much you understand.

Keep in mind that highlighters and sticky notes are *indexing tools;* they can help you find information, but they can't help you *learn* the information unless you do some follow-up work. Whenever you mark a section of your book, make sure you do something with it later, such as writing a summary of highlighted information or drawing a chart or diagram to summarize the information.

Zooming in.   Every chapter has a central premise, and every paragraph within that chapter presents at least one main idea. The main ideas and supporting details of each paragraph support the central premise of the chapter.

In a typical paragraph, the *topic sentence* tells you the main idea. The topic sentence usually appears at the beginning or end of the paragraph but may appear anywhere. Pay particular attention to topic sentences, highlighting the sentence or parts of the sentence as appropriate.

So what you're saying is...   Take notes while you read. If you can rephrase the material, then you probably understand it. Comprehension builds on itself. Some concepts (in math, for example) must be understood before you can move on. One method of note "rephrasing" involves drawing graphics of the material. Graphics are sometimes more memorable than words, and the act of drawing them will give your memory an extra boost.

Getting personal.   The active reader assimilates information to relate to her own experience, thus making the information more easily remembered because it's more personal. The more personal the information, the more meaningful the material. Make the material more meaningful.

- Make associations of personal relevance. For example, perhaps an important date can be associated with a birth date.
- Allow it to evoke an emotional response. A deep emotional response to information or even something that strikes you as funny can make the information more interesting and, therefore, more entrenched in memory.
- Take advantage of your brain's ability to recall pictures, graphics, and illustrations. Draw out what you learn; make patterns, doodles, and drawings that make sense to *you*.

Criticism counts.   Read critically, asking yourself questions about the text. Question the authority of the author or the reliability of the information provided. Questioning the content forces you to think critically about the information, which may open doors to greater understanding of the content and improve retention. Here are examples of critical questions:

- How can I apply this information to the care of a patient?
- How does this information relate to what I studied last week?
- Does the information validate ideas in other resources or contradict other reading?
- Under what circumstances were the data collected?
- How was the information verified?
- Do inconsistencies exist in the information?
- How does the author answer his own questions?
- Has the author made any assumptions?
- Are the author's statements based on knowledge, facts, experiences, or opinions?
- Is the author being objective?
- Do I disagree with the author? Why?
- If I were playing "devil's advocate," what questions would I ask the author? What examples would I include that the author hasn't?
- What do I want to know that the author hasn't told me?

Calling Mr. Webster... stat!   If you come across a word you've never seen, don't understand, or can't pronounce, look it up in a dictionary. However, first try to derive the meaning of the word from its context in the sentence and from its root words, prefixes, and suffixes. Try to pronounce it. Then read the dictionary meaning and pronunciation of the word, noting both in the margin of your notes. Keep in mind that if the author used the word once, he'll probably use it again.

If the text contains a lot of difficult words, you may want to read through some of the material first, marking the difficult words or making a list of the words that need to be looked up. Then go back for a second pass with a dictionary close at hand.

It's especially important to understand the meaning of technical terms when reading scientific material. Technical terms are integral to understanding scientific principles being discussed. By building your vocabulary, you not only better understand the material, but also become better able to express yourself, both verbally and in writing.

Summarizing the Material

In general, textbooks use the same method in every chapter to summarize the chapter's content. This information may be contained in a summary paragraph or a group of summary questions. After reading your assignment, look at the chapter summary and table of contents again to be sure you understood the material in the format intended by the author. If there's an area you're unsure of, read through that information again or ask for clarification from your instructor, who can probably explain it better.

Slow and steady.   If you need to read the material again to understand it better, do it differently the second time. Read the material more slowly, perhaps, concentrating on one sentence at a time. Or, read the material aloud. Make sure you understand each sentence before moving to the next. Try to relate the new idea to what the author has already covered.

Can we talk?   After you've finished the assignment, find ways to apply your newly acquired knowledge, even if just by talking about it. Share what you read with others. Talking about the material reflects your ability to restate what you've learned, which reinforces your comprehension.

Increasing Your Reading Rate

The average college student reads fiction and nontechnical materials at a rate of 250 to 350 words per minute. To reach peak efficiency in reading, experts say your reading speed should approach 500 to 700 words per minute. Some people can read at a rate of 1,000 words per minute or even faster.

Increasing the rate at which you read can help you move through assignments more quickly, thus improving your study efficiency. However, keep in mind that when it comes to reading speed, faster isn't better if you don't understand what you've read. The trick is to read faster *and* comprehend the material.

Rapid Eye Movement

The key to rapid reading is to sweep your eyes from left to right across the page, making as few stops — called *fixations* — as possible. Readers who can see a full phrase at a time can read faster than those who see one word at a time.

When you read, your eyes tend to jump toward information you've already read. In some situations, you can spend as much as 90% of your reading time with your eyes looking away from what you think you're looking at. Training your eyes to reduce eye movement can double reading speed almost immediately.

Optimum optics. To train your eyes to stay where you want them when reading, hold a blank index card above each line you read. As you progress down the page, use the card to cover each line after you've finished reading it. At first you might find this process physically different because your eyes naturally want to scan back up the page, but after a few weeks you'll find that you're reading faster than ever.

Role of Speed in the Reading Process

Does reading faster compromise comprehension? Researchers say no, particularly if the technique used to improve the reading rate focuses on improving basic reading habits. Most adults are able to increase their rate of reading without lowering comprehension. In fact, an increase in rate is typically paralleled by an increase in comprehension. Furthermore, people who increase their reading speed don't understand material better if they slow down. So, reading faster is, in many instances, a win-win situation.

What's slowing you down? A number of factors play a role in keeping the reading rate slower than it could be, including:

- reading word by word
- slow reaction time
- slow recognition and response to the material
- reading aloud
- faulty eye movements, including wrong placement on the page, faulty return sweep (movement from line to line), and irregular rhythm and movement
- habitual rereading
- inattention
- impaired retention
- lack of practice
- deliberate rate suppression out of fear of losing comprehension

MEMORY JOGGER

Play your **CARDs** right when increasing your reading rate. Remember to do these four key steps:

Correct vision problems.
Avoid rereading.
Read silently.
Develop a wider eye span.

- habitual slow reading
- poor differentiation between important aspects and those that can be safely skimmed over
- inability to remember critical details.

Preparing to increase your reading rate. Certain conditions should be met before trying to increase your reading rate:

- Have your eyes checked; slow reading is sometimes related to uncorrected vision defects. To ease eye strain and lessen eye movement while reading, hold your book 4″ to 6″ farther away from your eyes than you normally do. Be sure to hold reading material at least 15″ away from your eyes.
- Avoid sounding out words as you read. Reading silently is two to three times faster than reading aloud. Concentrate on key words and ideas rather than on whispering each word to yourself.
- Avoid rereading. Rereading is generally just a bad habit rather than a symptom of the need to improve comprehension. Many of the ideas that may need further explanation are explained later in the text. Slower readers tend to reread more often, possibly due to an inability to concentrate or a lack of confidence in their ability to comprehend the material.
- Develop a wider eye span by focusing on taking in more words on a line as you read. Most people read one word at a time, but the brain can assimilate several words at once. Developing a wider eye span helps you reduce the number of reading stops, which, in turn, yields a faster reading rate.

Adjusting your reading rate. Your reading rate shouldn't be the same for all the material you read. Adjust your reading rate according to the difficulty level and the specific purpose for reading. Use a faster rate for easy, familiar, or interesting material, and a slower rate for unfamiliar content or language. (See *Calculating average reading speed* on next page.) Keep in mind that as your vocabulary improves, so does your reading speed. The fewer stops you make to stumble over an unknown word, the faster you can move through the material.

EXERCISE YOUR MIND

Widening your eye span

Readers whose eyes take in more than one word at a time can read faster and retain just as much information as a reader whose eyes take in only one word at a time. Try this exercise to help you see the whole page rather than zooming in on single words. Perform this exercise 5 minutes per day, every day for several weeks. Use a large book when practicing.

1. Flip through the pages of the book quickly, turning them from the top with your left hand and scrolling left to right down each page with the edge of your right hand.
2. Follow your right hand down each page with your eyes, trying to see as many words as possible. Start by drifting down each page for 2 or 3 seconds, gradually reducing the time spent on each page until you can go as fast as you can turn pages.
3. Start by reading at a rate of 20 pages per minute. Slowly increase this rate over a period of 1 to 2 months to as many as 100 pages per minute.

What's your purpose?   Avoid planning to read your assignments at your maximum reading rate. Take into account those areas of the reading assignment that may be difficult to read as well as those that may be easier. Decide on your purpose in reading, and then read at a rate that best provides the level of comprehension you require.

Know when to slow down...   In general, you should slow your reading speed when you encounter:

- complex sentence or paragraph structure
- material that must be remembered in detail
- detailed or highly technical material, including complicated instructions and statements of difficult principles
- unfamiliar or unclear terminology (Try to understand the material in context, and then continue reading, returning to that section later.)
- unfamiliar or abstract concepts. (Try to internalize the information by making it applicable to your personal life.)

...and when to speed up.   In general, accelerate your reading speed when you encounter:

- simple material that contains few new ideas
- broad or generalized ideas or statements of ideas already explained

ADVICE FROM THE EXPERTS

Calculating average reading speed

Use your average reading rate when planning your reading schedule. To figure your average reading rate, perform this calculation:

- Count the total number of words in 10 lines of text. Divide this figure by 10 to get the average number of words per line.
- Count the total number of lines on a full page of text.
- Multiply the average number of words per line by the number of lines on a page. This is the *word density* of the material. Keep in mind that word density can vary from book to book.
- Read for exactly 10 minutes. (Time yourself.)
- Multiply the number of pages read in 10 minutes by the word density to get an approximate number of words read.
- Divide the total number of words read by 10 (the number of minutes read). This is your *reading rate* for this text.

Sample calculation

Here's a sample calculation of a person's average reading speed for a textbook that consists of about 125 words in 10 lines and holds 52 lines on each page.

$$\frac{125 \text{ words}}{10 \text{ lines}} = 12.5 \text{ words/line}$$

$$52 \text{ lines/page} \times 12.5 \text{ words/line} = 650 \text{ words/page}$$

$$\frac{650 \text{ words/page} \times 3.5 \text{ pages read in 10 minutes}}{10 \text{ minutes}} = 227.5 \text{ words/minute}$$

- detailed explanations and elaborations of ideas that aren't necessary for your purpose
- examples and illustrations that cover material you already understand.

So many words, so little time. Of the more than 600,000 words in the English language, 400 of them are used over and over again in most of the material you'll ever read. These 400 words, called *structure words,* make up 65% of printed works. Structure words include such words as *the, and, to, from, but,* and *however.* Even though you shouldn't completely skip words in a sentence, you shouldn't stop on structure words either. Let your eye take them in along with neighboring words to speed reading along.

Practice, practice, practice. As you practice reading faster, you'll become more adept at it. However, always read all of the words in a passage; otherwise, you may misinterpret the author's meaning or miss a relevant point. In addition, reading faster than you can understand the material can provoke frustration and anxiety.

If you're concerned that reading faster will make you miss words, remember that practice makes perfect — or at least better. You may also find it helpful to visualize yourself as an improved, faster reader. Visualizing yourself as you would like to be can help you attain your goal.

BASIC CLASSROOM SKILLS

The instructor's goal in giving a lecture is to make the content easier to understand. The instructor includes explanations and clarifies ideas and information included in your textbook. To improve your ability to retain information provided in the classroom, you'll need to take specific steps before and during class and to organize your notes and other class materials for maximum efficiency.

Preparing for Class

To prepare properly for a lecture, look at the reading assignment. Use the skimming techniques you learned at the beginning of this chapter.

First things first. Read the section headings. Then look at charts or illustrations in the chapter, and read the captions for each. Skim the main text to identify basic concepts and the most important information. Look for words emphasized in boldface or italics print.

At this point, your goal is to gain a general understanding of the content. Try not to get bogged down in difficult sections; the lecture may clarify those sections for you.

Write questions that come to mind as you read, but keep the questions brief — most of them will probably be answered during the lecture. If they aren't, you'll be better prepared to ask the instructor for clarification.

A second look. After you finish your first reading, look again at the headings and illustrations. This quick review increases your long-term memory and allows you to more effectively integrate what you learn in class with what you read before class.

CLASSROOM LEARNING

During class, pay special attention to:

- contents of handouts
- anything written on the board
- anything the instructor stresses or repeats
- the instructor's response to questions from classmates
- your own thoughts, questions, or reactions to lecture material
- anything the instructor takes a long time to explain
- anything discussed that isn't covered in the textbook, particularly the instructor's personal views
- how the instructor presents the information — for instance, whether she presents the "big picture" or the details
- the beginning and end of the lecture. Instructors commonly summarize their entire lecture during the first few minutes; in the last few minutes, they summarize major points and other important points that weren't covered earlier.

Learning from Lectures

In a lecture, communication takes place primarily between the instructor and the students. How well you listen to your instructor depends on your background knowledge, the difficulty of the concepts being covered, and your purpose for listening. (See *Levels of listening,* page 36.)

How well you listen may also be affected by the instructor's teaching style. For most students, listening to lectures is a passive activity — but it doesn't have to be. Try to stay involved in the lecture, thinking of questions as the speaker lectures. Jot down a key word or two about each question in the margin of your notes. Then, when the instructor asks whether anyone has questions, refer to your notes to ask the questions you raised earlier.

Slow down — you move too fast! When the instructor seems to run through a lecture quickly, covering a lot of material in a limited time, it may be wise to interrupt and ask for clarification, particularly if you familiarized yourself with the material beforehand but still don't understand it. When asking for clarification, be as specific as possible. Try to show that you understood some of what was said by rephrasing the information in your own words.

Pick up the pace. Daydreaming is more likely to be a problem when a class is slow. To stave off boredom and loss of concentration, try to rephrase, repeat, and apply what has

LEVELS OF LISTENING

Listening occurs on several levels, depending on the effort expended by the listener. This chart describes the different levels of listening.

Level	Description
Reception	Hearing without thought
Attention	Listening passively; no effort to understand what's being said
Definition	Lowest level of active listening; giving meaning to isolated facts and details; no overall organizational plan
Integration	Relating new information to old learning
Interpretation	Synthesizing information; putting information into your own words
Implication	Drawing conclusions
Application	Applying information to personal experience; using information in new situations
Evaluation	Judging information in terms of accuracy and relevance

been said. Use slow parts of the class to review material in your head. Review concepts and definitions that the instructor has introduced and try rephrasing them in your own words. Then repeat new phrases and definitions to yourself and try to memorize them. Or, try to anticipate the instructor's next move. This keeps you involved in the class and trains you to follow the instructor's thought processes, which helps you to perform better on assignments.

In too deep?   If you aren't understanding the material well, you may not have the background that other students in the class have. The feeling of being lost usually comes from the lack of a sufficient foundation of knowledge in a particular area. In each class, the instructor assumes a certain amount of knowledge on the part of the students, and tries to build on that knowledge.

If that foundation doesn't exist, it's easy to tune out what the instructor is saying. Instead of tuning out the instructor, focus on tuning in even more carefully. Keep taking notes even though you don't comprehend everything. Jot down words and phrases that you don't understand. Look them up right after the class, or ask the instructor for clarification.

Keeping the lines open.   Maintaining communication between you and your instructor can help her clarify points of misunderstanding. In addition, your respectful feedback can help reinforce the instructor's method or point out places a lecture may be weak.

If it's a bore, try not to snore.   Contrary to popular opinion, your instructor is actually a human being! She may be brilliant in her field, but that's no guarantee that she's equally brilliant at communicating all the facts, ideas, and concepts she wants her students to learn.

You may need to compensate for a less effective speaker by defining, integrating, and interpreting information and drawing

conclusions for yourself. Finding ways to apply information and judge its value then becomes one of your primary jobs.

In a lecture, the speaker controls what information is conveyed to the class. Your job is to determine what the instructor expects and to keep that purpose in mind while listening and reacting to the lecture. To help you maintain active listening during a lecture, follow these steps:

- keep your purpose for listening in mind
- pay careful attention to the instructor's introductory and summary statements, which usually state main points.
- continue to take notes
- sit comfortably erect to convey your interest and stave off sleepiness
- keep your eyes on the instructor
- concentrate on what the instructor is saying to ignore external distractions and eliminate internal ones
- question the material
- listen for transition words that signal main points.
- mark words or references you don't understand for later investigation
- adjust your listening and note-taking pace to the lecture
- avoid being a distraction yourself by sitting still and remaining silent.

Active listening

Active listening occurs when you consciously think about how you're listening and use strategies to improve and maximize your listening skills. To improve your active listening skills, you need to:

- avoid behaviors that can interfere with listening
- recognize main ideas
- use transition cues effectively
- differentiate more important information from less important information.

OVERCOMING OBSTACLES

Compensating for an ineffective lecturer

Does this student's problem sound familiar? Read and learn.

Question

I'm taking a course, and the instructor isn't a very good lecturer. I'm having a hard time understanding, and I'm getting frustrated. Do you have any tips?

If your instructor fails to do this	Then you do this
Explain goals of the lecture	Use your text and syllabus to set objectives.
Review previous lecture material before beginning a new lecture	Set aside time before each class to review notes.
State main ideas in an introduction and summary of the lecture	Write short summaries of the day's lecture immediately after class.
Provide an outline of the lecture	Preview assigned readings before class, or outline notes after class.
Provide "wait time" for writing notes	Politely ask the instructor to repeat information or to speak more slowly.
Speak clearly with appropriate volume	Politely ask the instructor to repeat information or to speak louder, or move closer to her.
Answer questions without sarcasm	Refrain from taking comments personally.
Stay on topic	Discover how anecdotes relate to the topic, or use anecdotes as a memory cue.

Words of wisdom

Your main task when faced with any lecturer is to get the most out of the class regardless of the lecturer's effectiveness. When a lecturer isn't effective, you can still obtain the knowledge you need by following a few guidelines. This chart explains what to do when an instructor falls short of expectations.

If your instructor fails to do this	Then you do this
Refrain from reading directly from the text	Mark passages in text as the instructor reads, or summarize or outline these passages in the text margin.
Emphasize main points	Supplement lectures through text previews and reading.
Use transition words	Supplement notes with terms listed in the text, and highlight information contained in the lecture.
Give examples to illustrate difficult ideas	Ask the instructor for a clarifying example, discuss idea with other students, or create an example yourself.
Write important words, dates, and other key information on the board	Use the text glossary or a dictionary.
Define important terms	Relate information to what you know about the topic, or create a clarifying example for yourself.

Do not disturb. A number of behaviors can interfere with your understanding when listening to a lecturer or other speaker, including:

- allowing yourself to be distracted
- zoning out when difficult material is presented
- becoming overexcited by something in the lecture
- considering the subject uninteresting
- criticizing the speaker's delivery or mannerisms
- daydreaming
- faking attentiveness
- letting emotion-laden words arouse personal antagonism
- listening primarily for facts instead of ideas
- trying to outline everything.

Heads up! Every lecture is structured to center around main ideas. This structure leads to certain patterns that vary with the instructor's purposes. Be aware that in a lecture an instructor may:

- introduce new topics or summarize information
- list or rank details
- present opposing sides of an issue
- identify causes and effects or problems and solutions
- discuss concepts using supporting details.

Take the hint. Signal words and other verbal markers help you identify and anticipate the flow of a lecture. Becoming familiar with *transition words* helps you organize lecture notes and listen more actively. For example, the word *conversely* probably indicates that the lecturer is about to present an opposing point of view. *Therefore* means the lecturer is summing up cause and effect. *Finally* means the instructor is getting to the end of her point or series of points.

Identifying important information.   Your ability to identify important information contributes to your ability to become a more active listener. Although instructors emphasize main points differently, they have similar ways of conveying important information. Some instructors, for instance, write key information on the board or present the information using a PowerPoint slide show. PowerPoint presentations allow instructors to present the information visually with an accompanying outline for note-taking.

Other instructors outline the entire lecture on the board before class begins. Some write key points or terms on the board as they lecture.

Be a copycat.   Copying outlines or lists of terms from the board aids learning in three ways. First, you learn as you write. Copying the outline also provides a nutshell view of the lecture's content and serves as a guide for later study.

Instructors also convey information by:

- pausing, which gives you more time to take comprehensive notes
- repeating information
- changing the tone or volume of their voices to make a point
- telling the class what's worth remembering for a test
- using body language (If your instructor gestures to stress a point, it's often an essential point for you to understand)
- using visual aids (The use of films, overhead transparencies, videotapes, and other audiovisual materials signals important topics)
- referring to specific text pages (Information an instructor knows by page number is worth noting and remembering.)

Listen with LISAN.   Active listening is the key to taking notes during a lecture. The *LISAN method* of taking notes encourages active listening and can improve understanding and retention. The LISAN method involves these guidelines:

- **L**ead; don't follow. Anticipate what the instructor is going to say.
- **I**deas. What's the main idea?
- **S**ignal words. Listen for words that indicate the direction the instructor is taking.
- **A**ctively listen. Ask questions, be prepared.
- **N**ote-taking. Write down key points; be selective.

DEVELOPING LEARNING SKILLS

You can also develop your learning skills as you listen. Developing these skills involves memorizing, applying knowl-

edge, interpreting information, and recognizing shifts in teaching styles.

Is it live, or is it memorized?   Introductory courses tend to demand a lot of memorization. Stay alert for information you should commit to memory. Such pieces of information as phrases, dates, and diagrams written on the board are probably items that the instructor expects you to remember. If the instructor takes the time to write a definition or prepare a handout or slide, that means the information is important and should be remembered. If the instructor speaks more slowly than usual or repeats information, she's probably giving you time to take notes on the material.

How can I apply it? Let me count the ways.   Many instructors arrange their classes and assignments to encourage you to apply the information they provide to practical situations. Pay attention to how the instructor structures the class. For instance, if the instructor gives written assignments on the material, you'll need to show in writing how well you can apply your new knowledge.

Does the instructor spend class time working through problems or cases? If so, you'll probably be expected to know how to work through such problems on a test. Does the instructor ask students to solve problems at the board? If so, expect to be asked to demonstrate your new knowledge in a practical situation.

Hmmm, how should I interpret that?   Many advanced science and health classes require that students use their interpretative skills. The instructor tries to foster development of those skills by asking a lot of general questions and offering guidance. In these kinds of classes, the students do most of the talking, and the assignments tend to consist primarily of reading and observing.

Heed the clues.   Be on the lookout for shifts in teaching style. For example, if an instructor stops a class discussion to write dates on the board, she has switched from an interpretive mode to a memorization mode. Write down the dates. Some instructors give obvious clues to what's important to study — for example, by saying something as clear and simple as "This is important."

Psychology 101.   Other clues aren't as obvious. Look for patterns in behavior, such as an instructor who gets up and paces whenever she begins warming up to an important point. The more attuned you are to the instructor's behaviors, the more knowledge you can gain from the material being presented.

Computer-assisted Instruction

Learning by computer, or *computer-assisted instruction (CAI)*, has become popular in the last few years to help fulfill a variety of educational goals. The most effective CAI programs require only basic computer skills. Many CAI applications combine a variety of formats to offer the student various ways to learn. Common CAI formats include:

- drill and practice
- tutorial
- simulation
- computer-managed instruction
- problem solving.

Repeat and improve.   *Drill-and-practice software* allows learners to master facts, relationships, problems, and vocabulary. The software usually offers groups of questions with similar content, which allows the student to hone specific skills. The software may be designed to offer more difficult questions as the student progresses through the application.

Tutor in a box.   *Tutorial software* aims to teach concepts rather than allow the practice of individual skills. This software presents concepts in several formats, including text and images, and commonly incorporates feedback to student responses. Tutorials may employ pretesting or posttesting to instruct students at the appropriate teaching level.

Simulated scenarios.   A *simulation* is a computer-generated visual and auditory experience. Computer simulations allow students to experience real-life events in the safety of the classroom. Because simulations usually demand decision-making skills, the student becomes directly involved in the outcomes.

Computer in charge.   *Computer-managed instruction* assesses the knowledge level and educational goals of students. Through computerized testing, this software can help instructors assess students and design a curriculum to fit students' needs.

Time to apply.   *Problem-solving software* is useful after students become familiar with basic necessary concepts. Problem-solving software can then help students use those concepts to solve difficult problems and advance their level of thinking.

Organizing Lecture Content

Lectures can be *text-dependent*, meaning that they follow the organization of the text closely, or *text-independent*, in which other media are used to enhance the delivery of information.

Lectures by the book.   During a text-dependent lecture, write notes and instructions emphasized during the lecture directly in your textbook, highlighting or underlining as the instructor speaks. This is an especially helpful technique if you read the text before class. You can also cross out information your instructor says is unnecessary and note important information in the margins of the chapter and in your notebook.

Working without backup.   When lectures are independent of the text, they're based on what the instructor thinks is most important about the topic. In those instances, your responsibility for taking notes increases. Because you don't have the text to use as a backup source, review or outline the lecture soon after class to give it some form of organization. Discuss your notes with other students, or augment the lecture with supplemental reading. Set some study objectives to help you create a purpose for learning and increase your recall.

Stimulating the senses.   Instructors use a variety of media — handouts, illustrations, PowerPoint presentations, videos or DVDs, models, and more — to stimulate students' senses during lectures. Media and advancing technology offer visually interesting ways to add knowledge and information, arouse emotion or interest, and increase skills and performance.

When an instructor creates or chooses the medium to be used, the information it contains tends to be course-specific and corresponds closely to what the instructor expects you to know.

Your responsibility is to recognize your instructor's purposes for using each particular medium, and judge its worth in meeting your learning needs. For example, if you have extensive knowledge of a topic, a film about that topic may serve only as a review. If the topic is new to you, the same film may be aimed at building background knowledge.

Student-teacher Conferences

Whenever you have questions about the content discussed in class, the instructor's expectations of you as a learner, or other important aspects of a course, you may want to set up a conference with the instructor. Before the conference, make sure you have a specific topic of discussion in mind. Your first test may make an ideal subject, particularly if you feel as if you're struggling with the course material.

Having a conference with your instructor helps you understand the instructor better. It also lets you demonstrate your interest in improving your performance. Even if you think you're doing well in a class, meeting with the instructor can help ensure that your perception is accurate, and can help you establish rapport.

EFFECTIVE NOTE-TAKING SKILLS

Taking notes may be the most crucial part of active listening during lectures. In your effort to capture everything significant said by the instructor, you'll not only need to use all of your listening ability and concentration during the lecture, but you'll also need a good system for recording what was said. Taking effective notes involves understanding why you take notes in the first place and following some practical guidelines for taking them.

Usefulness of Notes

Notes commonly trigger your memory of the lecture or the text. In general, students who review notes achieve more than those who don't. Researchers have found that if important information was contained in notes, students tended to remember that information 34% of the time. Information not found in notes was remembered only 5% of the time. Even if you understand your instructor's lecture fully and have no questions, take notes anyway. Later, you'll want to know what the instructor thought was important, and you'll use the notes to refresh your memory.

Listen up!   Taking notes also makes you pay more attention to the new material, thereby allowing you to become more familiar with it. Note-taking requires more effort than reading and therefore requires you to take an active role in class. By paraphrasing and condensing information as you take notes, you show your understanding of the information and your ability to relate the information to your background knowledge.

Tips for Taking Notes

To take effective notes, you'll need to use your own form of note-taking shorthand, organize your notes after class, keep your notes personal, avoid using a tape recorder, and employ other notetaking strategies.

Shrthnd spds note tkng.   Taking notes rapidly involves doing as little writing as possible while capturing all of the facts, principles, and ideas expressed by the lecturer. Fast note-taking can be enhanced by:

- abbreviating common words consistently (See *Common note-taking abbreviations and symbols*)
- leaving out conjunctions, prepositions, and other words not essential to understanding a thought
- thinking before you write (but without thinking so long that you fall behind)
- creating a shorthand word or symbol for something used repeatedly in a lecture
- marking for emphasis, such as through the use of asterisks, exclamation points, underlining, color coding, or highlighting
- using shapes or varying handwriting size to stay organized (You're more likely to recall information supplemented with visual clues, such as geometric shapes or different-sized handwriting.)

Postclass organization.   After class, organize your notes. Write down the date at the beginning of each lecture, and number the pages so you can keep track of what you're doing. Make a note of your assignments, what they involve, and when they're due.

Keep 'em personal.   The most effective notes are personal, reflecting the note-taker's background knowledge and understanding. Borrowed or bought notes require no effort or action on the part of the learner; thus they do little to help the student learn. To get the most out of notes for a class, make sure you attend the class yourself and take your own notes.

Borrowed notes do have a place, however, when they're all that's available. If you've been absent from class, you may have no choice but to borrow someone else's notes.

Taping is a sticky business.   Tape-recording a lecture can be useful, but only if you also take notes during the lecture, allowing the taped material to pick up any important points you miss. If you can't attend a class, asking a classmate to audiotape the class may prove the next-best thing to being there. Otherwise, using a tape recorder to record lectures is probably not a good idea. Here's why:

- listening to the tape takes as long as, if not longer than, listening to the lecture itself
- to record the main ideas and highlights of the lecture, you have to make notes from the tape, which takes even longer
- taped material doesn't reflect diagrams or additional written material the instructor may have used during the class
- technical difficulties, such as a flawed tape or a dead battery, sometimes arise, causing you to miss part or all of a lecture
- some instructors may not allow tape-recorder use. Ask the instructor before class whether it's permissible to record a lecture.

Other Note-taking Strategies

Most students take reasonably good notes but then don't use them properly. They tend to wait until just before an examination to review their notes; by then, the notes have lost much of their meaning. Remember that active listening and note-taking go hand in hand. To help you keep your notes specific, organized, and comprehensive, follow these pointers:

- even if you disagree with a point being made by the instructor, write it down
- raise questions whenever appropriate
- develop and use a standard method of note-taking, including punctuation and abbreviations
- keep notes in a large, loose-leaf binder, which allows you to more easily use an outline form for your notes. The binder also allows you to reorganize your notes easily when preparing for a test or quiz (See *Cornell system of note-taking*)
- leave a few spaces blank as the lecture progresses, so that additional points can be filled in later.

MEMORY JOGGER

Remember the mnemonic **CATTLE** when taking effective notes:

Create a shorthand for repeated words.
Abbreviate common words.
Think before writing.
Try using shapes or varying handwriting.
Leave out unessential words.
Emphasize important words or topics.

ADVICE FROM THE EXPERTS

Common note-taking abbreviations and symbols

To speed note taking, get in the habit of using abbreviations and symbols. This chart lists common abbreviations and symbols used for taking notes.

Abbreviations		Symbols	
abt	about	®	right
b/c	because	Ⓛ	left
dx	diagnose or diagnosis	↑	increase, increased, or increasing
e.g.	for example	↓	decrease, decreased, or decreasing
h/a	headache	→	leads to or causes
hx	history	>	more than
imp	important	<	less than
incl	including	Δ	change
pt	patient	~	about, approximately
px	physical	+	and, in addition
rx	treat or treatment	#	pounds or number
s/e	side effects	☆	important or stressed by instructor
s/s	signs and symptoms	p̄	after
w/	with	ā	before
w/o	without	−	negative
		c̄	with
		s̄	without

- don't write down every word the lecturer says. Spend more time listening; try to write down the main points, but know that sometimes it's more important to think than to write
- listen for transition cues, such as a change in vocal inflection, that signify important points or a transition from one point to the next
- make your original notes legible enough for you to read later
- copy everything your instructor writes on the board. You may not be able to integrate the information with your lecture notes, but you'll have the information in your notes for later referral
- sit at the front of the class, where there are fewer distractions.

That's entertainment.   Taking notes from films, slides, or television differs from traditional note-taking because these types of media are associated with entertainment. As a result, you may not realize the importance of the information they provide. Furthermore, these types of media are usually shown in a darkened room, which is hardly conducive to note-taking.

The fast pace of these formats is another stumbling block to note-taking. A film or television show doesn't provide many pauses for taking notes. For this reason, taking notes immediately after the presentation is sometimes the best alternative for recording new information. If a presentation was on film or slides, ask whether you can watch the presentation again or check to see if the instructor puts the presentation on reserve in the library.

Take a note on note-taking outlines.   Making a *note-taking outline* before the lecture gives you a basis for understanding the lecture and a chance to locate important terms, concepts, and dates beforehand. To construct a note-taking outline, divide each page of notes vertically into two sections, with one-third of the space to the left and two-thirds to the right. Then record the chapter title and major and minor headings on the left side, estimating the amount of space that each section may require.

When previewing the material, survey the physical characteristics of the chapter, including length, text structure, visual aids, and term identification. Read the chapter introduction or first paragraph. Survey graphs, maps, charts, and diagrams. Look for such typographic aids as **boldface,** underlining, and *italics,* used to highlight important new terms or ideas. Record the terms in the outline. Lastly, read the last paragraph or summary, which generally reviews the main points or conclusions of the chapter.

OVERCOMING OBSTACLES

Cornell system of note-taking

Are your notes a mess like this student's? Look over her shoulder for some words of wisdom.

Question

My instructor doesn't use a PowerPoint slide show to present new information. After class, I look at my notes and they're a mess. How can I take better notes?

Words of wisdom

The *Cornell system* can help you develop organized notes. Before the lecture, obtain a large, loose-leaf binder. Use only one side of the paper. Divide your paper as shown in the illustration at right.

During the lecture

Use the "Notes" area on the right side of the page to take notes in paragraph form. Capture general ideas, not illustrative ideas. Skip a line to show the end of an idea or thought. Use abbreviations whenever possible to save time. Write legibly.

After the lecture

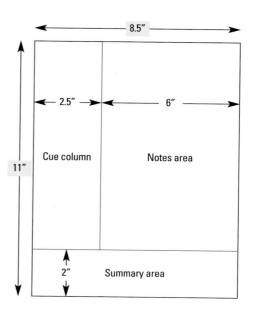

Read through your notes and make them more legible as needed. Use the "Cue" column to jot down ideas or key words that highlight the main aspects of the lecture. Cover the "Notes" area with a blank piece of paper and describe the general ideas and concepts of the lecture using the notes in the "Cue" column. Use the "Summary" area to summarize your notes in one or two sentences.

I'll note it myyyy way.   Develop a system for taking notes that best fits your learning style and course content. Date each day's notes to serve as a reference point if you need to compare notes with someone else's or ask your instructor for clarification. If you're absent, the missing dates identify which notes you need. Other steps to personalizing your notes include:

- keeping your notes together in a notebook, preferably one with pockets that can be used to save class handouts
- bringing all necessary note-taking materials to each class
- knowing how to interpret your own shorthand
- grouping and labeling information to aid recall
- writing down facts and diagrams written on the board
- leaving room in your notes to fill in later
- skipping lines to separate important groups of ideas and writing on only one side of the paper, both of which will make it easier to read your notes later
- keeping your notes neat and your writing legible so you can read your own writing later
- organizing your notes after class
- using color coding to mark important ideas and concepts
- reading over your notes as soon as possible after class, while the material is still fresh in your mind, and correcting your notes as needed

- refraining from rewriting the text verbatim. If the instructor refers to a specific text page, go to the book and mark the information there. Remember to jot the page number in your notes and to write a brief summary later.

How much is enough?   How many notes are enough? That depends on your own confidence and your instructor's teaching style. Notes must be accurate and useful for refreshing your memory on important points.

You're probably making too few notes if you simply write down a list of facts without tying them together. Conversely, if you spend all your time writing notes, you don't have time to think about or question the material. Furthermore, you may miss an important point while writing down something less significant. Try to find an effective medium.

Style is everything.   Be flexible enough to adapt your note-taking style to best fit the style of the instructor. One format for note-taking may work well for one instructor but not for another. Some possible note formats follow:

- *Outline.* If the lecture is highly organized, an outline will probably work well. Mark main section headings with uppercase roman numerals. Mark important points under each section with capital letters and supporting points under the important points with Arabic (regular) numerals. Subordinate sets of ideas can be indented and bulleted beneath the preceding higher level.

- *Thin-fat columns.* On your note paper, draw one thin column and one fat column. Use the thin column to keep track of extra notes to yourself, such as "See page 53 of text" or "Test on Tuesday." Also use this column for important facts to remember. Use the fat column to record lecture notes.
- *Equal columns.* Divide your note paper into two equal columns when comparing two concepts. Put notes about one concept on one side and notes about the other on the opposite side. You'll then have information about both concepts in addition to a visual way to compare and contrast the concepts.
- *Idea tree.* Start with the main idea circled in the center of the writing, and then branch off facts like branches from the tree. Branch off subordinate ideas like twigs branching off of larger branches. This format is also called *concept mapping.*

Reviewing Notes

After class, review your notes for clarity. Rewrite anything you think you may not be able to read later, particularly if you've used many abbreviations in your notes. Finish up open-ended notes that you didn't finish before moving on to the next topic.

Reviewing class notes can be particularly important after a disorganized lecture or one in which the instructor stated certain intentions at the beginning of the lecture but never fulfilled them. Reviewing these notes may take time and research because you may need to fill in blank spots with material from the textbook.

Reviewing your notes within 24 hours after taking them can help establish the information in your memory. If you don't look over your notes within a day, they may not make sense anymore. In addition, read your notes again before the next class to give yourself a sense of continuity.

TAKE A BREAK!

Term searching

Take a break from your reading material and find these 20 terms that help your reading and classroom strategies. Hint: Go up, down, across, and diagonal! The answers are on the next page.

- Abbreviate
- Clarity
- Classroom
- Columns
- Comprehension
- Dictionary
- Eye span
- Lectures
- Listening
- Notes
- Outline
- Prepare
- Rapid eye movement
- Reading
- Review
- Shorthand
- Skimming
- Sweeping
- System
- Textbook

Answer Key

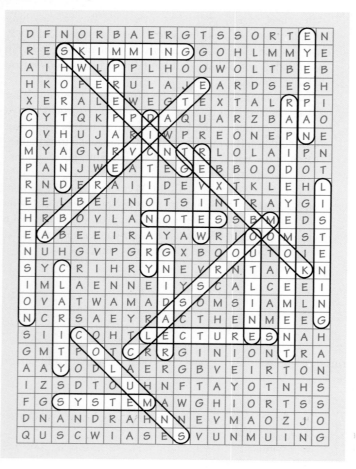

D	F	N	O	R	B	A	E	R	G	T	S	S	O	R	T	E	N
R	E	S	K	I	M	M	I	N	G	G	O	H	L	M	M	Y	E
A	I	H	W	L	P	P	L	H	O	O	W	O	L	T	B	E	B
H	K	O	F	E	R	U	L	A	J	E	A	R	D	S	E	S	H
X	E	R	A	L	E	W	E	G	T	E	X	T	A	L	R	P	I
C	Y	T	Q	K	P	P	D	A	Q	U	A	R	Z	B	A	A	O
O	V	H	U	J	A	R	I	W	P	R	E	O	N	E	P	N	E
M	Y	A	G	Y	R	V	C	N	T	R	L	O	L	A	I	P	N
P	A	N	J	W	E	A	T	E	G	E	B	B	O	O	D	O	T
R	N	D	E	R	A	I	I	D	E	V	X	T	K	L	E	H	L
E	E	L	B	E	I	N	O	T	S	I	N	T	R	A	Y	G	I
H	R	B	O	V	L	A	N	O	T	E	S	S	B	M	E	D	S
E	A	B	E	E	I	R	A	Y	A	W	R	I	O	O	M	S	T
N	U	H	G	V	P	G	R	G	X	B	O	O	U	T	O	I	E
S	Y	C	R	I	H	R	Y	N	E	V	R	N	T	A	V	K	N
I	M	L	A	E	N	N	E	I	Y	S	C	A	L	C	E	E	I
O	V	A	T	W	A	M	A	D	S	O	M	S	I	A	M	L	N
N	C	R	S	A	E	Y	R	A	C	T	H	E	N	M	E	E	G
S	I	I	C	O	H	T	L	E	C	T	U	R	E	S	N	A	H
G	M	T	P	O	T	C	R	R	G	I	N	I	O	N	T	R	A
A	A	Y	O	D	L	A	E	R	G	B	V	E	I	R	T	O	N
I	Z	S	D	T	O	U	H	N	F	T	A	Y	O	T	N	H	S
F	G	S	Y	S	T	E	M	A	W	G	H	I	O	R	T	S	S
D	N	A	N	D	R	A	H	N	N	E	V	M	A	O	Z	J	O
Q	U	S	C	W	I	A	S	E	S	V	U	N	M	U	I	N	G

Tips on Test-Taking

CHAPTER OBJECTIVES

In this chapter, you'll learn:

1. How to prepare mentally for a test, including how to construct a study plan, relax, and develop a positive attitude.
2. How to prepare physically for a test.
3. How objective examinations focus on recalling specific information.
4. How subjective examinations focus on your ability to explain ideas.
5. How learning about the results of a test can help you prepare for future tests.

PREPARING FOR A TEST

Being a top test-taker demands preparation. The first step in that preparation is to recognize elements of test-related anxiety that may be preventing you from reaching your optimum performance level. After you've identified test anxiety elements, you can prepare your mind and body for the test.

Recognizing Test Anxiety

Test anxiety comes in many forms and may occur before the test or during the test itself. Types of test anxiety include:

- freezing up, in which your brain doesn't register the meaning of questions or you have to read test questions several times to comprehend them
- panicking about a difficult question or the thought of time running out
- worrying about the test
- being easily distracted, or spending time daydreaming about ways to escape rather than completing the test itself
- feeling nervous, which can prevent you from putting in the time necessary to succeed
- experiencing physical effects, such as nausea, muscle tension, headache, and sweating
- feeling a lack of interest in the test or topic. Some students find it easier not to care than to face their anxiety about performing well.

A little is OK. Feeling slightly anxious — but not *too* anxious — can improve your mental clarity and provide greater focus. Complacency, on the other hand, is more likely to result in falling short of your goals. If you find that you're consistently underperforming or feeling the physical effects of test anxiety — such as exhaustion, vague discomfort, and an inability to remember information — test anxiety may be getting the best of you.

Preparing the Mind

Most successful students use a combination of techniques to prepare themselves mentally to perform well on tests. To cope with test anxiety, you need to study well, relax, stay positive, and take well-planned breaks.

Anxiety antidote. Studying well can be the best antidote for test anxiety. The feeling of accomplishment that comes with an effective study regimen can banish many of the fears that cause test anxiety.

I've got rhythm, I've got clarity. Relaxation and other stress-reduction techniques can reduce test anxiety and give you the clarity of mind necessary to study effectively. Rhythmic breathing and meditation are two of the many techniques you may consider to reduce test anxiety.

Accentuate the positive. Test anxiety commonly stems from low self-esteem. Make an effort to think positively about the test experience. Tell yourself, "I can do it!" You'll be amazed how often positive results follow positive thinking.

Take a breather! Mild, short-term test anxiety can commonly be reduced by taking a short break. If you feel anxious during a test, sharpen your pencil or get a drink of water. If you feel anxious while studying, give yourself a quick break away from studying. Sometimes anxiety is your body's way of saying, "I need a few minutes off."

Preparing the Body

Many students, even those with rigorous study habits, neglect their bodies when preparing for a test. Maximum test performance depends on meeting the need for proper rest, nutrition, and overall health. Physical preparedness is basic to improving your test-taking skills.

R and R. Rest and relaxation can overcome fatigue after intense mental or physical exertion. You can accomplish more when you feel rested and relaxed than when you're fatigued. To make sure you get enough rest and relaxation:

- get a sufficient amount of sleep
- change activities periodically
- exercise regularly
- relax periodically by watching television, listening to music, talking to friends, or reading a book (other than your textbook).

Mom was right! Your posture during studying and examinations can affect your mood. Slouching not only hurts your back but also can make you feel sluggish and uninterested. Maintain good posture, and watch your focus improve.

Feed your brain. Because nutrition affects your physical well-being, it also affects your study habits and test-taking skills. Because class time, work time, and study time may conflict with eating on a regular schedule, counterbalance odd mealtimes with nutritious snacks or meals. Avoid excessive intake of caffeine or sugar, because these substances will cause your energy level to peak and trough.

Fever procedure. Even when you're in strong physical condition, you may become too ill to study properly to take a test. Don't neglect symptoms of illness in favor of studying for an upcoming test; you'll most likely feel ill during the test and, as a result, perform poorly. If you become ill, contact the instructor as soon as possible. This communicates your concern about missing the test and helps alleviate your own anxiety about missing it. Follow all of your doctor's guidelines for getting well again, including taking medications as prescribed and resting as much as the doctor advises.

Healthy habits. When a test is coming up, don't do anything that will upset your sense of normalcy. If you normally walk 30 minutes each day after lunch, don't jog during that time to relieve stress; you'll probably end up being sore, tired, *and* stressed. If you normally sleep 8 hours per night, avoid pulling an all-nighter. You may end up throwing off your sleep pattern and becoming sleep-deprived — not a healthy state for your brain just before a test.

PLANNING FOR A TEST

Successful students think about upcoming tests long before the day of the examination. They learn all they can about the test itself and then construct their study time accordingly.

Learning About the Test

Before studying for a test, find out what kind of test it's going to be. If you know what kind of test to expect, your studying time will be more focused. For *objective tests* (short-answer, sentence-completion, multiple-choice, matching, and true-false tests), focus your studying on knowing facts and details and being able to recognize related material. For *essay* or *oral tests,* preparation includes being able to argue persuasively about several general topics and being able to back up those arguments with details.

In any case, you'll need to find out key pieces of information about the test to prepare properly, including facts about the test format and objectives, the availability of past tests, and the overall structure of the class.

Size it up. To find out about a test, ask the instructor. Many instructors explain the format of their tests to the whole class. Others inform only those students who ask these questions. For the latter instructors especially, make sure to ask about test format. When faced with an upcoming test, ask:

- Will the test be comprehensive, or will it cover certain chapters only? (See *That wasn't in the book.*)
- How many questions will it contain?
- How will the questions be weighted?
- Will it be subjective or objective?
- Will it require that I apply knowledge or just know facts?
- How important is this test to my final grade?
- What can I bring to the test? Will calculators be allowed? Will formulas be supplied?
- Who is making the test?
- Who will grade the test?
- Will it be a special type of examination, such as a take-home test or an open-book test?

Look to the past. If you've previously taken tests in this course, you may already have an idea of what the upcoming test will be like. Past experience may tell you that the previous test focused on details rather than principles or that it contained an occasional "trick" question.

If this is your first test in the course, check for copies of past examinations. These may be available from the instructor

---

OVERCOMING OBSTACLES

That wasn't in the book

Are you having trouble deciding what to study? Heed the advice that this student receives.

Question
It seems that there's always something on the test that wasn't covered in the textbook. So how do I prepare for the test?

Words of wisdom
Some instructors give their lecture material more weight than textbook material when composing test questions. Don't assume that a test will cover mostly information found in the textbook. Attempt to get the most from your lecture notes by considering these guidelines:

- listen carefully to the instructor and take frequent notes
- try to identify what the instructor thinks is important, especially when she repeats or emphasizes information
- play an active role by digging deep into each lecture and applying the information to a real-life situation
- attend all lectures. If missing a lecture can't be avoided, get the class notes or PowerPoint presentation from a classmate
- sit in the front two or three rows so you can see and hear well.

---

or may be on file with the instructor's department or college library. Study the examinations for ideas about what to expect, but don't expect identical questions or directions.

Look to the class. The class structure can also yield clues about an upcoming test. Which topics have been singled out for greater emphasis or more detailed explanation? Does the instructor emphasize details or global ideas? Does she refer to the book often, or do her lectures tend to stray from, or greatly enhance, the textbook material?

Some instructors give optional review sessions before an examination. In such a case, attend the session and be prepared. Write down questions you want to ask before the examination. If you have a study guide that accompanies your textbook, use these questions and activities to study. Some test questions may be directly taken from the study guide.

Creating a Study Plan

Get started early when studying for an upcoming test. Most instructors explain at the beginning of the semester when tests will be administered. Note test dates in your semester calendar. If the dates haven't been announced, ask the instructor for approximate dates of the examinations.

What, where, when? Create an organized, continuous study plan. Each day, plan how much time you'll devote to studying, what time of day you'll study, and where you'll study. If you plan to study with a partner, set up the meeting times early. Plan enough time to review lecture notes several times and to rehearse the information.

Give yourself at least a week to study for an examination. Studying every day of the week before a test keeps the material fresh and clear in your mind. Reviewing your notes after each class is recommended for helping you understand and keep up with the material but, when preparing for a test, more intense review is also needed.

Pop goes the pop quiz. Sometimes instructors will give an unannounced in-class quiz. In case of a pop quiz, you'll be glad you reviewed material covered in each class.

Let's get together. Gather review materials together. Compile information about the main terms, facts, concepts, themes, problems, questions, and issues stressed in the lectures. The most likely sources for this information include course notes and the textbook.

The textbook's index and glossary are valuable resources for finding important topics and definitions of key terms. Supplementary reading and handouts supplied by the instructor should also be available for review. Keep in mind that material assigned by the instructor — but not discussed in class — may appear on the test in addition to information covered in class.

Once is never enough! When you begin reviewing your class notes in preparation for an examination, make sure to go over your notes and reading materials more than once. Don't expect to remember everything about a topic in one reading.

The first pass at the material serves to refresh your recall of the information and lay a foundation for subsequent passes. Each review becomes easier than the last because the information is fresh and you can anticipate the next topic or sequence of ideas. Take a break between review sessions to let your brain ponder relationships within the material.

Legal cheat sheets. Condense your notes to a one-page summary sheet. Then reconstruct the notes from memory, picturing the placement of notes on the page. Gain command of the material by reciting details. Using these review techniques for various types of tests will help boost your memory:

- for math or science testing, drill yourself by rewriting equations and graphs. Practice writing mathematical symbols so you can reproduce them easily. Practice solving sample problems. If you have particular trouble with certain mathematical expressions or graphs, write them out separately and keep them with you to look at from time to time

- for short-answer tests, make a list of important terms and write the definition of each. Think of an example for each term
- for essay questions, look at old essay assignments and examinations. Choose a topic that relates to what you've been learning in class. Write an outline and thesis statement; then flesh out the essay, giving yourself as much time as you would have for a real examination.

Dress rehearsal. For every test, try to compile a simulated test based on material from your instructor or review questions in your textbook. Administer the test under testlike conditions, in a quiet room where you will not be disturbed or distracted, allowing yourself the length of time alloted for the actual test. This dress rehearsal will familiarize you with the testing conditions and may alleviate some of your anxiety about facing an unfamiliar situation.

Forming a Study Group

Many students find that studying in a group setting helps in reviewing and learning class content — especially for difficult subject matters. Teaching is a good way to learn. Explaining the material to another student not only helps that student, but also gives the person explaining the information an effective way to review the material. A study group is as productive and successful as the group wishes to make it, and following some guidelines will help to ensure its success.

It isn't a party. Use caution when joining or forming a study group. It helps to review the material with others and hear their interpretation of material, but the membership and format of the group need to be conducive to learning. The size of the group is important; four or five members is best. A group that's too big can easily break into smaller groups to discuss different topics and will likely turn into a loud get-together.

Keep your eye on the prize. The members must be committed to learning the material and contributing to discussions to help the group accomplish the task at hand. The members must be compatible and able to put aside differences and concentrate on the work. They must also be reliable and punctual, and be available to attend most of the study meetings.

It helps to assign a time-keeper and a gate-keeper for the study sessions. The time-keeper can alert group members when they need to move on to a different topic. The gate-keeper can help the group stay focused on the subject and keep each meeting from becoming a visiting session.

Come to the group meeting prepared to study and with a basic understanding of the material to be covered. Don't expect the group members to do all the studying for you. Come prepared to explain the material in your own words. If you're having a hard time understanding parts of the material, write down specific questions to ask the group.

Test Day

On the day of the test, you can take several actions to make sure you do your best on the examination, including:

- resting
- eating small meals
- avoiding caffeinated drinks and foods
- exercising briefly
- having your test materials ready to go
- getting to class on time, without rushing
- reading the test directions carefully
- budgeting test time efficiently.

Pretest care and feeding. You should get at least 6 hours of sleep the night before a test. In addition, try to wake up at your regular time and eat a normal breakfast without breaking routine. Don't overeat; doing so will cause your body to work harder on digesting the meal than on coming up with correct test answers.

Be careful as well not to overstimulate yourself with caffeinated drinks and foods. Caffeine-related stimulation can distract you and make you jittery for the test.

Brief exercise before a test can invigorate your mind by increasing cerebral circulation. Be careful not to exercise too much, though; exercise just enough to get your blood moving.

Last-minute fact check. Review your summary sheet casually. If you have last-minute facts or formulas to remember, commit them to memory as close to examination time as possible. This information will most likely be stored in short-term memory and won't last long. Jot these facts down as soon as the test begins.

Be prepared. Gather all the supplies you'll need for the examination, especially a watch and extra pencils. During a timed test, you may worry excessively if you don't know how long you've been working and how much time is left. Bring pencils, erasers, paper, a calculator, and other items as needed and allowed.

Make sure to prepare your supplies well in advance of the test so you aren't rushing around immediately before you head to the examination. In fact, you might consider keeping these items in a test kit, which you can grab before each test and restock afterward. The night before a test, put the test kit with your car keys or other items you know you'll be taking to the test, so you won't forget it.

Dress for success. Dress comfortably in layers. If the room is hot, peel off a layer. If it's cold, add a sweater. Bring an easy-to-eat snack and some water if you think you may become distracted by hunger or thirst.

The early bird catches the best seat. Arrive 5 to 10 minutes early for your test. Select the seat you want, preferably one with the least potential for distractions. If the room is poorly lit, sit beneath a light fixture. Stay away from seats near the door. If you still have time, continue reviewing your con-densed notes. Avoid listening to other students chat among themselves, especially if they're discussing the examination. Their conversation may make you unduly anxious and needlessly concerned about material you already know well.

Get the 411. When you take your first look at the test, don't let your eye jump to the first question. Instead, read the instructions and listen carefully to verbal instructions. Underline, circle, or otherwise mark important instructions, such as "fill in the circles," "copy the question," or "show your work." Look at the sample questions if there are any, and work them through. (See *Facts and formulas*.)

Next, skim through the test for an overall sense of the questions and their level of difficulty. Read the questions that require lengthy writing. By reviewing the questions in advance, your brain can work on answers to longer questions while you're addressing shorter questions.

In essay questions, underline key words and jot down notes you don't want to forget when you come back to answer the questions completely. For example, you may want to write dates or points you want to make for a question you plan to answer last.

So many questions, so little time. After reading the instructions and previewing the test, determine a budget for your test time. Consider:

- how much time you've been given to complete the examination

---

OVERCOMING OBSTACLES

Facts and formulas

Do you have questions about the best way to remember formulas for a test? If you do, you can probably relate to this student's question — and learn from the answer!

Question
When I get to the calculations on the test, I spend a lot of time trying to remember the correct formulas. This wastes a lot of my time. Any suggestions?

Words of wisdom
When you're in the process of taking a test, you may need to concentrate for a while when trying to remember complicated formulas, facts, conversions, or equations. Prepare to answer such questions before you ever see the first question on the test. Immediately after receiving the test and test instructions, turn your test over and, on the back of the page, write down any conversions, formulas, dates, or facts that you've committed to short-term memory or that you think you may forget. You can then focus on answering the test questions, confident that you can refer back to these notes when necessary.

- the total number of questions
- the type and difficulty of each question
- the point value for each question.

If you have a choice of questions, decide which ones you intend to answer and in which order you plan to answer them. If, during the test, you start to lag behind the schedule you set, be flexible. Rebound by deciding how you can best use your remaining time.

TYPES OF TESTS

You may be faced with any combination of test formats, each of which requires its own strategies. Types of tests include:

- objective tests
- subjective tests
- other types of tests (vocabulary, reading comprehension, open-book, take-home, oral, and standardized tests).

Objective Tests

In an *objective test,* only one correct answer to a question is possible. These tests primarily measure your ability to recall information. Objective questions are commonly used in standardized examinations. Types of objective tests include:

- multiple-choice
- true-false
- short-answer
- sentence-completion
- problem-solving.

First things first. For all objective tests, start by looking over the entire test to determine the number of questions you'll need to answer. Try to answer the questions in the order they appear. Mark difficult questions, and then move on; you can return to them in the time you have left after you've reached the end of the test. You may be better able to handle these difficult questions at the end of the test, after your brain has had a chance to think about them. In addition, other questions may prompt you to remember the correct answers to the more difficult questions.

Multiple-Choice Tests

Observe these principles when taking a multiple-choice test:

- Read each question carefully. *Qualifying phrases,* such as *except* and *all of the following,* provide important clues to the correct answer.
- Think of an answer before looking at the options. Then try to match your answer to one of the options. Even if you find a match right away, read all the answers anyway. You may find that another option comes closer to the answer you originally thought correct.

> ## MEMORY JOGGER
>
> **REAP** your rewards of great grades when taking multiple-choice tests! Remember these steps:
>
> **R**ead each question carefully.
> **E**liminate wrong answers.
> **A**ttempt to match your answer with an option.
> **P**ace yourself.

- Use the process of elimination to narrow your choices. Eliminating clearly wrong options greatly improves your odds of selecting the correct answer.
- Work at a good pace. Read each question through, answer it, and then move on to the next question.

Is that your final answer? Sometimes, test instructions tell you to select the "best" answer. In such a case, there may be more than one correct answer, but one may be better or more appropriate than the others. In these cases, prioritize to determine which response best answers the question.

When prioritizing, think of well-known principles or theories. For example, for a question that asks what you would do first, think of Maslow's hierarchy of needs. Physical needs are always more important than psychological needs, so meeting nutritional demands would automatically come before establishing a trusting relationship.

Anything's possible. In a well-constructed test, all options are plausible. Therefore, go back to the question and look for a clue that makes one answer better than the others (such as the word *first* in the question: "What should the allied health professional do first?").

Don't be rash. Some test makers deliberately put a plausible — but incorrect — answer first. To avoid simply picking the first answer that appears, read all answers before deciding which is correct.

When it's right, it's right. Sometimes, questions and correct responses are taken directly out of the textbook, review guides, computer programs, or lecture notes. If you recognize particular words or phrases in one of the options, or if the question and one option seem like the right combination, choose that option; it's probably the correct one.

Be alert for "attractive distracters," words that *look like* the word to be defined but aren't. For example, if *illusion* is the correct answer, *allusion* might be used as a "decoy" among the answers.

The homestretch. When you've finished the test:

- go back and read the instructions again to make sure you've followed them
- check that you've answered the questions in the areas where they were supposed to be answered

- check the questions you flagged for further review
- review all the questions if you have time.

Change answers only if you're convinced they need to be changed to be correct. Trust your first impressions; they're usually accurate.

True-False Tests

In general, *true-false questions* assess your recognition of information rather than your ability to recall it and concentrate on simple facts and details. Most true-false statements are straightforward and are based on key words or phrases from the textbook or lectures. Always decide whether the statement is completely true before you mark it true. If only part of it is true, then the whole statement is false.

Take the hint. One word can turn an otherwise true statement into a false one, or a false statement into a true one. Pay special attention to these words:

- all
- always
- because
- generally
- never
- none
- only
- sometimes
- usually.

Short-Answer and Sentence-Completion Tests

Short-answer test items usually consist of one or two specific sentences after which you're asked to give a definition or formula. *Sentence-completion items* typically consist of a single sentence in which you're asked to fill in a specific word or phrase.

Plan of attack. To take a short-answer or sentence-completion test, break the items into these three categories:

1. Items you know without hesitation
2. Questions you should be able to answer if you think for a minute
3. Items about which you have no idea.

Answer the questions you know first. Then attack the questions that need more thought. Lastly, answer all remaining questions as best you can.

Don't blank out on blanks. Sentence-completion, or *fill-in-the-blank,* questions generally ask for an exact wording from memory. Make sure the grammar is consistent. When in doubt, guess; even if you make a generalized guess, you may receive partial credit. Many times, the question itself will contain a clue to the correct answer. For example, a date may help you narrow the scope of answers simply by providing a point of historical reference.

The numbers game. Look at the number and length of blanks in the question, and use them as clues to the correct answer. Is there more than one blank? Are the blanks long or short? Many instructors deliberately indicate when they expect one word, two words, or three words by using that number of blanks. The instructor may also use long blanks for long answers and short blanks for short answers.

Problem-Solving Tests

Tests that require problem-solving skills are used mainly in quantitative subjects, such as math and science. To approach a problem-solving examination, first read through all of the problems before answering them. Underline key words in the instructions and important data in the problems. Jot down thoughts that come to mind, such as specific formulas or possible approaches to solving the problems. As you move from question to question, repeat the same procedure.

Easy does it. Work on the easiest problems first; return to the more difficult ones later. Working on simple problems first will help build your confidence and warm up your brain for the more difficult problems to come.

Nothing to hide. Show all of your work. If you make a mistake, the instructor can see where you went wrong and may at least give you partial credit. Be careful and deliberate about your calculations so you don't make computational errors. Check that your answer meets all of the requirements of the problem. In addition, check that your answer makes sense.

If at first you don't succeed... If you have trouble solving a problem, approach it in a different manner. Think about similar problems from class or homework and the methods used to solve them. These are typically the methods used in the test, except that the ones in the test use different numbers or scenarios. Keep in mind that there's usually more than one way to solve a problem. If one method doesn't work, try another.

Subjective Tests

In a *subjective test,* such as an essay test, no single correct answer exists. Instead, the person grading the test judges how well each essay demonstrates understanding of the material. Follow these steps for successfully completing an essay test:

1. Read all instructions, underlining important words and phrases.
2. Read all questions even if you need to answer only some of them. Jot down facts and thoughts about each topic.

3. Mark the time you estimate it will take to complete each question.
4. Outline your answer.
5. Write the answer.
6. Read the instructions and question again. Review your answer. Proofread, and make corrections.

Stop and get directions. Read all instructions first. Failure to do so can result in points being deducted. For instance, the instructions may state to supply three supporting facts for each point of view. If you provide only one or two facts, you may lose points.

When reading the instructions for the first time, underline key points so you can refer to them quickly as you write. Unless the instructions state otherwise, double-space your essay and write only on the right-hand pages of the test booklet. Both techniques provide room for information to be added and for comments from the instructor.

Leave no question unread. After reading all instructions, read all the questions, quickly jotting down what you know about each topic, including facts, formulas, names, dates, ideas, and impressions. Later, when you write your outline, you'll have facts and figures handy to plug into the essay quickly. In addition, if you have a choice of questions for the test, you'll know which topics you know the most about by looking at how many notes you've written for each.

Time is money — and 90% of your grade. If a single essay question is worth, say, 50% of your grade, plan to spend 50% of your time on that question. Break this time allotment down further to include the time required to organize an outline, write the essay, and check your work.

Birth of an outline. When creating an outline, first write your thesis statement to guide you in writing the rest of the essay. Choose a title, even if one isn't required. The title, like the thesis, helps guide the direction of your arguments.

When organizing your outline, use the five-paragraph format as a guide. (See *Five-paragraph format.*) Content and organization typically account for most of your test grade. If you run out of time while writing an essay, you may be able to submit your outline, which shows your organization and intent.

Get to the point. Follow your outline when you write, and get to the point quickly. Your thesis statement should restate the question or answer the question succinctly. Use the

---

ADVICE FROM THE EXPERTS

Five-paragraph format

The *five-paragraph format* is an easy-to-follow structure for answering an essay question that asks you to state and support an opinion. Use it to get yourself started, especially when pressed for time.

Paragraph	Content
1	Introduction, in which you briefly outline the direction your argument will take and list the three main points you'll illustrate
2	First point, including at least two supporting facts
3	Second point, including at least two supporting facts
4	Third point, including at least two supporting facts
5	Conclusion, which pulls together the three main points into one final summary statement

---

EXERCISE YOUR MIND

Essay checklist

After completing an essay question, check your work. Ask yourself these questions to determine whether you've covered all the points you intended to cover.

Content
- Did you stick to your original point of view?
- Have you proven each argument?
- Have you provided examples?
- Have you clearly distinguished facts from opinions?
- Have you mentioned exceptions to your general statements?

Organization
- Did you open with a topic sentence?
- Does the topic sentence address the question?
- Did you follow your outline?
- Did you cover all the points in your original outline?
- Does your ending pull together all points without adding new information?

Writing mechanics
- Does every sentence state what you intended it to state?
- Are you sure of the meanings of all the words?
- Are spelling, grammar, punctuation, and sentence structure correct?
- Is your work neat and your handwriting legible?

introduction to tell the instructor what you're going to say. If the question states to "explain" or "summarize," for example, be sure to do just that. (See *Essay checklist* on page 52.)

Guided by your outline, make your points and supporting statements in the body of the essay. Each paragraph should have a topic statement, which, in turn, should relate to your thesis statement. Incorporate the facts and thoughts you jotted down at the beginning of the test. Write simple, direct, specific sentences that follow one another logically.

The conclusion should restate your thesis, drawing together the points made in the body of the essay. The conclusion tells the instructor that you had a point to make and that you made it.

Nips and tucks. When you've finished writing your essay, go back and read the question and instructions again. Make sure you've answered the question and that you've addressed all the points in the instructions. Then read your essay slowly and carefully, proofreading for grammatical errors and legibility. (See *Writing mechanics for essay questions.*) Make corrections where necessary.

Know when to fold 'em. After you've reviewed your completed essay and you've corrected errors and made needed changes, stop writing! Additional, extraneous verbiage will be viewed by your instructor as just that. When the question has been answered as it was intended to be, any other additions or changes are more likely to hurt your grade than to help. They'll also obscure the main points your instructor will be looking for.

Other Types of Tests

Other types of tests include:

- vocabulary
- reading comprehension
- open-book and take-home
- oral
- standardized.

Vocabulary Tests

A *vocabulary test* assesses your ability to remember the meaning of a word or use it correctly. Vocabulary tests are commonly used when studying foreign languages or in fields that employ specialized terminology.

Winning with words. These strategies are useful when you're faced with a vocabulary test:

- Avoid decoy options that look like the correct answer but aren't.
- Choose grammatically correct answers only.
- If you don't know the meaning of a word, try to remember where you've heard it and how it was used in a sentence. Select the answer that seems closest in meaning.
- Try to determine what part of speech the word is — for example, is it a noun or verb? Knowing a word's part of speech helps put the word into grammatical context and give you a clue about the meaning.

ADVICE FROM THE EXPERTS

Writing mechanics for essay questions

Answering an essay question involves providing the correct information, of course, but it also involves presenting the information in a readable format. Like a finely tuned car, a finely crafted essay shows that the author pays attention to mechanical details. Following certain tips for mechanically precise writing will help you write clear, compelling answers to essay questions.

Punctuation and word choice

- Avoid semicolons, exclamation marks, and parenthetical statements. Many inexperienced writers use semicolons incorrectly and exclamation marks too frequently. Parenthetical statements can knock a sentence off track.
- Avoid using a big word when a smaller one will do. Using unnecessarily long words or jargon can confuse your reader and detract from the clarity of your response. Keep it simple, and your instructor will be able to judge your knowledge more clearly.
- Avoid fragments and run-ons. A *fragment* is an incomplete sentence, such as *Because the laboratory technologist is responsible for monitoring blood bank supplies.* A *run-on* is a long sentence typically formed by joining two or three other sentences without using proper punctuation or linking words.
- Avoid slang, nonstandard language, and profanity. Keep your tone professional throughout.

Content and transitions

- Support all opinions with facts or other supporting information.
- Use transitions properly to give your writing a smooth flow. For example, if you introduce a term or concept at the end of one paragraph, use the term or refer to the concept in the first sentence of the next paragraph.
- When working on lined paper, skip every other line as you write. Skipping lines makes it easier for the instructor to read your response and also allows for extra room in which to write additional information later.

- Apply your knowledge of other languages. If you studied Latin, for instance, you may be able to derive the correct answer by looking at the unknown word's root. Look also at the word's prefix or suffix for clues.

Reading Comprehension Tests

In a *reading comprehension test,* you'll be asked to read a particular passage and then answer questions based on the passage. For these tests, read the *questions* first and then the passage. That way, you can focus on finding answers to the questions as you read.

Just the facts, Ma'am. After you read the passage, base your answers entirely on facts given in the passage. Applying outside knowledge can cost you points. Check your answers to make sure you've answered the questions completely.

Open-Book and Take-Home Tests

In an *open-book* or *take-home examination,* you're allowed to refer to your textbooks or notes. These tests deemphasize memorization and encourage critical thinking. They're often graded more strictly than tests based on your ability to eliminate factual errors. Neatness and grammar may count more heavily because you're given time to find and correct those errors.

Getting to know all about you. Here are some strategies for taking an open-book or take-home examination:

- Use the index and table of contents extensively.
- Don't copy your essays from the book. Use as many sources and resources as you're allowed. Treat the assignment like writing a paper.
- For some open-book tests, the instructor may allow students to bring only one page of notes. In such a case, organize and condense as much information as possible onto that one paper.
- Check your answers. Make sure you answered the questions without adding new, unsupported thoughts at the end.
- Proofread your work.

Oral Examinations

In an oral examination, you need to speak clearly, fluently, and without much time to prepare an answer. If you're allowed to choose a topic in advance, prepare as completely as if you were writing an essay. Choose a relatively narrow topic on which you can remain focused and for which you can give many supporting details. Try to make at least three points during the examination, and support each point with three pieces of evidence.

Say it again, Sam. Practice for an oral examination the same way you would prepare for a written test. Rehearse your answers in a simulated testing situation. Practice public speaking so you feel comfortable speaking in front of an audience.

Here are some tips to help you get through your oral examinations:

- Dress appropriately and look neat. Your physical appearance can make a positive or negative impression on your audience.
- Maintain control of your voice. Speak clearly and in measured tones. Avoid speaking quickly, mumbling, or letting your voice become too excited and "squeaky."
- Look at your audience. If you can't look directly at someone in the audience, look at a reference point in the audience. Looking at a reference point gives audience members the impression that you're looking at them. You might also look just above the heads of the people in the audience.
- If the oral examination involves giving a speech, prepare notes and do most of your speaking without reading. If you read directly from your notes, you might sound ill-prepared.
- Use language you're comfortable with. Don't use offensive language or words you don't know how to pronounce. In preparing, practice pronouncing the names of people or places that may come up during your test.
- Treat questions seriously. If you're allowed to take notes, write down questions asked of you. This is particularly helpful if the question contains several parts. If you don't understand what the questioner is asking, request clarification. Always repeat or rephrase the question yourself so you're sure you understand it.
- Unless you know how to answer a question immediately, take a moment to organize your thoughts before you begin your response.
- If you don't know the answer to a question, explain why. Perhaps the answer falls outside your realm of expertise.
- Exit gracefully. When your oral examination is finished, collect yourself and your papers and thank the audience members for their attention.

Standardized Tests

Standardized tests — for example, the Scholastic Aptitude Test (SAT) — are used for placement and admissions purposes. The test scores for standardized tests become a permanent part of your academic record. Always prepare before taking a standardized test by practicing under simulated test conditions. Use materials prepared by the same people who publish the actual test or materials designed specifically to replicate the actual test.

Numerous practice books and software are available for nearly every major standardized test. Take advantage of these books, using their self-tests to practice under simulated test conditions. Practice questions may also be available on the Internet, depending on the test.

TEST REVIEW

Tests provide you and your instructor with valuable information to evaluate your performance and judge your progress. Most instructors review the tests with the class after the examination. Review your examination when it's returned to you. (See *Test review checklist*.) Reflect carefully on instructor comments on the test, especially comments on an essay test. They can tell you not only about mistakes you've made but also how you can better fulfill that particular instructor's expectations and better perform on the final examination.

EXERCISE YOUR MIND

Test review checklist

Reviewing your test after it has been corrected can help clarify where you went wrong and what areas you need to concentrate on for the next test. After your test is returned to you, ask yourself these questions:

- What was my biggest problem overall?
- In general, what types of comments did the instructor make?
- Did I prepare for this test properly?
- Did I make careless errors? If so, how can I avoid doing the same in the future?
- What else can I learn from my mistakes?

TAKE A BREAK!

Scrambled or over-easy

Do you experience anxiety before a test? Fill in the blanks and then unscramble the circled letters to reveal a technique you can use to cope with your anxiety. Find the answers on the next page.

1. This is the best antidote for test anxiety.
   — — —◯— — — — —

2. This is the minimum number of hours of sleep advised the night before a test.
   —◯—

3. Avoid consuming this before a test to prevent jitteriness.
   — — — —◯— — —

4. This type of test has only one correct answer per question.
   ◯— — — — — — — —

5. No single correct answer exists when taking this type of test.
   — — — — —◯— —

6. Creating one of these will help you organize your thoughts to answer a question.
   — —◯— — — —

7. This pulls together the three main points of an essay.
   — — — — — — — —◯

8. This is the first thing you should read when you get a test.
   — — — — — —◯— —

9. This type of test assesses your ability to remember the meaning of a word.
   — — —◯— — — —

10. Problem-solving skills are commonly used for testing in this subject.
    ◯— — —

Answer: _____

Answer Key

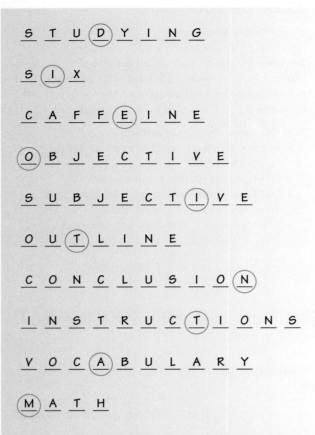

S T U (D) Y I N G

S (I) X

C A F F (E) I N E

(O) B J E C T I V E

S U B J E C T (I) V E

O U (T) L I N E

C O N C L U S I O (N)

I N S T R U C (T) I O N S

V O C (A) B U L A R Y

(M) A T H

You can use MEDITATION to cope with your anxiety before a test.

6

Stress?
What Stress?

CHAPTER OBJECTIVES

In this chapter, you'll learn:
1. How stress is the body's response to a demand.
2. How the body responds to stress.

3. How stress management techniques can be directed at the body or the mind.

WHAT IS STRESS?

Stress, according to the famed neuropsychologist Hans Selye, is "the nonspecific response of the body to any demands made upon it." When faced with a stimulus, the body seeks to adapt. These adaptations provoke a variety of physical and psychological reactions that, collectively, we recognize as stress.

People typically think of stress as being negative or unpleasant, but that isn't always the case. The way we react to stress will, in large part, determine the type of impact stress will have on our lives. We can react to stress positively or negatively, depending on the type of stress and our ability to manage it.

Eureka! Eustress!   People commonly encounter situations that cause them to react in a positive way. This response to beneficial environmental stimuli, called *eustress*, helps keep us alert, motivates us to face challenges, and drives us to solve problems. These low levels of stress are manageable and may be thought of as necessary and normal stimulation.

Stop the insanity!   *Distress*, on the other hand, results when our bodies overreact to events. Distress leads to what has been called the *fight-or-flight response*, a reaction deeply rooted in human physiology and behavior. The fight-or-flight response evolved as a mechanism to deal with life-or-death situations faced by primitive humans.

Lions, and tigers, and bears — oh my!   Nowadays, truly life-or-death situations tend to occur rarely for most people. Yet the human body continues to react to day-to-day situations the way our ancestors did, as if our lives depended on our reactions. For instance, your body can't physiologically differentiate between the threat of a saber-toothed tiger and that of a boss in a gray tweed suit. How we perceive and interpret the events of life dictates how our body reacts. If we think something is scary or worrisome, our bodies react accordingly.

Rating your reaction.   Exposing two people to the same stressor can provoke very different reactions. One possible explanation for these differences is that people have varying levels of what psychologists call *coherence*, or a sense of fitting into the environment. People with a strong sense of coherence feel more in control of themselves and react more positively to stress than do people with a weaker sense of coherence. Understanding how you tend to react to stress can help you gain control of your reactions and cope with stress more effectively.

REACTING TO STRESS

Selye categorized the body's reactions to environmental stress in three phases, together called the *general adaptation syndrome (GAS)*. The phases of GAS are:

1. alarm
2. resistance
3. exhaustion.

All hands on deck!   In the first stage, *alarm*, a nonspecific, general alarm occurs. In this response, the hypothalamus in the brain activates the autonomic nervous system, which, in turn, sparks activity in the pituitary gland and leads to an arousal of body defenses. At this point, the person experiences an increase in alertness and anxiety.

Call in the hormones.   During the second phase of the GAS, *resistance*, the hormone epinephrine is released from the adrenal glands. Epinephrine helps the body counteract the stressor directly or take flight to avoid the stressor's harmful effects.

Stress overload.   If exposure to the same stressor continues over a long period, the body will no longer be able to adapt to or resist the stressor's effects, and *exhaustion* sets in. Regardless of the inner strength of an individual, prolonged, unrelenting stress eventually breaks down the body's resistance, and disease, or even death, can result.

Recognizing Stress

Signs and symptoms of stress vary, depending on whether the stress reaction is of short duration or prolonged. Stress can also cause a number of psychological effects.

Stress, I know you all too well.   Short-term signs and symptoms of stress are easy to recognize and differ little from person to person. When a person is faced with stress, her:

- breathing becomes rapid and shallow
- heart rate increases
- muscles in the shoulders, forehead, and back of the neck tighten
- hands and feet become cold and sweaty.

Stress can also lead to disturbances in the GI system, such as a "butterfly" stomach or diarrhea, vomiting, and frequent urination. The mouth may become parched, and the hands and knees may begin to shake or tremble. These short-term effects disappear soon after the stressor is removed.

Enough is enough!   Extended exposure to stress can have lasting or even permanent effects on the body. Chronic stress suppresses the immune system by destroying white blood cells (WBCs) and suppressing WBC production, thus diminishing the body's disease-fighting capabilities. In addition, stress causes the release of free fatty acids into the bloodstream. These fatty acids can eventually accumulate as fatty deposits on arterial walls and lead to coronary artery disease, stroke, or heart attack.

Matters of the mind.   A number of psychological changes also occur because of stress. Memory becomes blocked, and clear thinking becomes difficult. A stressed individual may also find it difficult to solve problems efficiently. If the situation persists, the person finds it difficult to concentrate and may experience a general sense of fear or anxiety, insomnia, early waking, changes in eating habits, excessive worrying, fatigue, or a frequent urge to escape from the stressor.

Characteristics of Anxious Students

Stress from classroom and test situations commonly results in anxiety. (See *Coping with test-taking anxiety*.) Study-related anxiety can affect your performance as a student in several ways. Anxiety appears to improve performance on simple tasks and heavily practiced skills, but it interferes with accomplishment of more complex tasks or skills that aren't thoroughly practiced.

If simple, practiced skills have become boring or rote, a small amount of anxiety can help keep you alert and eager to finish. If a task is difficult or new, however, anxiety can prove distracting, making it more difficult to complete the task successfully.

A stress-filled brain. Highly anxious students seem to divide their attention between the new material and a preoccupation with how nervous they're feeling. So instead of concentrating on a lecture or on what she's reading, an anxious student keeps noticing the tight feelings in her chest, thinking something like, "I'm so tense; I'll never understand this stuff!" Because much of an anxious student's attention is occupied with negative thoughts about performing poorly, being criticized, or feeling embarrassed, she may miss information to be learned.

Distracting distractions. Anxious students tend to have poor study habits. They commonly have trouble learning material if it's somewhat disorganized or difficult to understand, or if it requires them to rely on their memory. Anxious students may be more easily distracted by irrelevant or incidental aspects of the task at hand. They seem to have trouble focusing on significant details and, as a result, waste time.

The deep freeze and forget. Anxious students often know more than they can demonstrate on a test, but because they commonly lack effective test-taking skills, they fail to demonstrate their knowledge when it really counts. They "freeze and forget" in a testing environment even though they may excel in nontest environments. (See *Recognizing the "freeze-up."*)

ADVICE FROM THE EXPERTS

Coping with test-taking anxiety

A test may cause undue anxiety. If you're experiencing worry and anxiety before a test, you can use a number of techniques to help you cope more effectively with your anxiety.

Before the test
- Discuss test content with your instructor and classmates.
- Develop effective study and test preparation skills.
- Spread your final studying over several days rather than cramming right before the test.
- Review your textbook, notes, and homework problems.
- Jot specific concepts or formulas on 3″ × 5″ cards and then study the cards.
- Take a practice test under examlike conditions.
- Continue your regular exercise program.
- Get sufficient rest the night before the test.
- Emphasize positive aspects of the test when you find yourself thinking negatively.
- Avoid studying immediately before the test.
- Relax or do something non-test-related immediately before the test.
- Arrive at the testing room about 5 minutes early to relax before the test is distributed. Arriving earlier may cause undue anxiety.

During the test
- Do something to break the test atmosphere, if allowed, such as getting a drink, sharpening a pencil, eating a snack, or asking a question.
- Alternately tense and relax muscles in several parts of your body, and then take several deep breaths with your eyes closed.
- Practice calming yourself by saying something like, "I have much more in my life than this test. I am calm and relaxed."
- Visualize a calm, soothing scene whenever you feel anxious.

ADVICE FROM THE EXPERTS

Recognizing the "freeze-up"

The most common symptom of test anxiety is experiencing a mental block or "freeze-up." A person with test anxiety may read the test questions and find the words meaningless. Or, the person may need to read test questions several times to fully comprehend them. Other symptoms include:

- feeling panic about not knowing the answer to a question or as time is running out of the test period
- worrying how your performance compares to the performance of other students
- feeling easily distracted during the examination
- plotting ways to escape from a test, such as sneaking out or faking an illness.

MANAGING STRESS

Stress management is a technique that can be useful on many levels. It can be as simple as taking a 5-minute break from studying and as comprehensive as reconsidering your life goals. To truly adjust your reaction to stress, choose the kinds of stress management techniques that will work for you. These techniques include:

- setting priorities
- caring for your body
- caring for your mind
- using social supports.

Setting Priorities

A key factor in stress management involves managing the limited amount of time you have. As a student, the activities and responsibilities you need to fit into each day may include going to classes, studying and preparing for class, working, participating in extramural activities, fulfilling family responsibilities, maintaining friendships and other personal relationships, engaging in your favorite hobbies, exercising, and attending social affairs.

Feeling the burden of fitting all those activities into a limited time is a source of significant stress. Setting priorities can help you manage activities and reduce the stress they cause.

The simple life.   It seems that we're always faced with more to do than can be accomplished. At times you may feel overwhelmed with responsibility, overextended, and out of control. The answer to a life that seems overwhelming is simplification. As Elaine St. James, a leader of the simplicity movement, states in her book *Simplify Your Life,* "Wise men and women in every major culture throughout history have found that the secret to happiness isn't in getting more but in wanting less." She encourages everyone to take some time out, examine their lives, and set some reasonable and specific goals that will simplify life.

Simplifying your life means identifying what you most want to have and most want to accomplish. Then determine how to reach those goals as simply as possible. For example, you may want to buy an expensive new car. Do you also want the high insurance rates that come with it? Are you ready for the added drain on your finances? Or would you prefer at this point to buy a solid, dependable secondhand car?

Here are some other ways to simplify your life:

- Run your errands all in one place. Don't hop from one shopping center to another; that takes time and energy. You might have to pay a little more for some of the things you need, but it will be worth it by making one stop instead of five or six.
- Turn off the television.
- Don't answer the phone every time it rings. If you have an answering machine, let it pick up sometimes. Give yourself a break.

- Stop sending greeting cards at the holidays.
- Resign from organizations whose meetings you hate to attend.
- Say no to one request each day or week.
- Every once in a while, just do nothing.

Remember, life isn't a race. Take it at your own pace, and simplify.

Those drop-dead deadlines.   If you can't reduce the number of demands you have, try to increase the time you allow yourself to perform them. Many deadlines are self-imposed. If you're overscheduled in your classes and, as a result, overwhelmed with responsibilities, perhaps you can aim to graduate a semester later. Sometimes it's necessary to differentiate between deadlines that can't be changed and those that can be extended without compromising goals.

Undo the urgency.   It's easy to mistake an urgency for an emergency. When you're feeling overwhelmed, sit down and divide a sheet of paper into three columns. Label the columns *Emergency, Urgent,* and *Non-urgent.*   Then prioritize all the tasks on your to-do list according to whether they're true emergencies (things that *must* be done immediately), urgencies (things that are important but aren't emergencies), or non-urgent. A bathtub that's leaking water through the ceiling into the kitchen is an emergency; handle it right away. If the tub is partly plugged but still drains and isn't leaking, it's urgent; handle it as soon as you have time. A bathtub that works fine but needs to be cleaned is non-urgent; handle it the next time you clean the bathroom.

Tasks that don't fit into any of the columns aren't important. Take them off your list, or put them on a separate list titled *Things to do sometime, maybe.* Above all, keep other people's needs in mind but don't sacrifice your needs and your health for things that aren't emergencies or urgencies.

Arranging the sock drawer.   Organize your schedule to make the most of what time is available. Identify and reduce wasted time, delegating certain activities to others in your social network and avoiding taking on too much yourself. Eliminate tasks if they aren't a high priority. That way you can schedule more time for high-priority tasks.

Nobody's perfect!   Another problem that affects optimal use of time is striving for perfection with each task, thereby delaying the task's completion. Give yourself permission to be imperfect. Not every task requires perfect effort. That doesn't mean you should do sloppy work, but it does mean you should avoid laboring over tasks until the outcome is what you consider perfect.

Delegate household tasks and chores to roommates or family members, such as your spouse or children. Don't expect perfection or that the task will be accomplished exactly as you would do it. Allow for imperfections, and be glad that someone else is taking care of things. This can also help your friends and family feel that they're helping you achieve your goals.

Baby steps. Be aware of procrastination that stems from feeling unable to complete a task. If a task seems overwhelming, break it down into smaller tasks that can be done individually. It's better to start with a small step than not to start at all.

Caring for Your Body

Because stress prompts a physical response from the body, caring for your body properly plays an important role in your ability to manage stress effectively. Caring for your body involves exercising, getting sufficient rest, eating well, and engaging in stressreducing breathing activities.

Exercise

Many students complain about not having enough time to study, let alone exercise. However, finding the time to exercise — even if it's just a daily regimen of stretches in the morning — can help lower stress, keep you looking and feeling trim, and make you feel better all around. Rather than draining energy, regular exercise actually replenishes your energy supply, allowing you to more easily manage all of the tasks you need to complete each day. Knowing what kinds of activities are best and how long and how often to exercise is the first step on the path to a healthy body.

Use it or lose it. Aerobic activities, such as swimming, jogging, brisk walking, cycling, or engaging in a vigorous racquet sport, not only strengthen your cardiovascular system but also provide numerous other physiologic benefits. For instance, people who engage in aerobic exercise tend to have more energy, feel less stress, sleep better, lose weight more easily, and experience an improved self-image.

The buddy system. In choosing your type of exercise, select an activity you enjoy. Unless you enjoy it, you won't continue with it. You might also look for an exercise partner to provide companionship, camaraderie, and motivation to exercise on a regular basis.

Take a day off. Exercise at least three times per week for at least 20 to 30 minutes at a time. You'll see even greater improvements if you build gradually to four to six times weekly. Give yourself at least one day per week free of exercise so your body can rest properly.

Rest

People experiencing high levels of stress tend to get insufficient amounts of sleep and become fatigued. Fatigue by itself is a stressor, which increases the amount of stress you feel, which leads to more fatigue, and so on. Sometimes it's more important to get some rest than to complete every task on your daily to-do list. Listen to your body when it tells you it's tired. After all, your body knows best when it's time to rest!

Eating Right

A balanced, nutritious diet is essential for maintaining good health. Diet also may influence your ability to cope with stress. Studies have shown that eating an adequate breakfast each day can improve the body's reaction to stress. Hunger can make an individual less able to cope effectively with stress.

An apple a day. During periods of stress, increase your intake of fruits and vegetables to supply vitamins B and C and folic acid, all of which enhance your body's ability to deal with the stress. Foods that can help elevate your mood include those that contain the amino acid tryptophan, such as milk, eggs, poultry, legumes, nuts, and cereal.

Got milk? Reducing your consumption of coffee, tea, cola soft drinks, and drugs containing caffeine can help control stress. Caffeine stimulates the sympathetic nervous system and promotes tension and anxiety. Avoid high-glucose foods as well; they can lead to sudden increases and decreases in blood glucose, which affect your ability to concentrate.

Stress-Reduction Techniques

A number of stress-reduction techniques — including conscious relaxation, massage, relaxation breathing, yoga, and other meditation-based activities — can be used to counteract your body's damaging reactions to stress.

Unwind those muscles. Relaxation is a conscious attempt to relax your muscles. Because tension tends to target muscles in the head, neck, and shoulders, many relaxation techniques focus on those parts of the body.

Here's an example of one relaxation technique. Relax your neck and shoulders. Slowly drop your head forward, roll it gently to the center of your right shoulder, and pause. Gently roll it to the center of your left shoulder, and pause. Roll it gently forward to the center of your chest, and pause. Reverse direction and go from left to right. Your goal for this and other forms of conscious relaxation is to slowly stretch muscles into relaxation. Similar techniques can be used to relax your entire body. (See *Full-body relaxation.*)

Therapeutic massage. *Therapeutic massage* today is used primarily for stress reduction and relaxation. The primary physiologic effect of therapeutic massage is improved blood circulation and muscle relaxation. As the muscles are kneaded and stretched, blood return to the heart increases and toxins such as lactic acid are carried out of the muscle tissue to be excreted from the body.

ADVICE FROM THE EXPERTS

Full-body relaxation

Relaxation exercises not only reduce stress but also send more blood and oxygen to the muscles. As muscles relax, they stretch, which allows more blood to flow into them. As a result, they gradually feel warmer and heavier. To relax your entire body in an attempt to reduce stress, try this exercise.

Start at the feet

Begin by settling back into a comfortable position. Start by focusing on relaxing your feet and ankles. Wiggle your feet or toes to help them to relax, and then allow that wave of relaxation to continue into the muscles of the calves. Continue the process up to the muscles of the thighs. Your legs should gradually feel more and more comfortable and relaxed.

Upper body

Next, concentrate on relaxing the muscles of your spine. Feel the relaxation spread into your abdomen. As you do this, you might feel a pleasant sense of warmth spreading to other parts of your body.

Focus on the muscles of the chest. Each time you exhale, your chest muscles should relax a little more. Let this relaxation flow into the muscles of the shoulders and then the arms and hands. Gradually, your arms and hands will become heavy, limp, and warm.

Neck and head

Now concentrate on relaxing the muscles of the neck, imagining that the muscles are as floppy as a handful of rubber bands. Next, relax the muscles of the jaws, cheeks, and sides of the face. Relax the eyes, nose, forehead, and scalp.

Cleansing breath

Lastly, take a long, slow, deep breath to eliminate tension that may remain.

Enter endorphins.   Improved circulation also results in increased perfusion and oxygenation of tissues. Improved oxygenation of the brain helps us think more clearly and, psychologically, helps us to feel relaxed and more alive. Massage also appears to trigger the release of endorphins, the body's natural pain relievers.

Qigong.   Qigong (pronounced "chee goong") is a system of gentle exercise, meditation, and controlled breathing used by millions of Chinese people daily to increase strength and relax the mind. Practitioners believe that when practiced daily over time, *qigong* can improve strength and flexibility, reverse damage due to injury or disease, relieve pain, restore energy, and induce relaxation and healing.

Yoga.   One of the oldest known health practices, *yoga* (which means *union* in Sanskrit) is the integration of physical, mental, and spiritual energies to promote health and wellness. The basic components of yoga include proper breathing, movement, and posture. While practicing specific postures, the practitioner pays close attention to his breathing, exhaling at certain times and inhaling at others. The breathing techniques are believed to promote relaxation and enhance the vital flow of energy known as *prana*.

Numerous scientific studies have shown that the regular practice of yoga can produce the same physiologic changes as meditation. Known as the *relaxation response*, these changes include decreased heart and respiratory rates, improved cardiac and respiratory function, decreased blood pressure, decreased oxygen consumption, increased alpha wave activity, and EEG synchronicity, a change in brain wave activity that occurs only in deep meditation.

Tai chi chuan.   A form of exercise built on the mind-body connection, *tai chi chuan* (or *tai chi*) combines physical movement, meditation, and breathing to induce relaxation and improve balance, posture, coordination, endurance, strength, and flexibility. Tai chi also benefits patients who suffer from anxiety, stress, restlessness, and depression. Tai chi can be practiced by people of all ages, sizes, and physical abilities because it relies more on technique than on strength. Participants perform a series of rhythmic movement patterns slowly and methodically.

Imagery.   In *imagery*, imagination is used to promote relaxation, relieve symptoms (or help to better cope with them), and heal disease. Imagery is based on the principle that the mind and body are interconnected and can work together to encourage healing. Imagery can lower blood pressure and decrease heart rate. It can also affect brain wave activity, oxygen supply to the tissues, vascular constriction, skin temperature, cochlear and pupillary reflexes, galvanic skin responses, salivation, and GI activity. According to imagery advocates, people with strong imaginations, including those who can literally worry themselves sick, are excellent candidates for using imagery.

Meditation.   Meditation reduces stress, which, in turn, results in decreased oxygen consumption, heart rate, and respiratory rate, and also leads to improved mood and a feeling of calmness. The most common form of meditation, called *concentrative meditation*, involves focusing on an object to eliminate distractions in the mind. The focus in a meditative exercise may be a repetitive sound (such as a word, phrase, or simple musical tune), a peaceful imaginary scenario, or the body itself, as in concentrated deep rhythmic breathing. (See *Relaxation breathing.*) The focus may also be a *mantra*, a word or phrase repeated over and over in a melodic rhythm.

Focusing on an object or thought of some kind prevents the undisciplined mind from flitting from subject to subject.

ADVICE FROM THE EXPERTS

Relaxation breathing

Relaxation breathing can increase lung capacity from the usual 15% to about 80% during the exercise. With daily practice, relaxation breathing and the resulting improvement in lung capacity can become automatic.

In with the good

To practice relaxation breathing, inhale through your nose but don't expand your chest. If your chest is expanding, you're breathing shallowly and actually constricting your lungs. When inhaling, your chest should remain unchanged but you should expand your belly. Imagine there's a balloon in your stomach and your job is to blow as much air into it as possible.

Inhalation should take about 6 seconds. For comparison, people typically inhale for only about 2 seconds. Inhaling more slowly brings more oxygen into the lungs.

Intermission

After inhaling, pause and hold your breath for a few seconds. Pausing exercises your diaphragm and internal muscles. When you first start doing relaxation breathing, you may feel a little out of breath from the pausing. If you feel uncomfortable, you can skip the pauses for now and insert them when you've become more comfortable with the basic pattern of inhaling and exhaling.

Out with the bad

Next, exhale slowly and evenly for 6 seconds by relaxing the abdomen and allowing the lungs to expel the air. The chest may expand slightly at this point.

Be aware that when you're practicing relaxation breathing as a conscious exercise, you should breathe through your mouth gently, not forcefully. When breathing this way during normal activity, exhale through your nose.

Putting it all together

Using this breathing technique, take 10 full, deep breaths. Inhale for 6 seconds, and then exhale for 6 seconds in a steady rhythm. After you learn the technique, there shouldn't be any pauses between inhalation and exhalation. If you have trouble with a 6-second cycle, find a cycle that's comfortable for you, such as a 3-second cycle, and gradually work your way up to 6 seconds.

Set aside 5 minutes three times each day to practice. If possible, practice your breathing while sitting comfortably in a chair with your feet flat on the floor and your arms resting loosely in your lap.

As you grow in experience with meditation, you'll find it easier to prolong and sustain concentration.

Let it go — the stress, that is. Another form of meditation involves "letting go" or "going with the flow" to become more sensitive to your environment. To do this, you need to be in a quiet, serene place, such as the shore, the woods, or a quiet place at home. Assume a comfortable position, such as the famous Lotus position or a similar meditative pose. Take some deep breaths, relaxing your body a little more each time you exhale.

Allow your thoughts to flow from one to the other without attempting to manipulate them. (See *Visualization.*) Allow

EXERCISE YOUR MIND

Visualization

Visualization is similar to meditation except that in visualization you're guiding your thoughts toward a set of specific images. Visualization can take many forms, but a common one involves focusing on being in a quiet, safe place.

Setting

To perform visualization, go to a quiet area with as few distractions as possible. Sit comfortably in a chair, and take at least 10 natural breaths. Close your eyes gently, and imagine the inside of your eyelids as a movie screen. Picture a physical setting that makes you feel calm and relaxed, such as a sunny clearing in the woods, a canoe ride on a still lake at sunrise, or a book-lined study with classical music playing in the background.

Colors and smells

Now sharpen your image of this place by using all of your senses to provide reality. See the flowers along the edge of the clearing. Feel the moisture in the morning mist. Listen to each note as the bassoons play off the sounds of the violins.

Sharpen the images with even more specific detail. What kind of trees are surrounding you? Are they old-growth or young trees? Is the clearing near a lake or stream? Can you hear the rushing water? Put as much detail as possible into your image.

Focus

As you work on the clarity of the vision, pay attention to your feelings. Focus on your sense of calm and restfulness. Let all the elements of the scene wash over your emotions. Remember your "place" when you finish your visualization session. When you visualize next, return to your place and add detail. Change its characteristics, if you like. Practice going to your quiet place on demand.

your distractions to be played out in your mind until you can gently bring your attention back to a calm, peaceful state. The aim of this sort of meditation is to lose self-consciousness and not to think in the perspective of "I."

Caring for Your Mind

Nearly every cultural tradition has techniques for promoting relaxation and reducing stress. You can turn your mind toward relaxation rather than stress and anxiety by controlling negative thoughts and building social supports.

Controlling Negative Thoughts

Some stress can be accentuated by imagining the worst possible scenario. The imagination can be highly creative. It can veer off in frightening directions if allowed to do so, creating images and events that increase anxiety.

You've got to accentuate the positive...   Positive, creative imagery can have a suggestive effect that starts the mind moving toward a goal and weakens or overcomes negative images. By imagining what goals you want to reach and visualizing how you'll achieve each goal, you can replace negative thoughts with positive ones. (See *The power of positive thinking*.) If you imagine failure, you're more

---

EXERCISE YOUR MIND

The power of positive thinking

If you plan to succeed and you visualize yourself succeeding, then you're more likely to ultimately succeed. Nurture your power of positive thinking by using these techniques:

- Psych yourself up for important events. Think about the upcoming situation, and visualize it as being a successful experience.
- Talk to yourself in a positive manner. Think of yourself as "The little engine that could." Repeat over and over, "I know I can. I know I can."
- Prepare properly. Develop a plan of action as well as contingency or alternative plans in case circumstances change.
- Label an upcoming event that could cause undue tension as a positive learning experience.
- Look at examinations and other potentially stressful events as opportunities to prove yourself by showing others what you know or what you can do. Avoid looking at these events as tests of what you don't know or can't do. Viewing them as positive opportunities can give you a feeling of power and accomplishment.

---

likely to fail; if you imagine success, you're more likely to succeed.

...and eliminate the negative.   To rid yourself of negative thoughts, find a quiet place, sit or lie down, close your eyes, and imagine your body as being two-dimensional with the interior completely dark. Slowly begin to inhale and exhale. Think of each exhalation as forcing some of the interior darkness from your body. Inhale and exhale the darkness until you feel that the interior of your body is no longer dark. You'll soon begin to feel the stress disappearing with each exhalation.

Another technique involves stopping yourself each time your inner voice says something negative. Replace these thoughts with positive thoughts or a mantra. You may have to repeat these thoughts several times until you conquer your anxiety, but gradually it may help you to eliminate angry or frightening thoughts.

Building Social Supports

A strong social network can help control and improve a person's ability to respond effectively to stress. Social networks can take many forms, including:

- family
- friends
- peers at work
- fellow students
- religious groups
- people with shared interests, such as sports, hobbies, or social causes.

These social supports give you an outlet for discussing problems with people who care for you and want to help you. Discussing stress-producing problems can also give you new perspectives on chronic problems. Some people find that prayer can provide quiet time and help focus priorities so they can better deal with stress-provoking situations.

Asking for Help

Stress is a normal part of daily life. Most of the time, the stressful situation passes or we're able to deal with it in a way that makes it manageable. At some point in our lives, however, most of us experience stress that's overwhelming. When stress interferes with your ability to do what you need — or want — to do, it's easy to feel helpless or even hopeless.

Reach out.   When stress gets to that point and you can't manage it effectively, it may be time to ask for help. Help comes in many forms — from family and friends, or from professionals, such as counselors, social workers, clergy, or community-based support groups. Remember that asking for help isn't a sign of weakness; it's a sign of strength and wisdom.

TAKE A BREAK!

Destress zone

Find your way out of this stress maze and into a warm, soothing bubble bath! Watch out for roadblocks along the way that can slow you down! Check out the next page for the correct trail!

Answer Key

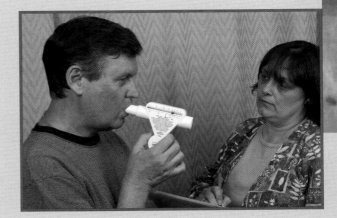

Medical Law and Ethics

7

Law and Ethics in the Health Care Setting

CHAPTER OBJECTIVES

In this chapter, you'll learn:

1. To spell and define the key terms.
2. To identify the two branches of the American legal system.
3. To list the elements and types of contractual agreements and describe the difference in implied and express contracts.
4. To list four items that must be included in a contract termination or withdrawal letter.
5. To list six items that must be included in an informed consent form and explain who may sign consent forms.
6. To list five legally required disclosures that must be reported to specified authorities.
7. To describe the purpose of the Self-Determination Act.
8. To describe the four elements that must be proven in a medical legal suit.
9. To describe four possible defenses against litigation for the medical professional.
10. To explain the theory of respondeat superior, or law of agency, and how it applies to the medical assistant.
11. To list ways that an allied health professional can assist in the prevention of a medical malpractice suit.
12. To outline the laws regarding employment and safety issues in the health care setting.
13. To list the requirements of the Americans with Disabilities Act relating to the health care setting.
14. To differentiate between legal issues and ethical issues.

KEY TERMS

abandonment
advance directive
age of majority
appeal
assault
battery
bench trial
bioethics
blood-borne pathogens
breach
certification
civil law
coerce
common law
comparative negligence
confidentiality

consent
consideration
contract
contributory negligence
cross-examination
damages
defamation of character
defendant
depositions
direct examination
durable power of attorney
duress
emancipated minor
ethics
expert witness
expressed consent

expressed contracts
fee-splitting
fraud
implied consent
implied contracts
informed consent
intentional tort
legally required disclosure
libel
licensure
litigation
locum tenens
malpractice
negligence
noncompliant
plaintiff

precedents
protocol
registered
res ipsa loquitur
res judicata
respondeat superior
slander
stare decisis
statutes
statute of limitations
tort
unintentional tort
verdict

DURING YOUR CAREER AS an allied health professional you will be involved in many medical situations with potential legal implications. You must uphold ethical standards to ensure the patient's well-being. Ethics deals with the concept of right and wrong. Laws are written to carry out these concepts. Medicare **fraud** (concealing the truth) and falsifying medical records can also result in a lawsuit. You may help to prevent many of these claims against your facility, and to protect yourself, by complying with medical laws, keeping abreast of medical trends, and acting in an ethical manner by maintaining a high level of professionalism at all times.

THE AMERICAN LEGAL SYSTEM

Our legal system is in place to ensure the rights of all citizens. We depend on the legal system to protect us from the wrongdoings of others. Many potential medical suits prove to be unwarranted and never make it into the court system, but even in the best relationships, **litigation** (lawsuits) between patients and health care facilities may occur. Litigation may result from a single medication error or a mistake that costs a person's life. It is essential that you have a basic understanding of the American legal system to protect yourself, your patients, and your employer by following the legal guidelines.

Sources of Law

Laws are rules of conduct that are enforced by appointed authorities. The foundation of our legal system is our rights outlined in the Constitution and the laws established by our Founding Fathers. These traditional laws are known as **common law**.

Common law is based on the theory of **stare decisis**. This term means "the previous decision stands." Judges usually follow these **precedents** (previous court decisions) but sometimes overrule a previous decision, establishing new precedent. **Statutes** are another source of law. Federal, state, or local legislators make laws or statutes, the police enforce them, and the court system ensures justice. Statutes pertaining to Medicare, Medicaid, and the Food and Drug Administration are common examples in the medical profession.

The third type of law is administrative. These laws are passed by governmental agencies, such as the Internal Revenue Service.

Branches of the Law

The two main branches of the legal system are public law and private or **civil law**.

Public Law

Public law is the branch of law that focuses on issues between the government and its citizens. It can be divided into four subgroups:

1. Criminal law is concerned with issues of citizen welfare and safety. Examples include arson, burglary, murder, and rape. Allied health professionals must stay within the boundaries of the profession. Failure to do so could result in a charge of practicing medicine without a license—an act covered under criminal law.
2. Constitutional law is commonly called the law of the land. The United States government has a constitution, and each state has a constitution of its own, laws, and regulations. State laws may be more restrictive than federal laws but may not be more lenient. Two examples of constitutional law are laws on abortion and civil rights.
3. Administrative law is the regulations set forth by governmental agencies. This category includes laws pertaining to the Food and Drug Administration, the Internal Revenue Service, and the Board of Medical Examiners.
4. International law pertains to treaties between countries. Related issues include trade agreements, extradition, boundaries, and international waters.

Private or Civil Law

Private or civil law is the branch of the law that focuses on issues between private citizens. The medical profession is primarily concerned with private law. The subcategories that pertain to the medical profession are contract, commercial, and tort law. Contract and commercial laws concern the rights and obligations of those who enter into contracts, as in a doctor–patient relationship. **Tort** law governs the righting of wrongs or injuries suffered by someone because of another person's wrongdoing or misdeeds resulting from a **breach** of legal duty. Tort law is the basis of most lawsuits against health care workers. Other civil law branches include property, inheritance, and corporation law.

 Checkpoint Question

1. Which branch of law covers an allied health professional charged with practicing medicine without a license?

The Rise in Medical Legal Cases

Since World War II, the number of medical malpractice cases brought to court has increased significantly. **Malpractice** refers to an action by a professional health care worker that harms a patient. A rise in the amounts of settlement awards has had a negative impact on the cost and coverage of malpractice insurance. With this rise, some doctors have actually changed the scope of their practice to reduce their costs. In an attempt to protect professionals, legislation designed to limit the amount a jury can award has been introduced in Congress. Legal issues involving the medical field are referred to as medicolegal, which combines the words medical and legal.

A government task force found four primary reasons for the rise in malpractice claims:

1. *Scientific advances.* As new and improved medical technology becomes available, the risks and potential for complications of these procedures escalate, making physicians more vulnerable to litigation.
2. *Unrealistic expectations.* Some patients expect miracle cures and file lawsuits because recovery was not as they hoped or expected, even if the health care provider is not at fault.
3. *Economic factors.* Some patients view lawsuits as a means to obtain quick cash. (In fact, the number of lawsuits filed has increased during economic recessions.)
4. *Poor communication.* Studies show that when patients do not feel a bond with their health care provider, they are more likely to sue. Attention to customer service helps develop a good rapport between patients, the provider, and the staff.

PHYSICIAN–PATIENT RELATIONSHIP

Rights and Responsibilities of the Patient and Physician

In any contractual relationship, both parties have certain rights and responsibilities. The rights of the patient include the ability to choose a physician. This right may be limited to a list of participating providers under a patient's insurance plan. Patients have the right to determine whether to begin medical treatment and to set limits on that treatment. The patient also has the right to know in advance what the treatment will consist of, what effect it may have, and what dangers are to be expected. The concept of informed consent is discussed later in the chapter.

Physicians have the right to limit their practice to a certain specialty or a certain location. For example, patients may not expect a physician to treat them at home. Physicians also have the right to refuse service to new patients or existing patients with new problems unless they are on emergency room call, in which case they must continue to treat patients seen during this time. Doctors have the right to change their policies or availability as long as they give patients reasonable notice of the change. This can be done through a local newspaper advertisement and/or a letter to each patient. Box 7-1 lists the patient's and physician's responsibilities.

Contracts

A **contract** is an agreement between two or more parties with certain factors agreed on among all parties. The physician–patient relationship is reinforced by the formation of a contract. All contractual agreements have three components:

1. **Offer** (contract initiation)
2. **Acceptance** (both parties agree to the terms)
3. **Consideration** (the exchange of fees for service)

Box 7-1

RESPONSIBILITIES OF THE PATIENT AND THE PHYSICIAN

Responsibilities of the Patient	Responsibilities of the Physician
Provide the physician with accurate data about the duration and nature of symptoms	Respect the patient's confidential information
Provide a complete and accurate medical history to the physician	Provide reasonable skill, experience, and knowledge in treating the patient
Follow the physician's instructions for diet, exercise, medications, and appointments	Continue treating the patient until the contract has been withdrawn or as long as the condition requires treatment
Compensate the physician for services rendered	Inform patients of their condition, treatments, and prognosis
	Give complete and accurate information
	Provide competent coverage during time away from practice
	Obtain informed consent before performing procedures (informed consent is a statement of approval from the patient for the physician to perform a given procedure after the patient has been educated about the risks and benefits of the procedure)
	Caution against unneeded or undesirable treatment or surgery

A contract is not valid unless all three elements are present. A contract offer is made when a patient calls the office to request an appointment. The offer is accepted when you make an appointment for the patient. You have formed a contract that implies that for a fee, the physician will do all in his or her power to address the health concerns of the patient.

Certain individuals, such as children and those who are mentally incompetent or temporarily incapacitated, are not legally able to enter contracts. Patients in this category do not have the capacity to enter into a contract, and therefore decisions about health care should be made by a competent party acting as a health care decision maker for the minor or incompetent person.

The two types of contracts between physicians and patients are implied and expressed.

Implied Contracts

Implied contracts, the most common kind of contract between physicians and patients, are not written but are assumed by the actions of the parties. For example, a patient calls the office and requests to see Dr. Smith for an earache. The patient arrives for the appointment, is seen by the physician, and receives a prescription. It is *implied* that because the patient came on his own and requested care that he wants this physician to care for him. The physician's action of accepting the patient for care *implies* that he acknowledges responsibility for his part of the contract. The patient *implies* by accepting the services that he will render payment even if the price was not discussed.

Expressed Contracts

Expressed contracts, either written or oral, consist of specified details. A mutual sharing of responsibilities is always stated in an expressed contract. The agreement you have with your creditors is an expressed contract. These kinds of contracts are not used as often in the medical setting as implied contracts.

Termination or Withdrawal of the Contract

A contract is ideally resolved when the patient is satisfactorily cured of the illness and the physician has been paid for the services. The patient may end the contract at any time, but the physician must follow legal **protocol** to dissolve the contract if the patient still seeks treatment and the physician wishes to end the relationship.

Patient-initiated termination.   A patient who chooses to terminate the relationship should notify the physician and give the reasons. You must keep this letter in the medical record. After the receipt of this letter, the physician should then send a letter to the patient stating the following:

- The physician accepts the termination.

- Medical records are available on written request.
- Medical referrals are available if needed.

If the patient verbally asks to end this relationship, the physician should send a letter to the patient documenting the conversation and again offering referrals and access to the medical records. Clear documentation is essential.

Physician-initiated termination.   The physician may find it necessary to end the relationship. A physician may terminate the contract if the patient is **noncompliant** or does not keep appointments or for personal reasons. The physician must send a letter of withdrawal that includes:

- A statement of intent to terminate the relationship
- The reasons for this action
- The termination date at least 30 days from the date of receipt of the letter
- A statement that the medical records will be transferred to another physician at the patient's request
- A strong recommendation that the patient seek additional medical care as warranted

The letter must be sent by certified mail with a return receipt requested. A copy of the termination letter and the return receipt are placed in the patient's record. Figure 7-1 shows a sample letter of intent to terminate a physician–patient relationship.

Amy Fine, MD
Charlotte Family Practice
220 NW 3rd Avenue
Charlotte, NC 25673

August 22, 2003

Regina Dodson
Jones Hill Road
Charlotte, NC 25673

Dear Ms. Dodson:

Due to the fact that you have persistently refused to follow my medical advice and treatment of your diabetes, I will no longer be able to provide medical care to you. Since your condition requires ongoing medical care, you must find another physician as soon as possible. I will be available to you until that time, but no longer than 30 days.

To assist you in continuing to receive care, we will make records available to your new physician as soon as you authorize us to send them.

Sincerely,

Amy Fine, MD

FIGURE 7-1.   Letter of intent to terminate physician–patient relationship.

Abandonment. If a contract is not properly terminated, the physician can be sued for abandonment. **Abandonment** may be charged if the physician withdraws from the contractual relationship without proper notification while the patient still needs treatment. Physicians must always arrange coverage when absent from the office for vacations, conferences, and so on. Patients may sue for abandonment in any instance that a suitable substitute is not available for care. Coverage may be provided by a **locum tenens**, a substitute physician.

Other examples of abandonment:

- The physician abruptly and without reasonable notice stops treating a patient whose condition requires additional or continued care.
- The physician fails to see a patient as often as the condition requires or incorrectly advises the patient that further treatment is not needed.

Checkpoint Question

2. What five elements must be in a physician's termination intent letter?

Consent

The law requires that patients must **consent** or agree to being touched, examined, or treated by the health care provider involved in the contractual agreement. No treatment may be made without a consent given orally, nonverbally by behavior, or clearly in writing. Patients have the right to appoint a health care surrogate or health care power of attorney who may make health care decisions when the patient is unable to make them. A health care surrogate may be a spouse, a friend, a pastor, or an attorney. A **durable power of attorney** for health care gives the patient's representative the ability to make health care decisions as the health care surrogate. A patient's physician should be aware of the power of attorney agreement, and a copy of the legal documentation should be kept in the office medical record.

Implied Consent

In the typical visit to a health care facility, the patient's actions represent an informal agreement for care to be given. A patient who raises a sleeve to receive an injection implies agreement to the treatment. **Implied consent** also occurs in an emergency. If a patient is in a life-threatening situation and is unable to give verbal permission for treatment, it is implied that the patient would consent to treatment if possible. As soon as possible, informed consent should be signed by either the patient or a family member in this type of situation. When there is no emergency, implied consent should be used only if the procedure poses no significant risk to the patient.

Informed or Expressed Consent

The physician is responsible for obtaining the patient's **informed consent** whenever the treatment involves an invasive procedure such as surgery, use of experimental drugs, potentially dangerous procedures such as stress tests, or any treatment that poses a significant risk to the patient. A federal law discussed later requires that health care providers who administer certain vaccines give the patient a current vaccine information statement (VIS). A VIS provides a standardized way to give objective information about vaccine benefits and adverse events (side effects) to patients. The VIS is available online through the Centers for Disease Control and Prevention (CDC) in 26 languages. Informed consent is also referred to as **expressed consent**.

Informed consent is based on the patient's right to know every possible benefit, risk, or alternative to the suggested treatment and the possible outcome if no treatment is initiated. The patient must voluntarily give permission and must understand the implications of consenting to the treatment. This requires that the physician and patient communicate in a manner understandable to the patient. Patients can be more active in personal health care decisions when they are educated about and understand their treatment and care.

A consent form must include the following information:

1. Name of the procedure to be performed
2. Name of the physician who will perform the procedure
3. Name of the person administering the anesthesia (if applicable)
4. Any potential risks from the procedure
5. Anticipated result or benefit from the procedure
6. Alternatives to the procedure and their risks
7. Probable effect on the patient's condition if the procedure is not performed
8. Any exclusions that the patient requests
9. Statement indicating that all of the patient's questions or concerns regarding the procedure have been answered
10. Patient's and witnesses' signatures and the date

As the medical assistant, you will frequently be required to witness consent signatures. A sample consent form is seen in Figure 7-2 on next page.

The informed consent form supplied for the patient's signature must be in the language that the patient speaks. Most physicians who treat multicultural patients have consent forms available in a variety of languages. Never ask a patient to sign a consent form if he or she:

- Does not understand the procedure
- Has unanswered questions regarding the procedure
- Is unable to read the consent form

Never coerce (force or compel against his or her wishes) a patient into signing a consent form.

I hereby authorize Dr. _____ , and such assistants as may be designated, to perform:

_____
(Name of treatment/procedure)

and any other related procedures or forms of treatment, including appropriate anesthesia, transfusions that they deem necessary for the welfare of:

_____
(Name of patient)

I consent to the administration of anesthesia and/or such drugs as may be necessary. I understand that all anesthetics involve risks of complications, serious injury, or rarely death from both known and unknown causes.

I consent to the examination and retention for educational, scientific and research purposes by the Medical Staff of

_____
of all body fluids, tissues and organs removed during the course of the above treatment/procedure with privilege of ultimate use and disposal resting with said medical staff.

The following has been explained to me and I understand:

A. The nature and character of the proposed treatment/procedure.
B. The anticipated results of the proposed treatment/procedure.
C. The recognized alternative forms of treatment/procedure.
D. The recognized serious possible risks and complications of the treatment/procedure and of the recognized alternative forms of treatment/procedure, including non-treatment.
E. The possible consequences of no treatment.
F. The anticipated date and time of the proposed treatment/procedure.

Additional M.D. comments: _____

_____

My physician has offered to answer all inquiries concerning the proposed treatment/procedure. I understand that I am free to withhold or withdraw consent to the proposed treatment/procedure at any time.

Witness			Signature of Person Giving Consent
Date Signed	Time	☐ A.M.	Relationship to patient (if applicable)
		☐ P.M.	

☐ Please check if this is a telephone monitored consent.
No treatment will be performed until this consent has been executed. This consent will be permanently filed in the patient's medical record.

Pt. No. _____	**Gastroenterology Associates** Anytown, PA
Name _____	
D.O.B. _____	**Special Consent to Treatment** (Diagnostic & Surgical Procedures, Anesthesia, Medical Treatment & Other Procedures)

F I G U R E   7 - 2 .   Sample consent form.

Who may sign a consent form?   An adult (usually someone over age 18) who is mentally competent and not under the influence of medication or other substances may sign a consent form. A minor may sign a consent form if he or she is:

- In the armed services
- Requesting treatment for communicable diseases (including sexually transmitted diseases)

F I G U R E   7 - 3 .   Using an interpreter, the allied health professional helps this patient understand the procedure.

WHAT IF

A well-meaning family member asks for information about her mother's condition. What should you say?

Tell the family member that you are not allowed to discuss the patient without his or her permission. No information should be released to anyone—friends, family, media, or insurance companies—without prior written approval from the patient.

At the first visit, you should establish the patient's wishes about giving information to family members and friends. If there is a particular family member who brings the patient to the office, the patient may sign a release form giving that person the right to receive information. Many health care providers provide the patient with a short progress report including the patient's test results, diagnosis, treatment, and next appointment. A form could be designed for this purpose. This gives the patient the opportunity to share complete and accurate information if they choose.

- Pregnant
- Requesting information regarding birth control, abortion, or drug or alcohol abuse counseling
- Emancipated

An **emancipated minor** is under the **age of majority** but is either married or self-supporting and is responsible for his or her debts. The age of majority varies from state to state and ranges from 18 to 21. Minors may give consent if any one of the above-listed criteria is present.

Legal guardians may also sign consent forms. A legal guardian is appointed by a judge when the court has ruled an individual to be mentally incompetent. Health care surrogates may also sign consent forms. Health care surrogates are discussed later in the chapter.

Checkpoint Question

3. Under what circumstances should a patient never be asked to sign a consent form?

Refusal of Consent

Patients may refuse treatment for any reason. Sometimes, patients make treatment choices based on religious or personal beliefs and preferences. For instance, a Jehovah's Witness may refuse a blood transfusion on religious grounds, or an elderly person may not want to undergo serious surgery because the potential complications may limit future lifestyle options. In this situation, the patient must sign a refusal of consent form indicating that the patient was instructed regarding the potential risks and benefits of the procedure as well as the risks if the procedure is not allowed. If the patient is a minor, the courts may become involved at the request of the health care provider and may award consent for the child. In this situation, the health care provider should follow legal counsel and document the incident carefully. In any instance that the patient refuses treatment, documentation must be made to protect the health care provider.

Releasing Patient Information

The health record is a legal document. Although the health record itself belongs to the physician, the information belongs to the patient. Patients have the right to their medical information, and they have the right to deny the sharing of this information.

Requests for health records are common. Other health care facilities, insurance companies, and patients themselves may need information from the health record.

Legally Required Disclosures

Even though patients have the right to limit access to their health records, health care facilities have a responsibility to report certain events to governmental agencies without the patient's consent, which are referred to as **legally required disclosures**. You and other health care providers must report to the department of public health the situations described in the following sections.

Vital Statistics

All states maintain records of births, deaths, marriages, and divorces. These records include the following:

- Birth certificates.
- Stillbirth reports. Some states have separate stillbirth forms; other states use a regular death certificate.
- Death certificates. These must be signed by a physician. The cause and time of death must be included.

You may assist in completing a death certificate and filing the finished report in the patient's chart.

Medical Examiner's Reports

Each state has laws pertaining to which deaths must be reported to the medical examiner's office. Generally, these include the following:

- Death from an unknown cause
- Death from a suspected criminal or violent act
- Death of a person not attended by a physician at the time of death or for a reasonable period preceding the death
- Death within 24 hours of hospital admission

PATIENT EDUCATION
Legally Required Disclosures

Patients who have conditions that require legal disclosure should be informed about the applicable law. Patients should be assured that all steps to ensure their confidentiality will be followed. Patients should be educated about why the disclosure is necessary, who receives the information, what particular forms will be completed, and any anticipated follow-up from the organization. For example, health care facilities are required to report to the local health department the name, address, and condition of a patient with sexually transmitted disease. It is the responsibility of the health department to contact the patient to acquire the names of the patient's sexual contacts. These contacts are notified and counseled by the health department official. Patients who are educated about these legally required disclosures will be more understanding and accepting of the need to file official reports.

Infectious or Communicable Diseases

These reports are made to the local health department. The information is used for statistical purposes and for preventing or tracking the spread of these diseases. Although state guidelines vary, there are usually three categories of reports:

- Telephone reports are required for diphtheria, cholera, meningococcal meningitis, and plague, usually within 24 hours of the diagnosis. Telephone reports must always be followed by written reports.
- Written reports are required for hepatitis, leprosy, malaria, rubeola, polio, rheumatic fever, tetanus, and tuberculosis. Sexually transmitted diseases must also be reported. Notification is usually required within 3 days of the date of discovery.
- Trend reports are made when your office notes an unusually high occurrence of influenza, streptococcal infections, or any other infectious diseases. Box 7-2 on next page, is a sample of reportable diseases and their time frames.

The CDC keeps a watchful eye on the public health. When necessary, the CDC establishes directives for the protection of the public. For example, when the public appeared to be at risk for contracting anthrax in 2001, the CDC mandated that documented anthrax cases be reported immediately. Fax machines and e-mail help facilitate such urgent public health communication.

Box 7-2

REPORTABLE CONDITIONS

acquired immune deficiency syndrome (AIDS)—
    7 days
amebiasis—7 days
anthrax—24 hours
blastomycosis—7 days
botulism—24 hours
brucellosis—7 days
Campylobacter infection—24 hours
chancroid—24 hours
chlamydial infection (laboratory confirmed)—7 days
cholera—24 hours
dengue—7 days
diphtheria—24 hours
E. coli infection—24 hours
encephalitis—7 days
food-borne disease, including but not limited to
    Clostridium perfringens, staphylococcal, and *Bacillus cereus*—24 hours
gonorrhea—24 hours
granuloma inguinale—24 hours
Haemophilus influenzae, invasive disease—24 hours
hepatitis A—24 hours
hepatitis B—24 hours
hepatitis B carriage—7 days
hepatitis non-A, non-B—7 days
human immunodeficiency virus infection (HIV)
    confirmed—7 days
legionellosis—7 days
leprosy—7 days
leptospirosis—7 days
Lyme disease—7 days
lymphogranuloma venereum—7 days
malaria—7 days
measles (rubeola)—24 hours
meningitis, pneumococcal—7 days
meningitis, viral (aseptic)—7 days
meningococcal disease—24 hours
mucocutaneous lymph node syndrome (Kawasaki
    syndrome)—7 days
mumps—7 days

Excerpt from the North Carolina Administrative Code Regarding
Reporting of Communicable Diseases

Box 7-3

VACCINATIONS REQUIRING VACCINE INFORMATION STATEMENTS

Anthrax
Chickenpox
Diphtheria, tetanus, and pertussis
Hib
Hepatitis A
Hepatitis B
Influenza
Lyme disease
Measles, mumps, and rubella
Meningococcal
Pneumococcal polysaccharide
Pneumococcal conjugate
Polio

following information:

1. Date the vaccine was administered
2. Lot number and manufacturer of vaccine
3. Any adverse reactions to the vaccine
4. Name, title, and address of the person who administered the vaccine

Box 7-3 lists the vaccines and toxoids covered by the National Childhood Vaccine Injury Act.

Abuse, Neglect, or Maltreatment

Abuse, neglect, or maltreatment of any person who is incapable of self-protection usually falls under this category and may include the elderly or the mentally incompetent. Each state has its own regulations regarding what must be reported. Patient confidentiality rights are waived when the law requires you to report certain conditions.

Abuse is thought to be the second most common cause of death in children under age 5. The Federal Child Abuse Prevention and Treatment Act mandates that threats to a child's physical and mental welfare be reported. Health care workers, teachers, and social workers who report suspected abuse are not identified to the parents and are protected against liability. State laws vary regarding the procedure for reporting abuse. Local regulations should be outlined in the policies and procedures manuals at any outpatient facility. If you suspect a child is being abused, relay your suspicions to your supervisor. The health care facility will make a formal report. When authorities receive a report from a health care provider, they follow up by investigating the situation. For assistance in reporting suspected child abuse, you may call the national 24-hour hotline at 800-4 A CHILD (800-422-4453).

National Childhood Vaccine Injury Act of 1986

Health care providers who administer certain vaccines and toxoids must report to the U. S. Department of Health & Human Services (DHHS) the occurrence of any side effects listed in the manufacturer's package insert. In addition, health care providers must record in the patient's record the

Spousal abuse is on the rise in this country. Many women and children are trapped in a cycle of abuse. Mothers who are financially dependent on their abusers may see no way out. You should record any information gathered in the patient interview or anything observed in the course of dealing with the patient that may indicate abuse. Report these observations to your supervisor. Most communities have anonymous safe places for victims of domestic abuse, and you should be familiar with these services. With proper referrals, you may be able to help break the cycle of domestic abuse.

This country is also undergoing a rise in elderly parents being cared for by their adult children who also have the responsibility of raising young children. This phenomenon can cause great stress among caregivers. Abuse of the elderly can be in the form of mistreatment or neglect (not providing appropriate care). You should pay attention to observations and information provided by your elderly patients. If mistreatment is suspected, alert your supervisor. Support groups for those caring for the elderly are useful in dealing with the challenges of caring for others.

Violent Injuries

Health care providers have the legal duty to report suspected criminal acts. Injuries resulting from weapons, assault, attempted suicide, and rape must be reported to local authorities.

Other Reports

A diagnosis of cancer must be reported to assist in tracking malignancies and identifying environmental carcinogens. Just as the CDC keeps track of all communicable diseases reported, a database of treated tumors is kept in hospitals through a tumor registry. Some states also require that epilepsy (a seizure condition) be reported to local motor vehicle departments. The testing of newborns for phenylketonuria (PKU), which can cause mental retardation, is required in all states. Some states require positive PKU results to be reported to the health department so that close observation and follow-up care are ensured to prevent serious complications for the infant. Infantile hypothyroidism is also a reportable condition in some states.

Checkpoint Question

4. What are six situations and conditions health care providers are legally required to report?

SPECIFIC LAWS AND STATUTES THAT APPLY TO HEALTH PROFESSIONALS

Licensure, Certification, and Registration

Medical professionals can be licensed, certified, or **registered**. Licensure is regulated by laws, such as medical prac-

tice acts and nursing practice acts. If a particular profession is a licensed one, it is mandatory that one maintain a license in each state where he or she works. Each state determines the qualifications and requirements for licensure of a particular profession. A state agency will be responsible for issuing and renewing licenses. Most professionals are licensed to practice their profession according to certain guidelines and are limited to specific duties.

The term *registered* indicates that a professional has met basic requirements, usually for education, has passed standard testing, and has been approved by a governing body to perform given tasks within a state. A national registry is available to verify a potential employee's status.

Certification is a voluntary process regulated through a professional organization. Standards for certification are set by the organization issuing the certificate.

Controlled Substances Act

The Controlled Substances Act of 1970 is a federal law enforced by the Drug Enforcement Agency (DEA). The act regulates the manufacture, distribution, and dispensing of narcotics and nonnarcotic drugs considered to have a high potential for abuse. This act was designed to decrease the illegal use of controlled substances and to prevent substance abuse by medical professionals. The law requires that any health professional who dispenses, administers, or prescribes narcotics or other controlled substances be registered with the DEA.

Health care facilities who maintain a stock of controlled substances in the office for dispensing or administration must use a special triplicate order form available through the DEA. A record of each transaction must be kept and retained for 2 to 3 years. The record must be available for inspection by the DEA at any time. The act requires that all controlled substances be kept in a locked cabinet out of the patients' view and that the keys be kept secure. Theft should be reported immediately to the local police and the nearest DEA office. Prescription pads used for prescribing controlled substances must remain in a safe place at all times.

This act also requires a health care facility to return all registration certificates and any unused order forms to the DEA if the facility is closed or sold. Violation of this act is a criminal offense. Penalties range from fines to imprisonment. Table 7-1 on the next page, outlines the classification of controlled substances.

Good Samaritan Act

As the number of lawsuits against doctors began to rise, many feared that giving emergency care to strangers outside the office could lead to malpractice suits. To combat that fear, all states now have Good Samaritan acts. Good Samaritan acts ensure that caregivers are immune from liability suits as long as

Table 7-1	CONTROLLED SUBSTANCES	
Schedule	Description	Examples
I	These drugs have the highest potential for abuse and have no currently accepted medical use in the United States. There are no accepted safety standards for use of these drugs or substances even under medical supervision, although some are used experimentally in carefully controlled research projects.	Opium Marijuana Lysergic acid diethylamide (LSD) Peyote Mescaline
II	These drugs have a high potential for abuse. They have accepted medicinal use in the United States but with severe restrictions. Abuse of these drugs can lead to dependence, either psychological or physiological. Schedule II drugs require a written prescription and cannot be refilled or called in to the pharmacy by a health care facility. Only in extreme emergencies may the doctor call in the prescription. A handwritten prescription must be presented to the pharmacist within 72 hours.	Morphine Codeine Seconal Cocaine Amphetamine Dilaudid Ritalin
III	These drugs have a limited potential for psychological or physiological dependence. The prescription may be called in to the pharmacist by the doctor and refilled up to 5 times in a 6-month period.	Paregoric Tylenol with codeine Fiorinal
IV	These drugs have a lower potential for abuse than those in Schedules II and III. They can be called in to the pharmacist by a medical office employee and may be refilled up to 5 times in a 6-month period.	Librium Valium Darvon Phenobarbital
V	These drugs have a lower potential for abuse than those in Schedules I, II, III, and IV.	Lomotil Dimetane expectorant DC Robitussin-DAC

they give care in good faith and in a manner that a reasonable and prudent person would in a similar situation. Each state has specific guidelines. Some even set standards for various professional levels, such as one set of standards for a physician and another set of standards for emergency medical technicians. Your state's Good Samaritan Act will not protect you if you are grossly negligent or willfully perform negligent acts.

You are not covered by the Good Samaritan Act while you are working at a medical facility, nor does it cover doctors in the performance of their duties. Liability and malpractice insurance policies are available to protect you in those situations. If you render emergency care and accept compensation for that care, the act does not apply.

The provisions only cover acts outside of the formal practice of the profession.

BASIS OF MEDICAL LAW

Tort Law

A tort is a wrongful act that results in harm for which restitution must be made. The two forms of torts are intentional and unintentional. An allegation of an **unintentional tort** means that the accuser (the **plaintiff**) believes a mistake has been made; however, the plaintiff believes the caregiver or accused party (the **defendant**) was operating in good faith and did not intend the mistake to occur.

Negligence and Malpractice (Unintentional Torts)

Most unintentional torts involve negligence. These are the most common forms of medical malpractice suits.

Negligence is performing an act that a reasonable health care worker or provider would not have done or the omission of an act that a reasonable professional or provider would have done. Failure to take reasonable precautions to prevent harm to a patient is termed **negligence**. If a doctor is involved, the term usually used is malpractice. Malpractice is said to have occurred when the patient is harmed by the professional's actions. There are three types of malpractice:

- Malfeasance—incorrect treatment
- Misfeasance—treatment performed incorrectly
- Nonfeasance—treatment delayed or not attempted

In a legal situation, the standard of care determines what a reasonable professional would have done. Standards of care are written by various professional agencies to clarify what the reasonable and prudent physician or health care worker would do in a given situation. Standards of care vary with the level of the professional. A registered nurse is not held to the same standards of care as a physician, nor is the medical assistant expected to perform by the same standards as the registered nurse. Each must practice within the scope of their training. The representing attorney may seek an **expert witness** to state under oath the standards of care for a specific situation. Expert witnesses may be physicians, nurses, physical therapists, or other specialized practitioners who have excellent reputations in their field.

Expert witnesses are always used in malpractice cases, except when the doctrine of **res ipsa loquitur** is tried. This doctrine means "the thing speaks for itself." In other words, it is obvious that the doctor's actions or negligence caused the injury. A judge must preapprove the use of this theory in pretrial hearings. An example of a case tried under this doctrine might be a fracture that occurred when the patient fell from an examining table.

For negligence to be proved, the plaintiff's attorney must prove four elements were present: duty, dereliction of duty, direct cause, and damage. The courts place the burden of proof on the plaintiff; the doctor is assumed to have given proper care until proven otherwise.

Duty

Duty is present when the patient and the doctor have formed a contract. This is usually straightforward and the easiest of the elements to prove.

Dereliction of Duty

The patient must prove that the doctor did not meet the standard of care guidelines, either by performing an act inappropriately or by omitting an act.

Direct Cause

The plaintiff must prove that the derelict act directly caused the patient's injury. This can be difficult to prove if the patient has an extensive medical history that may have contributed to the injury.

Damage

The plaintiff must prove that an injury or **damages** occurred. Documentation must be available to prove a diagnosis of an injury or illness.

Jury Awards

There are three types of awards for damages:

1. *Nominal.* Minimal injuries or damages occurred and compensation is small.
2. *Actual (compensatory).* Money is awarded for the injury, disability, mental suffering, loss of income, or the anticipated future earning loss. This payment is moderate to significant.
3. *Punitive.* Money is awarded to punish the practitioner

for reckless or malicious wrongdoing. Punitive damages are the most costly.

Checkpoint Question

5. What four elements must be proved in a negligence suit?

Intentional Torts

An **intentional tort** is an act that takes place with malice and with the intent of causing harm. Intentional torts are the deliberate violation of another person's legal rights. Examples of intentional torts are assault and battery, use of duress, invasion of privacy, defamation of character, fraud, tort of outrage, and undue influence. These are described next.

Assault and Battery

Assault is the unauthorized attempt or threat to touch another person without consent. **Battery** is the actual physical touching of a patient without consent; this includes beating and physical abuse. By law, a conscious adult has the right to refuse medical care. An example of battery might be suturing a laceration against the patient's expressed wish.

Duress

If a patient is coerced into an act, the patient can possibly sue for the tort of **duress**. Following is an example in which a patient may be able to sue successfully for assault, battery, and duress: A 22-year-old woman arrives at a pregnancy center. She is receiving public assistance and has five children. Her pregnancy test is positive. The staff persuades her to have an abortion. She signs the consent form, and the abortion is performed. Later she sues, stating that she was verbally coerced into signing the consent form (duress) and that the abortion was performed against her wishes (assault and battery).

Invasion of Privacy

Patients have the right to privacy. Most offices have patients sign an authorization to release information to their insurance company on their first visit. This covers each return visit unless the insurance carrier changes. Written permission must be obtained from the patient to:

- Release health records or personal data
- Publish case histories in medical journals
- Make photographs of the patient (exception: suspected cases of abuse or maltreatment)
- Allow observers in examination rooms

For example, a 57-year-old woman is seen in a medical office for a skin biopsy. Her insurance company calls asking for information regarding the bill and asks for the biopsy report. The office releases the requested information and then finds that the patient never signed a release form. She has a valid case for invasion of privacy.

Defamation of Character

Making malicious or false statements about a person's character or reputation is **defamation of character**. **Libel** refers to written statements and **slander** refers to oral statements. For example, a patient asks for a referral to another doctor. She states that she has heard "Dr. Rogers is a good surgeon." You have heard that he has a history of alcoholism. You tell the patient that he is probably not a good choice because of his drinking. That is defamation of his character, and you could be sued for saying it.

Fraud

Fraud is any deceitful act with the intention to conceal the truth, such as:

- intentionally raising false expectations regarding recovery
- not properly instructing the patient regarding possible side effects of a procedure
- filing false insurance claims.

Tort of Outrage

Tort of outrage is the intentional infliction of emotional distress. For this tort to be proved, the plaintiff's attorney must show that the physician:

- intended to inflict emotional distress
- acted in a manner that is not morally or ethically acceptable
- caused severe emotional distress.

Undue Influence

Improperly persuading another to act in a way contrary to that person's free will is termed undue influence. For instance, preying on the elderly or the mentally incompetent is a common type of undue influence. Unethical practitioners who gain the trust of these persons and persuade them to submit to expensive and unnecessary medical procedures are practicing undue influence.

Checkpoint Question

6. What is the difference between assault and battery?

THE LITIGATION PROCESS

The litigation process begins when a patient consults an attorney because he or she believes a health care provider has done wrong or becomes aware of a possible prior injury. The patient's attorney obtains the health records, which are reviewed by medicolegal consultants. (Such consultants may be nurses or physicians who are considered experts in their field.) Then the plaintiff's attorney files a complaint, a written statement that lists the claim against the health care provider and the remedy desired, usually monetary compensation.

The defendant and his or her attorney answer the complaint. The discovery phase begins with interrogatories and **depositions**. During this phase, attorneys for both parties gather relevant information.

Next, the trial phase begins. A jury is selected unless the parties agree to a **bench trial**. In a bench trial, the judge hears the case without a jury and renders a **verdict** (decision or judgment). Opening statements are given, first by the plaintiff's attorney, then by the defendant's attorney. The plaintiff's attorney presents the case. Expert witnesses are called, and the evidence is shown. Examination of the witnesses begins. **Direct examination** involves questioning by one's own attorney; **cross-examination** is questioning by the opposing attorney. When the plaintiff's attorney is finished, the defense presents the opposing arguments and evidence. The plaintiff's attorney may cross-examine the defendant's witnesses. Closing arguments are heard. Finally, a verdict is made.

If the defendant is found guilty, damages are awarded. If the defendant is found not guilty, the charges are dismissed. The decision may be appealed to a higher court. An **appeal** is a process by which the higher court reviews the decision of the lower court.

DEFENSES TO PROFESSIONAL LIABILITY SUITS

The objective of all court proceedings is to uncover the truth. Many defenses are available to a health care worker who is being sued. These include the health record, statute of limitations, assumption of risk, res judicata, contributory negligence, and comparative negligence, discussed next.

Health Records

The best and most solid defense the caregiver has is the health record. Every item in the record is considered to be a part of a legal document. Juries may believe a health record regardless of testimony. Juries tend to believe these records because they are tangible items from the actual time the injury occurred. There is a common saying in the medicolegal world: "If it's not in the chart, it did not happen." This means that even negative findings should be listed. For example, instead of saying that the patient's neurological history is negative, the documentation might say the patient reports no headaches, seizures, one-sided weakness, and so on. Entries in the medical record refresh the memory of the defendant and provide documentation of care. You must make sure that all of your documentation is timely, accurate, and legible.

Statute of Limitations

Each state has a statute that defines the length of time during which a patient may file a suit against a caregiver. When the **statute of limitations** expires, the patient loses the right to file a claim. Generally, the limits vary from 1 to 3 years following the alleged occurrence. Other states use a combination rule. Some states allow 1 to 3 years following the patient's discovery of the occurrence. States vary greatly when an alleged injury involves a minor. The statute may not take effect until the minor reaches the age of majority and then may extend 2 to 3 years past this time. Some states have longer claim periods in wrongful death suits.

Assumption of Risk

In the assumption of risk defense, the health care provider will claim that the patient was aware of the risks involved before the procedure and fully accepted the potential for damages. For example, a patient is instructed regarding the adverse effects of chemotherapy. The patient fully understands these risks, receives the chemotherapy, and wants to sue for alopecia (hair loss). Alopecia is a given risk with certain forms of chemotherapy. A signed consent form indicating that the patient was informed of all of the risks of a procedure proves this point.

Res Judicata

The doctrine of **res judicata** means "the thing has been decided." Once the suit has been brought against the health care provider or patient and a settlement has been reached, the losing party may not countersue. If, for instance, the health care provider sues a patient for not paying bills and the court orders the patient to pay, the patient cannot sue for malpractice. The opposite may occur as well. If the health care provider is sued for malpractice and loses, he cannot countersue for defamation of character.

Contributory Negligence

With the **contributory negligence** defense, the health care provider usually admits that negligence has occurred; he or she will claim, however, that the patient aggravated the injury or assisted in making the injury worse. Most states do not grant damage awards for contributory negligence. If an award is granted, the courts assess **comparative negligence**.

Comparative Negligence

In comparative negligence, the award of damages is based on a percentage of the contribution to the negligence. If the patient contributed 30% to the damage, the damage award is 30% less than what was granted. For example, the courts may decide that the negligence is shared at 50%. Therefore, if the court assessed damages of $20,000, the health care provider would be responsible for $10,000.

In the past, contributory negligence, such as a patient not returning for appointments, was seen as absolute defense for the doctor. Since the 1970s, however, the trend has been toward using the defense of comparative negligence, with the responsibility shared between the doctor and the patient.

Immunity

The Federal Tort Claim Act of 1946 prohibits suits against any U. S. governmental facility, such as veterans hospitals or military bases. This provides immunity to all of their employees for ordinary negligence but not for intentional torts.

DEFENSE FOR THE MEDICAL ASSISTANT

Respondeat Superior or Law of Agency

The doctrine of **respondeat superior** literally means "let the master answer." This may also be called law of agency. This doctrine implies that physicians are liable for the actions of their employees. The physician is responsible for your actions as a medical assistant as long as your actions are within your scope of practice. If your actions exceed your abilities or training, the physician is not generally responsible for any error that you make. You must understand that you can be sued in this instance and that respondeat superior does not guarantee immunity for your actions.

To protect yourself, have your job description in written form and always practice within its guidelines. Do not perform tasks that you have not been trained to do. Never hesitate to seek clarification from your supervisor. If you are not sure about something, such as a medication order, ask!

Malpractice insurance is available to allied health care professionals for further protection. Malpractice premiums are inexpensive and afford protection against losing any personal assets if sued. The insurance company would pay damages as assessed by a jury. Of course, as with any insurance policy, there will be conditions of coverage and maximum amounts the company will pay. Box 7-4 provides some additional tips for preventing lawsuits.

 Checkpoint Question
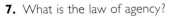
7. What is the law of agency?

EMPLOYMENT AND SAFETY LAWS

Civil Rights Act of 1964, Title VII

Title VII of the Civil Rights Act of 1964 protects employees from discrimination in the workplace. The Equal Employment Opportunity Commission (EEOC) enforces the provisions of

---

Box 7-4

YOU CAN AVOID LITIGATION

- Keep medical records neat and organized. Always document and sign legibly.
- Stay abreast of new laws and medical technology.
- Keep your CPR and first aid certification current.
- Never give any information over the telephone unless you are sure of the caller's identity and you have patient consent.
- Limit waiting time for patients. If an emergency arises, causing a long wait, explain to the patients in a timely and professional manner.
- Practice good public relations. Always be polite, smile, and show genuine concern for your patients and their families.

---

the act and investigates any possible infractions. Employers may not refuse to hire, limit, segregate or classify, fire, compensate, or provide working conditions and privileges on the basis of race, color, sex, religion, or national origin. This act determines the questions that may be asked in a job interview. For example, a potential employee cannot be asked questions that would reveal age, marital status, religious affiliation, height, weight, or arrest record. It is acceptable, however, to ask if an applicant has ever been convicted of a crime. In the health care setting, employers can require a criminal records check and even drug screening to ensure the safety of the patients.

Sexual Harassment

In recent years, Title VII has been expanded to include sexual harassment. Sexual harassment is defined by the EEOC as unwelcome sexual advances or requests for sexual favors in the workplace. The definition includes other verbal or physical conduct of a sexual nature when such conduct is made a condition of an individual's employment, is used as a basis for hiring or promotion, or has the purpose or effect of unreasonably interfering with an individual's work performance. If such behavior creates an intimidating, hostile, or offensive working environment, it is considered sexual harassment. In the past two decades court decisions have confirmed that this form of harassment is a cause for both criminal prosecution and civil litigation.

Americans with Disabilities Act

Title VII also includes the Americans with Disabilities Act (ADA), which prohibits discrimination against people with substantial disabilities in all employment practices, including job application procedures, hiring, firing, advancement, compensation, training, benefits, and all other privileges of employment. The ADA applies to all employers with 15 or more employees. The law covers those with impairments that limit their major life activities. The statute also protects those with AIDS or HIV-positive status and individuals with a history of mental illness or cancer. ADA also requires that employers provide basic accommodations for disabled employees. Those basic accommodations include extra-wide parking spaces close to the door, ramps or elevators, electric or easily opened doors, bathroom facilities designed for the disabled, an accessible break room, and a work area with counters low enough for a person in a wheelchair.

The ADA also takes safety into consideration. Employers are permitted to establish qualification standards that will exclude individuals who pose a direct threat to others if that risk cannot be lowered to an acceptable level by reasonable accommodations. In the medical field, technical standards are established that outline physical requirements of a certain job. If a particular job requires reaching a certain height, it is unreasonable to expect an employer to hire a person who is too short. The law is designed to protect employees, not to require unreasonable accommodations.

The ADA also requires that all public buildings be accessible to physically challenged people. Following is a partial list of ways the medical office can comply with this act:

- Entrance ramps
- Widened rest rooms to be wheelchair accessible
- Elevated toilet bowls for easier transferring from wheelchairs
- Easy-to-reach elevator buttons
- Braille signs
- Access to special telephone services to communicate with hearing-impaired patients

Occupational Safety and Health Act

Employers must provide safe environments for their employees. In accordance with the Occupational Safety and Health Act of 1970, the Occupational Safety and Health Administration (OSHA) controls and monitors safety for workers. Specific OSHA rules and regulations protect the clinical worker from exposure to **blood-borne pathogens**. Blood-borne pathogens are organisms that can be spread through direct contact with blood or body fluids from an infected person. Universal precautions are designed to protect health care workers from blood and body fluids contaminated with HIV, hepatitis, or any contagious "bugs" by requiring that those in direct contact with patients use protective equipment (e.g., gloves, gowns, face mask). In days past, health care workers felt that they needed protection only from patients with known risk factors (sharing needles, having unprotected sexual intercourse). OSHA's regulations ensure protection from contracting a contagious disease from *any* body fluids handled.

Your training will include an extensive study of safety issues and protection against accidental exposure to blood-borne pathogens. Box 7-5 on page 83, outlines OSHA rules governing all free-standing health care providers. Box 7-6 outlines the laws governing employer and employee rights and responsibilities.

Box 7-5

OCCUPATIONAL SAFETY AND HEALTH ACT OF 1970 RULES GOVERNING HEALTH CARE PROVIDERS

OSHA defines body fluids as semen, blood, amniotic fluids, vaginal secretions, synovial fluid (from joint spaces), pleural fluid (from the lungs), pericardial fluid (from the heart), cerebrospinal fluid (from the spinal cord), and saliva. OSHA employs inspectors who may conduct inspections and issue citations for violations and recommend penalties. Under specific rules, OSHA requires that health care facilities provide:

- A list of all employees who might be exposed to blood-borne diseases on either a regular or an occasional basis.
- A written exposure control plan that outlines steps to be taken in the event of an employee's accidental exposure to blood-borne pathogens.
- One employee who is responsible for OSHA compliance.
- Availability of protective clothing that fits properly.
- An employee training program in writing and records of sessions and participants.
- Warning labels and signs denoting biohazards (potentially dangerous materials).
- Written guidelines for identifying, containing, and disposing of medical waste, including housecleaning and laundry decontamination.
- Written guidelines and procedures to follow if any employee is exposed to blood or other potentially infectious materials, as well as a policy for reporting incidents of exposure and maintaining records.
- Postexposure evaluation procedures, including follow-up testing of the exposed employee.
- Material safety data sheets (MSDS) listing each ingredient in a product used in the office Manufacturers provide an MSDS for every product they sell Information included in the sheets includes any hazards involved or necessary precautions that must be taken when handling materials.
- Hepatitis B vaccine free of charge to employees working with body fluids.

Box 7-6

LAWS GOVERNING EMPLOYER AND EMPLOYMENT RIGHTS AND RESPONSIBILITIES

Fair Labor Standards Act of 1939
- Regulates wages and working conditions including
- Federal minimum wage, overtime compensation, equal pay requirements, child labor, hours, requirements for record keeping.

Civil Rights Act of 1964, Title VII
- Applies to employers with 15 or more employees for at least 20 weeks of the year.
- Federal regulation forbids discrimination on the basis of race, color, sex, religion, or national origin. Some state laws also prohibit discrimination for sexual orientation, personal appearance, mental health, mental retardation, marital status, parenthood, and political affiliation.

Americans with Disabilities Act of 1990
- Applies to employers with 15 or more employees.
- Prohibits discrimination against individuals with substantial impairments in all employment practices.

Age Discrimination in Employment Act of 1967
- Applies to employers with 15 or more employees.
- Regulates discrimination against workers on the basis of age. Protects those 40–65.

Family and Medical Leave Act of 1993
- Employees are covered after 1 year or 1,250 hours of employment over the past 12 months.
- Provides up to 12 weeks per year of unpaid, job-protected leave to eligible employees for certain family and medical reasons.

Immigration Reform and Control Act of 1986
- Applies to employers with four or more employees.
- Prohibits employment of illegal aliens and protects legal aliens from discrimination based on national origin or citizenship.

specific laws regarding patient care, insurance billing, collections, and such matters.

Checkpoint Question

8. What are blood-borne pathogens? Which government agency governs their control in the medical office?

MEDICAL ETHICS

Medical **ethics** are principles of ethical and moral conduct that govern the behavior and conduct of health professionals.

Other Legal Considerations

The Clinical Laboratory Improvement Amendments (CLIA) of 1988 contain specific rules and regulations regarding laboratory safety.

The Joint Commission on Accreditation of Healthcare Organizations (JCAHO) is a private organization that sets standards for health care administration. Each state also has

These principles define proper medical etiquette, customs, and professional courtesy. Ethics are guidelines specifying right or wrong and are enforced by peer review and professional organizations. Laws are regulations and rules that are enforced by the government. **Bioethics** are issues and problems that affect a patient's life; many bioethical issues have arisen from the advances of modern medicine.

Allied Health Professional's Role in Ethics

As an allied health professional, you are also governed by ethical standards and are responsible for:

- Protecting patient confidentiality
- Following all state and federal laws
- Being honest in all your actions

You must apply ethical standards as you perform your duties. You must realize that your personal feelings of right and wrong should be kept separate if they differ from the ethics of your profession. The care you give patients must be objective, and personal opinions about options must not be shared.

Patient Advocacy

Advocacy requires that you consider the best interests of the patient above all other concerns. This often means setting aside your own personal beliefs, values, and biases and looking at a given situation in an objective manner. You should never, however, be asked or forced to compromise your own value system.

Patient Confidentiality

Confidentiality of patient information is an important ethical principle. As discussed earlier, information obtained in the care of the patient may not be revealed without the permission of the patient unless required by law. Whatever you say to, hear from, or do to a patient is confidential. Patients will reveal some of their innermost thoughts, feelings, and fears. This information is not for public knowledge. Family members, friends, pastors, or others may call the physician's office to inquire about a patient's condition. Many of these calls are made with good intentions; NO INFORMATION, however, should be released to anyone—friends, family, media, or insurance companies—without prior written approval from the patient.

Honesty

We all make mistakes at times; how we handle our mistakes is the indication of our ethical standards. If you make a mistake, you must immediately report the error to your supervisor. The mark of a true professional is the ability to admit mistakes and take full responsibility for all actions. When speaking to patients concerning medical issues, be honest;

WHAT IF

A patient is hearing impaired, and you cannot communicate with him or her. What should you do?

If the patient does not understand the procedure, he or she is not *informed*. Legally, you have not met your responsibilities to obtain informed consent if the patient does not understand the information you are trying to convey. If the patient cannot provide his or her own assistance, it is the legal responsibility of the health care provider to provide the means for effective communication.

Most community colleges offer courses in sign language. The Internet offers a site for the deaf community that will direct you to resources in your area. Handspeak is a site that provides a visual language dictionary. These websites are listed at the end of this chapter.

give the facts in a straightforward manner. Never offer false expectations or hope. Never minimize or exaggerate the risks or benefits of a procedure. If you do not know the answer to a question, say, "I don't know, but I will find out for you," or refer the question to your superior. Treating the patient with dignity, respect, and honesty in all interactions will build trust in you and your professional abilities.

BIOETHICS

Bioethics deals specifically with the moral issues and problems that affect human life. As a result of advances in medicine and research, many situations require moral decisions for which there are no clear answers. Abortion and genetic engineering are examples. The goal is to make the right decision in each specific instance as it applies to an individual's specific circumstances. What may be right for one patient may be wrong for another; that is the foundation of bioethics.

Allocation of Resources

The term *allocate* means set aside or designate for a purpose. Allocation of resources in the medical profession may refer to many health needs:

- *Organs for transplantation.* Who gets this heart, the college professor or the young recovering addict whose heart was damaged by his lifestyle? Should lifestyle or perceived worth be considered in the decision?
- *Funds for research.* Which disease should receive more funding for research, cancer or AIDS?

- *Funds for health care.* Where should the money be spent, for keeping alive extremely premature infants or making preventive health care available for a greater number of poor children?
- *Hospital beds and professional care.* With hospital care at a premium, who will pay for the indigent? How is it decided which patient is entitled to the last bed in the intensive care unit?

Obstetric Dilemmas

Advances in technology have created legal and ethical situations that have polarized opinions and are difficult to bring to consensus. Issues such as the beginning of life, genetic testing and engineering, sex determination, the rights of the fetus, ownership of the fertilized egg, and so forth will not be easily answered.

Organ Transplantation

Organ transplantation became a medical option in the mid 1950s, although at that time there were many problems with rejection of the organs by the recipient's immune system. When this postoperative complication was corrected by antirejection drugs, the practice became more common. Organs are viable (able to support life) for varying lengths of time, but most can be used successfully if transplanted within 24 to 48 hours. An organization in Richmond, Virginia, the United Network of Organ Sharing, coordinates local organ procurement teams that will fly to areas where organs are to be harvested to assist with the surgery if needed and to ensure the integrity of the organ. There are far fewer organs available than are needed, and every year thousands of patients die who could have lived if an organ had been available. The scarcity of organs has caused many Third World countries to become sources of organs as poor people sell parts of their bodies to meet their basic needs.

The use of organs from a baby born without a brain (anencephaly) raises serious ethical issues. The council states that everything must be done for the infant until the determination of death can be made. For infant organs to be transplanted, both parents must consent. Box 7-7 highlights the Uniform Anatomical Gift Act.

Withholding or Withdrawing Treatment

Health care professionals have a professional and ethical obligation to promote quality of life, which means sustaining life and relieving suffering. Sometimes, these obligations conflict with a patient's wishes. Patients have the right to refuse medical treatment and to request that life support or life-sustaining treatments be withheld or withdrawn. Withholding treatment means that certain medical treatments may not be initiated. Withdrawing treatment is terminating a treatment that has already begun. In 1991, congress passed the

Box 7-7

UNIFORM ANATOMICAL GIFT ACT

Approximately 60 American citizens die each day waiting for an organ transplant. Many organs can be transplanted, including the liver, kidney, cornea, heart, lung, and skin. To meet the growing need for organs and to allay the concern over donor standards, the National Conference of Commissioners for Uniform State Laws passed legislation known as the Uniform Anatomical Gift Act.

All acts include the following clauses:
- Any mentally competent person over age 18 may donate all or part of his or her body for transplantation or research.
- The donor's wishes supersede any other wishes except when state laws require an autopsy.
- Physicians accepting donor organs in good faith are immune from lawsuits against harvesting organs.
- Death of the donor must be determined by a physician not involved with the transplant team.
- Financial compensation may not be given to the donor or survivors.
- Persons wishing to donate organs can revoke permission or change their minds at any time.

In most states the Department of Motor Vehicles asks applicants for a driver's license about organ donation and indicates their wishes on their license. In addition, an individual may declare the wish to donate all or parts of the body in a will or any legal document, including a Uniform Donor Card. Organ donors should make their families aware of their wishes to ensure they will be carried out.

Self-Determination Act, which gave all hospitalized patients the right to make health care decisions on admission to the hospital. These decisions may be referred to as advance directives. Today, everyone is encouraged to participate in his or her own end-of-life decisions. We can go online and complete an advance directive. An **advance directive** is a statement of a person's wishes for medical decisions prior to a critical event. Advance directives may include specific wishes, such as whether a ventilator can be used, whether cardiopulmonary resuscitation (CPR) should be initiated, and whether a feeding tube should be inserted. Just completing an advance directive does not ensure that the patient's wishes will be carried out. It is important to make family members aware of these wishes. The patient's next of kin should keep a copy of the advance directive, and one should be placed in the medical office chart with special notation. Figure 7-4 on next page, is a sample of an advance directive.

ADVANCE DIRECTIVE

UNIFORM ADVANCE DIRECTIVE OF [list name of declarant]

To my family, physician, attorney, and anyone else who may become responsible for my health, welfare, or affairs, I make this declaration while I am of sound mind.

If I should ever become in a terminal state and there is no reasonable expectation of my recovery, I direct that I be allowed to die a natural death and that my life not be prolonged by extraordinary measures. I do, however, ask that medication be mercifully administered to me to alleviate suffering, even though this may shorten my remaining life.

This statement is made after full reflection and is in accordance with my full desires. I want the above provisions carried out to the extent permitted by law. Insofar as they are not legally enforceable, I wish that those to whom this will is addressed will regard themselves as morally bound by this instrument.

If permissible in the jurisdiction in which I may be hospitalized I direct that in the event of a terminal diagnosis, the physicians supervising my care discontinue feeding should the continuation of feeding be judged to result in unduly prolonging a natural death.

If permissible in the jurisdiction in which I may be hospitalized I direct that in the event of a terminal diagnosis, the physicians supervising my care discontinue hydration (water) should the continuation of hydration be judged to result in unduly prolonging a natural death.

I herewith authorize my spouse, if any, or any relative who is related to me within the third degree to effectuate my transfer from any hospital or other health care facility in which I may be receiving care should that facility decline or refuse to effectuate the instructions given herein.

I herewith release any and all hospitals, physicians, and others for myself and for my estate from any liability for complying with this instrument.

Signed:

_____

[list name of declarant]

City of residence: _____

[city of residence]

County of residence: _____

[county of residence]

State of residence: _____

[state of residence]

Social Security Number: _____

[social security number]

Date: _____

_____

Witness

_____

Witness

STATE OF _____

COUNTY OF _____

This day personally appeared before me, the undersigned authority, a Notary Public in and for _____ County, _____ State,

_____   _____

(Witnesses)

who, being first duly sworn, say that they are the subscribing witnesses to the declaration of [list name of declarant], the declarant, signed, sealed, and published and declared the same as and for his declaration, in the presence of both these affiants; and that these affiants, at the request of said declarant, in the presence of each other, and in the presence of said declarant, all present at the same time, signed their names as attesting witnesses to said declaration.

Affiants further say that this affidavit is made at the request of [list name of declarant], declarant, and in his presence, and that [list name of declarant] at the time the declaration was executed, in the opinion of the affiants, of sound mind and memory, and over the age of eighteen years.

Taken, subscribed and sworn to before me by _____(witness) and

_____ (witness) this _____ day of_____, 20_____.

My commission expires: _____

_____ Notary Public

F I G U R E   7 - 4 .   Sample advance directive.

Procedure 7-1

Performing within Legal and Ethical Boundaries

Equipment/Supplies: Paper, writing utensil, computer with Internet access, textbook, Medical Assistants' Creed, AAMA Code of Ethics.

Steps

1. Read and understand the Medical Assistants' Creed.

2. Read and understand the five principles of the American Association of Medical Assistants Code of Ethics.

3. Identify the legal implications of this action.

4. Identify the ethical implications of this action.

5. Identify three resources that support your conclusions.

6. Based on this information, resolve the issue in a legal and ethical manner.

Checkpoint Question

9. What is an advance directive? How can a patient be sure his or her wishes will be followed?

CHAPTER SUMMARY

The fields of medicine and law are linked in common concern for the patient's health and rights. Increasingly, health care professionals are the object of malpractice lawsuits. You must keep abreast of medicolegal issues to protect yourself and other health care professionals from legal action. You can help prevent medical malpractice by acting professionally, maintaining clinical competency, and properly documenting in the medical record. Promoting good public relations between the patient and the health care team can avoid frivolous or unfounded suits and direct attention and energy toward optimum health care.

Medical ethics and bioethics involve complex issues and controversial topics. There will be no easy or clear-cut answers to questions raised by these issues. Your first priority must be to act as your patients' advocate with their best interests and concerns foremost in your actions and interactions. You must always maintain ethical standards and report the unethical behaviors of others.

Many acts and regulations affect health care organizations and their operations. All health care setings must keep current on all legal updates. Most states publish a monthly bulletin that reports on new legislation. Every state has a website that will link you to legislative action. Read these on a regular basis. Each facility should have legal counsel who can assist in interpreting legal issues.

Critical Thinking Challenges

1. An acquaintance who knows you work in the medical field asks you to diagnose her rash. What do you say?
2. A patient owes a big bill at your facility. She requests copies of her records. What do you do?
3. You suspect that a new employee in the facility is misusing narcotics. What do you do?

Answers to Checkpoint Questions

1. Criminal law deals with the act of practicing medicine without a license.
2. The following elements must be in a physician's termination intent letter: statement of intent, explanation

of reasons, termination date, availability of medical records, and a recommendation that the patient seek medical help as needed.

3. Never ask a patient to sign a consent form if the patient does not understand the procedure, has questions about the procedure, or is unable to read the consent form.
4. The six situations or conditions legally requiring disclosure are vital statistics, medical examiner reports, infectious diseases, abuse or maltreatment, violent injuries, and others according to state laws.
5. The four elements that must be proved in a negligence suit are duty, dereliction of duty, direct cause, and damages.
6. Assault is the attempt or threat to touch another person without permission; battery is the actual touching.
7. The law of agency implies that physicians are liable for the actions of their employees. The physician is responsible for your actions as a medical assistant, as long as your actions are within your scope of practice and you practice the standard of care required for your assigned duties and responsibilities.
8. Blood-borne pathogens are organisms that can be spread through direct contact with blood or body fluids from an infected person. OSHA governs their control in the medical office.
9. An advance directive is a statement of a person's wishes for medical decisions prior to a critical event. Letting family know of these wishes and keeping a copy in the medical office chart will help ensure that these wishes are carried out.

WWW.GO   Websites

To keep abreast of changes in the medical field:

- Go to your state's home page and click on the link to the state legislature to view pending state legislation
- Go to The Library of Congress to view federal legislation to be considered in the coming week via the website http://Thomas.loc.gov

Equal Employment Opportunity Commission
    www.eeoc.gov
For a complete text of Title VII of the Civil Rights Act
    www.eeoc.gov/laws/vii.html
U. S. Department of Labor, Bureau of Labor Statistics
    http://stats.bls.gov
To complete an advance directive
    www.LegalZoom.com

Spanish Terminology

¿Usted entiende la información que acaba de recibir?	Do you understand the information I have given?
¿Usted nos autoriza a llevar a cabo este procedimiento médico?	Do you give us permission to perform this procedure?
Firme aquí, por favor. Please sign here.	

8

Health Records and Records Management

CHAPTER OBJECTIVES

In this chapter, you'll learn:

1. To spell and define the key terms.
2. To describe standard and electronic health record systems.
3. To explain the process for releasing health records to third-party payers and individual patients.
4. To list and explain the EHR guidelines established to protect computerized records.
5. To list the standard information included in health records.
6. To identify and describe the types of formats used for documenting patient information in outpatient settings.
7. To explain how to make an entry in a patient's health record, using abbreviations when appropriate.

8. To explain how to make a correction in a standard and electronic health record.
9. To identify the various ways health records can be stored.
10. To compare and contrast the differences between alphabetic and numeric filing systems and give an example of each.
11. To explain the purpose of the Health Insurance Portability and Accountability Act.

PERFORMANCE OBJECTIVE
Upon successfully completing this chapter, you will be able to:

1. To prepare and file a health record file folder.

KEY TERMS

alphabetic filing
chief complaint
chronological order
cross-reference
demographic data

electronic health records (EHR)
flow sheet
microfiche
microfilm

narrative
numeric filing
present illness
problem-oriented medical record (POMR)

reverse chronological order
SOAP
subject filing
workers' compensation

HEALTH RECORDS HAVE A VITAL role in ensuring quality patient care. Proper health records management requires adherence to certain legal, moral, and ethical standards. If these standards are disregarded, a breach of contract between patient and health care provider may occur, exposing the patient to potential embarrassment and making the health care provider vulnerable to lawsuits.

Health records have many uses, including research, quality assurance, and patient education. Information gathered from health records aids the government in planning for future health care needs and protecting the health of the public.

A thorough and accurate health record furnishes documented evidence of the patient's evaluation, treatment, change in condition, and communication with the health care provider.

STANDARD HEALTH RECORDS

The standard practice of recording and filing patient information in a folder and labeling it with the patient's name or a number is gradually being replaced by the use of **electronic health records (EHR)**, but in the meantime, a medical facility accumulates mounds of paper every day. There are a variety of options for record keeping. The best systems are those that have been tried, revised, and revised again. No matter how the records are stored, make sure that the information is:

- Easily retrievable
- Kept in an orderly manner
- Complete
- Legible
- Accurate
- Brief

Whether a record is on paper or a computer disk, all health records have the same contents.

Contents of the Record

A health record, often called a chart or a file, contains confidential clinical information about the patient's health and treatment in addition to billing and insurance information.

General information such as name, address, telephone number, date of birth, social security number, credit history, and next of kin is vital to a complete chart but should never be intermingled with the clinical information. Metal fasteners can be used to keep certain pages on one side of the chart.

The following information is typically found in the clinical section of the medical chart:

- *Chief complaint*—A description of the symptoms that led the patient to seek care. This information is supplied by the patient during the interview at the beginning of the visit. It is usually stated in the patient's own words in quotation marks. For example, the patient complains of "something stuck in my throat."

- *Present illness*—A more specific account of the chief complaint, including time frames and characteristics. For example, the patient says it started 2 days ago. She describes the pain as severe and stabbing and reports taking Tylenol with no relief.
- *Family and personal history*—A review of any major illnesses of family members, including grandparents, parents, siblings, aunts, and uncles. Any previous major illnesses and surgeries of the patient are listed under personal history.
- *Review of systems*—A systematic review of the body's ten systems to detect problems not yet identified. For example, problems with the integumentary system (skin) may be identified if the patient reports a rash, areas of discoloration, or change in a mole.
- *Progress notes*—Documentation of each patient encounter, including information obtained in phone calls and refills of prescriptions.
- *Radiographic reports*— Reports of any x-ray studies.
- *Laboratory results*—A copy of the results of any laboratory work.
- *Consultation reports*—Any reports from other health care professionals regarding consultations with the patient.
- *Medication administration*—Some facilities use a separate sheet to log medications given in the facility.
- *Diagnosis or medical impression*—The most recent entry on the progress note will contain the provider's opinion of the patient's problems.
- *Provider's identification and signature*—Experts have suggested that you sign your entire name instead of initials, with your credentials written after the name.
- *Documented advance directives, such as living will and power of attorney for medical care*—A copy of any instructions from the patient regarding end-of-life decisions or the appointment of another person who can give consent for treatment for the patient.
- *All correspondence pertaining to the patient*—Any letters or memos generated in the facility and sent out are copied and placed in the chart. Correspondence from other health care professionals is also included in the chart.

 Checkpoint Question

1. What is the chief complaint?

ELECTRONIC HEALTH RECORDS

Some facilities often use computers for storing patient **demographic data** (e.g., address, phone number), insurance billing, printing statements, managing appointments, and word processing. Data are saved, backed up, and stored electronically. In addition to accounting and tracking, computer charting in the clinical area is becoming more common. Such systems often use a touch screen, making it easy to store a patient's history, vital signs, and any other information. Documents such as letters from other providers are scanned and become a part of the permanent electronic record. Computer record keeping has many advantages, including legibility, easy storage and retrieval, and improved documentation. Documentation is improved because the computer will require that specific information be inserted. For example, when completing a patient history form, the computer will ask, "Is this patient male or female?" The question must be answered before you can move to the next screen, which prevents missed documentation. A paperless system eliminates the need for paper and storage space, and the possibility of losing a chart is nonexistent. Computer charting takes less time than handwriting notes. Health record software will continue to expand and integrate data in ways that will further revolutionize health documentation.

Computers do have some disadvantages, however, including downtime, cost, security issues, equipment failure, and the need for more in-depth staff training. In some facilities, the setup may consist of a mainframe with various terminals placed throughout the office.

Electronic Health Record Security

With computer records, confidential health information is at risk for being seen by unauthorized persons. The Health Insurance Portability and Accountability Act of 1996 (HIPAA) was passed to ensure the privacy of patients' records without creating problems transferring information between health professionals, which might harm the quality of care. HIPAA's privacy rule applies to health insurance plans, insurance clearinghouses, and health care providers who perform administrative transactions electronically (e.g., electronic billing, electronic claims submission). After review and some changes, HIPAA's final rule took effect in April 2003.

Many risk management companies have published guidelines for the EMR. Following are suggestions and guidelines based on HIPAA's requirements for practices using computers to transfer or store patient information. Experts advise facilities considering software programs to look for the following capabilities:

- User friendly commands that allow users to move easily within the system.
- Spell check, free text fields for inserting corrections and late entries. The electronic record is corrected by using the same rules as in the standard record. Entries are not deleted but corrected, with an explanation to avoid the appearance of hiding information.
- Security levels to limit entry to all functions.
- A system to repel hackers. Evidence shows that persons with access to technology can invade patients' records stored on computer databases. This is a gross breach of confidentiality and is illegal.

To maintain security, facilities are urged to do the following:

- Keep all computer backup disks in a safe place away from the practice.
- Store disks in a bank safe-deposit box.
- Use passwords with characters other than letters and encrypt the passwords.
- Change log-in codes and passwords every 30 days.
- Prepare a backup plan for use when the computer system is down.
- Turn terminals away from areas where information may be seen by patients.
- Keep the fax machines and printers that receive personal medical information in a private place.
- Ensure that each user is restricted to the information needed to do his or her job.
- Train employees on confidentiality and each person's responsibility. With HIPAA's final rule, effective April 2003, training is available from vendors of medical software.
- Design a written confidentiality policy that employees sign.
- Conduct routine audits that produce a trail of each employee's movement through the EMR system.
- Include disciplinary measures for breaches of confidentiality.

In this era of paperless health care settings, care must be taken to protect the privacy of the patient as carefully as in the world of paper.

Other Technologies for Health Record Maintenance

Providers may use a handheld personal data device (PDA), laptop, or personal computer (PC) in central areas or examination rooms. The same security measures apply to these items. Patients should not have access to computer screens in the examination room. The health care provider should take care in keeping a personal data system.

HEALTH RECORD ORGANIZATION

Information in the paper health record is usually organized in a standard chart order and placed in a specially designed folder. The order in which documents are placed in the health record depends on the provider's preference. As mentioned earlier, the demographic information is kept separate from the clinical information. The clinical portion of the health record is organized in either a source-oriented or a problem-oriented format. In source-oriented health records, all similar categories or sources of information are grouped together. The typical groupings:

- Billing and insurance information
- Physician orders

- Progress notes
- Laboratory results
- Radiographic results (magnetic resonance imaging, computed tomography, ultrasound)
- Patient education

All documentation in these categories is placed in **reverse chronological order**; that is, the most recent documents are placed on top of previous sheets.

Provider Encounters

Whether or not the patient is seen by a health professional, the visit is documented.

Narrative Format

Some providers document visits in the narrative form. **Narrative** is the oldest documentation form and the least structured. It is simply a paragraph indicating the contact with the patient, what was done for the patient, and the outcome of any action. In the sample page shown in Figure 8-1, the chart entries are in narrative format.

Some offices record new patients' encounters in the history and physical format. Visits of established patients returning for follow-up are documented in a different format. Although some facilities use the same format for new and established patients, the most common formats used to document each established patient encounter are narrative, SOAP, and POMR.

SOAP Format

The **SOAP** (subjective-objective-assessment-plan) format is one of the most common methods for documenting patient visits. The *subjective* component is a statement of what the patient says. Whenever possible, actual quotations by the patient should be used. The *objective* component is what is observed about the patient when the allied health professional begins the assessment and when the provider does the examination. The *assessment* portion is a phrase stating the impression of what is wrong or the patient's diagnosis. If a final diagnosis cannot be made yet, the provider lists possible disorders to be ruled out, called the differential diagnosis. The *plan* is a list of interventions that are to be carried out.

POMR Format

The **problem-oriented medical record (POMR)** lists each problem of the patient, usually at the beginning of the folder, and references each problem with a number throughout the folder. This method was developed by Dr. Lawrence Week and is a common method of compiling information because of its logical flow and the ease with which information can be reviewed. In group practices where patients may be seen by more than one doctor, the POMR format makes it easier to track the patient's treatment and progress. For instance, if Mr. Jones has hypertension and hyperglycemia, each diagnosis will be assigned a problem number as soon as the diagnosis is made:

2/4/9 **#**1. Hypertension
2/4/9 **#**2. Hyperglycemia

At each subsequent visit made by Mr. Jones, these problems will be referenced by these numbers. If a problem develops and is resolved, the problem number will be terminated by a single strike-through with a date beside it or by adding an X to a heading that indicates resolution of problems. Chronic problems, such as hypertension and hyperglycemia, will be retained by number for as long as the patient remains with the practice. These may be divided by headings of acute and chronic or short-term and long-term for convenience.

POMR documents are divided into four components:

1. *Database.* This contains the following:
   - Chief complaint (Fig. 8-2 on next page, shows charting for a chief complaint and history of present illness)
   - Present illness
   - Patient profile
   - Review of systems
   - Physical examination
   - Laboratory reports

Mamie Parrish

| 10/17/03 | Pt. Called c/o fever, sore throat. Asked to speak to Dr. Johnson. Instructed patient to come in for exam; explained that Dr. Johnson cannot treat her over the phone. Given appt for tomorrow at 10:00 a.m. |
| 10/18/03 | Pt. called and stated that she felt "90% better". Appt. canceled.
Jennifer Wise, CMA |

12/05/03	Office Visit
SUBJECTIVE:	Pt presents c/o of bad pain in RLQ x 2 days.
OBJECTIVE:	Vital signs: T-101.3, P-94, R-16, BP-112/76. Urine pregnancy test was done, negative. Urine dip was negative for blood and WBC, pH 7.0. Urine was clear. Blood was sent to the laboratory for CBC with diff.
ASSESSMENT:	Pain in RLQ. Possible appendicitis vs. ovarian cyst.
PLAN:	Tylenol 650 mg suppository given now. Will await lab results and notify patient with further instructions at that time.
James Owens, MD

| 12/16/03 | Lab work normal. Called pt. Per Dr. Johnson and instructed to notify us if her fever is not gone tomorrow. Patient states, "I guess I feel some better." Pt. will call office p.r.n.
Melissa Hurley, RMA |

FIGURE 8-1. Sample page from patient's progress record.

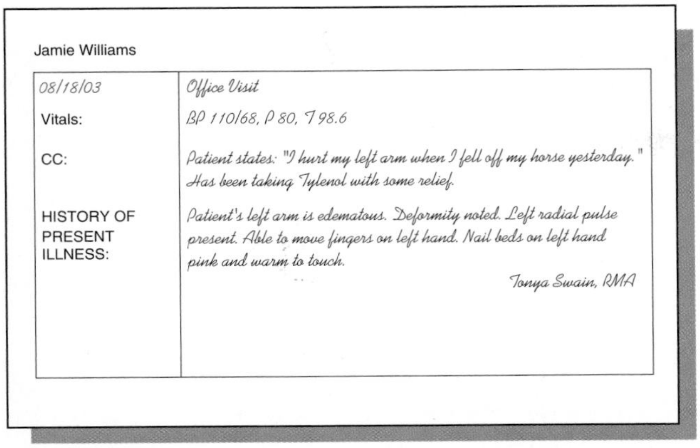

Jamie Williams

08/18/03	Office Visit
Vitals:	BP 110/68, P 80, T 98.6
CC:	Patient states: "I hurt my left arm when I fell off my horse yesterday." Has been taking Tylenol with some relief.
HISTORY OF PRESENT ILLNESS:	Patient's left arm is edematous. Deformity noted. Left radial pulse present. Able to move fingers on left hand. Nail beds on left hand pink and warm to touch.
	Tonya Swain, RMA

FIGURE 8-2. Charting a chief complaint and history of present illness.

2. *Problem list.* This includes every problem the patient has that requires evaluation, including social, demographic, medical, and surgical problems. (Demographic problems relate to statistical characteristics of certain populations.)
3. *Treatment plan.* This includes management, additional workups that may be necessary, and therapy.
4. *Progress notes.* These are structured notes corresponding to each problem.

Checkpoint Question

2. What are three common formats used to document patient–provider encounters?

DOCUMENTATION FORMS

Using printed forms and flowcharts in the health record saves space and time and allows for easy retrieval of information. They are usually customized to meet the needs of the individual facility. Some forms, like vaccination records, are required by federal law. In the paperless facility, these forms are completed by the patient and transferred to the patient's electronic record by data entry, and then the completed form is shredded.

Patient History Forms

Patient history forms are commonly used to gather information from the patient before the visit. Many facilities mail these forms to new patients and have them bring the completed form to their visit. This gives the patient the opportunity to concentrate on the questions, gather information about the family history, and give a more complete history. Whether the patient brings the completed form or fills out the history form in the facility, you will review the information with the patient to clarify any questions and add additional information gathered in the interview. Specialty practices

use forms designed to gather the type of information they will need to manage the patient's care. For example, an orthopedist's history form might include fields for prior orthopedic injuries, accident information, and flow sheets for physical therapy visits.

Flow Sheets

The **flow sheet** is designed to limit the need for long, handwritten care notes by allowing information to be recorded in either graphic or table form. Generally, flow sheets are designed for a given task. Color-coded sheets for medication administration, vital signs, pediatric growth charts, and so on eliminate the need to read through the pages of a chart to retrieve information. An advantage of using electronic health records is the capability of converting such information to charts, graphs, and flow sheets. In a computer health record, clicking an icon for a growth chart takes you to a screen that allows you to enter the information. The software transfers the numbers to a graph. When you refill a patient's daily blood pressure medication, you enter the information into the computer record, and it is transferred to the medication record. The record of all entries related to the patient's medications can then be easily retrieved by clicking on the medication icon. Figure 8-3 on the following page, is an example of a medication flow chart from a fictitious patient's electronic chart.

Progress Notes

Progress notes are written statements about various aspects of patient care. Some facilities use a lined piece of paper with two columns. The left column is used to document the date and time, and the right column is used to write the note. Others use a plain or lined piece of paper without columns. The progress notes will reflect each encounter with the patient chronologically, whether by phone, by e-mail, or in person. No matter what form is used for documenting, you must always include the date, time, your signature, and credential.

Checkpoint Question

3. List three advantages of using flow sheets in a health chart.

HEALTH RECORD ENTRIES

Proper health record entries are necessary for efficient communication and for legal considerations. The health record allows health care practitioners to communicate among themselves and therefore provide the best care possible for the patient. Good communication fosters continuity of patient care.

The health record is a legal document that can be subpoenaed in a malpractice suit. If the documentation is accurate, timely, and legible, it can help win a lawsuit or prevent one

Ardmore Family Practice, P.A.
2805 Lyndhurst Avenue
Winston-Salem, NC 27103
PHONE: 336-659-0076
FAX: 336-659-0272

Patient: MICHAEL FIELDS   **Date:**   02-12-2003 9:06 AM

MEDICATIONS

Date	Drug Name	Strength/Form	Dispense	Refill	Sig	Last Dose/ Disc Date	Status
1/28/03	SINGULAIR	10 MG TABS	5	0	1 PO BID		NEW
1/28/03	ZITHROMAX	200 MG/5ML SUSR	5	0	1 P.O Q DAY		NEW
1/22/03	ACCUPRIL	10 MG TABS	34	4	1 PO QD	1/28/03	CONTINUE
1/22/03	ADVIL	200 MG TABS	1	1	1/2 Q A.M.	1/25/03	NEW
1/22/03	ALTACE	5 MG CAPS	60	5	ONE TWICE DAILY	1/28/03	CONTINUE
1/22/03	MACROBID	100 MG CAPS	14	0	1 PO BID	1/28/03	CONTINUE
8/26/02	ALTACE	5 MG CAPS	60	5	ONE TWICE DAILY		CONTINUE
8/7/02	PRECOSE	25 MG CAPS	60	0	1/2 B.I.D.	10/5/02	NEW
5/2/01	ACCUPRIL	10 MG TABS	34	4	1 PO QD		NEW
5/2/01	ACCUPRIL	20 MG TABS	30	0	1 PO QD		NEW
5/2/01	ACCUPRIL	40 MG TABS	30	5	1 PO QD		NEW
4/25/01	ACCUPRIL	20 MG TABS	30	0	1 PO QD	4/25/01	NEW
4/25/01	ACCUPRIL	40 MG TABS	30	5	1 PO QD		NEW
4/25/01	MACROBID	100 MG TABS	14	0	1 PO BID	5/1/01	NEW
3/2/01	ACIPHEX 20 MG	TABS	30	6	1 PO QD		NEW
3/2/01	ACTOS 30 MG	TABS	30	2	1 PO QD		NEW
1/23/01	ENTEX PSE	120-600 MG TB12	45	0	1 PO BID		NEW
1/23/01	NASONEX	50 MCG/ACT SUSP	1	3	2 SPRAYS EACH NOSTRIL QD		NEW
8/24/99	ADALAT CC	60 MG TBCR	34	5	1 PO QD	8/24/99	NEW
7/8/99	NITROGLYCERIN	0.4 MG/DOSE AERS	100	1	1 TAB SL Q 5 MIN X 3, IF CHEST PAIN PERS	7/8/99	NEW
6/26/99	CLARITIN	10 MG TABS	30	5	ONE EVERY MORNING		NEW
6/23/99	CELEBREX 100 MG	CAPS	90	3	1 PO Q AM AND 2 PO Q PM		NEW
6/3/99	GLUCOPHAGE	850 MG TABS	90	6	ONE 3 TIMES DAILY	6/3/99	NEW
6/3/99	HYTRIN	5 MG CAPS	30	6	ONE EVERY DAY	6/3/99	NEW

F I G U R E 8 - 3 .   Medication administration flow sheet.

Correct

| 9-15-03 | Pt. Called to cancel appt. for recheck of UTI on 9-16-03. States she is feeling better. Advised to keep appointment, since Dr. Smith wants to repeat a urinalysis to see if her bladder infection has cleared up. Pt. states, "I don't see any sense in that; I'm not coming". Advised Dr. Smith.   Fred Lane, CMA |

Incorrect

| 9-15-03 | Pt. Called to cancel appt.   Fred Lane, CMA |

FIGURE 8-4. Right and wrong chart entries.

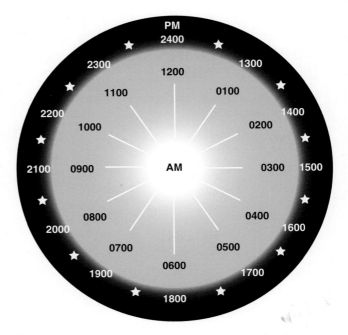

FIGURE 8-5. Military time.

altogether. If the documentation is messy, inaccurate, or improperly done, however, it can raise questions that might cause the practice to lose a malpractice suit. Figure 8-4 shows the difference between a well-written chart note and one that leaves in question what really happened. The golden rule in documentation is that if it is not documented, it was not done. Therefore, all patient procedures, assessments, interventions, evaluations, teachings, and communications must be documented.

Follow these guidelines for documenting in patients' health records:

1. Make sure you know the facility's policy regarding charting. Find out who is allowed to write in the chart and the procedures for doing so.
2. Make sure you have the correct patient chart. If the patient's name is common, ask for a birth date or social security number as a double check.
3. Always document in ink.
4. Always sign your complete name and credential.
5. Always record the date of each entry. Some outpatient facilities record the time as well. Using military time will eliminate the need to use A.M. and P.M. (Fig. 8-5).
6. Write legibly. Printing is more legible than cursive writing.
7. Check spelling, especially medical terms, before entering them into the chart.
8. Use only abbreviations that are accepted by your facility. Abbreviations can cause confusion and errors in patient care if they are overused, used incorrectly, or open to interpretation. For instance, the abbreviation BS might stand for bowel sounds, breath sounds, or blood sugar. Box 8-1 shows abbreviations used in charting.
9. When charting the patient's statements, use quotation marks to signify the patient's own words.
10. Do not attempt to make a diagnosis. For example, if the patient says, "My throat is sore," do not write pharyngitis. It is not within the scope of your training to diagnose.
11. Document as soon as possible after completing a task to promote accuracy.

12. Document missed appointments in the patient's chart. Chart your attempts to reach the patient to remind him or her of the appointment.
13. Document any telephone conversations with the patient in the chart.
14. Be honest. If you have given a wrong medication or performed the wrong procedure, as soon as the appropriate supervisor is notified, document it, then complete an incident report. State only the facts; do not draw any conclusions or place blame.
15. Never document for someone else, and never ask someone else to document for you.
16. Never document false information.
17. Never delete, erase, scribble over, or white-out information in the health record because this can be construed as attempting to cover the truth and tampering with a legal document. If you do make an error, draw a single line through it, initial it, and date it. Then write the word "correction" and document the correct information (Fig. 8-6). You can click on an icon to make a correction in the electronic chart, but the original information is not deleted. For example, if you discover that you have entered the wrong date of birth after the patient's information has been saved, you can correct it, but most systems allow only certain users to make changes in the saved database.

Charting Communications With Patients

In addition to documenting patient visits to the facility, other encounters and communications may occur and should

Box 8-1

ABBREVIATIONS USED IN CHARTING

In office charting, use these common abbreviations to save time and space.

Abbreviation	Meaning
ā	before
abd	abdomen
ant.	anterior
AP	anteroposterior
Ax	axillary
b.i.d.	twice a day
BP	blood pressure
C	Celsius
c̄	with
CC	chief complaint
C/o	complains of
CPX	complete physical examination
Cx	canceled
D/C	discontinue
F	Fahrenheit
Fx	fracture
h.s.	bedtime, hour of sleep
Hx	history
L	left
LLE	left lower extremity
LLQ	left lower quadrant
LUE	left upper extremity
LUQ	left upper quadrant
NKDA	no known drug allergies
noct.	nocturnal
p̄	after
p.c.	after a meal
PE	physical examination
p.r.n.	as needed
pt.	patient
R	right
R/O	rule out
RLE	right lower extremity
RUE	right upper extremity
RLQ	right lower quadrant
RUQ	right upper quadrant
R/s	rescheduled
s̄	without
SOB	shortness of breath
spec	specimen
s/p	status post
STAT	immediately
t.i.d.	3 times a day
TPR	temperature, pulse, respiration

When correcting a charting error, draw a single line through the error, initial it, date it, and document the correct information.

left 05/15/03 TW

05/15/03 Patient presents today complaining of pain in ~~right~~ eye. Tracy Wiles, CMA

FIGURE 8–6. Correcting an error.

become a part of the permanent record. To ensure continuity of care and patient safety, charts should contain a progress sheet or some sort of tool to record each communication with a patient. Actions taken by health care professionals on behalf of the patient should be charted. For example, when a prescription is phoned to a pharmacy, the action is recorded. The doctor may give instructions to be carried out regarding a patient, such as calling the patient with normal test results. This should be concisely explained in the chart. These entries should appear in **chronological order**. Dates that are out of order and gaps between entries may confuse the reader and give the appearance of poor service. For this reason, entries should be made immediately after communications with the patient.

Telephone communications with patients are typically recorded in a narrative manner. When a patient calls or e-mails the facility, the conversation must be documented in the chart immediately. Phone calls should be documented with the time and date of the call, patient's problem or request, and actions taken by the person making the entry. If special telephone message pads are used, a copy should be placed in the patient's chart. E-mails from patients should be printed and kept in the chart. Replies to a patient's e-mail should be printed out and included with the progress sheet. Remember, care must be taken to protect the patient's privacy when using electronic means to communicate.

Additions to Health Records

Any additions to a health record, such as laboratory results, that are smaller than the standard 8.5 × 11 inches should be transcribed onto a full sheet of paper or shingled and placed in the appropriate area of the chart. Shingling is taping the paper across the top to a regular-size sheet. Each sheet is then added under the current one with a piece of tape across the top. Each sheet can be lifted to view the entire document. Most laboratory reports are computer generated and will come ready to insert into the chart. All additions to the health record (e.g., laboratory results, radiographic reports, consultation reports) should be read and initialed by the doctor before you put them in the chart.

Checkpoint Question

4. What is the golden rule in documentation?

WORKERS' COMPENSATION RECORDS

From time to time, a patient who is active in your practice may seek treatment for a **workers' compensation** case or an injury or illness related to employment. The government requires employers to provide insurance for care when an injury occurs at work. When this occurs, do not simply add the information to the patient's health record. Instead, start a new record. A workers' compensation health record actually belongs to the employer, so the data in that record can be reviewed by the employer's insurance carrier. No information about the patient's previous health or family history that is not pertinent to the workplace incident should be made available to the insurance carrier.

Before treating a patient for a possible workers' compensation case, you must first obtain verification from the employer unless the situation is life-threatening. Be sure to document the name of the person who authorizes treatment as well as any other information that becomes available during the verification process.

Workers' compensation cases are kept open for 2 years after the last date of treatment for any follow-up care that may be required. After that time, care may not be covered under the same case. Even after the care is complete, the separate record is kept with the patient's other record, and information is incorporated into the original record as needed.

HEALTH RECORD PREPARATION

To start filing, you need folders, labels, and any other appropriate supplies. Keep these supplies on hand and follow the same steps every time you put together and file a health record. Over the course of many years, you may have to replace worn-out folders or peeling labels and stickers. Do so before the folder tears or the labels fall off.

After preparing the folders, you may also want to prepare several out guides, that is, plastic sheets with a tab (projection) and a pocket for index cards. Type "Out guide" on the tabbed edge of the sheet. Then, when you remove a chart, write the date, name of the patient, your initials, and where the chart can be found on an index card. Place the card inside the out guide, and put the out guide in the spot in the file cabinet where the chart was. An out guide indicates that the chart has been removed and where it can be found. Larger facilities often use a wand to keep track of charts and radiographs. When a chart arrives in a certain location, a wand is passed over a bar code. When the patient's number is entered into the computer, the screen shows the location of the patient's chart at the moment. If it is in the file cabinet, that is also indicated.

FILING PROCEDURES

Every day information is added to a patient's chart. It is best to keep this information filed on a daily basis. Pieces of paper to be added can be kept in a central location until filed so that employees can retrieve it if needed before the patient's next visit. This holding area should be used only until the daily filing can be done. In a paperless office, these additions to the health record are scanned into the system and the original paper is shredded.

To ensure efficient and speedy filing and document retrieval, follow these four steps:

1. *Condition.* Prepare items by removing loose pieces of tape or paper clips. Make sure each sheet of paper includes the patient's name in case a second page gets separated from the first page.
2. *Index.* Separate business records from patient records.
3. *Sort.* Put each group of records in proper order to be filed on shelves, either alphabetic or numeric. This makes actual filing go much faster because you are not moving up and down and back and forth to find the proper letter area; you will just move down in order.
4. *Store.* Place each record in the proper storage area, as described next.

 Checkpoint Question

5. Why is it necessary to make a new chart for an established patient who is being seen for an injury sustained at work?

FILING SYSTEMS

The two main filing systems are alphabetic and numeric. In some practices you may use both systems, each for different types of files.

Alphabetic Filing

As the name implies, **alphabetic filing** is a system using letters. Begin alphabetic filing by distinguishing the first, second, and third unit as described in Box 8-2. (A unit is each part of a name or title that is used in indexing.) Using the first letter of the first unit, place your records in small groups in order from A to Z. After that, take each small group and gradually work through the second and consecutive letters to put the small groups in order. Using this process allows you to work in a progressive order as you add records to existing files.

If the entire first unit is the same, move onto the second unit. If the second unit is still the same, move onto the third unit. Occasionally, you will have records whose units one, two, and three are identical. In such cases, it does not matter which one is filed first; use extreme caution, however, when retrieving records with identical units to prevent errors. Asking the patient to provide his or her birthday will ensure that you have the right patient and avoid confusion.

With alphabetic filing, color coding may also be used. Letters of the alphabet are color-coded and affixed to each folder, or a color-coded bar is placed next to the label with

Box 8-2

INDEXING RULES FOR ALPHABETIC FILING

When filing records alphabetically, use these indexing rules to help you decide the placement of each record. Indexing rules apply whether you use the title of the record's contents or a person's name.

File by name according to last name, first name, and middle initial, and treat each letter in the name as a separate unit. For example, Jamey L. Crowell should be filed as Crowell, Jamey L. and should come before Crowell, Jamie L.

- Make sure professional initials are placed after a full name. John P. Bonnet, D.O., should be filed as Bonnet, John P., D.O.
- Treat hyphenated names as one unit. Bernadette M. Ryan-Nardone should be filed as Ryan-Nardone, Bernadette M. not as Nardone, Bernadette M. Ryan.
- File abbreviated names as if they were spelled out. Finnigan, Wm. should be filed as Finnigan, William, and St. James should be filed as Saint James.
- File last names beginning with Mac and Mc in regular order or grouped together, depending on your preference, but be consistent with either approach.
- File a married woman's record by using her own first name. Helen Johnston (Mrs. Kevin Johnston) should be filed as Johnston, Helen, not as Johnston, Kevin Mrs.
- Jr. and Sr. should be used in indexing and labeling the record. Many times a father and son are patients at the same facility.
- When names are identical, use the next unit, such as birth dates or the mother's maiden name. Use Durham, Iran (2-4-94) and Durham, Iran (4-5-45).
- Disregard apostrophes.
- Disregard articles (a, the), conjunctions (and, or), and prepositions (in, of) in filing. File *The Cat in the Hat* under Cat in Hat.
- Treat letters in a company name as separate units. For ASM, Inc., "A" is the first unit, "S" is the second unit, and "M" is the third unit.

Numeric Filing

Numeric filing uses digits, usually six. The digits are typically run together but read as three groups of two digits. For example, the record filed as 324478 is read as 32, 44, 78. Commas are not placed or any separation used when applying the labels to the tabbed edge of the file folder. The records are placed in numeric order without concern for duplication, which may sometimes happen with the alphabetic system. If you use this technique, it is called straight digit filing because you are reading the number straight out from left to right.

Sometimes, the file label will look the same, 324478, but will be read in the reverse order: 78, 44, 32. This technique is called terminal digit filing; that is, the groups of numbers are read in pairs from right to left. Be careful not to mix the two filing systems. If using both techniques within your office, be sure to keep them separate by changing the folder color or some other means to prevent errors. The chart is filed by using the last pairs of digits.

Numeric filing plays an important role in the medical office. With tests for human immunodeficiency virus (HIV) and acquired immunodeficiency syndrome (AIDS) and their results being held in strict confidence, the use of numeric filing is becoming even more popular. When this technique is used, it is important to keep a **cross-reference** in a secure area, away from patient areas, listing the numeric code and the name of the patient. Such a reference is called a master patient index. This way limited numbers of people know who the patient is, which maintains privacy. Boxes 8-3 and 8-4 on the next page, show how to file patient records alphabetically or numerically.

Other Filing Systems

Most facilities keep files other than patient records. An office manager keeps files on employees, insurance policies, accounts payable, and so on. For this type of filing, systems include **subject filing**, in which documents are arranged alphabetically according to subject (e.g., insurance, medications, referrals); geographic filing, in which documents are grouped alphabetically according to locations, such as state, county, or city; and chronological filing, in which documents are grouped in the order of their date.

Checkpoint Question

6. What are the two main filing systems? Briefly describe each.

CLASSIFYING HEALTH RECORDS

Records are classified in three categories: active, inactive, or closed. Active records are those of patients who have been seen within the past few years. The exact amount of time is designated within each practice; it usually ranges from 1 to 5 years. Keep these records in the most accessible storage spot available because you will be using them regularly.

the patient's name. For example, names beginning with A to F may be blue; G to L, green; M to T, yellow; and U to Z, purple. Using this system, Michele Beals would have a blue strip, Laurie Palmer would have a yellow strip, Lauren Kayser's would be green, and Dana Warbeck would have purple. Finding misfiled charts is easier. With one glance at the cabinet, for example, you can spot one purple tab in the middle of the green ones.

Box 8-3

ALPHABETIC FILING EXAMPLES

The following patient records are to be filed alphabetically:

Mary P. Martin
Floyd Pigg, Sr.
Susan Bailey
Ellen Eisel-Parrish
Anita Putrosky
Susan R. Hill
Sister Mary Catherine
Cher
Stephen Dorsky, MD
Mrs. John Moser (Donna)

The proper order is:

Susan Bailey
Cher
Stephen Dorsky
Ellen Eisel-Parrish
Susan R. Hill
Mary P. Martin
Donna Moser
Floyd D. Pigg
Anita Putrosky
Sister Mary Catherine

Box 8-4

NUMERIC FILING EXAMPLES

The following patient records are to be filed numerically:

LeRoy Flora	213456
Ramsey Curtis	334387
Sharon Moore	979779
Cathy King	321138

In straight digit filing, the proper order is:

213456
321138
334387
979779

In terminal digit filing, the proper order is:

321138
213456
979779
334387

With files in which one or two groups of numbers are the same numbers, you refer to the second or third groups or numbers. For example, in straight digit filing (reading from left to right) the number 003491 comes before 004592. The first group of numbers (00) is the same for both files, so you determine the order of filing by the second group of numbers; in this case, 34 comes before 45.

In terminal digit filing (reading from right to left), 456128 would come before 926128. The first two groups of numbers (28 and 61) are the same for both files, so you go to the third group of numbers; in this case, 45 comes before 92.

Inactive records are those of patients who have not been seen in more than the designated time set aside for active records. You will still keep these records in the facility, but they do not have to be as accessible as the active files. Usually, they are placed on bottom shelves to eliminate constant bending when reaching for active files, or they may be stored in another room within the office. "Inactive" patients have not formally terminated their contact with the provider, but they have either not needed the provider's services or have not informed the facility regarding a move, change in provider, or death.

Closed records are those of patients who have terminated their relationship with the provider. Reasons for such termination might include the patient moving, termination of physician–patient relationship by letter, no further treatment necessary, or death of the patient.

INACTIVE RECORD STORAGE

Inactive records can be stored in the facility in an out-of-the-way area, such as a basement or attic. Many practices use **microfilm** or **microfiche** to store closed records. Microfilm and microfiche are ways to photograph documents and store them in a reduced form. Microfilm, a popular method for storing large volumes of records, uses a photographic process that develops health records in miniature on film. Information is stored on cards holding single film frames or in reels or strips for projection on compact electric viewers placed at convenient office locations. The cost of the equipment is declining, making this a more practical method for storing and retrieving inactive files.

Microfiche is a miniature photographic system that stores rows of images in reduced size on cards with clear plastic sleeves rather than on film strips. Information can be handled manually, examined on a viewer that enlarges the record, or reproduced as hard copy on a high-speed photocopier. A standard microfiche card holds more than 60 pages of information. The microfiche process allows 3,200 papers to be reduced to fit on a single 4×6-inch transparency.

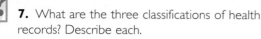

Checkpoint Question

7. What are the three classifications of health records? Describe each.

STORING ACTIVE HEALTH RECORDS

Facilities use a variety of storage methods for active files that are used on a daily basis. Shelf files are stationary shelves. Shelving units are stacked on each other or placed side by side. These shelves may also be custom-ordered to the width you need. Records are stored horizontally, and labels are read from the side. Figure 8-7 shows such shelving units.

Drawer files are a type of filing cabinet. The drawer pulls out for easy access and visibility of all records. This type of filing system allows you easier access to all sides of files, which can help in searches for missing files that may have been pushed to the back or behind other files. Drawer files also allow easier filing because you can read from above the files, rather than squatting to read the labels from the sides as you work your way down to the lower shelves. A disadvantage is that these files take up a great deal of space.

Rotary circular or lateral files allow records to be stored in units that either spin in a circle or stack one behind the other, enabling you to rotate different units to the front. This system allows for maximum use of office space and is suggested for a facility with large quantities of records to be stored. With shelf or drawer units, more wall space is needed to spread out each unit, but with rotary files, less wall space is needed.

Even the paperless health care setting must consider storage because backup copies of computerized records must be made daily and stored in a safe, fireproof location. Security experts advise storing backup disks off-site.

Record Retention

The statute of limitations is the legal time limit set for filing suit against an alleged wrongdoer. The time limit varies from state to state. You must observe the statute of limitations in your particular state to know how long health and business records should be kept in storage.

It is recommended that health records be stored permanently, because in some states malpractice lawsuits can be filed within 2 years of the date of discovery of the alleged malpractice. The statute of limitations for minors is extended until the child reaches legal age in every state; the time given past the legal age varies, however.

Tax records and liability plans, including old and new policies, should be permanently stored in a fireproof cabinet. Older liability plans may provide coverage should a malpractice lawsuit be filed later, after that policy expires and a new policy takes effect.

Insurance policies should also be stored in a fireproof cabinet. You can keep the newest policy and discard the older one.

Canceled checks should be kept in fireproof storage for at least 3 years. After that, keep them indefinitely in regular storage.

Receipts for equipment should be kept until each item listed on the receipt is no longer being used.

Checkpoint Question

8. How long should health records be kept?

RELEASING HEALTH RECORDS

Although the physical health record legally belongs to the physician, the information belongs to the patient. Any release of records must first be authorized by the patient or the patient's legal guardian. When releasing a health record, provide a copy only. *Never* release the original health record except in limited circumstances.

LEGAL TIP

The only time an original record should be released is when it is subpoenaed by a court of law. In such situations, the physician may wish to have the judge sign a document stating that he or she will temporarily take charge of the health record. This signed document should be filed in the medical office until the record is returned. To further ensure the record's safety, a staff member can transport the original record to court on the day it is requested, then return the record at the end of the court session that day. As soon as it is known that a record will be part of a court case, the record should be kept in a locked cabinet. When the court orders that a record be submitted to the court at a given date and time, the legal order is termed *subpoena duces tecum*.

FIGURE 8-7. File cabinets.

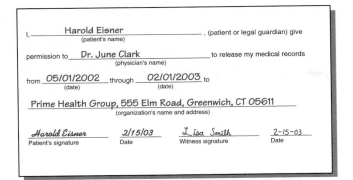

I, _____Harold Eisner_____ , (patient or legal guardian) give
       (patient's name)

permission to __Dr. June Clark__ to release my medical records
       (physician's name)

from _05/01/2002_ through _02/01/2003_ to
   (date)   (date)

__Prime Health Group, 555 Elm Road, Greenwich, CT 05611__
       (organization's name and address)

Harold Eisner   _2/15/03_   _Lisa Smith_   _2-15-03_
Patient's signature   Date   Witness signature   Date

FIGURE 8-8. Sample authorization to release information.

Insurance companies, lawyers, other health care practitioners, and patients themselves may request copies of health records. All requests should be made in writing, stating the patient's name, address, and social security number, and must contain the patient's *original* signature authorizing the release of records. Never release information over the telephone. You will have no way of verifying that the person with whom you are speaking is actually the person who has authorization. Unless the request is made by the patient, state laws allow facilities to charge a fee for copying the health record.

You must follow certain guidelines even with a signed authorization release form (Fig. 8-8). The authorization form must give the patient the opportunity to limit the information to be released. Patients may release only information relating to a specific disorder, or they may specify a time limit. They may not, however, ask that the doctor leave out information pertinent to the situation. References to mental health diagnosis or treatments, drug or alcohol abuse, HIV, AIDS, or any other sexually transmitted disease may not be released without specific mention on the signed authorization form. If it is not specifically requested, when you are copying the

record, place a piece of blank white paper over any such areas of information. Never white-out these areas on the original document or mention what these blank areas are.

Releasing Records to Patients

When patients request copies of their own records, the doctor makes the decision about what to copy. Patients aged 17 and under cannot get copies of their own health records without a signed consent from a parent or legal guardian, except for emancipated minors. They may obtain certain services independently (check your state's law regarding treatment of minors), however; in such cases, under the law, you are not permitted to contact the parent or guardian. Some states allow minors to seek treatment for sexually transmitted diseases and birth control without parental knowledge or consent. Sometimes, the parent or guardian may still be billed for these services without the bill being itemized. The billing statement should include only the treatment dates and amount due.

Checkpoint Question

9. What is required for a legal disclosure of a patient's HIV status?

Reporting Obligations

Although patients' records are confidential, in certain situations concerning the public's health and safety, the law requires reporting information to particular authorities. Requirements for reporting vary among states. Generally, the following types of items must be reported: vital statistics, communicable diseases, child and elderly abuse or maltreatment, and certain violent injuries.

Spanish Terminology

Por firmar aquí, usted nos da permiso de compartir su información medical con su compañía de seguro.	By signing here, you are giving us permission to share your medical information with your insurance company.

Procedure 8-1

Preparing a Health File

Equipment/Supplies

- File folder
- Title, year, and alphabetic or numeric labels

Step	Reason
1. Decide the name of the file (a patient's name, company name, or name of the type of information to be stored).	Properly naming a file allows for easy retrieval.
2. Type a label with the title *in unit order* (e.g., Lynn, Laila S., *not* Laila S. Lynn).	Typing the label in unit order helps avoid filing errors.
3. Place the label along the tabbed edge of the folder so that the title extends out beyond the folder itself. (Tabs can be either the length of the folder or tabbed in various positions, such as left, center, and right.)	This ensures easy readability.
4. Place a year label along the top edge of the tab before the label with the title. This will be changed each year the patient has been seen. *Note:* Do not automatically replace these labels at the start of a new year; remove the old year and replace with a new one only when the patient comes in for the first visit of the new year.	Doing this makes removing inactive files more time efficient. At the beginning of each new year, you can easily spot the records that are years beyond your storage time limit in the active file area. Doing this also can help you locate inactive files if patients return years later. (By determining the last year the patient was seen, you can narrow your search to files with a matching year label.)
5. Place the appropriate alphabetic or numeric labels below the title.	This aids in accurate filing and retrieval.
6. Apply any additional labels that your office may decide to use.	Labels noting special information (e.g., insurance, drug allergies, advanced directives) act as quick and easy reminders.

Procedure 8-2

Maintaining Medication and Immunization Records

Equipment/Supplies: Medication record, immunization record, list of medications prescribed for an adult patient, list of immunizations administered to a pediatric patient, black or blue ink pen, red ink pen, highlighter pen.

Steps

1. Assemble the appropriate materials for completing a medication record and an immunization record.

2. Using the adult patient information sheet, complete the top of the medication record in black or blue ink.

3. Write the medications noted on the patient information sheet on the medication record.

4. Note any allergies on the medication record in red ink.

5. Check the medication record for accuracy.

6. Highlight any medications on the record that the patient is no longer taking.

7. Using the pediatric patient information sheet, complete the top of the immunization record in black or blue ink.

8. Write the immunizations noted on the patient information sheet on the immunization record.

9. Note any allergies on the immunization record in red ink.

10. Check the immunization record for accuracy.

CHAPTER SUMMARY

Health records not only are a means of communication among health care providers but also are legal documents depicting the quality of patient care. Preparing and maintaining health records is an important responsibility. To ensure efficient recording and retrieval, you must be familiar with the varied documentation forms as well as the different kinds of filing systems. In addition, you must adhere to strict guidelines when releasing any information in patients' health records. Electronic health records are giving rise to new issues in protecting health records. The patient's privacy must be protected at all times. The quality, use, and care of the health record are reflections of the quality of the facility itself.

Critical Thinking Challenges

1. Interview a fellow student with a hypothetical injury. Document the incident with the chief complaint and the present illness.
2. Compare and contrast alphabetic filing with numeric filling. Which system do you think works better? Explain your response.
3. Instruct a fellow student in the requirements of your office regarding the release of health records.
4. Write an office policy for maintaining confidentiality with electronic modalities, such as fax machines, printers, laptops, and computer screens.

Answers to Checkpoint Questions

1. The patient's chief complaint is the reason the patient is seeing the health care provider.

2. Narrative, SOAP, and POMR are three common formats for recording patient–provider encounters.

3. The advantages of using flow sheets in the health chart are that they limit the need for long handwritten notes, save time and space, and make it easier to locate information.

4. The golden rule in documenting is that if it is not documented, it was not done.

5. The chart of the patient injured on the job has information that should not be available to the employer, who has access only to the information about the worker's injury.

6. The two main filing systems are alphabetic (using letters to file records) and numeric (using digits to file records).

7. The three classifications of health records are active (seen within the past few years), inactive (not currently being seen but still patients), and closed (relationship is terminated because of death, patient moved, or change in physician).

8. Health records should be kept forever.

9. Permission to release information about a patient's HIV status must be specifically given on the release form that is signed by the patient.

9

Quality, Privacy, and HIPAA

CHAPTER OBJECTIVES

In this chapter, you'll learn:

1. To spell and define the key terms.
2. To list four regulatory agencies that require health care facilities to have quality improvement programs.
3. To describe the accreditation process of the Joint Commission on Accreditation of Healthcare Organizations.
4. To describe the intent of the Clinical Laboratory Improvement Amendments Act.
5. To describe the intent of the Health Insurance Portability and Accountability Act.

6. To describe the steps to developing a quality improvement program.
7. To list five guidelines for completing incident reports.
8. To explain how quality improvement programs and risk management work together in a health care facility. to improve overall patient care and employee needs.

PERFORMANCE OBJECTIVE

Upon successfully completing this chapter, you will be able to:

1. To complete an incident report.

KEY TERMS

Centers for Medicare & Medicaid
Clinical Laboratory Improvement Amendments Act

expected threshold
incident reports
Health Insurance Portability and Accountability Act

Joint Commission on Accreditation of Healthcare Organizations
Occupational Safety and Health Administration

outcomes
quality improvement
sentinel event
task force

QUALITY IMPROVEMENT (QI) is the commitment and plan to improve every part of an organization. Its goal is both to meet and to exceed customers' (patients') expectations and employees' needs. QI plans examine the way care is delivered, analyze problems in the delivery system, and investigate methods to correct the problems. Although quality medical care has been a concern of health care providers for many years, formal QI plans were not always required. In the mid 1980s, health care settings were required to develop quality assurance (QA) plans. The purpose of a QA plan was to "assure" patients that they received good medical care. QA plans often created mounds of statistical data to prove that the staff was doing a good job. QA plans did not focus on improving care, only on acquiring statistical data. Therefore, health care facilities now focus on QI plans. These plans require that you collect the data and then use the information to improve and provide quality health care.

In this chapter, we discuss why health care organizations have QI programs, the process for developing and maintaining QI plans in a medical office setting, and risk management. We also discuss the agencies that mandate health care facilities to have QI programs.

QUALITY IMPROVEMENT PROGRAMS IN THE HEALTH CARE SETTING

Quality improvement programs let an organization scientifically measure the quality of its products and services. A health care organization's success depends on patient satisfaction and patient **outcomes**. The patient's outcome is the final result of the care that he or she received. Patient outcomes are reported to various regulatory agencies. At present, only hospitals are required to post report cards about patient outcomes. Legislative bills now in Congress would require all health care settings to report patient outcomes. Patients can review report cards and other regulatory agencies' reports on various websites. Then, patients can select the health care organization that best meets their needs in terms of professional services and personal care.

Quality improvement programs have many other benefits for all health care organizations. These benefits include the following:

- Identifying system failures or delays in patient care
- Improving patient and family customer service
- Improving patient outcomes and satisfaction
- Improving employee efficiency and productivity
- Improving company morale
- Encouraging teamwork within the institution or organization

Regulatory Agencies

Quality improvement programs exist in health care facilities because of these benefits and because regulatory agencies require such programs. The primary regulatory agencies that mandate QI programs are the Joint Commission on Accreditation of Healthcare Organizations (JCAHO), Occupational Safety and Health Administration (OSHA), Centers for Medicare & Medicaid (CMS), and state public health departments. Some other organizations and associations have requirements for QI programs. These associations require QI data along with applications for research or grant money and for specific accreditation of services. For example, the American Diabetes Association may require an endocrinologist to receive a certification in diabetes care to provide QI data on diabetic patient outcomes. The three major agencies are discussed next.

Joint Commission on Accreditation of Healthcare Organizations (JCAHO)

The JCAHO is a private agency that sets health care standards and evaluates an organization's implementation of these standards for health care settings. Prior to the mid 1990s, the primary focus of the JCAHO was on evaluating hospitals and in-patient care institutions such as nursing homes. In 1996, the JCAHO expanded its jurisdiction to outpatient and ambulatory care settings. This change was, in part, due to the shift of patient care from inpatient to outpatient services. The JCAHO sets standards and evaluates the care in the various health care settings. Box 9-1 lists various

---

Box 9-1

TYPES OF FACILITIES

The Joint Commission on Accreditation of Healthcare Organizations accredits a variety of health care settings. These are some types of centers that can be accredited:

- Ambulatory care centers
- Birthing centers
- Chiropractic clinics
- Community health organizations
- Corporate health services
- County jail infirmaries
- Dental clinics
- Dialysis centers
- Endoscopy centers
- Group practices
- Imaging centers
- Independent practitioner practices
- Lithotripsy centers
- Magnetic resonance imaging centers
- Oncology centers
- Ophthalmology surgery centers
- Pain management centers
- Podiatry centers
- Physician offices
- Rehabilitative centers
- Research centers
- Sleep centers
- Student health centers
- Women's health centers

types of freestanding facilities for which the JCAHO sets standards and provides accreditation.

The JCAHO surveys these centers and then assigns them an accreditation title. A survey is on-site evaluation of the organizations facility and policies. Participation in the JCAHO is voluntary for health care organizations; without accreditation, however, the health care organization may not be eligible to participate in particular federal and state funding programs, such as Medicare and Medicaid. In addition, accreditation indicates to the community that an organization has met basic practice standards, which is important for marketing its services.

Checkpoint Question

I. What are the benefits to a health care organization that has obtained an accreditation from the JCAHO?

JCAHO accreditation process. The process of obtaining and maintaining accreditation by the JCAHO occurs in various stages:

1. The health care organization files a survey application and a business associate agreement with the JCAHO. The business associate agreement is a new requirement that is part of the Health Insurance Portability and Accountability Act regulations. These regulations are discussed later in the chapter. The application, which is sent from the JCAHO headquarters, consists of inquiries regarding the following:
   • Ownership of the organization
   • Demographics (e.g., address and phone number)
   • Types of services provided
   • Volume of patients served per year
2. The health care organization prepares for the survey by reviewing each JCAHO standard and assessing its own compliance. JCAHO standards can be found in its publications or on its website. In addition, the organization to be inspected reviews and updates all policy and procedure manuals. Personnel records are checked for accuracy and completion. Staff members are taught about the survey process and provided with sample questions that they may be asked during the survey.
3. The JCAHO informs the health care organization of the date, time, and duration of the survey. The length of the survey depends on the size and complexity of the setting. A first-time survey visit usually lasts 2 to 4 days. The JCAHO surveyors who specialize in health care standards conduct the survey.
4. The JCAHO conducts the survey, which consists of reviewing patient records, interviewing patients and family members, and touring the facility. Employees are interviewed to determine whether they know

where the policy and procedure manuals are kept, what is in the manuals, and safety rules. An exit conference in which preliminary findings are discussed is held between the surveyors and the administration (leadership) of the health care organization.

5. The JCAHO mails the accreditation decision to the health care organization within 60 days after the survey. An organization can appeal to the JCAHO for reevaluation of its assigned title. The organization receives a certificate indicating the level of accreditation that it has achieved. The certificate is posted at the facility.
6. If the initial site review identified some unsatisfactory areas, a second survey, called a focus survey, may be required to prove that corrections have been made. This type of survey generally lasts 1 to 2 days. After 3 years (the period for which accreditation by the JCAHO is valid), the health care organization submits a renewal application, resuming the cycle. Approximately 50% of the JCAHO standards are directly related to patient safety issues. As of January 2003, all site surveys are based on a new set of national goals aimed at improving the overall safety of patient care in hospitals and in other health care settings. All settings must show that they have reached these six goals:
   • Improved accuracy of patient identification. (Always use two methods to identify patients.)
   • Improved effectiveness of communication among caregivers. (Physician offices and hospitals must standardize abbreviations, acronyms, and symbols used in documentation. All sites must also have a policy stating what abbreviations and symbols cannot be used.)
   • Improved safety of using high-alert medications. (These medications are given only in hospitals by registered nurses. Examples of high-alert medications are chemotherapy agents and potassium injections.)
   • Eliminate wrong-site, wrong-patient, and wrong-procedure surgeries. (All steps must be taken to prevent procedures on a wrong patient. Wrong procedures can be simple errors, such as drawing blood from a wrong patient, to serious life-changing mistakes.)
   • Improved safety of infusion pumps. (Examples of infusion pumps are pain management devices and insulin administration devices.)
   • Improved effectiveness of clinical alarm systems. (All alarms must be checked on a regular basis and must be audible to everyone.)

   In addition, the JCAHO requires accredited health care organizations to have a **sentinel event** policy and alert forms. A sentinel event is an unexpected death or serious physical or psychological injury to a patient. Box 9-2 lists some examples of sentinel events. Anytime a sentinel event occurs, the

Box 9-2

EXAMPLES OF SENTINEL EVENTS

These are examples of sentinel events that are reportable to the JCAHO:

- Any patient's death, paralysis, coma, or other major loss of function associated with a medication error
- Any suicide of a patient in a setting where the patient is housed around the clock, including suicides following elopement from such a setting
- Any procedure on the wrong patient, wrong side of the body, or wrong organ
- Any intrapartum maternal death and any death of a newborn weighing more than 2500 g that is not due to a congenital condition
- Any fall by a patient that directly results in death or major permanent loss of function
- Hemolytic transfusion reactions involving major blood group incompatibilities

organization must determine the cause, implement improvements to prevent a repeat occurrence, and monitor the effectiveness of its plan. The JCAHO publishes a newsletter, *The Sentinel Event Alert*, discussing reported events to alert other facilities to potential problems, and copies can be viewed on its website. *The Sentinel Event Alert* has raised awareness in the health care community and in the federal government about the occurrences of adverse events and ways these events can be prevented.

Checkpoint Question

2. What is a sentinel event?

Occupational Safety and Health Administration

OSHA is a federal agency that regulates health and safety concerns in the workplace. OSHA requires that QI programs be in place to protect the health and welfare of patients and employees. OSHA's mission is to save lives, prevent injuries, and protect the health of America's workers. Many rules under OSHA affect the allied health professional's job. Examples are rules for blood-borne pathogen protection, use of personal protective equipment (PPE), tuberculosis prevention, management of biohazardous waste, ergonomics, and laser protection. Laser protection is needed if you are working with a health care provider who is operating a laser in the office. These rules and other guidelines can be found on the OSHA website. Unlike the JCAHO, compliance with OSHA regulations is not voluntary. Noncompliance with OSHA regulations can result in fines and closure of the health care organization.

Checkpoint Question

3. What is the mission of OSHA?

Centers for Medicare & Medicaid Services

The Centers for Medicare & Medicaid Services (CMS) [formerly the Health Care Financing Administration (HCFA)], a division of the United States Department of Health and Human Services, regulates and runs various departments and programs, including Medicare and Medicaid. This group is assigned to monitor and follow two key regulations that will affect your job as a medical assistant. These two laws are the **Clinical Laboratory Improvement Amendments Act** (CLIA) and the **Health Insurance Portability and Accountability Act** (HIPAA).

Clinical Laboratory Improvement Amendments Act.   CLIA (Public Law 100-578) was originally written in 1988 and was aimed a streamlining the standards and quality of all laboratory settings. There are three levels of testing complexity. Laboratory sites and physician offices may perform tests only to the level of their certification. The three levels are low complexity, moderate complexity, and high complexity. Most physician offices perform only low- to moderate-complexity tests. Examples of low-complexity tests are urine dipsticks, fecal occult blood packets, urine pregnancy tests, ovulation kits, centrifuged microhematocrits, and certain blood glucose determinations. Examples of moderate-complexity tests are white blood cell counts, Gram staining, packaged rapid strep test, and automated cholesterol testing.

As the CMS has expanded, many amendments have occurred, with the latest one (CMS-2226F) occurring on January 24, 2003. The amendments aim at further reducing the potential for errors. Most laboratory errors occur in specimen collection and handling. Laboratory settings must have a complete and comprehensive QI program that studies and corrects problems associated with specimen collection and handling. Box 9-3 lists examples of errors in collecting and handling specimens.

Health Insurance Portability and Accountability Act.   The HIPAA has four main objectives. They are to ensure health insurance portability for all people, reduce health care fraud and abuse, enforce standards of health information, and guarantee security and privacy of health information. Health insurance portability ensures that all working Americans have access to health insurance and can take that insurance along if they leave the job. Some key requirements of the HIPAA are:

- each health care facility must designate a privacy officer. This person is responsible for maintaining the privacy and security of all patients and ensuring compliance with the HIPAA

Box 9-3

ERRORS IN SPECIMEN COLLECTION

Errors in handling specimens or collecting them can occur in many ways. These errors can lead to errors in patient care. In most of these cases, the laboratory will not do the test and will dispose of the specimen. Another specimen will have to be collected from the patient. Here are some common errors:

- Wrong container used for specimen.
- Container's expiration date passed.
- Wrong patient's name on the label.
- Wrong doctor's name on the label.
- No date or time on the label.
- Patient's identification number not matched to laboratory slip.
- Messy or illegible label.
- Specimen label not matched to laboratory slip.
- Specimen not stored at right temperature.
- Laboratory slip not completely filled out.

- health care facilities must post a note in all waiting room areas that explains the practice's privacy policies
- policies and procedures must ensure that patients' safety and confidentiality are protected.

You will need to focus and guarantee security and privacy of all patient health information. There are specific guidelines on how you can transmit electronic transactions. Information must be encrypted before it is sent electronically. Many software programs can help physician offices to comply with these new regulations. The government is planning on implementing new laws that will require digital signatures to be sent with electronic data to decrease the potential for fraudulent Medicare claims. You can stay abreast of these new changes and regulations through the CMS website.

Health care facilities must take appropriate steps to ensure that any company they are associated with also follows HIPAA regulations. Health care facilities often have a variety of business partnerships that help keep the office flowing professionally and effectively. Some examples of business partnerships are cleaning services, document-shredding companies, laboratory and specimen transport personnel, and temporary staffing agencies. Contracts among health care facilities and their business partners should reflect that the business adheres to HIPAA regulations. For the JCAHO to meet HIPAA regulations and ensure security and privacy of patient information during the site visit, health care settings being surveyed must sign a business associate agreement prior to inspection.

Checkpoint Question

4. What governmental agency would you look to for additional information on HIPAA and CLIA regulations?

State Health Departments

Each state has a specific agency to license and monitor health care organizations. Each state has specific guidelines for required QI programs. As in participation with OSHA regulations, participation with state regulations is not optional. The rules and regulations vary among states. It is important that you be aware of the regulations in your state. Using your Internet search engine, type in key words "public health department" and look for your state's health department website.

DEVELOPING A QUALITY IMPROVEMENT PROGRAM

The size and complexity of an organization's QI program depends on the organization's particular needs. In large facilities, numerous committees may be assigned to monitor and implement QI plans. Examples of QI plans are fall prevention, needlestick surveillance, and laboratory contamination rates. The committees will consist of staff members, including doctors.

QI programs tend to be more informal. Usually the office manager or senior smaller facilities doctor is responsible for monitoring and implementing QI plans. As more facilities become accredited by the JCAHO, however, QI programs have become more structured. A few examples of quality issues that can be monitored in a small health care facility are:

- Patient waiting times
- Unplanned returned patient visits for the same ailment or illness
- Misdiagnosed illnesses that are detected by another partner in the practice
- Patient or family complaints
- Timely follow-up telephone calls to patients
- Patient falls in facility
- Mislabeled specimens sent to the laboratory
- Blood specimens that are coagulated or contaminated

Seven Steps for a Successful Program

The following seven steps are essential for creating an effective QI program:

1. *Identify the problem or potential problem.* All organizations can improve their delivery of patient care. Suggestions for improving care can come from many resources, including the following:
   - office managers

- other employees (e.g., doctors, allied health professionals)
- patients (interviews)
- incident report trending (discussed later)

The person responsible for QI in the medical office reviews all QI problems or potential problems and selects the one to be addressed first. Problems given top priority are those that are high risk (most likely to occur) and those that are most likely to cause injury to patients, family members, or employees.

2. *Form a task force.* A task force is a group of employees with different roles within the organization brought together to solve a given problem.

3. *Assign an expected threshold.* The task force establishes an **expected threshold** (numerical goal) for a given problem. Thresholds must be realistic and achievable. For example, if the problem is needlestick injuries, the expected threshold is a realistic number of employee needlestick injuries that the task force considers acceptable in a given period. For instance, the threshold may be one employee stick per month. It is not realistic to set the goal at zero; this may be optimal but is not achievable.

4. *Explore the problem and propose solutions.* The task force investigates the problem thoroughly to determine all potential causes and possible solutions. After various solutions are discussed, the task force decides what solution or solutions are to be implemented.

5. *Implement the solution.* The key to successful implementation of the solution is staff education. All staff members must be taught about the problem and the plan to decrease the problem. The type of implementation will be based on the problem. For example, if the problem is patients falling at the entrance to the building, fixing the problem is likely to be complex and expensive. It may involve reengineering and construction of new walkways. If the problem is mislabeling or misspelling patient's names on laboratory specimens, the implementation will be simpler, possibly printing labels from the computer database.

6. *Establish a QI monitoring plan.* After implementation, the solution must be evaluated to determine whether it worked and if so, how well. QI monitoring plans have three elements:
   - source of monitoring, that is, where the numerical data will be obtained (e.g., health record review, incident reports, laboratory reports, office logs)
   - frequency of monitoring, that is, how often the data will be monitored and tallied (e.g., once a week, once a month)
   - person responsible for monitoring, that is, who collects the data and presents the results in graphic form, allowing for easy comparison of data from before and after implementation of the solution.

7. *Obtain feedback.* The members of the task force must review the graphs in relation to their expected threshold. Did they meet the threshold? If yes, the problem has been resolved. If the threshold was not met, the task force must determine whether the expected threshold was unrealistic or the solutions were inadequate. In either case, the problem has not been resolved; therefore, the task force must review each of the steps and make appropriate changes.

 Checkpoint Question

5. How does an organization select problems for a QI program?

RISK MANAGEMENT

Risk management is an internal process geared to identifying potential problems before they cause injury to patients or employees. Potential problems are related to risk factors. A risk factor is any situation or condition that poses a safety or liability concern for a given practice. Examples of risk factors are poor lighting, unlocked medication cabinets, failure to dispose of needles properly, and faulty patient identification procedures. Such factors may lead to patient falls, medication errors, employee needlesticks, and mistakes in therapeutic intervention. Risk factors for a particular health care organization are identified through the trending of incident reports.

One of the most challenging problems for risk managers is to prevent noncompliance with regulatory agencies. As discussed earlier, numerous agencies regulate health care settings, and these rules and regulations change frequently. You can stay up-to-date with new changes by reading newsletters from these organizations, attending your state and local professional meetings, and frequently visiting various professional websites.

Incident Reports

Incident reports, sometimes referred to as occurrence reports, are written accounts of untoward (negative) patient, visitor, or staff events. Such events may be minor or life or limb threatening. The insurance company that provides the institution's liability insurance often requires incident reports.

An incident report is written or completed by the staff member involved in or at the scene of the incident. The report is reviewed by a supervisor for completion and accuracy and is then sent to a central location. In medical facilities, incident reports are sent to the risk manager. In a medical office, incident reports are usually given to the office manager or the physician. Depending on the type of event and organizational policy, a physician may or may not document the event on the incident report. If an unusual event happens to a patient, however, the physician should assess the patient and document the findings on the incident report.

Box 9-4

MYTHS ABOUT COMPLETING AN INCIDENT REPORT

Myth	Fact
If I complete an incident report, I will get fired.	Employers want incident reports to be completed for documentation of events. You are more likely to get fired for *not* completing one.
Incident reports go into my personnel file.	They are not placed in your file. They are stored separately. Supervisors may document discussions or education that you were given about the incident.
If I complete the incident report, I am admitting that I am at fault.	Incident reports do not imply fault. They document the evidence.
I need to photocopy the incident report and save it at home for my own legal protection.	You may find yourself in more trouble if you copy the document and store it at home. Most incident reports contain confidential patient information, and it is illegal to copy private patient information and store it at home.

Checkpoint Question

6. What is an incident report?

When to Complete an Incident Report

Even in the safest settings, undesirable things can happen to patients. These events sometimes result from human error (e.g., giving the wrong medication), or they may be idiopathic. Idiopathic means that something occurred for unknown reasons and was unavoidable (e.g., an allergic reaction). Incident reports must be completed even if no injury resulted from an event. A few examples of situations requiring an incident report are:

- all medication errors
- all patient, visitor, and employee falls
- drawing blood from a wrong patient
- mislabeling of blood tubes or specimens
- incorrect surgical instrument counts following surgery
- employee needlesticks
- workers' compensation injuries.

The rule of thumb is, when in doubt, always complete an incident report. Many health care professionals are reluctant to complete incident reports, owing to various myths, which are discussed in Box 9-4.

Information Included on an Incident Report

Although every agency has its own form, the following data are always included on an incident report (Fig. 9-1):

- name, address, and phone number of the injured party
- date of birth and sex of the injured party
- date, time, and location of the incident
- brief description of the incident and what was done to correct it

- any diagnostic procedures or treatments that were needed
- patient examination findings, if applicable
- names and addresses of witnesses, if applicable
- signature and title of person completing form
- supervisor's signatures as per policy.

Guidelines for Completing an Incident Report

When completing an incident report, follow these guidelines:

1. State only the facts. Do not draw conclusions or summarize the event. For example, if you walk into the reception room and find a patient on the floor, do not write, "Patient tripped and fell in reception area," because that draws a conclusion. Instead, document the incident as follows: "Patient found on the floor in the reception area. Patient states that he fell" (Fig. 9-2).
2. Write legibly and sign your name legibly. Be sure to include your title.
3. Complete the form in a timely fashion. In general, incident reports should be completed within 24 hours of the event.
4. Do not leave any blank spaces on the form. If a particular section of the report does not apply, write n/a (not applicable).
5. Never photocopy an incident report for your own personal record.
6. Never place the incident report in the patient's chart. Never document in the patient's chart that an incident report was completed. Only document the event in the patient's chart. (By writing in the health record that an incident report was completed, it opens the potential for lawyers to subpoena the incident report, should there be a lawsuit.)

INCIDENT REPORT FORM
PRIVILEGED & CONFIDENTIAL

Patient Stamp

☐ Inpatient ☐ Outpatient ☐ Visitor ☐ Volunteer ☐ Other   *NOT A PART OF THE MEDICAL RECORD–FORWARD TO RISK MANAGER WITHIN 72 HOURS*

Name		Age	Sex	Admit Date	Location of Incident	Room #
Diagnosis	Date of Incident	Time AM/PM		Date of Report	Person Reporting & Title (print)	

CONDITION BEFORE INCIDENT
☐ Alert   ☐ Disoriented ☐ Unconscious   ☐ Agitated
☐ Confused ☐ Sedated   ☐ Uncooperative ☐ Other

Activity Orders
☐ Adib   ☐ BRP   ☐ BRP c help
☐ With assist   ☐ CBR
☐ Up in chair   ☐ BSC

Signature

INCIDENT (please check all items that apply)   **FALLS**

FALLS	PREFALL FACTORS	RESTRAINTS	RISK CONDITIONS	CURRENT MEDICATIONS
☐ Fall from Bed	☐ Bed Up	Restraints Ordered ☐Y ☐N	☐ Weakness ☐ Decreased Mobility	☐ None
☐ Fall from Chair	☐ Bed Down	Restraints in Use ☐Y ☐N	☐ Confusion	☐ NTG ☐ Diuretics
☐ Fall from Bedside Commode	☐ Brake On ☐Y ☐N	Type: ☐ Vest ☐ Wrist ☐ Ankle	☐ Neuro/ortho diagnosis	☐ Cathartic preps/enemas
☐ Fall from Stretcher	☐ Not working	☐ Secured Mittens	☐ Cardiovascular diagnosis	☐ Antihypertensives
☐ Fall from Wheelchair	☐ Siderails Down	☐ Tied ☐ Untied by:	☐ Inpaired Vision	☐ Antiseizure
☐ Fall from Toilet	____ 2 Up	____ Staff	☐ History of Syncope	☐ Antidepressants
☐ Fall while Ambulatory	____ 3 Up	____ Patient	☐ Poor Nutritional Status	☐ Antiemetics
☐ Other_____	____ 4 Up	____ Family/S.O.	☐ Incontinence	☐ Antipsychotics
	____ Climbed Out	Call light in reach ☐Y ☐N	☐ History of fall last 6 months	☐ Analgesics/Hypnotics
		Fall follow-up program initiated	Safety Education given prior to fall:	☐ Narcotics
		prior to fall ☐Y ☐N	☐ None ☐ Patient ☐ Family/S.O.	☐ Cardiovascular

Environment: ☐ Floor wet ☐Y ☐N   ☐ Free from obstacles ☐Y ☐N Describe: _____
          ☐ Night light on ☐Y ☐N ☐N/A   ☐ Objects not in reach-searching for _____

MEDICATION VARIANCE, Including IV & Blood Product(s)		PROCEDURE VARIANCE		MISCELLANEOUS
☐ Incorrect Pt. Identification	☐ Incorrect IV Solution	☐ Record Error ☐ Transcription	☐ Documentation Error	☐ AMA/Elopement
☐ Incorrect Dosage	☐ Incorrect IV Rate	☐ Incorrect Pt. Identification	☐ Consent Variance	☐ Admitted c Pressure Sore
☐ Incorrect Route	☐ Incorrect Count/Missing Med	☐ Omitted Treatment	☐ Improper Prep of Pt.	☐ Damaged/Lost Teeth/ Denture
☐ Incorrect Time	☐ Topical Substance Reaction,	☐ Delayed Treatment	☐ NPO Violated	☐ Injury During Transport
☐ Incorrect Med Given	including Tape	☐ Omitted Diagnostic/Lab	☐ Radiation/Toxic Chemical Exposure	☐ Self Inflicted Injury/Suicide
☐ Incorrect Med Dispensed	☐ Allergy Not Documented	☐ Delayed Diagnostic/Lab	☐ X-ray Interpretation Discrepancy	☐ Malpositioning/Incorrect
☐ Med Omitted	☐ Contrast Reaction/Complication	☐ Traumatic Venipuncture	☐ Airway/Intubation Problem	Body Alignment
☐ Med Transcription Error	☐ Medication Past Due 1 hour	☐ Break in Sterile Technique	☐ Incorrect Level of Heat/Cold Applied	☐ Pt. Self Extubation
☐ Incorrect Blood Given	or more	☐ Incorrect Surgical Count–Sponge	☐ Incorrect Procedure/Treatment	☐ Tube/IV Catheter Out
☐ Pharmacy Notified	☐ Other_____	☐ Incorrect Surgical Count–Needle	☐ Unordered Procedure/Treatment	☐ Accidental Strking Against
☐ Infiltration		☐ Incorrect Surgical Count–Instrument	☐ Equip./Product Malfunction	an Object
☐ Blood Reaction		☐ Retained Foreign Body	☐ User Error	☐ Fainted
☐ Med Reaction		☐ Other:	☐ Equipment Unavailable	☐ Pt. Dissatisfied/Pt. Threatened Law Suit
				☐ Transfer to Critical Care p incident
				☐ Behavior Out of Norm.
				☐ Other:_____

INJURY (please check all items that apply) All serious/significant injuries must be described on reverse side   **PROCEDURE/LABOR & DELIVERY/NURSERY**

SERIOUS	SIGNIFICANT	SUPERFICIAL	PROCEDURE/LABOR & DELIVERY/NURSERY
☐ None	☐ None	☐ None	☐ Newborn with apparent Cerebral dysfunction
☐ Spinal Cord Injury	☐ Major Infiltration	☐ Unknown	☐ Newborn with APGAR of four (4) or less at five (5) minutes
☐ Injury to Nerves	☐ Hospital Acquired Decubiti	☐ Abrasion	☐ Newborn with serious birth trauma
☐ Brain Injury	☐ Burn	☐ Bruising	☐ Precipitous Delivery
☐ Surgery to Wrong Pt.	☐ Fracture	☐ Blister/Skin Tear	☐ Unattended Delivery
☐ Incorrect Surgical Procedure	☐ Sprain/Strain Joint/Muscle	☐ Skin Prick	**MEDICAL DEVICE/EQUIPMENT RELATED**
☐ Shock	☐ Injury to Blood Vessel	☐ Laceration	Equipment involved: _____
☐ Trauma Causing Internal Injury	☐ Dislocation of Joint	☐ Rash/Hives	Manufacturer: _____
☐ Hemorrhage	☐ Open Wound Needing Medical Care	☐ Other:	Serial #: _____
☐ Death	☐ Adverse Effect Due to Med/Anesthesia/Transfusion		Asset #: _____
☐ Unscheduled Return to OR	☐ Adverse Effect Due to Exposure to Toxic Chemical		Biomedical Dept. Notified: _____
☐ Other:	☐ Complication Due to Mechanical Device		Tagged & Removed from Service: _____ Date
	☐ Prolongation of Hospital Stay		Date/Time
	☐ Anoxia/Respiratory Distress		**Maintain all components of device such as connectors, adaptors, tubings, etc. Document all readings/settings.**
	☐ Cancellation of or after induction of anesthesia		**DO NOT ADJUST OR CLEAR ANY READINGS.**

AMA FOLLOW-UP

Reason for leaving: _____
Patient admitted <24 hours ☐ Yes ☐ No
Patient/S.O. Teaching: ☐ Completed ☐ Partial ☐ None ☐ Patient Uncooperative

F I G U R E   9 – 1.   Sample incident report.

(continued)

Description of event: _____
_____
_____
_____
_____
_____
_____
_____
_____
_____
_____
_____
_____
_____
_____
_____

Physician notified: ☐ Yes ☐ No Name of Physician (print): _____
Physician Remarks: _____
_____
_____
_____
_____
_____
_____
_____
_____

_____
Physician Signature   Date

Supervisor/Manager Investigation/Follow-up Action: _____
_____
_____
_____
_____
_____
_____

_____
Supervisor/Manager Signature   Date

Witness: Name (print)	Department/Shift	Address	Phone

_____
Risk Manager Signature   Date

F IGURE 9 – I . *(Continued)*

FIGURE 9-2. When writing an incident report, document only the facts. Do not draw conclusions. Always be honest, and never falsify the information.

corrected through QI programs. Examples of statistical data that can be found in incident reports follow:

- Particular days of the week when most negative events happen (if most events occur on Friday afternoons, perhaps staffing on Friday afternoon should be reevaluated)
- Most common area for patient falls (if most falls happen in the lobby, a QI program may need to be established to assess why falls occur there)
- Medications that are routinely given incorrectly (educating staff and using colored labels to highlight similar drug names may correct this)
- The age group most likely to have problems (if most of your incident reports reflect problems in the geriatric population, a QI program focusing on geriatric care may be needed)
- Incident reports should be kept in a special file in the manager's office (some managers file these reports according to dates, whereas others file them according to the problem)

Trending Incident Reports

After incident reports are completed, they are reviewed and tracked to highlight specific patterns. The resulting statistical data can be used to identify problem areas, which can be

ñSpanish Terminology

¿Vio usted lo que pasó?	Did you see what happened?
¿Cayo usted?	Did you fall?
¿Está lastimado usted?	Are you hurt?
¿Quiere usted ver un doctor?	Do you want to see a doctor?
Usted necesita obtener una radiografía.	You need an x-ray.

Procedure 9-1

Demonstrating Knowledge of Federal and State Health Care Legislation and Regulations

Equipment/Supplies: Paper, writing utensil, computer with Internet Access.

Steps

1. Find the American Association of Medical Assistants (AAMA) internet site and explain what resources they have available regarding health care regulations.

2. Explain the actions you can take to stay current and aware of new federal and state health care legislation and regulations.

3. Locate your state's Department of Health internet site and explain

   - the laws and/or regulations they cover
   - the resources they have available to help you understand these regulations
   - the potential fines or other consequences of not following these regulations

4. Locate the Occupational Safety and Health Administration internet site and explain

   - the laws and/or regulations they cover
   - the resources they have available to help you understand these regulations
   - the potential fines or other consequences of not following these regulations

5. Locate the Medicare internet site and explain

   - the laws and/or regulations they cover
   - the resources they have available to help you understand these regulations
   - the potential fines or other consequences of not following these regulations

6. Locate the Joint Commission of Accreditation of Hospitals internet site and explain

   - the laws and/or regulations they cover
   - the resources they have available to help you understand these regulations
   - the potential fines or other consequences of not following these regulations

(continued)

Procedure 9-1 *(continued)*

Demonstrating Knowledge of Federal and State Health Care Legislation and Regulations

Steps

7. Locate information on the Health Insurance Portability and Accountability Act and explain

    *   the intent of this regulation
    *   the resources available to help you understand this regulation
    *   the legal implications of not following this regulation

8. Locate information on the Clinical Laboratory Improvement Ammendments and explain

    *   the intent of this regulation
    *   the resources available to help you understand this regulation
    *   the legal implications of not following this regulation

CHAPTER SUMMARY

Quality improvement programs have many benefits to heath care organizations. They can identify potential problems for patients and employees. After identifying the problem, the task force can create solutions to resolve them. QI programs are also required by various agencies. Four important agencies are the JCAHO, OSHA, CMS, and your state health department. You must stay alert to new regulations from these agencies. More information about various health care regulations can be found through their websites, newsletters, and professional organizations. Patients place trust in all health care workers and health care settings. We must all work hard to provide good quality care to all patients every time they are treated.

Critical Thinking Challenges

1. Create a list of potential patient or employee problems that could be solved with a QI program. Then select three problems and develop a list of solutions for each problem.
2. List 10 reasons to complete an incident report. Select one of these reasons and complete the incident report. (Photocopy the incident report from the chapter.) Be sure to review the guidelines for completing an incident report. Make sure your description of events follows these guidelines.
3. Search the JCAHO website. What information can you find regarding sentinel events? What steps can be taken to prevent them?
4. Privacy of patient information is essential. Write a policy that aims at protecting patients' privacy. What steps can you take to ensure patients' privacy? Would you make a good privacy officer? Why or why not?

Answers to Checkpoint Questions

1. The benefits of being accredited by the JCAHO are that the health care organization is eligible for state and federal funding programs and that accreditation proves to the community that the facility has met basic standards of care.
2. A sentinel event is an unexpected occurrence involving a death or serious physical or physiological injury to a patient.
3. OSHA's mission is to save lives, prevent injuries, and protect the health of America's workers.
4. Centers for Medicare & Medicaid (CMS) are responsible for HIPAA and CLIA regulations.
5. QI programs should be selected to address problems that are high risk and those most likely to cause injury to patients, family members, or employees.
6. An incident report is a written account of untoward or negative events involving patients, visitors, or employees.

 ## Websites

Centers for Medicare & Medicaid Services
    www.cms.gov
Clinical Laboratory Improvement Amendments Act
    www.cms.hhs.gov/clia/
Health Care Report Cards
    www.healthgrades.com
Health Insurance Portability and Accountability Act
    www.cms.hhs.gov/hipaa
Joint Commission on Accreditation of Healthcare Organizations
    www.jcaho.org
Occupational Health and Safety Administration
    www.osha.gov

Math
Fundamentals

10

Math Fundamentals

CHAPTER OBJECTIVES

In this chapter, you'll learn:

1. To multiply and divide whole numbers, fractions, and decimals.
2. To read decimals.
3. To clear decimal points.
4. To round off decimals.
5. To solve ratio and proportion.
6. Proficiency test in arithmetic.

THIS CHAPTER COVERS those common arithmetic functions needed to work as an allied health professional.

Examples and learning aids demonstrate how calculations are performed; self-tests provide practice and drill. The proficiency exam should be taken after mastering the content.

Why perform arithmetic operations when calculators are readily available? Solving the arithmetic forces one to think logically about the task at hand and to evaluate the answer. One must also know what numbers and functions to enter when using a calculator. There may be occasions when a problem that requires a calculator arises; however, all arithmetic problems in this chapter can be completed without a calculator.

MULTIPLYING WHOLE NUMBERS

The multiplication table (Fig. 10-1 on next page) is provided for review. Study the table for the numbers 1 through 12. You should achieve 100% accuracy without referring to the table.

EXAMPLE

Multiply 8 by 7 (8×7).

1. Find row number 8.
2. Find column number 7.
3. Read across row 8 until you intersect column number 7. The answer is 56.

SELF-TEST 1 | Multiplication

After studying the multiplication table, write the answers to these problems. Answers are given at the end of the chapter; if you do not achieve 100%, you need more study time.

1.	2×6 = _____	13.	4×6 = _____
2.	9×7 = _____	14.	9×6 = _____
3.	4×8 = _____	15.	8×8 = _____
4.	5×9 = _____	16.	7×8 = _____
5.	12×9 = _____	17.	2×9 = _____
6.	8×3 = _____	18.	8×11 = _____
7.	11×10 = _____	19.	4×9 = _____
8.	2×7 = _____	20.	3×8 = _____
9.	8×6 = _____	21.	12×11 = _____
10.	8×9 = _____	22.	9×5 = _____
11.	3×5 = _____	23.	9×9 = _____
12.	6×7 = _____	24.	7×5 = _____

DIVIDING WHOLE NUMBERS

The multiplication table is also helpful when dividing large numbers by smaller ones. Study the table for the division of numbers 2 through 12 (Fig. 10-2 on next page). Again, you should be able to achieve 100% accuracy without referring to the table; if not, study it again.

EXAMPLE

Divide 108 by 12 ($108 \div 12$).

1. Find 12 (the smaller number) in the left row.
2. Read across that row until you find 108 (the larger number).
3. The number at the top of that column is the answer: 9.

Remember, because $9 \times 12 = 108$, then $108 \div 12 = 9$ (see Fig. 10-2).

SELF-TEST 2 | Division

After studying the division of larger numbers by smaller numbers, write the answers to the following problems. Answers are given at the end of the chapter.

1.	$63 \div 7$ = _____	13.	$28 \div 7$ = _____
2.	$24 \div 6$ = _____	14.	$21 \div 7$ = _____
3.	$36 \div 12$ = _____	15.	$24 \div 8$ = _____
4.	$42 \div 6$ = _____	16.	$84 \div 12$ = _____
5.	$35 \div 5$ = _____	17.	$81 \div 9$ = _____
6.	$96 \div 12$ = _____	18.	$32 \div 8$ = _____
7.	$12 \div 3$ = _____	19.	$36 \div 6$ = _____
8.	$27 \div 9$ = _____	20.	$18 \div 9$ = _____
9.	$49 \div 7$ = _____	21.	$21 \div 3$ = _____
10.	$18 \div 3$ = _____	22.	$48 \div 4$ = _____
11.	$72 \div 8$ = _____	23.	$144 \div 12$ = _____
12.	$48 \div 8$ = _____	24.	$56 \div 8$ = _____

FRACTIONS

A *fraction* is a portion of a whole number. The top number is called the *numerator*. The bottom number is called the *denominator*.

EXAMPLE

$\dfrac{1}{4}$ → numerator
→ denominator

Learning Aid

The line between the numerator and the denominator is a division sign. Therefore, the fraction can be read as one divided by four.

Types of Fractions

In a *proper* fraction, the numerator is smaller than the denominator.

EXAMPLE

$\frac{2}{5}$ (Read as two fifths.)

In an *improper* fraction, the numerator is larger than the denominator.

1	2	3	4	5	6	⑦	8	9	10	11	12
2	4	6	8	10	12	14	16	18	20	22	24
3	6	9	12	15	18	21	24	27	30	33	36
4	8	12	16	20	24	28	32	36	40	44	48
5	10	15	20	25	30	35	40	45	50	55	60
6	12	18	24	30	36	42	48	54	60	66	72
7	14	21	28	35	42	49	56	63	70	77	84
⑧	16	24	32	40	48	㊿6	64	72	80	88	96
9	18	27	36	45	54	63	72	81	90	99	108
10	20	30	40	50	60	70	80	90	100	110	120
11	22	33	44	55	66	77	88	99	110	121	132
12	24	36	48	60	72	84	96	108	120	132	144

FIGURE 10-1. The multiplication table. The numbers going down the left side (from 1 to 12) are the row numbers. The numbers going across the top (from 1 to 12) are the column numbers. To multiply any two numbers from 1 to 12, find the column for one number, find the row for the other number, and read across the row until you intersect the column.

EXAMPLE

$\frac{5}{2}$ (Read as five halves.)

A *mixed number* has a whole number plus a fraction.

EXAMPLE

$1\frac{2}{3}$ (Read as one and two thirds.)

In a *complex* fraction, both the numerator and the denominator are already fractions.

EXAMPLE

$\frac{\frac{1}{2}}{\frac{1}{4}}$ (Read as one half divided by one fourth.)

RULE   Reducing Fractions

Find the largest number that can be divided evenly into the numerator *and* the denominator. ■

EXAMPLE

Example 1:

Reduce $\frac{4}{12}$

$\frac{\overset{1}{\cancel{4}}}{\underset{3}{\cancel{12}}} = \frac{1}{3}$

Example 2:

Reduce $\frac{7}{49}$

$\frac{\overset{1}{\cancel{7}}}{\underset{7}{\cancel{49}}} = \frac{1}{7}$

Learning Aid

Check to see if the denominator is evenly divisible by the numerator. The number 7 can be evenly divided into 49.

1	2	3	4	5	6	7	8	⑨	10	11	12
2	4	6	8	10	12	14	16	18	20	22	24
3	6	9	12	15	18	21	24	27	30	33	36
4	8	12	16	20	24	28	32	36	40	44	48
5	10	15	20	25	30	35	40	45	50	55	60
6	12	18	24	30	36	42	48	54	60	66	72
7	14	21	28	35	42	49	56	63	70	77	84
8	16	24	32	40	48	56	64	72	80	88	96
9	18	27	36	45	54	63	72	81	90	99	108
10	20	30	40	50	60	70	80	90	100	110	120
11	22	33	44	55	66	77	88	99	110	121	132
⑫	24	36	48	60	72	84	96	⑩⑧	120	132	144

FIGURE 10-2. Division table. The numbers going down the left side (from 1 to 12) are the row numbers. The numbers going across the top (from 1 to 12) are the column numbers. To divide, find the divisor (the number performing the division) in the row. Read across the row to the dividend (the number to be divided). The number at the top of that column is the answer.

Sometimes fractions are more difficult to reduce because the answer is not obvious.

EXAMPLE

Example 1:

Reduce $\frac{56}{96}$

$$\frac{56}{96} = \frac{\overset{1}{\cancel{8}} \times 7}{\underset{1}{\cancel{8}} \times 12} = \frac{7}{12}$$

Example 2:

Reduce $\frac{54}{99}$

$$\frac{54}{99} = \frac{\overset{1}{\cancel{9}} \times 6}{\underset{1}{\cancel{9}} \times 11} = \frac{6}{11}$$

Learning Aid

Your knowledge of the multiplication table can help you. Change the numbers to their multiples.

Patience is required to reduce a very large fraction. It may be difficult to find the largest number that will divide evenly into the numerator and the denominator, and you may have to reduce several times.

EXAMPLE

Example 1:

Reduce $\frac{189}{216}$

Try to divide both by 3 $\dfrac{\overset{63}{\cancel{189}}}{\underset{72}{\cancel{216}}} = \dfrac{63}{72}$

Then use multiples $\dfrac{63}{72} = \dfrac{\overset{1}{\cancel{9}} \times 7}{\underset{1}{\cancel{9}} \times 12} = \dfrac{7}{8}$

Example 2:

Reduce $\frac{27}{135}$

Try to divide both by 3 $\dfrac{\overset{9}{\cancel{27}}}{\underset{45}{\cancel{135}}} = \dfrac{\overset{1}{\cancel{9}}}{\underset{5}{\cancel{45}}} = \dfrac{1}{5}$

Learning Aid

Certain numbers are called prime numbers because they cannot be reduced further. Examples are 2, 3, 5, 7, and 11.

When reducing, if the last number is even or a zero; try 2.

If the last number is a zero, or 5, try 5.

If the last number is odd, try 3, 7, or 11.

SELF-TEST 3 | Reducing Fractions

Reduce these fractions to their lowest terms. Answers are given at the end of the chapter. Be patient!

1. $\frac{16}{24}$

2. $\frac{36}{216}$

3. $\frac{18}{96}$

4. $\frac{70}{490}$

5. $\frac{18}{81}$

6. $\frac{8}{48}$

7. $\frac{12}{30}$

8. $\frac{68}{136}$

9. $\frac{55}{121}$

10. $\frac{15}{60}$

Multiplying Fractions

There are two ways to multiply fractions.

First Way

Multiply the numerators across. Multiply denominators across. Reduce the answer to its lowest terms.

EXAMPLE

$$\frac{2}{7} \times \frac{3}{4} = \frac{2 \times 3}{7 \times 4} = \frac{6}{28}$$

$$\frac{6}{28} = \frac{3 \times \overset{1}{\cancel{2}}}{14 \times \underset{1}{\cancel{2}}} = \frac{3}{14}$$

Learning Aid

When multiplying fractions, sometimes one way will be easier. Use whichever method is more comfortable for you.

Second Way (When There Are Several Fractions)

Reduce by dividing numerators into denominators evenly. Multiply the remaining numerators across. Multiply the remaining denominators across. Check to see if further reductions can be made.

EXAMPLE

Example 1:

$$\frac{3}{14} \times \frac{7}{10} \times \frac{5}{12} = \frac{\overset{1}{\underset{2}{\cancel{3}}}}{\underset{2}{\cancel{14}}} \times \frac{\overset{1}{\cancel{7}}}{\underset{2}{\cancel{10}}} \times \frac{\overset{1}{\cancel{5}}}{\underset{4}{\cancel{12}}} = \frac{1}{16}$$

Learning Aid

$$12 \div 3 = 4$$

$$14 \div 7 = 2$$

$$10 \div 5 = 2$$

Example 2:

$$1\frac{1}{2} \times \frac{4}{6} = \frac{\overset{1}{\underset{1}{\cancel{3}}}}{\cancel{2}} \times \frac{\overset{2}{\cancel{4}}}{\underset{2}{\cancel{6}}} = \frac{2}{2} = 1$$

Learning Aid

Mixed numbers must be changed to improper fractions. Multiply the whole number by the denominator and add the numerator.

$$1\frac{1}{2} = 1 \times 2 + 1 = \frac{3}{2}$$

Example 3:

$$\frac{4}{5} \times 6\frac{2}{3} = \frac{4}{\underset{1}{\cancel{5}}} \times \frac{\overset{4}{\cancel{20}}}{3} = \frac{16}{3}$$

Learning Aid

Change the mixed number to an improper fraction.

$$6 \times 3 = 18 + 2 = \frac{20}{3}$$

SELF-TEST 4 | Multiplying Fractions

Multiply these fractions. Answers are given at the end of the chapter.

1. $\frac{1}{6} \times \frac{4}{5} \times \frac{5}{2} =$

2. $\frac{4}{15} \times \frac{3}{2} =$

3. $1\frac{1}{2} \times 4\frac{2}{3} =$

4. $\frac{1}{5} \times \frac{15}{45} =$

5. $3\frac{3}{4} \times 10\frac{2}{3} =$

6. $\frac{7}{20} \times \frac{2}{14} =$

7. $\frac{9}{2} \times \frac{3}{2} =$

8. $6\frac{1}{4} \times 7\frac{1}{9} \times \frac{9}{5} =$

Dividing Fractions

Fractions can be divided by inverting the number after the division sign then changing the division sign to a multiplication sign.

EXAMPLE

Example 1:

$$\frac{1}{75} \div \frac{1}{150} = \frac{1}{\underset{1}{\cancel{75}}} \times \frac{\overset{2}{\cancel{150}}}{1} = 2$$

Example 2:

$$\frac{\frac{1}{4}}{\frac{3}{8}} = \frac{1}{4} \div \frac{3}{8} = \frac{1}{\underset{1}{\cancel{4}}} \times \frac{\overset{2}{\cancel{8}}}{3} = \frac{2}{3}$$

Example 3:

$$\frac{1\frac{1}{5}}{\frac{2}{3}} = \frac{6}{5} \div \frac{2}{3} = \frac{\overset{3}{\cancel{6}}}{5} \times \frac{3}{\underset{1}{\cancel{2}}} = \frac{9}{5}$$

Learning Aid

Complex fractions such as

$$\frac{\frac{1}{4}}{\frac{3}{8}} \text{ may be read as } \frac{1}{4} \div \frac{3}{8}$$

Remember, the long line represents a division sign.

SELF-TEST 5 | Dividing Fractions

Divide these fractions. This operation is important in calculating doses correctly. Answers are given at the end of the chapter.

1. $\frac{1}{75} \div \frac{1}{150} =$

2. $\frac{1}{8} \div \frac{1}{4} =$

3. $2\frac{2}{3} \div \frac{1}{2} =$

4. $75 \div 12\frac{1}{2} =$

5. $\frac{7}{25} \div \frac{7}{75} =$

6. $\frac{1}{2} \div \frac{1}{4} =$

7. $\frac{3}{4} \div \frac{8}{3} =$

8. $\frac{1}{60} \div \frac{7}{10} =$

Changing Fractions to Decimals

This can be accomplished by dividing the numerator by the denominator. Remember that the line between the numerator and the denominator is a division sign; hence, $\frac{1}{4}$ can be read as $1 \div 4$.

In division, the number being divided is called the *dividend;* the number that does the dividing is called the *divisor;* the answer is called the *quotient.*

$$\text{divisor} \rightarrow 16\overline{)640.} \leftarrow \text{dividend} \atop \underset{0}{\underline{64}}$$

with quotient $40.$ above.

1. Look at the fraction $\frac{1}{4}$

$\frac{1}{4}$ ← numerator = dividend
   ← denominator = divisor

2. Write

$4\overline{)1}$

3. If you have difficulty setting this up, you can continue the line for the fraction and place the number above the line into the box.

$\frac{1}{4} = \frac{1}{4\overline{)1}}$

4. Once the division problem is set up, place a decimal point immediately after the dividend and also bring the decimal point up to the quotient.

$\frac{1}{4} \begin{array}{c} . \leftarrow \text{quotient} \\ \overline{)1.} \leftarrow \text{dividend} \end{array}$

Important! Failure to place decimal points carefully can lead to serious medical errors.

5. Carry out the division.

$$\frac{1}{4}\overline{)1.00} \begin{array}{c} .25 = 0.25 \\ \underline{8} \\ 20 \\ \underline{20} \\ 0 \end{array}$$

Learning Aid

If the answer does not have a whole number; place a zero before the decimal. This prevents misreading the answer; .25 is incorrect; 0.25 is correct.

The number of places to report your answer will vary depending on the way the stock drug comes and the equipment you use. For these exercises, carry answers to three decimal places.

EXAMPLE

Example 1:

$$\frac{5}{16} = 16\overline{)5.000} \begin{array}{c} 0.312 = 0.312 \\ \underline{4\,8} \\ 20 \\ \underline{16} \\ 40 \\ \underline{32} \\ 8 \end{array}$$

Example 2:

$$\frac{640}{8} = \frac{640}{8}\;8\overline{)640.} \begin{array}{c} 80. \\ \end{array} = 80$$

Example 3:

$$\frac{1}{75} = 75\overline{)1.000} \begin{array}{c} 0.013 = 0.013 \\ \underline{75} \\ 250 \\ \underline{225} \\ 25 \end{array}$$

Learning Aid

Note that there is a space between the 8 and the decimal point in the answer. When this occurs, place a zero in the space to complete the answer.

SELF-TEST 6 | Converting Fractions to Decimals

Divide these fractions to produce decimals. Answers are given at the end of the chapter. Carry decimal places to three if necessary.

1. $\frac{1}{6}$
2. $\frac{6}{8}$
3. $\frac{4}{5}$
4. $\frac{9}{40}$
5. $\frac{1}{8}$
6. $\frac{1}{7}$

DECIMALS

Most medication orders are written in the metric system, which uses decimals.

Reading Decimals

Count the number of places after the decimal point. As you read the decimal, you also create a fraction.

0.1 is read as one tenth $\left(\frac{1}{10}\right)$.

0.01 is read as one hundredth $\left(\frac{1}{100}\right)$.

0.001 is read as one thousandth $\left(\frac{1}{1000}\right)$.

Learning Aid

The first number after the decimal point is the tenth place.

The second number after the decimal point is the 100th place.

The third number after the decimal point is the 1000th place.

EXAMPLE

0.56 = fifty-six hundredths $\left(\frac{56}{100}\right)$

0.2 = two tenths $\left(\frac{2}{10}\right)$

0.194 = one hundred ninety-four thousandths $\left(\frac{194}{1000}\right)$

0.31 = thirty-one hundredths $\left(\frac{31}{100}\right)$

1.6 = one and six tenths $\left(1\frac{6}{10}\right)$

17.354 = seventeen and three hundred fifty-four thousandths $\left(17\frac{354}{1000}\right)$.

Learning Aid

When reading decimals, read the number first, then count off the decimal places.

Whole numbers preceding decimals are read in the usual way.

SELF-TEST 7 | Reading Decimals

Write these decimals in longhand and as fractions. Answers are given at the end of the chapter.

1. 0.25 _____
2. 0.004 _____
3. 1.7 _____
4. 0.5 _____
5. 0.334 _____
6. 136.75 _____
7. 0.1 _____
8. 0.150 _____

Dividing Decimals

Again, in division the number that is being divided is called the *dividend;* the number that does the dividing is called the *divisor;* and the answer is called the *quotient.*

$$\text{divisor} \rightarrow 16\overline{)5.000} \begin{array}{l} 0.312 \rightarrow \text{quotient} \\ \rightarrow \text{dividend} \end{array}$$

Note that a decimal point is placed immediately after the dividend is written and is moved up to the quotient as well.

EXAMPLE

$$\frac{13}{16} \quad 16\overline{)13.}$$

Division is then completed.

EXAMPLE

$$\begin{array}{r} 0.812 \\ 16\overline{)13.000} \\ \underline{12\,8} \\ 20 \\ \underline{16} \\ 40 \\ \underline{32} \\ 8 \end{array}$$

Clearing the Divisor of Decimal Points

Before dividing one decimal by another, clear the divisor of decimal points. To do this, move the decimal point to the far right. Move the decimal point in the dividend *the same number of places* and bring the decimal point up to the quotient in the same place.

EXAMPLE

Example 1:

$$0.2 \overline{)0.004} = 0.2 \overline{)0.004}$$

$$\text{Hence, } 2 \overline{)00.04} \quad \frac{0.02}{}$$

Example 2:

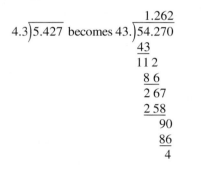

$$4.3 \overline{)5.427} \text{ becomes } 43. \overline{)54.270}$$

Learning Aid

When dividing, the answer may not "come out even." Instructions are usually given as to how many places to carry out the answer. In Example 2, you could keep dividing and end up with an answer that is very long (1.262093). In this example, the answer is carried out to three decimal places.

SELF-TEST 8 | Division of Decimals

Do these problems in division of decimals. The answers are given at the end of this chapter. If necessary, carry the answer to three places.

1. $24 \overline{)0.0048}$
2. $0.004 \overline{)0.1}$
3. $0.02 \overline{)0.2}$
4. $7.8 \overline{)140}$
5. $6 \overline{)140}$
6. $0.025 \overline{)10}$

Rounding Off Decimals

How do you determine the number of places to carry out division? First, let us review the general rule for rounding off decimals.

RULE   Rounding Off Decimals

When the number to be dropped is 5 or more, drop the number and add 1 to the previous number. When the last number is 4 or less, drop the number. ■

EXAMPLE

0.864 becomes 0.86

1.55 becomes 1.6

0.33 becomes 0.3

4.562 becomes 4.56

2.38 becomes 2.4

Suppose you want answers to the nearest tenth. Look at the number in the hundredth place and follow the rules for rounding off.

EXAMPLE

0.12 becomes 0.1

0.667 becomes 0.7

1.46 becomes 1.5

Suppose you want answers to the nearest hundredth. Look at the number in the thousandth place and follow the rules for rounding off.

EXAMPLE

0.664 becomes 0.66

0.148 becomes 0.15

2.375 becomes 2.38

Suppose you want answers to the nearest thousandth. Look at the number in the ten-thousandth place and follow the rules for rounding off.

EXAMPLE

1.3758 becomes 1.376

0.0024 becomes 0.002

4.5555 becomes 4.556

SELF-TEST 9 | Rounding Decimals

Round off these decimals as indicated. Answers are given at the end of the chapter.

Nearest Tenth

1. 0.25 = _____
2. 1.84 = _____
3. 3.27 = _____
4. 0.05 = _____
5. 0.63 = _____

Nearest Hundredth

6. 1.268 = _____
7. 0.750 = _____
8. 0.677 = _____
9. 4.539 = _____
10. 1.222 = _____

Nearest Thousandth

11. 1.3254 = _____
12. 0.0025 = _____
13. 0.4520 = _____
14. 0.7259 = _____
15. 0.3482 = _____

Comparing the Value of Decimals

Understanding which decimal is larger or smaller is often a help in the health care facility.

RULE Determining the Value of Decimals

The decimal with the higher number in the tenth place has the greater value. ■

EXAMPLE

Compare 0.25 with 0.5.
    It is clear that 0.5 is greater because the number 5 is higher than the number 2.

SELF-TEST 10 | Value of Decimals

In each pair, underline the decimal with the greater value. Answers are given at the end of the chapter.

1. 0.125 and 0.25
2. 0.04 and 0.1
3. 0.5 and 0.125
4. 0.1 and 0.2
5. 0.825 and 0.44
6. 0.9 and 0.5
7. 0.25 and 0.4
8. 0.7 and 0.350

PERCENT

Percent means parts per hundred. Percent is a fraction, with the number becoming the numerator and 100 becoming the denominator. Whole numbers, fractions, and decimals may be written as percents. Percents may be changed to decimals or to fractions.

EXAMPLE

Whole number: 4% (four percent)

Decimal: 0.2% (two-tenths percent)

Fraction: $\frac{1}{4}$% (one-fourth percent)

Percents That Are Whole Numbers

EXAMPLE

Example 1:

Change to a fraction.

$$4\% = \frac{4}{100} = \frac{1}{25}$$

Example 2:

Change to a decimal.

$$4\% = \frac{4}{100} \quad 100\overline{)4.00}^{.04} = 0.04$$

Learning Aid

Note that 4% means four parts per 100. The one hundredth place has two decimal points. A quick rule to change a percent to a decimal is to move the decimal point two places to the left.

$$4\% = 0.04$$
$$25\% = 0.25$$

Percents That Are Decimals

These may be changed in three ways:

1. By using the quick rule (see Learning Aid)

$$0.2\% = 00.2 = 0.002$$

Learning Aid

Quick rule: To remove a percent sign, move the decimal point two places to the left.

2. By keeping the decimal (see Learning Aid)

$$0.2\% = \frac{0.2}{100} \overset{0.002}{\big)0.200} = 0.002$$

Learning Aid

Method 2: Place the number over 100.

---

3. By changing to a complex fraction

$$0.2\% = \frac{\frac{2}{10}}{100} =$$

$$\frac{2}{10} \div \frac{100}{1} =$$

$$\frac{2}{10} \times \frac{1}{100} = \frac{2}{1000}$$

$$\frac{\overset{1}{\cancel{2}}}{\underset{500}{\cancel{1000}}} = \frac{1}{500}$$

Learning Aid

Remember that the number after a division sign is inverted. The sign is changed to a multiplication sign.

Every whole number is understood to have a denominator of 1.

$$\frac{2}{10} \div 100 = \frac{2}{10} \times \frac{1}{100}$$

Percents That Are Fractions

EXAMPLE

Example 1:

$$\frac{1}{4}\% = \frac{\frac{1}{4}}{100} = \frac{1}{4} \div \frac{100}{1} = \frac{1}{4} \times \frac{1}{100} = \frac{1}{400}$$

Example 2:

$$\frac{1}{2}\% = \frac{\frac{1}{2}}{100} = \frac{1}{2} \div \frac{100}{1} = \frac{1}{2} \times \frac{1}{100} = \frac{1}{200}$$

Alternative way. Because $\frac{1}{2} = 0.5$, $\frac{1}{2}\%$ could also be written as 0.5%. By using the quick rule of moving the decimal point two places to the left to clear a percent, you have $00.5\% = 0.005$. Note that 0.005 is $\frac{5}{1000} = \frac{1}{200}$. You could also write $\frac{0.5}{100}$.

Change these percents to both a ***fraction*** and a ***decimal***. Answers are given at the end of the chapter.

1. 10% _____ _____
2. 0.9% _____ _____
3. $\frac{1}{5}$% _____ _____
4. 0.01% _____ _____
5. 2/3% _____ _____
6. 0.45% _____ _____
7. 20% _____ _____
8. 0.4% _____ _____
9. $\frac{1}{10}$% _____ _____
10. 2 1/2% _____ _____
11. 33% _____ _____
12. 50% _____ _____

RATIO AND PROPORTION

A ratio indicates the relationship between two numbers. Ratios can be written as a fraction $\left(\frac{1}{10}\right)$ or as two numbers separated by a colon (1:10). (Read as *one is to ten.*)

Proportion indicates a relationship between two ratios. Proportions can be written as fractions or as two ratios separated by a double colon.

EXAMPLE

$\frac{2}{8} = \frac{10}{40}$ (Read as *two is to eight as ten is to forty.*)

5:30 :: 6:36 (Read as *five is to thirty as six is to thirty-six.*)

Proportions written with colons can be written as fractions; therefore 5:30 :: 6:36 becomes

$$\frac{5}{30} = \frac{6}{36}$$

Solving Proportion with an Unknown

When one of the numbers in a proportion is unknown, the letter x is substituted. There are three steps in determining the value of x in a proportion.

Step 1. Cross-multiply.
Step 2. Clear x.
Step 3. Reduce.

Let's see how this is done.

Proportions Expressed as Decimals

Suppose you had to solve this proportion:

$$\frac{1}{0.125} = \frac{x}{0.25}$$

Step 1. Cross-multiply the numerators and denominators.

$0.125x = 0.25$

Learning Aid

How to cross-multiply

$$\frac{1}{0.125} \diagdown\diagup \frac{x}{0.25}$$

Step 2. Clear x by dividing both sides of the equation with the number preceding x.

$$x = \frac{0.25}{0.125}$$

Learning Aid

$$\frac{0.125x}{0.125} = \frac{0.25}{0.125}$$

Step 3. Reduce the number.

$$0.125 \overline{)0.250.}^{\,2.}$$

$x = 2$

Learning Aid

Remember, the line between the two numbers in a fraction is a division sign.

$$\frac{0.25}{0.125}$$

This can be read as 0.25 divided by 0.125.

Proportions Expressed as Two Ratios Separated by Colons

Suppose you had this proportion:

$4 : 3.2 :: 7 : x$

Step 1. Cross-multiply the two outside numbers (called *extremes*) and the two inside numbers (called *means*).

$4 : 3.2 :: 7 : x$

$4x = 22.4$

Step 2. Clear x by dividing both sides of the equation with the number preceding x.

$$x = \frac{22.4}{4}$$

Learning Aid

$$\frac{4x}{4} = \frac{22.4}{4}$$

Remember that the line between two numbers in a fraction is a division sign. This can be read as 22.4 divided by 4.

Step 3. Reduce the number.

$x = 5.6$

Learning Aid

$$4 \overline{)22.4}^{\,5.6}$$

EXAMPLE

$$\frac{45}{180} \diagdown\diagup \frac{3}{x}$$

$45x = 540$

$x = 12$

Learning Aid

$$45 \overline{)540.}^{\,12.}$$
$$\underline{45}$$
$$\;\;90$$
$$\;\;\underline{90}$$

EXAMPLE

$11x = 363$

$x = 33$

$11 : 121 :: 3 : x$

Learning Aid

$$11 \overline{)363.}^{\,33.}$$
$$\underline{33}$$
$$\;\;33$$
$$\;\;\underline{33}$$

SELF-TEST 12 | Solving Proportions

Solve these prboportions. Answers are given at the end of the chapter.

1. $\frac{120}{4.2} = \frac{16}{x}$

2. $750 : 250 :: x : 5$

3. $\frac{14}{140} = \frac{22}{x}$

4. $2 : 5 :: x : 10$

5. $\frac{81}{3} = \frac{x}{15}$

6. $0.125 : 0.5 :: x : 10$

Ratio and Proportion in Dosage

When the amount of drug ordered differs from the supply, ratio and proportion are used to solve the problem.

EXAMPLE

Order: 0.5 mg of a drug

Supply: A liquid labeled 0.125 mg per 4 mL

We know the liquid comes as 0.125 mg in 4 mL. We want 0.5 mg. We don't know what amount of liquid will contain 0.5 mg. We have three pieces of information. We need the fourth, which is X.

This arithmetic operation can be set up and solved as a fraction–ratio or as two ratios separated by colons.

Fraction–Ratio

$$\frac{0.5}{0.125} \diagdown \frac{X}{4}$$

$$0.125X = 2$$

$$\downarrow$$

$$\frac{0.125X}{0.125} = \frac{2}{0.125}$$

$$\downarrow$$

$$X = \frac{2}{0.125}$$

$$\downarrow$$

$$X = \frac{2}{0.125}\quad \frac{16.}{0.125\,\big)2.000.}$$
$$\frac{1\,25}{750}$$
$$\frac{750}{}$$

$$X = 16$$

Two Ratios Using Colons

$$0.5 : 0.125 :: X : 4$$

$$0.125X = 2$$

$$\downarrow$$

$$\frac{0.125X}{0.125} = \frac{2.0}{0.125}$$

$$\downarrow$$

$$X = \frac{2}{0.125}$$

$$\downarrow$$

$$X = \frac{2}{0.125}\quad \frac{16.}{0.125\,\big)2.000.}$$
$$\frac{1\,25}{750}$$
$$\frac{750}{}$$

In the previous examples, several steps are needed to solve ratio and proportion. This procedure can be simplified.

EXPONENTIAL NOTATION

Many physical and chemical measurements deal with either very large or very small numbers. Because it often is difficult to handle these numbers when performing even the simplest arithmetic operations, it is best to use exponential notation or *powers of 10* to express them.

EXAMPLE

121 becomes 1.21×10^2

1210 becomes 1.21×10^3

1, 210,000 becomes 1.21×10^6

Likewise, you may express 0.0121 as 1.21×10^{-2}, 0.0000121 as 1.21×10^{-6}.

When you write numbers this way, the first part is called the *coefficient*. It is usually written with one figure to the left of the decimal point.

The second part is the *exponential factor* or *power of 10*. The exponent represents the number of places that the decimal point has been moved — positive to the left and negative to the right — to form the exponential.

EXAMPLE

When you convert 19,000 to 1.9×10^4, move the decimal point 4 places to the left. So, the exponent is 4.

When you convert 0.0000019 to 1.9×10^{-6}, move the decimal point 6 places to the right. So, you have a *negative* exponent $^{-6}$.

SELF-TEST 13 | Writing Exponentials

Write each of the following in exponential form. Answers are given at the end of the chapter.

1. 12,650
2. 0.0000000055
3. 451
4. 0.065
5. 625,000,000

Write each of the following in the usual numeric form. Answers are given at the end of the chapter.

6. 4.1×10^6
7. 3.65×10^{-2}
8. 5.13×10^{-6}
9. 2.5×10^5
10. 8.6956×10^3

Multiplying Exponentials

When multiplying exponentials, the exponents are *added*.

EXAMPLE

$10^2 \times 10^4 = 10^6$.

In the multiplication of numbers that are expressed in exponential form, the *coefficients* are multiplied in the usual manner, and then this product is multiplied by the power of *10* found by algebraically *adding* the exponents.

EXAMPLE

$(2.5 \times 10^2) \times (2.5 \times 10^4) = 6.25 \times 10^6$, or 6.3×10^6

$(2.5 \times 10^2) \times (2.5 \times 10^{-4}) = 6.25 \times 10^{-2}$, or 6.3×10^{-2}

$(2.5 \times 10^2) \times (4.5 \times 10^3) = 24.3 \times 10^5$, or 2.4×10^6

Dividing Exponentials

When dividing exponentials, the exponents are *subtracted*.

EXAMPLE

$10^2 \div 10^5 = 10^{-3}$

In the division of numbers that are expressed in exponential form, the *coefficients* are divided in the usual way, and the result is multiplied by the power of *10* found by algebraically *subtracting* the exponents.

EXAMPLE

$(7.5 \times 10^5) \div (2.5 \times 10^3) = 3.0 \times 10^2$

$(7.5 \times 10^{-4}) \div (2.5 \times 10^6) = 3.0 \times 10^{-10}$

$(2.8 \times 10^{-2}) \div (8.0 \times 10^{-6}) = 0.35 \times 10^4 = 3.5 \times 10^3$

Note that in each of these examples, the result is rounded off to the number of *significant figures* contained in the *least* accurate factor, and it is expressed with only one figure to the left of the decimal point.

SELF-TEST 14 | Multiplying and Dividing Exponentials

Multiply or divide the exponentials. Answers are given at the end of the chapter.

1. $(3.5 \times 10^3) \times (5.0 \times 10^4)$
2. $(8.2 \times 10^2) \times (2.0 \times 10^{-6})$
3. $(1.5 \times 10^{-6}) \times (4.0 \times 10^6)$
4. $(1.5 \times 10^3) \times (8.0 \times 10^4)$
5. $(9.3 \times 10^3) \div (5.0 \times 10^4)$
6. $(3.6 \times 10^{-4}) \div (1.2 \times 10^6)$

Adding Exponentials

When adding and subtracting exponentials, the expressions must be changed (by moving the decimal points) to forms having any common power of 10. Then the coefficients only are added or subtracted.

The result should be rounded off to the number of *decimal places* contained in the *least* precise component, and it should be expressed with only one figure to the left of the decimal point.

Suppose you had to solve this problem:

$$(1.4 \times 10^4) + (5.1 \times 10^3)$$

Step 1. Move the decimal points to have common powers of ten.

$$5.1 \times 10^3 = 0.51 \times 10^4$$

Step 2. Add the coefficients only.

$$\begin{array}{r} 1.4 \times 10^4 \\ + \underline{0.51 \times 10^4} \\ 1.91 \times 10^4 \end{array}$$

Step 3. Round off to the number of decimal places contained in the least precise component.

$$1.9 \times 10^4.$$

Subtracting Exponentials

Follow the same steps that you did for adding exponentials, except subtract the coefficients.

Suppose you had to solve this problem:

$$(1.4 \times 10^4) - (5.1 \times 10^3)$$

Step 1. Move the decimal points to have common powers of ten.

$$1.4 \times 10^4 = 14.0 \times 10^3$$

Step 2. Subtract the coefficients only.

$$\begin{array}{r} 14.0 \times 10^3 \\ - \ \underline{5.1 \times 10^3} \\ 8.9 \times 10^3 \end{array}$$

SELF-TEST 15 | Adding and Subtracting Exponentials

Add or subtract the exponentials. Answers are given at the end of the chapter.

1. $(9.2 \times 10^3) + (7.6 \times 10^4)$
2. $(1.8 \times 10^{-6}) + (3.4 \times 10^{-5})$
3. $(6.5 \times 10^6) - (5.9 \times 10^4)$
4. $(7.4 \times 10^3) - (4.6 \times 10^2)$

Answers

Self-Test 1: Multiplication

1. 12	9. 48	17. 18
2. 63	10. 72	18. 88
3. 32	11. 15	19. 36
4. 45	12. 42	20. 24
5. 108	13. 24	21. 132
6. 24	14. 54	22. 45
7. 110	15. 64	23. 81
8. 14	16. 56	24. 35

Self-Test 2: Division

1. 9	9. 7	17. 9
2. 4	10. 6	18. 4
3. 3	11. 9	19. 6
4. 7	12. 6	20. 2
5. 7	13. 4	21. 7
6. 8	14. 3	22. 12
7. 4	15. 3	23. 12
8. 3	16. 7	24. 7

Self-Test 3: Reducing Fractions

1. $\frac{16}{24} = \frac{4}{6} = \frac{2}{3}$ (Divide by 4, then 2.)

   Alternatively: $\frac{16}{24} = \frac{2}{3}$ (Divide by 8.)

2. $\frac{36}{216} = \frac{6}{36} = \frac{1}{6}$ (Divide by 6, then 6.)

3. $\frac{18}{96} = \frac{9}{48} = \frac{3}{16}$ (Divide by 2, then 3.)

4. $\frac{70}{490} = \frac{7}{49} = \frac{1}{7}$ (Divide by 10, then 7.)

5. $\frac{18}{81} = \frac{2}{9}$ (Divide by 9.)

6. $\frac{8}{48} = \frac{1}{6}$ (Divide by 8.)

7. $\frac{12}{30} = \frac{6}{15} = \frac{2}{5}$ (Divide by 2, then 3.)

   Alternatively: $\frac{12}{30} = \frac{2}{5}$ (Divide by 6.)

8. $\frac{68}{136} = \frac{34}{68} = \frac{1}{2}$ (Divide by 2, then 34.)

9. $\frac{55}{121} = \frac{5}{11}$ (Divide by 11.)

10. $\frac{15}{60} = \frac{1}{4}$ (Divide by 15.)

    Alternatively: $\frac{15}{60} = \frac{3}{12} = \frac{1}{4}$ (Divide by 5, then 3.)

Self-Test 4: Multiplying Fractions (Two Ways to Solve)

First Way

1. $\frac{1}{6} \times \frac{4}{5} \times \frac{5}{2} = \frac{20}{60} = \frac{1}{3}$

Second Way

1. $\frac{1}{\underset{3}{6}} \times \frac{\overset{1}{4}}{5} \times \frac{\overset{1}{5}}{2} = \frac{2}{\underset{3}{6}} = \frac{1}{3}$

2. $\frac{4}{15} \times \frac{3}{2} = \frac{\overset{2}{12}}{\underset{5}{30}} = \frac{2}{5}$ 2. $\frac{4}{\underset{5}{15}} \times \frac{\overset{1}{3}}{2} = \frac{2}{5}$

(Divide by 6)

3. $1\frac{1}{2} \times 4\frac{2}{3} = \frac{3}{2} \times \frac{14}{3} = \frac{\overset{7}{42}}{\underset{1}{6}} = 7$ 3. $1\frac{1}{2} \times 4\frac{2}{3} = \frac{\overset{1}{3}}{\underset{1}{2}} \times \frac{\overset{7}{14}}{\underset{1}{3}} = 7$

4. $\frac{1}{5} \times \frac{15}{45} = \frac{\overset{3}{15}}{\underset{45}{225}} = \frac{3}{45} = \frac{1}{15}$ 4. $\frac{1}{5} \times \frac{\overset{1}{15}}{\underset{3}{45}} = \frac{1}{15}$

(Divide by 5.)

5. $3\frac{3}{4} \times 10\frac{2}{3} = \frac{15}{4} \times \frac{32}{3}$ 5. $\frac{\overset{5}{15}}{\underset{1}{4}} \times \frac{\overset{8}{32}}{\underset{1}{3}} = 40$

(Too confusing! Use the second way.)

6. $\frac{7}{20} \times \frac{2}{14}$ 6. $\frac{\overset{1}{7}}{\underset{10}{20}} \times \frac{\overset{1}{2}}{\underset{2}{14}} = \frac{1}{20}$

(Too difficult. Use the second way.)

7. $\frac{9}{2} \times \frac{3}{2} = \frac{27}{4}$

(Cannot reduce.)

8. $6\frac{1}{4} \times 7\frac{1}{9} \times \frac{9}{5} = \frac{25}{4} \times \frac{64}{9} \times \frac{9}{5}$ 8. $\frac{\overset{5}{25}}{\underset{1}{4}} \times \frac{\overset{16}{64}}{\underset{1}{9}} \times \frac{\overset{1}{9}}{\underset{1}{5}} = 80$

(Too difficult. Use the second way.)

Self-Test 5: Dividing Fractions

1. $\frac{1}{75} \div \frac{1}{150} = \frac{1}{75} \times \frac{\overset{2}{150}}{\underset{1}{1}} = 2$

2. $\frac{1}{8} \div \frac{1}{4} = \frac{1}{\underset{2}{8}} \times \frac{\overset{1}{4}}{1} = \frac{1}{2}$

3. $2\frac{2}{3} \div \frac{1}{2} = \frac{8}{3} \times \frac{2}{1} = \frac{16}{3}$

4. $75 \div 12\frac{1}{2} = 75 \div \frac{25}{2} = \frac{3}{\underset{1}{75}} \times \frac{2}{25} = 6$

5. $\frac{7}{25} \div \frac{7}{75} = \frac{\overset{1}{7}}{\underset{1}{25}} \times \frac{\overset{3}{75}}{\underset{1}{7}} = 3$

6. $\frac{1}{2} \div \frac{1}{4} = \frac{1}{\underset{1}{2}} \times \frac{\overset{2}{4}}{1} = 2$

7. $\frac{3}{4} \div \frac{8}{3} = \frac{3}{4} \times \frac{3}{8} = \frac{9}{32}$

8. $\frac{1}{60} \div \frac{7}{10} = \frac{1}{\underset{6}{60}} \times \frac{\overset{1}{10}}{7} = \frac{1}{42}$

Self-Test 6: Converting Fractions to Decimals

1. $\dfrac{1}{6}\overline{)\begin{array}{l}.166\\1.000\end{array}} = 0.166$

$$\begin{array}{r}6\\\hline 40\\36\\\hline 40\\36\\\hline 4\end{array}$$

2. $\dfrac{\overset{3}{\cancel{6}}}{\underset{4}{\cancel{8}}} = \dfrac{3}{4}\,\overline{)\begin{array}{l}.75\\3.00\end{array}} = 0.75$

$$\begin{array}{r}2\,8\\\hline 20\\20\\\hline 0\end{array}$$

3. $\dfrac{4}{5}\overline{)\begin{array}{l}.8\\4.0\end{array}} = 0.8$

$$\begin{array}{r}4\,0\\\hline 0\end{array}$$

4. $\dfrac{9}{40}\overline{)\begin{array}{l}.225\\9.000\end{array}} = 0.225$

$$\begin{array}{r}8\,0\\\hline 1\,00\\80\\\hline 200\\200\\\hline 0\end{array}$$

5. $\dfrac{1}{8}\overline{)\begin{array}{l}.125\\1.000\end{array}} = 0.125$

$$\begin{array}{r}8\\\hline 20\\16\\\hline 40\\40\\\hline 0\end{array}$$

6. $\dfrac{1}{7}\overline{)\begin{array}{l}.145\\1.000\end{array}} = 0.142$

$$\begin{array}{r}7\\\hline 30\\28\\\hline 20\\14\\\hline 6\end{array}$$

Self-Test 7: Reading Decimals

1. Twenty-five hundredths $\left(\dfrac{25}{100}\right)$
2. Four thousandths $\left(\dfrac{4}{1000}\right)$
3. One and seven tenths $\left(1\dfrac{7}{10}\right)$
4. Five tenths $\left(\dfrac{5}{10}\right)$

5. Three hundred thirty-four thousandths $\left(\dfrac{334}{1000}\right)$
6. One hundred thirty-six and seventy-five hundredths $\left(136\dfrac{75}{100}\right)$
7. One tenth $\left(\dfrac{1}{10}\right)$
8. One hundred fifty thousandths $\left(\dfrac{150}{1000}\right)$. The zero at the end of 0.150 is not necessary. The number could be read as fifteen hundredths $\left(\dfrac{15}{100}\right)$.

Self-Test 8: Division of Decimals

1. $24\overline{)\begin{array}{l}0.0002\\0.0048\end{array}}$ No decimals in the divisor, so no need to move the decimal in the dividend.

2. $0\underbrace{.004}\,\overline{)\,0\underbrace{.100}}$ Now it is $4\overline{)\begin{array}{l}25.\\100\end{array}}$

3. $0\underbrace{.02}\,\overline{)\,0\underbrace{.20}}$ Now it is $2\overline{)\begin{array}{l}10.\\20\end{array}}$

4. $7\underbrace{.8}\,\overline{)\,140\underbrace{.0}}$ Now it is $78\overline{)\begin{array}{l}17.948\\1400.000\end{array}}$

$$\begin{array}{r}78\\\hline 620\\546\\\hline 74\,0\\70\,2\\\hline 3\,80\\3\,12\\\hline 680\\624\\\hline 56\end{array}$$

5. $6\overline{)\begin{array}{l}23.333\\140.000\end{array}}$

$$\begin{array}{r}12\\\hline 20\\18\\\hline 20\\18\\\hline 20\\18\\\hline 20\\18\\\hline 2\end{array}$$

6. $0\underbrace{.025}\,\overline{)\,10\underbrace{.000}}$ Now it is $25\overline{)\begin{array}{l}400.\\10000\end{array}}$

Note that because there are two places between the 4 and the decimal, you had to add two zeros.

Self-Test 9: Rounding Decimals

Nearest Tenth

1. 0.3   4. 0.1
2. 1.8   5. 0.6
3. 3.3   6. 1.27

Nearest Hundredth

7. 0.75
8. 0.68

9. 4.54
10. 1.22

Nearest Thousandth

11. 1.325
12. 0.003
13. 0.452

14. 0.726
15. 0.348

Self-Test 10: Value of Decimals

1. 0.25
2. 0.1
3. 0.5
4. 0.2

5. 0.825
6. 0.9
7. 0.4
8. 0.7

Self-Test 11: Conversion of Percents

1. Fraction $10\% = \dfrac{\frac{1}{10}}{\frac{100}{10}} = \dfrac{1}{10}$

   Decimal $10\% = \dfrac{10}{100} \overset{.1}{)10.0} = 0.1$

   Quick-rule decimal $10.\% = 0.1$

2. Fraction $0.9\% = \dfrac{\frac{9}{10}}{100} = \dfrac{9}{10} \div 100 = \dfrac{9}{10} \times \dfrac{1}{100} = \dfrac{9}{1000}$

   Decimal $0.9\% = \dfrac{0.9}{100} \overset{.009}{)0.900} = 0.009$

   Quick-rule decimal $00.9\% = 0.009$

3. Fraction $\dfrac{1}{5}\% = \dfrac{\frac{1}{5}}{100} = \dfrac{1}{5} \div 100 = \dfrac{1}{5} \times \dfrac{1}{100} = \dfrac{1}{500}$

   Decimal $\dfrac{1}{5}\% = \dfrac{1}{5} \div 100 = \dfrac{1}{500} \overset{.002}{)1.000} = 0.002$

   Quick-rule decimal $\dfrac{1}{5}\% = \dfrac{1}{5} \overset{.2}{)1.0} = 0.2\%$

   $00.2 = 0.002$

4. Fraction $0.01\% = \dfrac{\frac{1}{100}}{100} = \dfrac{1}{100} \div \dfrac{100}{1}$

   $= \dfrac{1}{100} \times \dfrac{1}{100} = \dfrac{1}{10000}$

   Decimal $0.1\% = \dfrac{0.01}{100} \overset{0.0001}{)\,.0100} = 0.0001$

   Quick-rule decimal $00.01 = 0.0001$

5. Fraction $\dfrac{2}{3}\% = \dfrac{\frac{2}{3}}{100} = \dfrac{2}{3} \div \dfrac{100}{1} = \dfrac{2}{3} \times \dfrac{1}{100}$

   $= \dfrac{2}{300} = \dfrac{1}{150}$

   Decimal $\dfrac{2}{3}\% = \dfrac{2}{3} \div \dfrac{100}{1} = \dfrac{2}{3} \times \dfrac{1}{100} = \dfrac{2}{300} \overset{.0066}{)2.000}$

   $= 0.0066$

   Quick-rule decimal $\dfrac{2}{3}\% = \dfrac{2}{3} \overset{.66}{)2.00} = 0.66\% = 00.66$

   $= 0.0066$

6. Fraction $0.45\% = \dfrac{\frac{45}{100}}{100} = \dfrac{45}{100} \div \dfrac{100}{1} = \dfrac{45}{100} \times \dfrac{1}{100}$

   $= \dfrac{45}{10000} = \dfrac{9}{2000}$

   Decimal $0.45\% = \dfrac{.45}{100} \overset{.0045}{)0.4500} = 0.0045$

   Quick-rule decimal $00.45\% = 0.0045$

7. Fraction $\dfrac{\frac{1}{20}}{\frac{100}{5}} = \dfrac{1}{5}$

   Decimal $20\% = \dfrac{20}{100} \overset{0.2}{)20.0}$

   Quick-rule decimal $20.\% = 0.2$

8. Fraction $0.4\% = \dfrac{\frac{4}{10}}{100} = \dfrac{4}{10} \div \dfrac{100}{1} = \dfrac{\frac{1}{4}}{10} \times \dfrac{1}{\underset{25}{100}} = \dfrac{1}{250}$

   Decimal $0.4\% = \dfrac{0.4}{100} \overset{0.004}{)0.400} = 0.004$

   Quick-rule decimal $00.4\% = 0.004$

9. Fraction $\dfrac{1}{10}\% = \dfrac{\frac{1}{10}}{100} = \dfrac{1}{10} \div \dfrac{100}{1} = \dfrac{1}{10} \times \dfrac{1}{100} = \dfrac{1}{1000}$

   Decimal $\dfrac{1}{10}\% = \dfrac{1}{10} \div \dfrac{100}{1} = \dfrac{1}{10} \times \dfrac{1}{100}$

   $= \dfrac{1}{1000} \overset{0.001}{)1.000} = 0.001$

   Quick-rule decimal $\dfrac{1}{10}\% = \dfrac{1}{10} \overset{0.1}{)1.0} = 0.1\%$

   $= 00.1 = 0.001$

10. Fraction $2\frac{1}{2}\% = 2.5\% = \frac{\frac{25}{10}}{100} = \frac{25}{10} \div \frac{100}{1}$

$$= \frac{25}{10} \times \frac{1}{100} = \frac{25}{1000} = \frac{1}{40}$$

Decimal $2.5\% = \frac{2.5}{100} \quad 100\overline{)2.50}^{\,0.025} = 0.025$

Quick-rule decimal $\underset{\smile}{000.}2.5\% = 0.025$

11. Fraction $33\% = \frac{33}{100}$

Decimal $33\% = \frac{33}{100} \quad 100\overline{)33.00}^{\,.33} = 0.33$

Quick-rule decimal $\underset{\smile}{33.}\% = 0.33$

12. Fraction $50\% = \frac{50}{100} = \frac{1}{2}$

Decimal $50\% = \frac{50}{100} \quad 100\overline{)50.0}^{\,.5} = 0.5$

Quick-rule decimal $\underset{\smile}{50.}\% = 0.5$

Self-Test 12: Solving Proportions

1. $\frac{120}{4.2} = \frac{16}{x}$
    $120x = 67.2$
    $x = 0.56$

    $120\overline{)67.20}^{\,0.56}$
    $\underline{60\ 0}$
    $7\ 20$
    $\underline{7\ 20}$

2. $750 : 250 :: x : 5$
    $250x = 750 \times 5$
    $x = 15$

    $\dfrac{750 \times 5}{\underset{1}{250}}^{\,3} = 15$

3. $\frac{14}{140} = \frac{22}{x}$
    $14x = 22 \times 140$
    $x = 220$

    $\dfrac{22 \times \overset{10}{140}}{\underset{1}{14}} = 220$

4. $2 : 5 :: x : 10$
    $5x = 20$
    $x = 4$

5. $\frac{81}{3} = \frac{x}{15}$
    $3x = 81 \times 15$
    $x = 405$

    $\dfrac{81 \times \overset{5}{15}}{\underset{1}{3}} = 405$

6. $0.125 : 0.5 :: x : 10$

    $0.5x = 0.125 \times 10 = \dfrac{\overset{1}{0.125}}{\underset{4}{0.500}} \times 10 = \frac{10}{4} \quad 4\overline{)10.0}^{\,2.5}$

    $x = 2.5$

Self-Test 13: Writing Exponentials

1. 1.265×10^4
2. 5.5×10^{-9}
3. 4.51×10^2
4. 6.5×10^{-2}
5. 6.25×10^8
6. $4,1000,000$
7. 0.0365
8. 0.00000513
9. $250,000$
10. $8,695.6$

Self-Test 14: Multiplying and Dividing Exponentials

1. $17.5 \times 10^7 = 1.75 \times 10^8$
2. $16.4 \times 10^{-4} = 1.64 \times 10^{-3}$
3. $6.0 \times 10^0 = 6.0$
4. $12 \times 10^7 = 1.2 \times 10^8$
5. 3.0×10^3
6. 3.0×10^{-10}

Self-Test 15: Adding and Subtracting Exponentials

1. 8.52×10^4 or 8.5×10^4
2. 3.58×10^{-5} or 3.6×10^{-5}
3. 6.441×10^6 or 6.4×10^6
4. 6.94×10^3 or 6.9×10^3

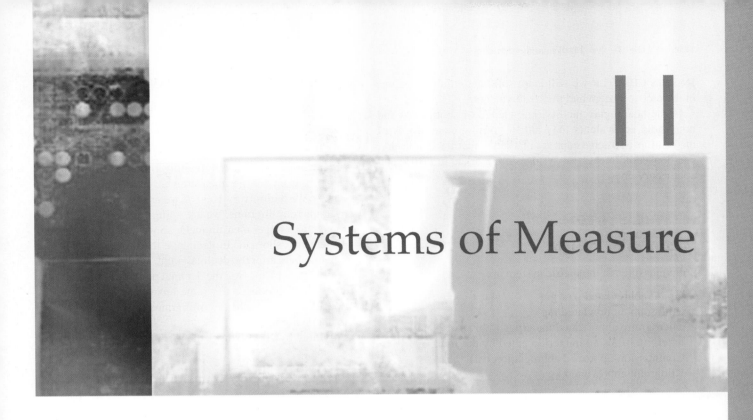

Systems of Measure

CHAPTER OBJECTIVES

In this chapter, you'll learn:

1. Metric solid and liquid measures.
2. Equivalents within the metric system.
3. Liquid household and apothecary measures.
4. Equivalents among metric, liquid apothecary, and household systems.

IN THIS CHAPTER we will learn solid and liquid measures in the metric system and their equivalents.

In the health care facility, knowledge of apothecary and household equivalents may aid in pouring exact doses of medication. Medicine cups are marked in metric, apothecary, and household measures; syringes are marked in metric and apothecary lines.

METRIC SYSTEM

Measures of Weight

Solid measures in the metric system are

Gram: abbreviated g or gm
Milligram: abbreviated mg
Microgram: abbreviated mcg (μg, which uses the Greek letter mu [μ], is no longer accepted by the Joint Commission-approved abbreviation list)
Kilogram: abbreviated kg

Weight Equivalents

The basic weight equivalents in the metric system are

1 g = 1000 mg
1 mg = 1000 mcg

Note that the gram is larger than a milligram. It takes 1000 mg to equal the weight of 1 g. A milligram is itself larger than a microgram; it takes 1000 mcg to equal the weight of 1 mg. These relationships can be indicated using the symbol >, which means "is greater than":

g > mg > mcg

Read: A gram is greater than a milligram, which is greater than a microgram.

Converting Solid Equivalents

The health care professional will have to calculate how much of a drug to give if the supply on hand is not in the same weight measure as the medication order.

EXAMPLE

Order: 0.25 g
Supply: tablets labeled 125 mg

We know the equivalent 1 g = 1000 mg. Therefore, we would change 0.25 g to milligrams by multiplying the number of grams by 1000.

$$
\begin{array}{r}
0.25 \\
\times\, 1000 \\
\hline
250.00
\end{array}
$$

The order, then, is that 0.25 g = 250 mg.

An easy rule to help you remember this type of conversion is

Large to small—multiply by 1000
Small to large—divide by 1000

For example, if we are converting grams to milligrams, we are going from a larger measurement to a smaller measurement, so we multiply by 1000. If we are converting from micrograms to milligrams, we are going from a smaller measurement to a larger measurement, so we divide by 1000.

There is a shortcut. In decimals, the thousandth place is three numbers after the decimal point. We can change grams to milligrams by moving the decimal point three places to the right, which produces the same answer as multiplying by 1000. We can also change milligrams to grams by moving the decimal point three places to the left, which is the same as dividing by 1000. This is the method we will learn.

RULE　Changing Grams to Milligrams

To multiply by 1000, move the decimal point three places to the right. ■

EXAMPLE

Example 1:

0.25 g = _____ mg
0 .250 = 250
0.25 g = 250 mg

Example 2:

0.1 g = _____ mg
0 .100 = 100
0.1 g = 100 mg

Grams to Milligrams Quick Rule: Some students have difficulty deciding whether to move decimal points to the left or to the right. Here is a method that might be helpful.

1. Write the order first.
2. Write the equivalent measure needed.
3. Use an arrow to show which way the decimal point should move.
4. The open part of the arrow always faces the *larger* measure.
5. In the equivalent 1 g = 1000 mg, the gram is the larger measure. It takes 1000 mg to make 1 g.

EXAMPLE

Example 1:

Order: 0.25 g
Supply: 125 mg

You want to convert grams to milligrams.

0.25 g > _____ mg

The arrow is telling you to move the decimal point three places to the right.

$0 .250 = 250$

Hence, 0.25 g = 250 mg

Example 2:

Order: 1.5 g
Supply: 500 mg
You want to convert grams to milligrams.

1.5 g > _____ mg
$1 .500 = 1500$

Hence, 1.5 g = 1500 mg

SELF-TEST 1 | Grams to Milligrams

Try these conversions from grams to milligrams. Answers are given at the end of the chapter.

1.	0.3 g = _____ mg	7.	0.08 g = _____ mg
2.	0.001 g = _____ mg	8.	0.275 g = _____ mg
3.	0.02 g = _____ mg	9.	0.04 g = _____ mg
4.	1.2 g = _____ mg	10.	0.325 g = _____ mg
5.	5 g = _____ mg	11.	2 g = _____ mg
6.	0.4 g = _____ mg	12.	0.0004 g = _____ mg

RULE   Changing Milligrams to Grams

To divide by 1000, move the decimal point three places to the left. ■

EXAMPLE

Example 1:

100 mg = _____ g
$100 . = 0.1$
100 mg = 0.1 g

Example 2:

8 mg = _____ g
$008 . = 0.008$
8 mg = 0.008 g

Milligrams to Grams Quick Rule: The arrow method also works to convert milligrams to grams. Remember the steps:

1. Write the order first.
2. Write the equivalent measure needed.

3. Use an arrow to show which way the decimal point should move.
4. The open part of the arrow always faces the *larger* measure.
5. In the equivalent 1 g = 1000 mg, the gram is the larger measure.

EXAMPLE

Example 1:

Order: 15 mg
Supply: 0.03 g
You want to convert milligrams to grams.

15 mg < g

The arrow tells you to move the decimal point three places to the left.

$015 . = 0. 015$
15 mg = 0.015 g

Example 2:

Order: 500 mg
Supply: 1 g
You want to convert mg to g.

500 mg = _____ g
500 mg < g

The arrow tells you to move the decimal point three places to the left.

$500 . = 0.5$
500 mg = 0.5 g

SELF-TEST 2 | Milligrams to Grams

Try these conversions from milligrams to grams. Answers are given at the end of the chapter.

1.	4 mg = _____ g	7.	50 mg = _____ g
2.	120 mg = _____ g	8.	600 mg = _____ g
3.	40 mg = _____ g	9.	5 mg = _____ g
4.	75 mg = _____ g	10.	360 mg = _____ g
5.	250 mg = _____ g	11.	10 mg = _____ g
6.	1 mg = _____ g	12.	0.1 mg = _____ g

The second major weight equivalent in the metric system is

1 mg = 1000 mcg.

Some medications are so powerful that minute microgram doses are sufficient to produce a therapeutic effect. It is easier to write orders in micrograms as whole numbers than to use milligrams written as decimals.

RULE   Changing Milligrams to Micrograms

To multiply by 1000, move the decimal point three places to the right. ■

EXAMPLE

Example 1:

0.1 mg = _____ mcg
0 .100 = 100
0.1 mg = 100 mcg

Example 2:

0.25 mg = _____ mcg
0 .250 = 250
0.25 mg = 250 mcg

Milligrams to Micrograms Quick Rule: Some students have difficulty deciding whether to move decimal points to the left or to the right.

1. Write the order first.
2. Write the equivalent measure needed.
3. Use an arrow to show which way the decimal point should move.
4. The open part of the arrow always faces the *larger* measure.
5. In the equivalent 1 mg = 1000 mcg, the milligram is the larger measure. It takes 1000 mcg to make 1 mg.

EXAMPLE

Example 1:

Order: 0.1 mg
Supply: 200 mcg
You want to convert milligrams to micrograms.

0.1 mg > _____ mcg

The arrow is telling you to move the decimal point three places to the right.

0 .100 = 100

Hence: 0.1 mg = 100 mcg

Example 2:

Order: 0.3 mg
Supply: 600 mcg
You want to convert milligrams to micrograms.

0.3 mg > _____ mcg
0 .300 = 300

Hence, 0.3 mg = 300 mcg

SELF-TEST 3 | Milligrams to Micrograms

Try these conversions from milligrams to micrograms. Use either method. Answers are given at the end of the chapter.

1.	0.3 mg = _____mcg	7.	5 mg = _____mcg
2.	0.001 mg = _____mcg	8.	0.7 mg = _____mcg
3.	0.02 mg = _____mcg	9.	0.04 mg = _____mcg
4.	0.08 mg = _____mcg	10.	10 mg = _____mcg
5.	1.2 mg = _____mcg	11.	0.9 mg = _____mcg
6.	0.4 mg = _____mcg	12.	0.01 mg = _____mcg

RULE   Changing Micrograms to Milligrams

To divide by 1000, move the decimal point three places to the left. ■

EXAMPLE

Example 1:

300 mcg = _____ mg
300 . = 0. 3
300 mcg = 0.3 mg

Example 2:

50 mcg = _____ mg
050 . = 0.05
50 mcg = 0.05 mg

Micrograms to Milligrams Quick Rule: The arrow method also works to convert micrograms to milligrams. Remember the steps:

1. Write the order first.
2. Write the equivalent measure needed.
3. Use an arrow to show which way the decimal point should move.
4. The open part of the arrow always faces the *larger* measure.
5. In the equivalent 1 mg = 1000 mcg, the milligram is the larger measure.

EXAMPLE

Example 1:

Order: 100 mcg
Supply: 0.1 mg
You want to convert micrograms to milligrams.

100 mcg < mg

The arrow tells you to move the decimal point three places to the left.

$$100. = 0.1$$

100 mcg = 0.1 mg

Example 2:

Order: 50 mcg
Supply: 0.1 mg
You want to convert micrograms to milligrams.

50 mcg = _____ mg
mcg < mg

The arrow tells you to move the decimal point three places to the left.

$$050. = 0.05$$

50 mcg = 0.05 mg

SELF-TEST 4 | Micrograms to Milligrams

Try these conversions from micrograms to milligrams. Answers are given at the end of the chapter.

1. 800 mcg = ____mg	7. 50 mcg = ____mg
2. 4 mcg = ____mg	8. 750 mcg = ____mg
3. 14 mcg = ____mg	9. 325 mcg = ____mg
4. 25 mcg = ____mg	10. 75 mcg = ____mg
5. 1 mcg = ____mg	11. 0.1 mcg = ____mg
6. 200 mcg = ____mg	12. 150 mcg = ____mg

SELF-TEST 5 | Mixed Conversions

Now try mixed conversions in metric weight measures. Be careful when reading, and take the time to think and apply the rules you have learned. Answers are given at the end of the chapter.

1. 0.3 mg = ____g	6. 50 mg = ____g
2. 0.03 g = ____mg	7. 0.014 g = ____mg
3. 15 mcg = ____mg	8. 200 mg = ____g
4. 0.1 g = ____mg	9. 0.2 mg = ____mcg
5. 100 mcg = ____mg	10. 0.65 mg = ____mcg

SELF-TEST 6 | Common Equivalents

Fill in the blanks to convert mg to g or to mcg.

1. 1000 mg = ____g	8. 30 mg = ____g
2. 600 mg = ____g	9. 15 mg = ____g
3. 500 mg = ____g	10. 10 mg = ____g
4. 300 mg = ____g	11. 0.6 mg = ____mcg
5. 200 mg = ____g	12. 0.4 mg = ____mcg
6. 100 mg = ____g	13. 0.3 mg = ____mcg
7. 60 mg = ____g	14. 0.25 mg = ____mcg

SELF-TEST 7 | Review of Grams to Milligrams

1. What is the short rule for converting grams to milligrams?_____

_____

2. 1 g = ____mg	9. 0.3 g = ____mg
3. 0.01 g = ____mg	10. 0.2 g = ____mg
4. 0.2 g = ____mg	11. 0.1 g = ____mg
5. 0.12 g = ____mg	12. 0.06 g = ____mg
6. 1 g = ____mg	13. 0.03 g = ____mg
7. 0.6 g = ____mg	14. 0.015 g = ____mg
8. 0.5 g = ____mg	15. 0.01 g = ____mg

APOTHECARY SYSTEM

The apothecary system was used in the past to write prescriptions. It has gradually been replaced by the metric system. Today, it is rare to see medication orders in apothecary notation. Table 11-1 on the next page contains a brief overview of the apothecary system.

Apothecary Abbreviations

The apothecary system has specific abbreviations. Table 11-1 presents the common apothecary abbreviations. Roman numerals are used to designate amounts.

Solid Apothecary Measure—The Grain

The only solid dosage measure in the apothecary system is the grain (abbreviated gr) followed by a Roman number (eg, gr v). Arabic numbers have been used (eg, gr 5; 5 gr). Do not confuse the apothecary grain (gr) with the metric gram (g, gm).

Solid Equivalents—Apothecary and Metric

Equivalents between the metric and apothecary systems are not exact (Table 11-2 on page 143).
   Three equivalents require explanation:

gr x = 0.6 g = 600 mg or 650 mg
gr v = 0.3 g = 300 mg or 325 mg
gr i = 0.06 g = 60 mg or 65 mg

Note that 15 grains = 1000 mg; 1 grain = 60 mg. If you multiply 15 × 60 the answer should be 1000 mg, but the answer is 900 mg. To remedy this discrepancy, some drug companies manufacture 1 grain to equal 65 mg. Aspirin and acetaminophen are made this way (5 grains = 325 mg; 10 grains = 650 mg.) When solving dosage problems when the order is written in one system and the stock comes in another system or conversion, use whichever equivalent is closer.

Table 11-1   APOTHECARY ABBREVIATIONS

Apothecary Abbreviation	Meaning	Learning Aid
ʒ	Dram	This is a liquid measure. It is slightly less than a household teaspoon. (One dram equals 4 milliliters; ʒi = 4 mL [see below].)
ʒ	Ounce	This is a liquid measure. It is slightly more than a household ounce. (One ounce equals 32 milliliters: ʒi = 32 mL.)
gr	Grain	Latin, *granum*. This solid measure was based on the weight of a grain of wheat in ancient times. There is no commonly used equivalent to the grain in the metric system.
gtt	Drop	Latin, *guttae*. This liquid measure was based on a drop of water. (One drop equals 1 minim.)
m (M, M$_x$)	Minim	Latin, *minim*. (One minim equals one drop: 1 m = 1 gtt.)
ss	One half	Latin, *semis*
i	One	*Example:* gr i = grains 1; ʒi = 4 mL
i ss	One and a half	*Example:* gr i ss = grains 1½
ii	Two	*Example:* gr ii = grains 2
iii	Three	*Example:* gr iii = grains 3
iv	Four	*Example:* gr iv = grains 4 ʒiv = drams 4
v	Five	*Example:* gr v = grains 5 m v = minims 5
vii	Seven	*Example:* gr vii = grains 7
vii ss	Seven and a half	*Example:* gr vii ss = grains 7½
x	Ten	*Example:* gr x = grains 10 m x = minims 10
xv	Fifteen	*Example:* gr xv = grains 15 m xv = minims 15

HOUSEHOLD SYSTEM

Household Measures

Household measures are used in preparing doses when a standard medication receptacle is used. Household measures are

Teaspoon: abbreviated tsp
Tablespoon: abbreviated tbsp
Ounce: abbreviated oz (or fl oz = fluid ounce)
Pint: abbreviated pt
Quart: abbreviated qt
Pound: abbreviated lb

Household equivalents are

1 tsp = 5 mL

1 tbsp = 15 mL
1 oz = 30 mL
1 pt = 500 mL
1 qt ≅ 1 L = 1000 mL
2.2 lb = 1 kg

Metric Liquid Measures

Liquid measures in the metric system are

Liter: abbreviated L
Milliliter: abbreviated mL (may be seen as ml)
Cubic centimeter: abbreviated cc (use is discouraged because it is not on the Joint Commission approved list of abbreviations)

Liquid equivalents in the metric system are

1 mL = 1 cc (acceptable in dosage; use is discouraged because it is not on the Joint Commission approved list of abbreviations)

1 L = 1000 mL

Table 11-2	METRIC AND APOTHECARY EQUIVALENTS		
Grain	**Milligram**	**Gram***	**Microgram**
gr xv	1000 mg	1 g	
gr x	(650)† 600 mg	0.6 g	
gr vii ss̄	500 mg	0.5 g	
gr v	(325)† 300 mg	0.3 g	
gr iii	200 mg	0.2 g	
gr i ss̄	100 mg	0.1 g	
gr i	(65)† 60 mg	0.06 g	
gr ss̄ or gr ½	30 mg	0.03 g	
gr ¼	15 mg	0.015 g	
gr ⅙	10 mg	0.01 g	
gr ¹⁄₁₀₀	0.6 mg		600 mcg
gr ¹⁄₁₅₀	0.4 mg		400 mcg
gr ¹⁄₂₀₀	0.3 mg		300 mcg

*g = gram.
†Alternative values.

SELF-TEST 8 | Converting Grains to Milligrams

Fill in the blanks to convert gr to mg; mg or g to gr. Answers are given in Arabic numbers.

1. gr iss _____
2. gr v _____
3. gr ¹⁄₁₅₀ _____
4. gr 15 _____
5. gr 4 _____
6. gr ¼ _____
7. Aspirin gr x _____
8. Tylenol gr v _____
9. 3 g _____
10. 325 mg _____
11. 15 mg _____
12. 0.5 mg _____
13. 9 g _____
14. Tylenol 650 mg _____
15. Aspirin 325 mg _____

Liquid Apothecary Measures

Although rarely used, in the apothecary system, the liquid measures are

Minim: abbreviated M or M͓ or m

Dram: abbreviated ʒ or dr
Ounce: abbreviated ℥ or oz
Drop: abbreviated gtt

Liquid equivalents in the apothecary system are

1 m = 1 gtt	1 minim = 1 drop
1 dr = 4 mL	1 dram = 4 mL
8 dr = 1 oz	8 drams = 1 ounce

Conversions Among Liquid Measures

Figure 11-1 shows a medicine cup with metric, apothecary, and household equivalents. Note that

5 mL = 1 tsp
15 mL = 1 tbsp = ½ fluid oz = 4 drams
30 mL = 2 tbsp = 1 fluid oz = 8 drams
500 mL = 1 pint
1000 mL = 1 L = 1 quart = 2 pints

Figure 11-2 shows a 3-mL syringe. Note that 1 mL = 16 minims.

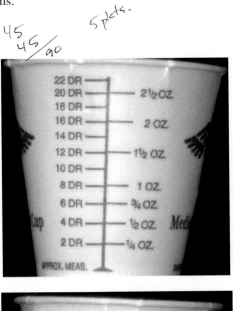

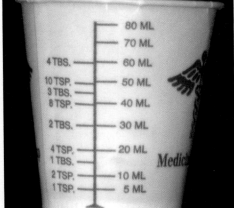

FIGURE 11-1. A medicine cup with apothecary, household, and metric equivalents.

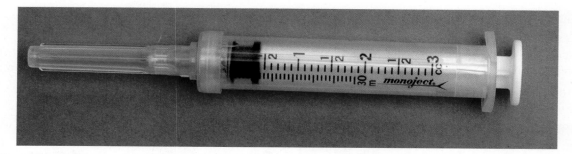

FIGURE 11-2. A 3-mL syringe with metric and apothecary measures. (© 2004 Lacey-Bordeaux Photography.)

SELF-TEST 9 | **Liquid Equivalents and Mixed Conversions**

Practice exercises in liquid equivalents and mixed conversions. Answers are given at the end of the chapter. Some equivalences may be approximate.

1. 1 oz = _____ mL
2. 1 tbsp = _____ mL
3. ½ fluid ounce = _____ mL
4. 2 fluid ounces = _____ mL
5. 1 mL = _____ minims
6. 5 mL = _____ tsp
7. 1 tsp = _____ mL
8. 1 fluid ounce = _____ tbsp
9. ½ tsp = _____ mL
10. 1 L = _____ mL
11. 1000 mL = _____ quart
12. 3 tbsp = _____ mL
13. 1½ fluid ounces = _____ mL
14. 5 mL = _____ tsp
15. 30 mL = _____ fluid ounce
16. 30 mL = _____ tbsp
17. 16 minims = _____ mL
18. 1 pt = _____ mL
19. 1 qt = _____ mL
20. 500 mL = _____ pint
21. 2 pints = _____ qt
22. 1 qt = _____ L
23. 15 mL = _____ tbsp
24. ½ qt = _____ pnt
25. 2 tbsp = _____ fluid ounce
26. 2.2 lb = _____ kg
27. 1 L = _____ mL
28. 3 tsp = _____ mL
29. 500 mL = _____ pt
30. 1 kg = _____ lb

CONVERSIONS AMONG SYSTEMS OF MEASUREMENT

All of the major measuring systems used in the practice of pharmacy have been introduced. Allied health professionals must study conversions in the metric system.

Table 11-3 CONVERSION EQUIVALENTS OF VOLUME

Apothecary Measure	Approximate Metric Equivalent (mL)	Exact Metric Equivalent (mL)
1 fl oz	**30**	29.57
4 fl oz	**120**	118.28
8 fl oz	240	236.56
1 pt (16 fl oz)	480	**473.00**
1 qt (2 pt)	960	**946.00**
1 gal (4 qt)	3840	**3785.00**
16.23 minims		1.00
1 minim		0.06

Items in bold must be committed to memory.

The household system is commonly used on prescription labels, and therefore conversions between the metric system and the household system must be memorized. Other equivalent measures that require memorization include specific apothecary and avoirdupois measures.

The example equivalents presented in Table 11-3 are useful in gaining perspective and in solving certain problems in the text, for example when it is necessary to convert fluidounces to milliliters or kilograms to pounds. The equivalents in **bold** print in Tables 11-3 to 11-5 must be memorized.

In the tables, not all of the exact equivalents are in bold; in many cases the approximate equivalent is commonly used in practice. For example, 30 mL and 30 g, *not* 29.57 mL, are commonly used as the equivalents for 1 fl oz and 1 oz. There is great variation in a pint; some manufacturers use 500-mL, others 480-mL, and still others 473-mL containers. The allied health professional should always refer to the manufacturer when there is a question. This text uses 473 mL as 1 pt. Grains are sometimes rounded up to 65 mg = 1 grain; other times 60 mg is used. The exact metric equivalent is 64.8 mg = 1 grain. For acetaminophen, aspirin, and iron products 65 mg = 1 grain. For codeine and thyroid 60 mg = 1 grain. Again, the allied health professional should refer to the manufacturer's label when there is a question.

Table 11-4	CONVERSION EQUIVALENTS OF WEIGHT	
Apothecary or Avoirdupois Measure	Approximate Metric Equivalent	Exact Metric Equivalent
1 grain	60 or 65 mg	64.8 mg
ss grain	30 mg	32.4 mg
$\frac{1}{60}$ grain	1 mg	1.08 mg
$\frac{1}{100}$ grain	0.6 mg (600 mcg)	0.648 mg
$\frac{1}{150}$ grain	0.4 mg (400 mcg)	0.432 mg
$\frac{1}{200}$ grain	0.3 mg (300 mcg)	0.324 mg
$\frac{1}{400}$ grain	0.15 mg (150 mcg)	0.162 mg
1 avoir oz	**30 g**	28.35 g
1 avoir lb (16 oz)		**454 g**
2.2 avoir ib	**1 kg**	1000 g

Items in bold must be committed to memory.

Table 11-5	COMMON HOUSEHOLD MEASURES		
Household Measure	Approximate Equivalent	Apothecary Equivalent	Other Equivalent
$\frac{1}{2}$ **tsp**	**2.5 mL**		
1 tsp	**5 mL**	**1 fluidram**	
2 tsp	10 mL	2 fluidrams	
3 tsp	**15 mL**		**1 tbsp or $\frac{1}{2}$ oz**
2 tbsp	**30 mL**	**1 fl oz**	1 oz

Items in bold must be committed to memory.

Conversions from other systems to the metric system must be thoroughly mastered by the allied health student.

SEE fluidounce → THINK mL
SEE teaspoon → THINK mL
SEE pound → THINK grams

All of the following example conversions can be solved with ratio-proporting.

EXAMPLE

Example 1:

Convert gr v to milligrams.

Step 1. List the equivalent.

gr i = 65 mg

Step 2. Set up ratio.

$$\frac{\text{gr i}}{\text{gr v}} = \frac{65 \text{ mg}}{X \text{ mg}}$$

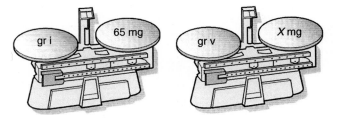

Step 3. Solve for X.

gr i (X) = 65 mg (gr v)
1 grain (X) = 65 mg (5 grains)

$$X = \frac{65 \text{ mg (5 grains)}}{1 \text{ grains}}$$

$X = 325$ mg, *answer*

Example 2:

Convert 12 fl oz to milliliters.

Step 1. List the equivalent.

1 fl oz = 30 mL

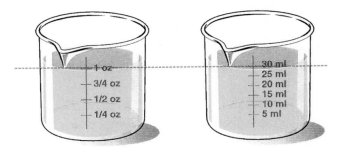

Step 2. Set up ratio.

$$\frac{1 \text{ fl oz}}{12 \text{ fl oz}} = \frac{30 \text{ mL}}{X \text{ mL}}$$

Step 3. Solve for X.

1 fl ox (X) = 30 mL (12 fl oz)

$$X = \frac{30 \text{ mL (12 fl oz)}}{1 \text{ fl oz}}$$

$X = 360$ mL, *answer*

SELF-TEST 10 | Conversions Among Systems of Measurement

Convert each amount to the unit indicated. Indicate the equivalent measure you used in each conversion.

Conversion	Equivalent Used
1. gr ii = _____ mg	_____
2. 3 tsp = _____ mL	_____
3. 325 mg = _____ grains	_____
4. 2 oz = _____ mL	_____
5. 90 1b = _____ kg	_____
6. 2 pints = _____ mL	_____
7. 7.5 mL = _____ tsp	_____
8. 45 mL = _____ tbsp	_____
9. 2.5 L = _____ mL	_____
10. 1 gal = _____ mL	_____
11. 2.5 kg = _____ lb	_____
12. gr X = _____ mg	_____
13. gr xxv = _____ g	_____
14. <uJ> = _____ mL	_____
15. ℨ = _____ tsp	_____
16. 60 mL = _____ oz	_____
17. 5 1b = _____ g	_____
18. 5 g = _____ mg	_____
19. i tsp = _____ mL	_____
20. 3 tbs = _____ mL	_____

21. Premature twins were born. The smaller weighted 1.2 kg, and the larger, 2 kg. Convert these weights to pounds.

22. How many 30-mg codeine capsules can be made from 0.0012 kg of codeine powder?

23. Calculate the total fluid intake in milliliters of a patient consuming the following:

Breakfast	4 oz orange juice
	6 oz milk
	4 oz water
Lunch	8 oz lemonade
Snack	12 oz diet soda
Dinner	6 oz chicken broth
	8 oz milk
	4 oz V-8 juice
	6 oz coffee
Snack	6 oz tea
	4 oz water

24. A patient was ordered to receive 2 tsp of Tylenol® Elixir every 4 hours. How many doses are contained in a 4-oz bottle of Tylenol® Elixir?

25. If a health care professional prescribed 4 g of aspirin to be taken by a patient daily, about how many 5-grain tablets should the patient take each day?

26. An allied health professional received a prescription calling for 30 capsules, each to contain $\frac{1}{200}$ grain of nitroglycerin. How many 0.4-mg nitroglycerin tablets would supply the amount required?

27. If a child accidentally swallowed 2 fl oz of Feosol® Elixir, containing $\frac{2}{3}$ grain of ferrous sulfate per 5 mL, how much ferrous sulfate in milligrams did the child ingest?

28. A health care professional advises an adult patient to take a children's aspirin (81 mg of aspirin per tablet) daily as a precaution against a heart attack. Instead, the patient decides to cut 5-grain aspirin tablets into dosage units. How many doses could be obtained from each 5-grain tablet?

29. Sustained-release tablets of nitroglycerin contain the following amounts of drug: $\frac{1}{25}$ grain, $\frac{1}{10}$ grain, and $\frac{1}{50}$ grain. Express these quantities as milligrams.

30. A health care professional instructs an adult patient to take 165-mg aspirin tablets. How much aspirin in grains does each tablet contain?

Answers

Self-Test 1: Grams to Milligrams

1. 300	5. 5000	9. 40
2. 1	6. 400	10. 325
3. 20	7. 80	11. 2000
4. 1200	8. 275	12. 0.4

Self-Test 2: Milligrams to Grams

1. 0.004	5. 0.25	9. 0.005
2. 0.12	6. 0.001	10. 0.36
3. 0.04	7. 0.05	11. 0.01
4. 0.075	8. 0.6	12. 0.0001

Self-Test 3: Milligrams to Micrograms

1. 300	5. 1200	9. 40
2. 1	6. 400	10. 10000
3. 20	7. 5000	11. 900
4. 80	8. 700	12. 10

Self-Test 4: Micrograms to Milligrams

1. 0.8	5. 0.001	9. 0.325
2. 0.004	6. 0.2	10. 0.075
3. 0.014	7. 0.05	11. 0.0001
4. 0.025	8. 0.75	12. 0.15

Self-Test 5: Mixed Conversions

1. 0.0003	4. 100	7. 14	9. 200
2. 30	5. 0.1	8. 0.2	10. 650
3. 0.015	6. 0.05		

Self-Test 6: Common Equivalents

1. 1	5. 0.2	9. 0.015	12. 400
2. 0.6	6. 0.1	10. 0.01	13. 300
3. 0.5	7. 0.06	11. 600	14. 250
4. 0.3	8. 0.03		

Self-Test 7: Review of Grams to Milligrams

1. Multiply grams by 1000, move decimal point three places to the right, or use an arrow with the open part toward gram to show movement of decimal point three places.

2. 1000	6. 1000	10. 200	13. 30
3. 10	7. 600	11. 100	14. 15
4. 200	8. 500	12. 60	15. 10
5. 120	9. 300		

Self-Test 8: Converting Grains to mg

1. 100 mg	3. 0.4 mg	5. 240 mg
2. 300 mg	4. 900 or 1000 mg	6. 15 mg
7. 650 mg	10. gr 5	13. gr 135
8. 325 mg	11. gr $\frac{1}{4}$	14. gr 10
9. gr 45 or gr 50	12. gr $\frac{1}{120}$	15. gr 5

Self-Test 9: Liquid Equivalents

1. 30	9. 2.5	17. 1	25. 1
2. 15	10. 1000	18. 500	26. 1
3. 15	11. 1	19. 1000	27. 1000
4. 60	12. 45	20. 1	28. 15
5. 16	13. 45	21. 1	29. 1
6. 1	14. 1	22. 1	30. 2.2
7. 5	15. 1	23. 1	
8. 2	16. 2	24. 1	

Self-Test 10: Conversions among Systems of Measurement

Conversion	Equivalent Used
1. gr ii = 120 mg or 130 mg	60 mg = gr i *Or* 65 mg = gr i
2. 3 tsp = 15 mL	1 tsp = 5 mL
3. 325 mg = gr v	65 mg = gr i
4. 2 oz = 60 mL	1 oz = 30 mL
5. 90 lb = 40.9 kg	1 kg = 2.2 lb
6. 2 pt = 946 mL	1 pt = 473 mL
7. 7.5 mL = 1½ tsp	1 tsp = 5 mL
8. 45 mL = 3 tbsp	1 tbsp = 15 mL
9. 2.5 L = 2500 mL	1 L = 1000 mL
10. 1 gal = 3785 mL	1 gal = 3785 mL
11. 2.5 kg = 5.5 lb.	1 kg = 2.2 lb.
12. gr x = 600 mg or 650 mg	60 mg = gr i or 65 mg = gr i
13. gr xxv = 1.5 g	60 mg = gr i
14. \<uJ\> = 30 mL	1 oz = 30 mL
15. \<uK\> = 1 tsp	1 dram = 1 tsp
16. 60 mL = 2 oz	1 oz = 30 mL
17. 5 lb. = 2270 g	1 lb = 454 g
18. 5 g = 5000 mg	1 g = 1000 mg
19. i tsp = 5 mL	1 tsp = 5 mL
20. 3 tbsp = 45 mL	1 tbsp = 15 mL

21. 1.2 kg convert to pounds: $\dfrac{1\,kg}{1.2\,kg} = \dfrac{2.2\,lb}{X}$

$X = 2.64$ lb *answer*

2 kg convert to pounds: $\dfrac{1\,kg}{2\,kg} = \dfrac{2.2\,lb}{X}$

$X = 4.4$ lb, *answer*

22. Step 1. Convert kg to mg by moving the decimal point 6 places left:

0.0012 kg = 1200 mg

Step 2. Divide 1200 mg by 30 mg (the amount in each capsule) to determine how many capsules can be made from 1200 mg:

1200 mg ÷ 30 mg = 40   40 caps, *answer*

23. Step 1. Convert all ounces to milliliters using 30 mL = 1 oz.

Step 2. Add all of the amounts in milliliters.

Step 3. Convert the total amount in milliliters to liters.

Step 4. 　4 oz = 120 mL
6 oz = 180 mL
4 oz = 120 mL
8 oz = 240 mL
12 oz = 360 mL
6 oz = 180 mL
8 oz = 240 mL
4 oz = 120 mL
6 oz = 180 mL
6 oz = 180 mL
4 oz = 120 mL

Total:　　2040 mL = 2.04 L

Or

Step 1. Add the volumes in ounces.

Step 2. Convert the ounces to milliliters, then liters:

68 oz <ts> 30 mL (per ounce) = 2040 mL = 2.04 L.

24. Step 1. Convert all volume measures to milliliters:

2 tsp = 10 mL (1 tsp = 5 mL)
4 oz = 120 mL (1 ounce = 30 mL)

Step 2. Divide 120 mL by 10 mL to determine the number of doses.

12 doses, *answer*

25. Step 1. Convert all measures to milligrams:

4 g = 4000 mg

gr v = 325 mg　　$\dfrac{\text{gr i}}{\text{gr v}} = \dfrac{65\,\text{mg}}{X}$　　$X = 325\,\text{mg}$

Step 2. Solve by Ratio-proportion:

$\dfrac{325\,\text{mg}}{1\,\text{tab}} = \dfrac{4000\,\text{mg}}{X}$

$X = 12$ tabs, *answer*

26. Step 1. Convert grains to milligrams:

gr 1/200 = 0.3 mg (see Table 10.9)

Step 2. 30 <ts> 0.3 mg = 9 mg.

Step 3. Solve by ratio-proportion: 0.4-mg tablets on hand; 9 mg needed.

$\dfrac{0.4\,\text{mg}}{1\,\text{tablet}} = \dfrac{9\,\text{mg}}{X}$　　$X = 22\frac{1}{2}$ tabs needed, *answer*

27. Step 1. Convert all units to metric measure:

2 oz = 60 mL
⅔ gr = 43.55 mg

Step 2. Solve by ratio-proportion:

$\dfrac{43.55\,\text{mg}}{5\,\text{mL}} = \dfrac{X}{60\,\text{mL}}$

$X = 522.6$ mg of Feosol® in 2 oz, *answer*

Or

Solve by dimensional analysis

$\dfrac{\frac{2}{3}\,\text{gr}}{5\,\text{mL}}$ <ts> $\dfrac{65\,\text{mg}}{1\,\text{gr}}$ <ts> $\dfrac{30\,\text{mL}}{1\,\text{oz}}$ <ts> 2 oz = 522.6 mg

28. Step 1. Convert apothecary measures to metric:

$\dfrac{\text{gr i}}{\text{gr v}} = \dfrac{65\,\text{mg}}{X}$　　$X = 325\,\text{mg}$

Step 2. Solve by ratio-proportion:

$\dfrac{325\,\text{mg}}{1\,\text{tab}} = \dfrac{81\,\text{mg}}{X}$　　$X = 4$ doses, *answer*

29. Step 1. Convert all grains to milligrams using 65 mg as your conversion factor:

1/25 gr = 2.6 mg, *answer*
1/10 gr = 6.5 mg, *answer*
1/50 gr = 1.3 mg, *answer*

30. Convert milligrams to grains

$\dfrac{65\,\text{mg}}{165\,\text{mg}} = \dfrac{\text{gr I}}{X}$　　$X = $ gr iiss, *answer*

Introduction to Pharmacology

12

Principles of Pharmacology

CHAPTER OBJECTIVES

In this chapter, you'll learn:

1. To define the chapter's key terms.
2. To identify the different names assigned to drugs.
3. To distinguish between prescription drugs, nonprescription drugs, and controlled substances.
4. To discuss the various types of drug reactions produced in the body.

5. To identify factors that influence drug action.
6. To discuss the types of drug interactions that may occur.
7. To discuss the use of herbal medicines.

KEY TERMS

additive drug reaction
adverse reaction
agonist
allergic reaction
anaphylactic shock
antagonist
antibodies

antigen
controlled substances
cumulative drug effect
drug idiosyncrasy
drug tolerance
hypersensitivity
nonprescription drugs

pharmaceutic phase
pharmacodynamics
pharmacogenetic disorder
pharmacokinetics
pharmacology
physical dependence
polypharmacy

prescription drugs
psychological dependence
receptor
synergism
teratogen
therapeutic response
toxic

PHARMACOLOGY is the study of drugs and their actions on living organisms. A sound knowledge of basic pharmacologic principles is essential for most health care professionals, especially those who interact with patients who receive medications. This chapter gives a basic overview of pharmacologic principles, drug development, federal legislation affecting the dispensing and use of drugs, and the use of herbal medicines.

DRUG DEVELOPMENT

Drug development is a long and arduous process, which takes anywhere from 7 to 12 years, and sometimes even longer. The United States Food and Drug Administration (FDA) has the responsibility of approving new drugs and monitoring drugs for adverse or toxic reactions. The development of a new drug is divided into the pre-FDA phase and the FDA phase (Fig. 12-1). During the pre-FDA phase, a manufacturer develops a drug that looks promising. In vitro testing (testing in an artificial environment, such as in a test tube) is performed using animal and human cells. This testing is followed by studies in live animals. The manufacturer then applies to the FDA for investigational new drug (IND) status.

With IND status, clinical testing of the new drug begins. Clinical testing involves three phases, each involving a larger number of people. All pharmacologic and biologic effects are noted. Phase I lasts 4 to 6 weeks and involves 20 to 100 individuals who are either "normal" volunteers or indi-

viduals in the intended treatment population. If phase I studies are successful, the testing moves to phase II, and if those results are positive, to phase III. Each successive phase has a larger subject population. Phase III studies generate more information on dosing and safety. The three phases last anywhere from 2 to 10 years, with an average of 5 years.

A new drug application (NDA) is submitted after the investigation of the drug in phases I, II, and III is complete and the drug is found to be safe and effective. With the NDA, the manufacturer submits all data collected during the clinical trials. A panel of experts, including pharmacologists, chemists, physicians, and other professionals, reviews the application and makes a recommendation to the FDA. The FDA then either approves or disapproves the drug for use. This process of review takes approximately 2 years.

After FDA approval, continued surveillance is performed to ensure safety after the manufacturer places the drug on the market. During this surveillance, an ongoing review of the drug occurs with particular attention given to adverse reactions. Health care professionals are encouraged to help with this surveillance by reporting adverse effects of drugs to the FDA by using the MedWatch system (Box 12-1).

SPECIAL FDA PROGRAMS

Although it takes considerable time for most drugs to get FDA approval, the FDA has special programs to meet certain needs, such as the orphan drug program, accelerated programs for urgent needs, and compassionate use programs.

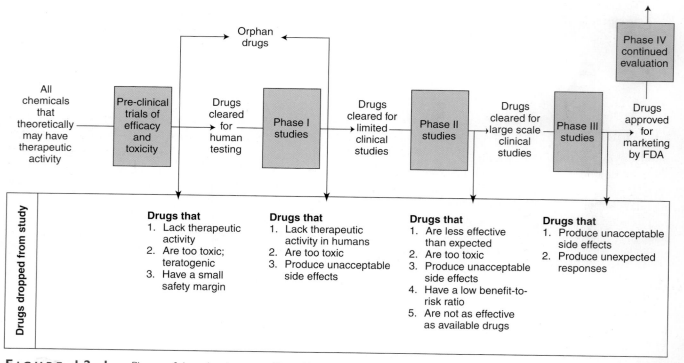

FIGURE 12-1.   Phases of drug development. (From Karch AM. *Focus on Nursing Pharmacology*. Philadelphia: Lippincott Williams & Wilkins; 2000.)

Box 12-1

HOW ADVERSE REACTIONS ARE REPORTED

A drug must be used and studied for many years before all of its adverse reactions are identified. The FDA established a reporting program called MedWatch, by which health care professionals can report observations of serious adverse drug effects by using a standard form (see Appendix D). The FDA protects the identity of those who voluntarily report adverse reactions. This form also is used to report an undesirable experience associated with the use of medical products (e.g., latex gloves, pacemakers, infusion pumps, anaphylaxis, blood, blood components, etc).

The FDA considers serious adverse reactions as those that may result in death, life-threatening illness, hospitalization, disability, or those that may require medical or surgical intervention.

Adverse drug reactions may be reported to the FDA by mail, fax, or e-mail. For more information, go to this website:

www.fda.gov/medwatch/index.html

Orphan Drug Program

The Orphan Drug Act of 1983 was passed to encourage the development and marketing of products used to treat rare diseases. The act defines a "rare disease" as a condition affecting fewer than 200,000 individuals in the United States. The National Organization of Rare Disorders reports that there are more than 6000 rare disorders that affect a total of approximately 25 million individuals. Examples of rare disorders include Tourette syndrome, ovarian cancer, acquired immunodeficiency syndrome (AIDS), Huntington disease, and certain forms of leukemia.

The act provides for incentives, such as research grants, protocol assistance by the FDA, and special tax credits, to encourage manufacturers to develop orphan drugs. If the drug is approved, then the manufacturer has 7 years of exclusive marketing rights. More than 100 new drugs have received FDA approval since the law was passed. Examples of orphan drugs include thalidomide for leprosy, triptorelin pamoate for ovarian cancer, tetrabenazine for Huntington disease, and zidovudine for AIDS.

Accelerated Programs

Accelerated approval of drugs is offered by the FDA as a means to make promising products for life-threatening diseases available on the market, based on preliminary evidence, before complete testing has demonstrated benefits for patients. A "provisional approval" may be granted, with a written commitment from the pharmaceutical company to complete clinical studies that formally demonstrate patient benefit. This program seeks to make life-saving investigational drugs available to treat diseases that pose a significant health threat to the public. One example of a disease that qualifies as posing a significant health threat is AIDS. Because AIDS is so devastating to the individuals affected, and because of the danger the disease poses to public health, the FDA and pharmaceutical companies are working together to shorten the IND approval process for some drugs that show promise in treating AIDS. This accelerated process allows health care providers to administer a drug with positive results in early phase I and II clinical trials, rather than wait until final approval is granted. If the drug continues to prove beneficial, then the process of approval is accelerated.

Compassionate Access to Unapproved Drugs

The compassionate access program allows patients to receive drugs that have not yet been approved by the FDA. This program provides experimental drugs for patients who could benefit from new treatments but who probably would die before the drug is approved for use. These patients are often too sick to participate in controlled studies. Drug manufacturers make a proposal to the FDA to target patients with the disease. The company then provides the drug free to these patients. The pharmaceutical company analyzes and presents to the FDA data about this treatment. This program can be beneficial but is not without problems. Because the drug is not in full production, quantities may be limited; the number of patients may be limited, and patients may be selected at random. Because patients receiving compassionate access often are sicker, they have an increased risk for toxic reactions. Thus, a newly developed drug may gain a bad reputation even before marketing begins.

DRUG NAMES

Throughout the process of development, drugs may have several names: a chemical name, a generic (nonproprietary) name, an official name, and a trade or brand name. These names can be confusing without a clear understanding of the different names used. Table 12-1 identifies the different names and explains each.

DRUG CATEGORIES

After approving a drug, the FDA assigns it to one of the following categories: prescription, nonprescription, or controlled substance.

Prescription Drugs

Prescription drugs are drugs that the federal government has designated to be potentially harmful unless their use is supervised by a licensed health care provider, such as a nurse

Table 12-1   DRUG NAMES

Drug Name and Example	Explanation
Chemical Name Example: ethyl 4-(8-chloro-5,6-dihydro-11H-benzo[5,6] cycloheptal[1,2-b]-pyridin-11-ylidene)-1-piperidinecardisplayylate	Gives the exact chemical makeup of the drug and placing of the atoms or molecular structure; it is not capitalized
Generic Name (nonproprietary) Example: loratadine	Name given to a drug before it becomes official; may be used in all countries, by all manufacturers; it is not capitalized
Official Name Example: loratadine	Name listed in *The United States Pharmacopeia-National Formulary;* may be the same as the generic name
Trade Name (brand name) Example: Claritin™	Name that is registered by the manufacturer and is followed by the trademark symbol; the name can be used only by the manufacturer; a drug may have several trade names, depending on the number of manufacturers; the first letter of the name is capitalized

practitioner, physician, or dentist. Although these drugs have been tested for safety and therapeutic effect, prescription drugs may cause different reactions in some individuals.

In hospitals and other institutional settings, patients are monitored for the therapeutic effect and adverse reactions of the drugs they are given. Some drugs have the potential to be **toxic** (harmful). When these drugs are prescribed to be taken at home, the patient and/or family members are educated about the drug.

Prescription drugs, also called legend drugs, are the largest category of drugs. Prescription drugs must be prescribed by a licensed health care provider. The prescription (Fig. 12-2) contains the name of the drug, the dosage, the method and times of administration, and the signature of the licensed health care provider prescribing the drug, along with other information.

Nonprescription Drugs

Nonprescription drugs are drugs that are designated by the FDA to be safe if taken as directed. They can be obtained without a prescription. These drugs are also referred to as over-the-counter (OTC) drugs and are available in many different settings, such as a pharmacy, drugstore, or supermarket. OTC drugs include those taken for symptoms of the common cold, headaches, constipation, diarrhea, and upset stomach.

Even nonprescription drugs, however, carry some risk and may produce adverse reactions. For example, acetylsalicylic acid, commonly known as aspirin, is potentially harmful and can cause gastrointestinal bleeding and salicylism. Product labels must give consumers important information regarding the drug, dosage, contraindications, precautions, and adverse reactions. Consumers are urged to read the directions carefully before taking OTC drugs.

Controlled Substances

Controlled substances are the most carefully monitored of all drugs. These drugs have a high potential for abuse and may cause physical or psychological dependence. **Physical dependence** is a compulsive need to use a substance repeatedly to avoid mild to severe withdrawal symptoms; it is the body's dependence on repeated administration of a drug. **Psychological dependence** is a compulsion to use a substance to obtain a pleasurable experience; it is the mind's dependence on the repeated administration of a drug. One type of dependence may lead to the other.

The Controlled Substances Act of 1970 regulates the manufacture, distribution, and dispensing of drugs that have abuse potential. Drugs under the Controlled Substances Act are categorized in five schedules, based on their potential for abuse and physical and psychological dependence. Box 12-2 describes the five schedules.

Prescriptions for controlled substances must be written in ink and include the name and address of the patient and the Drug Enforcement Agency number of the health care provider. Prescriptions for these drugs cannot be filled more than 6 months after the prescription was written and cannot be refilled more than five times. Under federal law, limited quantities of certain schedule C-V drugs may be purchased without a prescription, with the purchase

DEA # _____

CHARLES FULLER M.D.
SUSAN LUNGLEY R.N., A.N.
1629 TREASURE HILLS
HOUSTON, TX 79635

NAME _____

ADDRESS _____ DATE _____

R$_X$

☐ Label

Refill _____ times PRN NR

_____ M.D.

To ensure brand name dispensing, prescriber must write 'Dispense As Written' on the prescription.

FIGURE 12-2. Example of a prescription form. (From Roach SS. *Introductory Clinical Pharmacology*, 7th ed. Baltimore: Lippincott Williams & Wilkins; 2004.)

Box 12-2

SCHEDULES OF CONTROLLED SUBSTANCES

Schedule I (C-I)
- High abuse potential
- No accepted medical use in the United States
- Examples: heroin, marijuana, LSD (lysergic acid diethylamide), peyote

Schedule II (C-II)
- Potential for high abuse with severe physical or psychological dependence
- Examples: narcotics such as meperidine, methadone, morphine, oxycodone; amphetamines; and barbiturates

Schedule III (C-III)
- Less abuse potential than schedule II drugs
- Potential for moderate physical or psychological dependence
- Examples: nonbarbiturate sedatives, nonamphetamine stimulants, limited amounts of certain narcotics

Schedule IV (C-IV)
- Less abuse potential than schedule III drugs
- Limited dependence potential
- Examples: some sedatives and anxiety agents, nonnarcotic analgesics

Schedule V (C-V)*
- Limited abuse potential
- Examples: small amounts of narcotics (codeine) used as antitussives or antidiarrheals

*Under federal law, limited quantities of certain schedule V drugs may be purchased without a prescription directly from a pharmacist if allowed under state law. The purchaser must be at least 18 years of age and must furnish identification. All such transactions must be recorded by the dispensing pharmacist.

recorded by the dispensing pharmacist. In some cases, state laws are more restrictive than federal laws and impose additional requirements for the sale and distribution of controlled substances. In hospitals or other agencies that dispense controlled substances, scheduled drugs are counted every 8 to 12 hours to account for each ampule, tablet, or other form of the drug. Any discrepancy in the number of drugs must be investigated and explained immediately.

FEDERAL DRUG LEGISLATION AND ENFORCEMENT

Many laws regarding drug distribution and administration have been enacted during the past century, including the Pure Food and Drug Act; Harrison Narcotic Act; Pure Food, Drug, and Cosmetic Act; and the Comprehensive Drug Abuse Prevention and Control Act. These laws control the use of prescription and nonprescription drugs and controlled substances.

Pure Food and Drug Act

The Pure Food and Drug Act, passed in 1906, was the first attempt by the government to regulate and control the man-

ufacture, distribution, and sale of drugs. Before 1906, any substance could be called a drug, and no testing or research was required before placing a drug on the market. Before this time, the potency and purity of many drugs were questionable, and some were even dangerous for human use.

Harrison Narcotic Act

The Harrison Narcotic Act, passed in 1914, regulated the sale of narcotic drugs. Before the passage of this act, any narcotic could be purchased without a prescription. This law was amended many times. In 1970, the Harrison Narcotic Act was replaced by the Comprehensive Drug Abuse Prevention and Control Act.

Pure Food, Drug, and Cosmetic Act

In 1938, Congress passed the Pure Food, Drug, and Cosmetic Act, which gave the FDA control over the manufacture and sale of drugs, food, and cosmetics. Previously, some drugs, as well as foods and cosmetics, contained chemicals that were often harmful to humans. This law requires that these substances are safe for human use. It also requires pharmaceutical companies to perform toxicology tests before submitting a new drug to the FDA for approval. After FDA review of the tests performed on animals and other research data, approval may be given to market the drug, as described earlier.

Comprehensive Drug Abuse Prevention and Control Act

Congress passed the Comprehensive Drug Abuse Prevention and Control Act in 1970 because of the growing problem of drug abuse. It regulates the manufacture, distribution, and dispensation of drugs with a potential for abuse. Title II of this law, the Controlled Substances Act, deals with control and enforcement. The Drug Enforcement Agency within the US Department of Justice is the leading federal agency responsible for the enforcement of this act.

Drug Enforcement Administration

The Drug Enforcement Administration (DEA) within the US Department of Justice is the chief federal agency responsible for enforcing the Controlled Substances Act. Failure to comply with the Controlled Substances Act is punishable by fine and/or imprisonment. With drug abuse so prevalent, all health care workers must diligently adhere to FDA and state regulations.

DRUG USE AND PREGNANCY

The use of any prescription or nonprescription medication carries a risk of causing birth defects in a developing fetus. Drugs administered to pregnant women, particularly during the first trimester (3 months), may cause teratogenic effects. A **teratogen** is any substance that causes abnormal development of the fetus, which may lead to a severely deformed fetus.

In an effort to prevent teratogenic effects, the FDA has established five drug categories based on the potential of a drug for causing birth defects (Box 12-3). Information regarding the pregnancy category of a specific drug is found in reliable drug literature, such as the inserts accompanying drugs and drug reference books. In general, most drugs are contraindicated during pregnancy or lactation unless the potential benefits of taking the drug outweigh the risks to the fetus or infant.

During pregnancy, no woman should consider taking any drug, legal or illegal, prescription or nonprescription, unless the drug is prescribed or recommended by her health care provider. Smoking and drinking alcoholic beverages also carry risks, such as low birth weight, premature birth, and fe-

---

Box 12-3

PREGNANCY CATEGORIES

Pregnancy Category A
- Controlled studies show no risk to the fetus.
- Adequate well-controlled studies in pregnant women have not demonstrated risk to the fetus.

Pregnancy Category B
- There is no evidence of risk in humans.
- Animal studies show risk, but human findings do not.
- If no adequate human studies have been performed, then animal studies are negative.

Pregnancy Category C
- Risk cannot be ruled out.
- Human studies are lacking, and animal studies are either positive for fetal risk or lacking.
- The drug may be used during pregnancy if the potential benefits of the drug outweigh its possible risks.

Pregnancy Category D
- There is positive evidence of risk to the human fetus.
- Investigational or postmarketing data show risk to the fetus.
- However, potential benefits may outweigh the risk to the fetus. If needed in a life-threatening situation or a serious disease, then the drug may be acceptable if safer drugs cannot be used or are ineffective.

Pregnancy Category X
- Use of the drug is contraindicated in pregnancy.
- Studies in animals or humans or investigational or postmarketing reports have shown fetal risk that clearly outweighs any possible benefit to the patient.

Regardless of the pregnancy category or the presumed safety of the drug, no drug should be administered during pregnancy unless it is clearly needed and the potential benefits outweigh potential harm to the fetus.

---

tal alcohol syndrome. Children born to mothers using addictive drugs, such as cocaine or heroin, often are born with an addiction to the drug, along with other health problems.

DRUG ACTIONS WITHIN THE BODY

Drugs act in various ways in the body. Drugs taken by mouth (except liquids) go through three phases: the pharmaceutic phase, pharmacokinetic phase, and pharmacodynamic phase. Liquid and parenteral drugs (drugs given by injection) go through the latter two phases only.

Pharmaceutic Phase

The **pharmaceutic phase** of drug action is the dissolution of the drug. Drugs must be in solution to be absorbed. Drugs that are liquid or drugs given by injection (parenteral drugs) do not go through the pharmaceutic phase because they are already in solution. A tablet or capsule (solid forms of a drug) goes through this phase as it disintegrates into small particles and dissolves into body fluids within the gastrointestinal tract. Enteric-coated tablets do not disintegrate until reaching the alkaline environment of the small intestine.

Pharmacokinetic Phase

Pharmacokinetics refers to activities involving the drug within the body after it is administered. These activities include absorption, distribution, metabolism, and excretion. Another pharmacokinetic component, the drug's half-life, is a measure of the rate at which it is removed from the body.

Absorption

Absorption follows administration and is the process by which a drug becomes available for use in the body. It occurs after dissolution of a solid form of the drug or after the administration of a liquid or parenteral drug. In this process, the drug particles within the gastrointestinal tract are moved into body fluids. This movement can be accomplished in several ways: active absorption, passive absorption, and pinocytosis. In active absorption, a carrier molecule such as a protein or enzyme actively moves the drug across a membrane. Passive absorption occurs by diffusion (movement from a higher concentration to a lower concentration). In pinocytosis, cells engulf the drug particle causing movement across the cell.

As the body transfers the drug from body fluids to tissue sites, absorption into body tissues occurs. Several factors influence the rate of absorption, including the route of administration, the solubility of the drug, and certain body conditions. Drugs are most rapidly absorbed when given by the intravenous (IV) route directly into the bloodstream, followed by the intramuscular (IM) route (injection into muscle tissue), the subcutaneous (SC) (injection under the skin), and, lastly, the oral route (Fig. 12-3). Some drugs are more soluble and thus are absorbed more rapidly than others. For example, water-soluble drugs are readily absorbed into the systemic circulation. Some body conditions, such as developing lipodystrophy (atrophy of the subcutaneous tissue) caused by repeated subcutaneous injections, inhibit absorption of a drug given in the site of lipodystrophy.

Distribution

The systemic circulation (blood flow throughout the body) distributes drugs to various body tissues or target sites.

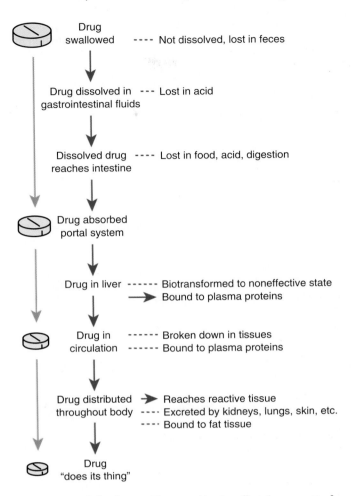

FIGURE 12-3. Pharmacokinetics affect the amount of a drug reaching reactive tissues. Very little of an oral dose of a drug actually reaches reactive sites. (From Karch AM. *Focus on Nursing Pharmacology.* Philadelphia: Lippincott Williams & Wilkins; 2000.)

There, drugs interact with specific receptors. Some drugs travel by binding to protein (albumin) in the blood. Drugs bound to protein are pharmacologically inactive. Only when the protein molecules release the drug can it diffuse into the tissues, interact with receptors, and produce a therapeutic effect.

As the drug circulates in the blood, a certain blood level must be maintained for it to be effective. When the blood level decreases to below the therapeutic level, the drug will not produce the desired effect. Should the blood level increase significantly above the therapeutic level, toxic symptoms may develop.

Metabolism

Metabolism, sometimes called biotransformation, is the process of chemical reactions by which the liver converts a drug to inactive compounds. Patients with liver disease may require lower dosages of a drug, or the health care provider may select a drug that does not undergo biotransformation in the liver. Frequent liver function tests are necessary when a patient has liver disease. The kidneys, lungs, plasma, and intestinal mucosa also aid in the metabolism of drugs.

Excretion

The elimination of drugs from the body is called excretion. After the liver renders a drug inactive, the kidney excretes the inactive compounds from the body in the urine. Some drugs are excreted unchanged by the kidney without liver involvement. Patients with kidney disease may require a lower dosage and careful monitoring of their kidney function. Because children have immature kidney function, they too may require dosage reduction and kidney function tests. Similarly, older adults have diminished kidney function and require careful monitoring and lower dosages. Other drugs are eliminated from the body through sweat, breast milk, breathing, or feces.

Half-Life

Half-life is the time required for the body to eliminate 50% of the drug. Drugs with a short half-life (2–4 hours) need to be administered frequently, whereas a drug with a long half-life (21–24 hours) requires less frequent dosing. For example, digoxin (Lanoxin) has a long half-life (36 hours) and requires once-daily dosing. However, aspirin has a short half-life and requires frequent dosing. It takes five to six half-lives to eliminate approximately 98% of a drug from the body. Although a drug's half-life is the same in most people, patients with liver or kidney disease may have problems excreting a drug; this increases its half-life and increases the risk of toxicity. Older patients or patients with impaired kidney or liver function require frequent diagnostic tests of their renal or hepatic function.

Pharmacodynamic Phase

Pharmacodynamics are the drug's actions and effects within the body. After administration, most drugs enter the systemic circulation and expose almost all body tissues to their possible effects. All drugs produce more than one effect in the body. The primary effect of a drug is the desired or therapeutic effect. Secondary effects are all other effects, whether desirable or undesirable, produced by the drug.

Most drugs have an affinity for certain organs or tissues and exert their greatest action at the cellular level in those specific areas, which are called target sites. The two main mechanisms of action are an alteration in cellular environment or cellular function.

Alteration in Cellular Environment

Some drugs act on the body by changing the cellular environment physically or chemically. Physical changes in the cellular environment include changes in osmotic pressures, lubrication, absorption, or conditions on the surface of the cell membrane. An example of a drug that changes osmotic pressure is mannitol, which produces a change in the osmotic pressure in brain cells, reducing cerebral edema. A drug that acts by altering the cellular environment by lubrication is sunscreen. An example of a drug that acts by altering absorption is activated charcoal, which is administered orally to absorb a toxic chemical ingested into the gastrointestinal tract. The stool softener docusate is an example of a drug that acts by altering the surface of the cellular membrane. Docusate has emulsifying and lubricating activity that causes a lowering of the surface tension in the cells of the bowel, permitting water and fats to enter the stool. This softens the fecal mass, allowing easier passage of the stool.

Chemical changes in the cellular environment include inactivation of cellular functions or an alteration of the chemical components of body fluid, such as a change in the pH. For example, antacids neutralize gastric acidity in patients with peptic ulcers.

Alteration in Cellular Function

Most drugs act on the body by altering cellular function. A drug cannot completely change the function of a cell, but it can alter its function. A drug that alters cellular function can increase or decrease certain physiologic functions, such as increase heart rate, decrease blood pressure, or increase urine output.

Receptor-mediated drug action.   The function of a cell alters when a drug interacts with a receptor. A **receptor** is a specialized macromolecule (a large group of molecules linked together) that attaches or binds to the drug molecule. This alters the function of the cell and produces the drug's **therapeutic response**. For a drug-receptor reaction to occur, a drug must be attracted to a particular receptor. Drugs bind to a receptor much like a piece of a puzzle. The closer the shape, the better the fit, and the better the therapeutic response. The intensity of a drug response is related to how good the "fit" of the drug molecule is and the number of receptor sites occupied.

Agonists are drugs that bind with a receptor to produce a therapeutic response. Drugs that bind only partially to the receptor generally have only a slight therapeutic response. Figure 12-4 identifies the different drug-receptor interactions. Partial agonists are drugs that have some drug receptor fit and produce a response but inhibit other responses.

Antagonists join with a receptor and thereby prevent the action of an agonist. When the antagonist binds more tightly than the agonist to the receptor, the action of the antagonist is strong. Drugs that act as antagonists produce no pharmacologic effect. An example of an antagonist is Narcan, a narcotic antagonist that completely blocks the effects of morphine. This drug is useful in reversing the effects of an overdose of narcotics.

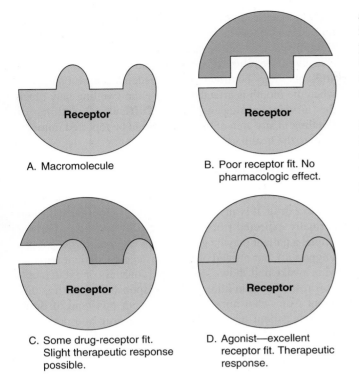

A. Macromolecule

B. Poor receptor fit. No pharmacologic effect.

C. Some drug-receptor fit. Slight therapeutic response possible.

D. Agonist—excellent receptor fit. Therapeutic response.

FIGURE 12-4. Drug–receptor interactions. (Adapted from Reiss & Evans. *Pharmacological Aspects of Nursing Care*, 3rd ed.)

Receptor-mediated drug effects. The number of available receptor sites influences the effects of a drug. If a drug occupies only a few receptor sites when many sites are available, then the response will be small. If the drug dose is increased, then more receptor sites are involved and the response increases. If only a few receptor sites are available, then the response does not increase if more of the drug is administered. However, not all receptors on a cell need to be occupied for a drug to be effective. Some extremely potent drugs are effective even when the drug occupies few receptor sites.

DRUG REACTIONS

Drugs produce many reactions in the body. The following sections discuss adverse drug reactions, allergic drug reactions, drug idiosyncrasy, drug tolerance, cumulative drug effect, toxic reactions, and pharmacogenetic reactions.

Adverse Drug Reactions

Patients may experience one or more adverse reactions (side effects) when they are given a drug (Fig. 12-5). **Adverse reactions** are undesirable drug effects. Adverse reactions may be common or rare. They may be mild, severe, or life-threatening. They may occur after the first dose, after several doses, or after many doses. An adverse reaction often is unpredictable, although some drugs are known to cause certain adverse reactions in many patients. For example, drugs used in the treatment of cancer are very toxic and are known to produce adverse reactions in many patients receiving them. Other drugs produce adverse reactions in fewer patients. Some adverse reactions are predictable, but many adverse drug reactions occur without warning.

Some texts use both the terms "side effect" and "adverse reaction." Often "side effects" refer to mild, common, and nontoxic reactions; "adverse reactions" refer to more severe or life-threatening reactions. In this text, only the term "adverse reaction" is used, referring to reactions that may be mild, severe, or life-threatening.

Allergic Drug Reactions

An **allergic reaction** also is called a **hypersensitivity** reaction. Allergy to a drug usually begins to occur after more than one dose of the drug has been given. Sometimes an allergic reaction may occur the first time a drug is given if the patient had received or taken the drug in the past.

A drug allergy occurs because the individual's immune system views the drug as a foreign substance, or **antigen**. The recognition of an antigen stimulates the antigen–antibody response that prompts the body to produce **antibodies,** which are immune system molecules that react with the antigen. If the patient takes the drug after the antigen–antibody response has occurred, then an allergic reaction results.

Even a mild allergic reaction can produce serious effects if it goes unnoticed and the drug is given again. Any indication of an allergic reaction must be reported to the health care provider before the next dose of the drug is given. Serious allergic reactions must be reported immediately because emergency treatment may be necessary.

Some allergic reactions occur within minutes (even seconds) after the drug is given; others may be delayed for hours or days. Allergic reactions that occur immediately are often the most serious.

Allergic reactions cause a variety of signs and symptoms that may be observed by health care workers or reported by the patient. Examples of some allergic signs and symptoms include itching, skin rashes, and hives (urticaria). Other signs and symptoms include difficulty breathing, wheezing, cyanosis, a sudden loss of consciousness, and swelling of the eyes, lips, or tongue.

Anaphylactic shock is an extremely serious allergic drug reaction that usually occurs soon after the administration of a drug to which the individual is sensitive. This type of allergic reaction requires immediate medical attention. The signs and symptoms of anaphylactic shock are listed in Table 12-2.

All or only some of these signs and symptoms may be present. Anaphylactic shock can be fatal if it not recognized and treated immediately. The treatment is to raise the patient's blood pressure, improve breathing, restore cardiac function, and treat other problems as they occur. Epinephrine (adrenalin) may be given by subcutaneous or intramuscular injection.

Table 12-2	**SIGNS AND SYMPTOMS OF ANAPHYLACTIC SHOCK**
Respiratory	Bronchospasm Dyspnea (difficult breathing) Feeling of fullness in the throat Cough Wheezing
Cardiovascular	Extremely low blood pressure Tachycardia (heart rate >100 bpm) Palpations Syncope (fainting) Cardiac arrest
Integumentary	Urticaria (rash) Angioedema Pruritus (itching) Sweating
Gastrointestinal	Nausea Vomiting Abdominal pain

Hypotension and shock may be treated with fluids and vasopressors. Bronchodilators are given to relax the smooth muscles of the bronchial tubes to improve breathing. Antihistamines may be given to block the effects of histamine.

Angioedema (angioneurotic edema) is another type of allergic drug reaction. It is manifested by the collection of fluid in subcutaneous tissues. The most commonly affected areas are the eyelids, lips, mouth, and throat, although other areas also may be affected. Angioedema can be dangerous when the mouth is affected because the swelling may block the airway causing asphyxia. Difficulty breathing or swelling in any area of the body should be reported immediately to the health care provider.

Drug Idiosyncrasy

Drug idiosyncrasy refers to any unusual or abnormal reaction to a drug. It is any reaction that is different from the one normally expected from a specific drug and dose. For example, a patient may be given a drug to promote sleep (e.g., a hypnotic), but instead of falling asleep the patient remains wide awake and shows signs of nervousness or excitement. This response is an idiosyncratic response because it is different from what normally occurs with this type of drug. Another patient may receive the same drug and dose, fall asleep, and after 10 hours be difficult to awaken. This, too, is an abnormal over-response to the drug.

The cause of drug idiosyncrasies is not clear. They are believed to occur because of a genetic deficiency that

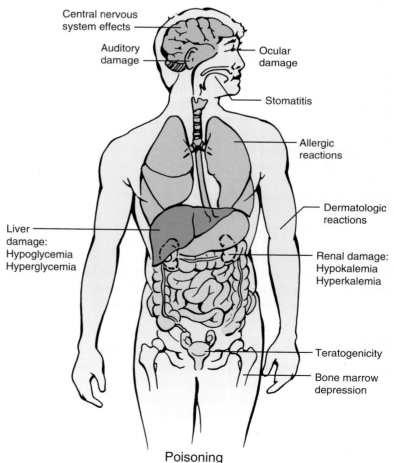

FIGURE 12-5. Various adverse effects may occur with drug use. (From Karch AM. *Focus on Nursing Pharmacology.* Philadelphia: Lippincott Williams & Wilkins, 2000.)

makes a patient unable to tolerate certain chemicals, including drugs.

Drug Tolerance

Drug tolerance is a decreased response to a drug, requiring an increase in dosage to achieve the desired effect. Drug tolerance may develop when a patient takes a certain drug, such as a narcotic or tranquilizer, for a long time. Someone who takes the drug at home may increase the dose when the expected effect does not occur. Drug tolerance is a sign of drug dependence. Drug tolerance may also occur in hospitalized patients. When a patient receives a narcotic for more than 10 to 14 days, drug tolerance (and possibly drug dependence) may be occurring. The patient may also begin to ask for the drug more frequently.

Cumulative Drug Effect

A **cumulative drug effect** may occur in patients with liver or kidney disease because these organs are the major sites for the breakdown and excretion of most drugs. This drug effect occurs when the body does not metabolize and excrete one (normal) dose of a drug before the next dose is given. Thus, if a second dose of this drug is given, some drug from the first dose remains active in the body. A cumulative drug effect can be serious because too much of the drug can accumulate in the body and lead to toxicity.

Patients with liver or kidney disease are usually given drugs with caution because a cumulative effect may occur. When the patient is unable to excrete the drug at a normal rate, the drug accumulates in the body, causing a toxic reaction. Sometimes the health care provider lowers the dose of the drug to prevent a toxic drug reaction.

Toxic Reactions

Most drugs can produce TOXIC or harmful reactions if administered in large dosages or when blood concentration levels exceed the therapeutic level. Toxic levels may also build if the patient's kidneys are not functioning properly and cannot excrete the drug. Some toxic effects are immediately visible; others may not be seen for weeks or months. Some drugs, such as lithium or digoxin, have a narrow margin of safety, even when given in recommended dosages. It is important to monitor these drugs closely to avoid toxicity.

Drug toxicity can be reversible or irreversible, depending on the organs involved. Damage to the liver may be reversible because liver cells can regenerate. An example of irreversible damage is hearing loss caused by damage to the eighth cranial nerve caused by toxic reaction to the anti-infective drug streptomycin. Sometimes drug toxicity can be reversed by the administration of another drug that acts as an antidote. For example, in serious instances of digitalis toxicity, the drug Digibind may be given to counteract the effect of digoxin toxicity.

Because some drugs can cause toxic reactions even in recommended doses, health care workers involved in direct patient care should be aware of the signs and symptoms of toxicity of commonly prescribed drugs.

Pharmacogenetic Reactions

A **pharmacogenetic disorder** is a genetically caused abnormal response to normal doses of a drug. This abnormal response occurs because of inherited traits that cause abnormal metabolism of a drug. For example, individuals with glucose-6-phosphate dehydrogenase (G6PD) deficiency have abnormal reactions to a number of drugs. These patients experience varying degrees of hemolysis (destruction of red blood cells) if they take these drugs. More than 100 million people are affected by this disorder. Examples of drugs that cause hemolysis in patients with a G6PD deficiency include aspirin, chloramphenicol, and the sulfonamides.

DRUG INTERACTIONS

Health care workers involved in patient care should be aware of the various drug interactions that can occur, most importantly drug–drug interactions and drug–food interactions. The following sections give a brief overview of drug interactions. Specific drug–drug and drug–food interactions are discussed in later chapters.

Drug–Drug Interactions

A drug–drug interaction occurs when one drug interacts with or interferes with the action of another drug. For example, taking an antacid with oral tetracycline causes a decrease in the effectiveness of the tetracycline. The antacid chemically interacts with the tetracycline and impairs its absorption into the bloodstream, thus reducing the effectiveness of the tetracycline. Drugs known to cause interactions include oral anticoagulants, oral hypoglycemics, anti-infectives, antiarrhythmics, cardiac glycosides, and alcohol. Drug–drug interactions can produce effects that are additive, synergistic, or antagonistic.

Additive Drug Reaction

An **additive drug reaction** occurs when the combined effect of two drugs is equal to the sum of each drug given alone. For example, taking the drug heparin with alcohol will increase bleeding. The equation "one + one = two" is sometimes used to illustrate the additive effect of drugs.

Synergistic Drug Reaction

Drug **synergism** occurs when drugs interact with each other and produce an effect that is greater than the sum of their separate actions. The equation "one + one = four" illustrates synergism. An example of drug synergism occurs when a person takes both a hypnotic and alcohol. When alcohol is taken simultaneously or soon before or after the hypnotic is taken, the action of the hypnotic increases. The individual experiences a drug effect that is much greater than that of either drug taken alone. A synergistic drug effect can be serious or even fatal.

Antagonistic Drug Reaction

An antagonistic drug reaction occurs when one drug interferes with the action of another, causing neutralization or a decrease in the effect of one drug. For example, protamine sulfate is a heparin antagonist. This means that the administration of protamine sulfate completely neutralizes the effects of heparin in the body.

Drug–Food Interactions

When a drug is given orally, food may impair or enhance its absorption. A drug taken on an empty stomach is absorbed into the bloodstream at a faster rate than when taken with food in the stomach. Some drugs must be taken on an empty stomach to achieve an optimal effect. Drugs that should be taken on an empty stomach are taken 1 hour before or 2 hours after meals. Other drugs, especially drugs that irritate the stomach, result in nausea or vomiting, or cause epigastric distress, are best given with food or meals to minimize gastric irritation. The nonsteroidal anti-inflammatory drugs and salicylates are examples of drugs given with food to decrease epigastric distress. Still other drugs combine with a food, forming an insoluble food–drug mixture. For example, when tetracycline is administered with dairy products, a drug–food mixture is formed that is unabsorbable by the body. When a drug cannot be absorbed by the body, no pharmacologic effect occurs.

FACTORS INFLUENCING DRUG RESPONSE

Various factors may influence a patient's drug response, including age, weight, gender, disease, and the route of administration.

Age

The age of the patient may influence the effects of a drug. Infants and children usually require smaller doses of a drug than adults do. Immature organ function, particularly the liver and kidneys, can affect the ability of infants and young children to metabolize drugs. An infant's immature kidneys are less able to eliminate drugs in the urine. Liver function is poorly developed in infants and young children. Drugs metabolized by the liver may produce more intense effects for longer periods. Parents must be taught the potential problems associated with administering drugs to their children. For example,

a safe dose of a nonprescription drug for a 4-year-old child may be dangerous for a 6-month-old infant.

Elderly patients may also require smaller doses, although this depends also on the type of drug administered. For example, an elderly patient may take the same dose of an antibiotic as a younger adult. However, the same older adult may require a smaller dose of a drug that depresses the central nervous system, such as a narcotic. Changes that occur with aging affect the pharmacokinetics (absorption, distribution, metabolism, and excretion) of a drug. Any of these processes may be altered because of the physiologic changes of aging. Table 12-3 summarizes changes that occur with aging and possible pharmacokinetic effects.

Polypharmacy is the taking of multiple drugs, which can potentially react with one another. When practiced by the elderly, polypharmacy leads to an increased potential for adverse reactions. Although multiple drug therapy is necessary to treat certain disease states, it always increases the possibility of adverse reactions.

Weight

In general, dosages are based on an average weight of approximately 150 lb for both men and women. A drug dose may sometimes be increased or decreased because the patient's weight is significantly higher or lower than this average. With narcotics, for example, higher or lower dosages may be necessary to produce relief of pain, depending on the patient's weight.

Gender

The person's gender may influence the action of some drugs. Women may require a smaller dose of some drugs than men because women have a body fat and water ratio different from that of men.

Disease

The presence of disease may influence the action of some drugs. Sometimes disease is a reason for not prescribing a drug or for reducing the dose of a certain drug. Both hepatic (liver) and renal (kidney) disease can greatly affect drug response.

In liver disease, for example, the ability to metabolize or detoxify a drug may be impaired. If the normal dose of the drug is given, then the liver may be unable to metabolize it at a normal rate. Consequently, the drug may be excreted from the body at a much slower rate than normal. The health care provider may then prescribe a lower dose and lengthen the time between doses.

Patients with kidney disease may experience drug toxicity and a longer duration of drug action. The dosage of drugs may be reduced to prevent the accumulation of toxic levels in the blood or further injury to the kidney.

Table 12-3 FACTORS ALTERING DRUG RESPONSE IN THE ELDERLY

Age-Related Changes	Effect on Drug Therapy
Decreased gastric acidity; decreased gastric motility	Possible decreased or delayed absorption
Dry mouth and decreased saliva	Difficulty swallowing oral drugs
Decreased liver blood flow; decreased liver mass	Delayed and decreased metabolism of certain drugs; possible increased effect, leading to toxicity
Decreased lipid content of the skin	Possible decrease in absorption of transdermal drugs
Increased body fat; decreased body water	Possible increase in toxicity of water-soluble drugs; more prolonged effects of fat-soluble drugs
Decreased serum proteins	Possible increased effect and toxicity of highly protein-bound drugs
Decreased renal mass, blood flow, and glomerular filtration rate	Possible increased serum levels, leading to toxicity of drugs excreted by the kidney
Changes in sensitivity of certain drug receptors	Increase or decrease in drug effect

Adapted from Eisenhauer L, Nichols L, Spencer R, Bergan F. *Clinical pharmacology and nursing management*, 5th ed. Philadelphia: Lippincott-Raven; 1998:189. Used with permission.

Route of Administration

Intravenous administration of a drug produces the most rapid drug action. Next in order of time of action is the intramuscular route, followed by the subcutaneous route. Giving a drug orally usually produces the slowest drug action.

Some drugs can be given only by one route; for example, antacids are given only orally. Other drugs are available in oral and parenteral forms. The health care provider selects the route of administration based on many factors, including the desired rate of action. For example, a patient with a severe cardiac problem may require intravenous administration of a drug that affects the heart. Another patient with a mild cardiac problem may have a good response to oral administration of the same drug.

HERBAL THERAPY AND NUTRITIONAL SUPPLEMENTS

Herbal therapy, also called botanical medicine, is a type of complementary or alternative therapy that uses plants or herbs to treat various disorders. People around the world use herbal therapy and nutritional supplements extensively. According to the World Health Organization (WHO), 80% of the world's population relies on herbs for a substantial part of their health care. Herbs have been used by virtually every culture in the world throughout known history. For example, Hippocrates prescribed St. Johns wort, an herbal remedy for depression that is still popular. Native Americans used plants such as coneflower, ginseng, and ginger for therapeutic purposes.

Herbal therapy is part of a group of nontraditional therapies commonly known as complementary/alternative medicine (CAM). Although CAM therapies have not been widely taught in medical schools, this is slowly changing. A 1998 survey revealed that 75 of 117 US medical schools offered elective courses in CAM or included CAM topics in required courses. Complementary therapies are therapies such as relaxation techniques, massage, dietary supplements, healing touch, and herbal therapy that can be used to "complement" traditional health care. Alternative therapies, however, are therapies used instead of conventional or Western medical therapies. The term "complementary/alternative therapy" often is used as an umbrella term for many therapies from all over the world.

Although herbs have been used for thousands of years, most of what we know has come from observation rather than clinical study. Most herbs have not been scientifically studied for safety and efficacy (effectiveness). Much of what we know about herbal therapy has come from Europe, particularly Germany. During the past several decades, European scientists have studied botanical plants in ways that seek to identify how they work at the cellular level, what chemicals are most effective, and what adverse effects are related to their use. Germany has compiled information on 300 herbs and has made recommendations for their use.

Dietary Supplement Health and Education Act

Because herbs cannot be sold and promoted in the United States as drugs, they are regulated as nutritional or dietary substances. Nutritional or dietary substances are terms used by the federal government to identify substances not regulated as drugs by the FDA but that are purported to promote health. Herbs, like vitamins and minerals, are classified as dietary or nutritional supplements. Because natural products cannot be patented in the United States, it is not profitable for drug manufacturers to spend millions of dollars and 8 to 12 years to study and develop these products as drugs.

In 1994, the US government passed the Dietary Supplement Health and Education Act (DSHEA). This act defines substances such as herbs, vitamins, minerals, amino acids, and other natural substances as "dietary supplements." The act permits general health claims such as "improves memory" or "promotes regularity" as long as the label also has a disclaimer stating that the supplements are not approved by the FDA and are not intended to diagnose, treat, cure, or prevent any disease. The claims must be truthful and not misleading and must be supported by scientific evidence. Some have abused the law by making exaggerated claims, but the FDA has the power to enforce the law, which it has done, and such claims have decreased.

Center for Complementary and Alternative Health

In 1992, the National Institutes of Health established an Office of Alternative Medicine to facilitate the study of alternative medical treatments and to disseminate information to the public. In 1998, the name was changed to National Center for Complementary and Alternative Medicine (NCCAM). This office was established partly because of the increased interest and use of these therapies in the United States. An estimated 40% of all individuals in the United States use some form of CAM therapy. In 1997, Americans spent more that $27 billion on these therapies. Among the various purposes of NCCAM, one is to evaluate the safety and efficacy of widely used natural products, such as herbal remedies and nutritional and food supplements. Although the scientific study of CAM is relatively new, the Center is dedicated to developing programs and encouraging scientists to investigate CAM treatments that show promise. NCCAM's budget has steadily grown from $2 million in 1993 to more than $68.7 million in 2000. This funding increase reflects the public's interest and need for CAM information based on rigorous scientific research.

Educating Patients on the Use of Herbs and Nutritional Supplements

The use of herbs and nutritional supplements to treat various disorders is common. Herbs are used for various effects, such as to boost the immune system, treat depression, or promote relaxation. People are becoming more aware of the benefits of herbal therapies and nutritional supplements. Advertisements, books, magazines, and Internet sites abound concerning these topics. Eager to cure or control various disorders, people take herbs, teas, megadoses of vitamins, and various other natural products. Although much information is available on nutritional supplements and herbal therapy, obtaining the correct information sometimes is difficult. Medicinal herbs and nutritional substances are available at supermarkets, pharmacies, health food stores, and specialty herb stores, and through the Internet. Much misinformation has been made public. Because these substances are "natural products," many individuals may incorrectly assume that they are without adverse effects. When a patient uses any herbal remedy or dietary supplement, it should be reported to the health care provider. Many of these botanicals have strong pharmacological activity, and some may interact with prescription drugs or be toxic in the body. For example, comfrey, an herb that was once widely used to promote digestion, can cause liver damage. Although it may still be available in some areas, it is a dangerous herb and is not recommended for use as a supplement.

When a patient's drug history is obtained, the patient should always be questioned about the use of any herbs, teas, vitamins, or other nutritional or dietary supplements. Many patients consider herbs as natural and therefore safe. It is also difficult for some to think of their use of an herbal tea as a part of their health care regimen. Box 12-4 identifies teaching points to consider when discussing the use of herbs and nutritional supplements with patients. Although a complete discussion about the use of herbs is beyond the scope of this book, sections on herbal remedies, including alerts, are included in all drug chapters in this text as relevant.

KEY POINTS

- Federal and sometimes state laws govern the development and sale of drugs to ensure public safety and to control prescription drugs and controlled substances whose effects could be harmful. Health care professionals are an important part of this process by monitoring patients' responses to drugs and reporting adverse reactions.
- Drugs may have several names: a chemical name, a generic (nonproprietary) name, an official name, and a trade or brand name.
- Drugs are categorized in a number of ways: (1) as prescription or nonprescription drugs; (2) in different classes of controlled substances; and (3) by pregnancy categories.
- After absorption and distribution in the body, drugs have therapeutic effects by binding to specific receptors on cells and altering cellular environment or function. Then the drug is metabolized and excreted.

Box 12-4

TEACHING POINTS WHEN DISCUSSING THE USE OF HERBAL THERAPY

- If you regularly use herbal therapies, then get a good herbal reference book such as *Guide to Popular Natural Products*, edited by Ara DerMarderosian (Facts and Comparisons Publishing Group, 2001).
- Store clerks are not experts in herbal therapy. Your best choice is to select an herbal product manufactured by a reputable company.
- Check the label for the word "standardized." This means that the product has a specific percentage of a specific chemical.
- Some herbal tinctures are 50% alcohol, which could pose a problem to individuals with a history of alcohol abuse.
- Use products with more than six herbs cautiously. It is generally better to use the single herb than to use a diluted product with several herbs.

- Do not overmedicate with herbs. The adage "if one is good, two must be better" is definitely not true. Take only the recommended dosage.
- Herbs are generally safe when taken in recommended dosages. However, if you experience any different or unusual symptoms, such as heart palpitations, headaches, rashes, or difficulty breathing, stop taking the herb and contact your health care provider.
- Inform your health care provider of any natural products that you take (e.g., herbs, vitamins, minerals, teas, etc). Certain herbs can interact with the medications that you take, causing serious adverse reactions or toxic effects.
- Allow time for the herb to work. Generally, 30 days is sufficient. If your symptoms have not improved within 30 to 60 days, then discontinue use of the herb.

Adapted from Fontaine KL. *Healing practices: Alternative therapies for nursing.* Upper Saddle River, NJ: Prentice Hall; 2000:126–127. Used with permission.

- Possible drug reactions include adverse reactions, allergic reactions, idiosyncratic reactions, tolerance, cumulative drug effect, and toxic reactions. All such observed patient responses should be reported to the health care provider.
- Drug interactions include additive reactions, synergistic reactions, antagonist reactions, and interactions with food.
- How an individual patient responds to a drug depends on factors such as age, weight, gender, disease conditions present, and the route of administration. Dose size and frequency may have to be adjusted for the individual.
- Herbal therapy may be an important complementary or alternative to drug therapy, but herbs can have many effects and interactions and should be used as carefully as drugs, based on available information and safety warnings. Patients frequently view herbs as harmless and may need to be taught cautions to take with any herbal product.

CASE STUDY

Jenny Davis, age 25, is pregnant. Jenny's health care provider tells her that she may not take any medication without first checking with her health care provider during the pregnancy. Jenny is puzzled and questions you about this. Discuss how you would address Jenny's concerns.

Review Questions

1. Mr. Carter has a rash and pruritus. You suspect an allergic reaction. What question would be most important to ask Mr. Carter?
   a. Are you having any difficulty breathing?
   b. Have you noticed any blood in your stool?
   c. Do you have a headache?
   d. Are you having difficulty with your vision?
2. Mr. Jones, a newly admitted patient, has a history of liver disease. Drug dosages must be based on the consideration that liver disease may result in a/an:
   a. increase in the excretion rate of a drug
   b. impaired ability to metabolize or detoxify a drug
   c. necessity to increase the dosage of a drug
   d. decrease in the rate of drug absorption
3. A patient asks you what a hypersensitivity reaction is. You might begin by telling the patient that a hypersensitivity reaction is also called a:
   a. synergistic reaction
   b. antagonistic reaction
   c. drug idiosyncrasy
   d. drug allergy
4. If a patient takes a drug on an empty stomach, the drug will be:
   a. absorbed more slowly
   b. neutralized by pancreatic enzymes
   c. affected by enzymes in the colon
   d. absorbed more rapidly

5. A synergistic drug effect may be defined as:
   a. an effect greater than the sum of the separate actions of two or more drugs
   b. a decrease in the action of one of the two drugs being given
   c. a neutralizing drug effect
   d. a comprehensive drug effect
6. An example of a schedule II controlled substance is:
   a. codeine cough medicine
   b. nonnarcotic analgesics
   c. morphine
   d. LSD
7. A drug's effect will occur most quickly if it is administered:
   a. subcutaneously
   b. intravenously
   c. orally
   d. intramuscularly
8. A drug that blocks the effect of another drug by binding to its receptors is called a/an:
   a. mediator
   b. receiver
   c. antagonist
   d. agonist
9. If you think a patient is experiencing anaphylactic shock, you should:
   a. write this in the patient's chart at the end of your shift
   b. ask the patient to call you in an hour if he/she feels the same
   c. report this to the health care provider as soon as you have a free moment
   d. call for help immediately
10. Health care providers care about patients' use of herbal remedies because:
    a. some herbs may interact with prescription drugs
    b. some patients may take herbs in too large a dose
    c. some herbs may be dangerous
    d. all of the above

www.GO   Websites

1. Go to the MedWatch website (www.fda.gov/medwatch/index.html). Navigate to the section on "Safety Information" and look for "Safety Alerts" for drugs. This information is organized by year; find the list of drugs for which safety alerts have been issued in the current year. Read the alerts for several different drugs and consider the following questions:
   a. Find a drug safety alert for which new adverse reactions are being reported. Look up that drug in this text or a drug reference such as the PDR. Does the alert add significant new information to what you would have known about the drug from only looking at this text or the reference?
   b. Explain the value of the alert for a health care provider who is prescribing this drug for a new patient.
2. Go the website of the National Center for Complementary and Alternative Medicine (http://nccam.nih.gov). Go to the "Health Information" section and then to Treatment Information "By Disease or Condition." Choose any medical condition (or a herb) and look for information on an herb used in treatment. Briefly answer these questions based on what you learn from this site:
   a. Name the herb and a medical condition for which it is used.
   b. How effective is this herb thought to be in the treatment of this condition?
   c. Are there any adverse effects of this herbal therapy?
   d. Does this herb interact with any drug or food to produce a negative effect?
   e. Are there any known problems with high doses of this herb?
   f. If this herb is recommended for treatment of this condition, are there certain patient types or other conditions that affect who should or should not use this herb?

13

Preparing and Administering Medications

CHAPTER OBJECTIVES

In this chapter, you'll learn:

1. To define the chapter's key terms.
2. To name the seven rights of drug administration.
3. To identify the different types of medication orders.
4. To describe the various types of medication dispensing systems.
5. To list the various routes by which a drug may be given.
6. To describe the administration of oral and parenteral drugs.
7. To describe the administration of drugs through the skin and mucous membranes.

KEY TERMS

buccal
drug error
extravasation
infiltration
inhalation

intradermal
intramuscular
intravenous
parenteral
standard precautions

subcutaneous
sublingual
transdermal
unit dose
Z-track

ALTHOUGH drugs are administered only by physicians, nurses, and, in some states, medical assistants or others, all health professionals who work with patients should understand the basics of drug administration to help ensure patient safety. The patient and often family members as well also need to understand how drugs are administered safely.

THE SEVEN RIGHTS OF DRUG ADMINISTRATION

Seven "rights" in the administration of drugs ensure that patients receive medications correctly and safely:

- Right patient
- Right drug
- Right dose
- Right route
- Right time
- Right documentation
- Right technique

Right Patient

The health care professional administering a drug must be certain that the patient receiving the drug is the patient for whom the drug has been ordered. With a hospitalized patient, this is accomplished by checking the patient's wristband containing the patient's name.

Right Drug

Drug names can be confused, especially when the names sound similar or the spellings are similar. Someone who hurriedly prepares a drug for administration or who fails to look up a questionable drug is more likely to administer the wrong drug. Table 13-1 gives examples of drugs that can easily be confused. The person administering the drug should compare the medication, container label, and medication record.

Right Dose, Route, and Time

The health care professional prescribing drugs for patients should write an order for the administration of all drugs. This written order must include the patient's name, the drug name, the dosage form and route, the dosage to be administered, and the frequency of administration. The health care provider must sign the drug order. In an emergency, a nurse or other qualified health care professional may administer a drug with a verbal order from the health care provider, who must then write and sign the order as soon as the emergency is over.

Right Documentation

After any drug is administered, the health care professional who administered it must record the process immediately. Immediate documentation is particularly important when

Table 13-1	EXAMPLES OF EASILY CONFUSED DRUGS
Accupril	Accutane
albuterol	atenolol
Alupent	Atrovent
Amikin	Amicar
Bentyl	Aventyl
Capitrol	captopril
Cefzil	Ceftin
Celebrex	Celexa
DiaBeta	Zebeta
dobutamine	dopamine
Elavil	Mellaril
Eurax	Serax
Flomax	Fosamax
Inderal	Isordil
K-Dur	Imdur
Klonopin	clonidine
Lodine	codeine
Nicobid	Nitro-Bid
nifedipine	nicardipine
prednisolone	prednisone
Prilosec	Prozac
Retrovir	ritonavir
Taxol	Paxil
TobraDex	Tobrex
Versed	VePesid
Zocor	Zoloft
Zyvox	Vioxx

drugs are given on an as-needed basis (PRN drugs). For example, most analgesics require 20 to 30 minutes before the drug begins to relieve pain. Patients may forget that they received a drug for pain, may not have been told that the administered drug was for pain, or may not know that pain relief is not immediate—and may then ask another health care worker for the drug. If the first administration of the analgesic had not been recorded, then the patient might receive a second dose soon after the first dose. This kind of situation can be extremely serious, especially with narcotics or other central nervous system depressants. Immediate documentation prevents accidental administration of a drug by another individual. Proper documentation is essential to the process of administering drugs correctly.

CONSIDERATIONS IN DRUG ADMINISTRATION

Drug Errors

Drug errors are any occurrence that can cause a patient to receive the wrong dose, the wrong drug, a drug by the wrong route, or a drug given at the incorrect time. Errors may occur in transcribing drug orders, dispensing the drug, or administering the drug. When a drug error occurs, it must be reported immediately so that any necessary steps can be taken to counteract the action of the drug or observe the patient for adverse effects. It is important that errors are reported even if the patient suffers no harm.

Drug errors occur when one or more of the seven "rights" has not been followed. Each time a drug is prepared and administered, the seven rights must be a part of the procedure. In addition to consistently practicing the seven rights, the person administering the drug should follow these precautions to help prevent drug errors:

- Confirm any questionable orders.
- When a dosage calculation is necessary, verify it with another person.
- Listen to the patient when he or she questions a drug, the dosage, or the drug regimen. Never administer the drug until the patient's questions have been adequately researched.
- Concentrate on only one task at a time.

Most drug errors are made during administration. The most common errors are a failure to administer a drug that has been ordered, administration of the wrong dose or strength of the drug, or administration of the wrong drug. Errors commonly occur, for example, with insulin and heparin.

The Medication Order

Before a medication can be administered to a patient, it must be ordered by a health care provider such as a physician, dentist, or, in some cases, a nurse practitioner. Common orders include the standing order, the single order, the PRN order, and the STAT order. Box 13-1 explains these types of orders, and Table 13-2 lists abbreviations commonly used in prescriptions and medication orders.

Once-per-Week Drugs

Increasingly available are drugs in once-per-week, or even twice-per-month, forms. These are designed to replace daily

---

Box 13-1

TYPES OF MEDICATION ORDERS

Standing order: This type of order is written when the patient is to receive the prescribed drug on a regular basis. The drug is administered until the physician discontinues it. Occasionally a drug may be ordered for a specified number of days, or in some cases a drug can only be given for a specified number of days before the order needs to be renewed.
Example: Lanoxin 0.25 mg PO QD.
Single order: An order to administer the drug one time only.
Example: Valium 10 mg IVP at 10:00 AM.
PRN order: An order to administer the drug as needed.
Example: Demerol 100 mg IM q4h PRN for pain.
STAT order: A one-time order given as soon as possible.
Example: Morphine 10 mg IV STAT.

---

doses of drugs. For example, in 2001 the FDA approved two new strengths for alendronate (Fosamax), a drug used to treat osteoporosis, to be given once per week. The 70-mg tablet is used to treat postmenopausal osteoporosis, and the 35-mg tablet is used for prevention of postmenopausal osteoporosis. Clinical trials showed that the once-per-week dosing caused no greater adverse reactions than the once-daily regimen. Once-per-week dosing may prove beneficial for those experiencing mild adverse reactions because they would experience the reactions only once per week rather than every day.

Drug Dispensing Systems

A number of drug dispensing systems are used to dispense medications after they have been ordered for patients. A brief description of three methods follows.

Computerized Dispensing System

Automated or computerized dispensing systems are used in many hospitals and other agencies dispensing drugs. Drugs are dispensed in the pharmacy for drug orders sent from the individual floors or units. Each floor or unit has a medication cart in which medications are placed for individual patients. Medication orders are filled in the hospital pharmacy and are placed in the drug dispensing cart. When orders are filled, the cart is delivered to the unit. The dispensing of the drugs is automatically recorded in the computerized system. After drugs are dispensed, the cart goes back to the pharmacy to be refilled and for new drug orders to be placed.

Table 13-2   ABBREVIATIONS COMMONLY USED IN PRESCRIPTIONS AND MEDICATION ORDERS

Abbreviation	Interpretation	Abbreviation	Interpretation
Route		**Frequency**	
IM	intramuscular	ac	Before meals
IV	intravenous	pc	After meals
IVPB	intravenous piggyback	ad lib	As desired, freely
SC	subcutaneous	prn	As necessary, when required, as needed
SL	sublingual, under the tongue	hs[a]	At the hour of sleep, at bedtime
GT	gastrostomy tube	stat	Immediately, at once
NG	nasogastric tube	q.d.[b]	Once a day, every day
po	By mouth, orally	qod[b]	Every other day
PR or R	rectally	bid	Twice a day
O.D.[a]	[a]Right eye	tid	Three times a day
O.S.[a]	[a]Left eye	qid	Four times a day
O.U.[a]	[a]Both eyes	h	Hour
A.D.[a]	[a]Right ear	qh	Every hour
A.S.[a]	[a]Left ear	q 4h	Every four hours
A.U.[a]	[a]Both ears	q 6h	Every six hours
		ATC	Around the clock
General		**General**	
a	before	mEq	Milliequivalent
aa	Of each	mg/m^2	Milligram (of drug) per square meter (of body surface area)
ad	Up to	mg/kg	Milligram (of drug) per kilogram of body weight
aq	water	mL	Milliliter
BSA	Body surface area	noct	Night
c	with	npo	Nothing by mouth (per oral)
cap	capsule	oint	Ointment
dil.	dilute	OJ	Orange juice
disp.	dispense	p	After
Disc. Or DC[a]	[a]discontinue	q	With
General		**General**	
d.t.d.	Give of such doses	qs	A sufficient quantity
div.	divide	qsad	A sufficient quantity to make
et	and	s	Without
fl	fluid	SiG	Write on label

Abbreviation	Interpretation	Abbreviation	Interpretation
ft	make	ss	One-half
g, Gm, gm	gram	Tab	Tablet
gtt	drop	tbs, tbsp	Tablespoonful
IU	International unit	tsp	Teaspoonful
m^2	Square meter	u.d.	As directed
mcg, μg	microgram	ung	Ointment
		RX, Rx	Prescription (recipe, you take)
		fʒi or flʒi	Teaspoonful (5 mL)
		fl<uJ>ss or fl<uJ>ss	Tablespoonful (15 mL)

Misc. Drugs and Conditions		**IV Products**	
ASA	Aspirin	DW	Distilled water
BP	Blood pressure	D5LR	Dextrose 5% in lactated Ringers solution
BS	Blood sugar	D5NS	Dextrose 5% in normal saline
CHD	Coronary heart disease	D10W	Dextrose 10% in water
CHF	Congestive heart failure	NS	Normal saline
HA	Headache		
HBP	High blood pressure	**Other**	
HC	Hydrocortisone	Gl	Gastrointestinal
NTG	Nitroglycerine	HRT	Hormone Replacement therapy
SOB	Shortness of breath		
URI	Upper respiratory tract infection		
UTI	Urinary tract infection		

^aOn the JCAHO suggested do *not* use list.
^bOn the JCAHO prohibited list.

All abbreviations in this chart must be memorized, even those on the JCAHO prohibited list, because not every facility is a JCAHO facility, and some prescribers are still using these abbreviations.

Many of these abbreviations are variously written as lowercase with or without periods, or all caps.

Unit Dose System

In the **unit dose** system, drug orders are filled and medications dispensed to fill each patient's medication order(s) for a 24-hour period. The pharmacist dispenses each dose (unit) in a package that is labeled with the drug name and dosage. The drug(s) are placed in drawers in a portable medication cart with a drawer for each patient. Many drugs are packaged by their manufacturers in unit doses; each package is labeled by the manufacturer and contains one tablet or capsule, a premeasured amount of a liquid drug, a prefilled syringe, or one suppository. Hospital pharmacists also may prepare unit doses. The pharmacist restocks the cart each day with the drugs patients need for the next 24-hour period (Fig. 13-1).

Some hospitals use a bar code scanner in the administration of unit dose drugs. A bar code is placed on the patient's hospital identification band when the patient is admitted to the hospital. This bar code, along with bar codes on the drug unit dose packages, is used to identify the patient and to record and charge routine and PRN drugs. The scanner also keeps an ongoing inventory of controlled substances, which eliminates the need for narcotic counts at the end of each shift.

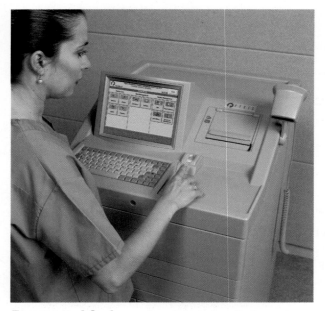

FIGURE 13-1.   An automated medication system.
(From Roach SS. *Introductory Clinical Pharmacology*, ed. 7. Baltimore:
Lippincott Williams & Wilkins; 2004.)

Floor Stock

Some agencies, such as nursing homes or small hospitals, use a floor stock method to dispense drugs. Some special units in hospitals, such as the emergency department, may use this method. In this system, the drugs most frequently prescribed are kept on the unit in containers in a designated medication room or at the nurses' station. Medication are taken from the appropriate container and administered to patients and recorded in the patient's administration record.

GENERAL PRINCIPLES OF DRUG ADMINISTRATION

Health care professionals involved in drug administration and patient care should know about each drug given, the reasons the drug is used, the drug's general action, its more common adverse reactions, special precautions in administration (if any), and the normal dose ranges.

With commonly used drugs, health care workers often become familiar with their pharmacologic properties. With less commonly used or new drugs, information can be obtained from reliable sources, such as the drug package insert or the hospital department of pharmacy.

Patient considerations are also important, such as allergy history, previous adverse reactions, the patient's comments, and any change in the patient's condition. Before a patient is given any drug for the first time, he or she should be asked about any known allergies and any family history of allergies. This includes allergies not only to drugs but also to food, pollen, animals, and so on. Patients with a personal or family history of allergies are more likely to experience additional allergies and must be monitored closely.

If the patient makes any statement about the drug or if the patient's condition changes, then the situation is carefully considered before the drug is given. Examples of such situations include:

- Problems that may be associated with the drug, such as nausea, dizziness, ringing in the ears, and difficulty walking. Any comments made by the patient may indicate the occurrence of an adverse reaction. The drug should be withheld until the health care provider is contacted.
- A patient's comment that the drug looks different from the one previously received, that the drug was just given by someone else, or that the health care provider had discontinued the drug therapy.
- A change in the patient's condition, a change in one or more vital signs (pulse, respiration, blood pressure, or temperature), or the appearance of new symptoms. Depending on the drug being given and the patient's diagnosis, such a change may indicate that the drug should be withheld and the health care provider contacted.

PREPARING A DRUG FOR ADMINISTRATION

Preparing a drug for administration should follow these guidelines:

- the health care provider's written orders should be checked and any questions answered
- drugs should be prepared in a quiet, well-lit area
- the label of the drug should be checked three times: (1) when the drug is taken from its storage area; (2) immediately before removing the drug from the container; and (3) before returning the drug to its storage area
- a drug should never be removed from an unlabeled container or from a container whose label is illegible
- the person preparing a drug for administration should wash hands immediately before the procedure
- capsules and tablets should not be touched with one's hands. The correct number of tablets or capsules is shaken into the cap of the container and from there into the medicine cup
- aseptic technique must be followed when handling syringes and needles
- some drugs have names that sound alike but are very different. Giving one drug when another is ordered could cause serious consequences. For example, digoxin and digitoxin sound alike but are different drugs
- the caps of drug containers should be replaced immediately after the drug is removed

- drugs requiring special storage must be returned to the storage area immediately after being prepared for administration. This rule applies mainly to the refrigeration of drugs but may also apply to drugs that must be protected from exposure to light or heat
- tablets must never be crushed or capsules opened without first checking with the pharmacist. Some tablets can be crushed or capsules opened and the contents added to water or a tube feeding when the patient cannot swallow a whole tablet or capsule. Some tablets have a special coating that delays the absorption of the drug. Crushing the tablet may destroy this drug property and result in problems such as improper absorption of the drug or gastric irritation. Capsules are made of gelatin and dissolve on contact with a liquid. The contents of some capsules do not mix well with water and therefore are best left in the capsule. If the patient cannot take an oral tablet or capsule, then the health care provider should be consulted because the drug may be available in liquid form.
- no one should ever give a drug that someone else prepared. The individual preparing the drug must administer the drug
- with a unit dose system, the wrappings of the unit dose should not be removed until the drug reaches the bedside of the patient who is to receive it. After the drug is administered, it is charted immediately on the unit dose drug form.

ADMINISTRATION OF DRUGS BY THE ORAL ROUTE

The oral route is the most frequent route of drug administration and rarely causes physical discomfort in patients. Oral drug forms include tablets, capsules, and liquids. Some capsules and tablets contain sustained-release drugs, which dissolve over an extended period of time. Administration of oral drugs is relatively easy for patients who are alert and can swallow.

Patient Care Considerations for Oral Drug Administration

- The patient should be in an upright position. It is difficult, as well as dangerous, to swallow a solid or liquid when lying down.
- A full glass of water should be available to the patient.
- The patient may need help removing the tablet or capsule from the container, holding the container, holding a medicine cup, or holding a glass of water. Some patients with physical disabilities cannot handle or hold these objects and may require assistance.
- The patient should be advised to take a few sips of water before placing a tablet or capsule in the mouth.
- The patient is instructed to place the pill or capsule on the back of the tongue and tilt the head back to

swallow a tablet or slightly forward to swallow a capsule. The patient is encouraged to take a few sips of water to move the drug down the esophagus and into the stomach, and then to finish the whole glass.
- The patient is given any special instructions, such as drinking extra fluids or remaining in bed, that are pertinent to the drug being administered.
- A drug is never left at the patient's bedside to be taken later unless the health care provider has ordered this. A few drugs (e.g., antacids and nitroglycerin tablets) may be ordered to be left at the bedside.
- Patients with a nasogastric feeding tube may be given their oral drugs through the tube. Liquid drugs are diluted and then flushed through the tube. Tablets are crushed and dissolved in water before administering them through the tube. The tube should be checked first for correct placement. Afterwards, the tube is flushed with water to completely clear the tubing.
- The patient is instructed to place a **buccal** drug against the mucous membranes of the cheek in either the upper or lower jaw. These drugs are given for a local, rather than systemic, effect. They are absorbed slowly from the mucous membranes of the mouth. Examples of drugs given buccally are lozenges.
- Certain drugs are given by the **sublingual** route (placed under the tongue). These drugs must not be swallowed or chewed and must be dissolved completely before the patient eats or drinks. Nitroglycerin is commonly given sublingually.

ADMINISTRATION OF DRUGS BY THE PARENTERAL ROUTE

Parenteral drug administration means the giving of a drug by the **subcutaneous** (SC), **intramuscular** (IM), **intravenous** (IV), or **intradermal** route. Other routes of parenteral administration include intralesional (into a lesion), intra-arterial (into an artery), intracardiac (into the heart), and intra-articular (into a joint).

Patient Care Considerations for Parenteral Drug Administration

- Gloves must be worn for protection from a potential blood spill when giving parenteral drugs. The risk of exposure to infected blood is increasing for all health care workers. The Centers for Disease Control and Prevention (CDC) recommends that gloves be worn when touching blood or body fluids, mucous membranes, or any broken skin area. This recommendation is one of the **Standard Precautions**, which combine the Universal Precautions for Blood and Body Fluids with Body Substance Isolation guidelines.
- At the site for injection, the skin is cleansed. Most hospitals and medical offices have a policy regarding the type of skin antiseptic used for cleansing the skin

before parenteral drug administration. The skin is cleansed with a circular motion, starting at an inner point and moving outward.

- After the needle is inserted for IM administration, the syringe barrel is pulled back to aspirate the drug. If blood appears in the syringe, the needle is removed so that the drug is not injected. The drug, needle, and syringe are discarded, and another injection prepared. If no blood appears in the syringe, the drug is injected. Aspiration is not necessary when giving an intradermal or SC injection.
- After the needle is inserted into a vein for IV drug administration, the syringe barrel is pulled back. Blood should flow back into the syringe. After a backflow of blood is obtained, it is safe to inject the drug.
- After the needle is removed from an IM, SC, or IV injection site, pressure is placed on the area. Patients with bleeding tendencies often require prolonged pressure on the area.
- Syringes are not recapped but are disposed of according to agency policy. Needles and syringes are discarded into clearly marked, appropriate containers. Most agencies have a "sharps" container located in each room for immediate disposal of needles and syringes after use (Fig. 13-2).
- Most hospitals and medical offices use needles designed to prevent accidental needle sticks. This needle has a plastic guard that slips over the needle as it is withdrawn from the injection site. The guard locks in place and eliminates the need to recap the syringe.

FIGURE 13-2.   A sharps container for disposal of used hypodermic needles.

Other models are available as well. These newer types of methods for administering parenteral fluids provide a greater margin of safety (see OSHA Guidelines).

Occupational Safety and Health Administration Guidelines

Each year between 600,000 and 1 million health care workers experience accidental needle sticks from conventional needles and sharps. Needle exposures can transmit hepatitis B, hepatitis C, and human immunodeficiency virus. Other infections, such as tuberculosis, syphilis, and malaria, also can be transmitted through needle sticks. More than 80% of needle stick injuries can be prevented with the use of safe needle devices.

In 2001 the Occupational Safety and Health Administration (OSHA) announced new guidelines for needle stick prevention. The revisions clarify the need for employers to select safer needle devices as they become available and to involve employees in identifying and choosing the devices. Employers with 11 or more employees must also maintain a Sharps Injury Log to help employees and employers track all needle stick incidents to help identify problem areas. In addition, employers must have a written Exposure Control Plan that is updated annually. As new safer devices become available, they should be adopted for use in the agency. The new OSHA guidelines help reduce needle stick injuries among health care workers and others who handle medical sharps. Safety-engineered devices such as self-sheathing needles and needleless systems are now commonly used.

Administration of Drugs by the Subcutaneous Route

A subcutaneous (SC) injection places the drug into the tissues between the skin and the muscle. Drugs administered in this manner are absorbed more slowly than are intramuscular injections. Heparin and insulin are two drugs most commonly given by the SC route.

Patient Care Considerations for Subcutaneous Drug Administration

- A small volume of 0.5 to 1 mL is used for SC injection. Larger volumes are best given as IM injections.
- The sites for SC injection are the upper arms, the upper abdomen, and the upper back. Injection sites are rotated to ensure proper absorption and to minimize tissue damage.
- When a drug is given by the SC route, the needle is generally inserted at a 45-degree angle. The needle length and angle of insertion depend on the patient's body weight.

Administration of Drugs by the Intramuscular Route

An intramuscular (IM) injection is the administration of a drug into a muscle. Drugs that are irritating to SC tissue can be given via IM injection. Drugs given by this route are absorbed more rapidly than drugs given by the SC route because of the rich blood supply in the muscle. In addition, a larger volume (1–3 mL) of drug can be given at one site.

Patient Care Considerations for Intramuscular Drug Administration

- With a large drug volume, the drug is divided and given as two separate injections. Volumes larger than 3 mL will not be absorbed properly at one site.
- The sites for IM administration are the deltoid muscle (upper arm), the ventrogluteal or dorsogluteal sites (hip), and the vastus lateralis (thigh). The vastus lateralis site is frequently used for infants and small children because it is more developed than the gluteal or deltoid sites. In children who have been walking for more than 2 years, the ventrogluteal site may be used.
- When a drug is given by the IM route, the needle is inserted at a 90-degree angle. When a drug is injected into the ventrogluteal or dorsogluteal muscles, the patient should be in a comfortable position, preferably in a prone position with the toes pointing inward. When the deltoid site is used, a sitting or lying down position may be used. The patient is placed in a recumbent position for injection of a drug into the vastus lateralis.
- The **Z-track** method of IM injection is used when a drug is highly irritating to SC tissues or may permanently stain the skin. In this technique, the skin and subcutaneous tissues are pulled to one side before the injection and an air bubble is injected from the syringe after the drug. This technique prevents the drug from oozing up through the small pathway created by the needle into the SC tissue.

Administration of Drugs by the Intravenous Route

A drug administered by the intravenous (IV) route is given directly into the blood by a needle inserted into a vein. Drug action occurs almost immediately. Drugs administered via the IV route may be given in a number of ways:

- slowly, over 1 or more minutes
- rapidly (IV push)
- by piggyback infusions (drugs are mixed with a compatible IV fluid and administered over 30–60 minutes piggybacked onto the primary IV line)
- into an existing IV line (the IV port)
- into an intermittent venous access device called a heparin lock (a small IV catheter in the patient's vein connected to a small fluid reservoir with a rubber cap through which the needle is inserted to administer the drug)
- by being added to an IV solution and allowed to infuse into the vein over a longer period.

When a drug is administered into a vein by a venipuncture, a tourniquet is placed above the vein and tightened so that venous blood flow is blocked but arterial blood flow is not. The vein is allowed to fill (distend) and the needle is inserted into the vein at a short angle to the skin. Blood should immediately flow into the syringe if the needle is properly inserted into the vein.

Some drugs are added to an IV solution, such as 1000 mL of dextrose 5% and water. The drug is usually added to the IV fluid container immediately before the fluid is added to the IV line. Whenever a drug is added to an IV fluid, the bottle must have an attached label indicating the drug and drug dose added to the IV fluid.

Intravenous Infusion Controllers and Pumps

Electronic infusion devices include infusion controllers and infusion pumps. The primary difference between the two is that an infusion pump administers the infused drug under pressure, whereas an infusion controller does not add pressure. An infusion pump can be set to deliver the desired number of drops of medication per minute. An alarm sounds if the IV rate is more than or less than the preset rate. Controllers and pumps have detectors and alarms that alert health care workers to problems such as air in the line, an occlusion, a low battery, the completion of an infusion, or an inability to deliver the drug at the preset rate. Whenever an alarm is activated, the device must be checked.

Patient Care Considerations for Intravenous Drug Administration

After an IV infusion is started, the type of IV fluid and the drug added to the IV solution are documented in the patient's chart. The infusion rate must be checked every 15 to 30 minutes. The needle site is inspected for signs of redness, swelling, or other problems. Swelling around the needle may indicate extravasation or infiltration. **Extravasation** is the escape of fluid from a blood vessel into surrounding tissues while the needle or catheter is in the vein. **Infiltration** is the collection of fluid in tissues (usually SC tissue) when the needle or catheter is out of the vein. Either problem necessitates stopping the infusion and inserting an IV line in another vein. Some drugs can cause severe tissue damage if extravasation or infiltration occurs. The health care provider should be contacted if such a drug escapes into the tissues surrounding the needle insertion site.

Administration of Drugs by the Intradermal Route

The intradermal route is usually used for sensitivity tests (e.g., the tuberculin test or allergy skin testing). Absorption is slow from this route, providing good results when testing for allergies or administering local anesthetics. The needle is inserted at a 15-degree angle between the upper layers of the skin. Injection produces a small wheal (raised area) on the outer surface of the skin. If a wheal does not appear, then the drug may have entered the SC tissue, making test results inaccurate.

Patient Care Considerations for Intradermal Drug Administration

- The inner part of the forearm and the upper back are used for intradermal injections. A hairless area should be chosen; areas near moles, scars, or pigmented skin areas should be avoided. The area is cleansed in the same manner as for SC and IM injections.
- Small volumes (usually <0.1 mL) are used for intradermal injections.

Other Parenteral Routes of Drug Administration

The health care provider may administer a drug by the intracardiac, intralesional, intra-arterial, or intra-articular routes. Special devices and materials are required for these routes of administration.

Venous access ports are implanted self-sealing ports attached to a catheter leading to a large vessel, usually the vena cava. These devices are most commonly used for chemotherapy or other long-term therapy. They require surgical insertion and removal. Drugs are administered through injections made into the portal through the skin.

ADMINISTRATION OF DRUGS THROUGH THE SKIN AND MUCOUS MEMBRANES

Drugs may be applied to the skin and mucous membranes using several routes: topically (on the outer layers of skin), **transdermally** through a patch in which the drug has been implanted, or inhaled through the membranes of the upper respiratory tract.

Administration of Drugs by the Topical Route

Most topical drugs act on the skin but are not absorbed through the skin. These drugs are used to soften, disinfect, or lubricate the skin. A few topical drugs are enzymes that remove superficial debris, such as the dead skin and purulent

---

> **Box 13-2**
>
> # TOPICAL APPLICATIONS AND LOCATIONS OF USE
>
> - Creams, lotions, or ointments applied to the skin with a tongue blade, gloved fingers, or gauze
> - Sprays applied to the skin or into the nose or oral cavity
> - Liquids inserted into body cavities, such as fistulas
> - Liquids inserted into the bladder or urethra
> - Solids (e.g., suppositories) or jellies inserted into the urethra
> - Liquids dropped into the eyes, ears, or nose
> - Ophthalmic ointments applied to the eyelids or dropped into the lower conjunctival sac
> - Solids (e.g., suppositories, tablets), foams, liquids, and creams inserted into the vagina
> - Continuous or intermittent wet dressings applied to skin surfaces
> - Solids (e.g., tablets, lozenges) dissolved in the mouth
> - Sprays or mists inhaled into the lungs
> - Liquids, creams, or ointments applied to the scalp
> - Solids (e.g., suppositories), liquids, or foams inserted into the rectum

---

matter present in skin ulcerations. Other topical drugs are used to treat minor superficial skin infections. The various forms of topical applications are described in Box 13-2.

Patient Care Considerations for Topical Drug Administration

- The health care provider may write special instructions for the application of a topical drug, such as to apply the drug in a thin even layer or to cover the area after the drug is applied to the skin.
- The manufacturer sometimes provides special instructions for drug administration, such as to apply the drug to a clean hairless area or to let the drug dissolve slowly in the mouth. All such instructions are important because drug action may depend on correct administration of the drug.

Administration of Drugs by the Transdermal Route

Drugs administered by the transdermal route are readily absorbed from the skin and have systemic effects. The drug dose is implanted in a small patch-type bandage. The backing is removed, and the patch is applied to the skin, where the drug is gradually absorbed into the systemic circulation. This

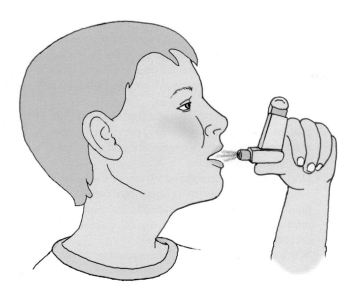

FIGURE 13-3. A respiratory inhalant is used to deliver a drug directly into the lungs. To deliver a dose of the drug, the patient takes a slow, deep breath while depressing the top of the canister. (From Roach SS. *Introductory Clinical Pharmacology*, ed. 7, Lippincott Williams & Wilkins; 2004.)

drug administration system maintains a relatively constant blood concentration and reduces the possibility of toxicity. In addition, drugs administered transdermally cause fewer adverse reactions. Nitroglycerin (used to treat cardiac problems) and scopolamine (used to treat dizziness and nausea) are two drugs commonly given by the transdermal route.

Patient Care Considerations for Transdermal Drug Administration

- Transdermal patches are applied to clean, dry, non-hairy areas of intact skin.
- The old patch is removed when the next dose is applied in a new site.
- Sites for transdermal patches are rotated to prevent skin irritation. The chest, flank, and upper arm are the most commonly used sites. The area of application should not be shaved because this may cause skin irritation.
- Ointments are sometimes used. They come with a special paper marked in inches. The correct length of ointment is measured onto the paper, and the paper is placed with the drug ointment side down on the skin and secured with tape. Before the next dose, the paper and tape are removed and the skin cleansed.

Administration of Drugs Through Inhalation

Drug droplets, vapor, and gas are administered through the mucous membranes of the respiratory tract. The patient breathes the drug in through a face mask, a nebulizer, or a positive-pressure breathing machine. Examples of drugs administered through **inhalation** include bronchodilators, mucolytics, and some anti-inflammatory drugs. These drugs primarily have a local effect in the lungs.

Patient Care Considerations for Drug Administration by Inhalation

The patient must be provided with proper instructions for taking the drug. For example, many patients with asthma use a metered-dose inhaler to dilate the bronchi and make breathing easier. Without proper instruction on how to use the inhaler, much of the drug may be deposited on the tongue rather than in the respiratory tract; this would decrease the therapeutic effect of the drug. The specific instructions are provided with the inhaler. Figure 13-3 illustrates the proper use of one type of inhaler.

PATIENT CARE CONSIDERATIONS AFTER DRUG ADMINISTRATION

- The administration of a drug to a patient is always documented. This should be performed as soon as possible.
- Other information concerning the administration of the drug is also often recorded, including information such as the IV flow rate, the site used for parenteral administration, any problems with administration, and the patient's vital signs taken immediately before administration.
- The patient's response to the drug is monitored and, when applicable, recorded. This evaluation may include such facts as relief of pain, decrease in body temperature, relief of itching, and decrease in the number of stools passed.
- The patient is observed for adverse reactions. The frequency of observation depends on the drug administered. All suspected adverse reactions are documented and reported to the health care provider. Serious adverse reactions must be reported immediately.

ADMINISTRATION OF DRUGS IN THE HOME

Often drugs are taken by patients in their homes or are administered by family members acting as caregivers. The patient or caregivers need to understand the treatment regimen and to be able to ask questions about their drug therapy, such as why the drug was prescribed, how to give or take it, and possible adverse reactions that may occur. Box 13-3 gives guidelines for drug use in the home by the patient or caregiver rather than by health care providers.

Box 13-3

ADMINISTERING DRUGS SAFELY IN THE HOME

Patients are often prescribed drugs to be taken at home. Because the home is not as controlled an environment as a health care facility, the patient's home environment should be considered:

- Does the home have a space that is relatively free of clutter and easily accessible to the patient or a caregiver?
- Do any small children live in or visit the home? If so, is there a place where drugs can be stored safely out of their reach?
- Does the drug require refrigeration? If so, does the refrigerator work?
- Does the patient need special equipment, such as needles and syringes? If so, where and how can the equipment be stored for safety and convenience? Does the patient have an appropriate disposal container? Will disposed items be safe from children and pets? Plastic storage containers with snap-on lids or clean, dry glass jars with screw tops can be used for needle disposal. A plastic milk jug with a lid or a heavy-duty, clean, cardboard milk or juice carton may be used if necessary. Patients should understand the importance of precautions to make sure discarded needles do not puncture the container.
- If the patient needs several drugs, can the patient or caregiver identify which drugs are used and when? Do they know how to use them and why?

- Health care professionals involved in drug administration and patient care should know about each drug given, the reasons the drug is used, the drug's general action, its more common adverse reactions, special precautions in administration, and the normal dose ranges.
- In drug administration, patient considerations are important, such as allergy history, previous adverse reactions, the patient's comments, and any change in the patient's condition.
- Drugs may be administered by any of the following routes, each with its own patient care considerations: the oral, parenteral (subcutaneous, intramuscular, intravenous, or intradermal), topical, transdermal, and inhalation routes.
- When drugs are taken by patients in their homes, the patients or caregivers need to understand the treatment regimen, such as why the drug was prescribed, how to give or take it, and possible adverse reactions that may occur.

Review Questions

1. To ensure a drug is given correctly, it should be administered:
   a. to the right patient
   b. at the right time
   c. by the right route
   d. all of the above
2. If a patient reports that the pill just given to him/her is a different color from the last one he/she received, you should:
   a. explain they should not worry because many pills come in different colors
   b. pretend you will check on it so he/she stop worrying
   c. report this to the health care provider
   d. try to get the patient to vomit up the pill as quickly as possible
3. A STAT medication order means the drug should be given:
   a. as soon as possible
   b. whenever the patient is having symptoms and requests it
   c. first thing in the morning
   d. following the daily staff meeting
4. Drugs can be administered to patients from the drug cart on the floor by:
   a. only the pharmacist
   b. only those allowed by law, such as physicians, nurses, some medical assistants, etc.
   c. any health care worker authorized by a nurse
   d. any staff person on duty at the time

KEY POINTS

- Seven "rights" in the administration of drugs ensure that patients receive medications correctly and safely: right patient, right drug, right dose, right route, right time, right documentation, and right technique.
- Drug errors are any occurrence that can cause a patient to receive the wrong dose, the wrong drug, a drug by the wrong route, or a drug given at the incorrect time. Errors may occur in transcribing drug orders, dispensing the drug, or administering the drug. When a drug error occurs, it must be reported immediately.
- Common medication orders include the standing order, the single order, the PRN order, and the STAT order.
- Drug dispensing systems include computerized dispensing systems, unit dose systems, and floor stock systems.

5. True or false: the administration of topical medications need not follow the "6 rights" of medication administration because the medication can be wiped off the skin if given incorrectly.
   a. true
   b. false
6. Why do health care workers watch patients for potential allergic reactions?
   a. allergic reactions can be uncomfortable for patients
   b. a different drug may need to be prescribed
   c. allergic reactions can be life-threatening
   d. all of the above
7. Which statement is true about the administration of oral medications?
   a. The patient should be in an upright position.
   b. The patient should not be allowed to drink water before a tablet or capsule is placed in the mouth.
   c. The pill or capsule to be swallowed should be placed under the tongue and the patient's head tilted forward.
   d. The patient should drink at least 3 glasses of water after taking the medication.

www.GO   Website

1. Go to the website of the U.S. Department of Labor Occupational Safety & Health Administration (OSHA) (http://www.osha.gov). Under "Safety/Health Topics" navigate to the section on Bloodborne Pathogens. Explore this page and find the OSHA material addressing the question, "What are some examples of possible solutions for workplace hazards?" In each of the following categories of how to prevent problems with infectious materials in the workplace, write in one example of a solution for control programs, safer needle devices, and decontamination.

Infection Control and Vital Signs

14

Medical Asepsis and Infection Control

CHAPTER OBJECTIVES

In this chapter, you'll learn:

1. To spell and define key terms.
2. To describe conditions that promote the growth of microorganisms.
3. To explain the components of the infectious process cycle.
4. To list the various ways microbes are transmitted.
5. To compare the effectiveness in reducing or destroying microorganisms using the four levels of infection control.
6. To describe the procedures for cleaning, handling, and disposing of biohazardous waste in the health care facility.
7. To explain the concept of medical asepsis.
8. To discuss risk management procedures required by the Occupational Safety and Health Administration guidelines for the health care setting.
9. To list the required components of an exposure control plan.
10. To explain the importance of following Standard Precautions.
11. To identify various personal protective equipment (PPE) items.
12. To describe circumstances when PPE items would be appropriately worn by allied health professionals.
13. To explain the facts pertaining to the transmission and prevention of the Hepatitis B virus and the Human Immunodeficiency Virus in the health care facility.
14. To describe how to avoid becoming infected with the Hepatitis B and Human Immunodeficiency viruses.

PERFORMANCE OBJECTIVES

In this chapter, you'll learn:

1. To perform a medical aseptic handwashing procedure (Procedure 14-1).
2. To remove and discard contaminated personal protective equipment appropriately (Procedure 14-2).
3. To clean and decontaminate biohazardous spills (Procedure 14-3).

KEY TERMS

aerobe	exposure control plan	OSHA	sanitization
anaerobe	exposure risk factors	pathogens	spore
asymptomatic	germicide	personal protective	standard precautions
bactericidal	immunization	equipment	sterilization
biohazard	infection	postexposure testing	transient flora
carrier	medical asepsis	resident flora	vector
disease	microorganisms	resistance	viable
disinfection	normal flora	sanitation	virulent

MANY PATIENTS ARE SEEN daily in health care facilities for a variety of reasons, including physical examinations for employment, reassurance about a current health problem, and follow-up care for a chronic condition or surgical procedure. In addition, many patients request appointments because of illness. It is important for you to protect patients from each other with regard to contagious diseases and for you to protect yourself from acquiring the many microorganisms with which you will come into contact every day.

To prevent the spread of **disease** in facilities, allied health professionals must meet two goals. First, you must understand and practice **medical asepsis** at all times, using specific practices and procedures to prevent disease transmission. These practices and procedures also allow you to work with ill patients while reducing the chances that you will spread disease to other patients or become infected yourself. Second, you must teach the patients and their families about techniques to use at home to prevent the transmission of disease. Handwashing, the cornerstone of infection control, is discussed in this chapter and is emphasized in all subsequent chapters wherever contact with infectious material might be expected. In addition, this chapter describes how disease is transmitted and most important, how to prevent the spread of disease.

MICROORGANISMS, PATHOGENS, AND NORMAL FLORA

Microorganisms, living organisms that can be seen only with a microscope, are part of our normal environment. In addition to our physical environment, many microorganisms can be found on your skin and throughout your gastrointestinal, genitourinary, and respiratory systems, and some of these are required for good health. These microorganisms are normal and are referred to as **normal flora** or **resident flora**. Some microorganisms, however, are not part of the normal flora and may cause disease or **infection.** Disease-producing microorganisms are referred to as pathogens and are classified as bacteria, viruses, fungi, or protozoa.

When normal flora become too many in number or are transmitted to an area of the body in which they are not normally found, they are referred to as **transient flora**, which can become pathogens under the right conditions. For example, *Staphylococcus aureus*, a microorganism commonly found on the skin, may get into underlying tissue if the skin is broken. In this situation, the normal flora of the skin has become transient flora and may cause disease. Decreased **resistance** in the host is one condition that may allow transient flora to become pathogenic. Individuals who are elderly, receiving certain drugs to treat cancer, or under unusual stress may have a lowered resistance and be particularly susceptible to infections.

Although the body is protected by many nonspecific defenses against disease, infection or illness may occur if the natural barriers are overpowered or breached. These are some of the body's natural defenses that may prevent the invasion of pathogens into various body organs:

- Skin. As long as the skin is kept clean and remains intact or unbroken, *staphylococcal* (Staph) bacteria are not considered dangerous. Washing the skin frequently will flush away many of these bacteria along with any other microorganisms.
- Eyes. The eyelashes act as a barrier by trapping dust that may carry microorganisms before they have an opportunity to enter the eye. If any microorganisms do enter the eye, the enzyme lysozyme normally found in tears will destroy some microorganisms, including bacteria.
- Mouth. The greatest variety of microorganisms in the body is in the mouth. Saliva is slightly **bactericidal**, and good oral hygiene will remove or prevent the growth of many of the pathogens in the mouth.
- Gastrointestinal tract. Hydrochloric acid normally found in the stomach destroys most of the disease-producing pathogens that enter the gastrointestinal system. One bacterium, *Escherichia coli* (*E. coli*), is resident flora found in the large intestine and is necessary for digestion. It does not usually cause disease as long it remains within the gastrointestinal tract. *Helicobacter pylori* also resides in the digestive tracts of some individuals and may cause gastric ulcers.
- Respiratory tract. Hairs and cilia on the membrane lining of the nostrils are early defenses against airborne microorganisms. If these physical barriers do not stop an invasion, mucus from the membranes lining the respiratory tract should trap the microorganisms and facilitate their removal from the respiratory system as the person swallows, coughs, or sneezes.
- Genitourinary tract. The reproductive and urinary systems provide a less hospitable environment for microorganisms. The slightly acidic environment of these body systems reduces the ability of many microorganisms to survive. In addition, frequent urination flushes the urinary tract and removes many transient microorganisms.

While these systems have protective mechanisms to prevent infection, any of them may be overpowered by a particularly **virulent** organism. Transient flora are not usually pathogenic unless the person's defenses are compromised by a decrease in resistance.

Checkpoint Question

1. What are pathogenic microorganisms? How does the body prevent an invasion and subsequent infection naturally?

Conditions That Favor the Growth of Pathogens

All microorganisms require certain conditions to grow and reproduce. To reduce the number of microorganisms and potential pathogens in the health care facility you must eliminate as many of their life requirements as possible. These requirements include the following:

- Moisture. Few microorganisms can survive with little water or moisture. However, some microorganisms form **spores** and remain dormant until moisture is available.
- Nutrients. Microorganisms depend on their environment for nourishment. Surfaces (tables, counters, equipment) that are contaminated with organic matter (food products, body fluids, or tissue) promote the growth of microorganisms.
- Temperature. Although some microorganisms can survive even in freezing or boiling temperatures, those that thrive at a normal body temperature of 98.6°F are most likely to be pathogenic to humans. Many microorganisms that leave an infected person can survive for a while at room temperature; therefore, surfaces that are contaminated with dried organic material should be considered possibly pathogenic.
- Darkness. Many pathogenic bacteria are destroyed by bright light, including sunlight.
- Neutral pH. The pH of a solution refers to the measurement of its acid-base balance on a scale of 1 to 14, with 7 being neutral. Many microorganisms are destroyed in an environment that is not neutral. The pH of blood, 7.35 to 7.45, is preferred by microorganisms that thrive in the human body.
- Oxygen. Microorganisms that need oxygen to survive are called **aerobes**. A few, however, do not require oxygen; these are called **anaerobes**. While most pathogens are aerobic, the microbes that cause tetanus and botulism are anaerobic.

If any one of these conditions is altered in any way, the growth and reproduction of the pathogen will be affected. Your role as an allied health professional in a health care facility includes using this knowledge of microbial growth to inhibit the growth and reproduction of microorganisms in the facility.

Checkpoint Question

2. Given the six conditions that favor the growth of pathogens, explain how you can alter the growth and reproduction of microorganisms by changing these factors.

The Infection Cycle

The infection cycle is often thought of as a series of specific links of a chain involving a causative agent or invading microorganism (Fig. 14-1). The first link in the chain is the reservoir host; this is the person who is infected with the

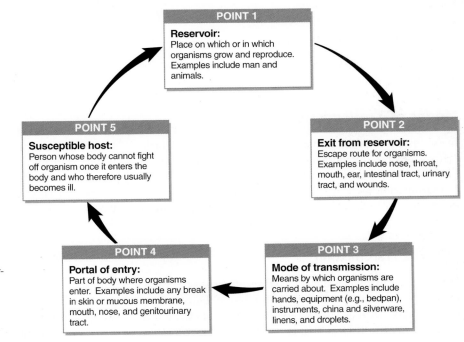

FIGURE 14-1. The infectious process cycle. Infections and infectious diseases are spread by starting from the reservoir (*point 1*) and moving in a circle to the susceptible host (*point 5*). Microorganisms can be controlled by interfering at any point in the cycle.

microorganism. While this person may or may not show signs of infection, his or her body is serving as a source of nutrients and an incubator in which the pathogen can grow and reproduce. These persons are also called **carriers**, or reservoirs, of disease.

The reservoir host may transmit disease only when the pathogen has a means of exit. The second link in the chain is the manner in which the pathogen leaves the reservoir host. Means of exit include the mucous membranes of the nose and mouth, the openings of the gastrointestinal system (mouth or rectum), and an open wound.

In addition to the means of exit, the microbe must have a vehicle in which to leave the host. This next link in the chain, the means of transmission, involves the vehicle that is used by the pathogen when it leaves the reservoir host and spreads through the environment. Vehicles include mucus or air droplets from the oral or nasal cavities and direct contact between an unclean hand and another person or object. Sneezing and coughing without covering the nose and mouth are excellent methods of transmitting microorganisms into the environment and potential hosts.

The fourth link in the chain of the infectious process cycle is the portal of entry. This is the route by which the pathogen enters the next host. With inhalation of contaminated air droplets the respiratory system is the portal of entry. Another portal of entry is the gastrointestinal system: the pathogen enters the body in contaminated food or drink. Any break in the skin or mucous membranes can be a portal of entry for pathogenic microorganisms.

The final link in the infectious process cycle is the susceptible host (Box 14-1). This host is one to whom the pathogen is transmitted after leaving the reservoir host. If the conditions in the susceptible host are conducive to reproduction of the pathogen, the susceptible host becomes a reservoir host and the cycle repeats.

Checkpoint Question

3. How are the first and fifth links of the infection cycle related?

Modes of Transmission

In the third link of the infectious process cycle, the vehicle that spreads the microorganism is often called the mode of transmission. It is important for you to understand the mode of transmission used by various pathogens so that you can break this link in the infectious cycle and prevent the spread of disease.

Direct Transmission

Direct contact between the infected reservoir host and the susceptible host produces direct transmission. Direct transmission may occur when one touches contaminated blood or body fluids, shakes hands with someone who has

---

Box 14-1

THE SUSCEPTIBLE HOST

The susceptible host is unable to resist the invading pathogens for a variety of reasons:

- *Age.* As the body ages, defense mechanisms begin to lose their effectiveness. The immune system is no longer as active or as efficient as in youth. The immune system may also not be fully functional in the very young.
- *Existing disease.* The stress of an existing illness may deplete the immune system and allow microorganisms to cause illness in someone who might otherwise be able to fight it naturally.
- *Poor nutrition.* A diet deficient in nutrients such as proteins, carbohydrates, fats, vitamins, or minerals will not allow cells of the body to repair or reproduce as they are weakened by disease.
- *Poor hygiene.* Although multitudes of microbes exist on our skin, keeping the numbers down by practicing good hygiene will reduce the numbers of pathogens.

---

contaminated hands, inhales infected air droplets, or has intimate contact, such as kissing or sexual intercourse.

Indirect Transmission

Indirect transmission may occur through contact with a vehicle known as a vector. Vectors include contaminated food or water, disease-carrying insects, and inanimate objects such as soil, drinking glasses, wound drainage, and infected or improperly disinfected medical instruments. While visible blood and body fluids are obvious sources of infection, many infectious organisms remain **viable** for long periods on inanimate surfaces that are not visibly contaminated.

Sources of Transmission

Most reservoir hosts are humans, animals, and insects. Human hosts include people who are ill with an infectious disease, people who are carriers of an infectious disease, and people who are incubating an infectious disease but are not exhibiting symptoms. This last group can transmit disease even though they are ambulatory and **asymptomatic** (have no symptoms). Animal sources, which are less common, include infected dogs, cats, birds, cattle, rodents, and animals that live in the wild. Diseases that may be transmitted to humans from infected animals include anthrax and rabies.

In addition to flies and roaches, which carry many diseases, other insect sources feed on the blood of an infected reservoir host and then pass the disease to another victim or susceptible host. Ticks and mosquitoes may transmit diseases, including

Table 14-1	COMMON COMMUNICABLE DISEASES
Disease	**Method of Transmission**
AIDS	Contact, or contact with contaminated sharps
Diphtheria	Airborne droplets, infected carriers
Rubella (German measles)	Airborne droplets, infected carriers
Influenza	Airborne droplets, infected carriers or direct contact with contaminated articles such as used tissues
Measles (rubeola)	Airborne droplets, infected carriers
Mumps	Airborne droplets, infected carriers or direct contact with materials contaminated with infected saliva
Mononucleosis	Airborne droplets or contact with infected saliva
Pneumonia	Airborne droplets or direct contact with infected mucus
Tuberculosis	Airborne droplets, infected carriers
Tetanus	Direct contact with spores or contaminated animal feces
Rabies	Direct contact with saliva of infected animal such as an animal bite
Cholera	Ingestion of contaminated food or water
Chicken pox (varicella)	Direct contact or droplets
Meningitis	Airborne droplets
Hepatitis B	Direct contact with infectious body fluid

Lyme disease (ticks) and malaria (mosquitoes). Table 14-1 lists some common diseases and their methods of transmission.

Checkpoint Question

4. The health care facility where you work has a policy of not opening screenless windows in examination rooms and the reception area. Why do you think this policy is or is not important?

PRINCIPLES OF INFECTION CONTROL

Most transmission of infectious disease in a health care facility can be prevented by strict adherence to guidelines issued by the Occupational Safety and Heath Administration (OSHA) and the Centers for Disease Control and Prevention (CDC). While most allied health professionals take extraordinary precautions when dealing with patients who are known carriers of infectious microorganisms, you may also treat an estimated five unknown carriers for each patient known to be infectious. Therefore, knowledge and use of effective infection control in relation to all patients is essential.

Medical Asepsis

Medical asepsis does not mean that an object or area is free from all microorganisms. It refers to practices that render an object or area free from pathogenic microorganisms. Commonly known as clean technique, medical asepsis prevents the transmission of microorganisms from one person or area to any other within the health care facility (Box 14-2 on next page).

PATIENT EDUCATION

Basic Aseptic Technique

While performing procedures, take the opportunity to instruct your patients in basic aseptic techniques they can use at home to reduce the spread of disease.

- *Handwashing.* This routine aseptic technique is particularly important for patients and families in preventing the spread of disease. Instruct patients to wash their hands before and after eating meals, after sneezing, coughing, or blowing the nose, after using the bathroom, before and after changing a dressing, and after changing diapers.
- *Use tissue.* Explain to patients with respiratory symptoms that using a disposable tissue to cover the mouth and nose when coughing and sneezing decreases the potential to transmit the illness throughout the household. In addition, immediate and proper disposal of the used tissue is essential to prevent the spread of infection.
- *Changing bandages.* Patients and family members who change dressings on wounds should be instructed in the proper procedure for using sterile dressings and clean bandages. Always demonstrate the procedure for the patient and have the patient or family member return the demonstration to ensure their understanding.
- *Sanitation.* Explain the proper techniques for disposing of waste from members of the household with communicable diseases. If in doubt, consult the local public health department for guidelines.

Box 14-2

GUIDELINES FOR MAINTAINING MEDICAL ASEPSIS

- Avoid touching your clothing with soiled linen, table paper, supplies, or instruments. Roll used table paper or linens inward with the clean surface outward.
- Always consider the floor to be contaminated. Any item dropped onto the floor must be considered dirty and be discarded or cleaned to its former level of asepsis before being used.
- Clean tables, counters, and other surfaces frequently and immediately after contamination. Clean areas are less likely than dirty ones to harbor microorganisms or encourage their growth.
- Always presume that blood and body fluids from any source are contaminated. Follow the guidelines published by OSHA and the CDC to protect yourself and to prevent the transmission of disease.

Handwashing is the MOST IMPORTANT medical aseptic technique to prevent the transmission of pathogens. The proper procedure for washing your hands is detailed in Procedure 14-1 at the end of this chapter. Always wash your hands:

- before and after every patient contact
- after coming into contact with any blood or body fluids
- after coming into contact with contaminated material
- after handling specimens
- after coughing, sneezing, or blowing your nose
- after using the restroom
- before and after going to lunch, taking breaks, and leaving for the day.

Because you should always assume that blood and body fluids are contaminated with pathogens, you should wear gloves when handling any specimens or when contact with contaminated material is anticipated. However, wearing gloves does not replace handwashing! In fact, your hands should be washed BEFORE you apply gloves and AFTER you remove them in all situations to prevent disease transmission.

Other medical aseptic techniques include general cleaning of the facility, including the examination and treatment rooms, waiting or reception area, and clinical work areas. Floors are always considered contaminated, and dust and dirt are vehicles for transmission of microorganisms and should be regularly cleaned from all surfaces, including the floor. In addition, you should teach patients and their caregivers proper medical aseptic techniques for use in the home to prevent the spread of disease.

Checkpoint Question

5. Explain why wearing examination gloves does not replace handwashing.

Levels of Infection Control

Sterilization, the highest level of infection control, destroys all forms of microorganisms, including spores, on an inanimate surfaces. Sterilization methods include exposing the articles to various conditions, including steam under pressure in an autoclave; specific gases, such as ethylene oxide; dry heat ovens; and immersion in an approved chemical sterilizing agent. Instruments or devices that penetrate the skin or come into contact with areas of the body considered sterile, such as the urinary bladder, must be sterilized using one of these methods. To save time, many facilities use disposable sterile supplies and equipment to eliminate the need for manual sterilization (Fig. 14-2).

The next highest level of infection control is **disinfection**. Disinfectants or **germicides** inactivate virtually all recognized pathogenic microorganisms except spores on inanimate objects. There are three levels of disinfection, high, intermediate, and low. Each is described in more detail in the following section.

The lowest level of infection control is **sanitization**, which is cleaning any visible contaminants from the item using soap or detergent, water, and manual friction.

Sanitation

Most instruments, equipment, and supplies used in health care facilities must be sanitized regularly according to the

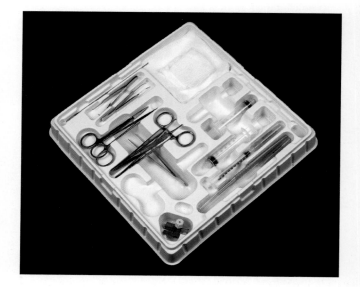

FIGURE 14-2. Equipment that must be sterile includes items that will penetrate the skin or come into contact with surgical incisions, such as surgical instruments. These items are disposable for one-time use only.

recommendations of the manufacturer. Sanitation maintenance of a healthful, disease-free, and hazard-free environment. Sanitation often involves sanitization procedures that reduce the number of microorganisms on an inanimate object to a safe or relatively safe level. This is accomplished by thoroughly cleaning items such as instruments and equipment with warm, soapy water with mechanical action to remove organic matter and other residue. Cleaning or sanitizing must precede disinfection and sterilization.

Disinfection

Disinfectants, or germicides, inactivate virtually all recognized pathogenic microorganisms but not necessarily all microbial forms, including spores, on inanimate objects. These factors may affect disinfection:

- prior cleaning of the object. Equipment and supplies that have been sanitized first are more effectively disinfected
- the amount of organic material on the object. The more organic matter, such as blood or body tissues, on the item, the more disinfectant agent you must use
- the type of microbial contamination. All blood and body fluids should be considered contaminated with blood-borne pathogens such as hepatitis B and HIV
- the concentration of the **germicide** or chemical disinfectant that kills pathogens. Disinfectants diluted with water are relatively ineffective at killing microbes
- the length of exposure to the germicide. The longer the disinfectant comes into contact with the contaminated object, the more thorough disinfection is likely to be
- the shape or complexity of the object being disinfected. Objects that have rough edges, corners, or otherwise difficult-to-clean areas may require special techniques to disinfect all surfaces
- the temperature of the process. Most disinfectants work adequately at room temperature.

Disinfection is categorized into three levels, high, intermediate, and low. High-level disinfection destroys most forms of microbial life except certain bacterial spores. This level of infection control, which is slightly less effective than sterilization, is commonly used to clean reusable instruments that come into contact with mucous membrane–lined body cavities that are not considered sterile, such as the vagina and the rectum. Methods of high-level disinfection include immersion in boiling water for 30 minutes and immersion in an approved disinfecting chemical, such as glutaraldehyde or isopropyl alcohol for 45 minutes or according to the guidelines in the disinfectant label.

Intermediate-level disinfection destroys many viruses, fungi, and some bacteria, including *Mycobacterium tuberculosis* (*M. tuberculosis*), the bacterium that causes tuberculosis. However, intermediate disinfection does not kill bacterial spores. Intermediate disinfection is used for surfaces and instruments that come into contact with unbroken skin surfaces, including stethoscopes, blood pressure cuffs, and

FIGURE 14-3. These products destroy many pathogenic microorganisms if used correctly.

splints. Commercial chemical germicides that kill *M. tuberculosis* and solutions containing a 1:10 dilution of household bleach (2 oz of chlorine bleach per quart of tap water) are effective intermediate disinfectants.

Low-level disinfection destroys many bacteria and some viruses, but not *M. tuberculosis* or bacterial spores. This type of disinfection is adequate in the health care facility for routine cleaning and removing surface debris when no visible blood or body fluids are on the items being disinfected. Disinfectants without tuberculocidal properties are used for low-level disinfection (Fig. 14-3). Table 14-2 on next page describes disinfection methods, uses, and precautions of various chemicals.

Checkpoint Question

6. What level of disinfection would you use to clean a reusable instrument that comes into contact with the vaginal mucosa, such as a vaginal speculum? Why?

OCCUPATIONAL SAFETY AND HEALTH ADMINISTRATION GUIDELINES

OSHA is the federal agency responsible for ensuring the safety of all workers, including those in health care. OSHA promulgates and enforces federal regulations that must be followed by all health care facilities. The practices of individual facilities regarding employees' health and safety must be put into either a policy and procedure manual or compiled separately as an infection control manual. Regardless of where the facility policies are kept, however, they must be readily available to both employees of the health care facility and OSHA representatives.

Table 14-2   Disinfection Methods

Method	Uses and Precautions
Alcohol (70% isopropyl)	Used for noncritical items (countertops, glass thermometers, stethoscopes) Flammable Damages some rubber, plastic, and lenses
Chlorine (sodium hypochlorite or bleach)	Dilute 1:10 (1 part bleach to 10 parts water) Used for a broad spectrum of microbes Inexpensive and fast acting Corrosive, inactivated by organic matter, relatively unstable
Iodine or iodophors	Bacteriostatic agent Not to be used on instruments May cause staining
Phenols (tuberculocidal)	Used for environmental items and equipment Requires gloves and eye protection Can cause skin irritation and burns
Formaldehyde	Disinfectant and sterilant Regulated by OSHA Warnings must be marked on all containers and storage areas
Hydrogen peroxide	Stable and effective when used on inanimate objects Attacks membrane lipids, DNA, and other essential cell components Can damage plastic, rubber, and some metals
Glutaraldehyde	Alkaline or acid Effective against bacteria, viruses, fungi, and some spores OSHA regulated; requires adequate ventilation, covered pans, gloves, masks Must display biohazard or chemical label

DNA, deoxyribonucleic acid; OSHA, Occupational Safety and Health Administration.

Exposure Risk Factors and the Exposure Control Plan

Health care facilities must provide clear instructions in the policy or infection control manual for preventing employee exposure and reducing the danger of exposure to biohazardous materials. The **exposure risk factor** for each worker by job description must be included in the written policy. It is based on the employee's risk of exposure to communicable disease. Some allied health professionals have a low exposure risk and require only minimal protection to perform the duties associated with their positions. However, other allied health professionals have a higher exposure risk and require access to a variety of **personal protective equipment** (**PPE**), such as gloves, goggles, and/or face shields, depending on the task at hand, and **immunization** against hepatitis B at no charge to the employee. The health care facility must provide the appropriate equipment and supplies as outlined in this facility policy according to OSHA.

Another written policy required by OSHA for facilities with 10 or more employees is the **exposure control plan**. The health care facility must have a written plan of action for all employees and visitors who may be exposed to **biohazardous** material despite all precautions. In the event of an exposure, you must first apply the principles of first aid and notify your immediate supervisor. The supervisor should provide guidance regarding **postexposure testing** and follow-up procedures. Next you should complete and file an incident report (or exposure report) form explaining the circumstances surrounding the exposure. This report form not only documents the incident but also allows management to establish a policy to prevent this type of exposure in the future. In addition, the employer must record the exposure on an OSHA 300 log (Fig. 14-4) and report the exposure to OSHA if one or more of the following criteria are present:

- the work-related exposure resulted in loss of consciousness or necessitated a transfer to another job
- the exposure resulted in a recommendation for medical treatment, such as vaccination or medication to prevent complications
- the exposure resulted in the conversion of a negative blood test for a contagious disease into a positive blood test in the employee who was exposed.

Box 14-3 on page 193 describes biohazard and safety equipment commonly used in health care facilities.

LEGAL TIP

BLOOD-BORNE PATHOGEN STANDARD TRAINING

According to OSHA, health care facilities must provide training to newly hired employees who will be exposed to blood or other possibly infectious material while caring for patients. This training must be repeated yearly and include any new issues or policies recommended by OSHA, the CDC, the Department of Health and Human Services, or the U.S. Public Health Service. Items that must be included in the training:

- A description of blood-borne diseases, including the transmission and symptoms.
- Personal protective equipment available to the employee and the location of the PPE in the health care facility.
- Information about the risks of contracting hepatitis B and about the HBV vaccine.
- The exposure control plan and postexposure procedures, including follow-up care in the event of an exposure.

Checkpoint Question

7. Explain the difference between exposure risk factors and the exposure control plan.

Standard Precautions

Standard precautions are a set of procedures recognized by the CDC to reduce the chance of transmitting infectious microorganisms in any health care setting. By presuming that all blood and body fluids except perspiration are contaminated and by following these precautions, you can protect yourself and prevent the spread of disease. Specifically, these precautions pertain to contact with blood, all body fluids except sweat, damaged skin, and mucous membranes and require that you:

- wash your hands with soap and water after touching blood, body fluids, secretions, and other contaminated items, whether you have worn gloves or not
- an alcohol-based hand rub (foam, lotion, or gel) is acceptable to decontaminate the hands if the hands are not visibly dirty or contaminated
- wear clean nonsterile examination gloves when contact with blood, body fluids, secretions, mucous membranes, damaged skin, and contaminated items is anticipated
- change gloves between procedures on the same patient after exposure to potentially infective material
- wear equipment to protect your eyes, nose, and mouth and avoid soiling your clothes by wearing a disposable

gown or apron when performing procedures that may splash or spray blood, body fluids, or secretions
- dispose of single-use items appropriately; do not disinfect, sterilize, and reuse
- take precautions to avoid injuries before, during, and after procedures in which needles, scalpels, or other sharp instruments have been used on a patient
- do not recap used needles or otherwise manipulate them by bending or breaking. If recapping is necessary to carry a used needle to a sharps container, use a one-handed scoop technique or a device for holding the needle sheath
- place used disposable syringes and needles and other sharps in a puncture-resistant container (sharps) as close as possible to the area of use
- use barrier devices (e.g., mouthpieces, resuscitation bags) as alternatives to mouth-to-mouth resuscitation.

Checkpoint Question

8. How will following standard precautions help to protect you against contracting an infection or communicable disease?

Personal Protective Equipment

In any area of the health care facility where exposure to biohazardous materials might occur, PPE must be made available and used by all health care workers. For instance:

- gloves must be available and accessible throughout the facility. If you or a patient is sensitive to the latex found in regular examination gloves, proper alternatives such as vinyl gloves must be available (Box 14-4 on page 193)
- disposable gowns, goggles, and face shields must be available in areas where splattering or splashing of airborne particles may occur (Fig. 14-5 on page 194)
- you must wear gloves when performing any procedure that carries any risk of exposure, such as surgical procedures or drawing blood specimens, disposing of biohazardous waste, touching or handling surfaces that have been contaminated with biohazardous materials, or if there is any chance at all, no matter how remote, that you may come into contact with blood or body fluids.

Employers who do not make this equipment available are not in compliance with OSHA regulations and may face significant fines. However, employees are responsible for using the PPE correctly and appropriately and washing their hands frequently throughout the day. Remember: pathogens may be carried home to family members and to other persons who come into contact with you or the patient. When removing PPE after a procedure, remove all protective barriers before removing your gloves. Once you have removed all PPE, including your contaminated gloves (Procedure 14-2 at the end of this chapter), always wash your hands.

OSHA's Form 300

Log of Work-Related Injuries and Illnesses

You must record information about every work-related death and about every work-related injury or illness that involves loss of consciousness, restricted work activity or job transfer, days away from work, or medical treatment beyond first aid. You must also record significant work-related injuries and illnesses that are diagnosed by a physician or licensed health care professional. You must also record work-related injuries and illnesses that meet any of the specific recording criteria listed in 29 CFR Part 1904.8 through 1904.12. Feel free to use two lines for a single case if you need to. You must complete an Injury and Illness Incident Report (OSHA Form 301) or equivalent form for each injury or illness recorded on this form. If you're not sure whether a case is recordable, call your local OSHA office for help.

Attention: This form contains information relating to employee health and must be used in a manner that protects the confidentiality of employees to the extent possible while the information is being used for occupational safety and health purposes.

Year 20 ____

U.S. Department of Labor
Occupational Safety and Health Administration

Form approved OMB no. 1218-0176

Establishment name _____

City _____ State _____

Identify the person

(A) Case no.	(B) Employee's name	(C) Job title (e.g., Welder)

Describe the case

(D) Date of injury or onset of illness	(E) Where the event occurred (e.g., Loading dock north end)	(F) Describe injury or illness, parts of body affected, and object/substance that directly injured or made person ill (e.g., Second degree burns on right forearm from acetylene torch)

(D) — month/day

Classify the case

Using these four categories, check ONLY the most serious result for each case:

Death (G)	Days away from work (H)	Remained at work — Job transfer or restriction (I)	Remained at work — Other recordable cases (J)

Enter the number of days the injured or ill worker was:

On job transfer or restriction (K)	Away from work (L)
____ days	____ days

Check the "injury" column or choose one type of illness:

(M)

Injury (1)	Skin disorder (2)	Respiratory condition (3)	Poisoning (4)	All other illnesses (5)

Page totals ▶

Be sure to transfer these totals to the Summary page (Form 300A) before you post it.

Injury (1)	Skin disorder (2)	Respiratory condition (3)	Poisoning (4)	All other illnesses (5)

Public reporting burden for this collection of information is estimated to average 14 minutes per response, including time to review the instructions, search and gather the data needed, and complete and review the collection of information. Persons are not required to respond to the collection of information unless it displays a currently valid OMB control number. If you have any comments about these estimates or any other aspects of this data collection, contact: US Department of Labor, OSHA Office of Statistics, Room N-3644, 200 Constitution Avenue, NW, Washington, DC 20210. Do not send the completed forms to this office.

Page ____ of ____

FIGURE 14-4. The OSHA 300 log. (Courtesy of the U.S. Department of Labor.)

BIOHAZARD AND SAFETY EQUIPMENT IN THE HEALTHCARE FACILITY

- *MSDS binder.* Material safety data sheets are forms prepared by the manufacturers of all chemical substances. The binder should contain sheets for all chemicals used in the facility. Each sheet describes how to handle and dispose of the chemical and most important, the health hazards of the chemical and safety equipment needed when using it.
- *Biohazard waste containers.* Only waste contaminated with blood or body fluids or other potentially infectious material (OPIM) should be placed in biohazard waste containers. Sharps containers are used for disposal of items that have the potential to puncture or cut the skin.
- *Personal protective equipment.* Employers are required to provide PPE appropriate to the risk of exposure. For example, employees who may come into contact with blood need be protected only by wearing gloves. However, situations that may cause a splash or splatter of blood require full coverage of the skin, eyes, and clothing.
- *Eyewash basin.* Pressing the lever on the basin and turning on the faucets produces a stream of water that forces open the caps of the eyewash basin. To remove contaminants or chemicals from the eyes, lower your face into the stream and continue to wash the area until the eyes are clear or for the amount of time recommended on the MSDS.
- *Immunization.* Employers are required by OSHA to provide immunization against blood-borne pathogens if vaccines are available.

WHAT IF

Your patient is offended that you are wearing gloves when drawing a blood specimen?

Sometimes patients become defensive and make statements to the effect that they are "disease free." If this happens to you, reassure the patient by saying that wearing gloves is a standard practice and is used for the protection of the patient also. Use this occasion to teach the patient about standard precautions and the importance of following these guidelines.

Handling Environmental Contamination

Although not all equipment or surfaces in the facility must be sterile (free from all microorganisms), all equipment and areas must be clean. Sanitization is cleaning or washing equipment or surfaces by removing all visible soil. Any detergent or low-level disinfectant can be used to clean and disinfect areas such as floors, examination tables, cabinets, and countertops. Because you may be expected to perform cleaning tasks routinely or when these surfaces become soiled with visible blood or body fluids, you should understand how these procedures are correctly performed.

Any surface contaminated with biohazardous materials should be promptly cleaned using an approved germicide or a dilute bleach solution. OSHA requires that spill kits or appropriate supplies be available, and commercial kits make cleaning contaminated surfaces relatively safe and easy. Commercial kits include clean gloves, eye protection if there is a risk of splashing, a gel to absorb the biohazardous material, a

LATEX ALLERGY AND PREVENTION

The incidence among health care workers of allergic reactions to proteins in latex has increased in recent years. The proteins in latex, a product of the rubber tree that is used to make many products, including gloves, may cause allergic reactions, especially with repeated exposure. The reactions can be mild (skin redness or rash, itching, or hives) or severe (difficulty breathing, coughing, or wheezing). Respiratory reactions often result when the powder in the gloves becomes airborne and is inhaled as the gloves are removed after use. To protect yourself from exposure and allergy to latex, the following guidelines may be useful:

- use gloves that are not latex for tasks that do not involve contact or potential contact with blood or body fluids
- when contact with blood or body fluids is possible, wear powder-free latex gloves. Powder-free gloves contain less protein than the powdered ones, reducing the risk of allergy
- avoid wearing oil-based lotions or hand creams before applying latex gloves. The oil in these products can break down the latex, releasing the proteins that cause the allergic reactions
- wash your hands thoroughly after removing latex gloves
- recognize the symptoms of latex allergy in yourself, your coworkers, and your patients.

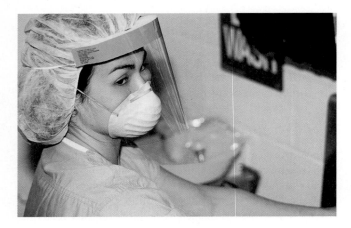

FIGURE 14-5. Personal protective equipment that must be provided for employees who may come into contact with contaminated materials includes gloves, goggles, face shields, and gowns or aprons to protect clothing.

FIGURE 14-6. A commercially prepared biohazard spill kit contains gloves, absorbent material, eye protection, and a biohazard bag for proper disposal. (Courtesy of Caltech Industries, Midland, MI)

scoop, towels, and a biohazard waste container to discard all used items (Fig. 14-6). If your facility does not purchase commercial kits, you should gather and store the following items together in the event that a biohazardous spill occurs:

- eye protection, such as goggles
- clean examination gloves
- absorbent powder, crystals, or gel
- paper towels
- a disposable scoop
- at least one biohazard waste bag
- a chemical disinfectant.

In some cases, you may need a sharps container (Fig. 14-7) and spill control barriers. If there is a large amount of contamination on the floor, you should put on disposable shoe coverings to avoid transmitting microorganisms on your shoes. All gloves, paper towels, eye protection, and shoe coverings should be discarded in the biohazardous waste bags, which must be disposed of properly. Procedure 14-3 at the end of this chapter outlines the procedure for an area contaminated with blood or body fluids.

Although most health care facilities use disposable patient gowns and drapes, some facilities use cloth. Hygienic storage of clean linens is recommended, and proper handling of soiled linens, disposable or not, is required. After applying clean gloves, handle soiled linen, including table paper, as little as possible by folding it carefully so that the most contaminated surface is turned inward to prevent contamination of the air. Contaminated linen should be placed in a biohazard bag in the room where the contamination occurred rather than carried through the hallways of the facility. Some facilities using cloth linens contract with an outside company for the laundering. If linen materials are laundered at the facility use normal laundry cycles following the recommendations of the washer, detergent, and fabric.

 Checkpoint Question

9. How would you respond to an employee in the facility who is unsure about how to clean up a spilled urine specimen? Is this biohazardous?

Disposing of Infectious Waste

Federal regulations from the Environmental Protection Agency (EPA) and OSHA set the policies and guidelines for disposing of hazardous materials, but individual states determine policies based on these guidelines. As a result, policies vary widely, and you should review your state and local regulations before making waste disposal decisions. Facilities that are considered small generators of waste produce less than 50 pounds of waste each month. Facilities

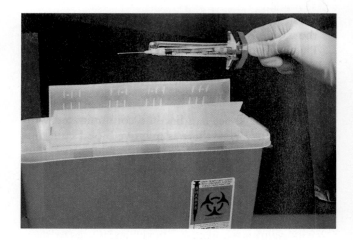

FIGURE 14-7. All sharps should be disposed of properly by placing them in a plastic puncture-resistant sharps container like the one shown here. Note the biohazard symbol on the sharps container.

that generate more than 50 pounds are considered large generators and must obtain a certificate of registration from the EPA and maintain a record of the quantity of waste and disposal procedures.

To remain compliant with any state and federal laws, facilities that are considered large generators of infectious waste and some smaller health care facilities use an infectious waste service to dispose of biohazardous waste appropriately and safely. These services supply the office with appropriate waste containers and pick up filled containers regularly (Box 14-5). Once the filled containers are picked up by the waste service, the infectious waste is disposed of according to EPA and OSHA guidelines. The service maintains a tracking record listing the type of waste, its weight in pounds, and the disposal destination. When the waste has been destroyed, a tracking form documenting the disposal is sent to the health care facility and should be retained in the facility records for 3 years. This documentation must be provided to the EPA should an audit be performed to assess compliance. States impose stiff penalties, including fines and/or imprisonment, for violations of regulations involving biohazardous waste.

Because the fee charged by an infectious waste service is based on the type and amount of waste generated, you should follow these guidelines to help keep the cost down while maintaining safety:

- use separate containers for each type of waste. Don't put bandages in sharps containers (puncture-resistant containers for needles or other sharp items) or paper towels used for routine handwashing in a biohazard bag
- fill sharps containers two-thirds full before disposing of them. Most containers have fill lines that must not be exceeded
- use only approved biohazard containers
- when moving filled biohazard containers, secure the bag or top with a closure for that specific container
- if the container is contaminated on the outside, wear clean gloves, secure it within another approved container, and wash your hands thoroughly afterward
- place biohazard waste for pick up by the service in a secure, designated area.

Hepatitis B and Human Immunodeficiency Viruses

One of the most persistent concerns in the health care setting is the transmission of hepatitis B virus (HBV) and human immunodeficiency virus (HIV). Although HIV is the most visible public concern, HBV has been an occupational hazard for health care professionals for many years. HBV is more viable than HIV and may survive in a dried state on equipment and counter surfaces at room temperature for more than a week. In this dried state, HBV may be passed

---

Box 14-5

PROPER WASTE DISPOSAL

Regular Waste Container

A regular waste container.

A regular waste container should be used only for disposal of waste that is not biohazardous, such as paper, plastic, disposable tray wrappers, packaging material, unused gauze, and examination table paper. To prevent leakage and mess, liquids should be discarded in a sink or other washbasin, not in the plastic bag inside the waste can. NEVER discard sharps of any kind in plastic bags; these are not puncture resistant, and injury may result even with careful handling. Bags should not be filled to capacity. When the plastic bag is about two-thirds full, it should be removed from the waste can, the top edges brought together and secured by tying or with a twist tie. Remove the bag from the area and follow the office policy and procedure for disposal. Put a fresh plastic bag into the waste can.

A biohazard waste container.

Biohazard Waste Container

The biohazard waste container is reserved for the disposal of waste contaminated with blood or body fluids, including soiled dressings and bandages, soiled gloves, soiled table paper and cotton balls and applicators that have been used on or in the body.

by way of contact with contaminated hands, gloves, or other means of direct transmission. Fortunately, HBV can be contained by the proper use of standard precautions, and it can be killed easily by cleaning with a dilute bleach solution.

HBV and HIV are both transmitted through exposure to contaminated blood and body fluids. Accidental punctures with sharp objects contaminated with blood are one way to become infected, but the viruses may also enter the body through broken skin. Disorders of the skin, including dry cracked skin, dermatitis, eczema, and psoriasis, also allow entrance into the body if contact with contaminated surfaces or equipment occurs.

While there is no vaccine to prevent infection with HIV, employers whose workers are at risk for HBV exposure are mandated by OSHA to provide the vaccine to prevent HBV at no cost to the employee. This vaccine is given in a series of three injections that normally produce immunity to the disease. It is recommended that a blood sample be drawn 6 months after the third injection of HBV vaccine to determine whether the person has developed immunity. The blood test can detect the presence, or titer, of antibodies against hepatitis B. The series is repeated if HBV immunity is not found, but the vaccine has been found to be very effective. The immunity may last as long as 10 years. Employees who choose not to receive the vaccine must sign a waiver or release form stating that they are aware of the risks associated with HBV. Individuals who contract hepatitis B may develop cirrhosis (destruction of the cells of the liver) and are at increased risk for developing liver cancer.

In the event of exposure to blood or body fluids infected with HBV, the postexposure plan should include an immediate blood test of the employee. Repeat blood titers should be obtained at specific intervals, usually 6 weeks, 3 months, 6 months, 9 months, and 1 year, as a comparison. If you have been immunized against HBV, usually no further treatment is required. However, if you waive the HBV series, hepatitis B immunoglobulin can be given by injection for immediate short-term protection, and the general series of three immunizations should be started.

The same schedule of evaluation is required after HIV exposure. Again, there is no vaccine to prevent HIV, but other HIV treatments for preventing transmission are being tested.

 Checkpoint Question

10. Which virus is more of a threat to the allied health professional: HIV or HBV? Why?

Handwashing for Medical Asepsis

Purpose: To prevent the growth and spread of pathogen

Equipment: Liquid soap, disposable paper towels, an orangewood manicure stick, a waste can

Standard: This task should take 2 to 3 minutes.

Steps	Reason
1. Remove all rings and your wristwatch if it cannot be pushed up onto the forearm.	Rings and watches may harbor pathogens that may not be easily washed away. Ideally, rings should not be worn when working with material that may be infectious.
2. Stand close to the sink without touching it.	The sink is considered contaminated, and standing too close may contaminate your clothing.
3. Turn on the faucet and adjust the temperature of the water to warm.	Water that is too hot or too cold will crack or chap the skin on the hands, which will break the natural protective barrier that prevents infection.
4. Wet your hands and wrists under the warm running water, apply liquid soap, and work the soap into a lather by rubbing your palms together and rubbing the soap between your fingers at least 10 times.	This motion dislodges microorganisms from between the fingers and removes transient and some resident organisms.

Step 4. Wet hands and wrists.

(continued)

Procedure 14-1 *(continued)*

Handwashing for Medical Asepsis

Steps	Reason
5. Scrub the palm of one hand with the fingertips of the other hand to work the soap under the nails of that hand; then reverse the procedure and scrub the other hand. Also scrub each wrist.  Step 5. Wash hands and wrists with firm rubbing and circular motions.	Friction helps remove microorganisms.
6. Rinse hands and wrists thoroughly under running warm water, holding hands lower than elbows; do not touch the inside of the sink.  Step 6. Rinse hands thoroughly.	Holding the hands lower than the elbows and wrists allows microorganisms to flow off the hands and fingers rather than back up the arms.
7. Using the orangewood stick, clean under each nail on both hands.	Nails may harbor microorganisms. Metal files and pointed instruments may break the skin and make an opening for microorganisms. This may be done at the beginning of the day, before leaving for the day, or after coming into contact with potentially infectious material.

(continued)

Handwashing for Medical Asepsis

Steps	Reason
8. Reapply liquid soap and rewash hands and wrists.	Rewashing the hands after using the orangewood stick washes away any microorganisms that may have been removed with the orangewood stick.
9. Rinse hands thoroughly again while holding hands lower than wrists and elbows.	
10. Gently dry hands with a paper towel. Discard the paper towel and the used orangewood stick when finished.	Hands must be dried thoroughly and completely to prevent drying and cracking.

Step 10. Dry hands gently with a paper towel.

11. Use a dry paper towel to turn off the faucets and discard the paper towel.	Your hands are clean and should not touch the contaminated faucet handles.

Procedure 14-2

Removing Contaminated Gloves

Purpose: To remove contaminated gloves to prevent the spread of pathogenic microorganisms
Equipment: Clean examination gloves; biohazard waste container
Standards: This task should take 1 to 2 minutes.

Steps	Reason
1. Choose the appropriate size gloves for your hands and put them on.	Gloves should fit comfortably, not too loose and not too tight.
2. To remove gloves, grasp the glove of your nondominant hand *at the palm* and pull the glove away.	To avoid transferring contaminants to the wrist, be sure not to grasp the glove at the wrist.

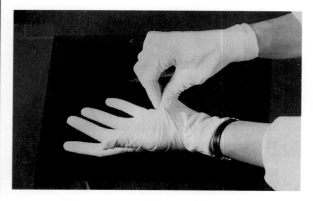

Step 2. Grasp the palm of the glove on your nondominant gloved hand.

Steps	Reason
3. Slide your hand out of the glove, rolling the glove into the palm of the gloved dominant hand.	You should avoid touching either glove with your ungloved hand.

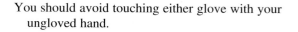

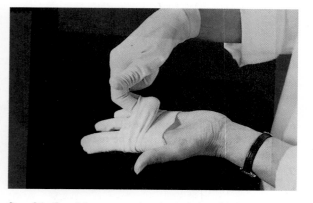

Step 3A. Carefully remove the glove and avoid contaminating your bare skin.

(continued)

Procedure 14-2 *(continued)*

Removing Contaminated Gloves

Steps	Reason
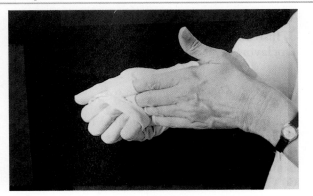 Step 3B. Grasp the soiled glove with your gloved dominant hand.	
4. Holding the soiled glove in the palm of your gloved hand, slip your ungloved fingers under the cuff of the glove you are still wearing, being careful not to touch the outside of the glove. 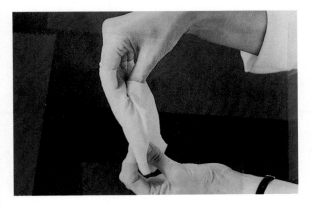 Step 4. Slip your free hand under the cuff of the remaining glove.	Skin should touch skin but never the soiled part of the glove.

(continued)

Procedure 14-2 *(continued)*

Removing Contaminated Gloves

Steps	**Reason**
5. Stretch the glove of the dominant hand up and away from your hand while turning it inside out, with the already removed glove balled up inside. 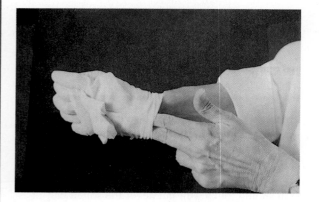 Step 5. Remove the glove by turning it inside out over the previously removed glove.	Turning it inside out ensures that the soiled surfaces of the gloves are enclosed.
6. Both gloves should now be removed, with the first glove inside the second glove and the second glove inside out.	
7. Discard both gloves as one unit into a biohazard waste receptacle.	
8. Wash your hands.	Wearing gloves is NOT a substitute for washing your hands!

Procedure 14-3

Cleaning Biohazardous Spills

Purpose: To clean contaminated surfaces

Equipment: Commercially prepared germicide OR 1:10 bleach solution, Gloves, Disposable towels, Chemical absorbent, Biohazardous waste bag, Protective eye wear (goggles or mask and face shield), Disposable shoe coverings. Disposable gown or apron made of plastic or other material that is impervious to soaking up contaminated fluids.

Standard: This task should take 3 to 5 minutes.

Steps	Reason
1. Put on gloves. Wear protective eyewear, gown or apron, and shoe coverings if you anticipate any splashing.	A plastic gown or apron will protect your clothing from contaminants.
2. Apply chemical absorbent material to the spill as indicated by facility policy. Clean up the spill with disposable paper towels, being careful not to splash.	
3. Dispose of paper towels and absorbent material in a biohazard waste bag.	The bag will alert anyone handling the waste that it contains biohazardous material.
4. Spray the area with commercial germicide or bleach solution and wipe with disposable paper towels. Discard towels in a biohazard bag.	
5. With your gloves on, remove the protective eyewear and discard or disinfect per facility policy. Remove the gown or apron and shoe coverings and put in the biohazard bag if disposable or the biohazard laundry bag for reusable linens.	
6. Place the biohazard bag in an appropriate waste receptacle for removal according to your facility's policy.	
7. Remove your gloves and wash your hands thoroughly.	Wearing gloves does not replace proper hand washing.

Procedure 14-4

Disposing of Biohazardous Materials

Equipment/Supplies: Biohazard waste container and liner provided by the infectious waste disposal service, a working biohazard trash can and liners, sharps container, a regular trash container, gloves, lab coat.

Steps

1. Wash your hands and put on gloves and a lab coat.

2. Discard any paper towels used for a routine handwashing procedure in the regular (not biohazardous) trash.

3. Pre-clean non-disposable hemostats that have been exposed to blood or body fluids, and follow the autoclave check-off procedure.

4. Dispose of urine or other body fluids by pouring specimen down a drain connected to a sanitary sewer, followed by a copious volume of water. Dispose of empty container in a clearly marked, impermeable, red biohazard waste bag.

5. Dispose of gauze that has been exposed to blood or body fluids in a clearly marked, impermeable, red biohazard waste bag.

6. When a biohazard waste bag is full, secure the bag with a closure and move it to the lined waste container provided by the infectious waste service company. Place an unused biohazard bag in the working biohazard trash container.

7. Dispose of a needle that has punctured a patient by activating any safety devices on the needle and placing it in a sharps container.

8. When a sharps container is two-thirds full, seal the sharps container and assemble a new one for disposal of used needles.

9. Remove the gloves and wash your hands.

Procedure 14-5

Practicing Standard Precautions

Equipment/Supplies: Faceshield or goggles and a mask, needle, sharps container, facility accident or incident report form, gloves, lab coat.

Steps

1. Locate and put on appropriate personal protective equipment including a lab coat, buttoned completely, and gloves. When handling fluids that may splash, put on either goggles and a mask or a faceshield.

2. When recapping dirty needle to transport to a sharps container, use the one handed scoop technique

3. If you accidentally stick yourself with a used needle take the following steps:

   • Immediately wash the area with soap and water.
   • Complete a facility accident or incident form documenting the exposure, including where on the body it occurred and how it happened.
   • Identify, if possible, the source patient of the exposure.
   • Report the exposure to your supervisor, who is responsible for following up.
   • Get tested for HIV and HBV. (You do have the right to refuse to be tested.)
   • Seek counseling from a physician regarding medication and vaccination options.

4. Remove and properly clean or dispose of all personal protective equipment and wash your hands.

CHAPTER SUMMARY

Following the principles of asepsis and infection control help ensure a safe environment for patients and health care providers in the health care setting.

If you fail to follow these principles consistently, you will place yourself and others at risk for infection that may impair patients' recovery and affect health care workers' performance. Although avoiding contact with microorganisms in the environment is impossible, sanitation and disinfection will reduce the numbers of microorganisms and potential pathogens, making the environment clean and as disease free as possible. In addition, OSHA and the CDC issue regulations and standards for health care workers who work with blood and body fluids, and you must always follow them, including wearing PPE. In case of exposure, your facility-must have an exposure control plan and a postexposure plan to assist you in receiving appropriate medical attention and follow-up care.

Remember: Handwashing is the single most effective measure to prevent the spread of infection.

Critical Thinking Challenges

1. Review Table 14-1 on common communicable diseases. Create a patient education brochure that focuses on the spread of these diseases.
2. A patient who comes into your facility has a leg wound that must be cared for at home. When asked about caring for the wound, he tells you that he knows how to do it, but you think he may be confused about the importance of using medical asepsis. How do you handle this situation?

Answers to Checkpoint Questions

1. Pathogenic microorganisms are microscopic organisms that cause disease. Natural ways that the body stops an invasion or destroys pathogens include tears (wash microbes away from the eyes and contain lysozyme, an effective disinfectant); hydrochloric acid in the stomach (produces a pH that kills many microbes that may get into the stomach); unbroken or intact skin (provides a barrier to invading microorganism); mucous membranes and cilia lining the respiratory tract (trap microorganisms that may be inhaled).
2. The conditions that favor the growth of microorganisms include moisture, nutrients, a warm temperature, darkness, a neutral or slightly alkaline pH, and oxygen. To prevent the growth of microbes, remove any moisture or sources of nutrition, use heat higher than 98.6°F, expose the area to light, or clean with acidic or alkaline chemicals.
3. The first link in the infection cycle (the reservoir host) provides nutrients and an incubation site for the pathogen. The fifth link (the susceptible host) allows the pathogen to enter and begin growing thus becoming the new reservoir host, repeating the cycle.
4. Opening screenless windows allows insects to come into the facility. Insects may be reservoir hosts to certain diseases and contaminate items in the health care facility.
5. Gloves are a barrier to prevent the skin from coming into contact with contaminated materials. However, once they are removed, standard precautions require that the hands be washed as an additional precaution.
6. Items or instruments that come into contact with unbroken mucous membranes in areas of the body that are not considered sterile (like the vagina) may be safely disinfected using a high-level disinfectant for the specified period.
7. Exposure risk factors are associated with specific jobs in terms of exposure to biohazardous or contaminated materials. The exposure control plan is a written document outlining the procedure that an employee or visitor should take to prevent contact with biohazardous material.
8. Following the standard precautions will help to protect you against contracting an infection or disease by preventing entrance of the pathogenic microorganisms into your body.
9. Urine may be biohazardous and should be cleaned up by applying clean gloves, using paper towels or absorbent powder to absorb the urine, and placing all items used for cleaning up the spill into a biohazardous waste container. Once the urine is absorbed and discarded appropriately, the area or floor should be disinfected.
10. The virus that is actually more of a threat is HBV. HBV may live in dried body secretions on an inanimate surface for up to 2 weeks. In the "right" circumstances, contact with these dried secretions may cause infection in the exposed individual. Hepatitis B is a serious disease and may cause scarring and destruction of the liver tissue (leading to liver failure), an increased risk for developing liver cancer, and death.

 Websites

OSHA www.osha.gov
Latex allergy prevention http://www.cdc.gov/niosh/98-113.html

15

Surgical Instruments and Sterilization

CHAPTER OBJECTIVES

In this chapter, you'll learn:
1. To spell and define key terms.
2. To describe several methods of sterilization.
3. To categorize surgical instruments based on use and identify each by its characteristics.
4. To identify surgical instruments specific to designated specialties.
5. To state the difference between reusable and disposable instruments.
6. To explain the procedure for storing supplies, instruments, and equipment.
7. To describe the necessity and procedure for maintaining documents and records of maintenance for instruments and equipment.

PERFORMANCE OBJECTIVES

In this chapter, you'll learn:
1. To sanitize equipment and instruments (Procedure 15-1).
2. To properly wrap instruments in preparation for sterilization in an autoclave (Procedure 15-2).
3. To operate an autoclave while observing for pressure, time, and temperature determined by the items being sterilized (Procedure 15-3).

KEY TERMS

autoclave	hemostat	ratchet	scissors
disinfection	needle holder	sanitation	serration
ethylene oxide	obturator	sanitize	sound
forceps	OSHA	scalpel	sterilization

THE GOAL OF SURGICAL ASEPSIS is to free an item or area from all microorganisms, both pathogens and others. The practice of surgical asepsis, also known as sterile technique, should be used during any facility surgical procedure, when handling sterile instruments to be used for incisions and excisions into body tissue, and when changing wound dressings. Surgical asepsis prevents microorganisms from entering the patient's environment; medical asepsis prevents microbes from spreading to or from patients.

In a health care facility your responsibilities may include assisting with minor surgical procedures while maintaining surgical asepsis. To manage this responsibility, you must do the following:

- become familiar with many types of surgical instruments
- understand the principles and practices of surgical asepsis
- understand and use **disinfection** and **sterilization** techniques
- use equipment designed for sterilization, treatment, and diagnostic purposes
- maintain accurate records and inventory of purchases related to surgical equipment and supplies.

You are expected to understand sterile technique and to be able to maintain sterility throughout procedures. Any break in sterile technique, no matter how small, can lead to infection the body cannot fight. Even small infections can delay the patient's recovery and are physically, mentally, and financially costly to the patient.

PRINCIPLES AND PRACTICES OF SURGICAL ASEPSIS

As an allied health professional you may be responsible for preventing infection in accordance with the principles and practices of asepsis as it relates to items used during minor surgical procedures. Surgical asepsis requires the absence of microorganisms, infection, and infectious material on instruments, equipment, and supplies. Disinfection, or medical asepsis, is different from sterilization (Table 15-1). By

becoming familiar with the manufacturer's recommendations for processing instruments according to the purposes for which the items will be used, you will be able to determine the appropriate level of asepsis.

Sterilization

While **sanitation** and disinfection are adequate for maintaining medical asepsis in the facility, these practices are not sufficient to process instruments and equipment used during sterile procedures. Objects requiring surgical asepsis must be **sanitized** first and sterilized by either a physical or chemical process. Procedure 15-1 describes the procedure for sanitizing instruments in preparation for sterilization. Sterilization is the complete elimination or destruction of all forms of microbial life, including spore forms. Steam under pressure, dry heat, **ethylene oxide** gas, and liquid chemicals are principle sterilizing agents. Although in health care facilities steam under pressure is the most frequently used method of sterilization, the method depends on the nature of the material to be sterilized and the type of microorganism to be destroyed. Table 15-2 describes the various methods of sterilization and the temperatures and time of exposure if applicable.

Checkpoint Question

1. How do sanitization, disinfection, and sterilization differ?

Sterilization Equipment

Several types of sterilization equipment are used in health care facilities. As an allied health professional, it may be your responsibility to do the following:

- Become familiar with the uses and operation of each piece of equipment
- Schedule periodic preventive maintenance or servicing of the equipment
- Maintain adequate supplies for general operational needs

Table 15-1   COMPARISON OF MEDICAL AND SURGICAL ASEPSIS

	Medical Asepsis	Surgical Asepsis
Definition	Destroys microorganisms after they leave the body	Destroys microorganisms before they enter the body
Purpose	Prevents transmission of microbes from one person to another	Prevents entry of microbes into the body in invasive procedures
When used	During contact with a body part that is not normally sterile	During contact with a normally sterile part of the body
Differences in handwashing technique	Hands and wrists are washed for 1 to 2 minutes	Hands and forearms are washed for 5–10 minutes with a brush

Table 15-2	STERILIZATION METHODS
Methods	**Concentration or Level**
Heat	
Moist heat (steam under pressure)	250°F or 121°C for 30 min
Boiling	212°F or 100°C for ≥ 30 min
Dry heat	340°F or 171°C for 1 hour
	320°F or 160°C for 2 hours
Liquids	
Glutaraldehyde	Follow manufacturer's recommendations or OSHA requirements and guidelines
Formaldehyde	Follow manufacturer's recommendations or OSHA requirements and guidelines
Gas	
Ethylene oxide	450–500mg/L 50°C

OSHA, Occupational Safety and Health Administration.

The Autoclave

The most frequently used piece of equipment for sterilizing instruments today is the autoclave (Fig. 15-1). The autoclave has two chambers: an outer one where pressure builds and an inner one where the sterilization occurs. Distilled water is added to a reservoir, where it is converted to steam as the preset temperature is reached. The steam is forced into the inner chamber, increasing the pressure and raising the temperature of the steam to 250°F or higher, well above the ordinary boiling temperature of water (212°F or 100°C). The pressure has no effect on sterilization other than to increase the temperature of the steam. The high temperature allows for destruction of all microorganisms, including viruses and spores.

An air exhaust vent on the bottom of the autoclave allows the air in the chamber to be pushed out and replaced by the pressurized steam. When no air is present, the chamber seals and the temperature gauge begins to rise. Most automatic autoclaves can be set to vent, time, turn off, and exhaust at preset times and levels. Older models may require that the steps be advanced manually. All manufacturers provide instructions for operating the machine and recommendations for the times necessary to sterilize different types of loads. These instructions should be posted in a prominent place near the machine.

Sterilization is required for surgical instruments and equipment that will come into contact with internal body tissues or cavities that are considered sterile. The autoclave is commonly used to sterilize minor surgical instruments, surgical storage trays and containers, and some surgical equipment, such as bowls for holding sterile solutions. Instruments or equipment subject to damage by water should not be sterilized in the autoclave. These items can be sterilized with gas. Items that are not subject to water damage but may be destroyed by heat can be cold-sterilized or soaked for a prescribed amount of time in a liquid such as glutaraldehyde or formaldehyde. Always follow the manufacturer's recommendations for sterilizing instruments or equipment and for using any chemical products for sterilization. Procedure 15-2 at the end of this chapter, describes preparation of instruments for sterilization in the autoclave.

Checkpoint Question

2. What is an autoclave, and how does it work?

Sterilization Indicators

Tape applied to the outside of the material used to wrap instruments or supplies for the autoclave indicates that the items have been exposed to steam, but the tape cannot ensure the sterility of the contents (Box 15-1 and Figure 15-2 on next page). Sterilization indicators placed inside the packs register that the proper pressure and temperature were attained for the required time to allow steam to penetrate the inner parts of the pack (Fig. 15-3). Improper wrapping, loading, or operation of the autoclave may prevent the indicator from registering properly.

FIGURE 15-1. (**A**) An autoclave that may be found in a health care facility; note the clearly marked dials and gauges. (**B**) The interior of the autoclave.

Box 15-1

AUTOCLAVE INDICATOR TAPE

Autoclave tape is designed to change color in the presence of heat and steam. In extreme instances the tape may change appearance when stored too close to heat sources. Most tapes have imprinted lines that darken after exposure, but sterilization of the package contents is not ensured by a color change on the autoclave tape. Proper sterilization can be assumed only if accompanying sterilization indicators have registered that all elements of the sterilization process (time and temperature) have been achieved.

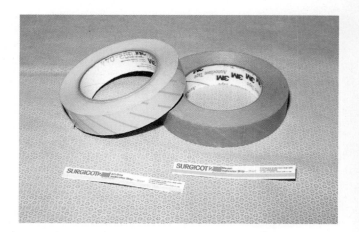

FIGURE 15-3. Sterilization indicators and autoclave indicator tape. Gas indicator tape (*left*) and steam indicator tape (*right*).

Types of indicators include those that change colors at high temperatures. Specially designed tubes containing wax pellets are also used to indicate that the required temperature was reached, as evidenced by the melted wax. Although most types of sterilization indicators work well, the best method for determining effectiveness of sterilization is the culture test. Strips impregnated with heat-resistant spores are wrapped and placed in the center of the autoclave between the packages in a designated load, such as the first load of the day. The strips are removed from their packets and placed in a broth culture to be incubated according to the instructions of the manufacturer. At the end of the incubation period, the culture is compared to a control to determine that all spores have been killed. If sterilization was not achieved, the load must be reprocessed.

 Checkpoint Question

3. What is the difference between a sterilization indicator and autoclave tape?

Loading the Autoclave

If you are responsible for loading the autoclave, follow these instructions. Load the autoclave loosely to allow steam to

FIGURE 15-2. The stripes on autoclave indicator tape change color, indicating that the pack has been exposed to steam.

circulate. If too many items are packed into the autoclave, steam will not penetrate the items in the center. Place empty wrapped containers or bowls on their sides with the lids wrapped separately. If containers are upright in the autoclave, air, which is heavier than steam, will settle into the interior of the container and keep steam from circulating to the inner surfaces. Place all packs on their sides to allow for the maximum steam circulation and penetration.

 Checkpoint Question

4. Why is the loading of the autoclave important? How would you load it?

Operating the Autoclave

All components of autoclaving — temperature, pressure, steam, and time — must be correct for the items to reach sterility. If you will be operating the autoclave, be sure to follow the instruction manual carefully. All machines use the same principles, but operation varies. Become familiar with the function of the machine in your facility. Instructions may be covered in plastic or laminated and posted beside the machine for easy reference.

The autoclave has a reservoir tank that should be filled with distilled water only. Tap water contains chemicals and minerals that would coat the interior chamber, clog the exhaust valves, and hinder the overall operation of the autoclave. When filling the internal chamber of the autoclave with distilled water from the reservoir, be sure the water level is at the fill line. If too much water is added to the chamber, the steam will be saturated and may not be efficient, and too little water will not produce the required amount of steam. Procedure 15-3 outlines the general steps for operating an autoclave.

The temperature, pressure, and time required vary with the items being sterilized. In most cases, 250°F at 15 pounds of pressure for 20 to 30 minutes will be sufficient, but you should follow the manufacturer's instructions for the load content. Solid or metal loads take slightly less time than soft, bulky loads. The timer should not be set until the proper temperature has been attained. Some microorganisms, such as spores, are killed only if exposed to high enough temperature for a specific amount of time.

When the items have been in the autoclave at the right temperature for enough time, the timer will sound, indicating that the cycle is finished. Be sure to vent the autoclave to allow the pressure to drop safely. After the pressure has dropped to a safe level, open the door of the autoclave slightly to allow the temperature to drop and the load to cool and dry. Newer autoclaves vent automatically. Do not handle or remove items from the autoclave until they are dry, because bacteria from your hands would be drawn through the moist coverings and contaminate the items inside the wrapping. Once the items are dry, remove the packages and store them in a clean, dry, dust-free area. Packs that are sterilized on site in the autoclave are considered sterile for 30 days and must be sterilized again after this period. Always store recently autoclaved items toward the back of the cabinet, rotating the previously autoclaved items to the front. In addition, maintenance should be performed on the autoclave at regular intervals. A schedule for this maintenance should be posted near the machine; it should allow for cleaning the lint trap, washing out the interior of the chamber with a cloth or soft brush, and checking the function of all components. This schedule can remind and document the service with space for initialing or signing after the maintenance has been done.

Checkpoint Question

5. Why is it important to set the timer on the autoclave during a cycle only after the correct temperature has been reached?

SURGICAL INSTRUMENTS

Allied health professionals may need to be able to identify surgical instruments according to their design and function. A surgical instrument is a tool or device designed to perform a specific function, such as cutting, dissecting, grasping, holding, retracting, or suturing. Surgical instruments are designed to perform specific tasks based on their shape; they may be curved, straight, sharp, blunt, serrated, toothed, or smooth. Many are made of stainless steel and are reusable; others are disposable. If you will be in contact with them, it is your responsibility to know the proper use and care of the surgical instruments in your facility.

Most instruments used in procedures can be identified by carefully examining the instrument. The most widely used surgical instruments are **forceps**, **scissors**, **scalpels**, and clamps. Table 15-3 shows the most commonly used instruments and equipment by specialty.

Forceps

Forceps are surgical instruments used to grasp, handle, compress, pull, or join tissue, equipment, or supplies.

The types of forceps include the following:

- **hemostat clamp** A surgical instrument with slender jaws used for grasping blood vessels and establishing hemostasis
- **Kelly clamp** A curved or straight forceps or hemostat; those with long handles are widely used in gynecological procedures
- **sterilizer forceps** Used to transfer sterile supplies, equipment, and other surgical instruments to a sterile field. May also be called sterile transfer forceps
- **needle holder** Used to hold and pass a needle through tissue during suturing
- **spring or thumb forceps** Used for grasping tissue for dissection or suturing, such as tissue forceps and splinter forceps.

A variety of forceps can be seen in Figure 15-4. All forceps are available in many sizes, with or without **serrations** or teeth, with curved or straight blades, and with ring tips, blunt tips, or sharp tips. Many have **ratchets** in the handles to hold the tips tightly together; these are notched mechanisms that click into position to maintain tension. Some have spring handles that are compressed between the thumb and index finger to grasp objects.

Scissors

Scissors are sharp instruments composed of two opposing cutting blades held together by a central pin at the pivot. Scissors are used for dissecting superficial, deep, or delicate tissues and for cutting sutures and bandages. Scissors have blade points that are blunt, sharp, or both, depending on the use of the instrument. The types of scissors include the following:

- **straight scissors** cut deep or delicate tissue and sutures
- **curved scissors** dissect superficial and delicate tissues
- **suture scissors** cut sutures; straight top blade and curved-out, or hooked, blunt bottom blade to fit under, lift, and grasp sutures for snipping.
- **bandage scissors** remove bandages; flattened blunt tip on the bottom longer blade safely fits under bandages; most common type is the Lister bandage scissors.

Figure 15-5 shows various types of scissors.

Scalpels and Blades

A scalpel is a small surgical knife with a straight handle and a straight or curved blade. A reusable steel scalpel handle can hold different blades for different surgical procedures. Straight or pointed blades are used for incision and drainage procedures, while curved blades are used to excise tissue. Reusable handles are used only with disposable blades. Many offices use disposable handles and blades packaged as one sterile unit. Figure 15-6 shows various scalpels and blades.

Table 15-3   COMMONLY USED INSTRUMENTS AND EQUIPMENT BY SPECIALTY

	Instruments	Use
Obstetrics, gynecology	Vaginal speculum	Open vagina to view vaginal walls, cervical os; perform procedures; sized; may be reusable metal or disposable plastic
	Tenaculum	Grasping and holding tissue with hooklike tips
	Uterine **sounds**	Assess depth of uterus; graduated in inches or centimeters
	Uterine dilator	Widens cervical os; usually 3–18 mm
	Curet	Blunt or sharp; for scraping endometrium
	Biopsy forceps	Secure pieces of tissue for microscopic study

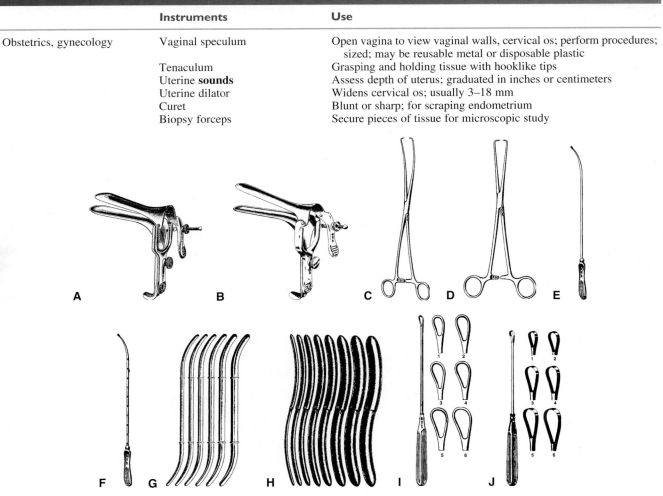

Gynecology instruments. (**A**) Graves vaginal speculum. (**B**) Pederson vaginal speculum. (**C**) Duplay tenaculum forceps. (**D**) Schroeder tenaculum forceps. (**E**) Sims uterine sound. (**F**) Simpson uterine sound, malleable. (**G**) Hand uterine dilator. (**H**) Hegar uterine dilator. (**I**) Thomas uterine curets. (**J**) Sims uterine curets.

	Instruments	Use
Orthopedics	Cast saw	Remove cast
	Cutters or spreaders	

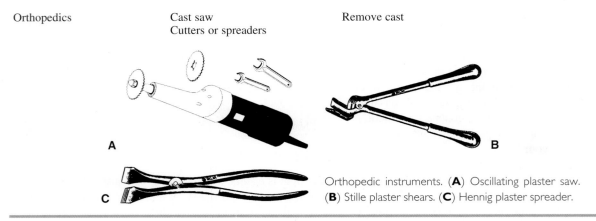

Orthopedic instruments. (**A**) Oscillating plaster saw. (**B**) Stille plaster shears. (**C**) Hennig plaster spreader.

Table 15-3　(CONTINUED)

	Instruments	Use
Urology	Urethral sounds	Explore bladder depth, direction; dilate urethral meatus in stenosis; sized Fr 8–26
	Prostate biopsy	Removes tissue for microscopic study

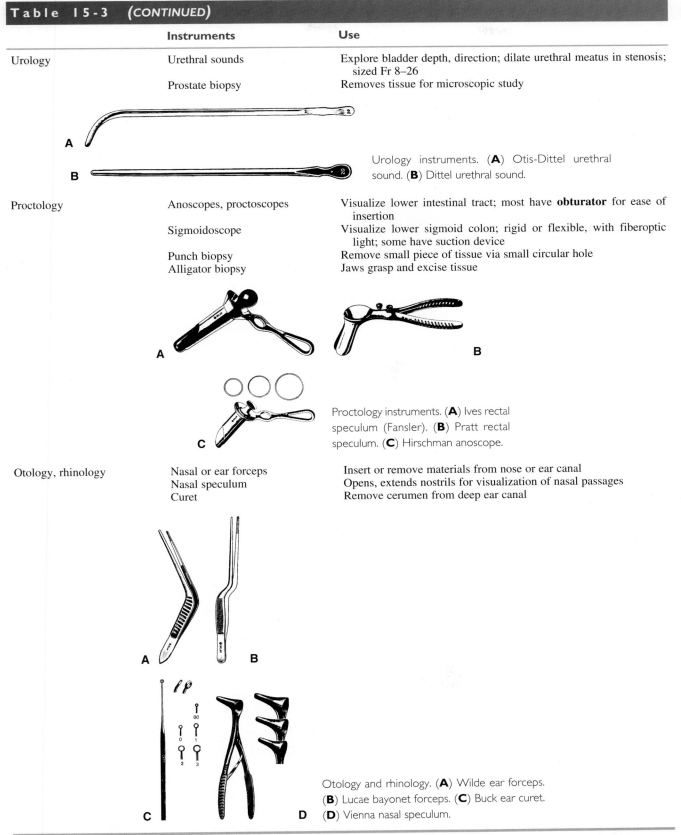

Urology instruments. (**A**) Otis-Dittel urethral sound. (**B**) Dittel urethral sound.

	Instruments	Use
Proctology	Anoscopes, proctoscopes	Visualize lower intestinal tract; most have **obturator** for ease of insertion
	Sigmoidoscope	Visualize lower sigmoid colon; rigid or flexible, with fiberoptic light; some have suction device
	Punch biopsy	Remove small piece of tissue via small circular hole
	Alligator biopsy	Jaws grasp and excise tissue

Proctology instruments. (**A**) Ives rectal speculum (Fansler). (**B**) Pratt rectal speculum. (**C**) Hirschman anoscope.

	Instruments	Use
Otology, rhinology	Nasal or ear forceps	Insert or remove materials from nose or ear canal
	Nasal speculum	Opens, extends nostrils for visualization of nasal passages
	Curet	Remove cerumen from deep ear canal

Otology and rhinology. (**A**) Wilde ear forceps. (**B**) Lucae bayonet forceps. (**C**) Buck ear curet. (**D**) Vienna nasal speculum.

(continued)

Table 15-3 (CONTINUED)

	Instruments	Use
Ophthalmology	Eye loop, lid retractor Tonometer	Hold eyelids open for removal of foreign bodies Measure intraocular pressure to diagnose glaucoma

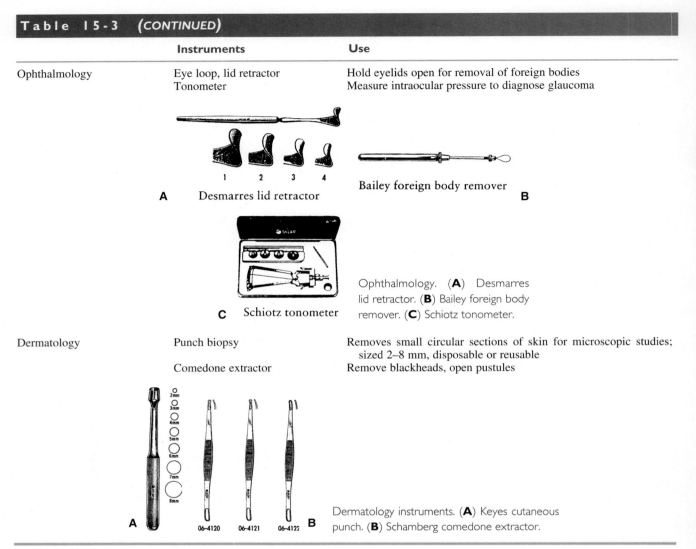

Ophthalmology. (**A**) Desmarres lid retractor. (**B**) Bailey foreign body remover. (**C**) Schiotz tonometer.

	Instruments	Use
Dermatology	Punch biopsy Comedone extractor	Removes small circular sections of skin for microscopic studies; sized 2–8 mm, disposable or reusable Remove blackheads, open pustules

Dermatology instruments. (**A**) Keyes cutaneous punch. (**B**) Schamberg comedone extractor.

Fr, French.

Towel Clamps

Towel clamps are used to maintain the integrity of the sterile field by holding the sterile drapes in place, allowing exposure of the operative site (Fig. 15-7). A sterile field is a specific area that is considered free of all microorganisms.

Probes and Directors

Before entering a cavity or site for a procedure, the physician may first probe the depth and direction of the operative area. A probe shows the angle and depth of the operative area, and a director guides the knife or instrument once the procedure has begun (Fig. 15-8).

Retractors

Retractors hold open layers of tissue, exposing the areas beneath. They may be plain or toothed; the toothed retractor may be sharp or blunt. Retractors may be designed to be held by an assistant or screwed open to be self-retaining. Figure 15-9 shows several types of retractors.

 Checkpoint Question

6. What types of instruments are used to remove tissue during a biopsy?

CARE AND HANDLING OF SURGICAL INSTRUMENTS

To ensure that surgical instruments always function properly, follow these guidelines:

1. Do not toss or drop instruments into a basin or sink. Surgical instruments are delicate, and the blade or tip is easily damaged by improper handling. Should

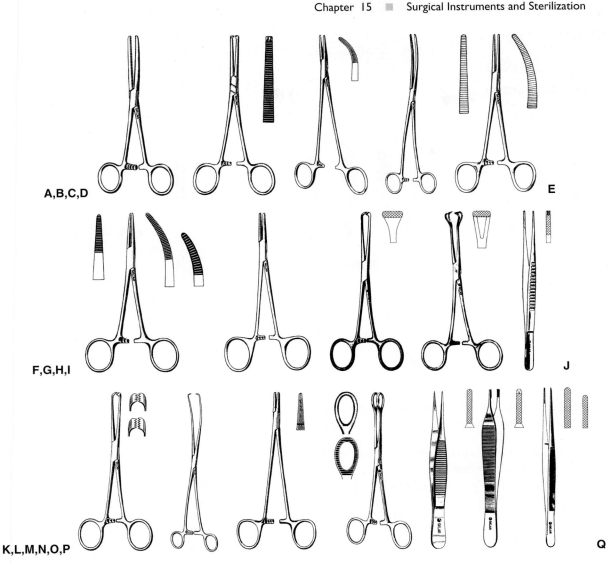

A,B,C,D

E

F,G,H,I

J

K,L,M,N,O,P

Q

FIGURE 15-4. (**A**) Rochester-Pean forceps. (**B**) Rochester-Ochsner forceps. (**C**) Adson forceps. (**D**) Bozeman forceps. (**E**) Crile hemostat. (**F**) Kelly hemostat. (**G**) Halsted mosquito hemostat. (**H**) Allis forceps. (**I**) Babcock forceps. (**J**) De-Bakey forceps. (**K**) Allis tissue forceps. (**L**) Duplay tenaculum forceps. (**M**) Crile-Wood needle holder. (**N**) Ballenger sponge forceps. (**O**) Fine-point splinter forceps. (**P**) Adson dressing forceps. (**Q**) Potts-Smith dressing forceps. (Courtesy of Sklar Instruments, West Chester, PA).

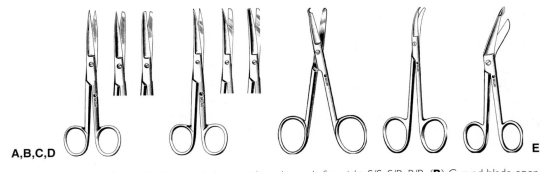

A,B,C,D

E

FIGURE 15-5. (**A**) Straight-blade operating scissors. *Left to right:* S/S, S/B, B/B. (**B**) Curved-blade operating scissors. *Left to right:* S/S, S/B, B/B. (**C**) Spencer stitch scissors. (**D**) Suture scissors. (**E**) Lister bandage scissors. S/S, sharp/sharp; S/B, sharp/blunt; B/B, blunt/blunt. (Courtesy of Sklar Instruments, West Chester, PA).

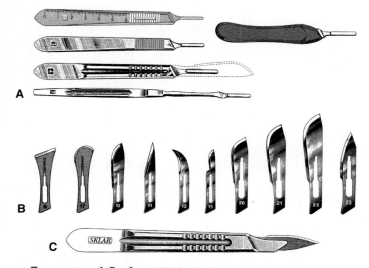

FIGURE 15-6. (**A**) Scalpel handles. (**B**) Surgical blades. (**C**) Complete sterile disposable scalpel. (Courtesy of Sklar Instruments, West Chester, PA).

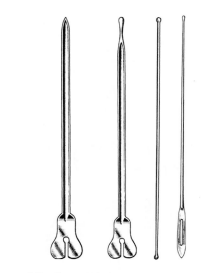

FIGURE 15-8. (**A**). Director and tongue tie. (**B**) Double-ended probe. (**C**) Probe with eye. (Courtesy of Sklar Instruments, West Chester, PA).

you drop an instrument accidentally, carefully inspect it for damage. Damaged instruments can usually be repaired and should not be discarded unless repair is not feasible.

2. Avoid stacking instruments in a pile. They may tangle and be damaged when separated.

3. Always store sharp instruments separately to prevent dulling or damaging the sharp edges and to prevent accidental injury. Disposable scalpel blades should

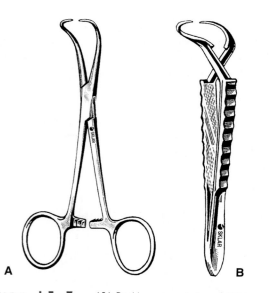

FIGURE 15-7. (**A**) Backhaus towel clamp. (**B**) Jones cross-action towel clamp. (Courtesy of Sklar Instruments, West Chester, PA).

be removed from reusable handles and placed in puncture-proof sharps biohazard containers. If a disposable scalpel is used, the whole unit is discarded into the sharps container. Syringes with needles attached and suture needles should also be discarded in a sharps container, never in the trash or with other instruments for processing. Delicate instruments, such as scissors or tissue forceps or those with lenses, are kept separate to be sanitized and sterilized appropriately.

4. Keep ratcheted instruments open when not in use to avoid damage to the ratchet mechanism.

5. Rinse gross contamination from instruments as soon as possible to prevent drying and hardening, which makes cleaning more difficult. Always wear gloves and follow OSHA standards to prevent contact with possibly infected blood or body fluids.

6. Check instruments before sterilization to ensure that they are in good working order and identify instruments in need of repair.

   A. Blades or points should be free of bends and nicks.

   B. Tips should close evenly and tightly.

   C. Instruments with box locks should move freely but should not be too loose.

   D. Instruments with spring handles should have enough tension to grasp objects tightly.

   E. Scissors should close in a smooth, even manner with no nicks or snags. (Scissors may be checked by cutting through gauze or cotton to be sure there are no rough areas).

   F. Screws should be flush with the instrument surface. They should be freely workable but not loose.

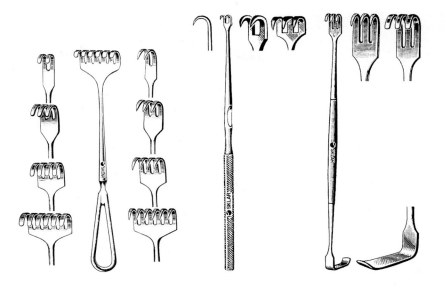

FIGURE 15-9. (**A**) Volkman retractor. (**B**) Lahey retractor. (**C**) Senn retractor. (Courtesy of Sklar Instruments, West Chester, PA).

WHAT IF

While pouring a liquid sterilization solution such as glutaraldehyde into a container, the chemical spills?

OSHA and state regulations have defined a specific law to protect you from hazardous materials. The law, The Right to Know, requires that all companies, including health care facilities, using hazardous materials have material safety data sheets (MSDS) available to their employees. MSDS are prepared by the chemical manufacturer and clearly state how to handle and dispose of the chemical. These forms also include a list of possible health hazards to workers and identify the safety equipment needed for using the chemical. Never handle any type of chemical spill without first reading the MSDS. You are required to add to the MSDS binder any MSDS that accompany any supplies or equipment containing hazardous materials. This notebook should be placed in a stationary area where it can be easily consulted in case of an emergency involving hazardous materials.

7. Use instruments only for the purpose for which they were designed. For instance, never use surgical scissors to cut paper or open packages, because this may damage the cutting edges.
8. Sanitize instruments before they are sterilized so that sterilization will work effectively.

Checkpoint Question

7. Why should you avoid dropping surgical instruments, and what should you do if one drops accidentally?

STORAGE AND RECORD KEEPING

When using and maintaining sterile instruments, equipment and supplies, staff are responsible for correctly storing these items, keeping accurate records of warranties and maintenance agreements and keeping reordering information on hand. Most offices have specific storage or supply areas for keeping sterile and other instruments and equipment. This area should be kept clean and dust free and should be close to the area of need. Clean and sterile supplies and equipment must be separated from soiled items and waste.

Allied health professionals may also be responsible for keeping accurate records of sterilized items and equipment. Information that must be recorded includes maintenance records and load or sterilization records. These records should include the following:

- date and time of the sterilization cycle
- general description of the load
- exposure time and temperature
- name or initials of the operator
- results of the sterilization indicator
- expiration date of the load (usually 30 days).

The maintenance records include service provided by the manufacturer's representative and daily or recommended maintenance to keep the equipment in optimum working condition.

Checkpoint Question

8. What six items should be included on a sterilization record?

MAINTAINING SURGICAL SUPPLIES

Up-to-date master lists of all supplies, including purchases and replacements, should be kept. Generally, one person is responsible for maintaining inventory, keeping maintenance schedules, and placing orders. If too many staff are involved, these tasks may be overlooked or efforts may be duplicated. Instruction manuals for all equipment should be kept on file and consulted when ordering supplies for replacement or maintenance. Equipment records for each item should include the following:

- date of purchase
- model and serial numbers of the equipment
- time of recommended service
- date service was requested

- name of the person requesting the service
- reason for the service request
- description of the service performed and any parts replaced
- name of the person performing the service and the date the work was completed
- signature and title of the person who acknowledged completion of the work.

Warranties and guarantees should be kept with the equipment records, along with the name of the manufacturer's contact person. A tickler file should be kept to remind the staff of the need for manufacturer service and concurrent or periodic maintenance by the staff.

Parts and supplies for items that are vital to the operation of the facility should always be kept on hand. The shelf life of the item, the storage space available, and the time required to order and receive an item should be considered when deciding what items to keep in inventory. If a piece of equipment cannot function without all of its components or if some of those components have a short life, replacements must be readily available. For example, an ophthalmoscope without a light is virtually useless.

Procedure 15-1

Sanitizing Equipment for Disinfection or Sterilization

Purpose: Properly sanitize instruments in preparation for disinfection or sterilization.

Equipment: Instruments or equipment to be sanitized, gloves, eye protection, impervious gown, soap and water, small handheld scrub brush.

Standard: This procedure should take 10 minutes.

Steps	Reason
1. Put on gloves, gown, and eye protection.	These devices protect against splattering and prevent contamination of your clothes.
2. Take any removable sections apart. If cleaning is not possible immediately, soak the instrument or equipment to prevent their sticking together.	
3. Check for operation and integrity of the equipment. Defective equipment should be repaired or discarded appropriately according to office policy.	
4. Rinse the instrument with cool water.	Hot water cooks proteins on, making the contaminants more difficult to remove.
5. After the initial rinse, force streams of soapy water through any tubular or grooved instruments to clean the inside as well as the outside.	
6. Use a hot, soapy solution to dissolve fats or lubricants on the surface. Use the soaking solution indicated by office policy.	
7. After soaking for 5 to 10 minutes, use friction with a soft brush or gauze to wipe down the instrument and loosen transient microorganisms. Abrasive materials should not be used on delicate instruments and equipment. Brushes work well on grooves and joints. Open and close the jaws of scissors or forceps several times to ensure that all material has been removed.	
8. Rinse well.	Proper rinsing removes soap or detergent residue and any remaining microorganisms.
9. Dry well before autoclaving or soaking in disinfectant.	Excess moisture decreases the effectiveness of the autoclave by delaying drying, and it dilutes the disinfectant.
10. Any items (brushes, gauze, solution) used in sanitation are considered grossly contaminated and must be properly disinfected or discarded.	

Procedure 15-2

Wrapping Instruments for Sterilization in an Autoclave

Purpose: Properly prepare and wrap instruments for sterilization in the autoclave.

Equipment: Instruments or equipment to be sterilized, wrapping material, autoclave tape, sterilization indicator, black or blue ink pen.

Standard: This procedure should take 10 minutes.

Steps	Reason
1. Assemble the equipment and supplies. Check the instruments being wrapped for working order.	Any instruments found to be defective, broken, or otherwise needing repair should not be wrapped or autoclaved.
2. Be sure that the wrapping material has these properties: • Permeable to steam but not contaminants • Resists tearing and puncturing during normal handling • Allows for easy opening to prevent contamination of the contents • Maintains sterility of the contents during storage	The wrap may be double layers of cotton muslin, special paper, or appropriately sized instrument pouches.

A

B

Step 2. Autoclave pouches are convenient and come in a variety of sizes.

3. Tear off one or two pieces of autoclave tape. On one piece, indicate in ink the contents of the pack or the name of the instrument that will be wrapped, the date, and your initials.	After the item is wrapped, the contents cannot be seen. Also, dating the package allows the user to determine the quality of the contents based on the amount of time (usually 30 days) that sterilized contents are considered sterile.

(continued)

Procedure 15-2 *(continued)*

Wrapping Instruments for Sterilization in an Autoclave

Steps	Purpose
4. When using autoclave wrapping material made of cotton muslin or special paper, begin by laying the material diagonally on a flat, clean, dry surface. Place the instrument in the center of the wrapping material with the ratchets or handles open. Include a sterilization indicator.	The ratchets should be left open during autoclaving to allow steam to penetrate and sterilize all surfaces.

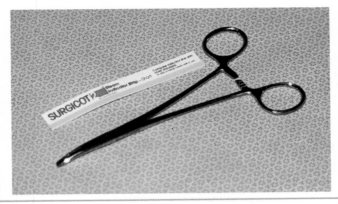

Step 4. The ratchets are open.

Steps	Purpose
5. Fold the first flap at the bottom of the diagonal wrap up and fold back the corner making a tab.	Making a tab allows for easier opening of the pack without contaminating the contents.

Step 5. Make a tab with the corner.

(continued)

Procedure 15-2   *(continued)*

Wrapping Instruments for Sterilization in an Autoclave

Steps	Purpose
6. Fold the left corner of the wrap, then the right, each making a tab for opening the package. Secure the package with autoclave tape.	

Step 6. The bottom, left, and right corners of the wrap are folded.

7. Fold the top corner down, making the tab tucked under the material.

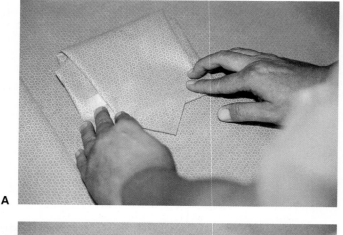

A

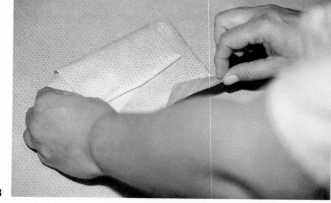

B

Step 7. **(A)** The top corner is folded down. **(B)** Secure the wrapped instrument package with autoclave tape.

Procedure 15-3

Operating an Autoclave

Purpose: Safely sterilize instruments or equipment using an autoclave.

Equipment: Sanitized and wrapped instruments or equipment, distilled water, autoclave operating manual

Standard: This procedure should take 1 hour.

Steps	Reason
1. Assemble the equipment, including the wrapped articles and the sterilization indicator in each package according to office policy.	Some offices want a separately wrapped indicator autoclaved with the load for checking that the procedure was performed properly without opening a pack.
2. Check the water level of the autoclave reservoir and add more if needed.	Use only distilled water in the reservoir tank.
3. Add water to the internal chamber of the autoclave to the fill line.	Too little water makes too little steam; too much water may cause saturated steam, extending drying time, and may wick microorganisms into the damp packages.
4. Load the autoclave:	
A. Place trays and packs on their sides 1 to 3 inches apart.	Air circulation is not possible if items are tightly packed. Vertical placement forces out heavier air rather than pooling in the containers.
B. Put containers on their side with the lid off.	Air can circulate in containers on their side with the lid off.
C. In mixed loads, place hard objects on the bottom shelf and softer packs on the top racks.	Hard objects may form condensation that will drip onto softer items and wet them.
5. Read the instructions and close to the machine. Most machines follow the same protocol: A. Close the door and secure or lock it. B. Turn the machine on. C. When the temperature gauge reaches the point required for the contents of the load (usually 250°F), set the timer. Many autoclaves can be programmed for the required time. D. When the timer indicates that the cycle is over, vent the chamber. E. After releasing the pressure to a safe level, crack the door of the autoclave to allow additional drying. Most loads dry in 5–20 mins. Hard items dry faster than soft ones.	

(continued)

Procedure 15-3   (continued)

Operating an Autoclave

Steps	Reason
6. When the load has cooled, remove the items.	
7. Check the separately wrapped sterilization indicator, if used, for proper sterilization.	If the indicator registers that the load was properly processed, the items in the additional packs are considered sterile; if not, the items should be considered not sterile and the load must be reprocessed.
8. Store the items in a clean, dry, dust-free area for 30 days.	After 30 days, reprocessing is necessary. The pack need not be rewrapped, but the autoclave tape should be replaced with new tape with the current date.
9. Clean the autoclave per manufacturer's suggestions, usually by scrubbing the interior chamber with a mild detergent and a soft brush. Attention to the exhaust valve will prevent lint from occluding the outlet. Rinse the machine thoroughly and allow it to dry.	Always follow the manufacturer's recommendations for cleaning the autoclave.

CHAPTER SUMMARY

Most areas of the health care facility require medical asepsis to maintain cleanliness and prevent the spread of infection to the patients and staff. However, when body tissues need repair or must be opened surgically, sterile technique or surgical asepsis is required. Allied health professionals may be responsible for maintaining surgical asepsis, which necessitates that they understand the principles and practices of medical and surgical asepsis, know disinfection and sterilization techniques, use equipment to sterilize and disinfect, and keep accurate records and adequate supplies on hand.

Critical Thinking Challenges

1. Create a record that can be used to document sterilization using the autoclave.
2. Research the various types of commercial cold chemical sterilization solutions. Design a step-by-step procedure for using the solution to disinfect and sterilize. Note any hazards or safety precautions that should be followed when working with the chemical.

Answers to Checkpoint Questions

1. Sanitation is maintenance of a healthful, disease-free environment by removing organic matter and other residue. Disinfection is destruction of pathogenic microorganisms but not their spores. Sterilization destroys all microorganisms and their spores on an item or instrument.
2. An autoclave is a steam pressure chamber for sterilizing medical instruments or supplies. Distilled water is converted to steam, and as the pressure increases, the temperature of the steam increases to allow for destruction of microorganisms and their spores.
3. Autoclave tape is used on the outside of a wrapped instrument or pack to identify the contents of the pack, the date the item was autoclaved, and the initials of the person who wrapped the pack. After exposure to steam, dark brown or black stripes will appear on the tape, acknowledging that the pack has been processed in the autoclave or exposed to steam. Sterilization indicators are placed inside the pack to indicate sterility of the contents.
4. Load the autoclave loosely; do not try to pack too many items in at once, because the steam cannot penetrate to items in the center of a crowded chamber. Place empty containers on their sides with the lids off and place all packs on their sides

to allow for maximum steam circulation and penetration.

5. The time indicated for sterilization should be started only after the appropriate temperature has been reached, since the temperature and time are both important for destruction of microorganisms and their spores. Items that have been exposed to the high temperature for less time than indicated by the manufacturer of the autoclave may not be sterile.

6. Forceps may be used to remove tissue for biopsy.

7. Because surgical instruments are delicate, improper handling may easily damage sharp blades or pointed tips. If you do drop an instrument, inspect it carefully for damage. Many instruments are expensive, but damaged instruments can usually be repaired.

8. The six items to include on a sterilization record are (1) date and time of the cycle, (2) a general description of the load, (3) time and temperature,(4) name or initials of the operator, (5) results of the sterilization indicator, and (6) load expiration date.

 Websites

Medical Resources New and Reconditioned Equipment: Midmark and Ritter Autoclaves
www.medicalresources.com

Amsco autoclaves and sterilizers: Alfa Medical
www.sterilizers.com

Sklar surgical instruments www.sklarcorp.com

Glutaraldehyde occupational hazards
www.cdc.gov/niosh/2001-115.html

Glutaraldehyde guidelines for safe use and handling in health care facilities
www.state.nj.us/health/eoh/survweb/glutar.pdf

Occupational Safety and Health Administration
www.governmentguide.com

The Clinical Laboratory

CHAPTER OBJECTIVES

In this chapter, you'll learn:

1. To spell and define the key terms.
2. To list reasons for laboratory testing.
3. To outline the allied health professional's responsibility in the clinical laboratory.
4. To name the kinds of laboratories where allied health professionals work and the functions of each.
5. To list the types of personnel in laboratories and describe their jobs.
6. To explain how to use a package insert to determine the procedure for a laboratory test.
7. To list the equipment found in most small laboratories and give the purpose of each.
8. To list and describe the parts of a microscope.
9. To explain the significance of the Clinical Laboratory Improvement Amendments and how to follow their regulations to ensure quality control.
10. To define OSHA and state its purpose.
11. To list the laboratory safety guidelines.

PERFORMANCE OBJECTIVE

In this chapter, you'll learn:

1. To care for the microscope (Procedure 16-1).

KEY TERMS

aerosol
calibration
capillary action
centrifugal force

Clinical Laboratory
  Improvement
  Amendments (CLIA)
material safety data sheet
  (MSDS)

National Committee for
  Clinical Laboratory
  Standards (NCCLS)
normal values

quality assurance (QA)
quality control (QC)
reagent
reportable range
specimen

THE MEDICAL LABORATORY provides the allied health professional with some of medicine's most powerful diagnostic tools. Laboratory staff analyze blood, urine, and other body samples to facilitate identification of diseases and disorders. Results of laboratory testing are compared with normal or reference values (acceptable ranges for a healthy population) to determine the relative health of body systems or organs. Blood levels of various medications are determined to adjust dosages to therapeutic levels. Bacteria, viruses, parasites, and other microorganisms are identified to begin the treatment process.

Laboratory testing is most commonly used for the following:

- Detecting and diagnosing disease
- Following the progress of a disease and its response to treatment
- Meeting legal requirements (e.g., drug testing, a marriage license)
- Monitoring a patient's medication and treatment
- Determining the levels of essential substances in the body
- Identifying the cause of an infection
- Determining a baseline value
- Preventing disease

As an allied health professional, you have an important role in laboratory analysis — even when testing is performed at sites other than the facility. In general, you may be responsible for the following:

- Informing patients of the proper procedure or preparation for obtaining laboratory **specimens** (samples, such as blood or urine, used to evaluate a patient's condition)
- Obtaining a quality specimen
- Arranging for appropriate transport if the specimen is to be analyzed at another site
- Performing common laboratory tests in the facility
- Documenting and maintaining a **quality assurance** (**QA**) program designed to ensure thorough patient care and a **quality control** (**QC**) protocol designed to monitor and evaluate testing procedures, supplies, and equipment to ensure accuracy in laboratory performance
- Maintaining laboratory instruments and equipment to manufacturers' standards

Allied health professionals also may control the purchase of laboratory supplies and selection of **reagents**, substances used to produce a reaction in tests. In addition, you may be in charge of biohazard safety and waste disposal for the workplace. This chapter outlines the basic information you will need to ensure the quality of the laboratory testing in your facility.

TYPES OF LABORATORIES

Three types of laboratories significant to the allied health professionals are reference, hospital, and physician office laboratories (POLs). Hospital and reference laboratories may perform hundreds of specialized tests and may process thousands of specimens per day. In contrast, POLs perform only a few types of tests on a limited number of patients.

Reference Laboratory

A reference or referral laboratory is a large facility, similar to a factory, in which thousands of tests of various types are performed each day. A reference laboratory's direct patient contact is limited to its own satellite specimen procurement stations. It also receives specimens from physicians' offices, hospitals, and clinics across the region it serves. The specimens are delivered by special courier, U.S. mail, or other ground or air transportation delivery service. Specimens sent to reference laboratories must be packaged to withstand rough handling, pressure changes, and temperature extremes during shipment. Packaging includes placement in a special leak-proof secondary transport container (Fig. 16-1) that meets federal regulations for transportation of biohazardous materials.

Tests are performed in bulk test runs, and results and reports are managed by information systems. Reference laboratories usually are not responsible for reporting test results to patients. Test results generally are returned to the referring health care professional, who relays the results to the patient.

Employees of reference laboratories have specific job descriptions. Specimen processors accept (receive) the specimens and log patient data and specimen information into the computer, which assigns each specimen an accession (testing) number. Processors also centrifuge, separate, and prepare aliquots (a portion of a specimen used for testing) if indicated and send them to the correct departments for testing.

Testing is performed by medical technologists, medical laboratory technicians, or laboratory assistants, depending on the complexity of the procedure. Most testing is performed in large batches on automated instruments. Test personnel are responsible for QC procedures, such as checking instruments, performing daily maintenance, and running

FIGURE 16-1. Transport containers are constructed to maintain the integrity of the specimen and to protect those who are responsible for the care and handling of possibly hazardous bodily fluids and substances.

FIGURE 16-2. Laboratory request forms.

control specimens. Test duties include loading specimens and reagents into the instruments to perform test runs and managing test results by accepting or rejecting, recording, and reporting results of QC and patient specimens.

Customer (or client) services personnel answer questions from sites submitting specimens, track specimens, report results, add or delete tests requested by health care providers, and troubleshoot problems primarily by phone. Allied health professionals may work in specimen processing or client services. They may also be employed in testing, provided they meet the Clinical Laboratory Improvements Amendments of 1988 (CLIA 1988) federal requirements, which include documented testing experience and supervision by a CLIA-qualified person.

Hospital Laboratory

The hospital laboratory serves inpatients (patients who stay overnight or longer) and outpatients (patients who come for services and leave the same day).

The hospital laboratory staff includes phlebotomists to collect and sometimes process blood specimens, laboratory assistants to collect and process specimens and perform limited testing, and medical laboratory technicians and medical technologists to perform most of the testing. Laboratories also have receptionists or secretaries, who process outpatients and manage the large volume of requisitions, test results, and other information and paperwork generated daily. Allied health professionals work as laboratory secretaries, receptionists, phlebotomists, or laboratory assistants.

Hospital test menus are restricted to the most commonly requested tests and tests for which results are needed immediately. Less commonly ordered tests are sent to reference laboratories. Whether the test is performed on site or sent to a reference laboratory, results generally are available within 24 to 48 hours. Results for some of the less common or more sophisticated tests may take a week or longer.

Laboratory Request Forms

Hospital and reference laboratories provide request forms appropriate to their individual operations (Fig. 16-2). All forms should be convenient to use, with clear instructions for complete patient and health care professionals identification to avoid errors. Most request forms cover a variety of tests, so that a single form can be used for tests in hematology, chemistry, immunology, and so on. Some forms serve as both request and report form, listing expected values by test. Many requisitions now contain bar codes that allow fast, accurate processing and reduce specimen identification errors. Most hospitals use computer-generated forms that also contain specimen labels. Box 16-1 lists the information required on all laboratory request forms.

Physician Office Laboratory

The most common type of laboratory is the POL, which may vary greatly in size and quality. POLs generally perform a limited number of waived (or low complexity) to moderate-complexity tests. Samples for less common or high-complexity tests may be obtained here but are sent to hospital or reference laboratories for testing.

The most common tests in this type of laboratory are urinalysis, blood cell counts, hemoglobin and hematocrit, and blood glucose or cholesterol levels. In POLs, pregnancy tests and quick screening tests for diseases such as mononucleosis and strep throat are also available. Like hospital and reference laboratories, POLs use forms that list normal ranges for various tests (Fig. 16-3 on page 229).

Box 16-1

LABORATORY REQUEST FORMS: COMMONLY REQUIRED INFORMATION

- Patient's database. This includes name, address, social security number, and the facility identification number to avoid errors with identical names. Other identifying information may be included.
- Patient's birth date and gender. Many test results vary with age and sex.
- Date and time of collection. Often test results are affected by the passage of time or the time of day the specimen was collected.
- Health care professional's name and address or identification number. Results may have to be reported immediately; this information also avoids errors in reporting.
- Checklist of the test or tests to be performed. These may be grouped under one heading as a profile, such as a thyroid profile or a liver profile, which includes more than one test to determine the state of health of one organ, or a general health profile, such as a complete blood count.

Other required information may include the source of the specimen, such as culture swabs for microbiology tests; medications the patient is taking that may alter certain test results (e.g., anticoagulants affecting prothrombin time); directions for reporting (e.g., an immediate need should be marked STAT); and total volume of a 24-hour urine specimen.

A POL may have allied health professionals who, in addition to other tasks, perform laboratory duties: collecting samples, performing tests, managing QC, maintaining instruments, keeping accurate records, and reporting results. Allied health professionals may perform all of these tasks, only if a supervisor monitors QC and abnormal results.

Checkpoint Question

1. What is a reference laboratory, and how does it differ from a POL? Name and describe the kinds of positions that an allied health professional may hold in a reference laboratory.

LABORATORY PERSONNEL

Within the various departments of reference and hospital laboratories, specially trained professionals oversee laboratory operations or perform testing required by allied health care professionals. Each professional position requires a particular level of education and training and has specific responsibilities (Box 16-2).

Box 16-2

LABORATORY PERSONNEL

- Pathologist. A physician who studies disease processes. Commonly, a pathologist oversees the technical aspects of a laboratory, a histology department, or an immunohematology department.
- Chief technologist or laboratory manager. A supervisor who manages the day-to-day operations of a laboratory, including staffing, test menu and pricing, purchasing, and QC.
- Medical technologist or clinical laboratory scientist. A graduate of a bachelor's (4-year) degree program (or equivalent) in medical laboratory science, who has been certified by a national certification agency. Laboratory technologists perform all levels of testing and often supervise laboratory departments.
- Medical laboratory technician or clinical laboratory technician. A graduate of an associate (2-year) degree program (or equivalent) in medical laboratory science who is nationally certified. Laboratory technicians perform specimen testing within limits defined by CLIA.
- Laboratory assistant. A person with a high school diploma or equivalent who is a graduate of a vocational or on-the-job laboratory assistant training program. Laboratory assistants collect and process specimens and can perform waived and certain moderately complex testing if CLIA qualified.
- Phlebotomist. A professional trained to draw blood and to process blood and other samples. A phlebotomist may be an allied health professional, or person trained specifically in phlebotomy. A nationally certified phlebotomist has a high school diploma or equivalent and either is a graduate of an approved training program or has a minimum of 1 year of full-time work in phlebotomy.
- Histologist. A technician trained to process and evaluate tissue samples, such as biopsy or surgical samples.
- Cytologist. A professional trained to examine cells under the microscope and to look for abnormal changes; Pap smears are generally examined by cytologists.
- Specimen processor or accessioner. A professional trained to accept shipments of specimens and to centrifuge, separate, or otherwise process the samples to prepare them for testing. In addition, this position usually includes numbering and labeling the specimens and entering specimen information into a computer.

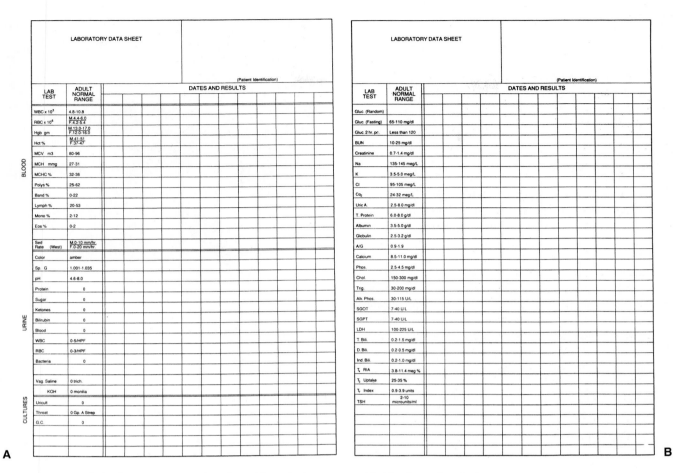

LAB TEST	ADULT NORMAL RANGE	DATES AND RESULTS

BLOOD

LAB TEST	ADULT NORMAL RANGE
WBC x 10³	4.8-10.8
RBC x 10⁶	M.4.4-6.0 F.4.2-5.4
Hgb gm	M.13.0-17.0 F.12.0-16.0
Hct %	M.41-51 F.37-47
MCV m3	80-96
MCH mmg	27-31
MCHC %	32-36
Polys %	25-62
Band %	0-22
Lymph %	20-53
Mono %	2-12
Eos %	0-2
Sed Rate (West)	M.0-10 mm/hr. F.0-20 mm/hr.

URINE

LAB TEST	ADULT NORMAL RANGE
Color	amber
Sp. G	1.001-1.035
pH	4.6-8.0
Protein	0
Sugar	0
Ketones	0
Bilirubin	0
Blood	0
WBC	0-5/HPF
RBC	0-3/HPF
Bacteria	0
Vag. Saline	0 trich.
KOH	0 monilia

CULTURES

LAB TEST	ADULT NORMAL RANGE
Uricult	0
Throat	0 Gp. A Strep
G.C.	0

LAB TEST	ADULT NORMAL RANGE
Gluc. (Random)	
Gluc. (Fasting)	65-110 mg/dl
Gluc. 2 hr. pc.	Less than 120
BUN	10-25 mg/dl
Creatinine	0.7-1.4 mg/dl
Na	135-145 meq/L
K	3.5-5.0 meq/L
Cl	95-105 meq/L
CO₂	24-32 meq/L
Uric A.	2.5-8.0 mg/dl
T. Protein	6.0-8.0 g/dl
Albumin	3.5-5.0 g/dl
Globulin	2.5-3.2 g/dl
A/G	0.9-1.9
Calcium	8.5-11.0 mg/dl
Phos.	2.5-4.5 mg/dl
Chol.	150-300 mg/dl
Trig.	30-200 mg/dl
Alk. Phos.	30-115 U/L
SGOT	7-40 U/L
SGPT	7-40 U/L
LDH	100-225 U/L
T. Bili.	0.2-1.5 mg/dl
D. Bili.	0.2-0.5 mg/dl
Ind. Bili.	0.2-1.0 mg/dl
T₄ RIA	3.8-11.4 meq %
T₃ Uptake	25-35 %
T₇ Index	0.9-3.9 units
TSH	2-10 microunits/ml

A   B

FIGURE 16-3. Laboratory data sheet. Normal values are provided for the various tests.

LABORATORY EQUIPMENT

Laboratory equipment and supplies come in hundreds of types and sizes. It is not necessary to become familiar with every possible type of laboratory equipment. However, a few basic pieces are common to most small laboratories.

LEGAL TIP

Test Results

People who work in laboratories have access to the results of many confidential blood and urine tests, such as tests for HIV, drugs, pregnancy, and sexually transmitted diseases. They have an ethical responsibility not to communicate any results to unauthorized persons. Only patients and their healthcare providers are entitled to the results. The only exception is the provision in state laws requiring the reporting of certain test results for public safety; however, reporting this information is not the responsibility of the allied health professional.

Box 16-3

UNDERSTANDING KIT PACKAGE INSERTS

Test package inserts provide the following basic pieces of information:

- Procedure. Explains the test method in numbered steps, usually with illustrations.
- Test principles. Outlines the test.
- Specimen required. Tells whether the test is done on blood, urine, or other body fluids and what collection method is acceptable.
- Reagents needed (or included). Lists the reagents in the kit and any other reagents or materials necessary to perform the test.
- Quality control. States recommendations for testing procedures to ensure that test results are accurate.
- Expected values. Lists **normal values** for comparison to results obtained.
- Interferences. Explains any factors that may alter test results or compromise test accuracy.

These include the following:

- Automated cell counter
- Microscope
- Chemistry analyzer
- Centrifuge
- Incubator
- Refrigerator or freezer
- Glassware

Cell Counter

A cell counter is an automated analyzer used to test blood specimens. The simplest cell counter counts only red and white blood cells and performs hemoglobin and hematocrit testing. Specimens are inserted individually, and results may be printed or read from a screen.

Cell counters also include more complex analyzers that accept hundreds of specimens and perform 12 to 15 tests and calculations on each specimen. Allied health professionals test specimens using a cell counter if they have received documented training in its use from a CLIA-qualified person.

Checkpoint Question

2. Why are package inserts crucial for safe and accurate testing?

Microscope

The microscope (see Fig. 16-4) is used to identify and count cells and microorganisms in blood and various other body specimens. Learning how to use a microscope properly requires time and repeated practice. The compound microscope is the type most commonly used in the health care facility. The compound microscope is a two-lens system in which ocular and objective lenses together provide the total magnification. A light source illuminates the objects as they are magnified. Figure 16-4 shows a microscope and its various parts.

The *frame*, which consists of the arm and base, is the basic structural component of the microscope. The ocular at the top of the instrument is for the user's eye. It is marked with its magnification, usually ×10. Binocular microscopes (two eyepieces) minimize eyestrain and have adjustments to allow for variations in spacing between the user's eyes.

To bring the object to be viewed into focus, the *coarse adjustment knob* is used with the lower-powered objective to focus on the object; the *fine adjustment knob* is used with the higher-powered objective or the oil immersion lens for the greatest definition. Always focus in two steps. First look at the slide and objective from the side (not through the ocular or oculars), bringing the slide very close to the lens. Then look through the ocular or oculars as you move the slide farther from the lens to bring it into focus. This procedure will prevent damage to the lens from contact with the slide.

The *nosepiece* houses three or four objective lenses and rotates to bring the objective into working position. Pressure to

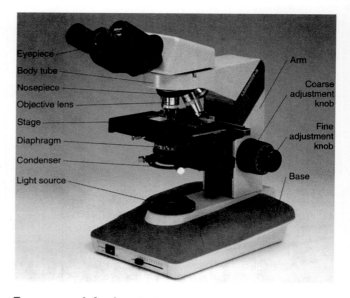

FIGURE 16-4. Basic components of the standard light microscope. (Courtesy of Nikon, Melville, NY.)

the objectives should never be used to rotate lenses. Only the grip should be used to make this adjustment. The magnification power is marked on each objective. The shorter, or low-power, objective, magnifies ×10. The higher power magnifies ×40 for closer observation. With the use of oil, the third objective, called the oil immersion lens, magnifies ×100. Some microscopes have a fourth objective with a ×4 lens to scan larger specimens. To determine the total magnification of a specimen, multiply the magnification of the working objective by the magnification of the ocular lens (×10):

Low power: $10 \times 10 = 100$
High power: $40 \times 10 = 400$
Oil immersion: $100 \times 10 = 1000$

The *stage* is the flat surface that holds the slide for viewing. An opening in the solid surface allows illumination of the slide from below. Many stages have clips to hold the slide in place and to allow manual movement of the slide as needed. Some stages mechanically adjust the position vertically or horizontally by moving adjustment knobs, also called X and Y axis knobs.

The *condenser* concentrates the light rays to focus on the slide. The condenser is adjustable. In the lower position, the light focus is reduced; in the higher position, it is increased.

The *diaphragm*, in the condenser, consists of interlocking plates that adjust into a variable-sized opening, or iris, to regulate the amount of light from the source in conjunction with the condenser. The more highly magnified the slide must be, the greater the need for light.

The *light source* is housed in the base.

Microscopes are delicate, expensive instruments. To ensure that the microscope used in your laboratory is kept in good working order, you must handle it properly and maintain it according to the manufacturer's standards (Procedure 16-1 at end of this chapter). Be sure to place it in a low-traffic area and away from any source of vibration, such as a centrifuge. It should always be covered when not in use.

Checkpoint Question

3. How do the three objective lenses of the microscope differ?

Chemistry Analyzers

Like cell counters, traditional chemistry analyzers vary from simple instruments that perform one or a few tests and require manual operation to complex analyzers that perform 30 or more tests per sample and are operated by computer.

Advances in laboratory instrumentation have led to the development of portable and even hand-held devices for point-of-care testing. These devices are especially suited to POL testing because they are simple to operate, require only small amounts of sample for testing, and provide results in minutes. The machine computes the result and displays it on a screen and/or provides a printout of results.

For high-volume testing and to perform a large variety of tests, a number of bench-top chemistry analyzers are suitable for POL testing. Several use dry reagent technology, in which all reagents are impregnated into a special strip or card. The strip or card is inserted into the machine and a drop of whole blood or serum is applied to the strip with an automated pipette. Other analyzers use wet reagent systems with special reagent packs required for each type of test. These machines can usually be interfaced with a computer to allow for storage and retrieval of results. Whatever the analyzer, the operator must follow the specific manufacturer's instructions for proper care and use.

Centrifuges

A centrifuge uses centrifugal force, or spinning to exert force outward, to separate liquids into their component parts. A whole blood specimen, when centrifuged, is separated into a bottom layer of heavy red blood cells, a thin middle layer of platelets and white blood cells called the buffy coat (Fig. 16-5), and a top liquid layer that is the lightest of the components. The top layer is serum if the specimen was allowed to clot before centrifuging or plasma if the specimen was anticoagulated and not allowed to clot.

Tubes must always be balanced in the centrifuge. If an uneven number of tubes are to be spun, a tube with water must counterbalance the odd tube. Try to place tubes with approximately the same level of liquid in opposing spaces. All tubes must be securely capped. Never start centrifugation until the lid is locked (many will not start until the lid is securely locked). NEVER open the centrifuge until all motion has stopped, and NEVER stop the spin with your hand. Follow the manufacturer's recommendations for cleaning, oiling, and

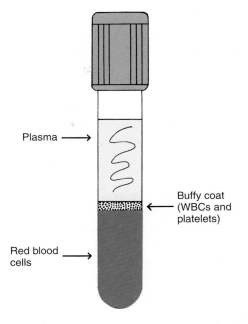

FIGURE 16-5. Centrifuged blood specimen. (Reprinted with permission from McCall R. *Phlebotomy Essentials.* Baltimore: Lippincott Williams & Wilkins, 2003.)

maintaining the equipment. As with all equipment, read the instructions before operation.

A special type of centrifuge called a microhematocrit centrifuge is used to perform a hematocrit test. A special capillary tube filled with blood is spun in the centrifuge. Clay is inserted to seal one end of the tube, and this end is positioned to the outside of the centrifuge to contain the specimen within the capillary tube. The percentage of packed red blood cells compared to the total volume of specimen is determined, and the result is the hematocrit. This is further discussed in the chapter on hematology.

Incubator

Microbiology specimens require a suitable environment to thrive and reproduce. Culture media inoculated with specimens are stored in an incubator for approximately 24 hours to allow microbes to reproduce to a large enough quantity to be identified. The incubator is set at about body temperature (99°F or 37°C), and a daily log is maintained to record the incubator temperature.

Refrigerators and Freezers

Laboratory refrigerators and freezers are similar to those used in the home, but their uses are very different. They are used to store reagents, kits, and specimens. The temperature is critical and must be measured and recorded daily. Food should never be stored in these refrigerators because of the possibility of biohazard contamination. These also vary in size and can be purchased according to office needs and space.

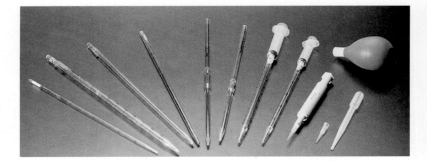

F IGURE 16-6. Assorted pipettes. Pipettes on the right have attached or integrated suction. The bulb at the tip is used for suction with standard pipettes.

Glassware

For general purposes, the term glassware also includes the disposable plastic supplies used in many health care facilities. As with all other medical supplies, sizes and shapes vary with the purpose. Many forms are named for their inventor or for their use. The term glassware includes the following items:

- Beaker. Container with wide mouth for mixing, holding, or heating liquids. Beakers come in various sizes and are used for measurements that need not be exactly precise.

- Flask. Container with narrow neck and a rounded base for holding or transporting liquid in a laboratory. Names include Florence, volumetric, and Erlenmeyer. Volumetric flasks, which have **calibration** lines etched on the neck, are used for critical measurements.
- Glass slide and coverslip. Used with the microscope for holding the specimen to be viewed and usually disposable.
- Graduated cylinder. Used for measuring substances or solutions.

Box 16-4

HOW TO USE A PIPETTE

Hold the pipette upright, not at an angle, with the tip slightly under the surface of the liquid. Use a slight suction on the suction apparatus until the meniscus is slightly above the desired level. Maintain the level by holding your finger over the top of the tube or maintaining constant pressure on the mechanical apparatus. Raise the pipette from the liquid and wipe the tip with a tissue. Allow the bottom of the meniscus curve to reach the desired calibration by releasing a small amount of the liquid into a waste receptacle. With the pipette vertical, place the side of the pipette against the receiving vessel and allow the contents to drain.

Some pipettes, such as the Unopette, have a premeasured amount of reagent supplied. The whole unit is discarded in a biohazard receptacle after use. Reusable glass pipettes and the mechanical components of automated pipettes should be cleaned according to the manufacturer's instructions. Some may be autoclaved after soaking and rinsing, whereas some require special chemical disinfection or sterilization.

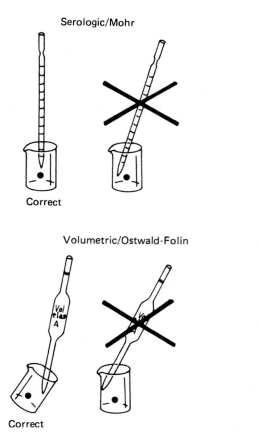

Correct and incorrect pipette positions.

(continued)

Box 16-4 (continued)

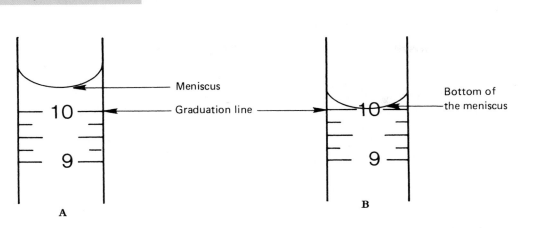

Pipette technique. (**A**) Meniscus is brought above the desired graduation line. (**B**) Liquid is allowed to drain until the bottom of the meniscus touches the desired calibration mark.

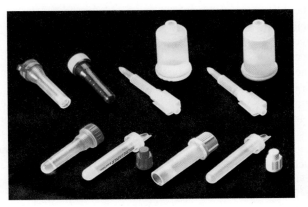

Unopettes are complete units that do not require additional equipment or supplies.

- Petri dish or plate. Shallow, covered dish filled with a solid medium to support the growth of microorganisms.
- Pipette (pipet). Narrow glass or plastic tube, sometimes graduated, open at both ends, used to transport or measure small amounts of liquid. Some pull liquid in by **capillary action**, others by mechanical suction (Fig. 16-6). Pipettes marked TC (to contain) are designed to hold a certain volume; those marked TD (to deliver) are designed to dispense a certain volume. Names include Pasteur, serological, volumetric, and Mohr. Box 16-4 describes how to use a pipette.
- Test tube. Cylindrical container open at one end and rounded or pointed on the other, used for holding laboratory specimens.

Figure 16-7 displays various kinds of glassware.

LABORATORY SAFETY

Allied health professionals must always be safety conscious when using laboratory equipment. All specimens studied in the laboratory should be considered hazardous and must be treated as such. An allied health professional who is aware of the types of hazards in the clinical laboratory is likely to work safely and avoid injury.

FIGURE 16-7. Glassware. *Left to right*: beakers, Erlenmyer flasks, graduated cylinders, volumetric flasks. *Front*: test tube.

There are three basic types of hazards in the laboratory:

- Physical hazards (fire, broken glass, liquid spills)
- Chemical hazards (acids, alkalis, chemical fumes)
- Biological hazards (diseases such as HIV, hepatitis, and tuberculosis)

Physical hazards include fires caused by an electrical malfunction. Staff must be able to find and operate fire extinguishers and identify fire escape routes. Maintaining and using electrical equipment by the manufacturer's instructions will reduce fire hazards. Avoid using extension cords and overloading electrical circuits. Before servicing any electrical equipment, unplug the instrument.

Chemical hazards can be minimized by labeling all chemicals with the **material safety data sheet** (**MSDS**) information. MSDS provide the manufacturer's instructions for storage, handling and disposal of the chemical. They describe the risks associated with the product and indicate steps necessary to prevent exposure. An up-to-date volume of MSDS for all chemicals used in the laboratory is the focal part of the facility's chemical hygiene plan. The plan should also include chemical safety protocols specific to that facility.

Hazardous chemicals may have additional labels of precaution. The National Fire Protection Association developed a classification system to identify areas where hazardous chemicals and other materials are stored. This system uses a diamond-shaped symbol, divided into four quadrants, to represent different types of hazards (Fig. 16-8 on page 235). The BLUE section indicates health hazards; the RED section indicates fire hazards; and the YELLOW section indicates reactive hazards. The WHITE is left blank unless there is a specific hazard such as an oxidizer, water reactive, or radiation hazard. There will be a number from 0 (no hazard) to 4 (serious hazard) in each colored section. Hazardous materials classification posters should be prominently displayed in all laboratory areas.

Biological hazards refer to specimens capable of transmitting disease. Personal protective equipment (PPE) used per Occupational Safety and Health Administration (OSHA) requirements and strict compliance with handwashing protocols are the best tools for preventing exposure.

Methods for handling each of these hazards must be outlined in detail in your facility's policy and procedure manual. Each member of the staff must be familiar with safety protocols to ensure that risks are kept to a minimum.

Occupational Safety and Health Administration

OSHA is a federal agency in the U.S. Department of Labor that monitors and protects the health and safety of workers. OSHA standards are federal regulations that protect workers by eliminating or minimizing chemical, physical, and biological hazards and preventing accidents. OSHA standards supersede all other regulatory agency requirements. Two OSHA standards of particular importance to medical laboratories are the Occupational Exposure to Blood-borne Pathogens Standard and the Hazardous Communication (Haz-Com) Standard, or the "right to know law."

Prevention of disease transmission in a health care facility is often called infection control or biohazard risk management. The OSHA Blood-borne Pathogens Standard requires all health care employers to provide training for their employees in techniques that will protect them from occupational exposure to infectious agents, including blood-borne pathogens. Safety manuals must be available or incorporated into the policies and procedures manual to guide employees in correct procedures and emergency protocols.

In addition, OSHA standards require that all workers who are at risk for exposure to potentially hazardous material wear PPE supplied by the employer and readily available for use. PPE includes the following:

- Gloves
- Gown
- Apron
- Face shield
- Goggles
- Glasses with side shields
- Mask
- Lab coat

Workers who are sensitive to allergens such as latex must be supplied with latex-free equipment.

All PPE must be appropriate to the level of exposure. An allied health professional performing phlebotomy or assisting with collection of most tissue samples is safe with glove protection. Situations that may result in splashes, splatters, or spreading of an **aerosol** (particles suspended in gas or air), however, require full coverage, including a face shield and footwear, such as shoe covers.

According to OSHA requirements, employers are required to provide free immunization against hepatitis B virus and other blood-borne pathogens if vaccines are available to employees within 10 days of being assigned to duties with possible exposure to blood-borne pathogens. Patient care and laboratory test duties carry the risk of exposure to blood-borne pathogens. Exposure can occur if the skin is pierced or if any body fluid splashes into the eyes, nose, mouth, other opening, or abrasion.

The OSHA HazCom Standard requires all hazardous materials to be labeled by their manufacturers. Hazardous chemicals must be labeled with a warning, such as "danger"; a statement of the hazard, such as "flammable"; precautions to avoid exposure; and first aid measures for exposure incidents. In addition, manufacturers must supply a MSDS for their products. Employers are responsible for obtaining or developing a protocol for each hazardous agent used on site. This protocol should include an MSDS supplied by the manufacturer for each substance used in the facility. The extensive information on the MSDS includes items such as storage guidelines, flammability, and exposure precautions. These sheets should be maintained in a binder near the site of use and should be reviewed routinely by all facility staff (Box 16-5 on page 236).

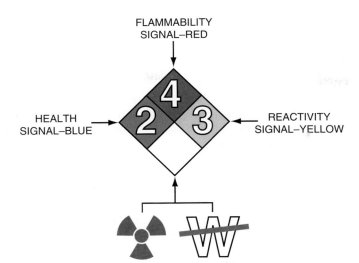

RADIOACTIVE OR WATER REACTIVE

Identification of Health Hazard Color Code: **BLUE**		Identification of Flammability Color Code: **RED**		Identification of Reactivity (Stability) Color Code: **YELLOW**	
	Type of possible injury		Susceptibility of materials to burning		Susceptibility to release of energy
SIGNAL		SIGNAL		SIGNAL	
4	Materials that on very short exposure could cause death or major residual injury even though prompt medical treatment was given.	4	Materials that will rapidly or completely vaporize at atmospheric pressure and normal ambient temperature, or that are readily dispersed in air and that will burn readily.	4	Materials that in themselves are readily capable of detonation or of explosive decomposition or reaction at normal temperatures and pressures.
3	Materials that on short exposure could cause serious temporary or residual injury even though prompt medical treatment was given.	3	Liquids and solids that can be ignited under almost all ambient temperature conditions.	3	Materials that in themselves are capable of detonation or explosive reaction but require a strong initiating source or that must be heated under confinement before initiation or that react explosively with water.
2	Materials that on intense or continued exposure could cause temporary incapacitation or possible residual injury unless prompt medical treatment is given.	2	Materials that must be moderately heated or exposed to relatively high ambient temperatures before ignition can occur.	2	Materials that in themselves are normally unstable and readily undergo violent chemical change but do not detonate. Also materials that may react violently with water or that may form potentially explosive mixtures with water.
1	Materials that on exposure would cause irritation but only minor residual injury even if no treatment is given.	1	Materials that must be preheated before ignition can occur.	1	Materials that in themselves are normally stable, but that can become unstable at elevated temperatures and pressures or that may react with water with some release of energy, but not violently.
0	Materials that on exposure under fire conditions would offer no hazard beyond that of ordinary combustible material.	0	Materials that will not burn.	0	Materials that in themselves are normally stable, even under fire exposure conditions, and that are not reactive with water.

FIGURE 16-8. Hazardous materials rating system. (Reprinted with permission from McCall R. Phlebotomy Essentials. Baltimore: Lippincott Williams & Wilkins, 2003.)

Checkpoint Question

4. What are three types of hazards found in the laboratory? Give suggestions for preventing exposure to them.

Safety Guidelines

These guidelines are some of the most important safety factors required in all laboratories. Follow them carefully to protect yourself, your coworkers, and your patients.

Box 16-5

MATERIAL SAFETY DATA SHEET

An MSDS is required for each of the hazardous materials at a particular site. In the laboratory, these can include disinfectants, cleaning compounds, laboratory chemicals, and some office supplies (e.g., toners, printing compounds). All of these must be labeled as hazardous, with the contents listed on the label. Protocols for each hazardous agent used on site must be listed on the MSDS with the following information:

- Product name and identification. Include all names (trade and generic) by which it may be known.
- Hazardous components. List all hazardous components if the agent contains more than one.
- Health hazard data. Note the risks to those using the agent.
- Fire and explosive data. If this is a volatile agent, note what precautions are necessary to prevent an accident.
- Spill and disposal procedures. Note how to handle spills and disposal to avoid danger.
- Recommendations for personal protection equipment. Note whether gloves, gown, face shield, or other equipment should be worn during use of this agent.
- Handling, storage, and transportation precautions. List any special precautions that must be observed.

1. Never eat, drink, or smoke in the laboratory area.
2. Never touch your face, mouth, or eyes with your gloves or with items such as a pen or pencil used in the laboratory.
3. Do not apply makeup or lipstick or insert contact lenses in the laboratory.
4. Wear gloves and appropriate protective barriers whenever contact with blood, body fluids, secretions, excretions, broken skin, or mucous membranes is possible. If splatters, splashes, spills, or exposure to aerosols is possible, wear appropriate PPE.
5. Label all specimen containers with biohazard labels.
6. Store all chemicals according to the manufacturer's recommendations. Discard any container with an illegible label. Never store chemicals in unlabeled containers.
7. Wash hands frequently for infection control. Always wash hands before and after gloving and before leaving the work site.
8. Clean reusable glassware and other containers with recommended disinfectant or soap and dry thoroughly before reuse. Wear gloves to prevent cuts.
9. Avoid inhaling the fumes of any chemicals found in the laboratory or wearing contact lenses when working with these types of chemicals. Use of chemicals with hazardous fumes should be limited to facilities equipped with a fume hood.
10. Know the location and operation of all safety equipment, such as fire extinguishers, eyewashes (Fig. 16-9), and safety showers. Keep fire extinguishers close at hand, because many chemicals are flammable.
11. Use safe practices when operating laboratory equipment. Read the manuals and know how to operate the equipment. Avoid contact with damaged electrical equipment.
12. Disinfect all laboratory surfaces concurrently and at the end of the day with a 10% bleach solution or appropriate disinfectant. Never allow clutter to accumulate.

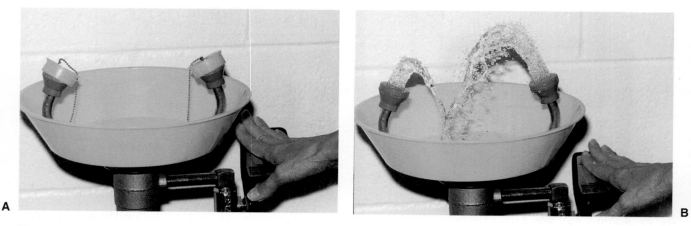

A   B

FIGURE 16-9.   Eyewash basin. (**A**) Press the lever at the right of the basin. (**B**) The stream of water forces the caps from the nozzles. Lower your face and eyes into the stream and continue to wash the area until the eyes are clear.

FIGURE 16-10. Spill cleanup kits. (Reprinted with permission from *McCall Phlebotomy Essentials.* Baltimore: Lippincott Williams & Wilkins, 2003.)

13. Dispose of needles and broken glass in sharps containers. Use biohazard containers for any other contaminated articles.
14. Use mechanical pipetters, but never the mouth, to apply suction to the pipette.
15. Use the proper procedure for removing chemical or biological spills. If the spill is chemical, follow the manufacturer's directions; commercial kits are available for such cleanups (Fig. 16-10). If the spill is biological:

   • Put on gloves.
   • Cover the area with disposable material, such as paper towels to soak up the spill; discard in a biohazard container.
   • Flood the area with disinfecting solution, allowing it to sit for 10 to 15 minutes.
   • Wipe up the solution.
   • Dispose of all waste in a biohazard container.

16. Avoid spills:

   • Pour carefully (palm the label).
   • Pour at eye level if possible or practical; never pour close to the face.
   • Tightly cap all containers immediately after use.

17. Use a splatter guard or splash shield whenever there is any risk of splatter or exposure to aerosols. Spills, splatters, and exposure to aerosols commonly occur in these circumstances:

   • Taking the stopper off a blood collection tube
   • Transferring blood from a collection syringe to a specimen receptacle
   • Conducting centrifugation
   • Preparing a smear
   • Flaming the inoculation loop

18. When removing a stopper, hold the opening away, use gauze around the cap, and twist gently. Avoid glove contact with the specimen.
19. Immediately report to your supervisor any work-related injury or biohazard exposure.
20. Follow all guidelines for standard precautions and the requirements of the various types of transmission-based precautions as described in Chapter 1.
21. When opening a tube or container, hold the mouth away from you to avoid aerosols, splashes and spills.

Checkpoint Question

5. How would you clean up a biological spill?

Incident Reports

When there is an occurrence in the facility for which liability could be considered, an incident report should be completed. An incident report is indicated if a patient, employee, or visitor is injured, if an employee is stuck with a contaminated needle, in case of medication error, or if blood is drawn from the wrong patient. The incident report should be completed by the staff member involved in the incident or closest to the patient or visitor involved in the incident.

Information necessary on an incident report includes the injured person's name, address, telephone number, and date of birth; the date and time; name and address of the facility where the incident occurred; and a brief description of the incident, including any diagnostic procedures or treatments performed. Witnesses to the incident should be listed with names, addresses, and phone numbers for insurance investigation if necessary. In addition to the signature of the person completing the form, a supervisor or doctor should review and sign the form in accordance with the facility's incident report policy.

CLINICAL LABORATORY IMPROVEMENT AMENDMENTS

With the goals of standardizing laboratory testing and enforcing quality protocols, Congress originally passed the **Clinical Laboratory Improvement Amendments (CLIA)** in 1988 to establish regulations governing any facility that performs testing for the diagnosis, prevention, or treatment of human disease or for assessment of patients' health status. While final modification of the amendments was made on January 24, 2003, with an effective date of April 24, 2003, the amendments maintain their original name, CLIA '88.

Standards were developed to cover all laboratories from large regional laboratories to the smallest POL. The Centers for Medicare and Medicaid Services (CMS) regulate all laboratory testing (except research) performed on humans in the United States through CLIA. The Division of Laboratory Services of the Survey and Certification Group in the Center for Medicaid and State Operations is responsible for implementing the CLIA program.

WHAT IF

Your laboratory is not in compliance with OSHA's safety regulations?

In such a situation, your health and that of your colleagues is in jeopardy. OSHA developed the guidelines to protect you from serious injury or death. OSHA can impose significant fines for noncompliance. Continued noncompliance may result in loss of the laboratory's license or large fines. To bring the laboratory back into compliance, any citations must be addressed and corrected. OSHA inspectors will revisit the site and reconsider licensure.

CLIA regulations set standards for the following:

- Laboratory operations
- Application and user fees
- Procedures for enforcement of the amendment
- Approval of programs for accreditation

Levels of Testing

CLIA regulations established the three levels of testing discussed next based on the complexity of the testing method.

Waived Tests

Waived tests are low-complexity tests that require minimal judgment or interpretation. They include many tests simple enough for the patient to perform at home (e.g., dipstick urinalysis and glucose monitoring). If these are the only types of tests performed on site, the laboratory can apply for a certificate of waiver (CLIA Waiver Registration), but it still must follow all manufacturers' recommendations for each piece of equipment or product used for testing.

Moderate-Complexity Tests

Most of the testing performed in large, established laboratories has moderate complexity.

A subcategory of moderate-complexity testing called provider-performed microscopy (PPM) requires POLs to have a special registration certificate. PPM can be performed only by a physician or dentist or by a nurse midwife, nurse practitioner, or physician assistant under the direct supervision of a physician.

High-Complexity Tests

If the level of testing to be performed is in question, it must be considered high complexity until its level can be designated by CMS. CMS publishes a list of all tests in the moderate-complexity category. States may establish stricter rules than those set by the governing body, but they may not adopt less strict rules.

Laboratory personnel must also meet the educational levels set forth by CLIA. These guidelines and their updates can be found in the Federal Register.

As a source of CLIA '88 compliance support for POLs, the Commission on Office Laboratory Accreditation (COLA) was established. COLA was subsequently granted deemed status under CLIA. The Joint Commission on Accreditation of Healthcare Organizations (JCAHO) also recognized COLA's laboratory accreditation program and granted it deemed status under JCAHO standards. COLA works to support the health care industry by providing knowledge and resources for maintaining quality laboratory operations.

LEGAL TIP

Chain of Custody

Laboratory personnel may be responsible for collecting drug screen specimens or other tests that become legal evidence with a documented chain of custody. Chain of custody (COC) systems are designed to account for each specimen at all times. Specimens in the system are documented with a COC form, a statement signed by each successive person in the chain of custody. COC collections should be completed following the step-by-step instructions on the testing laboratory's COC requisition. The instructions are similar to this:

- Client name's and identification.
- Which urine drug screen test is requested.
- Client's signature with date and time of collection.
- Collector's signature with date and time of collection.
- Whether or not specimen collection was witnessed.
- Specimen temperature (90.5–99.8°F is acceptable).
- Tamper seals affixed and signed as indicated on the requisition. The seal should be attached to one side of container, go across the lid, and attach again to the other side of the container.
- COC requisition in packet of tamper-proof bag.
- Specimen in pouch of tamper-proof bag.
- Tamper-proof bag sealed and transported to testing facility.

These requirements for collection of the specimen must also be fulfilled:

- Client must present picture identification. Client must empty pockets prior to specimen collection.
- Water supply must be turned off to the restroom used for specimen collection and a dye added to the toilet water to prevent client from using toilet water to replace specimen.
- Minimum required specimen volume is usually 35 mL.

Laboratory Standards

Laboratories that perform moderate- or high-complexity testing may be inspected in an unannounced visit every year by representatives from CMS or the Centers for Disease Control and Prevention (CDC) under the direction of the Department of Health and Human Services. As discussed later, they must meet all standards set by CLIA.

Patient Test Management

It must be proved that a system is in place to ensure that the specimens are properly maintained and identified and that the results are accurately recorded and reported. Policies must be written for standards of patient care and employee conduct. Each test performed will be evaluated for safety, reliability, and diagnostic indication for its performance.

Policy and procedure manuals will clearly outline patient preparation, specimen handling, how tests are to be performed, alternatives to the usual testing methods for specific situations, and what to do in the event of questionable testing results.

Quality Control

A comprehensive QC program monitors each phase of the laboratory process, including specimen collection, specimen processing, testing, and reporting results. The programs also monitor reagents, instruments, and personnel in addition to actual test performance. Each laboratory must have its own written policies and procedures that include instructions to ensure that all QC standards for monitoring the accuracy and quality of each test are in place for all levels of testing the laboratory conducts. The protocols ensure reliable findings and identification and elimination of errors.

Control sample. Manufacturers provide specimens comparable to human specimens with known reference ranges. Testing control samples at the same time the patient specimen is tested or when a new reagent kit is received ensures that all components are performing as required. Reagent and instrument manufacturers document frequencies for performing QC on their products. The performance of these controls must be recorded in the QC log book.

The **National Committee for Clinical Laboratory Standards (NCCLS)** establishes rules to ensure the safety, standards, and integrity of all testing performed on human specimens. Fig. 16-11 is an example of an NCCLS form on which control sample testing can be recorded. If controls do not fall in the range given in the manufacturer's package insert, testing *cannot* be conducted. The cause must be discovered and corrected before reporting any patient results. Start by checking the reagents and controls for expiration dates, accurate reconstitution, and expiration dates once reconstituted. Next check to see that the testing instrument is clean and functioning properly. If all of this has been done, reconstitute or open a new control sample or reagent and begin the process again.

Management of reagents. Reagents are chemicals used to produce a reaction. All reagents have a manufacturer's lot

Quality Control Log

Test: ______________________ Control Lot Number: ______________________

Date	Control Value	Performed By	Accept	Reject	Corrective Action Taken

FIGURE 16-11. Quality control log. (Reprinted with permission from *Physician's Office Laboratory Guidelines and Procedure Manual*, 3rd ed. Wayne, PA: National Committee for Clinical Laboratory Standards, 1995.)

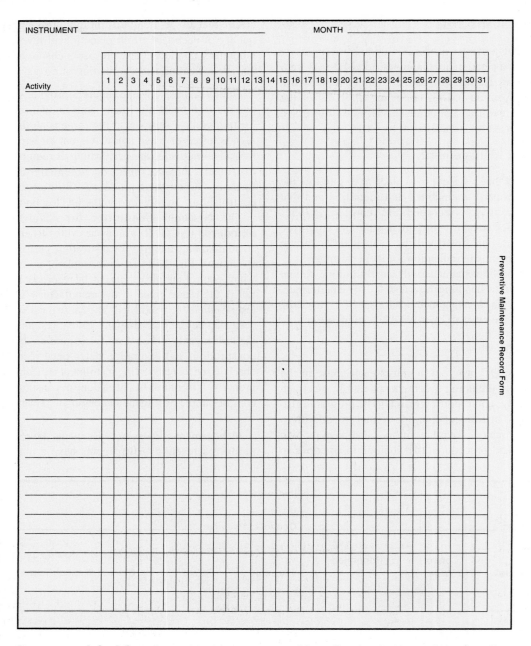

INSTRUMENT _____   MONTH _____

Activity | 1 | 2 | 3 | 4 | 5 | 6 | 7 | 8 | 9 | 10 | 11 | 12 | 13 | 14 | 15 | 16 | 17 | 18 | 19 | 20 | 21 | 22 | 23 | 24 | 25 | 26 | 27 | 28 | 29 | 30 | 31

Preventive Maintenance Record Form

FIGURE 16-12. Preventive maintenance record form. (Reprinted with permission from *Physician's Office Laboratory Guidelines and Procedure Manual*, 3rd ed. Wayne, PA: National Committee for Clinical Laboratory Standards, 1995.)

number and expiration date. These must be recorded in a QC log book with the date received, the date opened, and the initials of the person who opened the package. If the reagent consistently performs inappropriately, the lot number will help the manufacturer identify defects. All supplies and equipment, reagents, and testing components must be labeled with identification, storage requirements, date of preparation or when opened, and expiration date.

Instrument calibration. Laboratory equipment is sensitive and requires strict compliance with operation and maintenance standards. Manufacturers provide maintenance schedules and

methods for evaluating performance. Maintenance of equipment and supplies must be documented in the QC log book; this includes maintenance either by an employee or by a manufacturer's representative. Any corrective action required for equipment or supply malfunction must be documented. Figures 16-12 and 16-13 show sample NCCLS forms on which this information can be recorded.

Instruments are designed to produce results within a documented **reportable range**. If the QC results are not within the stated reference range, the instrument's calibration should be checked by the manufacturer's instructions, and patients' and QC specimens should be retested. If the calibration is correct

```
┌──────────────────────────────────────────────────────────────────────────────────┐
│                                                                                    │
│  Instrument History Record          Instrument: _____   │
│                                                                                    │
│  Model No.: _____      Serial No.: _____  │
│                                                                                    │
│  Date Purchased: _____      Cost: _____   │
│                                                                                    │
│  Manufacturer: _____                                                    │
│                                                                                    │
│  _____      State: _____  Zip: _____   │
│                                                                                    │
│  Telephone: _____      Contact                                       │
│                                      Person: _____   │
│                                                                                    │
│  Dealer: _____                                                    │
│                                                                                    │
│  _____      State: _____  Zip: _____   │
│                                                                                    │
│  Telephone: _____      Contact                                       │
│                                      Person: _____   │
│                                                                                    │
│  Warranty: _____      Expiration Date: _____   │
│                                                                                    │
│                                                                                    │
│  Technical Service Representative: _____   │
│                                                                                    │
│  Telephone: _____   │
│                                                                                    │
│                                    Service Record                                  │
│                                                                                    │
│  Date              Comments   Who was contacted, action taken                      │
│  _____  │
│                                                                                    │
│  _____  │
│                                                                                    │
│  _____  │
│                                                                                    │
└──────────────────────────────────────────────────────────────────────────────────┘
```

FIGURE 16-13. Instrument history record. (Reprinted with permission from *Physician's Office Laboratory Guidelines and Procedure Manual*, 3rd ed. Wayne, PA: National Committee for Clinical Laboratory Standards, 1995.)

and the results of QC specimens run in the same manner as the patients' specimens are within the stated reference range, the patients' results are correct. The flow chart in Figure 16-14 shows how you can evaluate test results for errors.

The laboratory's procedure manual must state the manufacturer's recommendation for the performance of calibration procedures, and supporting documentation must show that controls are performed as directed. Some procedures may require that controls be performed at each testing. Documentation must show the action taken to verify results, what was done when a problem arose, what the solution to the problem was, when the testing equipment was serviced and by whom, and what was done.

Quality Assurance

The laboratory's policy and procedure manual should cover recommendations for continuing education for the laboratory personnel and evaluation methods for ensuring that workers are competent. The qualifications and responsibilities of all laboratory workers are specified by CLIA, with education and training requirements for all levels of personnel. Employers must ascertain the educational background of employees, provide opportunities for continuing education, and conduct or provide for proficiency testing. This information

must be documented and available for inspection by CLIA representatives.

Proficiency Testing

Proficiency testing facilitates external evaluation of the laboratory. To continue testing and maintain Medicare eligibility, all laboratories, even those conducting only waived tests, must participate in three proficiency tests a year and must be available for at least one on-site inspection. Three times a year, the laboratory is shipped specimens prepared by an approved agency. These specimens must be tested by the same procedures used for patients' evaluation and the results mailed to the proficiency testing agency. The proficiency testing agency evaluates the results and provides feedback on performance.

Quality Control Log Book

To record compliance with CLIA measures, a record must be kept of each control sample and standard test. The log must show the date and time of the test, the control or standard results expected, what results were obtained, and the action taken for correction, if any. Documentation must be consistent, and the records must be retained for at least 2 years. Computer software programs are also available for maintaining this data.

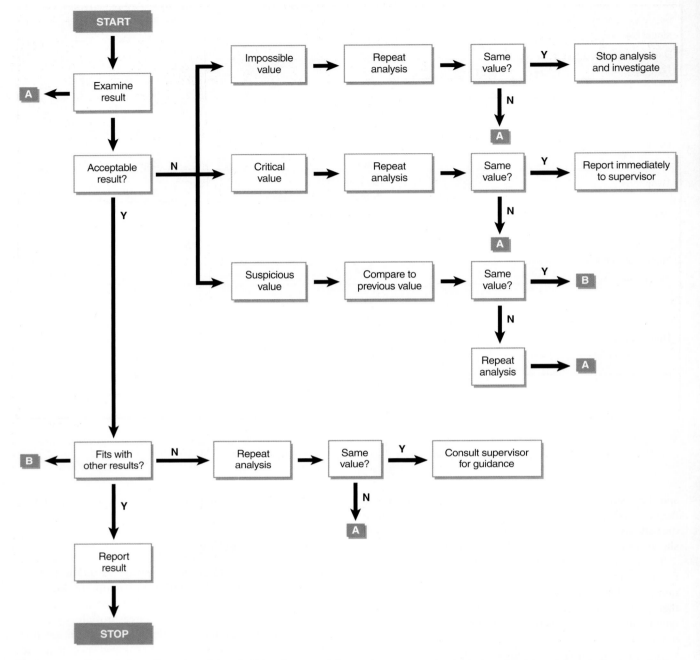

FIGURE 16-14.   Flow chart for evaluation of test result for random error: a simple strategy for determining whether an individual test result is reasonable and correlates with other results. Y, yes; N, no. A and B (far left) show interconnection between evaluation of repeat testing and where decision-making strategy should resume. For example, if an impossible value is obtained and repeat analysis does not show same value, uppermost horizontal line of chart says that testing procedure should return to symbol A, where the steps are begun again with examine result. (Adapted from Cembrowksi GS. Use of patient data for quality control. Clin Lab Med 6:715, 1986).

Procedure 16-1

Caring for a Microscope

Purpose: To protect the integrity and function of laboratory equipment

Equipment: Lens paper, lens cleaner, gauze, mild soap solution, microscope

Steps	Reason
1. Wash your hands.	Handwashing aids infection control.
2. Assemble the equipment.	
3. If you need to move the microscope, carry it in both hands, one holding the base and the other holding the arm.	
4. Clean the ocular areas, following these steps:	
A. Place a drop or two of lens cleaner on a piece of lens paper. Never use tissue or gauze, because either may scratch the ocular areas.	
B. Wipe each eyepiece thoroughly with the lens paper. To prevent transfer of oils from your skin, do not touch the ocular areas with your fingers.	
C. Wipe each objective lens, starting with the lowest power and continuing to the highest power (usually an oil immersion lens). If the lens paper appears to have dirt or oil on it, use a clean section of the lens paper or a new piece of lens paper with cleaner.	Wiping in this manner ensures that you progress from the cleanest area (eyepieces) to the least clean area (oil immersion lens).
D. Using a new piece of dry lens paper, wipe each eyepiece and objective lens so that no cleaner remains.	Removing the cleaner completely prevents distortion by residue.
5. Clean the areas other than the oculars:	This removes oil and dirt from mechanical and structural surfaces.
A. Moisten gauze with mild soap solution and wipe all areas other than the oculars, including the stage, base, and adjustment knobs.	
B. Moisten another gauze with water and rinse the washed areas.	
6. To store the cleaned microscope, ensure that the light source is turned off. Rotate the nosepiece so that the low-power objective is pointed down toward the stage. Cover the microscope with the plastic that came with it or a small trash bag.	This protects the mechanism and surfaces between uses.

Note: To maintain precision focusing, the microscope should be used in a low-traffic area and away from any source of vibration, such as a centrifuge.

Note: Follow the manufacturer's recommendations for changing the light bulb and servicing the microscope.

Procedure 16-2

Using the Principles of Quality Control

Equipment/Supplies: Test information, control sample, QC manual, laboratory equipment, QC Log.

Steps

1. Correctly identify QC manual.

2. Identify expiration date.

3. Locate manufacturer's control sample.

4. Test control sample.

5. Calibrate machine accordingly.

6. Document test results on Log.

Procedure 16-3

Performing Routine Maintenance on a Glucose Meter

Equipment/Supplies: Glucose meter, instrument manual, supplies indicated in instrument manual

Steps

1. Locate glucose meter and the instrument manual specific to that meter.

2. Read the manufacturer's instructions for performing routine maintenance on the meter as listed in the manual.

3. Assemble the necessary supplies as described in the instructions.

4. Perform the listed routine maintenance procedures.

5. Complete maintenance by successfully performing quality control analysis to verify working condition of meter.

6. Document maintenance and quality control in Equipment Maintenance Log according to office policy.

7. Clean work area, discarding used supplies as appropriate.

CHAPTER SUMMARY

As the CLIA list of waived tests continues to grow, allied health professionals can provide numerous laboratory findings to aid diagnosis. By maintaining an up-to-date working knowledge of the CLIA standards, allied health professionals can validate and document the quality and dependability of the results they report. Maintaining awareness of the types of hazards in the clinical laboratory allows the allied health professional to perform these critical tasks safely.

Critical Thinking Challenges

1. Review the laboratory safety rules and create a poster summarizing these rules for display in the laboratory.
2. List all items that must be documented in the laboratory. Design a form to meet these requirements. Who should complete the form? Where should it be kept? Explain your responses.
3. Working with another student, develop a plan of action to use in case your controls do not come into range and how to go about correcting a problem.

Answers to Checkpoint Questions

1. A reference laboratory is a large facility that serves a particular region, performing thousands of specialized tests daily. In contrast, the POL performs only a few kinds of common tests; some specimens may be sent to a reference laboratory for testing. Allied health professionals working in reference laboratories may be employed as specimen processors, sorting specimens and entering data into computers. They may also work as customer service personnel, answering telephones, tracking specimens, and reporting results to the centers from which the specimens were collected.
2. Because tests vary among manufacturers, the package insert is the best source of information on performing the test and evaluating the results.
3. The low-power objective lens magnifies objects $\times 10$ and is used for scanning. The high-power objective lens magnifies objects $\times 40$ and is used for close observation. The oil immersion lens magnifies objects $\times 100$ for close visualization.
4. The three basic types of hazards are physical (e.g., fire, broken glass, and liquid spills), chemical (e.g., acids, alkalis, and chemical fumes), and biological (e.g., diseases such as HIV, hepatitis, and tuberculosis).
5. To clean up a biological spill, first put on gloves. Cover the area with disposable material, such as paper towels; discard these in an appropriate container. Next, flood the area with disinfecting solution and allow it to sit for 10 to 15 minutes. Wipe up the spill. Dispose of all waste in a biohazard container.

 **Websites**

Commission on Office Laboratory Accreditation
    www.cola.org
Centers for Medicare and Medicaid Services
    www.cms.hhs.gov/clia/waivetbl.pdf

17

Measurements and Vital Signs

CHAPTER OBJECTIVES

In this chapter, you'll learn:

1. To spell and define key terms.
2. To explain the procedures for measuring a patient's height and weight.
3. To identify and describe the types of thermometers.
4. To compare the procedures for measuring a patient's temperature using the oral, rectal, axillary, and tympanic methods.
5. To list the fever process, including the stages of fever.
6. To describe the procedure for measuring a patient's pulse and respiratory rates.
7. To identify the various sites on the body used for palpating a pulse.
8. To define Korotkoff sounds and the five phases of blood pressure.
9. To identify factors that may influence the blood pressure.
10. To explain the factors to consider when choosing the correct blood pressure cuff size.

PERFORMANCE OBJECTIVES

In this chapter, you'll learn:

1. To measure and record a patient's weight (Procedure 17-1).
2. To measure and record a patient's height (Procedure 17-2).
3. To measure and record a patient's oral temperature using a glass mercury thermometer (Procedure 17-3).
4. To measure and record a patient's rectal temperature using a glass mercury thermometer (Procedure 17-4).
5. To measure and record a patient's axillary temperature using a glass mercury thermometer (Procedure 17-5).
6. To measure and record a patient's temperature using an electronic thermometer (Procedure 21-6).
7. To measure and record a patient's temperature using a tympanic thermometer (Procedure 21-7).
8. To measure and record a patient's radial pulse (Procedure 17-8).
9. To measure and record a patient's respirations (Procedure 17-9).
10. To measure and record a patient's blood pressure (Procedure 17-10).

KEY TERMS

afebrile	cardinal signs	intermittent	remittent fever
aneroid	diastole	palpation	sphygmomanometer
anthropometric	febrile	postural hypotension	sustained fever
baseline	hyperpyrexia	pyrexia	systole
calibrated	hypertension	relapsing fever	tympanic thermometer
cardiac cycle			

VITAL SIGNS, also known as **cardinal signs**, are measurements of bodily functions essential to maintaining life processes. Vital signs frequently measured and recorded by allied health professionals include the temperature (T), pulse rate (P), respiratory rate (R), and blood pressure (BP). In addition, allied health professionals take **anthropometric** measurements, or the height and weight, of patients and document them in the medical record. This information is essential for the health care provider to diagnose, treat, and prevent many disorders.

Measurements taken at the first visit are recorded as **baseline** data and are used as reference points for comparison during subsequent visits. After the first visit, the height is usually not taken; however, the vital signs and weight are taken and recorded for each adult patient at each visit to the health care facility.

ANTHROPOMETRIC MEASUREMENTS

Weight

An accurate weight is always required for pregnant patients, infants, children, and the elderly. In addition, weight monitoring may be required if the patient has been prescribed medications that must be carefully calculated according to body weight or for a patient who is attempting to gain or lose weight.

Since most facilities have only one scale, placement of the scale is important. Many patients are uncomfortable if they are weighed in a place that is not private. Types of scales used to measure weight include balance beam scales, digital

scales, and dial scales (Fig. 17-1). Weight may be measured in pounds or kilograms, depending upon the preference of the health care provider and the type of scale in the facility. Procedure 17-1 describes how to measure and record a patient's weight.

Height

Height can be measured using the movable ruler on the back of most balance beam scales. Some facilities use a graph ruler mounted on a wall (Fig. 17-2), but more accurate measures can be made with a parallel bar moved down against the top of the patient's head. Height is measured in inches or centimeters, depending upon the health care provider's preference. Procedure 17-2 describes how to measure an adult patient's height. Refer to Chapter 39 for the procedure for measuring the height and weight of infants and children.

Checkpoint Question

1. Why is it important to measure vital signs accurately at every patient visit?

VITAL SIGNS

Temperature

Body temperature reflects a balance between heat produced and heat lost by the body (Fig. 17-3). Heat is produced during normal internal physical and chemical processes called

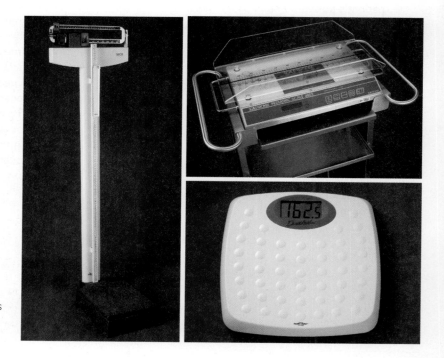

FIGURE 17-1. The three types of scales used in medical offices include the digital, dial, and balance scales.

FIGURE 17-2. A wall-mounted device to measure height and the sliding bar on the balance scale.

metabolism and through muscle movement. Heat is normally lost through several processes, including respiration, elimination, and conduction through the skin (Table 17-1). Normally, the body maintains a constant internal temperature of around 98.6° Fahrenheit (F) or 37.0° Celsius (C) (centigrade). A patient whose temperature is within normal limits is said to be **afebrile**, while a patient with a temperature above normal is considered **febrile** (has a fever).

Thermometers are used to measure body temperature using either the Fahrenheit or Celsius scale. Box 17-1 compares temperatures taken a variety of ways in Celsius and in Fahrenheit. Since glass thermometers used in the facility

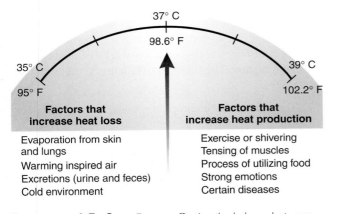

FIGURE 17-3. Factors affecting the balance between heat loss and heat production.

Box 17-1

TEMPERATURE COMPARISONS

	Fahrenheit	Celsius
Oral	98.6	37.0
Rectal	99.6	37.6
Axillary	97.6	36.4
Tympanic	98.6	37.0

may be marked in either scale, you should be able to convert from one scale to another. The patient's temperature can be measured using the oral, rectal, axillary, or **tympanic** method. The oral method is most commonly used, but use of the tympanic thermometer is increasing; if used accurately, it gives a reading that is comparable to the oral temperature. A reading of 98.6°F orally is considered a normal average for body temperature. Rectal or axillary readings will vary slightly. Rectal temperatures are generally 1°F higher than the oral temperature because of the vascularity and tightly closed environment of the rectum. Axillary temperatures are usually 1°F lower because of lower vascularity and difficulty in keeping the axilla tightly closed. When recording the body temperature, you must indicate the temperature reading and the method used to obtain it, such as oral, rectal, axillary, or tympanical. A rectal temperature reading of 101°F is equivalent to 100°F orally, and an axillary reading of 101°F is equivalent to 102°F orally.

Checkpoint Question

2. How does an oral temperature measurement differ from a rectal measurement? Why?

Fever Processes

Although a patient's temperature is influenced by heat lost or produced by the body, it is regulated by the hypothalamus in the brain. When the hypothalamus senses that the body is too warm, it initiates peripheral vasodilation to carry core heat to the body surface via the blood and increases perspiration to cool the body by evaporation. If the temperature registers too low, vasoconstriction to conserve heat and shivering to generate more heat will usually maintain a fairly normal core temperature. Temperature elevations and variations are often a *sign* of disease but are not a disease in themselves. These factors may cause the temperature to vary:

- *Age.* Children usually have a higher metabolism and therefore a higher body temperature than adults. The elderly, with a slower metabolism, usually have lower readings than younger adults. Temperatures of both the very young and the elderly are easily affected by the environment.

Table 17-1   MECHANISMS OF HEAT TRANSFER

Mechanism	Definition	Example
Radiation	Diffusion or dissemination of heat by electro-magnetic waves	The body gives off waves of heat from uncovered surfaces.
Convection	Dissemination of heat by motion between areas of unequal density	An oscillating fan blows cool air across the surface of a warm body.
Evaporation	Conversion of liquid to vapor	Body fluid (perspiration and insensible loss) evaporates from the skin.
Conduction	Transfer of heat during direct contact between two objects.	The body transfers heat to an ice pack, melting the ice.

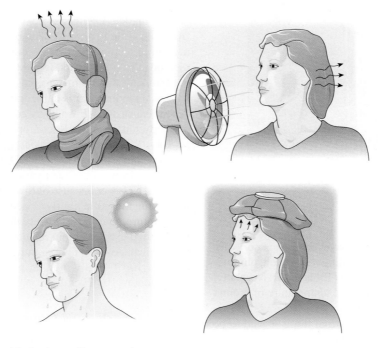

Mechanisms of heat transfer.

Adapted with permission from Taylor C, Lillis C, Le Mone P. *Fundamentals of Nursing*, 2nd ed. 388. Philadelphia: Lippincott, 1993; 388.

- *Gender.* Women usually have a slightly higher temperature than men, especially at the time of ovulation.
- *Exercise.* Activity causes the body to burn more calories for energy, which raises the body temperature.
- *Time of day.* The body temperature is usually lowest in the early morning, before physical activity has begun.
- *Emotions.* Temperature tends to rise during times of stress and fall with depression.
- *Illness.* High or low body temperatures may result from a disease process.

Stages of Fever

An elevated temperature, or fever, usually results from a disease process, such as a bacterial or viral infection. Body temperature may also rise during intense exercise, anxiety, or dehydration unrelated to a disease process, but these elevations are not considered fevers. **Pyrexia** refers to a fever of 102°F or higher rectally or 101°F or higher orally. An extremely high temperature, 105° to 106°F, is **hyperpyrexia** and is considered dangerous, since the intense internal body heat may damage or destroy cells of the brain and other vital organs. The fever process has several clearly defined stages:

1. The *onset* may be abrupt or gradual.
2. The *course* may range from a day or so to several weeks. Fever may be **sustained** (constant), **remittent** (fluctuating), **intermittent** (occurring at intervals), or **relapsing**, (returning after an extended period of normal readings). Table 17-2 describes and illustrates these courses of fever.
3. The *resolution*, or return to normal, may occur as either a *crisis* (abrupt return to normal), or *lysis* (gradual return to normal).

Table 17-2   VARIATIONS IN FEVER PATTERNS

Type of Fever	Description
Sustained	Remains elevated, with very little fluctuation.
Remittent	Fluctuates several degrees but never reaches normal.
Intermittent	Cycles frequently between periods of normal or subnormal temperatures and spikes of fever.
Relapsing	Recurs after a brief but sustained period of normal temperature.

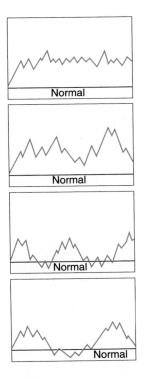

Variations in fever patterns.

Adapted with permission from Timby BK. *Fundamental Skills and Concepts in Patient Care*, 6th ed. Philadelphia: Lippincott-Raven, 1996.

Checkpoint Question

3. Explain why the body temperature of a young child may be different from that of an adult.

Types of Thermometers

Glass mercury thermometers. Oral, rectal, and axillary temperatures have traditionally been measured using the mercury glass thermometer. This thermometer consists of a glass tube divided into two major parts. The bulb end is filled with mercury and may have a round or a slender tip. Glass thermometers have different shapes for oral and rectal use. Rectal thermometers have a rounded, or stubbed, end and are usually color coded red on the opposite flat end of the thermometer. Thermometers with a long, slender bulb are used for axillary or oral temperatures and are color-coded blue (Fig. 17-4). When the glass thermometer is placed in position for a specified period, body heat expands the mercury, which rises up the glass column and remains there until it is physically shaken back into the bulb.

The long stem of the Fahrenheit thermometer is calibrated with lines designating temperature in even degrees: 94°, 96°, 98°, 100°, and so on. Uneven numbers are marked only with a longer line. Between these longer lines, four smaller lines designate temperature in 0.2° increments. The thermometer is read by noting the level of the mercury in the glass column. For example, if the level of the mercury falls on the second smaller line past the large line marked 100, the reading is 100.4°F. Celsius thermometers are marked for each degree (35°, 36°, 37°, and so on), with 10 markings between the whole numbers (Fig. 17-5). If the mercury falls on the third small line past the line marked 37, the temperature reading is recorded as 37.3°C.

Before using an electronic thermometer, place it in a disposable clear plastic sheath (Fig. 17-6). When you take the thermometer from the patient, remove the sheath by pulling the thermometer out, which turns the sheath inside out and traps the saliva inside it. Dispose of the sheath in a biohazard container and sanitize and disinfect the thermometer according to the office policy. Usually, washing the thermometers with warm—not hot—soapy water and soaking in a solution of alcohol is sufficient. The procedures for measuring oral, rectal, and axillary temperatures using glass mercury thermometers are described in Procedures 17-3 to 17-5.

Electronic thermometers. Electronic thermometers are portable battery-operated units with interchangeable probes (Fig. 17-7). The base unit of the thermometer is battery operated, and the interchangeable probes are color-coded blue for oral or axillary and red for rectal. When the probe is properly positioned, the temperature is sensed and a digital readout shows in the window of the handheld base. Electronic thermometers are usually kept in a charging unit between uses to ensure that the batteries are operative at all times. The procedure for taking and recording an oral temperature using an electronic thermometer is described in Procedure 17-6.

Tympanic thermometers. Another type of thermometer used in health care facilities today is the tympanic, or aural, thermometer. This device is usually battery powered. The end is fitted with a disposable cover that is inserted into the ear (Fig. 17-8). With the end of the thermometer in place, a button is pressed and infrared light bounces off the tympanic membrane, or eardrum. When correctly positioned, the sensor in the thermometer determines the temperature of the blood in the tympanic membrane. The temperature reading is displayed on the unit's digital screen within 2 seconds. This device is considered highly reliable for temperature measurement. Procedure 17-7 describes the complete process for obtaining a body temperature with a tympanic thermometer.

FIGURE 17-4. Glass mercury thermometers. **Front.** Slender bulb, oral. **Center.** Rounded bulb, red tip, rectal. **Back.** Blue tip, oral.

Disposable thermometers. Single-use disposable thermometers are fairly accurate but are not considered as reliable as electronic, tympanic, or glass thermometers. These thermometers register quickly by indicating color changes on a strip. They are not reliable for definitive measurement, but they are acceptable for screening in settings such as day care centers and schools (Fig. 17-9). Other disposable thermometers are available for pediatric use in the form of sucking devices, or pacifiers, but these are not used in the health care facility.

 ### Checkpoint Question

4. Why is a tympanic membrane temperature more accurate than an axillary temperature?

Pulse

As the heart beats, blood is forced through the arteries, expanding them. With relaxation of the heart, the arteries relax also. This expansion and relaxation of the arteries can be felt at various points on the body where you can press an artery against a bone or other underlying firm surface. These areas are known as pulse points. With **palpation**, each expansion of the artery can be felt and is counted as one heartbeat. A pulse in specific arteries supplying blood to the extremities also indicates that oxygenated blood is flowing to that extremity.

The heartbeat can be palpated (felt) or auscultated (heard) at several pulse points. The arteries most commonly used are the carotid, apical, brachial, radial, femoral, popliteal, posterior tibial, and dorsalis pedis (Fig. 17-10). Palpation of the pulse is performed by placing the index and middle fingers, the middle and ring fingers, or all three fingers over a pulse

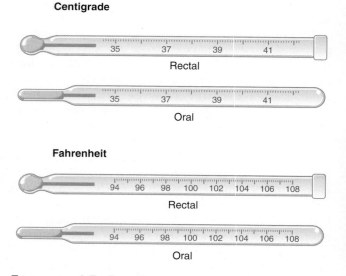

Centigrade

Rectal

Oral

Fahrenheit

Rectal

Oral

FIGURE 17-5. The two glass thermometers on the top are calibrated in the Celsius (centigrade) scale, and the two on the bottom use the Fahrenheit scale. Note the blunt bulb on the rectal thermometers and the long thin bulb on the oral thermometers.

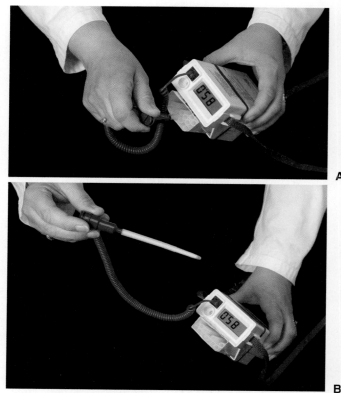

FIGURE 17-6. (**A** and **B**) An electronic thermometer is placed in a disposable sheath before use.

WHAT IF

You have been assigned to disinfect the glass mercury thermometers used in your facility?

Although glass thermometers are always placed in a disposable sheath before use, the thermometer should be sanitized and disinfected after each use. The procedure should be outlined in the facility policy and procedure manual, but the following steps can be used as a guide:

• Wearing gloves, wash the thermometer with cool or tepid soapy water. Do not use hot water, since too much heat may break the thermometer.
• After rinsing with cool water, dry the thermometer to avoid diluting your disinfecting solution.
• Pour a disinfecting soaking solution (70% alcohol is commonly used) into a tray or container with a lid. The lid will prevent the soaking solution from evaporating.
• Soak the thermometers for a prescribed period, usually 3 to 4 hours, before rinsing, drying, and storing.

FIGURE 17-8. The tympanic thermometer in use.

ber can be determined by palpating the pulse and counting each heartbeat while watching the second hand of your watch either for 30 seconds and then multiplying that number by 2 or for 1 minute. In healthy adults, the average pulse rate is 60 to 100 beats per minute. At other ages, there is a large variance of pulse rates as shown in Table 17-3.

The rhythm is the interval between each heartbeat or the pattern of beats. Normally, this pattern is regular, with each heartbeat occurring at a regular, consistent rate. An irregular rhythm should be counted for 1 full minute to determine the rate, and the irregular rhythm should be documented with the pulse rate.

Volume, the strength or force of the heartbeat, can be described as soft, bounding, weak, thready, strong, or full. Usually the volume of the pulse is recorded only if it is weak, thready, or bounding.

point (Fig. 17-11). The thumb is not used to palpate a pulse. The apical pulse is auscultated using a stethoscope with the bell placed over the apex of the heart (Fig. 17-12), and a Doppler unit is used to amplify the sound of peripheral pulses that are difficult to palpate.

Pulse Characteristics

While palpating the pulse, you also assess the rate, rhythm, and volume as the artery wall expands with each heartbeat. The *rate* is the number of heartbeats in 1 minute. This num-

Factors Affecting Pulse Rates

Many factors affect the force, speed, and rhythm of the heart. Young children and infants have a much faster heart rate

FIGURE 17-7. Two types of electronic thermometers and probes.

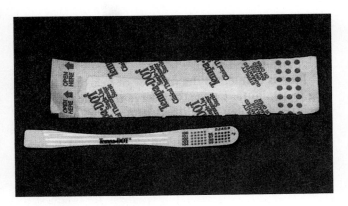

FIGURE 17-9. Disposable paper thermometer. The dots change color to indicate the body temperature.

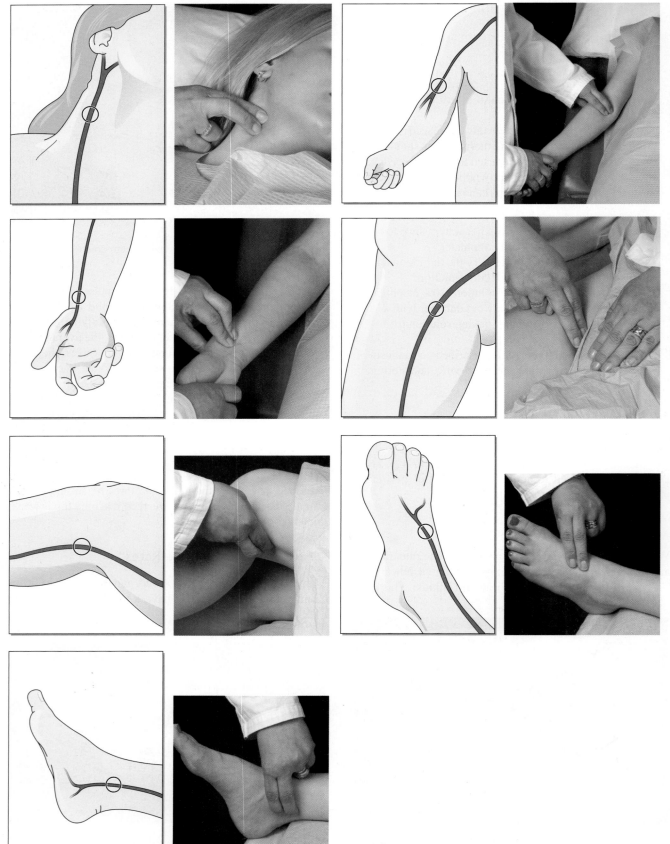

FIGURE 17-10. Sites for palpation of peripheral pulses.

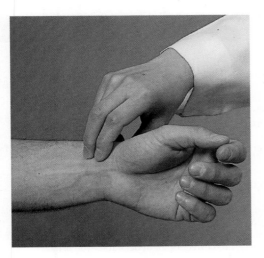

FIGURE 17-11. Measuring a radial pulse. (Reprinted with permission from Bickely LS. *Bates' Guide to Physical Examination and History Taking*, 8th ed. Philadelphia: Lippincott Williams & Wilkins, 2003.)

Table 17-3	VARIATIONS IN PULSE RATE BY AGE
Age Minute	**Beats p**
Birth to 1 year	110–170
1–10 years	90–110
10–16 years	80–95
16 years to midlife	70–80
Elderly adult	55–70

than adults. A conditioned athlete may have a normal heart rate below 60 beats per minute. Older adults may have a faster heart rate, as the myocardium compensates for decreased efficiency. Other factors that affect pulse rates are listed in Table 17-4.

The radial artery is most often used to determine pulse rate because it is convenient for both the allied health professional and the patient (Procedure 17-8). If the radial pulse is irregular or hard to palpate, the apical pulse is the site of choice (Fig. 17-13). Peripheral pulses that are difficult to palpate may also be auscultated with a Doppler unit (Fig. 17-14), a small battery-powered or electric device that consists of a main box with control switches, a probe, and an earpiece unit

that plugs into the main box and resembles the earpieces to a stethoscope. The earpiece may be detached so the sounds can be heard by everyone in the room if desired. Follow these steps to use a Doppler device:

1. Apply a coupling or transmission gel on the pulse point before placing the end of the probe, or transducer, on the area. This gel creates an airtight seal between the probe and the skin and facilitates transmission of the sound.
2. With the machine on, hold the probe at a 90° angle with light pressure to ensure contact. Move the probe as necessary in small circles in the gel until you hear the pulse (Fig. 17-14). When contact with the artery is made, the Doppler will emit a loud pumping sound with each heartbeat. Adjust the volume control on the Doppler unit as necessary.
3. After assessing the rate and rhythm of the pulse, clean the patient's skin and the probe with a tissue or soft cloth. Do not clean the probe with water or alcohol, as this may damage the transducer.

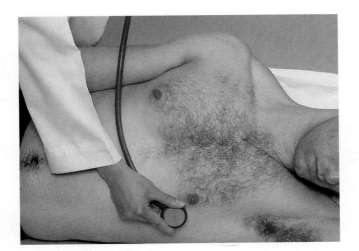

FIGURE 17-12. Measuring an apical pulse. (Reprinted with permission from Bickely LS. *Bates' Guide to Physical Examination and History Taking*, 8th ed. Philadelphia: Lippincott Williams & Wilkins, 2003.)

Table 17-4	FACTORS AFFECTING PULSE RATES
Factor	**Effect**
Time of day	The pulse is usually lower early in the morning than later in the day.
Gender	Women have a slightly higher pulse rate than men.
Body type and size	Tall, thin people usually have a lower pulse rate than shorter, stockier people.
Exercise	The heart rate increases with the need for increased cardiac output (the amount of blood ejected from either ventricle in one minute).
Stress or emotions	Anger, fear, excitement, and stress will raise the pulse; depression will lower it.
Fever	The increased need for cell metabolism in the presence of fever raises the cardiac output to supply oxygen and nutrients; the pulse may rise as much as 10 beats/minute per degree of fever.
Medications	Many medications raise or lower the pulse as a desired effect or an undesirable side effect.
Blood volume	Loss of blood volume to hemorrhage or dehydration will increase the need for cellular metabolism and will increase the cardiac output to supply the need.

 Checkpoint Question

5. What characteristics of a patient's pulse should be assessed, and how should they be recorded in the health record?

Respiration

Respiration is the exchange of gases between the atmosphere and the blood in the body. With respiration, the body expels carbon dioxide (CO_2) and takes in oxygen (O_2). External respiration is inhalation and exhalation, during which air travels through the respiratory tract to the alveoli so that oxygen can be absorbed into the bloodstream. Internal respiration is the exchange of gases between the blood and the tissue cells. Respiration is controlled by the respiratory center in the brainstem and by feedback from chemosensors in the carotid arteries that monitor the CO_2 content in the blood.

As the patient breathes in (inspiration), oxygen flows into the lungs and the diaphragm contracts and flattens out, lifting and expanding the rib cage. During expiration, air in the lungs flows out of the chest cavity as the diaphragm relaxes, moves upward into a dome-like shape, and allows the rib cage to contract. Each respiration is counted as one full inspiration and one full expiration.

Observing the rise and fall of the chest to count respirations is usually performed as a part of the pulse measurement. Generally you should not make the patient aware that you are counting respirations, because patients often change the voluntary action of breathing if they are aware that they are being watched. Respirations can be counted for a full minute or for 30 seconds with the number multiplied by 2. When appropriate, a stethoscope may be used to auscultate respirations.

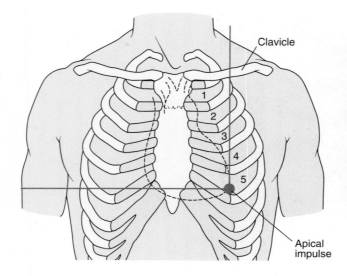

FIGURE 17-13. Finding the apical pulse.

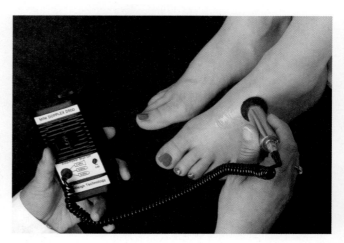

FIGURE 17-14. The dorsalis pedis pulse being auscultated using a Doppler device.

Respiration Characteristics

The characteristics of respirations include rate, rhythm, and depth. *Rate* is the number of respirations occurring in 1 minute. *Rhythm* is time, or spacing, between each respiration. This pattern is equal and regular in patients with normal respirations. Any abnormal rhythm is described as irregular and recorded as such in the patient's record after the rate.

Depth is the volume of air being inhaled and exhaled. When a person is at rest, the depth should be regular and consistent. There are normally no noticeable sounds other than the regular exchange of air. Respirations that are abnormally deep or shallow are documented in addition to the rate. Abnormal sounds during inspiration or expiration are usually a sign of a disease process. These abnormal sounds are usually recorded as crackles (wet or dry sounds) or wheezes (high-pitched sounds) heard during inspiration or expiration.

Factors Affecting Respiration

In healthy adults, the average respiratory rate is 14 to 20 breaths per minute. Table 17-5 shows the normal variations in respiratory rates according to age. Patients with an elevated body temperature usually also have increased pulse and respiratory rates. A respiratory rate that is much faster than average is called tachypnea, and a respiratory rate that is slower than usual is referred to bradypnea. Further descriptions of abnormal or unusual respirations include the following:

dyspnea   difficult or labored breathing.
apnea   no respiration.
hyperpnea   abnormally deep, gasping breaths.
hyperventilation   a respiratory rate that greatly exceeds the body's oxygen demand.
hypopnea   shallow respirations.
orthopnea   inability to breathe lying down; the patient usually has to sit upright to breathe.

Procedure 17-9 lists the steps for counting and recording respirations.

Checkpoint Question

6. What happens within the chest cavity when the diaphragm contracts?

Table 17-5	Variations in Respiration Ranges by Age
Age	**Respirations per Minute**
Infant	20 +
Child	18–20
Adult	12–20

Blood Pressure

Blood pressure is a measurement of the pressure of the blood in an artery as it is forced against the arterial walls. Pressure is measured in the contraction and relaxation phases of the cardiac cycle, or heartbeat. When the heart contracts, it forces blood from the atria and ventricles in the phase known as **systole**. This highest pressure level during contraction is recorded as the systolic pressure and is heard as the first sound in taking blood pressure (Procedure 17-10).

As the heart pauses briefly to rest and refill, the arterial pressure drops. This phase is known as **diastole**, and the pressure is recorded as the diastolic pressure. Systolic and diastolic pressure result from the two parts of the **cardiac cycle**, the period from the beginning of one heartbeat to the beginning of the next. When measured using a stethoscope and **sphygmomanometer**, or blood pressure cuff, these two pressures constitute the blood pressure and are written as a fraction, with the systolic pressure over the diastolic pressure. The normal adult systolic blood pressure is 100 to 140, and the normal diastolic pressure is 60 to 90, with an average adult blood pressure of 120/80. A lower pressure may be normal for athletes with exceptionally well-conditioned cardiovascular systems. Blood pressure that drops suddenly when the patient stands from a sitting or lying position is **postural hypotension**, or orthostatic hypotension; it may cause symptoms including vertigo. Some patients with postural hypotension may faint. Extra precautions should be taken when assessing patients going from lying down to sitting or standing.

Two basic types of sphygmomanometers are used to measure blood pressure: the **aneroid**, which has a circular dial for the readings, and the mercury, which has a mercury-filled glass tube for the readings (Fig. 17-15). Although only one type actually contains mercury, both types are calibrated and measure blood pressure in millimeters of mercury (mm Hg). A blood pressure of 120/80 indicates the force needed to raise a column of mercury to the 120 calibration mark on

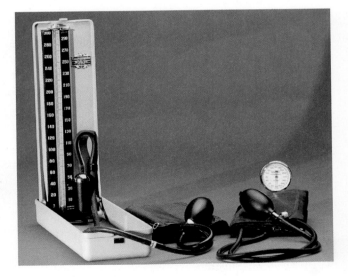

FIGURE 17-15.   A mercury column sphygmomanometer and an aneroid sphygmomanometer.

the glass tube during diastole and 80 during diastole. The elasticity of the person's arterial walls, the strength of the heart muscle, and the quantity and viscosity (thickness) of the blood all affect the blood pressure.

The sphygmomanometer is attached to a cuff by a rubber tube. A second rubber tube is attached to a hand pump with a screw valve. This device is used to pump air into the rubber bladder in the cuff. When the screw valve is turned clockwise, the bladder in the cuff around the patient's arm is inflated by multiple compressions of the pump. As the bladder inflates, the pressure created against the artery at some point prohibits blood from passing through the vessel. When the screw valve is slowly opened by turning it counterclockwise, the blood pressure can be determined by listening carefully with the stethoscope placed on the artery to the sounds produced as the blood begins to flow through the vessel. Procedure 17-10 describes the steps for correctly obtaining a patient's blood pressure using the radial artery.

Checkpoint Question

7. What happens to the heart during systole? Diastole?

Korotkoff Sounds

Korotkoff sounds can be classified into five phases of sounds heard while auscultating the blood pressure as described by the Russian neurologist Nicolai Korotkoff. Only the sounds heard during phase I (represented by the first sound heard) and phase V (represented by the last sound heard) are recorded as blood pressure. You may hear other Korotkoff sounds during the procedure, but it is not necessary to record them. Table 17-6 describes the five phases of Korotkoff sounds that may be heard when auscultating blood pressure.

Pulse Pressure

The difference between the systolic and diastolic readings is known as the pulse pressure. For example, with the average adult blood pressure of 120/80, the difference between the numbers 120 and 80 is 40. The average normal range for pulse pressure is 30 to 50 mm Hg. Generally the pulse pressure should be no more than one-third of the systolic reading. If the pulse pressure is more or less than these parameters, the physician should be notified.

Table 17-6	FIVE PHASES OF BLOOD PRESSURE
Phase	**Sounds**
I	Faint tapping heard as the cuff deflates (systolic blood pressure)
II	Soft swishing
III	Rhythmic, sharp, distinct tapping
IV	Soft tapping that becomes faint
V	Last sound (diastolic blood pressure)

Auscultatory Gap

Patients with a history of **hypertension**, or elevated blood pressure, may have an auscultatory gap heard during phase II of the Korotkoff sounds. An auscultatory gap is the loss of any sounds for a drop of up to 30 mm Hg (sometimes more) during the release of air from the blood pressure cuff after the first sound is heard. If the last sound heard at the beginning of the gap is recorded as the diastolic blood pressure, the documented blood pressure is inaccurate and may result in misdiagnosis and treatment of a condition that the patient does not have. As a result, it is important for you to listen and watch carefully as the dial or column of mercury falls until you are certain that you have heard the last sound, or diastolic pressure.

Factors Influencing Blood Pressure

Atherosclerosis and arteriosclerosis are two disease processes that greatly influence blood pressure. These diseases affect the size and elasticity of the artery lumen. The general health of the patient is also a major factor. General health includes dietary habits, alcohol and tobacco use, the amount and type of exercise, previous heart conditions such as myocardial infarctions, and family history of cardiac disease. These other factors normally affect blood pressure:

* *Age.* As the body ages, vessels begin to lose elasticity and more force is needed to expand the arterial wall. The buildup of atherosclerotic patches inside the artery also increases the force needed for blood flow.

Ñ Spanish Terminology

Voy a tomar su pulso radial.	I am going to take your radial pulse.
Voy a tomar su presión de sangre.	I am going to take your blood pressure.
Voy a tomar la temperatura.	I am going to take your temperature.
Fiebre?	Fever?

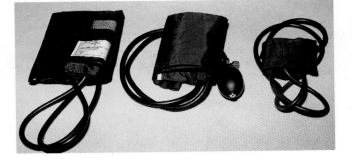

FIGURE 17-17. Three sizes of blood pressure cuffs (from left): a large cuff for obese adults, a normal adult cuff, and a pediatric cuff.

WHAT IF

A patient has a dialysis shunt (a surgically made venous access port that allows a patient with little or no kidney function to be connected to a dialysis machine) in his left arm? Should you use that arm to take his blood pressure?

No! Taking blood pressure in that arm might permanently damage the shunt, and the patient would not be able to receive dialysis until another shunt was prepared by a surgeon. A patient who has had a mastectomy should also not have a blood pressure taken in the arm on the affected side, since the lymphatic circulation in that extremity is impaired. The patient with a dialysis shunt or mastectomy should have the health record clearly marked indicating that no blood pressure or blood draws are to be performed on the designated arm. Most patients are aware of the importance of not taking blood pressure or specimens from the affected arm and will alert you before you mistakenly perform the procedure.

- *Activity.* Exercise raises the blood pressure temporarily, and inactivity or rest usually lowers the pressure.
- *Stress.* The sympathetic nervous system stimulates the release of the hormone epinephrine, which raises the pressure in the fight or flight response.
- *Body position.* Blood pressure normally falls when a person lies supine.
- *Medications.* Some medications lower the pressure, and others may cause an elevation.

Because so many variables can affect a patient's blood pressure, a diagnosis of hypertension is usually not made by the health care professional unless a pattern of three or four elevated pressures are documented over time.

Blood Pressure Cuff Size

Before beginning to take a patient's blood pressure, assess the size of the patient's arm and choose the correct size accordingly. The width of the cuff should be 40% to 50% of the circumference of the arm. To determine the correct size, hold the narrow edge of the cuff at the midpoint of the upper arm. Wrap the width, not the length, around the arm. The cuff width should reach not quite halfway around the arm (Fig. 17-16). Varying widths of cuffs are available from about 1 inch for infants to 8 inches for obese adults (Fig. 17-17). The blood pressure measurement may be inaccurate by as much as 30 mm Hg if the cuff size is incorrect. Box 17-2 lists causes of errors in blood pressure readings.

 Checkpoint Question

8. How are the pulse pressure and the auscultatory gap different?

> **Box 17-2**
>
> ## CAUSES OF ERRORS IN BLOOD PRESSURE READINGS
>
> - Wrapping the cuff improperly
> - Failing to keep the patient's arm at the level of the heart while taking the blood pressure
> - Failing to support the patient's arm on a stable surface while taking the blood pressure
> - Recording the auscultatory gap for the diastolic pressure
> - Failing to maintain the gauge at eye level
> - Applying the cuff around the patient's clothing and attempting to listen through the clothing
> - Allowing the cuff to deflate too rapidly or too slowly
> - Failing to wait 1 to 2 minutes before rechecking using the same arm
> - Improper size of cuff

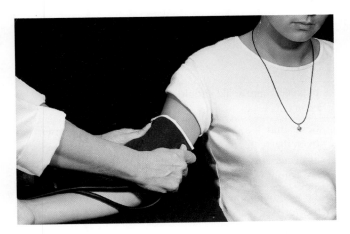

FIGURE 17-16. Choosing the right blood pressure cuff.

Procedure 17-1

Measuring Weight

Purpose: Accurately measure and record a patient's weight.

Equipment: Calibrated balance beam scale, digital scale, or dial scale; paper towel.

Standard: This procedure should take 5 minutes.

Steps	Reason
1. Wash your hands.	Handwashing before contact with patients aids in infection control.
2. Ensure that the scale is properly balanced at zero.	This helps prevent an error in measurement.
3. Greet and identify the patient. Explain the procedure.	Identifying the patient prevents errors, and explaining the procedure promotes cooperation.
4. Escort the patient to the scale and place a paper towel on the scale.	Since the patient will be standing in bare feet or stockings, the paper towel minimizes microorganism transmission.
5. Have the patient remove shoes and heavy outerwear and put down purse.	Unnecessary items must be removed to get an accurate reading.
6. Assist patient onto scale facing forward, standing on paper towel, without touching or holding on to anything if possible while watching for difficulties with balance.	Some patients may feel unsteady as the plate of the scale settles.
7. Weigh the patient: A. *Balance beam scale:* Slide counterweights on bottom and top bars (start with heavier bars) from zero to approximate weight. Each counterweight should rest securely in notch with indicator mark at proper calibration. To obtain measurement, balance bar must hang freely at exact midpoint. To calculate weight, add top reading to bottom one. (Example: If heavier counterweight reads 100 and lighter one reads 16 plus three small lines, record weight as 116.75 lb.). B. *Digital scale:* Read and record weight displayed on digital screen. C. *Dial scale:* Indicator arrow rests at patient's weight. Read this number directly above the dial.	Reading at an angle would result in an incorrect measurement.
8. Return the bars on the top and bottom to zero.	A balance beam scale should be returned to zero after each use.
9. Assist the patient from the scale if necessary and discard the paper towel.	Patients may lose balance and fall when stepping down from the scale; they should be observed and assisted as necessary. The paper towel may be left in place if the height is going to be obtained.
10. Record the patient's weight.	If the weight and height are measured at the same time, they are recorded together.

Procedure 17-2

Measuring Height

Purpose: Accurately measure and record a patient's height.

Equipment: A scale with a ruler.

Standards: This procedure should take less than 5 minutes.

Steps	Purpose
1. Wash your hands if this procedure is not done at the same time as the weight.	Typically, height is obtained with weight; your hands are already washed.
2. Have the patient remove shoes and stand straight and erect on the scale, heels together, eyes straight ahead. (Patient may face the ruler, but a better measurement is made with the patient's back to the ruler).	The posture of the patient must be erect for an accurate measurement.
3. With measuring bar perpendicular to the ruler, slowly lower it until it firmly touches the patient's head. Press lightly if the patient's hair is full or high.	Hair that is full should not be included in the height measurement.

(continued)

Procedure 17-2   *(continued)*

Measuring Height

Steps	Purpose
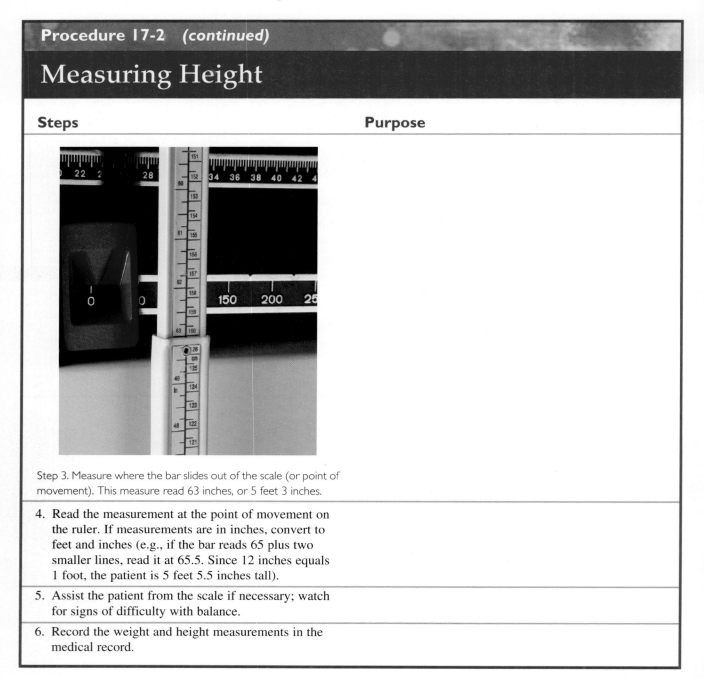 Step 3. Measure where the bar slides out of the scale (or point of movement). This measure read 63 inches, or 5 feet 3 inches.	
4. Read the measurement at the point of movement on the ruler. If measurements are in inches, convert to feet and inches (e.g., if the bar reads 65 plus two smaller lines, read it at 65.5. Since 12 inches equals 1 foot, the patient is 5 feet 5.5 inches tall).	
5. Assist the patient from the scale if necessary; watch for signs of difficulty with balance.	
6. Record the weight and height measurements in the medical record.	

Procedure 17-3

Measuring Oral Temperature Using a Glass Mercury Thermometer

Purpose   Accurately measure and record a patient's oral temperature using a glass mercury thermometer.

Equipment: Glass mercury oral thermometer; tissues or cotton balls; disposable plastic sheath; gloves; biohazard container; cool, soapy water; disinfectant solution

Standard: This procedure should take 10 minutes.

Steps	Reason
1. Wash your hands and assemble the necessary supplies.	Handwashing aids infection control.
2. Dry the thermometer if it has been stored in a disinfectant solution by wiping it from the bulb and going up the stem with a tissue or cotton ball.	Removing the wet disinfectant allows the thermometer to slip easily into the sheath.
3. Carefully check the thermometer for chips or cracks.	A chipped or cracked thermometer could injure the patient.
4. Check the reading by holding the stem horizontally at eye level and turning it slowly.	It is easiest to see the mercury in the column in this position.
5. If the reading is above 94°F, shake down the thermometer by securely grasping it at the end of the stem with your thumb and forefinger and snapping your wrist several times. Avoid hitting the thermometer against anything while snapping your wrist.	The reading must begin below 94°F to provide an accurate temperature reading. The reading will never decrease in the thermometer unless the mercury is physically forced into the bulb.
6. Insert the thermometer into the plastic sheath.	Follow the package instructions for placing the thermometer correctly in the sheath.
7. Greet and identify the patient. Explain the procedure and ask about any eating, drinking of hot or cold fluids, gum chewing, or smoking within the past 15 minutes.	Eating, drinking, gum chewing, or smoking may alter the oral reading. If the patient has done any of these within 15 minutes, wait 15 minutes or select another route.
8. Place the thermometer under the patient's tongue to either side of the frenulum.	This is the area of highest vascularity and will give the most accurate reading.
9. Tell the patient to keep the mouth and lips closed but not to bite down on the thermometer.	Keeping the mouth and lips closed prevents air from entering the mouth and causing an inaccurate reading. Biting down on the thermometer may break it.
10. Leave the thermometer in place for 3 to 5 minutes. *Note*: The patient's pulse, respirations, and blood pressure may be taken during this time (See Procedures 17-8 to 17-10).	The thermometer may be left in place for 3 minutes if there is no evidence of fever and the patient is compliant. It should be left in place for 5 minutes if the patient is febrile or noncompliant (talks or opens mouth frequently).
11. At the appropriate time, remove the thermometer from the patient's mouth while wearing gloves. Remove the sheath by holding the very edge of the sheath with your thumb and forefinger and pulling down from the open edge over the length of the thermometer to the bulb. Discard the sheath into a biohazard container.	

(continued)

Procedure 17-3   *(continued)*

Measuring Oral Temperature Using a Glass Mercury Thermometer

Steps	Reason

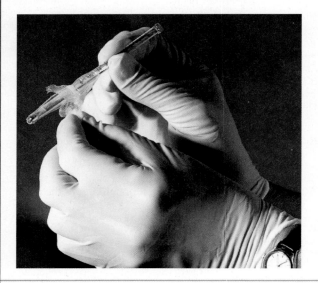

Step 11. Remove the sheath by grasping the end nearest the tip and inverting the plastic toward the bulb. The soiled area should now be inside the sheath.

Steps	Reason
12. Hold the thermometer horizontal at eye level and note the level of mercury that has risen into the column.	
13. Sanitize and disinfect the thermometer according to the facility policy and wash your hands.	Wash the thermometer with cool or tepid soapy water, rinse with cool water, and dry well. Place the thermometer in a disinfectant solution, such as 70% isopropyl alcohol, according to facility policy.

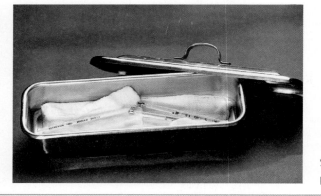

Step 13. Store clean thermometers in a covered instrument tray padded with gauze to prevent chipping or cracking of the glass.

Steps	Reason
14. Record the patient's temperature.	Procedures are considered not done if they are not recorded. The vital signs (temperature, pulse, respirations, and blood pressure) are usually recorded together.

Procedure 17-4

Measuring a Rectal Temperature

Purpose: Accurately measure and record a rectal temperature using a glass mercury thermometer.

Equipment: Glass mercury rectal thermometer; tissues or cotton balls; disposable plastic sheath; surgical lubricant; biohazard container; cool, soapy water; disinfectant solution; gloves.

Standard: This procedure should take 5 minutes.

Steps	Reason
1. Wash your hands and assemble the necessary supplies.	Handwashing aids infection control.
2. Dry the thermometer if it has been stored in a disinfectant solution by wiping it from the bulb up the stem with a tissue or cotton ball.	Removing the wet disinfectant allows the thermometer to slip easily into the sheath.
3. Carefully check the thermometer for chips or cracks.	A chipped or cracked thermometer may injure the patient.
4. Check the reading in the thermometer by holding the stem horizontally at eye level and turning it slowly to see the mercury column.	It is easiest to see the mercury in the column in this position.
5. If the reading is above 94°F, shake down the thermometer by securely grasping it at the end of the stem with your thumb and forefinger and snapping your wrist several times. Avoid hitting the thermometer against anything while snapping your wrist.	The mercury must begin below 94°F to get an accurate temperature reading.
6. Insert the thermometer into the plastic sheath.	Follow the package instructions.
7. Spread lubricant onto a tissue and then from the tissue onto the sheath of the thermometer.	When using a tube of lubricant, avoid cross-contamination by not applying lubricant directly to the thermometer. A lubricant should always be used for rectal insertion to prevent patient discomfort.
8. Greet and identify the patient and explain the procedure.	

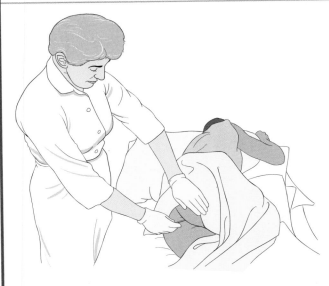

Step 9. The patient in a side-lying position draped appropriately. (Reprinted with permission from LifeART. Philadelphia: Lippincott Williams & Wilkins, 2004.)

(continued)

Procedure 17-4   (continued)

Measuring a Rectal Temperature

Steps	Reason
9. Ensure the patient's privacy by placing the patient in a side-lying position facing the examination room door and draping appropriately.	If the examination room door is opened, a patient facing the door is less likely to be exposed. The side-lying position facilitates exposure of the anus.
10. Apply gloves and visualize the anus by lifting the top buttock with your nondominant hand.	Never insert the thermometer without first having a clear view of the anus.
11. Gently insert the thermometer past the sphincter muscle about 1.5 inches for an adult, 1 inch for a child, and 0.5 inch for an infant.	Inserting the thermometer at these depths helps prevent perforating the anal canal.
12. Release the upper buttock and hold the thermometer in place with your dominant hand for 3 minutes. Replace the drape without moving the dominant hand.	The thermometer will not stay in place if it is not held. Replacing the drape will ensure the patient's privacy.
13. After 3 minutes, remove the thermometer and sheath. Discard the sheath into a biohazard container.	The lubricant or sheath may obscure the mercury column and should be removed before you read the thermometer.
14. Note the reading with the thermometer horizontal at eye level.	
15. Give the patient a tissue to wipe away excess lubricant and assist with dressing if necessary.	
16. Sanitize and disinfect the thermometer according to the facility policy.	
17. Remove your gloves and wash your hands.	This prevents the spread of microorganisms.
18. Record the procedure and mark the letter R next to the reading, indicating that the temperature was taken rectally.	Temperatures are presumed to have been taken orally unless otherwise noted in the health record. The vital signs (temperature, pulse, respirations, and blood pressure) are usually recorded together.

Note: Infants and very small children may be held in your lap or over your knees for this procedure. Hold the thermometer and the buttocks with your dominant hand while securing the child with your nondominant hand. If the child moves, the thermometer and your hand will move together, avoiding injury to the anal canal.

Procedure 17-5

Measuring an Axillary Temperature

Purpose: Accurately measure and record an axillary temperature using a glass mercury thermometer.

Equipment: Glass mercury (oral or rectal) thermometer; tissues or cotton balls; disposable plastic sheath; biohazard container; cool, soapy water; disinfectant solution.

Standard: This procedure should take 15 minutes.

Steps	Reason
1. Wash your hands and assemble the necessary supplies.	Handwashing aids infection control.
2. Dry the thermometer if it has been stored in a disinfectant solution by wiping it from the bulb up the stem with a tissue or cotton ball.	Removing the wet disinfectant allows the thermometer to slip easily into the sheath.
3. Carefully check the thermometer for chips or cracks.	A chipped or cracked thermometer may injure the patient.
4. Check the reading in the thermometer by holding the stem horizontally at eye level and turning it slowly to see the mercury column.	It is easiest to see the mercury in the column in this position.
5. If the reading is above 94°F, shake down the thermometer by securely grasping it at the end of the stem with your thumb and forefinger and snapping your wrist several times. Avoid hitting the thermometer against anything while snapping your wrist.	The mercury must begin below 94°F to get an accurate temperature reading.
6. Insert the thermometer into the plastic sheath.	Follow the package instructions.
7. Expose the patient's axilla without exposing more of the chest or upper body than is necessary.	The patient's privacy must be protected at all times.
8. Place the bulb of the thermometer deep in the axilla and bring the patient's arm down, crossing the forearm over the chest. Drape the patient as appropriate for privacy.	This position offers the best skin contact with the thermometer and maintains a closed environment.

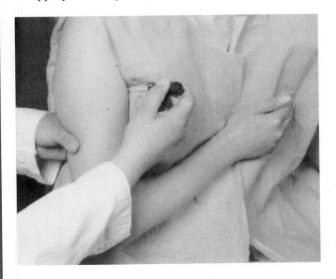

Step 8. With the thermometer in the axilla, the arm should be down and the forearm should be crossed across the chest.

(continued)

Procedure 17-5   (continued)

Measuring an Axillary Temperature

Steps	Reason
9. Leave the thermometer in place for 10 minutes.	Axillary temperatures take longer than oral or rectal ones. Since the thermometer is secure in the axilla, it is not necessary to hold it in place unless the patient does not understand to leave the arm down.
10. At the appropriate time, remove the thermometer from the patient's axilla and remove the sheath by holding the very edge of the sheath with your thumb and forefinger, pulling down from the open edge over the length of the thermometer to the bulb. Discard the sheath into a biohazard container.	
11. Hold the thermometer horizontal at eye level and note the level of mercury that has risen into the column.	
12. Sanitize and disinfect the thermometer according to the facility policy.	
13. Wash your hands.	This prevents the spread of microorganisms.
14. Record the procedure and mark a letter A next to the reading, indicating that the reading is axillary.	Temperatures are presumed to have been taken orally unless otherwise noted in the health record. The vital signs (temperature, pulse, respirations, and blood pressure) are usually recorded together.

Procedure 17-6

Measuring Temperature Using an Electronic Thermometer

Purpose: Accurately measure and record a patient's temperature using an electronic thermometer.

Equipment: Electronic thermometer with oral or rectal probe, lubricant and gloves for rectal temperatures, disposable probe cover, biohazard container.

Standard: This task should take 5 minutes.

Steps	Reason
1. Wash your hands and assemble the necessary supplies.	Handwashing aids infection control.
2. Greet and identify the patient and explain the procedure.	Identifying the patient prevents errors.
3. Choose the most appropriate method (oral, axillary, or rectal) and attach the appropriate probe to the battery-powered unit.	
4. Insert the probe into a probe cover. Covers are usually carried with the unit in a specially fitted box attached to the back of the unit.	All probes fit into one size probe cover. If using the last probe cover, be sure to attach a new box of covers to the unit to be ready for the next patient.
5. Position the thermometer appropriately for the method.	If measuring the temperature rectally, be sure to apply lubricant to the probe cover and hold the probe in place.
6. Wait for the electronic unit to beep when it senses no signs of the temperature rising further. This usually occurs within 20 to 30 seconds.	
7. After the beep, remove the probe and note the reading on the digital display screen on the unit.	
8. Discard the probe cover in a biohazard container by depressing a button, usually on the end of the probe. Most units automatically shut off when the probe is reinserted into the unit.	Always note the temperature reading before replacing the probe in the slot on the unit.
9. Remove your gloves if any, wash your hands, and record the procedure.	Record the temperature exactly as if taken with a glass mercury thermometer. Be sure to indicate a rectal or axillary reading by recording an R or A next to the reading in the documentation. The vital signs (temperature, pulse, respirations, and blood pressure) are usually recorded together.
10. Return the unit and probe to the charging base.	Although the unit is battery powered, it should be kept in the charging base so that the battery is always adequately charged.

Procedure 17-7

Measuring Temperature Using a Tympanic Thermometer

Purpose: Accurately measure and record a patient's temperature using a tympanic thermometer.

Equipment: Tympanic thermometer, disposable probe covers, biohazard container.

Standard: This task should take 5 minutes.

Steps	Reason
1. Wash your hands and assemble the necessary supplies.	Handwashing aids infection control.
2. Greet and identify the patient and explain the procedure.	Identifying the patient prevents errors.
3. Insert the ear probe into a probe cover.	Always put a clean probe cover on the ear probe before inserting it.
4. Place the end of the ear probe in the patient's ear canal with your dominant hand while straightening out the ear canal with your nondominant hand.	Straighten the ear canal of most patients by pulling the top posterior part of the outer ear up and back. For children under 3 years of age, pull the outer ear down and back.
5. With the ear probe properly placed in the ear canal, press the button on the thermometer. The reading will be displayed on the digital display screen in about 2 seconds.	
6. Remove the probe and note the reading. Discard the probe cover in a biohazard container.	The probe covers are for one use only.
7. Wash your hands and record the procedure.	Record the temperature as if using a glass mercury thermometer. Be sure to indicate that the tympanic temperature was taken. The vital signs (temperature, pulse, respirations, and blood pressure) are usually recorded together.
8. Return the unit and probe to the charging base.	The unit should be kept in the charging base so that the battery is always adequately charged.

Procedure 17-8

Measuring the Radial Pulse

Purpose: Accurately measure and record a patient's radial pulse.

Equipment: A watch with a sweep second hand.

Standard: This procedure should take 3 to 5 minutes.

Steps	Reason
1. Wash your hands.	Handwashing aids infection control.
2. Greet and identify the patient and explain the procedure.	In most cases, the pulse is taken at the same time as the other vital signs.
3. Position the patient with the arm relaxed and supported either on the lap of the patient or on a table.	If the arm is not supported or the patient is uncomfortable, the pulse may be difficult to find and the count may be affected.
4. With the index, middle, and ring fingers of your dominant hand, press with your fingertips firmly enough to feel the pulse but gently enough not to obliterate it.	Do not use your thumb; it has a pulse of its own that may be confused with the patient's. You may place your thumb on the opposite side of the patient's wrist to steady your hand.
5. If the pulse is regular, count it for 30 seconds, watching the second hand of your watch. Multiply the number of pulsations by 2, since the pulse is always recorded as beats per minute. If the pulse is irregular, count it for a full 60 seconds.	Counting an irregular pulse for less than 60 seconds may give an inaccurate measurement.
6. Record the rate in the patient's health record with the other vital signs. Also, note the rhythm if irregular and the volume if thready or bounding.	Procedures are considered not to have been done if they are not recorded. The vital signs (temperature, pulse, respirations, and blood pressure) are usually recorded together.

Procedure 17-9

Measuring Respirations

Purpose: Accurately measure and record a patient's respirations.

Equipment: A watch with a sweeping second hand.

Standard: This procedure should take 3 to 5 minutes.

Steps	Reason
1. Wash your hands.	Handwashing aids infection control.
2. Greet and identify the patient and explain the procedure.	In most cases, the respirations are counted at the same time as the other pulse.
3. After counting the radial pulse and still watching your second hand, count a complete rise and fall of the chest as one respiration. *Note:* Some patients have abdominal movement rather than chest movement during respirations. Observe carefully for the easiest area to assess for the most accurate reading.	A patient who is aware that you are observing respirations may alter the breathing pattern. It is best to begin counting respirations immediately after counting the pulse without informing the patient.
4. If the breathing pattern is regular, count the respiratory rate for 30 seconds and multiply by 2. If the pattern is irregular, count for a full 60 seconds.	Counting an irregular respiratory pattern for less than 60 seconds may give an inaccurate measurement.
5. Record the respiratory rate in the patient's health record with the other vital signs. Also, note the rhythm if irregular along with any unusual or abnormal sounds, such as wheezing.	Procedures are considered not to have been done if they are not recorded. The vital signs (temperature, pulse, respirations, and blood pressure) are usually recorded together.

Procedure 17-10

Measuring Blood Pressure

Purpose: Accurately measure and record a patient's blood pressure.

Equipment: Sphygmomanometer, stethoscope

Standard: This procedure should take 5 minutes.

Steps	Purpose
1. Wash your hands and assemble your equipment.	Handwashing aids infection control.
2. Greet and identify the patient and explain the procedure.	Identifying the patient prevents errors, and explaining the procedure eases anxiety.
3. Position the patient with the arm to be used supported with the forearm on the lap or a table and slightly flexed, with the palm upward. The upper arm should be level with the patient's heart.	Positioning the arm with the palm upward facilitates finding and palpating the brachial artery. If the upper arm is higher or lower than the heart, an inaccurate reading may result.
4. Expose the patient's arm.	Any clothing over the area may obscure the sounds. If the sleeve is pulled up, it may become tight and act as a tourniquet, decreasing the flow of blood and causing an inaccurate blood pressure reading.
5. Palpate the brachial pulse in the antecubital area and center the deflated cuff directly over the brachial artery. The lower edge of the cuff should be 1 to 2 inches above the antecubital area.	If the cuff is placed too low, it may interfere with the placement of the stethoscope and cause noises that obscure the Korotkoff sounds.
6. Wrap the cuff smoothly and snugly around the arm and secure with the Velcro edges.	
7. With the air pump in your dominant hand and the valve between your thumb and forefinger, turn the screw clockwise to tighten. Do not tighten it to the point that it will be difficult to release.	The cuff will not inflate with the valve open. If the valve is too tightly closed, it will be difficult to loosen with one hand after the cuff is inflated.

Step 7. Holding the bulb and the screw valve properly allows you to inflate and deflate the cuff easily.

(continued)

Procedure 17-10   *(continued)*

Measuring Blood Pressure

Steps	Reason
8. While palpating the brachial pulse with your nondominant hand, inflate the cuff and note the point or number on the dial or mercury column at which you no longer feel the brachial pulse.	The dial or mercury column should be at eye level. Noting this number gives you a reference point for reinflating the cuff when taking the blood pressure.

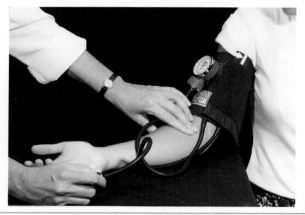

Step 8. Palpate the brachial pulse before auscultating the blood pressure.

Steps	Reason
9. Deflate the cuff by turning the valve counterclockwise. Wait at least 30 seconds before reinflating the cuff.	Always wait at least 30 seconds after deflating the cuff to allow circulation to return to the extremity.
10. Place the stethoscope earpieces in your ears with the openings pointed slightly forward. Stand about 3 feet from the manometer with the gauge at eye level. The stethoscope tubing should hang freely without touching or rubbing against any part of the cuff.	With the earpieces pointing forward in the ears, the openings follow the natural opening of the ear canal. The manometer should be at eye level to decrease any chance of error when it is read. If the stethoscope rubs against other objects, environmental sounds may obscure the Korotkoff sounds.
11. Place the diaphragm of the stethoscope against the brachial artery and hold it in place with your nondominant hand without pressing too hard.	If not pressed firmly enough, you may not hear the sounds. Pressing too firmly may obliterate the pulse.

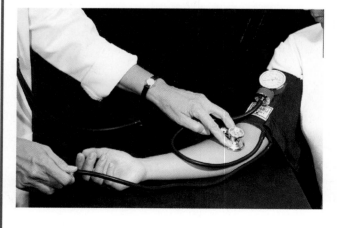

Step 11. Hold the stethoscope diaphragm firmly against the brachial artery.

(continued)

Procedure 17-10 *(continued)*

Measuring Blood Pressure

Steps	Reason
12. With your dominant hand, turn the screw on the valve just enough to close the valve; inflate the cuff. Pump the valve bulb to about 30 mm Hg above the number noted during step 8.	Inflating more than 30 mm Hg above baseline is uncomfortable for the patient and unnecessary; inflating less may produce an inaccurate systolic reading.
13. Once the cuff is appropriately inflated, turn the valve counterclockwise to release the air at about 2 to 4 mm Hg per second.	Releasing the air too fast will cause missed beats, and releasing it too slowly will interfere with circulation.
14. Listening carefully, note the point on the gauge at which you hear the first clear tapping sound. This is the systolic sound, or Korotkoff I.	Aneroid and mercury measurements are always made as even numbers because of the way the manometer is calibrated.

Step 14A. The meniscus on the mercury column in this example reads 120 mm Hg.

Step 14B. The gauge on the aneroid manometer reads 80 mm Hg.

Steps	Reason
15. Maintaining control of the valve screw, continue to listen and deflate the cuff. When you hear the last sound, note the reading and quickly deflate the cuff. *Note:* Never immediately reinflate the cuff if you are unsure of the reading. Totally deflate the cuff and wait 1 to 2 minutes before repeating the procedure.	The last sound heard is Korotkoff V and is recorded as the bottom number or diastolic blood pressure.
16. Remove the cuff and press the air from the bladder of the cuff.	

(continued)

Procedure 17-10 *(continued)*

Measuring Blood Pressure

Steps	Reason
17. If this is the first recording or a new patient, the health care professional may also want a reading in the other arm or in another position.	Blood pressure varies in some patients between the arms or in different positions such as lying or standing.
18. Put the equipment away and wash your hands.	
19. Record the reading with the systolic over the diastolic, noting which arm was used (120/80 LA). Also record the patient's position if other than sitting.	Procedures are considered not done if they are not recorded. The vital signs (temperature, pulse, respirations, and blood pressure) are usually recorded together.

CHAPTER SUMMARY

Anthropometric measurements include height and weight. Vital signs include temperature (T), pulse (P), respirations (R), and blood pressure (BP). When a patient first visits the health care facility, these measurements are recorded as a baseline and used as a comparison for data collected at subsequent visits. These measurements, which provide important data for the health care professional to use in diagnosing and treating illnesses, are very frequently performed by allied health professionals.

Critical Thinking Challenges

1. Ms. Black arrived late for her appointment, frantic and explaining that she had car trouble on the way to the office, could not find a parking place, and just locked her keys inside her car. How do you expect these events to affect her vital signs? Explain why.
2. What size cuff do you choose for Mrs. Cooper, an elderly woman who is 5 feet 3 inches tall and weighs approximately 90 pounds? Why?
3. An elderly woman with osteoporosis requests that her height be taken and recorded today, since she "feels shorter." Do you explain that the facility policy requires measuring height only at the first visit and give her the previously recorded measurements, or do you comply with her request?

Answers to Checkpoint Questions

1. Accurately measuring vital signs assists the physician in diagnosing and treating various disorders.

2. Rectal temperature measurements are usually 1° higher than oral measurements because of the vascularity and tightly closed environment of the rectum.
3. A child's body temperature may be slightly higher than an adult's because of the faster metabolism in a child.
4. Tympanic thermometers measure the temperature of the blood in the eardrum. The ear canal is a closed environment with the probe in place, providing a rapid, noninvasive, and accurate reading when performed correctly.
5. Measuring a patient's pulse entails assessing and recording the rate (number of heartbeats in 1 minute), rhythm (regular or irregular), and volume (thready, bounding).
6. Contraction of the diaphragm causes negative pressure in the lungs, which respond by filling with inhaled air.
7. During systole, the heart contracts and forces blood out and through the arteries. In diastole, the heart relaxes and fills with blood.
8. The pulse pressure is the difference between the systolic and diastolic blood pressures, and the auscultatory gap is an abrupt but temporary end to the tapping sound heard when auscultating the blood pressure.

 Websites

National Reye's Syndrome Foundation
    www.reyessyndrome.org
American Society of Hypertension www.ash-us.org
American Lung Association www.lungusa.org

Unit 6

Complementary and Alternative Medicine

Overview of Complementary and Alternative Medicines

CHAPTER OBJECTIVES

In this chapter, you'll learn:

1. To define complementary, alternative, and integrative medicine.
2. To discuss the history, cultural context and current use of alternative healing.
3. To identify the major types of complementary and alternative medicine as defined by the National Center for Complementary and Alternative Medicine (NCCAM).

4. To discuss approaches for evaluating evidence for therapeutic efficacy of CAM and conventional care.

IN 1997, four out of ten adults in the United States used at least one form of complementary or alternative medicine (CAM), according to Eisenberg et al. (1998). Among people between ages 35 and 49, the numbers increased to one out of two. The most frequently used therapies were relaxation techniques, herbal medicine, massage, and chiropractic manipulation. Eisenberg and colleagues also estimated that visits to alternative health care providers increased from 427 million in 1990 to 629 million in 1997, creating a $21.2 billion industry. In fact, the number of visits to CAM providers exceeded visits to primary care physicians by approximately 243 million, with an estimated $12.2 billion paid out of pocket. Burg's study (1998) found similar usage rates among health care professionals; more than half of his respondents had used at least one type of alternative therapy at some time. A 1998 study by Wetzel et al. revealed that almost two-thirds of medical schools have integrated alternative and complementary approaches into their curricula.

Neck and back problems were the most frequently cited (42%) medical problems for which CAM was sought. People also sought CAM for the treatment of anxiety and depression, headaches, arthritis, GI problems, fatigue, insomnia, sprains and strains, allergies, lung problems, and hypertension. One out of three people who visited a medical doctor also consulted a CAM provider for the same medical problem. Most patients, however, didn't discuss their plans to combine CAM with conventional treatment with their medical doctor (Eisenberg et al., 1998). According to Astin (1998), the following qualities served as indicators of those most likely to use CAM: higher level of education, poorer health status, interest in spirituality or personal growth psychology, history of a transformational experience that altered the individual's world view, and identification with a cultural group committed to environmentalism or feminism.

Why has the use of CAM risen so sharply? To understand the answer to that question, it is first necessary to understand what CAM is and where it came from.

WHAT IS CAM?

A 1998 study by Eskinazi proposed that alternative medicine be defined as "a broad set of health care practices that are not readily integrated into the dominant health care model because they pose challenges to diverse societal beliefs and practices (cultural, economic, scientific, medical, and educational)." The National Center for Complementary and Alternative Medicine (NCCAM) defines alternative medicine as "a broad range of healing philosophies (schools of thought), approaches, and therapies that mainstream Western (conventional) medicine does not commonly use, accept, study, understand, or make available." But it was NCCAM that took the definition a step further by adding "complementary" to the general definition to arrive at "complementary and alternative medicine, or CAM." This is an important distinction, because CAM may be used either as an *adjunct* to modern medicine (hence "complementary") or *in place of* conventional therapy (hence "alternative").

HISTORY OF CAM

Many of the myriad philosophies and therapies falling under the general heading of CAM actually date back thousands of years. Long before university-trained doctors became the providers of healing, a society's religious leaders were also its healers. Shamanism, a spiritual philosophy in which the individual is believed to be a unit composed of equally important physical and spiritual elements, is a system of spiritual practice dating back 40,000 years to the Stone Age. The tie between physical health and spirituality is also at the core of many of the world's spiritual and philosophical practices, including those of Tibet, India, Japan, and the cultures of Native American peoples.

Priest (or shaman) and healer remained the same person for centuries, even into the European society of the early 1600s. It was in this period that French philosopher Rene Descartes proposed that the study of spirit belonged to the discipline of philosophy (or religion), while the study of the physical body was the province of science. This rejection of the relationship between spirit and body set the stage for the division between practitioners of then-traditional medicine and those who believed that science should be the basis for all health care. This concept took some time to catch on, however.

Prior to the Industrial Revolution, which began in the late 1700s and lasted until the mid-1800s, science — particularly medical science — was still primarily viewed through a haze of superstition and suspicion. In fact, some nations had laws forbidding certain forms of research; for example, in Victorian England it was illegal to dissect a human cadaver for research purposes. During the course of the Industrial Revolution, however, a more tolerant view of science began to surface. By the end of the 19th century this newfound tolerance had grown into enthusiastic acceptance as people began to take pride in their willingness to embrace new technologies.

Like many other sciences, modern health care was in its infancy in the early 1900s. Surgical techniques were primitive at best, cellular understanding of disease was very basic, and hospitals were where people went to die. Aside from sulfur, antibiotics were unavailable, making infectious disease the most common cause of death. Although cities were growing, and with them a more impersonal way of life, most people still lived in close proximity to their families, and a strong sense of family responsibility was still the cornerstone of most lives. People still relied on family members or acknowledged healers to provide health care, and treatment typically took the form of traditional home or cultural remedies, herbal preparations, and other methods that supported the body's own recuperative powers.

As the decades passed, though, the modernization of health care gained momentum until it became a revolution. A better understanding of disease and its etiology made treatments more effective. Drugs and immunizations eradicated many infectious diseases, once-fatal illnesses were now curable or at least controllable, and the expected lifespan of Americans lengthened beyond that of individuals in any other country. Whereas local healers, usually trained by their predecessors, once provided most, if not all, of a community's medical care, formally trained physicians became the center of the new health care system. With the increasing availability — and variety — of scientific health care methods and the growing number of practitioners familiar with those methods, modern health care supplanted traditional medicine.

In the past two to three decades, attitudes toward health care issues have started to come full circle. Conventional (or "modern") medicine uses pharmaceuticals, surgery, radiation, chemotherapy, or apparatus such as dialysis machines to treat disease. Many of the methods were developed first in research laboratories rather than by practitioners. There are times when such methods may be preferable to CAM. Often, however, expensive, invasive, or side-effect-fraught treatments are used before other treatments are considered.

Spiraling health care costs, dissatisfaction with the "cost effective" practice methods dictated by insurance companies, and general disillusionment with a high-tech, low-touch health care system that so often treats symptoms without regard for the cause (Eliopoulos, 1999) have caused many people to seek alternatives to the modern form of health care. Information that wasn't previously accessible — for example, therapeutic modalities that are standard in one country, but not in another — is now widely distributed via the Internet and other media. The accessibility of a broader range of options has empowered people to seek alternative treatments for illnesses and chronic conditions unresponsive to conventional treatment, and the result is the resurgence of CAM.

FOUNDATIONS OF CAM

One of the difficulties in defining CAM is the broad range of therapies that the term encompasses. This section describes and defines some of the basic principles and domains of CAM.

Holism

One of the most significant aspects of the resurgence of CAM is the reunion of science and philosophy (or religion) as Western culture once again recognizes the importance of inner experiences to the health of the individual. Nowhere is this concept more apparent than in the notion of holism, which is one of the cornerstones of CAM. Holism is the view that individuals are composed of four interdependent and interrelated elements — physiological, psychological, sociological, and spiritual — which must be addressed as a unit when treating illness and promoting good health. Note that holism isn't a recently formulated concept; before the discovery and development of pharmacotherapeutic treatments for tuberculosis, Canadian physician Sir William Osler (1849–1919) believed

that a patient's recovery was more dependent on what went on in his or her mind than in the lungs (Siegel, 1986).

Holism has gained popularity since Osler embraced the concept at the turn of the 20th century, and now many organizations and individuals involved in CAM share a common belief in the importance of the holistic view. The health care model of the American Holistic Nurses Association (AHNA) is framed on a holistic approach. Central to holistic nursing is the necessity to identify the interrelationship of the four elements and the knowledge that the individual is a unitary whole in mutual process with his or her environment (Dossey et al., 2000).

The concept of holism was both expanded and refined by Eliopoulos (1999), and is also a key component of at least one of the five health care domains described by NCCAM, as discussed below.

Five Basic Principles

Eliopoulos' 1999 study identified five basic principles underlying CAM:

- the body has the ability to heal itself
- health and healing are related to a harmony of mind, body, and spirit
- basic, good health practices build the foundation for healing
- healing practices are individualized
- people are responsible for their own healing (Eliopoulos, 1999).

The notion that mind, body, and spirit are interrelated and that stress on one dimension invariably places stress on the others is reflected in Eliopoulos' principles and, indeed, is the foundation of many CAM therapies. The core of many CAM practices is teaching patients the importance of taking a holistic view of the healing process.

NCCAM's Five Domains

Because there are almost as many forms of CAM as there are people walking the earth, it is helpful to categorize the various systems into domains based on how they are used. NCCAM has identified CAM practices in five primary domains: alternative medical systems, biologically based treatments, manipulative and body-based methods, energy therapies, and mind-body interventions (NCCAM, 2000).

Alternative Medical Systems

Alternative medical systems include complete systems of theory and practice that exist outside conventional biomedicine and are frequently practiced by cultures in other parts of the world. The alternative medical systems most familiar to many Westerners are Chinese medicine and Ayurveda, or Indian medicine. Both Chinese medicine and Ayurveda approach healing from a holistic standpoint.

Biologically Based Therapies

Biologically based therapies include the use of dietary supplements, herbal preparations, special diets, and orthomolecular and biological therapies. Examples of orthomolecular therapies are administration of megadoses of vitamins or other chemical supplements, such as magnesium and melatonin. Biological therapies include the use of preparations derived from nature, such as shark cartilage for cancer or bee pollen for autoimmune and inflammatory disorders.

Manipulative, Body-based, and Energy Therapies

Manipulative and body-based therapies include chiropractic manipulation as well as massage, Rolfing, and the Feldenkrais method. Energy therapies focus on energy fields that either surround or penetrate the body, or consist of outside sources such as electromagnetic fields. Therapeutic Touch is an energy therapy originated in the United States by Dolores Krieger, a registered nurse. It's performed by a trained practitioner who assesses, and subsequently attempts to manipulate and balance, the energy field surrounding the patient (Krieger, 1993).

Mind-body Interventions

Mind-body interventions are based on the existence of a mind-body connection and the ability of the mind to affect bodily functions and symptoms. Examples of mind-body therapies are meditation, hypnosis, visual imagery, prayer, and mental healing. Many of these therapies can be said to include a holistic approach.

AN OVERVIEW OF CAM SYSTEMS

This section provides an expanded view of several of the most widely used CAM systems.

Chinese and Indian Medicine

Two of the most well known and ancient systems of CAM are Chinese medicine and Indian medicine (or *Ayurveda*), both of which have been in use for thousands of years.

The core of Chinese medicine is the notion of an energy force called *qi* (pronounced "chee"), which flows through the body along paths called *meridians*. The unimpeded flow of qi is necessary for the restoration and maintenance of health. If an individual's qi is stagnant, accumulations occur in the body and can lead to poor health — mental, spiritual, and physical. Physical manifestations of stagnant qi can include obesity, cancers, and other problems that manifest as immune or degenerative diseases.

To understand qi, one should also be familiar with the principles of *yin* and *yang*. The yin-yang symbol may be familiar: it depicts two fish, intertwined head to tail. One fish is dark with a white eye (yin); the other, white with a dark eye (yang). The intertwined fish form a circle representing a universe that's made up of unlimited pairs of opposites interacting with each other. Qi is a yang force, associated with energy of the body, and yin is considered the "mother of qi" because it's associated with body fluids, specifically blood. One method that facilitates the flow of qi is acupuncture, a practice that has been the mainstay of Chinese medicine for centuries. (Acupuncture is described in detail in the section below devoted to energetic manual healing.) Other methods for maintaining or restoring the balance of qi include diet, exercise, meditation, spiritual practices, and herbal therapy. Qi is synonymous with *prana* in India and *ki* in Japan.

Another complex and ancient system of medicine is *Ayurveda*, practiced in India. Ayurveda means "science of life" and has been practiced as the medical model in India for over 5,000 years. As with Chinese medicine, Ayurvedic medicine is highly individualized, using therapies that bring the body, mind, and spirit back into harmony within the individual and within nature. It's also based on the concept of energy flow, called prana, which is facilitated by a balancing of *doshas* (body types). *Constitution* is the term used to describe an individual's character, temperament, and overall health profile, including strengths and weaknesses. Ayurvedic medicine identifies three major doshas: *vata*, *pitta*, and *kapha*.

The vata dosha is changeable and unpredictable. Vata individuals tend to be erratic in both thought processes and behavior, to be anxious, and to suffer from insomnia. People who are vata tend toward slenderness. Although vatas have a lot of energy, they often fail to follow a project through to completion.

Pitta individuals, as opposed to vatas, tend to be quite predictable. They are of medium build and possess strength and endurance. Pittas tend to be intelligent and so passionate as to be unduly critical or display explosive outbursts.

The kapha individual is relaxed, solid, heavy, and strong. Kaphas have a tendency to be overweight. For kaphas, everything related to thinking and behavior is slow, and for this reason they often procrastinate.

The purpose of Ayurvedic medical treatment is to bring the patient back into harmony within himself and within nature. Disease management in Ayurvedic medicine concentrates on cleansing and detoxifying (*shodan*), palliation (*shaman*), rejuvenation (*rasayana*), and mental hygiene and spiritual healing (*satvajaya*). Specific therapies may include diet, exercise, yoga, meditation, massage, tonics, baths, enemas, or aromatherapy.

Both Chinese medicine and Ayurveda are sophisticated systems based on the assumption of a mind-body connection and the body's innate ability to heal itself if provided the proper tools and environment.

Homeopathic Medicine

Homeopathy, derived from the Greek words *homeo*, meaning similar, and *pathos*, meaning suffering, is a form of

CAM that has been practiced for only around 200 years. Samuel Hahnemann, a German physician, was the first person to posit the concept of homeopathic medicine. Hahnemann tested hundreds of different minerals and herbs, carefully recording the response or symptoms that each produced. From his findings he drew three primary conclusions: first, that like cures like, a notion first proposed by Hippocrates and termed the Law of Similars; second, that substances gain rather than lose potency as they are diluted, a concept referred to as the Law of Infinitesimal Dose; and third, that illnesses are specific to individuals and can't be treated with a universal panacea.

The Law of Similars manifests in the development of vaccines against illnesses such as measles, influenza, pneumonia, and so forth, and is also the basis for the practice of immunotherapy for allergy patients. According to this ancient principle, giving a patient a very minute quantity of the substance responsible for his disease awakens the immune system, forcing it to produce antibodies against the disease.

Homeopathic medicine, as outlined by Dr. Hahnemann, is widely practiced in Europe, including the United Kingdom, France, and Germany. The British Royal family is known to use homeopathic remedies, and homeopathy is considered a postgraduate medical specialty in Britain. Homeopathy is also practiced in India, Mexico, Argentina, and Brazil. Underscoring the importance of homeopathic medicine worldwide, the World Health Organization called for it to be integrated with conventional medicine by the year 2000 to ensure adequate provision of global health care. Interestingly, however, the reason homeopathic medicine works can't be explained, even by homeopaths — the practice doesn't follow any known laws of chemistry, physics, or pharmacology.

Naturopathic Medicine

Naturopathic medicine — cures derived from nature — is based on the principle that disease is a manifestation of natural systems the body uses to heal itself. This philosophy is a derivation of the ancient medical systems, including traditional Chinese medicine, Ayurveda, Native American medicine, and ancient Greek medicine. From these disciplines, naturopathic medicine borrows its basic principles: treat the cause rather than the effect, do no harm, treat the whole person, and prevention is the best cure. Father Sebastian Kneipp, a priest who credited his recovery from tuberculosis to bathing in the Danube, popularized naturopathy. Naturopathy further developed and spread through Kneipp's student, Benedict Lust, who carried the discipline of naturopathy to the United States in the 1890s and founded the first naturopathic college in the United States in New York City in 1902.

Treatment and prevention modalities used by naturopaths include nutrition, homeopathy, acupuncture, electrotherapy, herbal medicine, hydrotherapy, exercise, manipulation, physical therapy, stress reduction, counseling, and pharma-

cology. Lust's program for curing included elimination of "evil" habits, incorporation of corrective habits, and development of new principles of living. In naturopathic medicine, the physician serves also as teacher and as such is responsible for educating, empowering, and motivating patients.

Diet, Nutrition, and Lifestyle Changes

The type of CAM falling under the heading of diet, nutrition, and lifestyle changes may be considered to overlap with the holistic approach to wellness because its basic premise is that a lack of appropriate diet and lifestyle habits contributes to the development of disease. Subcategories within this broad category include dietary changes; supplemental therapy with vitamins, minerals, or other nutritional supplements; exercise for the mind and body; relaxation for the mind and body; and lifestyle changes.

Diet and Nutrition

Throughout history, people have used food to aid the healing process and to promote good health; the Greek physician, Hippocrates, referred to food as medicine. However, it was not until 1988 that the Surgeon General of the United States publicly acknowledged the connection between diet and health. Possible reasons for modern society's failure to recognize the importance of proper nutrition may include a lack of extensive study of the topic in the typical medical school curriculum and the convenience of "fast" and "junk" foods. However, with each passing day, more people recognize the connection between today's poor food sources and disease.

The nutritional value of modern food is affected in two ways: by processing or altering with chemical additives, and by the degeneration of the environment itself. Food is routinely altered by any of over 2,000 additives used for flavoring, coloring, preserving, texturizing, and stabilizing. Adulteration also includes hydrogenation of oils, thereby producing trans fatty acids, which are implicated in the development of degenerative diseases. The very environment in which they're produced also contributes to the poor nutritional value of most modern foods. Minerals in the soil, clean water, and pure air are essential to the growth of whole, healthy foods, but all are in dangerously short supply. Crops are exposed to any of more than four hundred pesticides that are approved for use in the United States. These pesticides penetrate soil, water, and both land and water animals — and thereby pervade much of the food we consume. Irradiation, which is used to combat bacteria, viruses, and fungi, may be effective in destroying these organisms, at the cost of forming toxins such as benzene and formaldehyde.

Dentist Weston A. Price (1997) determined the relationship between eating habits and degenerative diseases. He observed that among primitive tribal populations, those who stuck to their native diets and consumed no processed or otherwise adulterated foods had healthy dentition: straight teeth, no caries, well-developed arches and nasal passages, with no evidence of degenerative diseases or cancers. Individuals who abandoned the tribal foods in favor of modern diets demonstrated poor dental health — as evidenced by crooked teeth, caries, and small arches leading to small nasal passages — and degenerative diseases.

Price's findings, when considered alongside the growing number of people afflicted with cancer, heart disease, obesity, and other diseases or disorders, add to the evidence that the modern diet of refined and processed food not only fails to protect against disease, but may well contribute to the development of many diseases. Recent studies have revealed the role of various foods in causing heart disease, cancer, osteoporosis, and other degenerative diseases.

For thousands of years, practitioners of Chinese medicine have used food to help people maintain health, balance, and well-being. Interestingly, food itself isn't the only important aspect of diet in the Chinese medical model. Preparation, combinations of foods eaten at a given meal, and the thoughts and feelings associated with the preparation and consumption of food are all important aspects of the way food contributes to harmony and health, reflecting the Chinese recognition of the interplay between humans and nature. Specific types of food also reflect this awareness of balance; for example, people who are affected by the summer heat can be brought back into balance by consuming foods considered to be "cooling," while those whose condition indicates the presence of toxins in their system may be given detoxifying foods and food substances to cleanse their bodies. Because food is valued for its harmonizing qualities as well as its nutrients, variety is an important aspect of meal preparation.

For many years, it was accepted practice not to feed patients in a critical care unit. However, systems of CAM that focus on diet and nutrition recognize the importance of nutrients to the healing process. As the use of CAM gains popularity, growing numbers of nutritionists and other health care practitioners are using nutrition to enhance patients' ability to heal.

Food therapies are abundant and include not only philosophies regarding food, such as those seen in Chinese, naturopathic, and Ayurvedic practices, but also specific treatments or cures that employ certain types of food. Treatments or cures for diseases using food include different types of fasts; juice therapies; enzyme therapy; yeast-combating diets; macrobiotic diets; elimination diets; low-fat, high-carbohydrate diets; high-protein or low-protein diets; Mediterranean diets; anticancer diets; cardiovascular diets; and numerous antiobesity diets.

Orthomolecular medicine is the use of vitamins and minerals, generally in the form of nutritional supplements, to prevent or cure diseases. The most well known use of orthomolecular medicine is the vitamin C research conducted by Nobel prizewinner Linus Pauling. Orthomolecular medicine has far-ranging implications, including the effect of antioxidants on cancer, heart disease, and other degenerative diseases; the use of supplements to cure deficiencies seen in psychiatric patients; and the prevention and reversal of osteoporosis. Other potential uses of orthomolecular medicine include the use of amino acids, essential fatty acids, or glucosamine to cure or prevent degenerative diseases.

Lifestyle Changes

Lifestyle changes include stimulating and relaxing the body and mind as well as ridding the body of toxic substances such as nicotine, alcohol, and drugs (both medicinal and illegal). Exercise and relaxation may boost the immune system in addition to building stronger bodies and minds. Price (1997) found that many tribal cultures knew the importance of exercise to strengthen the body, mind, and spirit, including the association between strong abdominal muscles and maximal breathing. A key element of Chinese medical and philosophical practice is the importance of breathing, movement, and meditation for overall balance between the individual and nature. Modern authorities are also beginning to recognize the relationship between lifestyle and health. For example, Hans Selye (1974) examined the relationship between stress and the development of degenerative diseases or distress. Norman Cousins' personal experience helped him to discover the stress-relieving benefits of laughter (Cousins, 1981).

Exercise bolsters the immune system and strengthens both body and mind. Relaxation also boosts the immune system; in addition, it lowers blood pressure and enables people to handle everyday stress. Popular relaxation techniques include tai chi, qigong, yoga, meditation, prayer, and journaling.

Qigong overlaps other therapeutic approaches in its use of movement, breathing, and meditation to enhance the flow of energy in the body for the purpose of enhancing circulation and strengthening the immune system. Both the ill and the well can use qigong, and its wide usefulness has made it the nucleus of the self-care health system of China. So important is qigong in China that it's estimated to be practiced daily by more than 200 million of China's citizens.

Eliminating toxic substances improves the health in myriad ways, including but not limited to improving cardiac and lung functions and perhaps extending life.

Herbal Medicine

An herb is a plant or part of a plant used as a food, spice, or medicine. Any part of an herb — the root, bark, leaf, berry, flower, fruit, stem, or seed — may be harvested for use.

Herbal medicine, or the use of herbs for medicinal purposes, is also referred to as phytomedicine or phytotherapy. Some conventional practitioners cringe at the thought of using herbs as medicine, when in fact at least a quarter of the pharmaceuticals used today are derived from plant sources. The very word "drug" is derived from an old Dutch word, *drogge*, meaning "to dry." Early medicines typically

TYPES OF MANUAL HEALING THERAPIES

The diagram below shows the different types of manual healing therapies and how they can overlap.

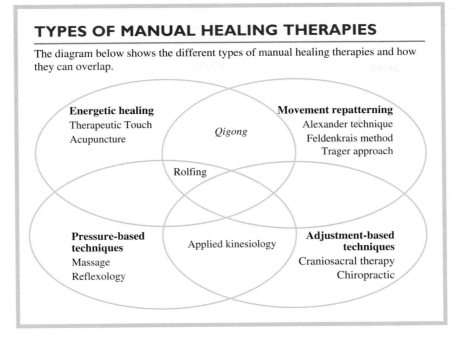

consisted of a single dried herb or a combination, usually administered in the form of a tea or sprinkled into some other beverage or on food. Two common examples are digoxin, which is derived from foxglove, and aspirin, which is derived from white willow bark. Because nature's products can't be patented, herbal pharmaceuticals are combined with other, mainly synthetic ingredients, the preparation is patented, and its herbal origins are forgotten.

Interest in herbal medicine is increasing because of drug interactions and side effects associated with conventional medications. Proponents of herbal medicine stress the decreased likelihood of interactions and untoward effects when such medicines are used properly. In Europe, herbal medicines share the mainstream with modern medications. Commission E in Germany is one notable pharmaceutical agency that produces a well-respected formulary of herbal medicines. As interest in herbs grows in the United States, informational resources for practitioners have become available.

Manual Healing

Manual therapy is a small term to describe the large array of therapies that have at their core the use of the practitioner's hands. These therapies use the therapist's hands directly to manipulate the patient, as energy fields to deliver healing to the patient, or in a combination of touch and energy. Manual therapies can be divided into four overlapping categories, including energetic healing, movement repatterning, pressure-based techniques, and adjustment-based techniques.

Energetic healing includes techniques such as therapeutic touch and acupuncture. Movement repatterning includes techniques such as the Alexander, Feldenkrais, and Trager methods. Massage, reflexology, and pressure-point therapies

are examples of pressure-based techniques. Chiropractic, osteopathic, and craniosacral therapy are forms of manipulative or adjustment-based techniques. Applied kinesiology overlaps the disciplines of pressure-based and adjustment-based techniques. Rolfing may be said to encompass the energetic healing, movement repatterning, and pressure-based categories. Qigong incorporates energetic healing and movement repatterning. The common factor shared by these techniques is that they are all used to reduce pain and stress, to enhance relaxation, and to stimulate circulation in order to promote healing.

Energetic Manual Healing

The energetic forms of manual healing are similar in that they use touch to transfer energy and healing into the patient. However, energetic healing may be either noninvasive, as in the form of Therapeutic Touch, or invasive, as in the case of acupuncture, which requires the use of needles.

Dolores Krieger, considered the founder of modern Therapeutic Touch, developed this therapy in 1972 as an interpretation of several ancient practices in which the practitioner modulates energy fields to decrease the patient's pain and anxiety. Therapeutic Touch is also used to correct problems with autonomic nervous system dysfunction. Rarely touching the patient, the practitioner's hands are kept approximately two to six inches above the body surface. They move along the patient to determine the locations of a blockage in the patient's energy fields. As blockages are identified, the practitioner works to relieve congestion and obstruction and to replenish energy flow.

Acupuncture is a complete system of healing that alleviates pain and boosts the immune system to both heal and prevent illness. Acupuncture theory and technique, based on balancing qi (the vital life energy) within the body, was developed in China thousands of years ago. Qi is mapped via meridians along the body and further divided into over 1,000 acupoints that enhance qi when stimulated with needles. The meridian system has been verified using Galvanic skin response, which detects energy flow along the meridians.

Acupuncture is used to treat pain, addictions, and illnesses. It's so effective in relieving pain that many insurance companies identify acupuncture as an accepted treatment intervention. Practitioners of Chinese medicine perform acupuncture in a very traditional style, using only defined meridians and acupoints; this method requires thousands of hours of practice before the practitioner becomes proficient. Chiropractors, anesthesiologists, and others may also practice a form of acupuncture that is similar to pressure-point therapy; in this method the needles are inserted into trigger points and the trigger point is stimulated either with the needle alone or by use of accompanying electrical stimulation.

Movement Repatterning

Movement repatterning includes the Alexander, Feldenkrais, and Trager techniques. The Alexander technique was devised by Fredrick Matthias Alexander, a Shakespearean actor who noticed a connection between posture and both physical and emotional problems. This therapy uses body awareness, movement, and touch to bring the posture and the body back into balance. The Alexander technique is especially helpful to those with chronic pain and back disorders.

Physicist Moshe Feldenkrais developed the technique bearing his name following a traumatic injury for which he refused surgical intervention. Studies of the nervous system and human behavior served as a jumping-off point for his method, into which he also incorporated martial arts, physiology, anatomy, psychology, and neurology. Feldenkrais determined that one's self-image is of utmost importance to one's health and well-being and that in order to overcome maladies, one must first redefine this image. The method also includes attention to breathing and movement and, as with the Alexander technique, the Feldenkrais method also considers posture to be the nucleus of movement. The practitioner uses touch to help the patient experience improved self-image and movement.

Milton Trager, a physician, developed the method that bears his name in the 1920s. The Trager method combines gentle and rhythmic touch with movement exercises. This method is also used to teach patients how to recognize posture and movement patterns indicating tension, and how to replace these patterns with healthy patterns. "Mentastics" is the term Trager coined for the increased awareness of movement gained by patients who practice his free-flowing and dancelike exercises.

Pressure-based Therapies

Pressure-based therapies include massage, reflexology, and pressure-point therapy. Massage has been shown to be beneficial in the treatment of pain and tension; massage also speeds recovery from illnesses and surgery. Massage therapy is relaxing, speeds recovery from exercise, helps break up scar tissue and adhesions, increases lymphatic drainage, reduces swelling, improves circulation, promotes respiratory drainage, and can increase peristalsis.

Reflexology is approximately 4,000 years old and is believed to have originated in Egypt. The Chinese have also used reflexology in conjunction with acupuncture. The purposes of reflexology include relief of congestion, inflammation, and tension. The modern method of reflexology evolved from zone therapy, which is practiced in Europe; laryngologist William Fitzgerald is credited with having brought reflexology to the United States. The guiding premise behind reflexology is that the hands and feet have reflex points corresponding to every part of the body, including the spine, organs, and glands. Nerve endings in the hands and feet seem to have an extensive interconnection to the spinal cord and brain, and therefore to all areas of the body. Therapy is administered by a practitioner who applies gentle pressure to the reflex points on the patient's hands or feet.

Bonnie Prudden, one of the cofounders of the President's Council on Physical Fitness and Sports, is credited with the development of pressure-point, or trigger-point, therapy. A trigger point is a point within a muscle that was once exposed to trauma. Long after the original trauma heals, the trigger point remains, and may cause spasm and tenderness within the muscle whenever the patient experiences emotional or physical stress. The pain associated with trigger points can be exacerbated by many physical and emotional stressors, including disease, aging, or poor lifestyle habits. In Prudden's method, pressure is applied to the trigger point until discomfort is noted, after which it is maintained for 5 to 7 seconds. Trigger-point therapy is combined with stretching to retrain the muscle into a more relaxed state.

Adjustment-based Therapies

Manipulative and adjustment-based therapies include chiropractic, osteopathic, and craniosacral methods. The discipline of chiropractic centers its theory of wellness on the relationship between nervous system, spinal column, and musculoskeletal system. The nervous system is thought to hold the key to health because it has the ability to coordinate and control all tissues of the body. If there is pressure on a nerve caused by subluxation, or misalignment, of a vertebra, pain can result and interfere with body function as well as with the immune system. The discipline of chiropractic was used in ancient Egypt, but the modern form was developed in 1895 by Daniel David Palmer. Palmer's first chiropractic patient reportedly had been deaf since a traumatic back injury. Palmer noted a misaligned vertebra in the patient's back and, after realigning it, the man regained his hearing.

Osteopathy is based on the premise that restoring the structural balance of the musculoskeletal system helps to restore health in the individual because structure equates to function. An osteopathic physician's patient evaluation may include observation of mechanical elements, such as posture, gait, motion, and symmetry, and an inspection of soft tissues. Osteopathic treatment can include mobilization, articulation, positional release methods, muscle energy techniques, and cranial manipulation. Physician Andrew Taylor Still founded the first school of osteopathy in the United States in 1892. Osteopathic training combines conventional medicine along with osteopathic techniques; however, today many osteopathic schools don't devote the same attention to osteopathic techniques that they do to conventional medicine.

Craniosacral therapy is used to manipulate the bones of the skull in an effort to treat a variety of health concerns, including headache, stroke, upper respiratory infection, and cerebral palsy. The three subdisciplines of craniosacral therapy are sutural, meningeal, and reflex; these approaches may also be combined in various ways. Osteopathic physician William Garner Sutherland developed the sutural approach, in which the practitioner manipulates the skull sutures to bring them back into alignment, thereby easing pressure and increasing the cranial bones' mobility. The meningeal approach was developed by osteopathic physician John Upledger; this method focuses on manipulating not only the cranial sutures but also the underlying meninges. Chiropractor George Goodheart devised the reflex approach, in which the nerve endings in the scalp and between the cranial sutures are stimulated to relieve stress. The sacro-occipital technique was developed by chiropractor M.B. DeJarnette and combines all three approaches — sutural, meningeal, and reflex.

George Goodheart also developed applied kinesiology. This approach is used to explain medical problems as they relate to detected, but often subtle, muscle weaknesses. After the muscles are tested, techniques designed either to stimulate or relax the afflicted muscles are performed to relieve the condition affected by the weakened muscle. Applied kinesiology is also used by many practitioners as a diagnostic tool to reveal a variety of problems, from specific pathology to specific food allergy.

Rolfing was developed in the 1970s by biochemist Ida Rolf and combines the disciplines of osteopathy and Hatha yoga. It is similar to other methods in the category of adjustment-based therapies in that it is based on the premise that proper alignment affects proper body functioning. Rolfing reestablishes alignment through manipulation and stretching of muscle structures, fascial layers, and connective tissue. Ida Rolf's ideas were expanded upon by Judith Aston, developer of Aston-Patterning, and Joseph Heller, creator of Hellerwork. Both Aston and Heller added their own styles of bodywork to Rolf's model, with the common purpose of realigning the body's structures to enhance health and well-being.

Mind-body Therapies

Mind-body therapies, like manual therapies, are numerous, and include such methods as art, dance, and music therapy; spirituality or religious practices; meditation, relaxation, and imagery; and hypnosis, biofeedback, and support groups. The interrelationship of mind and body, and how that interrelationship affects the whole person, is an integral element of mind-body therapies.

Importance of Attitude

Another important aspect of mind-body therapies is the realization that attitude makes a difference to a person's physical and emotional well-being. Negative feelings beget negative internal workings and promote the development of disease. Positive attitudes and feelings help healing and seem to boost the immune system. Norman Cousins' *Anatomy of an Illness* (1981) is an account of the author's healing process, in which he employed laughter as a recovery tool. Studies have shown that an individual's opinion about his or her health is the best predictor not only of current health status but of future health status as well. Investigation into this relationship between health, the body, and the mind grew into a new field of study, called psychoneuroimmunology, in the 1970s. Psychoneuroimmunologic research has revealed the presence of neurochemicals such as endorphins and other neuropeptides that link emotions with physical well-being. Mind-body therapies employ a variety of techniques to control stress-related illnesses, such as tension headaches, hypertension, and irritable bowel syndrome. These techniques are also used to treat incontinence, muscle spasms, dyskinesia, and other illnesses. Mind-body therapies empower individuals to become active participants in their health care rather than passive recipients who rely solely on practitioners.

Art, Biofeedback, Hypnosis

Art forms such as painting or drawing, dancing, or playing a musical instrument can have stimulating or relaxing effects and seem to affect the immune system. Prayer, either for one's self or for others, has been shown to create literal miracles. Recent studies have shown prayer to influence healing even when the person praying was unknown to the person for whom the prayer was intended. Meditation, relaxation, and imagery all employ techniques to slow breathing, improve energy flow, and visualize a positive outcome.

Biofeedback teaches people how to use electronic monitors as an aid to exerting conscious control over various autonomic functions. By observing the fluctuations of a particular body function — such as breathing, heart rate, or blood pressure — on the monitor, patients eventually learn how to adjust their thinking and other mental processes in order to control that function. As with other mind-body techniques, biofeedback gives the individual an active role in self-care management.

Hypnosis uses a more passive approach by having the therapist offer suggestions to patients while they are in an altered level of consciousness. The suggestions are intended to effect positive changes in behavior or enhance well-being; for example, hypnosis may be used to overcome habits such as smoking or overeating. The hypnotic suggestions are used, as with biofeedback, to give the patient control over autonomic or conditioned responses.

Pharmacologic and Biological Therapies

Pharmacologic and biological therapies use chemically or biologically active entities for treatment of diseases. These treatment modalities include antineoplaston therapy, chelation therapy, oxygen therapy, light therapy, neural therapy, apitherapy, aromatherapy, and biologicals such as shark cartilage.

Pharmacologic Therapies

Antineoplaston therapy is used to eradicate cancer by injecting polypeptides into the body that convert cancerous cells into normal cells. This form of cancer therapy was developed by Dr. Stanislaw Burzynski and has been in use for the past 20 years.

Chelation therapy uses I.V. administration of ethylenediaminetetraacetic acid (EDTA) to draw out toxins and metabolic wastes to promote healing. It has been used to rid the body of calcium plaques in heart disease. By removing toxins, chelation acts as an anti-inflammatory agent that removes free radicals in order to reduce the pain and disability associated with degenerative diseases such as arthritis, lupus, and scleroderma. EDTA is not FDA-approved for chelating anything except for heavy metal toxins, such as lead; however, this therapeutic approach has been in use in the United States for almost 50 years.

Oxygen therapy is used primarily to destroy microbes such as viruses, bacteria, fungi, and amoebas in patients with acute myocardial infarction or poor circulation syndromes, such as those seen in diabetes, chronic fatigue syndrome, arthritis, allergies, cancer, and multiple sclerosis. Antioxidant enzymes such as superoxide dismutase, glutathione peroxidase, methionine reductase, and catalase are often recommended for use in combination with hyperoxygenation therapies. Oxygen therapies make use of many oxygen derivatives, such as hydrogen peroxide, ozone, glyoxylide, and stabilized oxygen compounds such as chlorine dioxide, magnesium oxide, and electrolytes of oxygen. Oxygen therapy can also be used in the form of hyperbaric oxygenation.

Ultraviolet (UV) light therapy, which is used to treat skin conditions such as psoriasis, is also based on oxygen therapy techniques because UV light activates oxidation at the dermis level. In the treatment of seasonal affective disorder, UV light is used to stimulate the neurochemical transmitters of the brain that affect depression and mood. Today, light in all its forms — full-spectrum, ultraviolet, colored, and laser — is considered an important source of healing.

Neural therapy uses anesthetic agents that are injected into nerve sites of the autonomic nervous system, acupuncture points, scars, glands, or other tissues to correct blockages present in these areas. Clearing the blockage restores energy, thereby reducing pain and improving function.

Biological Therapies

One of the most well-known forms of biological CAM is the use of shark cartilage to arrest cancer. Hypothetically, it works by inhibiting angiogenesis. Proponents of this therapy often claim that shark cartilage may cure almost any illness.

Substances such as the venom and honey produced by honeybees are at the center of apitherapy, a method that has been in use since the time of Hippocrates. The most common modern use of apitherapy is in the treatment of inflammatory conditions such as arthritis.

Aromatherapy is based on the premise that odors stimulate the limbic system to release neurochemicals that affect the autonomic nervous system, help control pain and stress, and may even affect the regulation of hormones such as insulin. The term was coined in the 1930s by French chemist René-Maurice Gattefosse, who studied plant oils and the beneficial effects they produced when inhaled or rubbed into the skin. Modern aromatherapy is used to reduce stress, thereby helping to prevent disease, and to treat certain illnesses of both mind and body.

Bioelectromagnetic Applications

The theory of bioelectromagnetics rests on the fact that every object in nature — earth, heavens, animals, and plants — produces an electric charge and that manipulation of the charge through the use of magnets can redirect the flow of the electrical field and result in diagnostic or healing benefits.

Electromagnetic technology, in the form of magnetic resonance imaging, magnetoencephalography, or positron emission tomography, is used in conventional medicine for the diagnosis of illness. The first application of electromagnetic fields in the treatment of disease occurred in 1974 when Albert Roy Davis, PhD, used magnets to destroy or arrest the growth of cancer cells in animals. Davis suggested that magnets could also be used to treat other diseases including arthritis, glaucoma, and infertility. He theorized that negative magnetic fields have beneficial effects and that positive magnetic fields are stressful to organisms. Negative magnetic fields, then, would be those that arrest disease and promote healing, whereas positive magnetic fields, of the type existing in manmade electromagnetic fields, may contribute to disease.

Magnetic fields, either positive or negative, are believed to affect organisms by increasing metabolism and the amount of oxygen available. Magnetic strength is measured in units of gauss or tesla, with 10,000 gauss equaling 1 tesla. All magnetic devices have a gauss rating; however, a magnet's strength at the skin's surface is often much lower — usually around 75% less — than the gauss rating. If magnets aren't placed directly on the skin, the gauss rating is even lower. Besides strength, magnets also contain a positive and negative pole and, as previously mentioned, negative poles seem to have beneficial effects whereas positive poles may prove to be deleterious. Magnets rated at a strength of 850 gauss or less are believed to reflect more nearly the strength of the earth's natural magnetic field. For this reason, practitioners consider them safe, even for prolonged periods, regardless of the polarity used.

Electromagnetic therapy can be used to reduce pain and speed the healing of fractures. Physician Robert Becker was instrumental in popularizing the use of weak electrical currents to help in the remineralization of orthopedic fractures. Others, including scientists from the Bio-Electro Magnetics Institute and the Institute for Biophysics in Germany, continue to research the efficacy of electromagnetic therapy.

Negative electromagnetic therapy is also being used in the treatment of many other human diseases, including cancer, rheumatoid diseases and other inflammatory processes, infections, headaches (particularly migraine), sleep disorders, and circulatory problems.

CAM TODAY

Despite parents' best efforts to teach their children basic health practices, those basic guidelines may fall by the wayside as children grow. If adults lose sight of the importance of nutrition, exercise, and rest and the avoidance of harmful substances, such as drugs, alcohol, and tobacco, they may rationalize this change in behavior and its subsequent effect on their body as a natural part of aging. Even when they realize it's time for a change, people may opt to use the kind of quick fixes — fad diets and medications for weight loss, analgesics for headache and arthritis pain relief, and anti-anxiety drugs to lessen or suppress the emotional response to chronic stress — that make lifestyle changes seemingly unnecessary. One of the greatest advantages of CAM is its stress on balancing a person's basic lifestyle and using preventive measures to maintain health and treat illness.

Each person's body reacts in its own way to stress and illness. Standardized protocols for specific diagnoses are not always the best treatment for everyone. CAM recognizes that people must be assessed individually, with treatment plans tailored to each person, an approach that is time-consuming and difficult to actualize in many conventional health care systems. Too often, symptoms are treated without identifying the underlying cause, which further delays accurate diagnosis and may even precipitate the evolution of a disease into a chronic state if the cause is an environmental factor or lifestyle-related behavior that isn't corrected.

Personal responsibility is the hub of much of CAM because it requires people to assume an active role in maintaining or restoring their health. While many people still prefer the "quick fix" of conventional medicine, CAM's ability to empower people to make their own health care decisions and lifestyle choices, and to draw on their own innate resources for health, is gaining popularity.

Modern Practitioners of CAM

As people become more active participants in their health care, CAM's popularity and that of its more famous practitioners is increasing. Physicians Bernie Siegel, Deepak Chopra, and Andrew Weil, to name only three, have written books that make information about CAM accessible to the public at large.

In *Love, Medicine, and Miracles* (1986), Bernie Siegel describes his transformation from a traditional surgeon to a proponent of the belief that the ability to fight disease and remain healthy resides in one's ability to love oneself and to love life. During the 10 years he practiced conventional modern medicine, Siegel was haunted by feelings of failure when his patients didn't get better and when they died. He said he felt like a "mechanic" because his attention was focused on the physical body with no provision for healing the spirit. Siegel also began to question the worth of his profession's attempts to prolong life unconditionally and to cure disease in the elderly or terminally ill. A shift to a highly personal method of practice, in which he let down his emotional barriers and began to feel for and love his patients, resulted in a feeling that he was able to offer them a deeper dimension of healing. Siegel's revised view is that his role as a surgeon is to buy people time, help them understand why they became ill, and help them learn how to heal themselves. His core philosophy is based on a patient's ability to facilitate the healing process by being an active participant and drawing on the inner energy that resides within every individual.

Deepak Chopra is a physician from India who was trained in Western medicine and served as chief-of-staff at a Boston hospital for several years. According to an interview in *Time* magazine (Van Biema, 1996), Chopra's lifestyle during his early years of practice included consuming pots of coffee on a daily basis, smoking packs of cigarettes, and drinking Scotch every night to relax. He reported feeling like a sort of "legalized drug pusher" who provided short-term cures without concern for long-term prevention. Chopra felt that he was fostering a diseased system — indeed, contributing to a diseased world — with himself in the center like a spider in a web. With the help of the Maharishi Mahesh Yogi, Chopra rediscovered his spirituality and its place in healing. His clinic today offers a combination of Western, Ayurvedic, and East Asian therapies, and he has written several books on Ayurveda, including *Quantum Healing: Exploring the Frontiers of Body-Mind Medicine*, and *Perfect Health*.

Andrew Weil is another traditionally educated physician who became disillusioned with traditional methods. He spent three years in Peru, Ecuador, and Columbia learning about herbal and alternative therapies, after which he established a program of what he calls "integrative medicine" at the University of Arizona. Weil practices both natural and preventive medicine, encouraging well people to come in for preventive health checks and providing advice about diet, exercise, and stress reduction. A critic of the public's blind faith in professional medicine, he believes that most individuals have no sense of their own health or their power to affect it for good or ill (Weil, 1995).

The focus of Weil's health care model is on helping people design a healthy lifestyle and reduce the risk of getting a disease (primarily those that cause premature death, such as heart attack, stroke, and cancer), and on educating people about natural forms of treatments they can use themselves. Weil has also written several books that focus on integrative health care, including *Eight Weeks to Optimum Health*; *Spontaneous Healing*; and *Natural Health, Natural Medicine*.

The influence that the mind and spirit have on health isn't limited to medical practice; those involved in research are also beginning to embrace the holistic notion of healing. In an article in *Time* magazine, David Felton, chairman of the department of neurobiology at Boston University, discussed research findings showing that meditation and controlling one's state of mind can alter hormone activity and potentially affect the immune system (Wallis, 1996). Holmes and Rahe (1967) provided the support for this relationship as far back as the 1960s with their Social Readjustment Scale, which they developed to measure the correlation between amounts of positive and negative stress and the likelihood of becoming sick. Psychoimmunology, the study of this phenomenon, is a growing area of research.

Regulation of CAM

The health care industry is striving to keep pace with the technological advances of the 21st century in a cost-effective manner. While keeping pace and controlling costs may appear to be mutually exclusive, combining the two seemingly disparate aims has nurtured the growing acceptance of CAM in our society. Many health care providers are finding that a combination of both conventional medicine and CAM may be a compatible marriage. Eighty percent of all disease in our society is chronic in nature, and such illnesses often respond better to CAM, which has the added advantages that it may be cheaper and cause fewer side effects over time. CAM has provided consumers a choice of options and, with those options, the opportunity to regain control of their health care. As CAM's popularity and use continue to grow, governments — particularly the United States government — are beginning to acknowledge the importance of alternative medicine and to formulate guidelines for its practice and use.

The National Institutes of Health created the Office of Alternative Medicine (OAM) in response to the U.S. Congress' recognition of the importance of CAM. As its scope and purview increased, the OAM was elevated to the status of "national center" and given its present name, NCCAM. Its modest 1993 budget of $2 million rose to $68.7 million for the year 2000. NCCAM was formed to conduct and support basic and applied clinical research and research training in various forms of CAM. It also houses a scientific database and serves as a central clearinghouse of information for researchers, health care providers, and consumers. Eleven research centers have been set up to evaluate alternative treatments in areas such as addiction, aging, arthritis, cancer, cancer and hyperbaric oxygen therapy, cardiovascular disease, cardiovascular disease and aging in African-Americans, chiropractic, craniofacial disorders, neurological disorders, and pediatrics. (See *NCCAM research sites and current studies*.)

Another important aspect of government involvement in the growing use of CAM is the regulation of practitioners, which varies according to the therapy employed. Some therapies are practiced by highly educated, clinically supervised practitioners of conventional medicine who have added some form of CAM to their models of care; such specialists include osteopaths, chiropractors, naturopaths, and medical doctors who have completed programs in acupuncture. Other practitioners may have been trained and certified in the use of a specific form of CAM in accordance with standards set by the certifying body for that form; examples include acupuncturists, massage therapists, or herbalists who received certification from the governing bodies of their respective specialties. Another group may have received training from practitioners within the same discipline, from continuing education, or from self-study without subsequent certification (Eliopoulos, 1999). While all 50 states require licensing for chiropractors, only half do so for acupuncture and massage therapists. Many states do not require licensing for homeopathy, naturopaths, or other CAM providers, allowing practitioners to operate freely (Jonas, 1998).

Medical clinicians committed to holistic practice formed the American Holistic Medical Association (AHMA) in 1978 to unite licensed physicians who practice holistic medicine. AHMA membership is open to licensed medical doctors (MDs), doctors of osteopathic medicine (DOs), and medical students studying for those degrees. Associate membership is also open to those health care practitioners certified, registered, or licensed in the state in which they practice. The mission of the AHMA is to support practitioners in their evolving personal and professional development as healers and to educate physicians about holistic medicine.

The American Holistic Nurses' Association (AHNA) was formed in 1981 to prepare nurses for holistic nursing practice, to standardize holistic nursing practice, and to unify holistic nursing care. The role of the holistic nurse is to incorporate mind-oriented therapies in all areas of nursing in order to treat the physiological, psychological, and spiritual sequelae of illnesses (Dossey et al., 2000). The association has established the underlying principles of holistic nursing practice, and sets standards of practice based on five core values.

The AHNA certification program provides a credential in holistic nursing to registered nurses who complete courses such as the Holistic Nurse Caring Process; Physical Fitness, Bodywork, and Movement; Energy Systems; Nutrition and Elimination; Communicating with the Whole Person; and Relaxation and Imagery. Information regarding the certification program is available on the AHNA Web site. The AHNA has also published *Holistic Nursing: A Handbook for Practice* (2000), a practice guide that is now in its third edition. The AHNA is also a good resource for locating instructional programs related to therapies such as Therapeutic Touch, imagery, aromatherapy, and so forth.

NCCAM RESEARCH SITES AND CURRENT STUDIES

Shown below are studies currently underway at research sites of the National Center for Complementary and Alternative Medicine (NCCAM).

Center	Objective	Current studies
Center for Addiction and Alternative Medicine Research, Minneapolis Medical Research Foundation	To scientifically evaluate complementary and alternative medicine (CAM) treatments for addictions	• Herbal compounds to help prevent alcoholic relapse • Electroacupuncture to map the neural substrates of opioids • Herbal compounds to treat hepatitis C symptoms
Center for CAM Research in Aging and Women's Health, Columbia University, New York	To analyze the effect herbal and dietary treatments have in the treatment of postmenopausal women	• Black cohosh to treat menopausal complaints • Safety of Chinese herbal preparations for women with or at risk for breast cancer • Comparison of a macrobiotic diet with an American Heart Association diet in relation to hormone and phytoestrogen metabolism, cardiovascular function, and bone metabolism
Center for Alternative Medicine Research on Arthritis, University of Maryland, Baltimore	To explore the potential efficacy, safety, and cost-effectiveness of CAM for arthritis-related illnesses	• Acupuncture to treat osteoarthritis of the knee • Mind-body therapies to treat fibromyalgia • Electroacupuncture to treat persistent pain and inflammation • Herbal therapies with possible immuno-modulatory properties
The Center for Cancer Complementary Medicine, Johns Hopkins University, Baltimore	To investigate CAM therapies in the treatment of cancer	• Antioxidant effects of herbs in cancer cells • Antioxidant and anti-inflammatory properties of soy and tart cherry on aspects of cancer pain • Safety and efficacy of PC-SPES* to treat prostate cancer • Impact of spiritual practices on disease recurrence and immune and neuroendocrine function in African-American women with breast cancer
Center for Research in Hyperbaric Oxygen Therapy, University of Pennsylvania, Philadelphia	To examine the mechanisms of action, safety, and clinical efficacy of hyperbaric oxygen therapy for head and neck tumors	• Benefits of hyperbaric oxygen after laryngectomy • Effects of hyperbaric oxygen on growth of blood vessels and tumors • Effects of hyperbaric oxygen on cell adhesion and growth of metastatic tumor cells in the lung • Effects of elevated oxygen pressures on cellular levels of nitric oxide
Center for Cardiovascular Diseases, University of Michigan, Ann Arbor	To investigate the use of CAM to treat and prevent cardiovascular disease as well as stressing education and promotion of validated CAM for cardiovascular well-being	• Hawthorn extract to treat congestive heart failure • Reiki biofield energy healing technique to treat diabetic peripheral vascular disease and autonomic neuropathy • Effects of spirituality on patients undergoing coronary artery bypass surgery • Effects of qi gong on pain and healing after coronary artery bypass graft

(continued)

NCCAM RESEARCH SITES AND CURRENT STUDIES

Center	Objective	Current studies
Center for Natural Medicine and Prevention, Maharishi University of Management, Fairfield, Iowa	To evaluate CAM for the prevention of cardiovascular disease in high-risk older African-Americans	• Effects of meditation on atherosclerotic cardiovascular disease • Effects of meditation on carotid atherosclerosis, cardiovascular disease risk factors, physiological mechanisms, psychosocial risk factors, and quality of life in older African-American women with cardiovascular disease • Comparison of effects of herbal antioxidants and conventional vitamin supplementation on carotid atherosclerosis, endothelial function, oxidative stress, cardiovascular disease risk factors, and quality of life
Consortial Center for Chiropractic Research, Palmer Center for Chiropractic Research, Davenport, Iowa	To examine the potential effectiveness and validity of chiropractic health care and to provide the appropriate clinical, scientific, and technical assistance to chiropractic researchers in developing high-quality research projects	• Development of research workshops and educational materials to provide an institutional focus for formal training in research methodology, bioethics, biostatistics, clinical trial design, epidemiological and health services studies, and basic laboratory methods • Establishment of a network of chiropractic clinicians and investigators in specific topic areas • Prioritization of research topics related to chiropractic treatment of musculoskeletal conditions • Development of a mechanism for scientific and technical merit review of research proposals • Implementation of selected research projects
Center for Complementary and Alternative Medicine Research in Craniofacial Disorders, Kaiser Foundation Hospitals, Portland, Oregon	To research the efficacy, effectiveness, effects on health care resource use, and psychosocial and other health outcomes associated with CAM for craniofacial disorders, as well as the physiological and psychological mechanisms underlying these practices	• Alternative approaches to pain management in temporomandibular disorders (TMD) • Alternative medicine approaches to treat TMDs in women • Complementary naturopathic medicine to treat periodontitis
Center for Complementary and Alternative Medicine in Neurological Disorders, Oregon Health Sciences University, Portland	To assess the use of antioxidants and stress reduction as treatments for neurodegenerative and demyelinating diseases	• Facilitation of four research projects and maintenance of four core facilities that integrate the research strengths of conventional medicine and CAM practitioners and researchers • Promotion of new areas of CAM research and spearheading of research on CAM therapies for neurologic disorders
Pediatric Center for Complementary and Alternative Medicine, University of Arizona, Tucson	To study integrative approaches in pediatrics	• Implementation of three projects to investigate alternative approaches to three common pediatric problems: recurrent abdominal pain, otitis media, and cerebral palsy • Establishment of a pediatric research fellowship in CAM and research methodologies

*PC-SPES is a formulation of seven plants and one fungus. The name is derived from the common abbreviation for prostate cancer (PC) and the Latin word *spes,* meaning hope. Don't confuse PC-SPES with a related herbal combination product called simply SPES, also under development as a potential cancer treatment.

Each day, more primary care physicians are changing the face of their practices by adding such specialists as acupuncturists, massage therapists, and chiropractic doctors to their staffs. Integration of conventional and CAM services into one office holds promise for combining the best of both worlds. As Andrew Weil wryly observed (1995), "If I'm in a car accident, don't take me to an herbalist. If I have bacterial pneumonia, give me antibiotics. But when it comes to maximizing the body's natural healing potential, a mix of conventional and alternative procedures seems like the only answer." The use of CAM in relation to conventional medicine isn't an either/or proposition; the greatest benefits to people both healthy and ill may be achieved using a judicious blend of both methods.

The present, inconsistent regulation of CAM dictates that practitioners must become familiar with the recommended certification for each particular treatment modality. They must also know how to access this information to ensure safe referrals. Books on CAM and integrative medicine provide excellent listings of national organizations devoted to CAM and its various specialties. The Internet is another good place to search for information on CAM, as many national organizations' Web sites list the recommended certifying body and certification level for a particular CAM practice.

Consumers and Integrated Practice

A new generation of consumers is demanding a more informed, active role in their health care. NCCAM established a clearinghouse in 1996 through which consumers can access information about CAM, NCCAM programs, conferences, and research activities. This information is accessed through a toll-free information line, fact sheets available from the NCCAM Clearing House, and a newsletter available through postal mail or online. While NCCAM provides a plethora of information on CAM, including the newest research findings, consumers can also find information at the library, bookstores, and Internet websites. However, sorting through this information can be challenging for the lay person without help from health care providers familiar with CAM.

THE FIVE CORE VALUES OF THE AMERICAN HOLISTIC NURSES' ASSOCIATION

1. Holistic philosophy and education
2. Holistic ethics, theories, and research
3. Holistic nurses' self-care
4. Holistic communication, therapeutic environment, and cultural diversity
5. Holistic caring process

In 1998, Eisenberg et al. recommended that "federal agencies, private corporations, foundations, and academic institutions adopt a more proactive posture concerning the implementation of clinical and basic science research, the development of relevant educational curricula, credentialing and referral guidelines, improved quality control of dietary supplements and the establishment of post-market surveillance of drug-herb (and drug supplement) interactions." In the meantime, health care providers must become informed about CAM and consider integrating them into conventional practice. Doing so will foster a model of health care, characterized by collaborative practice, that provides patient-focused, individualized care in a cost-efficient, self-responsible manner. The renewed interest in CAM shown by health care consumers and the increased political and financial support offered by the NIH indicate that CAM's resurgence isn't a trend that will pass with time.

CHAPTER SUMMARY

It's time to recognize the power of the mind and its effect on the body — for example, studies show that the placebo effect works in 25% of people regardless of what intervention they're undergoing. As increasing numbers of patients turn to CAM, it behooves practitioners to familiarize themselves with these alternative approaches to healing and wellness in order to intelligently direct patients to the best possible care and prevention strategies. Even if no scientific evidence supports a particular therapy, if it produces measurable outcomes in patients, then either the therapy works or the placebo effect is in place.

As we learn about the various forms of CAM, we must remember that conventional Western medicine as it exists today was once viewed with the kind of suspicion with which many modern practitioners now view CAM. Traditional practices that had long been abandoned as archaic — for example, bloodletting by the application of leeches — are now being reassessed and found to have some validity. Perhaps we'll find that the most important aspects of wellness and the prevention of disease, as well as the treatment of disease, are based upon natural elements — foods and food substances, personal lifestyle, interaction with nature, and spiritual well-being — that our ancestors once embraced and later abandoned. We may find that the use of these basic elements affects our physical and emotional well-being more than any conventional medicine ever could.

Not long ago, osteopathy, chiropractic, and naturopathy were not considered accepted disciplines for diagnosing and treating illness, yet now insurance companies reimburse all three. Also, Medicare is considering the use of acupuncture for treating pain. Therapeutic Touch and reflexology are used in well-respected teaching hospitals. Music therapy and prayer are also being mainstreamed into hospitals. So many things about this world still lie beyond our understanding; who can say that what isn't currently considered mainstream lacks credibility?

GLOSSARY OF KEY TERMS

A

abandonment withdrawal by a physician from a contractual relationship with a patient without proper notification while the patient still needs treatment.

additive drug reaction a reaction that occurs when the combined effect of two drugs is equal to the sum of each drug given alone.

advance directive a statement of a patient's wishes regarding health care prior to a critical medical event.

adverse reaction undesirable drug effect.

aerobe microorganism that requires oxygen to live and reproduce.

aerosol suspended particles in gas or air.

afebrile body temperature not elevated above normal.

age of majority age at which an individual is considered to be an adult (usually 18–21 years of age).

agonist drug that binds with a receptor to produce a therapeutic response.

allergic reaction a drug reaction that occurs because the individual's immune system views the drug as a foreign substance.

alphabetic filing arranging of names or titles according to the sequence of letters in the alphabet.

anaerobe bacterium that does not require oxygen for growth and reproduction.

anaphylactic shock a severe form of hypersensitivity reaction.

aneroid sphygmomanometer that measures blood pressure without using mercury.

antagonist a drug that joins with a receptor to prevent the action of an agonist at that receptor.

anthropometric pertaining to measurements of the human body.

antibodies molecules with the ability to bind with a specific antigen responsible for the immune response.

antigen a substance that the immune system perceives as foreign and that causes production of antibodies.

appeal process by which a higher court reviews the decision of a lower court.

assault an attempt or threat to touch another person without his or her consent.

asymptomatic without any symptoms.

autoclave appliance used to sterilize medical instruments with steam under pressure.

B

bactericidal substance that kills or destroys bacteria.

baseline original or initial measure with which other measurements will be compared.

battery actual touching of a person without his or her consent.

bench trial trial in which the judge hears the case and renders a verdict; no jury is present.

bioethics moral issues and concerns that affect a person's life.

biohazard substance that is a risk to the health of living organisms.

blood-borne pathogens viruses that can be spread through direct contact with blood or body fluids from an infected person.

breach an infraction, such as breach of contract, in which the agreed-on terms are violated.

buccal within the cheek.

C

calibrated marked in units of measurement, as a thermometer calibrated in Celsius.

calibrations measurements for size or volume, as in calibrations on a syringe or pipette.

capillary action the raising or lowering of a liquid at the point of contact with a solid; used to pull blood into a capillary tube or small pipette.

cardiac cycle period from the beginning of one heartbeat to the beginning of the next; includes systole and diastole.

cardinal signs usually, vital signs; signifies their importance in assessment.

carrier person infected with a microorganism but without signs of disease; a company that assumes the risk of an insurance company.

Centers for Medicare & Medicaid federal agency that regulates Medicare and Medicaid along with the Clinical Laboratory Improvement Amendments Act and Health Insurance Portability and Accountability Act.

centrifugal force a spinning motion to exert force outward, heavier components of a solution are spun downward.

certification voluntary process that involves a testing procedure to prove an individual's baseline competency in a particular area.

chief complaint main reason for the visit to the medical office.

chronological order placing in the order of time; usually the most recent is placed foremost.

civil law a branch of law that focuses on issues between private citizens.

Clinical Laboratory Improvement Amendments Act (CLIA) guidelines established by Congress in 1988 to standardize and improve laboratory testing.

coerce to force or compel a person to do something against his or her wishes.

common law traditional laws that were established by the English legal system.

comparative negligence a percentage of damage awards based on the contribution of negligence between two parties.

confidentiality protection of patient data from unauthorized personnel.

consent an agreement between a patient and physician to do a given medical procedure.

consideration the exchange of fees for a service.

contract an agreement between two or more parties for a given act.

contributory negligence a defense strategy in which the defendant admits to negligence but claims that the plaintiff assisted in promoting the damages.

controlled substances drugs with a high potential for abuse that are controlled by special regulations.

cross-examination questioning of a witness by the opposing attorney.

cross-reference notation in a file telling that a record is stored elsewhere and giving the reference; verification to another source; checking the tabular list against the alphabetic list in ICD-9 coding.

cumulative drug effect a drug effect that occurs when the body has not fully metabolized a dose of a drug before the next dose is given.

D

damages the resulting injury or suffering that resulted from negligence.

defamation of character making false or malicious statements about a person's character or reputation.

defendant the party that is accused.

demographic data relating to the statistical characteristics of populations.

denominator the bottom number in a fraction.

deposition a process in which one party questions another party under oath.

diastole relaxation phase of the cardiac cycle.

direct examination questioning of a witness by the attorney for the individual the witness is representing.

disease definite pathological process having a distinctive set of symptoms and course of progression.

disinfection killing or rendering inert most but not all pathogenic microorganisms.

dividend the number to be divided (eg, 40 divided by 5, 40 is the dividend).

divisor the number by which the dividend is divided; in the previous example, 5 is the divisor.

drug error any incident in which a patient receives the wrong dose, the wrong drug, a drug by the wrong route, or a drug given at the incorrect time.

drug idiosyncrasy any unusual or abnormal reaction to a drug.

drug tolerance a decreased response to a drug, requiring an increase in dosage to achieve the desired effect.

durable power of attorney a legal document giving another person the authority to act in one's behalf.

duress the act of compelling or forcing someone to do something that they do not want to do.

E

electronic health records (EHR) information about patients that is recorded and stored on computer.

emancipated minor a patient under the age of majority but who is legally considered to be an adult.

ethics guidelines for moral behavior that are enforced by peer groups.

ethylene oxide gas used to sterilize surgical instruments and other supplies.

expected threshold a numerical goal.

expert witness a professional who testifies on the standard of care in a trial.

exposure control plan written plan required by the Occupational Safety and Health Administration that outlines an employer's system for preventing infection.

exposure risk factors conditions that tend to put employees at risk for contact with biohazardous agents such as blood-borne pathogens.

expressed consent a statement of approval from the patient for the physician to perform a given procedure after the patient has been educated about the risks and benefits of the particular procedure; also referred to as informed consent.

expressed contracts formal agreements between two or more people.

extravasation escape of fluid from a blood vessel into surrounding tissue.

F

febrile having above-normal body temperature.

fee-splitting sharing of fees between physicians for patient referrals.

flow sheet color-coded sheets that allow information to be recorded in graphic or tabular form for easy retrieval.

forceps surgical instrument used to grasp, handle, compress, pull, or join tissues, equipment, or supplies.

fraction division of one number by another.

fraud a deceitful act with the intention to conceal the truth.

G

germicide chemical that kills most pathogenic microorganisms; disinfectant.

H

Health Insurance Portability and Accountability Act federal law that requires all health care settings to ensure privacy and security of patient information. Also requires health insurance to be accessible for working Americans and available when changing employment.

hemostat surgical instrument with slender jaws used for grasping blood vessels.

hyperpyrexia dangerously high temperature, 105° to 106°F.

hypersensitivity being allergic to a drug.

hypertension morbidly high blood pressure.

I

immunization act or process of rendering an individual immune to specific disease.

implied consent an informal agreement of approval from the patient to perform a given task.

implied contracts contracts between physician and patient not written but assumed by the actions of the parties.

improper fraction a fraction with the numerator larger or equal to the denominator.

incident report a form used by an organization to document an unusual occurrence to a patient, visitor or employee.

infection invasion by disease-producing microorganisms.

infiltration the collection of fluid in a tissue.

informed consent a statement of approval from the patient for the physician to perform a given procedure after the patient has been educated about the risks and benefits of the procedure; also referred to as expressed consent.

inhalation route of administration in which drug droplets, vapor, or gas is inhaled and absorbed through the mucous membranes of the respiratory tract.

intentional tort an act that takes place with malice and with the intent of causing harm; a deliberate violation of another person's legal rights.

intermittent occurring at intervals.

intradermal route of administration in which the drug is injected into skin tissue.

intramuscular route of administration in which the drug is injected into muscle tissue.

intravenous route of administration in which the drug is injected into a vein.

J

Joint Commission on Accreditation of Health Care Organizations (JCAHO) a voluntary organization that sets and evaluates the standards of care for health care institutions; based on the JCAHO evaluation, an accreditation title will be given to the organization.

L

legally required disclosure reporting of certain events to governmental agencies without the patient's consent.

libel written statements that defame a person's reputation or character.

licensure the strictest form of professional accreditation.

litigation process of filing or contesting a lawsuit.

locum tenens a substitute physician.

M

malpractice a tort in which the patient is harmed by the actions of a health care worker.

Material Safety Data Sheet (MSDS) a detailed record of all hazardous substances kept within a site.

medical asepsis removal or destruction of microorganisms.

microfiche sheets of microfilm.

microfilm photographs of records in a reduced size.

microorganisms microscopic living organisms.

mixed number a whole number and a fraction (*e.g.*, $1\frac{1}{2}$).

N

narrative a paragraph indicating the contact with the patient, what was done for the patient, and the outcome of any action.

National Committee for Clinical Laboratory Standards (NCCLS) a committee appointed to establish rules to ensure the safety, standards and integrity of all testing performed on human specimens.

needle holder type of surgical forceps used to hold and pass suture through tissue.

negligence performance of an act that a reasonable health care worker would not have done or the omission of an act that a reasonable person would have done.

noncompliant describes a patient who refuses or is unable to follow prescribed orders.

nonprescription drugs drugs designated by the FDA to be obtained without a prescription.

normal flora microorganisms normally found in the body; also known as resident flora.

normal values acceptable range as established for an age, a population, or a sex; variations usually indicate a disorder.

numerator the top number in a fraction.

numeric filing arranging files by a numbered order.

O

obturator smooth, rounded, removable inner portion of a hollow tube, such as an anoscope, that allows for easier insertion.

Occupational Safety and Health Administration (OSHA) a federal agency with a mission to protect employees from work related hazards.

outcomes final results of patient care.

P

palpation technique in which the examiner feels the texture, size, consistency, and location of parts of the body with the hands.

parenteral   a general term for drug administration in which the drug is injected inside the body.

pathogens   disease-causing microorganisms.

personal protective equipment   equipment used to protect a person from exposure to blood or other body fluids.

pharmaceutic phase   the dissolution of the drug.

pharmacodynamics   a drug's actions and effects within the body.

pharmacogenetic disorder   a genetically determined abnormal response to normal doses of a drug.

pharmacokinetics   activities occurring within the body after a drug is administered, including absorption, distribution, metabolism, and excretion.

pharmacology   the study of drugs and their action on living organisms.

physical dependence   a compulsive need to use a substance repeatedly to avoid mild to severe withdrawal symptoms.

plaintiff   the party who initiates a lawsuit.

polypharmacy   taking a large number of drugs (may be prescribed or over-the-counter drugs).

postexposure testing   laboratory tests that may be performed after a person comes into contact with a biohazard.

postural hypotension   sudden drop in blood pressure upon standing.

precedent   the use of previous court decisions as a legal foundation.

prescription drugs   drugs the federal government has designated as potentially harmful unless supervised by a licensed health care provider.

present illness   a specific account of the chief complaint, including time frames and characteristics.

problem-oriented medical record (POMR)   a common method of compiling information that lists each problem of the patient, usually at the beginning of the folder, and references each problem with a number throughout the folder.

proper fraction   a fraction with a numerator smaller than the denominator.

protocol   a code of proper conduct; a treatment plan.

psychological dependence   a compulsion to use a substance to obtain a pleasurable experience.

pyrexia   body temperature of 102°F or higher rectally or 101°F or higher orally.

Q

quality assurance (QA)   an evaluation of health care services as compared to accepted standards.

quality control (QC)   method to evaluate the proper performance of testing procedures, supplies or equipment in a laboratory.

quality improvement   a plan that allows an organization to scientifically measure the quality of its product and service.

quotient   the answer in division.

R

ratchet   notched mechanism, usually at the handle end of an instrument, that clicks into position to maintain tension on the opposing blades or tips of the instrument.

reagent   a substance used to react in a certain manner in the presence of specific chemicals to obtain a diagnosis.

receptor   a specialized macromolecule that binds to the drug molecule, altering the function of the cell and producing the therapeutic response.

registered   indicates that a professional has met basic requirements, usually for education; has passed standard testing; and has been approved by a governing body to perform given tasks within a state.

relapsing fever   fever that returns after extended periods of being within normal limits.

remittent fever   fever that is fluctuating.

reportable range   range in which instruments are designed to produce results.

res ipsa loquitur   "the thing speaks for itself".

res judicata   "the thing has been decided".

resident flora   microorganisms normally found in the body; also known as normal flora.

resistance   body's immune response to prevent infections by invading pathogenic microorganisms.

respondeat superior   "let the master answer".

reverse chronological order   items placed with oldest first.

S

sanitation   maintenance of a healthful, disease-free environment.

sanitization   processes used to lower the number of microorganisms on a surface by cleansing with soap or detergent, water, and manual friction.

sanitize   reduce the number of microorganisms on a surface by use of low-level disinfectant practices.

scalpel   small, pointed knife with a convex edge for surgical procedures.

scissors   sharp instrument composed of two opposing cutting blades, held together by a central pin on which the blades pivot.

sentinel event   an unexpected occurrence or event that results in death or serious physical or psychological injury.

serration   groove, either straight or criss-cross, etched or cut into the blade or tip of an instrument to improve its bite or grasp.

slander   oral statements that defame a person's reputation or character.

SOAP   a style of charting that includes subjective, objective, assessment, and planning notes.

sound   long instrument for exploring or dilating body cavities or searching cavities for foreign bodies.

specimen   a small portion of anything used to evaluate the nature of the whole.

sphygmomanometer   device used to measure blood pressure.

spore   bacterial life form that resists destruction by heat, drying, or chemicals. Spore-producing bacteria include botulism and tetanus.

standard precautions   usual steps to prevent injury or disease.

stare decisis   "the previous decision stands".

statute of limitations   a legal time limit; e.g., the length of time in which a patient may file a lawsuit.

statutes   laws that are written by federal, state or local legislators.

sterilization   process, act, or technique for destroying microorganisms using heat, water, chemicals, or gases.

subcutaneous   route of administration in which the drug is injected just below the layer of skin.

subject filing   arranging files according to their title, grouping similar subjects together.

sublingual   route of administration in which the drug is placed under the tongue for absorption.

sustained fever   fever that is constant or not fluctuating.

synergism   a drug interaction that occurs when drugs produce an effect that is greater than the sum of their separate actions.

systole   contraction phase of the cardiac cycle.

T

task force   a group of employees that works together to solve a given problem.

teratogen   any substance that causes abnormal development of the fetus.

therapeutic response   the intended (beneficial) effect of a drug.

tort   the righting of wrongs or injuries suffered by someone because of another person's wrongdoing.

toxic   harmful drug effect.

transdermal   route of administration in which the drug is absorbed through the skin from a patch.

transient flora   microorganisms that do not normally reside in a given area; transient flora may or may not produce disease.

tympanic thermometer   device for measuring the temperature using the blood flow through the tympanic membrane, or eardrum.

U

unintentional tort   describes an honest mistake by a person operating in good faith.

unit dose   a single dose of a drug packaged ready for patient use.

V

vector   (biological) a living, nonhuman carrier of disease, usually an arthropod; (mechanical) a carrier of disease that does not support growth; examples include contaminated inanimate objects.

verdict   a decision of guilty or not guilty based on evidence presented in a trial.

viable   capable of growing and living.

virulent   highly pathogenic and disease producing; describes a microorganism.

W

workers' compensation   employer insurance for treatment of an employee's injury or illness related to the job.

Z

Z-track   a technique of intramuscular injection used with drugs that are irritating to subcutaneous tissues.

INDEX

Page numbers followed by a "f" indicate figures, those followed by a "t" indicate tables, those followed by a "b" indicate boxes, those followed by a "p" indicate procedures.

A

Abandonment, of contract, 73
Abbreviations
    apothecary, 141, 142t
    in charting, 96b
    in medication orders, 169, 170t–171t
    for note-taking, 41
    in prescriptions, 169, 170t–171t
Absorption, drug, 157
Abuse
    child, 76
    drug, 77, 78t, 154–155, 155b
    elder, 77
    legally required disclosure of, 76
    spousal, 77
Acceptance, 71
Acronyms, 17
Acrostics, 17
Active heath records, 98–99
Active listening, 36–38
Active reading skills, 30–32
Acupuncture, 289–290
Additive drug reaction, 161
Adjustment-based therapies, 290–291
Adjustment knobs, microscope, 234, 234f
Administration
    drug, 168–178 (*See also* Drug administration)
    route of, 163
Advance directive, 85, 86f
Adverse reactions, 152, 153b, 159, 160f
Advocacy, patient, 84
Aerobes, 187
Aerosol, 238
Afebrile patient, 253
Age
    on blood pressure, 262
    on drug response, 162, 163t
    on pulse, 259t
    on respiration, 261t
Age Discrimination in Employment Act, 83b
Age of majority, 74
Agonists, 158
Alarm, in general adaptation syndrome, 58
Alcohol, 192t
Alexander technique, 290
Allergic reactions, to drugs, 159–160, 160t
Alligator biopsy instrument, 215f
Allocation of resources, 84–85
Alphabetic filing, 97–98, 98b, 99b
Alternative medicine, 284, 285. *See also* Complementary and alternative
    medicine (CAM)
American Association of Medical Assistants (AAMA), 115p

American Holistic Medical Association (AHMA), 294
American Holistic Nurses' Association (AHNA), 294, 297
American legal system, 70–72
Americans with Disabilities Act (ADA), 82, 83b
Anaerobes, 187
Anaphylactic shock, 159–160, 160t
Aneroid sphygmomanometer, 261, 261f, *279p
Angioedema, 160
Anoscope, 215f
Antagonistic drug reaction, 162
Antagonists, 158
Anthropometric measurements, 252
Antibodies, 159
Antigen, 159
Antineoplaston therapy, 292
Anxiety
    characteristics of, 59
    freeze-up and, 59
    test, 46
    test-taking, coping with, 59
Apical pulse, 257, 259, 259f, 260f
Apitherapy, 292
Apnea, 261
Apothecary abbreviations, 141, 142t
Apothecary system, 141
    abbreviations in, 142t
    liquid measures in, 143, 143f, 144f
        converting, 143–144, 143f, 144f
    metric equivalents of, 143t
Appeal, 80
Applied kinesiology, 289, 291
Aromatherapy, 292
Art, as therapy, 291
Arteriosclerosis, on blood pressure, 262
Asepsis
    medical, 189–190, 189b, 190b (*See also* Infection control, medical)
        guidelines for maintaining, 190b
        handwashing in, 189b, 190, 199p–201p
        sterilization in, 190
        vs. surgical asepsis, 210t
    surgical, 210–226 (*See also* Sterilization, surgical)
        goal of, 210
        vs. medical sepsis, 210t
        sterilization in, 210–213 (*See also* Sterilization, surgical)
Assault, 79
Assistance, asking for, 64
Assistant, laboratory, 232b
Associations
    developing, 17
    in memory, 15
    in studying, 16–17
Assumption of risk, 81

Asymptomatic patients, disease transmission from, 188
Atherosclerosis, on blood pressure, 262
Attendance, class, 21–22
Attitude
    in health, 291
    in learning, 4
Attitude meter, 4
Auscultatory gap, 262
Authorization, for release of health records, 100–101, 101f
Autoclave, 211–213
    equipment in, 211, 211f
    loading of, 212
    operation of, 212–213, 225p–226p
    wrapping instruments for sterilization in, 211, 222p–224p
Autoclave indicator tape, 211–212, 212b, 212f
Automated dispensing systems, 169, 172f
Axillary temperature, 253, 253b
Axillary temperature measurement, 271p–272p
Ayurveda, 286, 293

B

Bactericidal, 186
Balance beam scales, 252, 252f
Bandage scissors, 213, 217f
Bandages, changing, 189b
Baseline, in vital signs, 252
Battery, 79
Beaker, 236, 237f
Belief, in yourself, 8
Bench trial, 80
Bioelectromagnetic therapies, 292–293
Bioethics, 84–87
    allocation of resources in, 84–85
    obstetric dilemmas in, 85
    organ transplantation in, 84–85
    Uniform Anatomical Gift Act in, 85, 85b
    withholding or withdrawing treatment in, 85, 86f
Biofeedback, 291
Biohazard risk management. See Infection control, medical
Biohazard spills
    kits for, 195–196, 196f, 205p, 241, 241f
    procedure for, 205p
Biohazard waste containers, 195b, 197, 197b
Biohazards, 238
    disposal of materials in, 210p
    in healthcare facility, 195b
    infection control for, 195–196, 196f, 197b, 205p
    material in, 192
    personal protective equipment as, 195b (See also Personal protective equipment (PPE))
Biologic therapies, 292
Biological hazards. See Biohazards
Biologically based therapies, 286
Biopsy forceps, 214f
Biotransformation, drug, 157–158
Blades, surgical, 213, 218f
Bleach, 192t
Blood-borne pathogens
    immunization against, 195b, 238
    OSHA regulations on, 82, 238
    standard training on, 193b
Blood pressure, 261–263
    auscultatory gap in, 262
    defined, 262
    with dialysis shunt, 263b
    errors in readings of, 263b
    factors in, 262–263
    Korotkoff sounds in, 262, *279p

phases of, 262, 262f
    pulse pressure in, 262
Blood pressure cuff sizes, 263, 263f
Blood pressure measurement, 261f, 262–263, *277p–280p
Blood specimen, centrifuged, 235, 235f
Body, caring for, 61–64
Body-based therapies, 286
Body-brain split, 22
Body temperature, 252–256. See also Temperature, body
Body temperature measurement
    axillary, 253, 253b, 271p–272p
    electronic thermometer, 255, 256f, 257f, 273p
    oral, 253, 253b, 267p–268p
    rectal, 253, 253b, 269p–270p
    tympanic thermometer, 253, 253b, 255, 257f, 274p
Botanical medicine, 163–164
Bradypnea, 261
Brand name, drug, 153, 154t
Breach, 70
Break, taking a, 27–28
Breathing, relaxation, 63
Buccal drug administration, 173

C

Calendar
    managing, 21
    in schedule planning, 20
Calibration
    of instruments, clinical laboratory, 244–245, 244f
    of thermometers, 255
Calibration lines, 236
Cancer diagnosis, legally required disclosure of, 77
Capillary action, 237
Cardiac cycle, 261
Cardinal signs. See Vital signs
Carrier, 188
Cast saw, 214f
Cell counter, 234
Center for Complementary and Alternative Health, 164
Centers for Medicare & Medicaid Services (CMS), 108, 115p
Centrifugal force, 235
Centrifuge, 235, 235f
Centrifuged blood specimen, 235, 235f
Certification, for health professionals, 77
Chain of custody, laboratory, 242b
Chart entries, 93–95, 95f
Charting. See also Records, health
    abbreviations in, 96b
    chronological order in, 96
    correcting errors in, 96, 96f
    entries in, 93–95, 95f
    of patient communications, 95–96, 96f
Chelation therapy, 292
Chemical hazards, 238, 239f
Chemical name, drug, 153, 154t
Chemical spills
    cleanup kits for, 241, 241f
    of glutaraldehyde, 219b
    of sterilization solutions, 219b
Chemistry analyzers, 235
Chi (qi), 286
Chief complaint, 90, 93f
Chief technologist, 232b
Child abuse, legally required disclosure of, 76
Chinese medicine, 286
    acupuncture in, 289–290
    diet in, 288
    lifestyle in, 288

Chiropractic, 290
Chlorine, 192t
Chopra, Deepak, 293
Chronological filing, 98
Chronological order, in charting, 96
Civil law, 70
Civil Rights Act of 1964, Title VII, 81–82, 83b
Clamps, 213, 217f
Class attendance, 21–22
Class preparation, 35
Class schedule, organizing, 20
Classroom learning, 35–38
    active listening in, 36–38
    lectures in, 35–36
    listening types in, 36
    overcoming obstacles in, 37
Classroom strategies, 35–44
    basic classroom skills in, 35
    classroom learning in, 35–38 (See also Classroom learning)
    computer-assisted instruction in, 38–39
    learning skill development in, 38–39
    lecture content in, organizing, 39
    student-teacher conferences in, 39
Clinical laboratory, 230–248
    answers to questions on, 256
    chain of custody in, 242b
    data sheet in, 231, 233f
    equipment in, 233–237 (See also Laboratory equipment)
    hospital laboratory as, 231
    improvement amendments for, 83, 115p, 241–246 (See also Clinical
        Laboratory Improvement Amendments (CLIA))
    kit package inserts for, 233b
    normal values for common tests from, 233f
    OSHA noncompliance in, 242b
    personnel in, 232, 232b
    physician office laboratory as, 231–232, 233f
    privacy of test results in, 233b
    purpose of, 230
    quality control log for, 243, 243f
    reference laboratory as, 230–231
    request forms for, 231, 231f, 232b
    safety in, 237–241 (See also Safety, laboratory)
    standards in, 243–246 (See also Laboratory)
    transport containers for, 230, 230f
    types of, 230–232
    use of testing in, 230
Clinical Laboratory Improvement Amendments (CLIA), 83, 108,
        115p, 241–246
    history of, 241
    levels of testing in, 242
Clinical laboratory technician, 232b
Closed health records, 99
Coarse adjustment knob, microscope, 234, 234f
Coefficient, 130
Coerce, 73, 79
Coherence, 58
Color, 17
Comedone extractor, 216f
Common law, 70
Communicable diseases
    legally required disclosures on, 75
    reportable conditions in, 75
Communications with patients, charting, 95–96, 96f
Comparative negligence, 81
Compassionate access, to unapproved drugs, 153
Complaint, chief, 90, 93f
Complementary and alternative medicine (CAM), 284–297
    alternative medical systems in, 285

American Holistic Medical Association in, 294
American Holistic Nurses' Association in, 294, 297
Ayurveda in, 286
bioelectromagnetic applications in, 292–293
biologic therapies in, 292
biologically based therapies in, 286
body-based therapies in, 286
Chinese medicine in, 286
consumers on, 297
current state of, 293–295
definition and scope of, 284
diet and nutrition in, 287–288
energy therapies in, 286
five basic principles of, 285
five domains of, 285–286
herbal medicine in, 288–289
herbal therapy in, 163, 164, 165b
history of, 284–285
holism in, 285
homeopathic medicine in, 286–287
Indian medicine in, 286
integrated practice in, 297
lifestyle changes in, 287, 288
manipulative therapies in, 286
manual healing in, 289–291, 289f
mind-body therapies in, 286, 291–292
modern practitioners of, 293–294
National Center for Complementary and Alternative Medicine in,
        284–286, 295t–296t
naturopathic medicine in, 287
pharmacologic therapies in, 292
regulation of, 294, 297
use of, 284
Complex fractions, 121, 123
Comprehension techniques, 30–32
Comprehensive Drug Abuse and Prevention and Control Act, 156
Computer, health records on, 91
Computer-assisted instruction (CAI), 38–39
Computerized dispensing systems, 169, 172f
Concentration
    improving, 13
    learning, 12–13
Concentrative meditation, 62–63
Condenser, microscope, 234, 234f
Conduction, 254t
Conferences, student-teacher, 39
Confidentiality, patient, 84
Consent, 73–75
    expressed, 73
    form for, 73–74, 74f
    implied, 73
    informed, 73
        in hearing impaired, 84b
    for minors, 74
    refusal of, 74–75, 74b
Consideration, 71
Constitution, 286
Containers, transport, 230, 230f
Contamination, environmental
    handling of, 195–196, 196f
    procedure for, 205p
Contracts, 71–73
    expressed, 72
    implied, 72
    termination or withdrawal of, 72–73
Contributory negligence, 81
Control sample, 243
Controlled substances, 77, 78t, 154–155, 155b

Controlled Substances Act, 77, 78t, 154, 155b
Convection, 254t
Conversions
    among systems of measurements, 144–146, 144t, 145t
    fractions to decimals, 124–125
    grains to milligrams, 143
    grams to milligrams, 138–139, 141
    metric, mixed, 141
    micrograms to milligrams, 140–141
    milligrams to grams, 139
    milligrams to micrograms, 140
    percents, 128
Converting liquid measures, 143–144, 143f, 144f
    in apothecary system, 143
    in household system, 143
    in metric system, 143
Converting solid measures, in metric system, 138
Cornell system of note-taking, 42
Coverslip, 236
Craniosacral therapy, 291
Cross-examination, 80
Culture test, for sterilization, 212
Cumulative drug effect, 161
Curet
    ear, 215f
    uterine, 214f
Curved scissors, 213, 217f
Cutaneous punch, 216f
Cutters, for orthopedics, 214f
Cylinder, graduated, 236, 237f
Cytologist, 232b

D
Damages, in lawsuits, 79
Data sheet, laboratory, 231, 233f
Deadlines, stress from, 60
Decimal places, 131
Decimal point, 124
Decimals, 125–127
    clearing divisor of decimal points in, 126
    comparing value of, 127
    determining value of, 127
    dividing, 125–126
    from fractions, 124–125
    as percents, 127–128
    proportion as, 128–129
    reading, 125
    rounding off, 126–127
Defamation of character, 80
Defendant, 78
Defenses
    for medical assistant, 81
    to professional liability suits, 80–81
Demographic data, 90–91
Denominator, 120
Dependence
    controlled substances in, 77, 78t, 154–155, 155b
    physical, 154
    psychological, 154
Deposition, 80
Dereliction of duty, 79
Dermatology instruments, 216f
Dial scales, 252, 252f
Dialysis shunt, blood pressure measurement with, 263b
Diaphragm, microscope, 234, 234f
Diastole, 261
Dictionary, 12

Diet, 287–288
Dietary Supplement Health and Education Act, 164
Digital scales, 252, 252f
Dilator, uterine, 214f
Direct cause, 79
Direct examination, 80
Direct transmission, 188, 189t
Directors, 216, 218f
Disclosures, legally required, 75–77
    of abuse, neglect, or maltreatment, 76
    of cancer diagnosis, 77
    of epilepsy diagnosis, 77
    of infectious or communicable diseases, 75, 76
    medical examiner's reports in, 75
    National Childhood Vaccine Injury Act on, 76, 76b
    patient education on, 75b
    of phenylketonuria diagnosis, 77
    of reportable conditions, 76b
    of violent injuries, 77
    vital statistics from, 75
Disease. *See also specific diseases*
    on drug response, 162
Disinfectants, 191, 191f
Disinfection, 190, 191, 191f, 192t, 210. *See also* Asepsis, medical
    sanitizing equipment for, 210, 221p
Disposable thermometers, 256, 257f
Distraction-free study areas, 24, 31
Distractions, 12, 59
Distress, 58. *See also* Stress
Distributed practice, 16
Distribution, drug, 157
Dividend, 124, 125
Dividing decimals, 125–126
Dividing exponentials, 131
Dividing fractions, 123–124
Dividing whole numbers, 120
Division sign, 120
Division table, 121f
Divisor, 124, 125
Documentation, drug administration, 168–169
Documentation forms, 93, 94f
Domino effect, 6
Doppler measurement, of pulse, 257, 259, 260f
Dosage, proportion and ratio in, 130
Doshas, 286
Dram, 142t, 143
Drill-and-practice software, 39
Drop, 142t, 143
Drug
    categories of, 153–155
    controlled substances, 77, 78t, 154–155, 155b
    easily confused, 168, 168t
    nonprescription, 154
    prescription, 153–154, 155f
Drug abuse, controlled substances and, 77, 78t, 154–155, 155b
Drug administration, 168–178, 173
    buccal, 173
    dispensing systems in, 169–172, 172f
    documentation of, 168–169
    on drug response, 163
    easily confused drugs in, 168, 168t
    errors in, 169
    in home, 177, 178b
    inhalation, 177, 177f
    medication order in, 169, 169b, 170t–171t
    oral, 173
    parenteral, 173–176 (*See also* Parenteral drug administration)

patient care considerations in, 173–174, 177
  preparation for, 172–173
  principles of, 172
  six rights of, 168–169
  sublingual, 173
  topical, 176, 176b
  transdermal, 176–177, 176b
  via mucous membranes, 176–177, 176b
Drug development, 152, 152f
Drug dispensing systems, 169–172, 172f
  computerized, 169, 172f
  floor stock, 172
  unit dose, 171, 172f
Drug Enforcement Administration (DEA), 156
Drug errors, 169
Drug idiosyncrasy, 160–161
Drug names, 153, 154t
Drug preparation, for administration, 172–173
Drug reactions, 159–161
  additive, 161
  adverse, 152, 153b, 159, 160f
  allergic, 159–160, 160t
  antagonistic, 162
  hypersensitivity, 159–160, 160t
  idiosyncrasy, 160–161
  reporting of, 152, 153b
  synergistic, 161–162
  toxic, 161
Drug response, factors in, 162–163, 163t
Drug tolerance, 161
Drug–drug interactions, 161–162
Drug–food interactions, 162
Drug–receptor interactions, 158–159, 159f
Durable power of attorney, 73
Duress, 79
Duty, 79
  dereliction of, 79
Dyspnea, 261

E
Ear curet, 215f
Ear forceps, 215f
Eating right, 61
Education, patient
  on herbs and nutritional supplements, 164, 165b
  on legally required disclosures, 75b
  on medical asepsis, 189–190, 189b
  on specimen collection, 231b
Elaboration, 17
Elder abuse, 77
Electromagnetic therapy, 292–293
Electronic health records (EHR), 90–91
Electronic thermometer, 255, 256f, 257f, 273p
Elimination, drug, 158
Emancipated minor, 74
Employer rights and responsibilities, 83b
Employment laws, 81–83
  Age Discrimination in Employment Act of 1967, 83b
  Americans with Disabilities Act, 82, 83b
  Civil Rights Act of 1964, Title VII, 81–82, 83b
  for employer and employment rights and responsibilities, 83b
  Fair Labor Standards Act of 1939, 83b
  Family and Medical Leave Act of 1993, 83b
  Immigration Reform and Control Act of 1986, 83b
  sexual harassment, 82
Employment rights and responsibilities, 83b
Endorphins, 62

Energetic manual healing, 289–290
Energy therapies, 286
Entries, in health records, 93–95, 95f. *See also* Charting
Environmental contamination, handling of, 195–196, 196f, 205p
Epilepsy diagnosis, legally required disclosure of, 77
Equal Employment Opportunity Commission (EEOC), 81–82
Equipment
  autoclave, 211–213, 211f, 222p–226p
  laboratory (*See* Laboratory equipment)
  personal protective (*See* Personal protective equipment (PPE))
  safety, 195b
  sanitization of, for surgical sterilization, 210, 221p
  sterile, 190, 190f
  for surgical sterilization, 210
Equivalents
  in apothecary system *vs.* metric system, 143t
  of household measures, 142, 144, 145t
  liquid
    in apothecary system, 143, 143f
    conversions among, 143–144, 143f, 144f
    of volume, 144, 144t
  in metric system, 141
  solid
    in apothecary system, 141, 142t, 143t
    in metric system, converting, 138
    in metric system *vs.* apothecary system, 141, 143t
    of volume, 144, 144t
    weight, 144, 145t
    in metric system, 138
Erlenmeyer flask, 236, 237f
Errors
  charting, correction of, 96, 96f
  drug, 169
  in specimen collection, 108, 109b
Escherichia coli (E. coli), in stomach, 186
Essay questions
  checklist for, 52
  writing mechanics for, 53
Essay tests, 47
Ethical boundaries, 87p
Ethics, medical, 83–88. *See also* Law
  allied health professional's role in, 84
  bioethics in, 84–87
  definition of, 83–84
  hearing impaired and, 84b
  honesty in, 84
  patient advocacy in, 84
  patient confidentiality in, 84
  performing within boundaries in, 87b
Ethylene oxide gas, 210, 211t
Eustress, 58. *See also* Stress
Evaporation, 254t
Examinations (legal). *See also* Test-taking tips; Tests
  cross-, 80
  direct, 80
  legal, 80
Excretion, drug, 158
Exercise, 61
Exhaustion, 58
Expected threshold, 110
Expert witness, 79
Exponential factor, 130
Exponential notation, 130–132
Exponentials, 130–132
  adding, 131
  dividing, 131
  multiplying, 131

Exponentials (*continued*)
  negative exponents, 130
  subtracting, 131–132
  writing, 131
Exposure control plan, 192
Exposure risk factors, 192
Expressed consent, 73
Expressed contracts, 72
Extravasation, 175
Extremes, 129
Extrinsic, 4
Eye loop, 216f
Eye span, widening, 33, 34
Eyelashes, as natural barrier, 186
Eyes, as natural barriers, 186
Eyewash basin, 195b, 240, 240f

F
Face shields, 193, 196f
Facts, memorization of, 49
Fair Labor Standards Act, 83b
Family and Medical Leave Act, 83b
Febrile patient, 253
Federal health care legislation, 115p–116p
Feldenkrais technique, 290
Fever
  process of, 253–254
  stages of, 254, 255t
  variations in pattern of, 254
Fight-or-flight response, 58
Filing procedures, for health records, 97
Filing systems, for health records, 97–99, 100f
  alphabetic, 97–98, 98b, 99b
  chronological, 98
  geographic, 98
  numeric, 98, 99b
  subject, 98
Fine adjustment knob, microscope, 234, 234f
Five-paragraph format, 53
Fixations, 33
Flasks, 236, 237f
Floor stock, 172
Flora, 186
Flow sheets, 93, 94f
Food, drug interactions with, 162
Food and Drug Administration (FDA), 152–153
  accelerated programs of, 153
  adverse reactions reporting to, 152, 153b
  compassionate access to unapproved drugs by, 153
  MedWatch of, 152, 152f
  orphan drug program of, 153
Food therapies, 288
Forceps, 213, 217f
Foreign body remover, for eye, 216f
Formaldehyde
  as disinfectant, 192t
  as sterilizing agent, 211t
Formulas, memorization of, 49
Fractions, 120–125
  complex, 121, 123
  to decimals, 124–125
  defined, 120
  dividing, 123–124
  improper, 121
  multiplying, 122–123
  as percents, 128
  proper, 120

reducing, 121–122
Frame, microscope, 234, 234f
Fraud, 70, 80
"Freeze-up," in test anxiety, 59
Freezers, laboratory, 235
Full-body relaxation, 61, 62

G
Gastrointestinal tract, as natural barrier, 186
Gender, in drug response, 162
General adaptation syndrome, 58
Generic name, drug, 153, 154t
Genitourinary tract, as natural barrier, 186
Geographic filing, 98
Germicides, 190, 191, 191f
Glass mercury and glass thermometers, 255, 256, 256f, 257f
  axillary temperature measurement with, 271p–272p
  disinfecting, 257b
  oral temperature measurement with, 267p–268p
  rectal temperature measurement with, 269p–270p
Glass slide, 236
Glassware, 236–237, 236b, 236f, 237f
Glossary, 293–297
Gloves, 193
  for drug administration, 173
  handwashing after removal of, 193
  latex allergy and prevention with, 193, 195b
  patient offense at, 195b
  removal procedure for, 202p–204p
Glucose meter, performing routine maintenance on, 249p
Glutaraldehyde
  chemical spill of, 219b
  as disinfectant, 192t
  as sterilizing agent, 211t
Goal structure, 6
Goals, 23
  accomplishing, 5–7
  belief in yourself and, 8
  evaluation of, 8
  grades and, 6
  intermediate, 6–7
  long-term, 6, 7
  procrastination and, 23–24
  reaching, 6
  setting, 5–8
  short-term, 5, 7
  staying on task for, 7–8
  structure of, 6
  types of, 6–7
"Going with the flow," 63–64
Good Samaritan Act, 77–78
Gowns, 193
Grades, goals and, 6
Graduated cylinder, 236, 237f
Grain, 141, 142t
  converting to milligrams, 143
Gram, 138
  converting to milligrams, 138–139, 141
Greater than sign, 138
Gynecology instruments, 214f

H
Habit, study as, 24
Half-life, 158
Handwashing, 189b, 190
  after glove removal, 193
  procedure for, 199p–201p

Harrison Narcotic Act, 155
Hazards
    biological (*See* Biohazards)
    chemical, 238
    physical, 238
HazCom Standard, 238
Health departments, state, 109, 115p
Health Insurance Portability and Accountability Act of 1996 (HIPAA),
        91–92, 108–109, 116p
Health records. *See* Records, health
Hearing impaired, patient confidentiality and, 84b
Heartbeat, palpation of, 256
Heat
    in body temperature, 252–253
    loss of, 253, 253t
    transfer mechanisms for, 253, 254t
Height measurement, 252, 252f, 253f, 265p–266p
Helicobacter pylori, 186
Help, asking for, 64
Hematocrit test, 235
Hemostat clamp, 213, 217f
Hepatitis B virus (HBV)
    immunization against, 192, 198, 238
    infection control for, 197–198
Herbal medicine (therapy), 163–164, 165b, 288–289
High-complexity tests, 242
Highlighting text, 31
Histologist, 232b
History
    instrument record on, 244, 245f
    patient form for, 93
HIV (human immunodeficiency virus), infection control for, 197–198
Home, drug administration in, 177, 178b
Homeopathic medicine, 286–287
Homework, 22
Honesty, 84
Hospital laboratory, 231
Hosts, susceptible, 188, 188b
Household system, 142–144
    converting liquid measures in, 143–144, 143f
    equivalents of, 142, 144, 145t
Hydrogen peroxide, 192t
Hyperpnea, 261
Hyperpyrexia, 254
Hypersensitivity reaction, to drugs, 159–160, 160t
Hypertension, 262
Hyperventilation, 261
Hypnosis, 291–292
Hypodermic needle disposal, 174, 174f, 196, 196f
Hypopnea, 261
Hypotension, postural, 261

I

Idiosyncrasy, drug, 160–161
Illness, present, 90, 93f
Imagery, 17
    in metalearning, 27
    in stress management, 62
Immigration Reform and Control Act, 83b
Immunity, in professional liability suits, 81
Immunization
    against blood-borne pathogens, 82, 195b, 238
    for hepatitis B virus, 192, 198
Immunization records, maintaining, 103p
Implied consent, 73
Implied contracts, 72
Improper fractions, 121

Inactive heath records, 98–99
Incident reports, 110–114
    for clinical laboratories, 241
    completion of
        guidelines for, 111, 114f
        necessity for, 111
    information included on, 111, 112f–113f
    myths about, 111b
    purpose and nature of, 110
    Spanish terminology for, 114
    trending of, 114
Incubator, 235
Indexing rules, for alphabetic filing, 98
Indian medicine, 286
Indicator tape, autoclave, 211–212, 212b, 212f
Indirect transmission, 188, 189t
Infection, 186
Infection control, medical, 190–207. *See also* Asepsis, medical
    for biohazards and environmental contamination, 195–196, 196f,
        197b, 205p
    in clinical laboratory, 238
    disinfection in, 191, 191f, 192t
    environmental contamination in, handling, 195–196, 196f, 205p
    flora types in, 186
    glove removal in, 202p–204p
    handwashing in, 189b, 190, 199p–201p
    for hepatitis B and HIV, 197–198
    host resistance and, 186
    infection cycle in, 187–188, 187f, 188b
    infectious waste disposal in, 174, 174f, 196–197, 196f, 197b
    levels of, 190, 190f
    medical asepsis in, 189–190, 189b, 190b
    microorganisms in, 186
    natural defenses in, 186
    OSHA guidelines for, 191–197 (*See also* Occupational Safety and
        Health Administration (OSHA) infection control guidelines)
    pathogen growth conditions and, 187
    pathogens in, 186
    personal protective equipment in, 192, 193, 196f
    principles of, 189–191
    resistance in, 186
    sanitation in, 190–191
    standard precautions in, 193
    vs. surgical asepsis, 210t
    susceptible hosts in, 188, 188b
    transmission in, 188–189, 189t
    virulence *vs.*, 186
Infection cycle, 187–188, 187f
Infectious diseases
    legally required disclosures on, 75
    reportable conditions in, 76b
Infectious waste disposal, 174, 174f, 196–197, 196f, 197b
Infiltration, 175
Influence, undue, 80
Informed consent, 73
    in hearing impaired, 84
Infusion controllers, intravenous, 175
Infusion pumps, intravenous, 175
Inhalation drug administration, 177, 177f
Injuries, violent, legally required disclosures on, 77
Instrument calibration and maintenance
    in clinical laboratories, 244–245, 244f
    of thermometers, 255
Instrument history record, 244, 245f
Intentional torts, 79
Interference, reduction of, 16
Intermittent fever, 254

Interpreter, 74, 74f
Intradermal drug administration, 176
Intramuscular (IM) drug administration, 175
Intravenous (IV) drug administration, 175
Intravenous (IV) infusion controllers, 175
Intravenous (IV) infusion pumps, 175
Intrinsic, 4
Invasion of privacy, 79–80
Investigational new drug (IND), 152
Iodine, 192t
Iodophors, 192t
Isopropyl alcohol, 192t

J

Jehovah's Witness, refusal of consent by, 74–75
Joint Commission on Accreditation of Healthcare Organizations
    (JCAHO), 83, 106–108, 106b, 115p
Jury awards, 79

K

Kapha, 286
Kelly clamp, 213, 217f
Kidney disease, on drug response, 162
Kilogram, 138
Kinesiology, applied, 289, 291
Kit package inserts, 233b
Knowing, *vs.* understanding, 15
Korotkoff sounds, 262, *279p

L

Labeling text, 31
Laboratory, clinical. *See* Clinical laboratory
Laboratory assistant, 232b
Laboratory data sheet, 231, 233f
Laboratory equipment, 233–237
    calibration and maintenance of, 244–245, 244f
    cell counter, 234
    centrifuge, 235, 235f
    chemistry analyzers, 235
    glassware, 236–237, 236b–237b, 236f, 237f
    incubator, 235
    instrument calibration and maintenance in, 244–245, 244f
    instrument history record for, 244, 245f
    microscope, 234–235, 234f, 247p
    preventive maintenance record form in, 244, 244f
    proficiency testing on, 245
    quality assurance for, 245
    quality control for, 243–245, 243f, 244f, 246f
    quality control log book for, 245
    random error with test result evaluation for, 245, 246f
    refrigerators and freezers, 235
Laboratory manager, 232b
Laboratory personnel, 232, 232b
Laboratory request forms, 231, 231f, 232b
Laboratory safety. *See* Safety, laboratory
Laboratory standards, 243–246
    instrument calibration and maintenance in, 244–245, 244f
    instrument history record in, 244, 245f
    patient test management in, 243
    preventive maintenance record form in, 244, 244f
    proficiency testing in, 245
    quality assurance in, 245
    quality control in, 243–245, 243f, 244f, 246f
    quality control log book in, 245
    random error with test result evaluation in, 245, 246f
Laboratory test package inserts, 233b
Laboratory testing. *See also* Clinical laboratory

use of, 230
Laptop computer, health records on, 91
Latex allergy and prevention, 193, 195b
Law, 69–83. *See also* Ethics, medical
    Age Discrimination in Employment Act of 1967, 83b
    American legal system in, 70–71
    avoiding litigation in, 81, 82b
    branches of, 70
    certification in, 77
    civil, 70
    Civil Rights Act of 1964, Title VII, 81–82, 83b
    Clinical Laboratory Improvement Amendments (CLIA) of 1988,
        83, 108, 115p
    common, 70
    Controlled Substances Act of 1970, 77, 78t, 154–155, 155b
    defense for medical assistant in, 81
    defenses to professional liability suits in, 80–81
    employment and safety, 81–83
    Fair Labor Standards Act of 1939, 83b
    Family and Medical Leave Act of 1993, 83b
    Good Samaritan Act, 77–78
    Health Insurance Portability and Accountability Act of 1996 (HIPAA),
        91–92, 108–109, 116p
    Immigration Reform and Control Act of 1986, 83b
    Joint Commission on Accreditation of Healthcare Organizations, 83,
        106–108, 106b, 115p
    licensure in, 77
    litigation process in, 80
    National Childhood Vaccine Injury Act of 1986, 76, 76b
    negligence and malpractice in, 78–79
    Occupational Safety and Health Act, 82, 83b, 115p (*See also*
        Occupational Safety and Health Administration (OSHA))
    physician–patient relationship in, 71–77 (*See also* Physician–patient
        relationship)
    private, 70
    public, 70
    registration in, 77
    rise in medical legal cases and, 70–71
    safety, 82–83
    sources of, 70
    specific laws and statutes in, 77–78
    tort, 70, 78
Law of agency, 81
Lawsuits, 70
Learning, 13
Learning skills development, 38–39
Lectures
    infective, overcoming obstacles in, 37
    learning from, 35–36
    organizing content of, 39
Legal boundaries, 87p
Legal cases, medical, 70–71. *See also* Law
    rise in, 70–71
Legal system, American, 70–71
Legally required disclosures, 75–77. *See also* Disclosures, legally
    required
Legend drugs, 153–154, 155f
Legislation, federal and state health care, 115p–116p
Lemon, 25
Lenses, microscope, 234, 234f
Letter of intent, to terminate physician–patient relationship, 72
"Letting go," 63–64
Liability suits
    defenses to, 80–81
    health records in, 80
Libel, 80
Licensure, for health professionals, 77

Lid retractor, 216f
Lifestyle changes, 287, 288
Light source, microscope, 234, 234f
Lighting, for studying, 24
Liquid measures
    in apothecary system, 143, 143f, 144f
    conversions among, 143–144, 143f, 144f
    in metric system, 142, 143–144, 143f, 144f
LISAN method, 38
Listening
    active, 36–38
    to lectures, 35–36
    with LISAN method, 38
    types of, 36
Lists, as memory aid, 17
Liter, 142
Litigation, 70
    avoiding, 81, 82b
Litigation process, 80
Liver disease, on drug response, 162
Locum tenens, 73

M
Magnets, as therapy, 292–293
Majority, age of, 74
Malfeasance, 78
Malpractice, 78–79
Malpractice insurance, 81
Maltreatment, legally required disclosure of, 76
Manipulative therapies, 286, 290. *See also* Complementary and
        alternative medicine (CAM)
Mantra meditation, 62
Manual healing, 289–291, 289f
    adjustment-based therapies, 290–291
    energetic, 289–290
    movement repatterning, 290
    pressure-based therapies, 290
Mapping, recall, 17
Marking text, 31
Massage, therapeutic, 61, 290
Material safety data sheet (MSDS), 219b, 238, 240b
Math fundamentals, 120–136
    answers to self-tests on, 133–136
    decimals, 125–127
    dividing whole numbers, 120, 121f
    exponential notation, 130–132
    fractions, 120–125 (*See also* Fractions)
    multiplying whole numbers, 120, 121f
    percent, 127–128
    ratio and proportion, 128–130
Means, 129
Measurements. *See also* Clinical laboratory; Vital signs; *specific tests*
    anthropometric, 252
    height, 252, 252f, 253f, 265p–266p
    weight, 252, 252f, 264p
Measuring systems, 138–148
    answers to self-tests on, 147–148
    apothecary system, 141, 142t, 143, 143f, 143t, 144f
    conversions among, 144–146, 144t, 145t (*See also* Conversions)
    household system, 142–144, 145t
    household system equivalents, 144, 145t
    liquid measure conversions, 143–144, 143f, 144f
    metric conversions, mixed, 141
    metric system, 138–141 (*See also* Metric system)
    solid equivalents, metric, 138
    solid measures conversions, metric system, 138
    volume equivalents, 144, 144t

    weight equivalents, 144, 145t
Medical asepsis. *See* Asepsis, medical; Infection control, medical
Medical ethics. *See* Ethics, medical
Medical examiner's reports, 75
Medical legal cases, rise in, 70–71
Medical records. *See* Records, health
Medical technologist, 232b
Medication administration flow sheet, 93, 94f
Medication orders, 169, 169b, 170t–171t
    abbreviations in, 169, 170t–171t
Medication records, maintaining, 103p
Meditation, for stress management, 62–63
MedWatch, 152, 153t
Memory and memorization, 13–16
    acronyms in, 17
    association in, 15, 16–17
    attention in, 18
    attitude in, 18
    color in, 17
    early, 13
    elaboration in, 17
    of facts and formulas, 49
    imagery in, 17, 18
    improving, 14, 17–18
    interference reduction in, 16
    lists in, 17
    long-term, 14
    lost, searching for, 15
    organization in, 15
    practice in, 16
    processing information in, 13–14
    rehearsal in, 15
    repetition in, 18
    retrieval of, 15–16
    rote, 15
    selection in, 14–15
    short-term, 14
    simplicity in, 18
    spaced study in, 16
    stress on, 58–59
    study strategies for, 16–17
    understanding in, 15, 18
    variety in, 18
    vivid images in, 18
    word games in, 17
    working, 14–15
Memory jogger
    CARDS, for reading rate, 33
    for memorization, 18
    REAP, for multiple-choice tests, 50
    RSVP, for goal setting, 7
    SALT, for study place, 24
Meniscus, in pipetting, 237b
Mercury glass thermometers, 255, 256f
    axillary temperature measurement with, 271p–272p
    disinfecting, 257b
    oral temperature measurement with, 267p–268p
    rectal temperature measurement with, 269p–270p
Mercury sphygmomanometer, 261, 261f, *279p
Meridians, 286
Metabolism
    of drugs, 157–158
    heat in, 253
Metalearning, 26–27
Metric system, 138–141
    common equivalents in, 141
    converting grains to milligrams, 143

Metric system (*continued*)
  converting grams to milligrams, 138–139, 141
  converting liquid measures in, 143–144, 143f, 144f
  converting micrograms to milligrams, 140–141
  converting milligrams to grams, 139
  converting milligrams to micrograms, 140
  converting mixed conversions in, 141
  converting solid equivalents in, 138
  liquid measures in, 142, 143–144, 143f, 144f
  weight equivalents, 138
  weight measures, 138
Microgram, 138
  converting milligrams to, 140
  converting to milligrams, 140–141
Microhematocrit centrifuge, 235
Microorganisms, 186
Microscope, 234–235, 234f, 247p
Microscopy, provider-performed, 242
Military time, 95
Milligram, 138
  converting grains to, 143
  converting grams to, 138–139, 141
  converting micrograms to, 140–141
  converting to grams, 139
  converting to microgram, 140
Milliliter, 142
Mind
  caring for, 64
  controlling, 11–18
    concentration in, 12–13
    memory in, 13–18 (*See also* Memory)
    meandering, 12
Mind-body therapies, 286, 291–292. *See also* Complementary and
  alternative medicine (CAM)
Minim, 142t, 143
Minor, emancipated, 74
Misfeasance, 78
Mixed numbers, 121
  multiplying, 123
Moderate-complexity tests, 242
Modes of transmission, 188–189, 189t
Motivation, 4–5
Motivators, 23
Mouth, as natural barrier, 186
Movement repatterning, 290
MSDS binder, 195b
Mucous membranes, drug administration through, 176–177
Multiple-choice tests, 50–51
Multiplication table, 120, 121f
Multiplying exponentials, 131
Multiplying fractions, 122–123
Multiplying mixed numbers, 123
Multiplying whole numbers, 120, 121f
Muscle relaxation, 61, 62

N
Narrative format, 92, 92f
Nasal forceps, 215f
Nasal speculum, 215f
National Center for Complementary and Alternative Medicine (NCCAM)
  on alternative medicine, 284
  five domains of, 284–285
  research cites and current studies of, 295t–296t
National Childhood Vaccine Injury Act, 76, 76b
National Committee for Clinical Laboratory Standards (NCCLS), 243,
  243f
Naturopathic medicine, 287

Needle disposal, 174, 174f, 196, 196f
Needle holder, 213, 217f
Needlestick prevention, OSHA guidelines for, 174
Negative electromagnetic therapy, 293
Negative exponent, 130
Negative thoughts, controlling, 64
Neglect, legally required disclosure of, 76
Negligence, 78–79
  comparative, 81
  contributory, 81
Neural therapy, 292
New drug application (NDA), 152
Noise, minimizing, 25
Noncompliant patient, 72
Nonfeasance, 78
Nonprescription drugs, 154
Normal flora, 186
Normal values, 233f
Nosepiece, microscope, 234, 234f
Note-taking skills, 39–43. *See also* Note-taking skills
  abbreviations and symbols for, 41
  Cornell system in, 42
  other strategies in, 40–42
  outlines in, 41
  overcoming obstacles in, 41
  personalization in, 42
  quantity in, 42–43
  reviewing notes in, 43
  tips for, 40
Notes, usefulness of, 39–40
Numerator, 120
Numeric filing, 98, 99b
Nutrition, 287–288
Nutritional supplements, 163–164

O
Objective tests, 47, 50–51
Obstacles, overcoming
  in fact and formula memorization, 49
  to infective lecturing, 37
  in note-taking, 41
  in studying for tests, 47
Obturator, 215f
Occupational Safety and Health Act, 82, 115p
Occupational Safety and Health Administration (OSHA), 108, 191
  drug administration guidelines of, 174
  HazCom Standard of, 238
  on laboratory safety, 238, 242b
  OSHA 300 log of, 192, 194f
  rules governing health care providers in, 83b, 115p
  on sterilization solution spills, 219b
Occupational Safety and Health Administration (OSHA) infection control
    guidelines, 191–197
  blood-borne pathogen regulations in, 195b, 238
  blood-borne pathogen standard training in, 193b
  exposure risk factors and exposure control plan in, 192
  infectious waste disposal in, 197–198, 197b
Occurrence reports, 110–114. *See also* Incident reports
Offer, 71
Office of Alternative Medicine (OAM), NIH, 294
Official name, drug, 153, 154t
Open-book tests, 54
Ophthalmology instruments, 216f
Oral examinations, 54
Oral route, of drug administration, 173
Oral temperature, 253, 253b
Oral temperature measurement, 267p–268p

Oral tests, 47
Organ transplantation, bioethics issues in, 84–85, 85b
Organization, in memory, 15
Orientation question, 27
Orphan drug program, 153
Orthomolecular medicine, 288
Orthopedics instruments, 214f
Otology instruments, 215f
Orthopnea, 261
OSHA 300 log, 192, 194f
OSHA HazCom Standard, 238
Osteopathy, 290–291
Otology instruments, 215f
Ounce, 142, 142t, 143
Outcomes, patient, 106
Outlines
    in note-taking, 41
    for subjective tests, 52
Outrage, tort of, 80
Over-the-counter (OTC) drugs, 154
Overcoming obstacles. *See* Obstacles, overcoming
Oxygen therapy, 292

P
Package inserts, kit (test), 233b
Palpation, of pulse, 256–257, 258f, 259f
Paper thermometers, 255, 257f
Paraphrasing, 27
Parenteral drug administration, 173–176
    intradermal, 176
    intramuscular (IM), 175
    intravenous (IV), 175
    OSHA guidelines on, 174
    patient care considerations in, 173–174
    subcutaneous (SC), 174
    venous access ports, 176
Pathogens, 186, 187
Pathologist, 232b
Patient advocacy, 84
Patient communications, charting, 95–96, 96f. *See also* Records, health
Patient confidentiality, 84
Patient history form, 93
Patient information
    family member inquiry on, 74b
    releasing, 75
Patient rights and responsibilities, 71, 71b
Patient test management, clinical laboratory, 243
Payload, personal, 6
Peppermint, 25
Percent, 127–128
    conversion of, 128
    decimals as, 127–128
    fractions as, 128
Perfection, stresses and, 60–61
Peripheral pulse, 257–258, 258f
Peroxide, 192t
Personal computer, health records on, 91
Personal data device (PDA), health records on, 91
Personal payload, 6
Personal protective equipment (PPE), 192, 193, 196f
    as biohazard, 195b
    in clinical laboratory, 238
    handwashing after removal of, 193
    latex allergy and prevention with, 193, 195b
    patient offense at, 195b
    removal of gloves in, 202p–204p
Petri dish, 237
Petri plate, 237

Pharmaceutic phase, 157
Pharmacodynamics, 158–159, 159f
Pharmacogenetic disorder, 161
Pharmacokinetic phase, 157–158, 157f
Pharmacokinetics, 157
Pharmacologic therapies, in complementary and alternative medicine, 292
Pharmacology, defined, 152
Pharmacology principles, 152–165
    additive drug reaction in, 161
    adverse drug reaction reporting in, 152, 153t
    adverse drug reactions in, 152, 153b, 159, 160f
    age in, 162, 163t
    allergic drug reactions in, 159–160, 160t
    anaphylactic shock in, 159–160, 160t
    antagonistic drug reaction in, 162
    Comprehensive Drug Abuse and Prevention and Control Act, 156
    cumulative drug effect in, 161
    drug absorption in, 157
    drug actions within body in, 156–159, 157f
    drug categories in, 153–155
    drug development in, 152, 152f
    drug distribution in, 157
    Drug Enforcement Administration, 156
    drug excretion in, 158
    drug idiosyncrasy in, 160–161
    drug interactions in, 161–162
    drug metabolism in, 157–158
    drug names in, 153, 154t
    drug reactions in, 159–161
    drug response in, 162–163, 163t
    drug tolerance in, 161
    drug–drug interactions in, 161–162
    drug–food interactions in, 162
    federal drug legislation and enforcement in, 155–156, 156b
    Food and Drug Administration in, 152–153
    gender in, 162
    half-life in, 158
    Harrison Narcotic Act, 155
    herbal therapy in, 163–164, 165b
    hypersensitivity drug reactions in, 159–160, 160t
    kidney disease in, 162
    liver disease in, 162
    nutritional supplements in, 163–164
    pharmaceutic phase in, 157
    pharmacodynamic phase in, 158–159, 159f
    pharmacogenetic reactions in, 161
    pharmacokinetic phase in, 157–158, 157f
    pregnancy and, 156
    pregnancy drug categories in, 156, 156b
    Pure Food, Drug, and Cosmetic Act, 156
    Pure Food and Drug Act, 155
    receptor-mediated drug actions in, 158
    receptor-mediated drug effects in, 159
    route of administration in, 163
    synergistic drug reactions in, 161–162
    toxic drug reactions in, 161
    weight in, 162
Phenols, 192t
Phenylketonuria, legally required disclosure of, 77
Phlebotomist, 232b
Physical dependence, 154
Physical hazards, 238
Physician contracts, 71–72
Physician office laboratory, 231–232, 233f
Physician rights and responsibilities, 71, 71b
Physician–patient relationship, 71–77
    consent in, 73–75, 74f

Physician–patient relationship (*continued*)
  contracts in, 71–73
  legally required disclosures in, 75–77
  releasing patient information in, 75
  rights and responsibilities in, 71, 71b
Pint, 142
Pipettes, 236b–237b, 236f, 237
Pitta, 286
Plaintiff, 78
Planning
  short- and long-range, 20
  for test taking, 47–50
Plaster saw, 214f
Plaster shears, 214f
Plaster spreader, 214f
Polypharmacy, 162
POMR format, 92, 93f
Ports, venous access, 176
Positive thinking, power of, 64
Postexposure testing, 192
Postural hypotension, 261
Pound, 142
Power of attorney, durable, 73
Power of positive thinking, 64
Power-reading symbols, 31
Powers of 10, 130
Practice
  distributed, 16
  as study strategy, 16
Prana, 62, 286
Precedents, legal, 70
Pregnancy drug categories, 156, 156b
Preparation
  for class, 35
  for test taking, 46–47
Prescription drugs, 153–154, 155f
Prescriptions, 154, 155f
  abbreviations in, 169, 170t–171t
  for controlled substances, 77, 78t, 154–155, 155b
Present illness, 90, 93f
Pressure-based therapies, 290
Pressure-point therapy, 290
Preventive maintenance record form, laboratory equipment, 244, 244f
Previewing material, 26–27
Prime numbers, 122
Priorities, 23
  setting, 21–22
    for stress management, 60–61
Privacy, invasion of, 79–80
Private law, 70
PRN order, 169, 169b
Probes, 216, 218f
Problem-oriented medical record (POMR) format, 92, 92f
Problem-solving software, 39
Problem-solving tests, 51
Procrastination, 22–24, 61
Proctology instruments, 215f
Proctoscope, 215f
Professional liability suits, health records in, 80
Proficiency testing, of clinical laboratories, 245
Progress notes, 93
Proper fraction, 120
Proportion, 128–130
  as decimal, 128–129
  in dosage, 130
  solving, 130
    with an unknown, 128

  as two ratios separated by colons, 129
Prostate biopsy instrument, 215f
Protocol, to terminate contract, 72
Provider encounters, medical records of, 92
Provider-performed microscopy (PPM), 242
PSQ5R method, 26
Psychological dependence, 154
Public law, 70
Pulse, 256–259
  age on, 257, 259t
  apical, 257, 259, 259f, 260f
  Doppler measurement of, 257, 259, 260f
  dorsal pedalis, 258f, 259, 260f
  factors in, 258–259, 260t
  origin of, 256–257
  palpation of, 256–257, 258f, 259f
  peripheral, 257–258, 258f
  radial, 256, 258f, 259, 259f, 275p
  rate of, 257
  rhythm of, 257
  volume of, 257
Pulse points, 257–258, 258f, 259f
Pulse pressure, 262
Punch biopsy instrument
  for dermatology, 216f
  for proctology, 215f
Pure Food, Drug, and Cosmetic Act, 156
Pure Food and Drug Act, 155
Pyrexia, 254

Q
Qi (chi), 286
Qigong, 62, 288, 289
Quality assurance
  in clinical laboratories, 230, 245
  plans for, 106
Quality control
  in clinical laboratories, 230, 243–245, 243f, 244f, 246f
  log book for, clinical laboratory, 245
  using principles of, 248p
Quality improvement, 106
Quality improvement programs, 106–109
  Centers for Medicare and Medicaid Services for, 108, 115p
  Clinical Laboratory Improvement Amendments for, 83, 108, 115p, 241–246 (*See also* Clinical Laboratory Improvement Amendments (CLIA))
  development of, 109–110
  Health Insurance Portability and Accountability Act on, 108–109
  Joint Commission on Accreditation of Healthcare Organizations for, 106–108, 106b
  Joint Commission on Accreditation of Healthcare Organizations in, 83, 115p
  Occupational Safety and Health Administration in, 83b, 108, 115p
  regulatory agencies for, 106–109
  state health departments for, 109, 115p
Quart, 142
Quotient, 124, 125

R
Radial pulse, 256, 258f, 259, 259f, 275p
Radiation, 254t
Random error, test result evaluation for, 245, 246f
Rapid eye movement, in reading rate, 33
Ratchets, in forceps, 213, 217f
Ratio, 128–130
  in dosage, 130
  proportions as, 129

Reaching out, 64
Reading comprehension
  techniques for, 30–32
  tests on, 54
Reading rate
  alterations in, 34–35
  average, 32
    calculating, 33, 34
  increasing, 32–35
    factors in, 33
    material on, 33
    practice of, 35
    preparation for, 33
    purpose in, 34
    rapid eye movement in, 33
    rationale for, 32–33
    widening eye span in, 33, 34
Reading skills, 30–35
  active, 30–32
  comprehension techniques in, 30–32
  increasing reading rate in, 32–35
  skimming for ideas in, 30
  summarizing material in, 32
Reagent management, 243–244
Reagents, 230
Recall, 13
Recall mapping, 17
Reception, 13
Receptor, 158
Receptor-mediated drug actions, 158
Receptor-mediated drug effects, 159
Receptor–drug interactions, 158–159, 159f
Reciprocal teaching, 26
Record keeping, on sterile instruments, 219
Records, health, 89–103
  abbreviations in, 96b
  active, 98–99
  additions to, 96
  charting patient communications in, 95–96, 96f
  classification of, 98–99
  closed, 99
  correction of, 96, 96f
  documentation forms in, 93, 94f
  electronic health records in, 90–91
  entries in, 93–96, 95f, 96b, 96f (See also Charting)
  file preparation in, 102p
  filing procedures for, 97
  filing systems for, 97–99, 100f
  inactive, 98–99
  medication and immunization, maintaining, 103p
  organization of, 91–93, 92f, 93f
  preparation of, 97
  in professional liability suits, 80
  release of, 100–101, 100b, 101f
  reporting obligations for, 101
  retention of, 100, 100f
  Spanish terminology on, 101
  standard medical records in, 90
  for workers' compensation, 97
Records storage, health
  of active records, 100
  of inactive records, 99
Rectal speculum, 215f
Rectal temperature, 253, 253b
Rectal temperature measurement, 269p–270p
Reflexology, 290
Refrigerators, laboratory, 235

Refusal of consent, 74–75
Registration, 13
  for health professionals, 77
Regulations, federal and state health care, 115p–116p
Regulatory agencies, health care, 106–109. See also specific agencies
Rehearsal, 15
Rehearsal forms, for memory, 16
Relapsing fever, 254
Relaxation, muscle and full-body, 61, 62
Relaxation breathing, 63
Relaxation response, 62
Release of health records, 100–101, 100b, 101f
Remittent fever, 254
Repatterning, movement, 290
Repetition, 16, 18
Reportable conditions, 76b
Reportable range, 244–245
Reporting obligations, 101
Request forms, laboratory, 231, 231f, 232b
Res ipsa loquitur, 79
Res judicata, 81
Resident flora, 186
Resistance
  disease, 186
  in general adaptation syndrome, 58
Resources, allocation of, 84–85
Respiration, 260–261, 261t
  defined, 260
  factors in, 261, 261t
  mechanisms of, 260
  rate, rhythm, and depth of, 261
Respiration measurement, 260, 276p
Respiratory tract, as natural barrier, 186
Respondeat superior, 81
Responsibilities. See Rights and responsibilities
Rest, 61
Retention of health records, 100, 100f
Retractors, 216, 219f
Reverse chronological order, 92
Review, after tests, 55
Reviewing notes, 43
Rewards, 23
Rhinology instruments, 215f
Rights and responsibilities
  employer and employment, 83b
  patient, 71, 71b
  physician, 71, 71b
Risk assumption, 81
Risk management, 110–114. See also Biohazards; Incident reports;
    Infection control, medical
Rolfing, 289, 291
Rote memorization, 15
Rounding off decimals, 126–127
Route of administration. See Drug administration

S
Safety, laboratory, 237–241
  biological hazards in, 238 (See also Biohazard)
  blood-borne pathogens in, 238
  chemical hazards in, 238, 239f
  eyewash basin in, 240, 240f
  guidelines for, 239–241
  incident reports in, 241
  material safety data sheet in, 219b, 238, 240b
  OSHA guidelines for, 238
  personal protective equipment in, 238 (See also Personal protective
    equipment (PPE))

Safety, laboratory (*continued*)
  physical hazards in, 238
  spill cleanup kits for, 241, 241f
Safety equipment, in healthcare facility, 195b
Safety guidelines, laboratory, 239–241
Safety laws, 82–83
  for employer and employment rights and responsibilities, 83b
  for health care providers, 83b
  in Occupational Safety and Health Act (OSHA), 82, 83b, 115p (*See also* Occupational Safety and Health Administration (OSHA))
Saliva, bactericidal properties of, 186
Sanitation, 189b, 190–191
Sanitization, 190, 212, 221p
Saw, cast, 214f
Scales, 252, 252f
Scalpels, 213, 218f
Scents, mind and, 25
Schedules, 20
  taking a break in, 27–28
Schiotz tonometer, 216f
Scissors, 213, 217f
Security, of electronic health records, 91
Selection, in memory, 14–15
Sentence-completion tests, 51
Sentinel event alert, JCAHO, 108
Sentinel events, 108, 108b
Serrations, in forceps, 213, 217f
Setting priorities, 21–22
  for stress management, 60–61
Sexual harassment, 82
Shark cartilage, 292
Sharps container, 174, 174f, 196, 196f
Shock, anaphylactic, 159–160, 160t
Short-answer tests, 51
Shorthand, in note taking, 40
Side effects, 159. *See also* Adverse reactions
Siegel, Bernie, 293
Sigmoidoscope, 215f
Sign language, 84b
Significant figures, 131
Simplicity, in stress management, 60
Simulation software, 39
Single order, 169, 169b
Six rights of drug administration, 168–169
Skimming for ideas, 30
Skin
  drug administration through, 176–177, 176b
  as natural barrier, 186
Slander, 80
SOAP format, 92
Social supports, building, 64
Sodium hypochlorite, 192t
Software, in computer-assisted instruction, 38–39
Solid equivalents
  in apothecary system, 141, 142t, 143t
  in metric system, converting, 138
  in metric system *vs.* apothecary system, 141, 143t
Spaced study, 16
Spanish terminology
  for health records, 101
  for incidents, 114
  for vital signs, 262
Specimen accessioner, 232b
Specimen collection. *See also* Clinical laboratory
  errors in, 108, 109b
  patient education on, 231b
Specimen processor, 232b

Speculum, vaginal, 214f
Sphygmomanometer
  aneroid, 261, 261f, *279p
  mercury, 261, 261f, *279p
  use of, 261f, 262–263, *277p–280p
Spill cleanup kits, 241, 241f
Spills. *See* Biohazard spills; Chemical spills
Spores, 187
Spousal abuse, 77
Spreaders, for orthopedics, 214f
Spring forceps, 213, 217f
SQ4R reading-study system, 26
Stage, microscope, 234, 234f
Standard medical records, 90
Standard precautions, 193
Standard training, on blood-borne pathogens, 193b
Standardized tests, 54–55
Standards, laboratory, 243–246
  instrument calibration and maintenance in, 244–245, 244f
  patient test management in, 243
  proficiency testing in, 245
  quality assurance in, 245
  quality control in, 243–245, 243f, 244f, 246f
  quality control log book in, 245
Standards of care, 78–79
Standing order, 169, 169b
Staphylococcus aureus, 186
Stare decisis, 70
STAT order, 169, 169b
State health care legislation, 115p–116p
State health departments, 109, 115p
Statistics, vital, 75
Statue of limitations, 81
Statutes, 70
Sterile equipment, 190, 190f
Sterile technique, 212
Sterile transfer forceps, 213, 217
Sterilization, 210
  surgical, 210–213
    answers to questions on, 226–227
    autoclave in, 211, 211f
    wrapping instruments for, 211, 222p–224p
    autoclave loading in, 212
    autoclave operation in, 212–213, 225p–226p
    equipment for, 212
    indicators of, 211–212, 212b, 212f
    Material Safety Data Sheets on chemicals for, 219b
    vs. medical asepsis, 210, 210t
    methods of, 211t, 212
    sanitizing equipment for, 212, 221p
Sterilization indicators, 211–212, 212b, 212f
Sterilization methods, 190
Sterilization solution spills, 219b
Sterilizer forceps, 213, 217f
Storage
  of health records
    active, 100
    inactive, 99
  of sterile instruments, 219
Straight scissors, 213, 217f
Stress, 57–59
  definition of, 58
  "freeze-up" in, 59
  reacting to, 58–59
  recognizing, 58–59
  test-taking anxiety in, coping with, 59
  types of, 58

Stress-free learning and recall, 13
Stress management, 60–66
    asking for help in, 64
    caring for body in, 61–64
    caring for mind in, 64
    endorphins in, 62
    imagery in, 62
    "letting go" and "going with the flow" in, 63–64
    meditation in, 62–63
    muscle and full-body relaxation in, 61, 62
    qigong in, 62
    relaxation breathing in, 63
    setting priorities in, 60–61
    tai chi chuan in, 62
    therapeutic massage in, 61
    visualization in, 63
    yoga in, 62
Stress maze, 65–66
Stress overload, 58
Stress-reduction techniques, 61–64
Structure words, 35
Student-teacher conferences, 39
Study area, selecting, 24–25
Study arrangement, 24
Study groups, 48
Study plan, creating, 47–48
Study strategies, 16–17
    for improving memory, 14 (*See also* Memory)
Studying
    attitude on, 4
    getting started with, 25–26
    motivation on, 4–5
    physical comfort in, 25
    preparing for, 24–26
    special programs for, 26–27
    study area in, 24–25
Subcutaneous (SC) drug administration, 174
Subject filing, 98
Subjective tests, 51–53
Sublingual drug administration, 173
Subpoena duces tecum, 100b
Supplements, nutritional, 163–164
Supplies, surgical, maintaining, 220
Surgical asepsis. *See* Asepsis, surgical; Sterilization, surgical
Surgical instruments, 213–220
    care and handling of, 216–219
    defined, 213
    in dermatology, 216f
    forceps, 213, 217f
    maintaining supplies for, 220
    in obstetrics and gynecology, 214f
    in ophthalmology, 216f
    in orthopedics, 214f
    in otology, 215f
    probes and directors, 216, 218f
    in proctology, 215f
    retractors, 216, 219f
    in rhinology, 215f
    scalpels and blades, 213, 218f
    scissors, 213, 217f
    storage and record keeping on, 219
    towel clamps, 216, 218f
    in urology, 215f
    wrapping of, for sterilization in autoclave, 211, 222p–224p
Surgical sterilization. *See* Sterilization, surgical
Surgical supplies, maintaining, 220
Surroundings, for studying, 25

Susceptible hosts, 188, 188b
Sustained fever, 254
Suture scissors, 213, 217f
Symbols
    for note-taking, 41
    for power-reading, 31
Synergistic drug reaction, 161–162
Systems of measure. *See* Measuring systems
Systole, 261

T
Tablespoon, 142
Tachypnea, 261
Tai chi (chuan), 62
Take-home tests, 54
Taking a break, 27–28
Task, staying on, 7–8
Task force, 110
Task management, 21
Teaching, reciprocal, 26
Teaspoon, 142
Technician, clinical laboratory, 232b
Technologist
    chief, 232b
    medical, 232b
Temperature
    body, 252–256
        defined, 252
        factors in, 253, 253f
        fever process in, 253–254
        fever stages in, 254, 255t
        heat transfer mechanisms in, 253, 254t
    for studying, 24–25
Temperature measurement, 253, 253b
    axillary, 253, 253b, 271p–272p
    electronic thermometer, 273p
    oral, 253, 253b, 267p–268p
    rectal, 253, 253b, 269p–270p
    tympanic thermometer, 253, 253b, 274p
Tenaculum forceps, 214f
Teratogen, 156
Termination of contract, 72–73
Test anxiety, 46
Test management, clinical laboratory, 243
Test package inserts, 233b
Test results
    evaluation of, for random error, 245, 246f
    privacy of, 233b
Test-taking tips, 45–55
    for anxiety, 59
    for freeze-up, 59
    planning in, 47–50
    preparation in, 46–47
    review in, 55
    for stress, 59
    types of tests in, 50–55 (*See also* Tests)
Test tube, 237, 237f
Tests
    essay or oral, 47
    objective, 47
Tests (academic), 50–55
    essay checklist for, 52
    essay writing mechanics for, 53
    five-paragraph format for, 52
    multiple-choice, 50–51
    objective, 50–51
    open-book, 54

Tests (academic) (*continued*)
oral, 54
problem-solving, 51
reading comprehension, 54
review after, 55
sentence-completion, 51
short-answer, 51
standardized, 54–55
subjective, 51–53
take-home, 54
true-false, 51
vocabulary, 53–54
Tests (laboratory). *See also* Clinical laboratory; *specific tests*
high-complexity, 242
moderate-complexity, 242
waived, 242
Textbook strategies, 30–35. *See also* Reading skills
Therapeutic massage, 61
Therapeutic response, 158
Therapeutic touch, 289
Thermometers, 253, 253b, 255–256
disposable, 256, 257f
electronic, 255, 256f, 257f, 273p
glass mercury, 255, 256f, 257b, 267p–272p
paper, 255, 257f
tympanic, 255, 257f, 274p
Thoughts, negative, 64
Threshold, expected, 110
Thumb forceps, 213, 217f
Time, military, 95
Time management, 19–28
day-to-day, 20–21
preparing to study in, 24–26
procrastination in, 22–24
schedules in, 20
setting priorities in, 21–22
special study programs in, 26–27
taking a break in, 27–28
in test taking, 50–53
Tissue use, 189b
Title VII (Civil Rights Act of 1964), 81–82
Tolerance, drug, 161
Tongue tie, 218f
Tonometer, 216f
Topical drug administration, 176, 176b
Tort
of duress, 79
intentional, 79
of outrage, 80
unintentional, 78–79
Tort law, 70, 78
Towel clamps, 216, 218f
Toxic reactions, to drugs, 161
Trade name, drug, 153, 154t
Traditional Chinese medicine (TCM), 286
acupuncture in, 289–290
diet in, 288
lifestyle in, 288
Trager technique, 290
Transdermal drug administration, 176–177, 176b
Transient flora, 186
Transition words, 37–38
Transmission
in common communicable diseases, 189t
direct, 188, 189t
indirect, 188, 189t
modes of, 188–189, 189t

sources of, 188–189
Transplantation, organ, bioethics issues in, 84–85
Transport containers, 230, 230f
Trigger-point therapy, 290
True-false tests, 51
Tutorial software, 39
Tympanic, 253
Tympanic temperature, 253, 253b, 274p
Tympanic temperature measurement, 253, 253b, 274p
Tympanic thermometer, 253, 253b, 255, 257f

U
Ultraviolet (UV) light therapy, 292
Understanding, *vs.* knowing, 15
Undue influence, 80
Uniform Anatomical Gift Act, 85, 85b
Unintentional torts, 78–79
Unit dose system, 171, 172f
Unopettes, 236b–237b
Urethral sounds, 215f
Urgency, reducing, 60
Urology instruments, 215f
Urticaria, from drugs, 159
Uterine curets, 214f
Uterine dilator, 214f
Uterine sounds, 214f

V
Vaccine
for hepatitis B virus, 192, 198
National Childhood Vaccine Injury Act on, 76, 76b
Vaccine information statement (VIS), 73, 76, 76b
Vaginal speculum, 214f
Variety, in memorization, 18
Vata, 286
Vector, 188
Venous access ports, 176
Verdict, 80
Viable, 188
Violent injuries, legally required disclosures on, 77
Virulent organism, 186
Visualization, 63
Vital signs, 252–263
baseline data in, 252
blood pressure in, 261–263, 261f, 263f, *277p–280p (See also* Blood pressure)
defined, 252
pulse in, 256–259, 258f–260f, 259t, 275p (*See also* Pulse)
respiration in, 260–261, 261t, 276p
Spanish terminology for, 262
temperature in, 252–256, 253b, 267p–273p (*See also* Temperature, body)
Vital statistics, 75
Vocabulary tests, 53–54
Volume equivalents, 144, 144t
Volumetric flask, 236, 237f

W
Waived tests, 242
Waste containers
biohazard, 195b, 196f, 197, 197b
regular, 197b
Waste disposal, infectious, 174, 174f, 196–197, 196f, 197b
Weight, in drug response, 162
Weight equivalents, 144, 145t
in metric system, 138
Weight measurement, 252, 252f, 264p

Weil, Andrew, 293–294, 297
White noise, 25
Withdrawal of contract, 72–73
Withdrawing treatment, bioethics of, 85, 86f
Withholding treatment, bioethics of, 85, 86f
Witness
    of consent signature, 73
    expert, 79
Word games, 17
Words
    structure, 35

transition, 37–38
    in vocabulary tests, 53–54
Workers' compensation records, 97
Writing, for essay questions, 53

Y
Yang, 286
Yin, 286
Yoga, 62

Z
Z-track method, 175

Introduction to HIPAA and the Privacy Rule

CHAPTER OBJECTIVES

In this chapter, you'll learn:

1. How rules related to HIPAA legislation are created.
2. How the Privacy Rule fits into HIPAA legislation.
3. Key terms in the Privacy Rule.
4. Significant points of the Privacy Rule.
5. Compliance dates for the Privacy Rule.

INTRODUCTION

April 14, 2003, was the "go-live" or compliance date of the HIPAA Privacy Rule. When I visited healthcare providers after that date, I noticed each handled the paperwork differently. Some gave the patient a four- or five-page document to read and sign. Others asked for a signature on a one-page form that said the **Notice of Privacy Practice**s had been received. After I read each of the documents given to me, I would say, "I'd like a copy of your Notice of Privacy Practices, please." Were they surprised! Had they not expected anyone to actually ask? Oops! I could see what they were thinking: HIPAA is really here.

If you visited your physician after April 14, 2003, you, too, were probably given papers related to the Privacy Rule. If you are a medical transcriptionist, perhaps your first notice of the rule came as a special training session arranged for you by your employer. Medical transcription students may have seen HIPAA for the first time when it was added to the curriculum. A transcription service company may have received new contracts from clients. They had to quickly make sure the contracts used terms that were covered by the rule and included conditions to which they could adhere.

The entire medical transcription industry scrambled to prepare for the Privacy Rule's compliance date. Where could we go to find the information we needed in terms we could easily understand? What should we do about the liability insurance our customers now required us to carry? What policies and procedures should we create? Where could we find examples that we could adapt to fit our needs? And how in the world would we find time to sleep!

This book is meant to help answer your questions. To begin, Chapter 1 offers a brief overview of HIPAA, explains how the Privacy Rule fits into that law, and lists some very important terms you need to know.

WHAT IS HIPAA?

I thought HIPAA was named after me!

The letters **HIPAA** stand for Health Insurance Portability and Accountability Act of 1996. As the name suggests, it is meant to make sure people can take their health insurance with them when they move from one job to another. The drafting of the HIPAA legislation began in 1993. At about the same time, a study was done by the Workgroup for Electronic Data Interchange (WEDI). It showed that the healthcare industry could save billions of dollars if it would record transactions electronically. Later, the huge savings predicted by the WEDI study became the primary benefit of the HIPAA legislation.

Many of WEDI's cost-saving ideas are spelled out in the rules of the Administrative Simplification provisions of the law. (See Figure 1.1.) Each of those rules includes standards

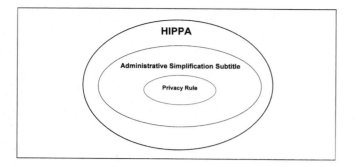

FIGURE 1-1.   The Privacy Rule is a subsection of the Administrative Simplification Subtitle, which is a part of HIPAA.

that help to improve electronic healthcare transactions. A good example of this is insurance billing. Before Administrative Simplification, a patient who had both Medicare and supplemental insurance had to have Medicare billed first. Once Medicare responded, the supplemental insurance company would then be billed. In addition, both had their own formats for how to submit bills, which required many hours to complete. With the new Administrative Simplification rules, the same bill would be sent to Medicare. It would then process the bill and send it on to the supplemental insurance company. Best of all, all the paperwork could be done in the same format.

Imagine having all billing formats standardized! That has been a dream in the medical transcription world for a long time. Standardizing could allow the same claim to be processed much faster, with fewer people. It also could provide reimbursement to the physician faster. All of this adds up to money saved.

The major rules of the Administrative Simplification part of HIPAA address topics such as development and implementation costs, timely testing and updating procedures, and adaptability to changes in infrastructure. The major rules are:

- *The Transactions and Code Sets Rule.* Insurance billing is similar to medical transcription in a service setting. That is, each insurance company uses its own forms in its own unique format. Those who are doing the billing must do it differently for every insurance company with which they interact. This rule is meant to standardize those transactions, so that the process is easier, more efficient, and cost effective.
- *The Privacy Rule.* The subject of this book, the Privacy Rule addresses the concerns people have about how their health information is used and stored.

THE REAL WORLD

Often, when someone refers to HIPAA, he or she may in fact be talking about the Privacy Rule. Keep in mind that the Privacy Rule is only one part of HIPAA.

- *The Security Rule.* This rule aims to make sure computer systems used in health care are accessible only to those who have a valid need to know. For example, it addresses the use of passwords to sign on and off computers. It explains how information transmitted electronically is encrypted. And it tells how servers and computers should be housed.
- *The National Identifier Rule.* This rule addresses unique identifiers for healthcare providers and employers. Still in development are standards for enforcement and health-plan identifiers, which at this time have no projected publication date.

- *The Enforcement Rule.* When this rule is ready, it will describe how all HIPAA rules are to be enforced. It will describe the penalties that may used when someone is in violation. It also will include procedures for both criminal and civil penalties.

The process for a rule to become effective is a long one. HIPAA's Privacy Rule was no exception. In 2000, the Privacy Rule was made available to the public for comment. As a result, the Department of Health and Human Services (DHHS) received over 50,000 responses. Each one on average included three different topics of concern—a total of over 150,000 comments. People were clearly worried about the privacy of their health information.

DHHS also sought comment on the workability of the rule in the complex healthcare industry. The department wanted to make certain that there were no unanticipated consequences

AHA!
The Process of Creating Rules

1 The Department of Health and Human Services (DHHS) publishes notice of a proposed rule in the *Federal Register*. The public has 60 days to comment.
2 DHHS responds to each comment by either making changes in the proposed rule or not.
3 The final rule is reviewed by DHHS and others who are affected by it.
4 If Congress approves after 60 days of its own review, the final rule is published.
5 Sixty days after that, the rule becomes effective.
6 Entities who are impacted by the rule have two years and two months in which to become totally compliant.

that might harm patients. So the industry was given one more month to comment.

In its final form, the Privacy Rule became effective April 14, 2001. There currently exists no other federal legislation that guarantees a patient the right to privacy of his or her health information.

AHA!
The HIPAA Privacy Rule Timeline

1999 Congress misses the deadline to pass legislation on protecting the privacy of health information. So the Privacy Rule is drafted by the Department of Health and Human Services (DHHS) and offered for public comment.
2000 The final Privacy Rule is published. The effective date is extended to 2001 in order to give Congress time to review it.
2001 Congress okays the Privacy Rule and re-publishes it for comment by the healthcare industry. One month later, it becomes effective.
2003 Effective date of compliance is April 14, 2003.

Stay abreast of any changes in the rules. Watch for notices of proposed rule making, and determine if compliance will impact your work setting. Notices can be tracked through the *Federal Register* as they are published. You can find a link to the *Federal Register* in the resources section of the appendices.

CAUTION
The Privacy Rule may be reviewed and modified on an annual basis. Stay up to date with changes to be sure you remain compliant.

THE PRIVACY RULE

Why should you as a medical transcriptionist care about the HIPAA Privacy Rule? Whether you are an independent contractor, a service owner, an educator, or a student, consider this scenario:

After examining a patient, a physician in *California* dictated his findings to a service in *Virginia*. The service used a medical transcriptionist who lives in *Florida*. She in turn relied on a quality assurance editor who is in *Minnesota*. Quite sometime later, the patient found out that the privacy of her medical records had been breached. Who could she turn to for help?

Do you know? Which of the four states involved, if any, do you think would have jurisdiction? Before the HIPAA Privacy Rule, there was no answer to this question. There was no federal law or rule that covered all states. HIPAA now offers a way to provide privacy for a patient's information in any state. Though it has not yet been tested in a court case, it is speculated that the state that would have jurisdiction in the scenario above is the one in which the patient resides.

HERE'S A HINT
"Is it HIPAA or HIPPO, and why should I care?" The answer is HIPAA—the Health Insurance Portability and Accountability Act of 1996—and you should care because it impacts YOU.

Again, why should you care? Because HIPAA impacts everyone working in the healthcare industry, including medical transcriptionists. Even you. Perhaps most important of all, a reason to care is that the Privacy Rule helps to ensure quality patient care. Always aim to maintain the integrity of the system, so that patients willingly give information to their healthcare providers, knowing that it will be protected.

CAUTION
The Privacy Rule outlines penalties for noncompliance, some of which include large fines and possible prison time.

Terminology

Trying to understand all of the terms in the Privacy Rule can be daunting. But learning just the important ones can help you figure out how the rule applies to your own work setting. Those terms are defined and discussed in the following paragraphs. The first one is:

- **Covered entities**—one of the two distinct healthcare groups identified in the Privacy Rule. (The other group is called *business associates*.) A covered entity may be a health plan. It may be a healthcare provider, such as a hospital or a physician. It also may be a healthcare clearinghouse. (A good definition for each of these covered entities is offered a bit later in this chapter.)

A medical transcriptionist is *never* a covered entity. If you work as an independent contractor, you are *not* a covered entity. If you are an employee of a medical transcription service, you are *not* a covered entity. If you are an employee of a hospital or a physician's office, you are a part of the "workforce" of a covered entity, but you are not the covered entity.

The next term for you to learn is *business associate*. Medical transcriptionists are often considered business associates.

If you are an independent medical transcriptionist who works directly for a covered entity, you are a business associate.

- **Business associate**—an individual who is not part of the workforce of a covered entity but who performs a function for the covered entity that involves protected health information. Examples include medical transcription companies and coding firms.

A medical transcriptionist who works as independent contractor may be a business associate, depending on who his or her client is. That is, if you are self-employed (an independent contractor) and your client is a covered entity, you are a business associate. Lawyers, accounting firms, and consultants may also be business associates.

You are *not* a business associate if you are a self-employed medical transcriptionist and your client is a transcription service company. In that case, you would be a *subcontractor*. The transcription service would be the business associate of its client, the covered entity.

There are times when a covered entity is a business associate. For example, when a hospital transcription department provides services to doctors, the doctor is the covered entity, and the hospital is his or her business associate.

Look at Table 1.1. It shows what roles a medical transcriptionist has in a variety of work settings. It also shows what contracts are necessary for each of those roles.

THE REAL WORLD

There is always a chance that a covered entity will be audited for compliance with the Privacy Rule. When this happens, your client, the covered entity, may ask you to prove you are compliant, too. One way to be prepared is to review your contracts and agreements annually and to keep them up to date.

More important terms from the Privacy Rule are defined below:

- **Protected health information (PHI)**—information about a patient's past, present, or future medical treatment that contains data that can reasonably identify the patient. Health information that has had all patient identifiers removed (that is, it has been de-identified) is *not* protected health information.
- **Health plan**—an insurance company or any program or plan that provides for payment of the cost of health care. Note that the government-funded health plans which are specifically listed in the Privacy Rule are considered covered entities.
- **Health care clearinghouse**—a covered entity that processes protected health information for others. For example, a clearinghouse that provides billing services will take information that is in a non-standard format or language and convert it to an acceptable standardized one. Medical transcription does *not* fit in this category.
- **Healthcare provider**—a physician or healthcare facility, both of which are covered entities. For them, all

Table 1-1 **MEDICAL TRANSCRIPTIONIST ROLES AND CONTRACTS**			
If you are a(n)...	**Then your role is ...**	**And you will need a ...**	**Will the Privacy Rule apply?**
Employee of a hospital or a physician and work either at home or in the office	Employee (workforce) of a covered entity	Normal confidentiality agreement for employees	YES
Medical transcription service	Business associate	Contract for services and a business associate agreement	YES
Employee of a medical transcription service	Employee of a business associate	Normal confidentiality agreement for employees	YES
Independent contractor who has a contract with physician offices and/or hospital	Business associate	Contract for services and a business associate agreement	YES
Independent contractor who has a contract with a medical transcription service	Subcontractor	Subcontractor agreement	YES

patient information is protected by the Privacy Rule, whether it is transmitted orally, electronically, or as a handwritten document. Note that the physician or healthcare facility is the covered entity, not the employees who work there. Employees—whether they work in the healthcare provider's office or from home—are considered a part of the "workforce."

- **Health care**—services or supplies related to the health of an individual. Health care includes:
  - Preventive, diagnostic, therapeutic, rehabilitative, maintenance, or palliative care.
  - Any counseling, service, assessment, or procedure related to either the physical or mental condition or functional status of an individual.
  - Any prescription drugs or prescribed devices, equipment, or other items.
- **Health information**—any information related to someone's past, present, or future mental or physical health, no matter what form it is created or received in. It also is information that relates to past, present, or future payment for the health care of an individual. The Privacy Rule protects all health information that can reasonably identify the patient.
- **Standard**—a condition or requirement that describes specific criteria for products, systems, services, or practices related to the privacy of health information. Criteria may include classification of components; specifications of materials, performance, or operations; or step-by-step procedures.
- **Standard-setting organization (SSO)** or standard development organization (SDO)—an organization accredited by the American National Standards Institute (ANSI) that develops and maintains standards for information transactions and data elements. One example of an SSO is an organization you are probably

familiar with—the American Society for Testing and Materials (ASTM).
- **Use**—sharing health information within an entity, which requires no authorization from the patient. An example of "use" would be transcribing a physician's recorded report for a patient's healthcare record.
- **Disclosure**—sharing information outside the covered entity's control, which requires authorization from the patient. An example of "disclosure" would be sending a patient's information to a pharmaceutical company for marketing purposes.
- **Business associate agreement (BAA)**—a contract that outlines the duties and responsibilities of a business associate in dealings with a covered entity, using the specific language outlined in the Privacy Rule. Any medical transcriptionist in the role of a business associate must have one of these contracts with his or her client.
- **Workforce**—employees and paid or unpaid volunteers, trainees, and other personnel whose conduct in the performance of work for a covered entity is under the direct control of that entity. If you are a medical transcriptionist who is an employee of a hospital or physician's office, you are a part of the workforce of that hospital or office. Independent contractors are not considered part of a workforce.

AHA!

If your client is a covered entity, the two of you must have a business associate agreement. It is the one thing in the entire Privacy Rule that you are absolutely required to have.

- **Independent contractor**—in medical transcription, this is a self-employed person who provides medical transcription services to others. This person is *not* an employee of the clients he or she serves. However, he or she might be a business associate (has contracted directly with a covered entity), or he or she might be a subcontractor (see the definition below).

The terms that follow are not part of the HIPAA Privacy Rule, but they are important to your business:

- **Subcontractor**—this is a medical transcriptionist who works as an independent contractor for a business associate. This transcriptionist does not have a contract with a covered entity. Instead, he or she has been hired by a service or by another independent contractor who actually has a contract with the client.
- **Confidentiality agreement**—a document that should be signed by all medical transcriptionists, whether an employee, independent contractor, or medical transcription service. It says that you will protect the confidential nature of the records you work with and will not divulge them to anyone who should not have access to them. If you are an independent contractor, this agreement may already be a part of your client contracts.
- **Contract for services**—a written agreement between someone who needs medical transcription service and someone who will provide it. It outlines how the relationship works, such as how payment will be made, and lists the specifics about the work to be done. It is an agreement that a business associate should have with all contractors. However, it is not a "business associate agreement" and should not be confused with one.

Other Significant Points

The Privacy Rule gives patients specific rights in regard to their health information. For example, a patient has the right to inspect and receive copies of his or her records and to request amendments or changes. However, there are exceptions. One such exception has to do with psychiatric records. They do not have to be given to the patient if the provider feels they could cause the patient harm. When this is the case, the provider must give a reason for not allowing the patient to see the information.

Note that it is the covered entity, not the business associate or subcontractor, who is responsible for providing records to a patient. Make sure your business associate contracts spell that out. This will help you avoid dealing directly with patients, should they become aware that you have access to their information.

Another point to keep in mind is that the Privacy Rule does not apply to a business associate. It applies only to the covered entity. Here is where it gets a bit tricky. When a covered entity gives a business associate protected health information, any breach in the privacy of that information is the covered entity's responsibility. Listen closely now. As a result, many covered entities require business associates to have liability insurance, so that any fees or fines related to a breach may be collected.

One final point to remember is that the Privacy Rule spells out the requirements for training in all matters related to protecting the privacy of health records. Covered entities must make sure their employees get that training. To prove it, they must describe all of their policies and procedures in writing. They also must document their training sessions.

You will learn more about these last three points in the following chapters.

THE REAL WORLD

April 14, 2003, was the compliance deadline for all covered entities, except small health plans. They had an additional year to comply.

Compliance Deadlines

The deadline for compliance with the Privacy Rule was April 14, 2003. This means all covered entities, such as a hospital or physician's office, should now have their own compliance plan in place and active. I hope with this "nuts and bolts" guide you, too, will be compliant—whether your role is as a student, subcontractor, business associate, or employee of a covered entity.

Rule Enforcement

Several government agencies are involved in the enforcement of the Privacy Rule. First, the *Secretary* of the Department of Health and Human Services (DHHS) has the right to delegate responsibility for monitoring compliance and accepting complaints. So, that responsibility is with the Office of Civil Rights (OCR), a branch of DHHS. OCR is responsible for all *civil* complaints and for imposing any fines related to violations of the Privacy Rule. The U.S. Department of Justice is responsible for investigating any *criminal* complaints related to the Privacy Rule and is empowered to prosecute offenders. For all other HIPAA rules, the Centers for Medicare and Medicaid Services (CMS) will be responsible for monitoring and investigating violations as well as imposing fines.

THE BOTTOM LINE
The Privacy Rule and HIPAA

- The Privacy Rule is one of four rules in the Administrative Simplification Subsection of the HIPAA legislation.

Main Groups Addressed by the Privacy Rule

- *Covered entities*—health plans, healthcare clearinghouses, and healthcare providers. Medical transcriptionists who work as employees of these groups are a part of the workforce and will follow policies developed by their employer.
- Business associates—those who perform a function for a covered entity that requires access to protected health information. Medical transcriptionists who are transcription service owners or independent contractors providing services directly to a covered entity are business associates.

Rights Recognized by the Privacy Rule

- The rule protects the privacy of health information.
- It also allows patients access to their health information.

Apply it

Multiple-choice questions are offered here to help you test your understanding. Answers are provided below.

1. The primary benefit of the Administrative Simplification Subsection of HIPAA is to:
   a. save billions of dollars in health care.
   b. protect the privacy of health information.
   c. outline a patient's rights to health information.
   d. protect covered entities and business associates.

2. Sarah provides volunteer services at the local hospital. According to the Privacy Rule, her position fits into which one of the categories listed below?
   a. covered entity
   b. business associate
   c. workforce
   d. healthcare provider

3. Dan is a medical transcriptionist who works as an independent contractor for a one-physician office. Does Dan need a business associate agreement with the physician?

   a. Yes, because Dan is part of the physician's workforce.
   b. Yes, because Dan is a self-employed transcriptionist.
   c. No, because the physician is not a covered entity.
   d. No, because the physician has a small practice.

4. Gabrielle is a medical transcriptionist who is an employee of Memorial Hospital. Her position fits into which one of the categories listed below?
   a. independent contractor
   b. business associate
   c. subcontractor
   d. workforce

5. The deadline for compliance with the Privacy Rule was in:
   a. 1996.
   b. 2001.
   c. 2002.
   d. 2003.

Answer to Apply it

1. **a.** The Privacy Rule protects health information. However, the Administrative Simplification Subsection was created in response to the WEDI study that showed billions of dollars in savings in health care.
2. **c.** The definition of "workforce" includes volunteers.
3. **b.** Dan is a medical transcriptionist who is an independent contractor—a self-employed person who contracts directly with a covered entity. So Dan must have a business associate agreement with the physician. Note that Dan's client, the physician, is a covered entity, no matter what the size of his or her practice.
4. **d.** Medical transcriptionists who are employees—not independent contractors—of a hospital or physician's office are a part of the workforce.
5. **d.** April 14, 2003, was the deadline for compliance with the Privacy Rule.

7

Law and Ethics in the Health Care Setting

CHAPTER COMPETENCIES

Review the information in your text that supports the following course objectives.

Learning Objectives

1. Spell and define the key terms

2. Identify the two branches of the American legal system

3. List the elements and types of contractual agreements and describe the difference in implied and expressed contracts

4. List four items that must be included in a contract termination or withdrawal letter

5. List six items that must be included in an informed consent form and explain who may sign consent forms

6. List five legally required disclosures that must be reported to specified authorities

7. Describe the purpose of the Self-Determination Act

8. Describe the four elements that must be proven in a medical legal suit

9. Describe four possible defenses against litigation for the medical professional

10. Explain the theory of respondeat superior, or law of agency, and how it applies to the medical assistant

11. List ways that a medical assistant can assist in the prevention of a medical malpractice suit

12. Outline the laws regarding employment and safety issues in the medical office

13. List the requirements of the Americans with Disabilities Act relating to the medical office

14. Differentiate between legal issues and ethical issues

15. List the seven American Medical Association principles of ethics

16. List the five ethical principles of ethical and moral conduct outlined by the American Association of Medical Assistants

17. List 10 opinions of the American Medical Association's Council pertaining to administrative office procedures

CHAPTER OUTLINE

CHAPTER OUTLINE	NOTES
The American Legal System	
Sources of Law	
Branches of the Law	
Public Law	
Private or Civil Law	
The Rise in Medical Legal Cases	
Physician–Patient Relationship	

CHAPTER OUTLINE *continued*	NOTES
Rights and Responsibilities of the Patient and Physician	
Contracts	
Implied Contracts	
Expressed Contracts	
Termination or Withdrawal of the Contract	
Consent	
Implied Consent	
Informed or Expressed Consent	
Refusal of Consent	
Releasing Medical Information	
Legally Required Disclosures	
Vital Statistics	
Medical Examiner's Reports	
Infectious or Communicable Diseases	
National Childhood Vaccine Injury Act of 1986	
Abuse, Neglect, or Maltreatment	
Violent Injuries	
Other Reports	
Specific Laws and Statutes That Apply to Health Professionals	
Medical Practice Acts	
Licensure, Certification, and Registration	
Controlled Substances Act	
Good Samaritan Act	
Basis of Medical Law	
Tort Law	
Negligence and Malpractice (Unintentional Torts)	
Duty	
Dereliction of Duty	
Direct Cause	
Damage	
Jury Awards	
Intentional Torts	
Assault and Battery	
Duress	
Invasion of Privacy	

CHAPTER OUTLINE *continued*

	NOTES
Defamation of Character	
Fraud	
Tort of Outrage	
Undue Influence	
The Litigation Process	
Defenses to Professional Liability Suits	
Medical Records	
Statute of Limitations	
Assumption of Risk	
Res Judicata	
Contributory Negligence	
Comparative Negligence	
Immunity	
Defense for the Medical Assistant	
Respondeat Superior or Law of Agency	
Employment and Safety Laws	
Civil Rights Act of 1964, Title VII	
Sexual Harassment	
Americans with Disabilities Act	
Occupational Safety and Health Act	
Other Legal Considerations	
Medical Ethics	
American Medical Association (AMA) Code of Ethics	
Medical Assistant's Role in Ethics	
Patient Advocacy	
Patient Confidentiality	
Honesty	
American Association of Medical Assistants (AAMA) Code of Ethics	
Principles	
Bioethics	
American Medical Association (AMA) Council on Ethical and Judicial Affairs	
Social Policy Issues	
Allocation of Resources	
Clinical Investigations and Research	
Obstetric Dilemmas	

CHAPTER OUTLINE *continued*	NOTES
Organ Transplantation	
Withholding or Withdrawing Treatment	
Professional and Ethical Conduct and Behavior	
Ethical Issues in Office Management	

LEARNING SELF-ASSESSMENT EXERCISES

Key Terms

Define the following key terms:

abandonment _____

advance directive _____

age of majority _____

appeal _____

assault _____

battery _____

bench trial _____

bioethics _____

blood-borne pathogens _____

breach _____

certification _____

civil law _____

coerce _____

common law _____

comparative negligence _____

confidentiality _____

consent _____

consideration _____

contract _____

contributory negligence _____

cross-examination _____

damages _____

defamation of character _____

defendant _____

depositions _____

direct examination _____

durable power of attorney _____

duress _____

emancipated minor _____

ethics _____

expert witness _____

expressed consent _____

expressed contracts _____

fee splitting _____

fraud _____

implied consent _____

implied contracts _____

informed consent _____

intentional tort _____

legally required disclosure _____

libel _____

licensure _____

litigation _____

locum tenens _____

malpractice _____

negligence _____

noncompliant _____

plaintiff _____

precedents _____

protocol _____

registered _____

res ipsa loquitur _____

res judicata _____

respondeat superior _____

slander _____

stare decisis _____

statute of limitations _____

statutes _____

tort _____

unintentional tort _____

verdict _____

Multiple Choice

1. Patient information may be released by permission of the
   a. Physician
   b. Patient
   c. Spouse
   d. Medical assistant

2. The mark of a true professional is a person's
   a. Level of education
   b. Salary
   c. Ability to admit mistakes
   d. Ability to problem solve

Matching

Match the definition in part 1 with the correct legal term in part 2.

PART 1

_____ 1. Previous decision stands

_____ 2. The thing has been decided

_____ 3. Let the master answer

_____ 4. Not having control over the mind or intellect

_____ 5. Under penalty you shall take with you

_____ 6. A court order requiring the recipient to appear

_____ 7. The thing speaks for itself

PART 2

a. Non compos mentis

b. Subpoena duces tecum

c. Respondeat superior

d. Stare decisis

e. Res ipsa loquitur

f. Res judicata

g. Subpoena

Multiple Choice

1. Common law principles are based on the theory of
   a. Stare decisis
   b. Res judicata
   c. Litigation
   d. Statute of limitations

2. The two main branches of the legal system are
   a. Criminal and administrative law
   b. Constitutional and international law
   c. Public and private law
   d. Commercial and tort law

3. Reasons for the escalation of medical malpractice cases include
   a. Unrealistic patient expectations
   b. Economic factors
   c. Scientific advances
   d. All of the above

4. What component or components do all contractual agreements have?
   a. Offer
   b. Consideration
   c. Durable power of attorney
   d. *a* and *b* only

5. Patients have the right to
   a. Obtain copies of their own medical records
   b. Refuse treatment
   c. Expect continuity of care
   d. All of the above

6. Minors may sign a consent form when
   a. They are 16 years old
   b. They become sexually active
   c. They request treatment for a communicable disease
   d. None of the above

7. Each state has laws pertaining to which deaths must be reported to the medical examiner's office. Generally, these include
   a. The death of anyone over 65 years old
   b. Deaths from unknown causes
   c. Deaths from terminal illnesses
   d. Any death occurring in a hospital

8. A narcotic inventory record must be kept for
   a. 4 to 6 years
   c. 5 to 7 years
   b. 2 to 3 years
   d. 10 years

8

Health Records and Records Management

CHAPTER COMPETENCIES

Review the information in your text that supports the following course objectives.

Learning Objectives

1. Spell and define the key terms

2. Describe standard and electronic health record systems

3. Explain the process for releasing health records to third-party payers and individual patients

4. List and explain the EHR guidelines established to protect computerized records

5. List the standard information included in health records

6. Identify and describe the types of formats used for documenting patient information in outpatient settings

7. Explain how to make an entry in a patient's health record, using abbreviations when appropriate

8. Explain how to make a correction in a standard and electronic health record

9. Identify the various ways health records can be stored

10. Compare and contrast the differences between alphabetic and numeric filing systems and give an example of each

11. Explain the purpose of the Health Insurance Portability and Accountability Act

Performance Objective

1. Prepare and file a health record file folder

CHAPTER OUTLINE

CHAPTER OUTLINE	NOTES
Standard Health Records	
Contents of the Health Record	
Electronic Health Records	
Electronic Health Record Security	
Other Technologies for Health Record Maintenance	
Health Record Organization	
Provider Encounters	
Narrative Format	
SOAP Format	
POMR Format	

CHAPTER OUTLINE *continued*	NOTES
Documentation Forms	
Patient History Forms	
Flow Sheets	
Progress Notes	
Health Record Entries	
Charting Communications With Patients	
Additions to Health Records	
Workers' Compensation Records	
Health Record Preparation	
Filing Procedures	
Filing Systems	
Alphabetic Filing	
Numeric Filing	
Other Filing Systems	
Classifying Health Records	
Inactive Record Storage	
Storing Active Health Records	
Record Retention	
Releasing Health Records	
Releasing Records to Patients	
Reporting Obligations	

LEARNING SELF-ASSESSMENT EXERCISES

Key Terms

Define the following key terms:

alphabetic filing _____

chief complaint _____

chronological order _____

cross-reference _____

demographic data _____

electronic health records (EHR) _____

flow sheet _____

microfiche _____

microfilm _____

narrative _____

numeric filing _____

patient history forms _____

present illness _____

problem-oriented medical record (POMR) _____

reverse chronological order _____

SOAP _____

subject filing _____

workers' compensation _____

Matching

Match the definition in part 1 with the correct term in part 2.

PART I

_____ 1. Uses digits to file records

_____ 2. Way to organize material

_____ 3. List of patients and matching numeric code

_____ 4. Use of letters to file records

_____ 5. Use of dates to file records

_____ 6. Use of topics to file

PART 2

a. Subject filing

b. Numeric filing

c. Filing system

d. Alphabetic filing

e. Cross-reference

f. Chronological filing

Multiple Choice

1. In source-oriented health records, all similar categories or sources of information are grouped together. Among such categories are
   a. Physician orders
   b. Progress notes
   c. Radiographic results
   d. *a* and *b* only

2. Problem-oriented health records are divided into four components. An example of primary components is
   a. Databases
   b. Treatment plans
   c. Progress notes
   d. All of the above

3. The oldest and least structured documentation form is
   a. Focus charting
   b. PIE charting
   c. Narrative charting
   d. SOAP charting

4. No matter what form is used for documentation, you must always include
   a. The date and time
   b. The procedure performed
   c. Your signature
   d. Both a and c

5. All additions to the health record (laboratory, radiography, consultations) should be
   a. Checked for spelling
   b. Initialed by the medical assistant
   c. Initialed by the physician
   d. None of the above

6. Workers' compensation cases are kept open
   a. For 2 years from the last date of treatment
   b. For 2 years from the initial date of treatment
   c. According to office protocol
   d. According to the employer's protocol

7. The golden rule refers to
   a. Legal documentation
   b. Abbreviation rules
   c. The principle that if it is not documented, it was not done
   d. Filing procedures

8. With the *terminal digit filing system*, the groups of numbers are read
   a. From right to left
   b. From left to right

9

Quality, Privacy, and HIPAA

CHAPTER COMPETENCIES

Review the information in your text that supports the following course objectives.

Learning Objectives

1. Spell and define the key terms
2. List four regulatory agencies that require medical office settings to have quality improvement programs
3. Describe the accreditation process of the Joint Commission on Accreditation of Healthcare Organizations
4. Describe the intent of the Clinical Laboratory Improvement Amendments Act
5. Describe the intent of the Health Insurance Portability and Accountability Act
6. Describe the steps to developing a quality improvement program
7. List five guidelines for completing incident reports
8. Explain how quality improvement programs and risk management work together in a medical office to improve overall patient care and employee needs.

Performance Objective

1. Complete an incident report

CHAPTER OUTLINE	NOTES
Quality Improvement Programs in the Medical Office Setting	
Regulatory Agencies	
Joint Commission on Accreditation of Healthcare Organizations (JCAHO)	
Occupational Safety and Health Administration	
Centers for Medicare & Medicaid Services	
State Health Departments	
Developing a Quality Improvement Program	
Seven Steps for a Successful Program	
Risk Management	
Incident Reports	
When to Complete an Incident Report	
Information Included on an Incident Report	

CHAPTER OUTLINE *continued*	NOTES
Guidelines for Completing an Incident Report	
Trending Incident Reports	
Putting It All Together: A Case Review	

LEARNING SELF-ASSESSMENT EXERCISES

Key Terms

Define the following key terms:

Centers for Medicare & Medicaid Services _____

Clinical Laboratory Improvement Amendments Act _____

expected threshold _____

Health Insurance Portability and Accountability Act _____

incident reports _____

Joint Commission on Accreditation of Healthcare Organizations _____

Occupational Safety and Health Administration _____

outcomes _____

quality improvement _____

sentinel event _____

task force _____

Matching

Match the definition in part 1 with the correct term in part 2.

PART 1

_____ 1. Assures the community that an organization has met basic practice standards

_____ 2. A second survey

_____ 3. Numerical goal

_____ 4. Occurred for unknown reasons

PART 2

a. Expected threshold

b. Accreditation

c. Focus survey

d. Idiopathic

Multiple Choice

1. The period for which JCAHO accreditation is valid is
   a. 5 years
   b. 2 years
   c. 3 years
   d. 4 years

2. The primary focus of IOP standards is for the organization to
   a. Do the right thing
   b. Do the right thing well
   c. Conduct a survey well
   d. *a* and *b*.

3. OSHA compliance is
   a. Not voluntary
   b. Voluntary
   c. Subject to review
   d. Required for facilities with 50 or more employees

4. How many elements do QI monitoring plans have?
   a. Four
   b. Five
   c. Three
   d. Six

5. Under risk management, risk factors for patients and employees are
   a. Safety concerns
   b. Financial accountability
   c. Liability concerns
   d. *a* and *c*

6. Incident reports are sometimes referred to as
   a. An employer liability
   b. A patient liability
   c. Occurrence reports
   d. Administrative reports

7. Incident reports should be completed within
   a. 12 hours
   b. 24 hours
   c. 48 hours
   d. 72 hours

8. Documentation in the patient's chart that an incident report has been completed is
   a. Always done
   b. Done only if the patient is injured
   c. Done on advisement of insurance company
   d. Never done

9. Patient care settings for which JCAHO is responsible include
   a. Ambulatory care
   b. Inpatient care
   c. Outpatient care
   d. All of the above

12

Principles of Pharmacology

CHAPTER COMPETENCIES

Review the information in your text that supports the following course objectives.

Learning Objectives

1. To define the chapter's key terms.
2. To identify the different names assigned to drugs.
3. To distinguish between prescription drugs, nonprescription drugs, and controlled substances.
4. To discuss the various types of drug reactions produced in the body.
5. To identify factors that influence drug action.
6. To discuss the types of drug interactions that may occur.
7. To discuss the use of herbal medicines.

CHAPTER OUTLINE	NOTES
Drug Development	
Special FDA Programs	
Orphan Drug Program	
Accelerated Programs	
Compassionate Access to Unapproved Drugs	
Drug Names	
Drug Categories	
Prescription Drugs	
Nonprescription Drugs	
Controlled Substances	
Federal Drug Legislation and Enforcement	
Pure Food and Drug Act	
Harrison Narcotic Act	
Pure Food, Drug, and Cosmetic Act	
Comprehensive Drug Abuse Prevention and Control Act	
Drug Enforcement Administration	
Drug Use and Pregnancy	
Drug Actions within the Body	
Pharmaceutic Phase	
Pharmacokinetic Phase	
Absorption	

CHAPTER OUTLINE *continued*	NOTES
Distribution	
Metabolism	
Excretion	
Half-Life	
Pharmacodynamic Phase	
Alteration in Cellular Environment	
Alteration in Cellular Function	
Drug Reactions	
Adverse Drug Reactions	
Allergic Drug Reactions	
Drug Idiosyncrasy	
Drug Tolerance	
Cumulative Drug Effect	
Toxic Reactions	
Pharmacogenetic Reactions	
Drug Interactions	
Drug–Drug Interactions	
Additive Drug Reaction	
Synergistic Drug Reaction	
Antagonistic Drug Reaction	
Drug-Food Interactions	
Factors Influencing Drug Response	
Age	
Weight	
Gender	
Disease	
Route of Administration	
Herbal Therapy and Nutritional Supplements	
Dietary Supplement Health and Education Act	
Center for Complementary and Alternative Health	
Educating Patients on the Use of Herbs and Nutritional Supplements	

LEARNING SELF-ASSESSMENT EXERCISES

Key Terms

Define the following key terms:

additive drug reaction _____

adverse reaction _____

agonist _____

allergic reaction _____

anaphylactic shock _____

antagonist _____

antibodies _____

antigen _____

controlled substances _____

cumulative drug effect _____

drug idiosyncrasy _____

drug tolerance _____

hypersensitivity _____

nonprescription drugs _____

pharmaceutic phase _____

pharmacodynamics _____

pharmacogenetic disorder _____

pharmacokinetics _____

pharmacology _____

physical dependence _____

polypharmacy _____

prescription drugs _____

psychological dependence _____

receptor _____

synergism _____

teratogen _____

therapeutic response _____

toxic _____

Matching

Match the term in Part 1 with the correct definition in Part 2.

PART I

_____ 1. additive drug reaction

_____ 2. antagonist

_____ 3. agonist

_____ 4. controlled substance

_____ 5. hypersensitivity

_____ 6. pharmaceutic phase

_____ 7. pharmacokinetics

_____ 8. polypharmacy

PART 2

a. The taking of numerous drugs that can potentially react with one another.

b. Any substance that causes abnormal development of the fetus.

c. Drugs with a high potential for abuse that are controlled by special regulations.

d. A specialized macromolecule that binds to the drug molecule, altering the function of the cell and producing the therapeutic response.

e. Activities occurring within the body after a drug is administered.

_____ 9. receptor

_____10. teratogen

f. Being allergic to a drug.

g. A drug that binds with a receptor to produce a therapeutic response.

h. A drug that joins with a receptor to prevent the action of an agonist at that receptor.

i. A reaction that occurs when the combined effect of two drugs is equal to the sum of each drug given alone.

j. The dissolution of the drug.

Matching

Match the term in Part 1 with the correct definition in Part 2.

PART 1

_____ 1. Pure Food and Drug Act 1906

_____ 2. Harrison Narcotic Act 1914

_____ 3. Pure Food, Drug, and Cosmetic Act 1938

_____ 4. Controlled Substance Act 1970

_____ 5. Comprehensive Drug Abuse Prevention and Control Act 1970

_____ 6. Drug Enforcement Agency (DEA)

_____ 7. Food and Drug Administration (FDA)

_____ 8. Dietary Supplement Health and Education Act (DSHEA)

_____ 9. Orphan Drug Act 1983

_____10. Investigational New Drug (IND)

PART 2

a. Chief federal agency responsible for enforcing the Controlled Substances Act.

b. Agency responsible for approving new drugs and monitoring drugs for adverse or toxic reactions.

c. Law that gives the FDA control over the manufacture and sale of drugs, food, and cosmetics.

d. First law that regulated the sale of narcotic drugs.

e. Regulates the manufacture, distribution, and dispensation of drugs with a potential for abuse.

f. First attempt by the U.S. government to regulate and control the manufacture, distribution, and sale of drugs.

g. Title II of the Comprehensive Drug Abuse Prevention and Control Act which deals with control and enforcement of the Act.

h. Act that defines herbs, vitamins, minerals, amino acids, and other natural supplements and permits general health claims as long as a disclaimer is present.

i. Encourages the development and marketing of products used to treat rare diseases.

j. The clinical testing phase of drug approval by the FDA.

True/False

Indicate whether each statement is True (T) or False (F).

_____ 1. A New Drug Application (NDA) is submitted immediately following Phase II of the clinical testing portion of the IND status.

_____ 2. The accelerated approval of drugs by the FDA seeks to make lifesaving investigational drugs available for healthcare providers to administer in early Phase I and II clinical trials.

_____ 3. The compassionate access program allows drugs to be given free of charge to patients in financial need.

_____ 4. Legend drugs can be prescribed by any healthcare provider.

_____ 5. Prescriptions for controlled substances must be written in ink, include the name and address of the patient, and the DEA number of the healthcare provider.

_____ 6. All drugs taken by mouth, except liquids, go through three phases: the pharmaceutic phase, the pharmacokinetic phase, and the pharmacodynamic phase.

_____ 7. The absorption of a drug is the process that refers to the activities involving the drug within the body after it is administered.

_____ 8. All drugs produce more than one effect on the body.

_____ 9. An allergic reaction to a drug occurs because the patient's immune system views the drug as an antibody.

_____ 10. Drug toxicity can be reversible or irreversible.

_____ 11. Apharmacogenetic disorder is a genetically caused abnormal response to a normal dose of a drug.

_____ 12. Herbs and nutritional supplements are "natural products" and therefore many individuals incorrectly assume they have no adverse effects.

Multiple Choice

1. The pre-FDA phase of drug development includes_____.
   a. in vitro testing
   b. development of a promising drug
   c. testing using animal and human cells
   d. testing using live animals
   e. all of the answers are correct

2. and 3. The FDA phase of drug development requires the manufacturer of the drug to apply first for (2)_____, and then after three phases of clinical testing to apply for a (3) _____.
   a. clinical trial phase I
   b. IND
   c. NDA
   d. clinical trial phase II
   e. clinical trial phase III

4. The Med Watch system allows healthcare professionals to _____.
   a. track drug use by patient
   b. obtain pharmacy records of patients
   c. monitor prescriptions written by a physician
   d. report observations of serious adverse drug reactions anonymously
   e. contact government officials about insurance fraud

5. The Orphan Drug Program allows manufacturers to produce drugs that treat rare disorders; in exchange, the manufacturer may receive _____.
   a. grants
   b. tax incentives
   c. protocol assistance by the FDA
   d. 7 years of exclusive production rights for the drug involved
   e. all of the answers are correct

6. A _____ is a drug that the FDA has designated to be potentially harmful unless its use is supervised by a licensed healthcare provider.
   a. controlled substance
   b. prescription drug
   c. nonprescription drug
   d. legend drug
   e. answers b and d are correct

7. The Drug Enforcement Agency (DEA) _____.
   a. is under the U.S. Department of Justice
   b. enforces the Controlled Substances Act of 1970
   c. requires compliance by all healthcare workers
   d. can punish those who fail to comply by imprisonment
   e. all of the answers are correct

8. Pregnancy Category D drugs, whether prescription or nonprescription, _____.
   a. have a risk that cannot be ruled out
   b. have controlled studies that show no risk
   c. have positive evidence of risk to the human fetus
   d. are contraindicated in pregnancy
   e. none of the answers are correct

9. Pharmacokinetics refers to _____.
   a. absorption
   b. excretion
   c. distribution
   d. metabolism
   e. all of the answers are correct

10. The therapeutic level of a drug is the level at which _____.
    a. toxic symptoms may develop
    b. the drug is pharmacologically inactive
    c. the drug is effective
    d. the liver biotransforms the drug
    e. occurs directly after administration

11. Drugs whose action alters the cellular environment act to _____.
    a. change the physical environment
    b. change the chemical environment
    c. change both the physical and chemical environment
    d. change the cellular genetics
    e. change the drug action itself

12. The number of receptor sites available at a target site can _____.
    a. influence the effects of a drug
    b. change as a person ages
    c. allow more potent drugs to be used
    d. keep other drugs from acting
    e. be chemically altered

13. Allergic or hypersensitivity reactions _____.
    a. usually begin to occur after more than one dose of a drug
    b. occur because the patient's immune system sees the drug as a foreign substance
    c. must be reported to the healthcare provider
    d. may occur within minutes after the drug is given
    e. all of the answers are correct

14. When a patient develops a tolerance to a drug, _____.
    a. they have a decreased response to the drug
    b. they will require an increase in dosage to achieve the desired effect
    c. it is an indicator of drug dependence
    d. the patient's body does not metabolize and excrete the drug before the next dose is given
    e. answers a, b, and c are correct

15. Drug interactions may occur _____.
    a. between two drugs
    b. between oral drugs and food
    c. answers a and b are correct
    d. between IV drugs and liquids
    e. often in young adults

16. A patient's response to a drug may be influenced by which of the following factors?
    a. disease
    b. age
    c. weight
    d. gender
    e. all of the answers are correct

17. The route of administration of a drug may influence a patient's drug response. The route order of response from most rapid to least rapid is _____.
    a. intravenous, intramuscular, subcutaneous, oral
    b. intramuscular, subcutaneous, oral, intravenous
    c. subcutaneous, oral, intravenous, intramuscular
    d. oral, intramuscular, subcutaneous, intravenous
    e. none of the answers are correct

18. The route of administration which results in the slowest drug action is _____.
    a. oral
    b. intravenous
    c. subcutaneous
    d. intramuscular
    e. transdermal

True/False

Indicate whether each statement is True (T) or False (F).

About Toxic Reactions/Levels

_____1. Can occur when drugs are administered in large doses

_____2. Some reactions are immediate while others may not be seen for months

_____3. Can be reversible or irreversible

_____4. Patients always know when a toxic reaction is going to occur

_____5. Can occur in recommended doses

_____6. Only licensed healthcare providers need to know the signs and symptoms of toxicity

About Herbal Therapy

_____1. Are regulated by the FDA

_____2. Cannot be sold or promoted as drugs in the United States

_____3. Are classified as dietary or nutritional supplements

_____4. Has not been widely taught in medical schools across the United States

_____5. Must have a disclaimer on the label that states that the supplements are not FDA approved

_____6. Can be important complementary or alternative therapy to drugs

About Controlled Substances

_____1. Have a high potential for abuse

_____2. May cause physical or psychological dependence

_____3. Prescriptions for these drugs cannot be filled more than 6 months after the prescription was written

_____4. Prescriptions for these drugs cannot be refilled more than five times.

_____5. Are the largest category of drugs

_____6. Are categorized in five schedules, C-I through C-V

About Drug Half-Life

_____1. 98% of drugs are eliminated in five to six half-lives

_____2. Increases with liver or kidney disease

_____3. Is the same for the same drug in most people

_____4. Can be altered by changing the dose

_____5. Is based on the frequency of administration

_____6. Is the time required for the body to eliminate 50% of the drug

13

Preparing and Administering Medications

CHAPTER COMPETENCIES

Review the information in your text that supports the following course objectives.

Learning Objectives

1. To define the chapter's key terms.
2. To name the seven rights of drug administration.
3. To identify the different types of medication orders.
4. To describe the various types of medication dispensing systems.
5. To list the various routes by which a drug may be given.
6. To describe the administration of oral and parenteral drugs.
7. To describe the administration of drugs through the skin and mucous membranes.

CHAPTER OUTLINE

CHAPTER OUTLINE	NOTES
The Seven Rights of Drug Administration	
Right Patient	
Right Drug	
Right Dose, Route, and Time	
Right Documentation	
Considerations in Drug Administration	
Drug Errors	
The Medication Order	
Once-per-Week Drugs	
Drug Dispensing Systems	
Computerized Dispensing Systems	
Unit Dose System	
Floor Stock	
General Principles of Drug Administration	
Preparing a Drug for Administration	
Administration of Drugs by the Oral Route	
Patient Care Considerations for Oral Drug Administration	
Administration of Drugs by the Parenteral Route	
Patient Care Considerations for Parenteral Drug Administration	

CHAPTER OUTLINE *continued*

	NOTES
Occupational Safety and Health Administration Guidelines	
Administration of Drugs by the Subcutaneous Route	
Patient Care Considerations for Subcutaneous Drug Administration	
Administration of Drugs by the Intramuscular Route	
Patient Care Considerations for Intramuscular Drug Administration	
Administration of Drugs by the Intravenous Route	
Intravenous Infusion Controllers and Pumps	
Patient Care Considerations for Intravenous Drug Administration	
Administration of Drugs by the Intradermal Route	
Patient Care Considerations for Intradermal Drug Administration	
Other Parenteral Routes of Drug Administration	
Administration of Drugs through the Skin and Mucous Membranes	
Administration of Drugs by the Topical Route	
Patient Care Considerations for Topical Drug Administration	
Administration of Drugs by the Transdermal Route	
Patient Care Considerations for Transdermal Drug Administration	
Administration of Drugs through Inhalation	
Patient Care Considerations for Drug Administration by Inhalation	
Patient Care Considerations after Drug Administration	
Administration of Drugs in the Home	

LEARNING SELF-ASSESSMENT EXERCISES

Key Terms

Define the following key terms:

buccal _____

drug error _____

extravasation _____

infiltration_____

inhalation _____

intradermal _____

intramuscular _____

intravenous _____

parenteral _____

standard precautions _____

subcutaneous _____

sublingual _____

transdermal _____

unit dose _____

Z-track _____

Matching

Match the term in Part 1 with the correct definition in Part 2.

PART 1

_____ 1. extravasation

_____ 2. inhalation

_____ 3. intradermal

_____ 4. intramuscular

_____ 5. intravenous

_____ 6. parenteral

_____ 7. subcutaneous

_____ 8. sublingual

_____ 9. transdermal

_____ 10. unit dose

PART 2

a. The escape of fluid from a blood vessel into surrounding tissues.

b. Route of administration in which the drug is injected into muscle tissue.

c. Route of administration in which the drug is injected into skin tissue.

d. Route of administration in which the drug is injected just below the layer of skin.

e. Route of administration in which the drug is absorbed through the skin from a patch.

f. Route of administration in which drug droplets, vapor, or gas is inhaled and absorbed through the mucous membranes of the respiratory tract.

g. Route of administration in which the drug is injected into a vein.

h. A single dose of a drug packaged ready for patient use.

i. Route of administration in which the drug is placed under the tongue for absorption.

j. A general term for drug administration in which the drug is injected inside the body.

True/False

Indicate whether each statement is True (T) or False (F).

_____ 1. A drug error is any occurrence that can cause a patient to receive the wrong dose, the wrong drug, the wrong route, or the drug at the wrong time.

_____ 2. A STAT order is an order to administer a drug as needed.

_____ 3. A standing order is an order written when a patient is to receive the prescribed drug on a regular basis.

_____ 4. An advantage of once-a-week dosing is that the patient who experiences mild adverse reactions would only have to experience them once a week rather than every day.

_____ 5. New OSHA guidelines help to reduce needle-stick injuries among healthcare workers and others who handle medical sharps.

_____ 6. 80% of needlestick injuries can be prevented with the use of safe needle devices.

_____ 7. A subcutaneous injection places the drug into tissues below the muscle level.

_____ 8. The Z-track method of IM injection is used when a drug is highly irritating to subcutaneous tissues or may permanently stain the skin.

_____ 9. Whenever a drug is added to an IV fluid, the IV bag must have an attached label indicating the drug and dose added.

_____ 10. After an IV infusion is started, if either extravasation or infiltration occurs the infusion must be stopped and restarted in another vein.

_____ 11. The administration of drugs by the intradermal route usually requires special equipment.

_____ 12. Topical drugs act on the skin but are not absorbed through the skin.

Multiple Choice

1. When a drug error occurs, the healthcare worker should _____.
   a. wait to see if any adverse effects occur
   b. report the incident immediately
   c. not tell anyone so they do not get into trouble
   d. tell the patient not to worry
   e. none of these answers are correct

2. In a computerized dispensing system the_____.
   a. drug orders are filled and medications are dispensed to fill each patient's medication order for a 24-hour period
   b. drugs that are dispensed are automatically recorded in a computerized system
   c. a bar code scanner is used to record and charge routine and PRN drugs
   d. the drugs most frequently ordered are kept on the unit in containers in a designated medication room
   e. all of these methods are part of the computerized dispensing system

3. Healthcare professionals involved in drug administration should know _____.
   a. the reason the drug is used
   b. the drug's general actions and adverse reactions
   c. special precautions in administration
   d. normal dose ranges
   e. all of this information should be known

4. Oral route drug administration _____.
   a. is the most frequent route of administration
   b. rarely causes physical discomfort
   c. is relatively easy for patients who are alert and can swallow
   d. can use drug forms such as tablets, capsules, or liquids
   e. all of the answers are correct

5. A method of parenteral drug administration is _____.
   a. subcutaneous
   b. intramuscular
   c. intravenous
   d. intradermal
   e. all of the answers are correct

6. Parenteral routes of administration can include _____.
   a. intra-articular
   b. intralesional
   c. intra-arterial
   d. intracardiac
   e. all of the answers are correct

7. Drugs administered by the subcutaneous route _____.
   a. are absorbed more slowly than are intramuscular drugs
   b. are delivered into the tissues between the skin and the muscle
   c. can be given in large amounts (greater than 1 mL)
   d. are generally given in the upper arm, upper back, or upper abdomen
   e. answers a, b, and d are correct

8. Sites for the administration of intramuscular drugs are _____.
   a. deltoid muscle
   b. ventrogluteal muscle
   c. dorsogluteal muscle
   d. vastus lateralis muscle
   e. all of the answers are correct

9. Infusion controllers and infusion pumps are electronic infusion devices. The primary difference between the two is that _____.
   a. an infusion pump administers the infused drug under pressure, and an infusion controller does not add pressure
   b. an infusion pump administers the infused drug without added pressure, whereas an infusion controllers adds pressure
   c. both devices administer the drug under pressure; the difference is the amount of pressure used
   d. there is no difference; the two devices are the same
   e. none of these answers are correct

10. Intradermal drug administration _____.
   a. usually results in the formation of a wheal
   b. requires a 90° angle of needle insertion
   c. provides good results for allergy testing or local anesthesia
   d. requires a portal to be implanted in the skin
   e. answers a and c are correct

True/False

Indicate whether each statement is True (T) or False (F).

About IV Drug Administration

_____ 1. Are given directly into the blood by a needle inserted into a vein.

_____ 2. Drug action occurs almost immediately.

_____ 3. May be given slowly (>1 minute) or rapidly (<1 minute).

_____ 4. Can be delivered by an IV port or through a heparin lock.

About Transdermal Drug Administration

_____ 1. Allows the drug to be readily absorbed from the skin and have systemic effects.

_____ 2. Allows for a relatively constant blood concentration.

_____ 3. Increases the risk of toxicity.

_____ 4. The sites are rotated to prevent skin irritation.

_____ 5. Should have the site shaved of hair before administration.

_____ 6. Old patches are removed before a new dose is applied.

About After a Drug Is Administered

_____ 1. Is always documented as soon as possible.

_____ 2. The patient's response to the drug is monitored.

_____ 3. The patient's vital signs are not taken until several hours after the drug is administered.

_____ 4. IV flow rate, site used, or problems with administration are recorded.

_____ 5. Adverse reactions are recorded at 15-minute intervals.

About Written Drug Orders

_____ 1. Should include the patient's name.

_____ 2. Should include the name of the drug to be administered.

_____ 3. Should include who is to administer the drug.

_____ 4. Should include what dosage route and form of the drug are to be used.

_____ 5. Should include the dose to be administered.

_____ 6. Should include the frequency of administration.

About Guidelines for Preparing a Drug for Administration

_____ 1. The written orders should be checked.

_____ 2. The drug label should be checked only once.

_____ 3. Never remove a drug from an unlabeled container.

_____ 4. Deposit capsules and tablets into clean hands then drop into medicine cup.

_____ 5. Replace the caps of drug containers immediately after the drug is removed.

_____ 6. Return drugs requiring special storage immediately to their storage area.

_____ 7. Follow aseptic technique when handling syringes and needles.

About Patient Care Considerations for Oral Drug Administration

_____ 1. A full glass of water should be given.

_____ 2. The patient may take the oral drug in any position.

_____ 3. The healthcare provider may safely leave the drug for the patient to take when convenient.

_____ 4. Patients with nasogastric feeding tubes may have their medication given through the tube.

_____ 5. Sublingual drugs must not be chewed or swallowed.

About Patient Care Considerations for Parenteral Drug Administration

_____ 1. Gloves must be worn for protection from a potential blood spill.

_____ 2. Cleanse the skin at the site of injection.

_____ 3. After insertion of the needle for an IM injection, blood should appear in the syringe after pulling back on the barrel.

_____ 4. After insertion of the needle for an IV drug administration, blood should appear in the syringe after pulling back on the barrel.

_____ 5. Syringes are not recapped but are disposed of according to policy.

_____ 6. There is no need to place pressure on an injection site from an IV, SC, or IM injection.

14

Medical Asepsis and Infection Control

CHAPTER COMPETENCIES

Review the information in your text that supports the following course objectives.

Learning Objectives

Upon successfully completing this chapter, you will be able to:

1. Spell and define key terms.

2. Describe conditions that promote the growth of microorganisms.

3. Explain the components of the infectious process cycle.

4. List the various ways microbes are transmitted.

5. Compare the effectiveness in reducing or destroying microorganisms using the four levels of infection control.

6. Describe the procedures for cleaning, handling, and disposing of biohazardous waste in the medical office.

7. Explain the concept of medical asepsis.

8. Discuss risk management procedures required by the Occupational Safety and Health Administration guidelines for the medical office.

9. List the required components of an exposure control plan.

10. Explain the importance of following Standard Precautions in the medical office.

11. Identify various personal protective equipment (PPE) items.

12. Describe circumstances when PPE items would be appropriately worn by the medical assistant.

13. Explain the facts pertaining to the transmission and prevention of the Hepatitis B virus and the Human Immunodeficiency Virus in the medical office.

14. Describe how to avoid becoming infected with the Hepatitis B and Human Immunodeficiency viruses.

Performance Objectives

Upon successfully completing this chapter, you will be able to:

1. Perform a medical aseptic handwashing procedure (Procedure 14-1).

2. Remove and discard contaminated personal protective equipment appropriately (Procedure 14-2).

3. Clean and decontaminate biohazardous spills (Procedure 14-3).

CHAPTER OUTLINE	NOTES
Microorganisms, Pathogens, and Normal Flora	
Conditions That Favor the Growth of Pathogens	
The Infection Cycle	
Modes of Transmission	
Principles of Infection Control	
Medical Asepsis	

CHAPTER OUTLINE *continued*

	NOTES
Levels of Infection Control	
Sanitation	
Disinfection	
Occupational Safety and Health Administration Guidelines for the Medical Office	
Exposure Risk Factors and the Exposure Control Plan	
Standard Precautions	
Personal Protective Equipment	
Handling Environmental Contamination	
Disposing of Infectious Waste	
Hepatitis B and Human Immunodeficiency Viruses	

LEARNING SELF-ASSESSMENT EXERCISES

Key Terms

Define the following key terms:

aerobe _____

anaerobe _____

asymptomatic _____

bactericidal _____

biohazard _____

carrier _____

disease _____

disinfection _____

exposure control plan _____

exposure risk factors _____

germicide _____

immunization _____

infection _____

medical asepsis _____

microorganisms _____

normal flora _____

OSHA _____

pathogens _____

personal protective equipment _____

postexposure testing _____

resident flora _____

resistance _____

sanitation _____

sanitization _____

spore _____

standard precautions _____

sterilization _____

transient flora _____

vector _____

viable _____

virulent _____

Matching

Match the term in Part 1 with the correct definition in Part 2.

PART I

_____ 1. Asymptomatic

_____ 2. Carrier

_____ 3. Medical asepsis

_____ 4. Microorganisms

_____ 5. OSHA

_____ 6. Use of topics to file

_____ 7. Pathogens

PART 2

a. Subject filing

b. Without any symptoms

c. A person infected with a microorganism

d. Microscopic living organisms

e. Removal or destruction of microorganisms

f. Occupational Safety and Health Administration

g. Disease-causing microorganisms

Multiple Choice

1. What is the cornerstone of infection control?
   a. Understanding and practicing medical asepsis
   b. Educating patients about the transmission of disease
   c. Handwashing
   d. Following policies of the medical facility where you work

2. Decreased resistance in a host is one condition that may allow transient flora to become pathogenic. Which of the following is least likely to be a factor in lowering a person's resistance to disease?
   a. Age (particularly the elderly)
   b. Chemotherapy (anticancer drugs)
   c. Experiencing an unusual amount of stress
   d. Low serum potassium and high serum sodium

3. One link in the infection cycle is the mode of transmission. Which of the following are examples of direct transmission?
   a. Inhaling infected droplets (from another person's cough or sneeze)
   b. Intimate contact with an infected person
   c. Sharing eating utensils
   d. a and b

4. Indirect transmission is another mode of spreading disease. Which of the following is not an example of indirect contact?
   a. Sharing eating or drinking utensils
   b. Disease-carrying insects
   c. Kissing an infected person
   d. Contact with a contaminated but inanimate object

5. Handwashing is one element of medical asepsis. Read the following list, and identify when you need to wash your hands.
   a. Before and after every patient contact
   b. Before and after putting on examination gloves
   c. Before and after every work break
   d. All of the above

6. Which of the following is the highest level of infection control?
   a. Sanitation
   b. Sterilization
   c. Disinfection
   d. Chemical immersion

7. Which of the following is not a category of disinfection?
   a. Ultramaximum
   b. Low
   c. High
   d. Intermediate

8. Intermediate-level disinfection kills all but one of the following. Identify the exception.
   a. Spores
   b. Viruses
   c. Fungi
   d. *Mycobacterium tuberculosis*

15

Surgical Instruments and Sterilization

CHAPTER COMPETENCIES

Review the information in your text that supports the following course objectives.

Learning Objectives

Upon successfully completing this chapter, you will be able to:

1. Spell and define key terms.

2. Describe several methods of sterilization.

3. Categorize surgical instruments based on use and identify each by its characteristics.

4. Identify surgical instruments specific to designated specialties.

5. State the difference between reusable and disposable instruments.

6. Explain the procedure for storing supplies, instruments, and equipment.

7. Describe the necessity and procedure for maintaining documents and records of maintenance for instruments and equipment.

Performance Objectives

Upon successfully completing this chapter, you will be able to:

1. Sanitize equipment and instruments (Procedure 15-1).

2. Properly wrap instruments in preparation for sterilization in an autoclave (Procedure 15-2).

3. Operate an autoclave while observing for pressure, time, and temperature determined by the items being sterilized (Procedure 15-3).

CHAPTER OUTLINE

	NOTES
Principles and Practices of Sterile Asepsis	
Sterilization	
Surgical Instruments	
Forceps	
Scissors	
Scalpels and Blades	
Towel Clamps	
Probes and Directors	
Retractors	
Care and Handling of Surgical Instruments	
Storage and Record Keeping	
Maintaining Surgical Supplies	

LEARNING SELF-ASSESSMENT EXERCISES

Key Terms

Define the following key terms:

autoclave _____

disinfection _____

ethylene oxide _____

forceps _____

hemostat _____

needle holder _____

obturator _____

OSHA _____

ratchet _____

sanitation _____

sanitize _____

scalpel _____

scissors _____

serration _____

sound _____

sterilization _____

Matching

Match the instrument in Part 1 with its common use in Part 2.

PART I

_____ 1. Straight scissors

_____ 2. Curved scissors

_____ 3. Thumb forceps

_____ 4. Probe or director

_____ 5. Retractor

_____ 6. Kelly clamp

PART 2

a. Holding open layers of tissue, exposing the areas beneath

b. Curved or straight forceps or hemostat for grasping vessels or tissue, etc.

c. Cutting deep or delicate tissue and cutting sutures

d. Dissecting superficial and delicate tissues

e. Probing depth and direction of an operative area

f. Grasping tissue for dissecting or suturing

Multiple Choice

1. The practice of sterile asepsis is also known as
   a. medical asepsis.
   b. sterile technique.
   c. clinical asepsis.
   d. hospital asepsis.

2. Some medical facilities expect medical assistants to be familiar with all but one of the following. Identify the exception.
   a. Many types of surgical instruments
   b. Use of disinfection and sterilization techniques
   c. Principles and practices of surgical technique
   d. Maintenance and repair of autoclave equipment

3. Identify the correct order of disinfection and sterilization practices.
   a. Sterilization, sanitation, disinfection
   b. Sanitation, disinfection, sterilization
   c. Disinfection, sanitization, sterilization
   d. None of the above

4. Sterilization by autoclave is achieved by which of the following combinations?
   a. Chemical disinfection followed by hot steam
   b. Chemical sanitation and exposure to gas under pressure
   c. Chemical sterilization then dried in the autoclave at high temperature
   d. Proper temperature, pressure, length of time

5. Which one of the following statements is not correct?
   a. Packs sterilized on site are considered sterile for 30 days.
   b. Adequate space between packs is necessary when autoclaving.
   c. Packs should dry before they are removed from the autoclave.
   d. Use of sterilization indicators or tape is optional.

6. Hemostat, Kelly clamp, sterilizer forceps, and needle holder are all part of which instrument group?
   a. Blades
   b. Punches
   c. Forceps
   d. Scissors

7. A scalpel is a very common instrument used in surgical procedures. Which statements are true about the scalpel?
   a. It has a straight handle with detachable, disposable blades.
   b. Disposable scalpels can be purchased and used once before discarding.
   c. Blades come with curved (convex) or straight cutting edges.
   d. All of the above

8. Straight, curved, suture, and bandage are some names of what group of instruments?
   a. Hemostats
   b. Retractors
   c. Scissors
   d. Probes

9. Serrations or teeth, curved or straight blades, ring tips, blunt tips, sharp tips, and ratchets are descriptions that may apply to what group of instruments?
   a. Scissors
   b. Scalpels
   c. Forceps
   d. Retractors

10. The autoclave is commonly used to sterilize all but one of the following. Identify the exception.
    a. Minor surgical instruments
    b. Latex surgical gloves
    c. Surgical bowls and cups
    d. Canisters of gauze sponges

16

The Clinical Laboratory

CHAPTER COMPETENCIES

Review the information in your text that supports the following course objectives.

Learning Objectives

Upon successfully completing this chapter, you will be able to:

1. Spell and define the key terms.

2. List reasons for laboratory testing.

3. Outline the medical assistant's responsibility in the clinical laboratory.

4. Name the kinds of laboratories where medical assistants work and the functions of each.

5. List the types of personnel in laboratories and describe their jobs.

6. Name the types of departments found in most large laboratories and give their purposes.

7. Explain how to use a package insert to determine the procedure for a laboratory test.

8. List the equipment found in most small laboratories and give the purpose of each.

9. List and describe the parts of a microscope.

10. Explain the significance of the Clinical Laboratory Improvement Amendments and how to follow their regulations to ensure quality control.

11. Define OSHA and state its purpose.

12. List the laboratory safety guidelines.

Performance Objective

Upon successfully completing this chapter, you will be able to:

1. Care for the microscope (Procedure 16-1).

CHAPTER OUTLINE	NOTES
Types of Laboratories	
Reference Laboratory	
Hospital Laboratory	
Physician's Office Laboratory	
Laboratory Departments	
Hematology	
Coagulation	
Clinical Chemistry	
Toxicology	
Urinalysis	
Immunohematology	

CHAPTER OUTLINE *continued*

	NOTES
Immunology	
Microbiology	
Anatomical and Surgical Pathology	
Laboratory Personnel	
Physician Office Laboratory Testing	
Laboratory Equipment	
Cell Counter	
Microscope	
Chemistry Analyzers	
Centrifuges	
Incubator	
Refrigerators and Freezers	
Glassware	
Laboratory Safety	
Occupational Safety and Health Administration (OSHA)	
Safety Guidelines	
Incident Reports	
Clinical Laboratory Improvement Amendments	
Levels of Testing	
Laboratory Standards	

LEARNING SELF-ASSESSMENT EXERCISES

Key Terms

Define the following key terms:

aerosol _____

calibration _____

capillary action _____

centrifugal force _____

Clinical Laboratory Improvement Amendments (CLIA) _____

material safety data sheet (MSDS) _____

National Committee for Clinical Laboratory Standards (NCCLS) ___

normal values _____

quality assurance (QA) _____

quality control (QC) _____

reagent _____

reportable range _____

specimen _____

Matching

Match the term in Part 1 with the correct definition in Part 2.

PART 1

_____ 1. POL

_____ 2. QC procedures

PART 2

a. Laboratory in a doctor's office that performs only a few types of tests on a limited number of patients

b. Checking instruments, performing daily maintenance, and running control specimens

Multiple Choice

1. What does the simplest cell counter count?
   a. Only red and white blood cells and performs hemoglobin and hematocrit testing
   b. Only white cells
   c. Only red cells
   d. Only hemoglobin and hematocrit determinations

2. What type of microscope is commonly used in the medical office?
   a. 7× to 45× trinocular stereo zoom boom microscope
   b. 3.75× to 35× stereo zoom boom microscope
   c. Articulating arm stereo zoom boom microscope
   d. Compound microscope—a two-lens system in which ocular and objective lenses together provide the total magnification.

3. Which of the following statements is a very important guideline for use of the centrifuge?
   a. Only spin two tubes at a time.
   b. It is permissible to open the lid before the spinning stops.
   c. Tubes must always be counterbalanced.
   d. Centrifuges require no routine cleaning.

4. Which statement is not correct?
   a. Refrigerators in laboratories are used to store reagents, kits, and patient specimens.
   b. The temperature is critical and must be measured and recorded daily.
   c. Food may be stored in these refrigerators if food containers are covered.
   d. They vary in size and can be purchased according to office needs and space.

5. Why is laboratory testing most commonly ordered?
   a. Detecting and diagnosing disease
   b. As part of pharmaceutical research project
   c. Meeting legal requirements (e.g., drug testing, a marriage license)
   d. *a* and *c* only

6. Which of the following is not accurate information about a reference laboratory?
   a. It is a large facility in which thousands of tests are performed each day.
   b. Direct patient contact is limited to its satellite specimen procurement stations.
   c. It receives specimens from hospitals and clinics from the region it serves.
   d. The specimens are mailed as low-priority shipments.

7. What are some of the most common tests done in a physician office laboratory?
   a. Blood glucose, Lyme disease, medication toxicity, mononucleosis and streptococcus tests
   b. Urinalysis, blood cell counts, blood glucose, rapid streptococcus and pregnancy tests
   c. Blood typing, Rh immune globulin (RhIg), and HIV testing
   d. Mononucleosis, streptococcus, diabetic testing, and kidney function

8. What are the three types of hazards found in a laboratory?
   a. Liquid, gas (flame), ergonomic
   b. Splash or spray, inhalation, skin contact
   c. Physical, chemical, and biological hazards
   d. Noise pollution, eyestrain, neck pain

9. What does BLUE represent in the National Fire Protection Association (NFPA) classification system section?
   a. Health hazard
   b. Fire hazard
   c. Reactive hazard
   d. Blank to list specific hazard

10. According to OSHA requirements, what are employers required to provide free to their employees?
    a. Hepatitis C vaccine series
    b. Testing for sexually transmitted diseases (STDs)
    c. Hepatitis B virus vaccine series
    d. Hepatitis laboratory screen to establish baseline of status

11. If there is a biological spill, what is the best order for safe cleanup?
    a. Cover spill, flood with disinfectant, put on gloves, wipe up, dispose of waste
    b. Put on gloves, cover spill, flood with disinfectant, wipe up, dispose of waste
    c. Flood with disinfectant, cover the area, put on gloves, wipe up, dispose of waste
    d. Put on gloves, cover the area with disposable towels, wipe up, dispose of waste

17

Measurements and Vital Signs

CHAPTER COMPETENCIES

Review the information in your text that supports the following course objectives.

Learning Objectives

Upon successfully completing this chapter, you will be able to:

1. Spell and define key terms.

2. Explain the procedures for measuring a patient's height and weight.

3. Identify and describe the types of thermometers.

4. Compare the procedures for measuring a patient's temperature using the oral, rectal, axillary, and tympanic methods.

5. List the fever process, including the stages of fever.

6. Describe the procedure for measuring a patient's pulse and respiratory rates.

7. Identify the various sites on the body used for palpating a pulse.

8. Define Korotkoff sounds and the five phases of blood pressure.

9. Identify factors that may influence the blood pressure.

10. Explain the factors to consider when choosing the correct blood pressure cuff size.

Performance Objectives

Upon successfully completing this chapter, you will be able to:

1. Measure and record a patient's weight (Procedure 17-1).

2. Measure and record a patient's height (Procedure 17-2).

3. Measure and record a patient's oral temperature using a glass mercury thermometer (Procedure 17-3).

4. Measure and record a patient's rectal temperature using a glass mercury thermometer (Procedure 17-4).

5. Measure and record a patient's axillary temperature using a glass mercury thermometer (Procedure 17-5).

6. Measure and record a patient's temperature using an electronic thermometer (Procedure 17-6).

7. Measure and record a patient's temperature using a tympanic thermometer (Procedure 17-7).

8. Measure and record a patient's radial pulse (Procedure 17-8).

9. Measure and record a patient's respirations (Procedure 17-9).

10. Measure and record a patient's blood pressure (Procedure 17-10).

CHAPTER OUTLINE	NOTES
Anthropometric Measurements	
Weight	
Height	

CHAPTER OUTLINE *continued*	**NOTES**
Vital Signs	
Temperature	
Pulse	
Respiration	
Blood Pressure	

LEARNING SELF-ASSESSMENT EXERCISES

Key Terms

Define the following key terms:

afebrile _____

aneroid _____

anthropometric _____

baseline _____

calibrated _____

cardiac cycle _____

cardinal signs _____

diastole _____

febrile _____

hyperpyrexia _____

hypertension _____

intermittent _____

palpation _____

postural hypotension _____

pyrexia _____

relapsing fever _____

remittent fever _____

sphygmomanometer _____

sustained fever _____

systole _____

tympanic thermometer _____

Matching

Match the term in Part 1 with the correct definition in Part 2.

PART 1

_____ 1. Diastole

_____ 2. Intermittent

_____ 3. Sustained

PART 2

a. Describes a fever that is constant or not fluctuating

b. The relaxation phase of the cardiac cycle

c. A fever that occurs at intervals

_____ 4. Systole

_____ 5. Anthropometric

d. The contraction phase of the cardiac cycle

e. Pertaining to measurements of the human body

Multiple Choice

1. Which of the following is not an example of why obtaining patient weights is important?
   a. Some patients are on medication prescribed according to weight.
   b. Some medications are prescribed for patients attempting to gain or lose weight.
   c. Some weight loss may be due to illness.
   d. It is a reality check showing that obese persons need to diet.

2. Which of the following is not true about tympanic temperature, when used accurately?
   a. Gives a reading comparable to oral
   b. Is also called an aural temperature
   c. Is positioned toward the tympanic membrane
   d. Gives a reading comparable to the axillary temperature

3. Fever process is explained by the following statements:
   a. Body temperature is regulated by the hypothalamus.
   b. When the hypothalamus senses the body is too warm, peripheral vasodilation is initiated.
   c. Core body heat is carried to the body surface via circulation, and perspiration increases to cool the body by evaporation.
   d. All of the above

4. Which of the following statements is not accurate?
   a. Fluctuations up or down in body temperature may be due to illness.
   b. Children have higher metabolisms than adults and tend to have higher temperatures than adults.
   c. Temperature of the very young and very old tends to be easily affected by environment.
   d. Exercise does not affect body temperature.

5. Heartbeat (pulse) can be felt at various points on the body where you can press an artery against a bone or other underlying firm surface. Which of the following is not a commonly used location:
   a. carotid, apical, brachial
   b. temporal
   c. popliteal, posttibial, dorsalis pedia
   d. radial, femoral

6. Pulse characteristics include
   a. rate—number of beats per minute.
   b. rhythm—time interval between beats.
   c. volume—strength of force against the heartbeat.

d. All of the above

7. Volume, the strength or force of the heartbeat, may be described as all but one of the following. Identify the exception.
   a. Soft, bounding
   b. Irregular or regular
   c. Strong or full
   d. Weak, thready

8. Many factors affect the force, speed, and rhythm of the heart. Which of the following does not affect these three factors?
   a. Youth—young children and infants have a faster heart rate than adults
   b. Being an athlete (conditioned)
   c. Age—older adults; decreased myocardial efficiency
   d. Nationality and cultural influence

9. Respiration is controlled by the respiratory center of the brainstem and by feedback from thermosensors in the carotid arteries that monitor the CO_2 content in the blood. The physiology of respiration also includes
   a. inspiration (oxygen brought into lungs).
   b. expiration (expels CO_2).
   c. alveoli of the respiratory tract that absorb O_2.
   d. All of the above

10. The radial artery is most often used to determine pulse rates, and which of the following statements does not apply?
    a. If the pulse is irregular, the apical pulse is the site of choice.
    b. If the pulse is irregular, the doctor should assess the rate.
    c. An irregular rhythm should be counted for a full minute to determine the rate.
    d. A Doppler unit is an appropriate choice to auscultate a pulse.

11. After taking a patient's blood pressure, take the opportunity to educate the patient with high blood pressure. What would you never say to a patient in this situation?
    a. Encourage the patient to keep a log of daily blood pressure readings.
    b. Emphasize that the patient should never stop taking the blood pressure medication without the doctor's permission.

c. Tell the patient that free-standing blood pressure machines in pharmacies and supermarkets are not always calibrated properly or calibrated on a regular basis. The readings may not be accurate.

d. Tell the patient that a relative, a registered nurse, may adjust a dose or prescribe a new medication if the doctor is unavailable.

12. A blood pressure that drops suddenly when the patient stands from a sitting or lying position is referred to as **postural hypotension,** or **orthostatic hypotension.** Which symptom is not associated with this condition?

a. Vertigo

b. Some patients with postural hypotension may faint.

c. This may occur as a patient moves from a position of lying down to sitting or standing.

d. Sudden onset of nausea and vomiting

13. Indicate which of the following factors does not influence blood pressure.

a. Age, activity

b. Stress, body position

c. Height

d. Medications

Notes

Notes

Notes

Critical Thinking Practice

1. Describe the difference between legal issues and ethical issues. Give an example of each.

_____

_____

_____

_____

2. Describe the difference between medical ethics and bioethics.

_____

_____

_____

_____

3. Describe the four steps that you can use to resolve an ethical dilemma.

_____

_____

_____

_____

4. Describe the opinions of the American Medical Association Council on Ethical and Judicial Affairs on social policy issues.

_____

_____

_____

Skill Drills

1. List three items that must be included in a contract.

_____

_____

_____

2. List six of the ten items that must be included in an informed consent form.

_____

_____

_____

3. List five incidents that must be reported to specified authorities.

_____

_____

_____

4. List six ways a medical assistant can help prevent a medical law suit.

_____

_____

_____

Critical Thinking Practice

1. Describe the purpose of the Self-Determination Act.

_____

_____

_____

2. What are intentional torts? Give four examples.

_____

_____

_____

3. Explain the theory of respondeat superior and describe how it applies to the medical assistant.

_____

_____

_____

4. A patient asks your opinion of a particular pediatrician's treatment of a certain illness and then tells you that she does not care for that physician's bedside manner. You know that the pediatrician is not well liked by his office staff because he is impatient and hard to get along with. How do you respond to this patient's question and statement so as to remain professional and to avoid defamation of character?

_____

_____

_____

Patient Education

1. An elderly patient being seen preoperatively in the medical office tells you that she has heard others talk about filling out advance directives, but she doesn't know what that means. How do you explain advance directives to this patient?

_____

_____

_____

Skill Drills

1. Identify the four ways that health records can be stored.

_____

_____

_____

_____

2. List the 13 standard topics of information included in a health record.

_____

_____

_____

_____

_____

_____

3. No matter how the records are stored, make sure that the information meets the following six criteria.

_____

_____

_____

_____

_____

Critical Thinking Practice

1. ABC Insurance Company has sent a written request for a copy of Mr. Johnson's medical records. Explain what information has to be included in the request for records *and* how you will process this request, including the guidelines for charging the insurance company for this type of processing.

_____

_____

_____

_____

2. Compare and contrast alphabetic and numeric filing systems; give an example of each.

_____

_____

_____

_____

Patient Education

1. Ms. Winters is 17 years old and still lives with her parents. She has been a patient of Dr. Wahlgren for many years. She comes into the office and asks you for a copy of her medical records. How do you respond?

_____

_____

_____

_____

Skill Drills

1. List the three regulatory agencies that require medical office settings to have quality improvement plans.

_____

_____

_____

_____

2. List six health care settings for which JCAHO presently sets standards and evaluates care.

_____

_____

_____

_____

3. Identify the six steps in the process of acquiring JCAHO accreditation.

_____

_____

_____

_____

_____

Critical Thinking Practice

1. An elderly patient slipped and fell in the waiting room. What type of report will you fill out, and what guidelines will you follow?

_____

_____

_____

2. You are a newly hired administrative medical assistant, and the physician has asked you to develop a QI program for the practice. How will you set up a successful program?

_____

_____

_____

3. There are many newly hired employees in your clinic, and you need to explain how quality improvement programs and risk management work together to improve overall patient care and employee needs. What will you tell this group?

_____

_____

_____

_____

Proficiency Test: Arithmetic

1. Multiply

   a) $\begin{array}{r} 647 \\ \times\, 38 \\ \hline \end{array}$

   b) $\frac{8}{9} \times \frac{12}{32}$

   c) $\begin{array}{r} 0.56 \\ \times\, 0.17 \\ \hline \end{array}$

2. Divide. If necessary, report to two decimal places.

   a) $82\overline{)793}$

   b) $5\frac{1}{4} \div \frac{7}{4}$

   c) $0.015\overline{)0.3}$

3. Change to a decimal. If necessary, report to two decimal places.

   a) $\frac{1}{18}$

   b) $\frac{3}{8}$

4. Change to a fraction and reduce to lowest terms.

   a) 0.35
   b) 0.08

5. In each set, which number has the greater value?

    a) _____ 0.4 and 0.162

    b) _____ 0.76 and 0.8

    c) _____ 0.5 and 0.83

    d) _____ 0.3 and 0.25

6. Reduce these fractions to their lowest terms as decimals. Report to two decimal places.

    a) $\frac{20}{12}$

    b) $\frac{7}{84}$

    c) $\frac{6}{13}$

7. Round off these decimals as indicated.

    a) nearest tenth   5.349 _____

    b) nearest hundredth   0.6284 _____

    c) nearest thousandth   0.9244 _____

8. Change these percents to a fraction.

    a) $\frac{1}{3}\%$

    b) 0.8%

9. Solve these ratios.

    a) $\frac{32}{128} = \frac{4}{X}$

    b) $8 : 72 :: 5 : X$

    c) $\frac{0.4}{0.12} = \frac{X}{8}$ (nearest whole number)

Proficiency Test: Exercises in Equivalents and Mixed Conversions

1. 100 mg = _____ gm

2. 1 oz = _____ mL

3. 1 L = _____ mL

4. 1 tsp = _____ mL

5. 0.015 g = _____ mg

6. 10 mg = _____ gm

7. 0.2 gm = _____ mg

8. 30 mg = _____ g

9. 500 mg = _____ g

10. 1 oz = _____ mL

11. 1 mL = _____ tsp

12. 1 tbsp = _____ mL

13. 1 kg = _____ lbs

14. 1 g = _____ mg

15. 60 mg = _____ g

16. 30 mL = _____ oz

17. 1 mL = _____ minims

18. 3 tbsp = _____ mL

19. 1000 mg = _____ gm

20. 0.1 gm = _____ mg

21. 5 mL = _____ tsp

22. 600 mg = _____ gm

23. 10 mcg = _____ mg

24. 0.5 mcg = _____ mg

25. 0.6 mg = _____ g

26. 250 mcg = _____ mg

27. 1 mg = _____ g

28. 0.125 mg = _____ mcg

29. 0.01 mg = _____ mcg

30. 0.001 mg = _____ mcg

31. 1 qt = _____ mL

32. gr $\frac{1}{100}$ = _____ mg

33. 30 mg = _____ gr

34. gr ii = _____ mg

35. 240 mg = _____ gr

36. gr $\frac{1}{125}$ = _____ mg

37. 1 g = _____ gr

38. gr $\frac{1}{200}$ = _____ mg

FILL IN THE BLANK

Fill in the blanks using words from the list below.

public   2–10
psychological   pharmacokinetics
8–12   physical
immediate   generic
small

1. The three phases of clinical testing of a new drug can last anywhere from_____years.
2. _____dependency is a compulsive need to use a substance repeatedly to avoid mild to severe withdrawal symptoms.
3. _____dependency is a compulsion to use a substance to obtain a pleasurable experience.
4. In hospitals or other agencies that dispense controlled substances, scheduled drugs are counted every_____ hours.
5. Enteric coated drugs do not disintegrate until they reach the_____intestine.
6. Changes that occur with aging affect the_____of a drug.
7. The National Center for Complementary and Alternative Medicine (NCCAM) disseminates information to the_____.
8. Anaphylactic shock is a serious allergic drug reaction that requires_____medical attention.
9. The_____name of a drug is defined as the name given to a drug before it becomes official and may be used in all countries, by all manufacturers, and is not capitalized.

LIST

List the requested number of items.

1. List the three categories to which the FDA assigns a new drug.
   a. _____
   b. _____
   c. _____

2. List four items that *must* be on a prescription for a drug.
   a. _____
   b. _____
   c. _____
   d. _____

3. List four items that *must* be on the product label of an OTC drug.
   a. _____
   b. _____
   c. _____
   d. _____

4. List the two phases that liquid and parenteral drugs go through in the body.
   a. _____
   b. _____

5. List the four activities that pharmacokinetics involves.
   a. _____
   b. _____
   c. _____
   d. _____

6. List the seven types of drug reactions in the body.
   a. _____
   b. _____
   c. _____
   d. _____
   e. _____

f. _____

g. _____

7. List the three effects of drug–drug interactions.

a. _____

b. _____

c. _____

8. List the five schedules of controlled substances and give a brief definition.

a. _____

b. _____

c. _____

d. _____

e. _____

9. List the four names that a drug may have.

a. _____

b. _____

c. _____

d. _____

10. List the five Pregnancy Categories and give a brief definition.

a. _____

b. _____

c. _____

d. _____

e. _____

CLINICAL APPLICATIONS

1. Mrs. C has recently discovered that she is pregnant. On her history and physical form you note that she takes many herbal remedies and dietary supplements as well as multiple over-the-counter medications. What might you suggest Mrs. C discuss with her healthcare provider?

2. Your overweight neighbor, knowing that you are in healthcare, wants to know why her prescription for antibiotics is the same strength as her elderly father who has kidney disease, but the other medication that they both take for cholesterol control have different dosages and schedules. What might you tell your neighbor in response?

FILL IN THE BLANK

Fill in the blanks using words from the list below.

11	15
circular	standing
outward	skin
inner	muscle
administration	surgical
45	topical
inhalation	90
immediately	

1. When a drug error occurs it must be reported _____ .
2. Most drug errors are made during _____.
3. A _____ order is one that is written when the patient is to receive the prescribed drug on a regular basis.
4. The skin site for parenteral drug administration is cleansed using a(n) _____ motion from a(n) _____ point and moving _____.
5. A Sharps Inquiry Log must be kept by employers with _____ or more employees.
6. A subcutaneous injection places the drug into the tissues between the_____ and the _____.
7. In an SC injection, the needle is placed at a _____ degree angle, in an IM injection the needle is inserted at a_____degree angle, and in an intradermal injection the needle is placed at a_____ degree angle.
8. A venous access port requires _____ implantation and removal.
9. Drugs that are used to soften, disinfect, or lubricate the skin are _____ drugs.
10. Examples of drugs administered by _____ include mucolytics, antiinflammatories, and bronchodilators.

LIST

List the requested number of items.

1. List the seven rights of drug administration.
   a. _____
   b. _____
   c. _____
   d. _____
   e. _____
   f. _____
   g. _____

2. List the three times that a drug label should be checked.
   a. _____
   b. _____
   c. _____

3. List the three forms of oral drugs.
   a. _____
   b. _____
   c. _____

4. List the four most commonly used routes of administration of parenteral drugs.
   a. _____
   b. _____
   c. _____
   d. _____

5. List six diseases that can be transmitted by needle exposures or sticks.

a. _____

b. _____

c. _____

d. _____

e. _____

f. _____

6. List three sites for SC injections.

a. _____

b. _____

c. _____

7. List four parenteral routes of drug administration that may be done by a healthcare provider.

a. _____

b. _____

c. _____

d. _____

8. List five items that should be known by the healthcare professional involved in the administration of drugs.

a. _____

b. _____

c. _____

d. _____

e. _____

9. List four precautions that should be followed to prevent drug errors before administration.

a. _____

b. _____

c. _____

d. _____

CLINICAL APPLICATION

1. Mr. T is being discharged from the hospital but will need to continue his medications at home. As a healthcare professional, what might you ask or suggest to Mr. T regarding his home environment and safe drug administration?

2. Today is the first day of employment for Miss C in a clinical setting of more than 20 persons. What OSHA guidelines should she be informed of before she begins using needles?

Skill Drills

1. List six of the body's natural defense systems.

   a. _____

   b. _____

   c. _____

   d. _____

   e. _____

   f. _____

2. List six conditions that microorganisms require for growth and reproduction.

   a. _____

   b. _____

   c. _____

   d. _____

   e. _____

   f. _____

3. Identify the five links in the chain of the infection cycle.

   a. _____

   b. _____

   c. _____

   d. _____

   e. _____

Critical Thinking Practice

1. A middle-aged man comes into the clinic with symptoms of low-grade fever and a productive cough that has lasted several weeks. The doctor orders a chest x-ray to aid in diagnosis. After the patient goes to the radiology department, you clean the room for the next patient. What level of disinfection will you use? What common household chemical will serve the purpose? If you have the chemical, but it is not diluted, how much water would you add to 1/2 cup of the chemical?

   _____

   _____

   _____

2. Every medical facility must have a written exposure control plan to help avoid coming into contact with biohazardous materials and to teach employees what to do in the event an exposure occurs. What equipment or medical preparation will you implement to protect yourself in the clinical setting?

   _____

   _____

   _____

Skill Drills

1. List six instruments used in obstetrics and gynecology practice and briefly state the use of each.

   a. _____

   b. _____

   c. _____

   d. _____

   e. _____

   f. _____

2. What six items should be included on a sterilization record?

   a. _____

   b. _____

   c. _____

   d. _____

   e. _____

   f. _____

Critical Thinking Practice

1. As you remove minor surgery packs from the autoclave and lay them on the counter, you notice some dampness remaining between them. What will you do? Why?

   _____

   _____

   _____

   _____

   _____

2. You notice a patient in the waiting room who is coughing frequently and who appears to be very ill. What would you say or do?

   _____

   _____

   _____

   _____

   _____

   _____

Patient Education

1. Dr. Day has just diagnosed a 10-year-old pediatric patient with a viral upper respiratory infection. What information about infection control could you share with the parents of the child that they can practice at home on a regular basis?

   _____

   _____

   _____

   _____

   _____

   _____

   _____

   _____

Skill Drills

1. List seven types of glassware used in a medical laboratory.

a. _____

b. _____

c. _____

d. _____

e. _____

f. _____

g. _____

2. List the seven important sections of a Material Safety Data Sheet.

a. _____

b. _____

c. _____

d. _____

e. _____

f. _____

g. _____

Critical Thinking Practice

1. Briefly explain who or what OSHA is and how the standards are meant to provide a safe work environment.

_____

_____

_____

_____

2. OSHA Bloodborne Pathogens Standard has set some specific training and safety provisions for the employer to make available for the employees. What are these provisions?

_____

_____

_____

_____

Patient Education

1. A patient has been sent to your medical clinic for a urine drug screen. She knows her employment may hinge on the results of the test, and she asks if there is any chance that someone else's laboratory results will be reported as hers. Explain the Chain of Custody procedure in lay terms. The purpose of having each person who has a role in processing the specimen rechecks the name on the sample and on the accompanying document before signing the Chain of Custody form. This extra precaution is to ensure the lab results will be hers.

_____

_____

_____

2. A patient phones your medical clinic and states that the surgeon he was referred to is going to be doing abdominal surgery in 2 weeks. The patient wants to come in to the clinic to have blood taken and held on reserve in case he has to have a blood transfusion. Explain to the patient why blood for transfusion is not taken in the clinic setting.

_____

_____

_____

Skill Drills

1. List four types of thermometers.

   a. _____

   b. _____

   c. _____

   d. _____

2. What are nine causes of errors in blood pressure readings?

   a. _____

   b. _____

   c. _____

   d. _____

   e. _____

   f. _____

   g. _____

   h. _____

   i. _____

Critical Thinking Practice

1. Ms. Green arrived at the office late for her appointment, frantic and explaining that her alarm clock had not gone off. She discovered that her car was almost out of gas, and she had to stop to refuel. Once she got to the clinic, she could not find a parking place in the parking lot and had to park a block down the street. How would you expect these events to affect her vital signs? Explain why.

_____

_____

_____

_____

_____

2. What size cuff would you likely choose for Mrs. Daily, an elderly female patient who is 5 feet, 4 inches tall and weighs approximately 200 pounds? Why?

_____

_____

_____

_____

_____

Patient Education

1. Ms. White, mother of a 6 month old and a 4 year old, would like to purchase a thermometer. She is not sure how to use them or what possible variations may occur in readings. Create a graph for her showing the types of thermometers and temperature comparisons. Include centigrade readings.

_____

_____

_____

_____

_____

PROCEDURE 7-1: **Performing within Legal and Ethical Boundaries**

Equipment/Supplies: Paper, writing utensil, computer with Internet access, textbook, Medical Assistants' Creed, AAMA Code of Ethics

Standards: Given the needed equipment and a place to work the student will perform this skill with _____ % accuracy in a total of _____ minutes. *(Your instructor will tell you what the percentage and time limits will be before you begin.)*

Key: 4 = Satisfactory   0 = Unsatisfactory   NA = This step is not counted

Procedure Steps

	Self	Partner	Instructor
1. Read and understand the Medical Assistants' Creed.	☐	☐	☐
2. Read and understand the five principles of the American Association of Medical Assistants Code of Ethics.	☐	☐	☐
3. Identify the legal implications of this action.	☐	☐	☐
4. Identify the ethical implications of this action.	☐	☐	☐
5. Identify three resources that support your conclusions.	☐	☐	☐
6. Based on this information, resolve the issue in a legal and ethical manner.	☐	☐	☐

Calculation

Total Possible Points: _____

Total Points Earned: _____   Multiplied by 100 = _____   Divided by Total Possible Points = _____ %

Pass ☐   Fail ☐

Comments:

Student signature _____ Date _____

Partner signature _____ Date _____

Instructor's signature _____ Date _____

Name_____   Instructor _____

PROCEDURE 8-1: Preparing a Health File

Equipment/Supplies: File folder, title, year, alphabetic or numeric labels

Standards: Given the needed equipment and a place to work the student will perform this skill with _____ % accuracy in a total of _____ minutes. *(Your instructor will tell you what the percentage and time limits will be before you begin.)*

Key: 4 = Satisfactory   0 = Unsatisfactory   NA = This step is not counted

Procedure Steps

	Self	Partner	Instructor
1. Decide the name of the file (a patient's name, company name, or the name of the type of information to be stored within the record).	☐	☐	☐
2. Type a label with the selected title on it *in unit order*.	☐	☐	☐
3. Place the label along the tabbed edge of the folder so that the title extends out farther than the file folder itself. (Tabs can either be the length of the folder or tabbed in various positions, such as left, center, and right, based on the type of filing system used.)	☐	☐	☐
4. Place a year label along the top edge of the tab before the label with the title. This will be changed each year that the patient has been seen.	☐	☐	☐
5. Place the appropriate alphabetic or numeric labels below the title.	☐	☐	☐
6. Apply any additional labels that your office may decide to use.	☐	☐	☐

Calculation

Total Possible Points: _____

Total Points Earned: _____   Multiplied by 100 = _____   Divided by Total Possible Points = _____ %

Pass   Fail

☐   ☐

Comments:

Student signature _____   Date _____

Partner signature _____   Date _____

Instructor's signature _____   Date _____

PROCEDURE 8-2: Maintaining Medication and Immunization Records

Equipment/Supplies: Medication record, immunization record, list of medications prescribed for an adult patient, list of immunizations administered to a pediatric patient, black or blue ink pen, red ink pen, highlighter pen

Standards: Given the needed equipment and a place to work the student will perform this skill with _____% accuracy in a total of _____ minutes. *(Your instructor will tell you what the percentage and time limits will be before you begin.)*

Key: 4 = Satisfactory   0 = Unsatisfactory   NA = This step is not counted

Procedure Steps	Self	Partner	Instructor
1. Assemble the appropriate materials for completing a medication record and an immunization record.	☐	☐	☐
2. Using the adult patient information sheet, complete the top of the medication record in black or blue ink.	☐	☐	☐
3. Write the medications noted on the patient information sheet on the medication record.	☐	☐	☐
4. Note any allergies on the medication record in red ink.	☐	☐	☐
5. Check the medication record for accuracy.	☐	☐	☐
6. Highlight any medications on the record that the patient is no longer taking.	☐	☐	☐
7. Using the pediatric patient information sheet, complete the top of the immunization record in black or blue ink.	☐	☐	☐
8. Write the immunizations noted on the patient information sheet on the immunization record.	☐	☐	☐
9. Note any allergies on the immunization record in red ink.	☐	☐	☐
10. Check the immunization record for accuracy.	☐	☐	☐

Calculation

Total Possible Points: _____

Total Points Earned: _____   Multiplied by 100 = _____   Divided by Total Possible Points = _____%

Pass   Fail

☐   ☐

Comments:

Student signature _____   Date _____

Partner signature _____   Date _____

Instructor's signature _____   Date _____

PROCEDURE 9-1: Demonstrating Knowledge of Federal and State Health Care Legislation and Regulations

Equipment/Supplies: Paper, writing utensil, computer with Internet Access

Standards: Given the needed equipment and a place to work the student will perform this skill with _____% accuracy in a total of _____ minutes. *(Your instructor will tell you what the percentage and time limits will be before you begin.)*

Key: 4 = Satisfactory   0 = Unsatisfactory   NA = This step is not counted

Procedure Steps	Self	Partner	Instructor
1. Find the American Association of Medical Assistants (AAMA) internet site and explain what resources they have available regarding health care regulations.	☐	☐	☐
2. Explain the actions you can take to stay current and aware of new federal and state health care legislation and regulations.	☐	☐	☐
3. Locate your state's Department of Health internet site and explain • the laws and/or regulations they cover • the resources they have available to help you understand these regulations • the potential fines or other consequences of not following these regulations	☐	☐	☐
4. Locate the Occupational Safety and Health Administration internet site and explain • the laws and/or regulations they cover • the resources they have available to help you understand these regulations • the potential fines or other consequences of not following these regulations	☐	☐	☐
5. Locate the Medicare internet site and explain • the laws and/or regulations they cover • the resources they have available to help you understand these regulations • the potential fines or other consequences of not following these regulations	☐	☐	☐
6. Locate the Joint Commission of Accreditation of Hospitals internet site and explain • the laws and/or regulations they cover • the resources they have available to help you understand these regulations • the potential fines or other consequences of not following these regulations	☐	☐	☐
7. Locate information on the Health Insurance Portability and Accountability Act and explain • the intent of this regulation • the resources available to help you understand this regulation • the legal implications of not following this regulation	☐	☐	☐

PROCEDURE 9-1:

Procedure Steps

Self   Partner   Instructor

☐   ☐   ☐

8. Locate information on the Clinical Laboratyr Improvement Ammendments and explain

- the intent of this regulation
- the resources available to help you understand this regulation
- the legal implications of not following this regulation

Calculation

Total Possible Points: _____

Total Points Earned: _____ Multiplied by 100 = _____ Divided by Total Possible Points = _____%

Pass   Fail

☐   ☐

Comments:

Student signature _____ Date _____

Partner signature _____ Date _____

Instructor's signature _____ Date _____

Name_____   Instructor _____

PROCEDURE 14-1: Handwashing for Medical Asepsis

Equipment/Supplies: Liquid soap, disposable paper towels, an orangewood manicure stick, a waste can

Standards: Given the needed equipment and a place to work, the student will perform this skill with _____% accuracy in a total of _____ minutes. *(Your instructor will tell you what the percentage and time limits will be before you begin practicing.)*

Key: 4 = Satisfactory   0 = Unsatisfactory   NA = This step is not counted

Procedure Steps

	Self	Partner	Instructor
1. Remove all rings and wristwatch.	☐	☐	☐
2. Stand close to the sink without touching it.	☐	☐	☐
3. Turn on the faucet and adjust the temperature of the water to warm.	☐	☐	☐
4. Wet hands and wrists, apply soap, and work into a lather.	☐	☐	☐
5. Rub palms together and rub soap between your fingers at least 10 times.	☐	☐	☐
6. Scrub one palm with fingertips, work soap under nails, and then reverse hands.	☐	☐	☐
7. Rinse hands and wrists under warm running water.	☐	☐	☐
8. Hold hands lower than elbows and avoid touching the inside of the sink.	☐	☐	☐
9. Using the orangewood stick, clean under each nail on both hands.	☐	☐	☐
10. Reapply liquid soap and rewash hands and wrists.	☐	☐	☐
11. Rinse hands again while holding hands lower than the wrists and elbows.	☐	☐	☐
12. Use a dry paper towel to dry your hands and wrists gently.	☐	☐	☐
13. Use a dry paper towel to turn off the faucets and discard the paper towel.	☐	☐	☐

Calculation

Total Possible Points: _____
Total Points Earned: _____   Multiplied by 100 = _____   Divided by Total Possible Points = _____%

Pass   Fail
☐   ☐

Comments:

Student signature _____   Date _____
Partner signature _____   Date _____
Instructor's signature _____   Date _____

PROCEDURE 14-2: Removing Contaminated Gloves

Equipment/Supplies: Clean examination gloves; biohazard waste container

Standards: Given the needed equipment and a place to work, the student will perform this skill with _____% accuracy in a total of _____ minutes. *(Your instructor will tell you what the percentage and time limits will be before you begin practicing.)*

Key: 4 = Satisfactory   0 = Unsatisfactory   NA = This step is not counted

Procedure Steps	Self	Partner	Instructor
1. Choose the appropriate size gloves and apply one glove to each hand.	☐	☐	☐
2. After "contaminating" gloves, grasp the glove palm of the nondominant hand with fingers of the dominant hand.	☐	☐	☐
3. Pull the glove away from the nondominant hand.	☐	☐	☐
4. Slide the nondominant hand out of the contaminated glove while rolling the contaminated glove into the palm of the gloved dominant hand.	☐	☐	☐
5. Hold the soiled glove in the palm of your gloved hand. a. Slip ungloved fingers under the cuff of the gloved hand. b. Stretch the glove of the dominant hand up and away from your hand while c. Turning it inside out with the nondominant hand glove balled up inside.	☐	☐	☐
6. Discard both gloves as one unit into a biohazard waste receptacle.	☐	☐	☐
7. Wash your hands.	☐	☐	☐

Calculation

Total Possible Points: _____
Total Points Earned: _____   Multiplied by 100 = _____   Divided by Total Possible Points = _____%

Pass   Fail
☐   ☐

Comments:

Student signature _____   Date _____
Partner signature _____   Date _____
Instructor's signature _____   Date _____

Name_____   Instructor _____

PROCEDURE 14-3: Cleaning Biohazardous Spills

Equipment/Supplies: Commercially prepared germicide OR 1:10 bleach solution, gloves, disposable towels, chemical absorbent, biohazardous waste bag, protective eyewear (goggles or mask and face shield), disposable shoe coverings, disposable gown or apron made of plastic or other material that is impervious to soaking up contaminated fluids

Standards: Given the needed equipment and a place to work, the student will perform this skill with _____% accuracy in a total of _____ minutes. *(Your instructor will tell you what the percentage and time limits will be before you begin practicing.)*

Key: 4 = Satisfactory   0 = Unsatisfactory   NA = This step is not counted

Procedure Steps	Self	Partner	Instructor
1. Put on gloves.	☐	☐	☐
2. Wear protective eyewear, gown or apron, and shoe covers if splashing is anticipated.	☐	☐	☐
3. Apply chemical absorbent to the spill.	☐	☐	☐
4. Clean up the spill using disposable paper towels.	☐	☐	☐
5. Dispose of paper towels and absorbent material in a biohazard waste bag.	☐	☐	☐
6. Further decontaminate using a commercial germicide or bleach solution. a. Wipe with disposable paper towels. b. Discard the towels used for decontamination in a biohazard bag.	☐	☐	☐
7. With gloves on, remove the protective eyewear and discard or disinfect.	☐	☐	☐
8. Remove the gown/apron and shoe coverings and place in biohazard bag.	☐	☐	☐
9. Place the biohazard bag in an appropriate waste receptacle.	☐	☐	☐
10. Remove contaminated gloves and wash hands thoroughly.	☐	☐	☐

Calculation

Total Possible Points: _____

Total Points Earned: _____   Multiplied by 100 = _____   Divided by Total Possible Points = _____%

Pass   Fail

☐   ☐

Comments:

Student signature _____   Date _____

Partner signature _____   Date _____

Instructor's signature _____   Date _____

PROCEDURE 14-4: Disposing of Biohazardous Materials

Equipment/Supplies: Biohazard waste container and liner provided by the infectious waste disposal service, a working biohazard trash can and liners, sharps container, a regular trash container, gloves, lab coat

Standards: Given the needed equipment and a place to work the student will perform this skill with _____ % accuracy in a total of _____ minutes. *(Your instructor will tell you what the percentage and time limits will be before you begin.)*

Key: 4 = Satisfactory   0 = Unsatisfactory   NA = This step is not counted

Procedure Steps

	Self	Partner	Instructor
1. Wash your hands and put on gloves and a lab coat.	☐	☐	☐
2. Discard any paper towels used for a routine handwashing procedure in the regular (not biohazardous) trash.	☐	☐	☐
3. Pre-clean non-disposable hemostats that have been exposed to blood or body fluids, and follow the autoclave check-off procedure.	☐	☐	☐
4. Dispose of urine or other body fluids by pouring specimen down a drain connected to a sanitary sewer, followed by a copious volume of water. Dispose of empty container in a clearly marked, impermeable, red biohazard waste bag.	☐	☐	☐
5. Dispose of gauze that has been exposed to blood or body fluids in a clearly marked, impermeable, red biohazard waste bag.	☐	☐	☐
6. When a biohazard waste bag is full, secure the bag with a closure and move it to the lined waste container provided by the infectious waste service company. Place an unused biohazard bag in the working biohazard trash container.	☐	☐	☐
7. Dispose of a needle that has punctured a patient by activating any safety devices on the needle and placing it in a sharps container.	☐	☐	☐
8. When a sharps container is two-thirds full, seal the sharps container and assemble a new one for disposal of used needles.	☐	☐	☐
9. Remove the gloves and wash your hands.	☐	☐	☐

Calculation

Total Possible Points: _____

Total Points Earned: _____   Multiplied by 100 = _____   Divided by Total Possible Points = _____ %

Pass   Fail

☐   ☐

Comments:

Student signature _____   Date _____

Partner signature _____   Date _____

Instructor's signature _____   Date _____

Name_____   Instructor _____

PROCEDURE 14-5: Practicing Standard Precautions

Equipment/Supplies: Faceshield or goggles and a mask, needle, sharps container, facility accident or incident report form, gloves, lab coat

Standards: Given the needed equipment and a place to work the student will perform this skill with _____ % accuracy in a total of _____ minutes. *(Your instructor will tell you what the percentage and time limits will be before you begin.)*

Key: 4 = Satisfactory   0 = Unsatisfactory   NA = This step is not counted

Procedure Steps	Self	Partner	Instructor
1. Locate and put on appropriate personal protective equipment including a lab coat, buttoned completely, and gloves. When handling fluids that may splash, put on either goggles and a mask or a faceshield.	☐	☐	☐
2. When recapping dirty needle to transport to a sharps container, use the one handed scoop technique.	☐	☐	☐
3. If you accidentally stick yourself with a used needle take the following steps:	☐	☐	☐

- Immediately wash the area with soap and water.
- Complete a facility accident or incident form documenting the exposure, including where on the body it occurred and how it happened.
- Identify, if possible, the source patient of the exposure.
- Report the exposure to your supervisor, who is responsible for following up.
- Get tested for HIV and HBV. (You do have the right to refuse to be tested.)
- Seek counseling from a physician regarding medication and vaccination options.

	Self	Partner	Instructor
4. Remove and properly clean or dispose of all personal protective equipment and wash your hands.	☐	☐	☐

Calculation

Total Possible Points: _____

Total Points Earned: _____   Multiplied by 100 = _____   Divided by Total Possible Points = _____ %

Pass   **Fail**

☐   ☐

Comments:

Student signature _____   Date _____

Partner signature _____   Date _____

Instructor's signature _____   Date _____

PROCEDURE 15-1: Sanitizing Equipment for Disinfection or Sterilization

Equipment/Supplies: Instruments or equipment to be sanitized, gloves, eye protection, impervious gown, soap and water, small hand-held scrub brush

Standards: Given the needed equipment and a place to work, the student will perform this skill with _____% accuracy in a total of _____ minutes. *(Your instructor will tell you what the percentage and time limits will be before you begin practicing.)*

Key: 4 = Satisfactory   0 = Unsatisfactory   NA = This step is not counted

Procedure Steps	Self	Partner	Instructor
1. Put on gloves, gown, and eye protection.	☐	☐	☐
2. For equipment that requires assembly, take removable sections apart.	☐	☐	☐
3. Check the operation and integrity of the equipment.	☐	☐	☐
4. Rinse the instrument with cool water.	☐	☐	☐
5. Force streams of soapy water through any tubular or grooved instruments.	☐	☐	☐
6. Use a hot, soapy solution to dissolve fats or lubricants left on the surface.	☐	☐	☐
7. Soak 5 to 10 minutes. a. Use friction (brush or gauze) to wipe down the instruments. b. Check jaws of scissors/forceps to ensure that all debris has been removed.	☐	☐	☐
8. Rinse well.	☐	☐	☐
9. Dry well before autoclaving if sterilizing or soaking in disinfecting solution.	☐	☐	☐
10. Items (brushes, gauze, solution) used in sanitation process must be disinfected or discarded.	☐	☐	☐

Calculation

Total Possible Points: _____
Total Points Earned: _____   Multiplied by 100 = _____   Divided by Total Possible Points = _____%

Pass   Fail
☐   ☐

Comments:

Student signature _____   Date _____
Partner signature _____   Date _____
Instructor's signature _____   Date _____

Name_____   Instructor _____

PROCEDURE 16-1: Caring for a Microscope

Equipment/Supplies: Lens paper, lens cleaner, gauze, mild soap solution, microscope

Standards: Given the needed equipment and a place to work, the student will perform this skill with _____% accuracy in a total of _____ minutes. *(Your instructor will tell you what the percentage and time limits will be before you begin practicing.)*

Key: 4 = Satisfactory   0 = Unsatisfactory   NA = This step is not counted

Procedure Steps

	Self	Partner	Instructor
1. Wash your hands.	☐	☐	☐
2. Assemble the equipment.	☐	☐	☐
3. If necessary to move the microscope, carry it in both hands, one holding the base and the other holding the arm.	☐	☐	☐
4. Clean the ocular areas, following these steps:	☐	☐	☐

4. Clean the ocular areas, following these steps:
   a. Place a drop or two of lens cleaner on a piece of lens paper.
      (1) Never use tissue or gauze because these may scratch the ocular areas.
      (2) Wipe each eyepiece thoroughly with the lens paper.
      (3) Avoid touching the ocular areas with your fingers.

   b. Wipe each objective lens.
      (1) Start with the lowest power and continue to the highest power.
      (2) If the lens paper has dirt or oil on it, use a clean section of the lens paper.

   c. Remove cleaner: using a new piece of dry lens paper, wipe each eyepiece and objective lens.

5. Clean the nonocular areas, following these steps: ☐   ☐   ☐
   a. Moisten gauze with mild soap solution and wipe all nonocular areas, including the stage, base, and adjustment knobs.
   b. Moisten another gauze pad with water and rinse the washed areas.

6. To store the cleaned microscope, make sure that the light source is turned off.   ☐   ☐   ☐
   a. Rotate the nosepiece, so the low-power objective is pointed down toward the stage.
   b. Cover the microscope with the plastic that came with it or a small trash bag.

Calculation

Total Possible Points: _____

Total Points Earned: _____   Multiplied by 100 = _____   Divided by Total Possible Points = _____%

Pass   Fail
☐   ☐

Comments:

Student signature_____   Date _____
Partner signature_____   Date _____
Instructor's signature_____   Date _____

PROCEDURE 16-2: Using the Principles of Quality Control

Equipment/Supplies: Test information, control sample, QC manual, laboratory equipment, QC Log

Standards: Given the needed equipment and a place to work the student will perform this skill with _____ % accuracy in a total of _____ minutes. *(Your instructor will tell you what the percentage and time limits will be before you begin.)*

Key: 4 = Satisfactory   0 = Unsatisfactory   NA = This step is not counted

Procedure Steps	Self	Partner	Instructor
1. Correctly identify QC manual.	☐	☐	☐
2. Identify expiration date.	☐	☐	☐
3. Locate manufacturer's control sample.	☐	☐	☐
4. Test control sample.	☐	☐	☐
5. Calibrate machine accordingly.	☐	☐	☐
6. Document test results on Log.	☐	☐	☐

Calculation

Total Possible Points: _____

Total Points Earned: _____   Multiplied by 100 = _____   Divided by Total Possible Points = _____%

Pass   Fail
☐   ☐

Comments:

Student signature _____ Date _____
Partner signature _____ Date _____
Instructor's signature _____ Date _____

PROCEDURE 16-3: Performing Routine Maintenance on a Glucose Meter

Equipment/Supplies: Glucose meter, instrument manual, supplies indicated in instrument manual

Standards: Given the needed equipment and a place to work the student will perform this skill with _____ % accuracy in a total of _____ minutes. *(Your instructor will tell you what the percentage and time limits will be before you begin.)*

Key: 4 = Satisfactory   0 = Unsatisfactory   NA = This step is not counted

Procedure Steps

	Self	Partner	Instructor
1. Locate glucose meter and the instrument manual specific to that meter.	☐	☐	☐
2. Read the manufacturer's instructions for performing routine maintenance on the meter as listed in the manual.	☐	☐	☐
3. Assemble the necessary supplies as described in the instructions.	☐	☐	☐
4. Perform the listed routine maintenance procedures.	☐	☐	☐
5. Complete maintenance by successfully performing quality control analysis to verify working condition of meter.	☐	☐	☐
6. Document maintenance and quality control in Equipment Maintenance Log according to office policy.	☐	☐	☐
7. Clean work area, discarding used supplies as appropriate.	☐	☐	☐

Calculation

Total Possible Points: _____

Total Points Earned: _____   Multiplied by 100 = _____   Divided by Total Possible Points = _____ %

Pass   Fail
☐   ☐

Comments:

Student signature _____   Date _____

Partner signature _____   Date _____

Instructor's signature _____   Date _____

PROCEDURE 17-1: Measuring Weight

Equipment/Supplies: Calibrated balance beam scale, digital scale, or dial scale; paper towel

Standards: Given the needed equipment and a place to work, the student will perform this skill with _____% accuracy in a total of _____ minutes. *(Your instructor will tell you what the percentage and time limits will be before you begin practicing.)*

Key: 4 = Satisfactory   0 = Unsatisfactory   NA = This step is not counted

Procedure Steps	Self	Partner	Instructor
1. Wash your hands.	☐	☐	☐
2. Ensure that the scale is properly balanced at zero.	☐	☐	☐
3. Escort the patient to the scale and place a paper towel on the scale.	☐	☐	☐
4. Have the patient remove shoes, heavy coats, or jackets.	☐	☐	☐
5. Assist the patient onto the scale facing forward.	☐	☐	☐
6. Ask patient to stand still, without touching or holding on to anything if possible.	☐	☐	☐
7. Weigh the patient.	☐	☐	☐
8. Return the bars on the top and bottom to zero.	☐	☐	☐
9. Assist the patient from the scale if necessary and discard the paper towel.	☐	☐	☐
10. Record the patient's weight.	☐	☐	☐

Calculation

Total Possible Points: _____
Total Points Earned: _____ Multiplied by 100 = _____ Divided by Total Possible Points = _____%

Pass ☐   Fail ☐

Comments:

Student signature _____ Date _____
Partner signature _____ Date _____
Instructor's signature _____ Date _____

Name_____   Instructor _____

PROCEDURE 17-2: Measuring Height

Equipment/Supplies: A scale with a ruler

Standards: Given the needed equipment and a place to work, the student will perform this skill with _____% accuracy in a total of _____ minutes. *(Your instructor will tell you what the percentage and time limits will be before you begin practicing.)*

Key: 4 = Satisfactory   0 = Unsatisfactory   NA = This step is not counted

Procedure Steps

	Self	Partner	Instructor
1. Wash your hands.	☐	☐	☐
2. Have the patient remove the shoes and stand straight and erect on the scale, heels together, and eyes straight ahead.	☐	☐	☐
3. With the measuring bar perpendicular to the ruler, slowly lower until it firmly touches patient's head.	☐	☐	☐
4. Read the measurement at the point of movement on the ruler.	☐	☐	☐
5. Assist the patient from the scale.	☐	☐	☐
6. Record the weight and height measurements in the medical record.	☐	☐	☐

Calculation

Total Possible Points: _____
Total Points Earned: _____   Multiplied by 100 = _____   Divided by Total Possible Points = _____%

Pass   Fail
☐   ☐

Comments:

Student signature _____   Date _____
Partner signature _____   Date _____
Instructor's signature _____   Date _____

PROCEDURE 17-3: Measuring Oral Temperature Using a Glass Mercury Thermometer

Equipment/Supplies: Glass mercury oral thermometer, tissues or cotton balls, disposable plastic sheath, gloves, biohazard waste container, cool soapy water, disinfectant solution

Standards: Given the needed equipment and a place to work, the student will perform this skill with _____% accuracy in a total of _____ minutes. *(Your instructor will tell you what the percentage and time limits will be before you begin practicing.)*

Key: 4 = Satisfactory   0 = Unsatisfactory   NA = This step is not counted

Procedure Steps

	Self	Partner	Instructor
1. Wash your hands and assemble the necessary supplies.	☐	☐	☐
2. Dry the thermometer if it has been stored in disinfectant.	☐	☐	☐
3. Carefully check the thermometer for chips or cracks.	☐	☐	☐
4. Check the level of the mercury in the thermometer.	☐	☐	☐
5. If the mercury level is above 94°F, carefully shake down.	☐	☐	☐
6. Insert the thermometer into the plastic sheath.	☐	☐	☐
7. Greet and identify the patient.	☐	☐	☐
8. Explain the procedure and ask about any eating, drinking hot or cold fluids, gum chewing, or smoking.	☐	☐	☐
9. Place the thermometer under the patient's tongue.	☐	☐	☐
10. Tell the patient to keep the mouth and lips closed but caution against biting down on the glass stem.	☐	☐	☐
11. Leave the thermometer in place for 3 to 5 minutes.	☐	☐	☐
12. At the appropriate time, remove the thermometer from the patient's mouth while wearing gloves.	☐	☐	☐
13. Remove the sheath by holding the very edge of the sheath with your thumb and forefinger.	☐	☐	☐
14. Discard the sheath into a biohazard waste container.	☐	☐	☐
15. Hold the thermometer horizontal at eye level and note the level of mercury in the column.	☐	☐	☐
16. Record the patient's temperature.	☐	☐	☐

Calculation

Total Possible Points: _____
Total Points Earned: _____   Multiplied by 100 = _____   Divided by Total Possible Points = _____%

Pass   Fail
☐   ☐

Comments:

Student signature _____   Date _____

Partner signature _____   Date _____

Instructor's signature _____   Date _____

PROCEDURE 17-4: Measuring a Rectal Temperature

Equipment/Supplies: Glass mercury rectal thermometer, tissues or cotton balls, disposable plastic sheaths, surgical lubricant, biohazard waste container, cool soapy water, disinfectant solution, gloves

Standards: Given the needed equipment and a place to work, the student will perform this skill with _____% accuracy in a total of _____ minutes. *(Your instructor will tell you what the percentage and time limits will be before you begin practicing.)*

Key: 4 = Satisfactory   0 = Unsatisfactory   NA = This step is not counted

Procedure Steps	Self	Partner	Instructor
1. Wash your hands and assemble the necessary supplies.	☐	☐	☐
2. Dry the thermometer if it has been stored in disinfectant.	☐	☐	☐
3. Carefully check the thermometer for chips or cracks.	☐	☐	☐
4. Check the level of the mercury in the thermometer.	☐	☐	☐
5. If the mercury level is above 94°F, carefully shake down.	☐	☐	☐
6. Insert the thermometer into the plastic sheath.	☐	☐	☐
7. Spread lubricant onto a tissue and then from the tissue onto the sheath of the thermometer.	☐	☐	☐
8. Greet and identify the patient and explain the procedure.	☐	☐	☐
9. Ensure patient privacy by placing the patient in a side-lying position facing the examination room door. Drape appropriately.	☐	☐	☐
10. Apply gloves and visualize the anus by lifting the top buttock with your nondominant hand.	☐	☐	☐
11. Gently insert thermometer past the sphincter muscle.	☐	☐	☐
12. Release the upper buttock and hold the thermometer in place with your dominant hand for 3 minutes.	☐	☐	☐
13. After 3 minutes, remove the thermometer and the sheath.	☐	☐	☐
14. Discard the sheath into a biohazard waste container.	☐	☐	☐
15. Note the reading with the thermometer horizontal at eye level.	☐	☐	☐
16. Give the patient a tissue to wipe away excess lubricant.	☐	☐	☐
17. Assist with dressing if necessary.	☐	☐	☐
18. Record the procedure and mark the letter R next to the reading.	☐	☐	☐

Calculation

Total Possible Points: _____

Total Points Earned: _____   Multiplied by 100 = _____   Divided by Total Possible Points = _____%

Pass   Fail

☐   ☐

Comments:

Student signature _____ Date _____

Partner signature _____ Date _____

Instructor's signature _____ Date _____

PROCEDURE 17-5: Measuring an Axillary Temperature

Equipment/Supplies: Glass mercury (oral or rectal) thermometer, tissues or cotton balls, disposable plastic sheaths, biohazard waste container, cool soapy water, disinfectant solution

Standards: Given the needed equipment and a place to work, the student will perform this skill with _____% accuracy in a total of _____ minutes. *(Your instructor will tell you what the percentage and time limits will be before you begin practicing.)*

Key: 4 = Satisfactory   0 = Unsatisfactory   NA = This step is not counted

Procedure Steps	Self	Partner	Instructor
1. Wash your hands and assemble the necessary supplies.	☐	☐	☐
2. Dry the thermometer if it has been stored in disinfectant.	☐	☐	☐
3. Carefully check the thermometer for chips or cracks.	☐	☐	☐
4. Check the level of the mercury in the thermometer.	☐	☐	☐
5. If the mercury level is above 94°F, carefully shake down.	☐	☐	☐
6. Insert the thermometer into the plastic sheath.	☐	☐	☐
7. Expose the patient's axilla, exposing as little of upper body as possible.	☐	☐	☐
8. Place the bulb of the thermometer well into the axilla.	☐	☐	☐
9. Bring the patient's arm down, crossing the forearm over the chest.	☐	☐	☐
10. Leave the thermometer in place for 10 minutes.	☐	☐	☐
11. After 10 minutes, remove the thermometer from the patient's axilla.	☐	☐	☐
12. Remove the sheath and discard the sheath into a biohazard waste container.	☐	☐	☐
13. Hold the thermometer horizontal at eye level and note the level of mercury.	☐	☐	☐
14. Record the procedure and mark a letter A next to the reading, indicating an axillary temperature.	☐	☐	☐

Calculation

Total Possible Points: _____
Total Points Earned: _____   Multiplied by 100 = _____   Divided by Total Possible Points = _____%

Pass   Fail
☐   ☐

Comments:

Student signature _____   Date _____
Partner signature _____   Date _____
Instructor's signature _____   Date _____

Name_____   Instructor _____

PROCEDURE 17-6: Measuring Temperature Using an Electronic Thermometer

Equipment/Supplies: Electronic thermometer with oral or rectal probe, lubricant and gloves for rectal temperatures, disposable probe covers, biohazard waste container

Standards: Given the needed equipment and a place to work, the student will perform this skill with _____% accuracy in a total of _____ minutes. (*Your instructor will tell you what the percentage and time limits will be before you begin practicing.*)

Key: 4 = Satisfactory   0 = Unsatisfactory   NA = This step is not counted

Procedure Steps	Self	Partner	Instructor
1. Wash your hands and assemble the necessary supplies.	☐	☐	☐
2. Greet and identify the patient and explain the procedure.	☐	☐	☐
3. Choose the method (oral, axillary, or rectal) most appropriate for the patient.	☐	☐	☐
4. Insert the probe into a probe cover.	☐	☐	☐
5. Position the thermometer.	☐	☐	☐
6. Wait for the electronic thermometer unit to "beep."	☐	☐	☐
7. Remove the probe and note the reading on the digital display screen on the unit.	☐	☐	☐
8. Discard the probe cover into a biohazard waste container.	☐	☐	☐
9. Record the procedure result.	☐	☐	☐
10. Return the unit and probe to the charging base.	☐	☐	☐

Calculation

Total Possible Points: _____
Total Points Earned: _____   Multiplied by 100 = _____   Divided by Total Possible Points = _____%

Pass   Fail
☐   ☐

Comments:

Student signature _____   Date _____
Partner signature _____   Date _____
Instructor's signature _____   Date _____

PROCEDURE 17-7: Measuring Temperature Using a Tympanic Thermometer

Equipment/Supplies: Tympanic thermometer, disposable probe covers, biohazard waste container

Standards: Given the needed equipment and a place to work, the student will perform this skill with _____% accuracy in a total of _____ minutes. *(Your instructor will tell you what the percentage and time limits will be before you begin practicing.)*

Key: 4 = Satisfactory   0 = Unsatisfactory   NA = This step is not counted

Procedure Steps	Self	Partner	Instructor
1. Wash your hands and assemble the necessary supplies.	☐	☐	☐
2. Greet and identify the patient and explain the procedure.	☐	☐	☐
3. Insert the ear probe into a probe cover.	☐	☐	☐
4. Place the end of the ear probe into the patient's ear.	☐	☐	☐
5. Press the button on the thermometer. Watch the digital display.	☐	☐	☐
6. Remove the probe at "beep" or other thermometer signal.	☐	☐	☐
7. Discard the probe cover into a biohazard waste container.	☐	☐	☐
8. Record the procedure result.	☐	☐	☐
9. Return the unit and probe to the charging base.	☐	☐	☐

Calculation

Total Possible Points: _____
Total Points Earned: _____   Multiplied by 100 = _____   Divided by Total Possible Points = _____%

Pass   Fail
☐   ☐

Comments:

Student signature _____   Date _____
Partner signature _____   Date _____
Instructor's signature _____   Date _____

Name_____   Instructor _____

PROCEDURE 17-8: Measuring the Radial Pulse

Equipment/Supplies: A watch with a sweeping second hand.

Standards: Given the needed equipment and a place to work, the student will perform this skill with _____% accuracy in a total of _____ minutes. *(Your instructor will tell you what the percentage and time limits will be before you begin practicing.)*

Key: 4 = Satisfactory   0 = Unsatisfactory   NA = This step is not counted

Procedure Steps	Self	Partner	Instructor
1. Wash your hands.	☐	☐	☐
2. Greet and identify the patient and explain the procedure.	☐	☐	☐
3. Position the patient with the arm relaxed and supported.	☐	☐	☐
4. Locate the radial artery.	☐	☐	☐
5. If the pulse is regular, count the pulse for 30 seconds (irregular, count 60 seconds).	☐	☐	☐
6. Multiply the number of pulsations in 30 seconds by 2 (record pulses in 60 seconds as is).	☐	☐	☐
7. Record the rate in the patient's medical record with the other vital signs.	☐	☐	☐
8. Also, note the rhythm if irregular and the volume if thready or bounding.	☐	☐	☐

Calculation

Total Possible Points: _____

Total Points Earned: _____   Multiplied by 100 = _____   Divided by Total Possible Points = _____%

Pass   Fail

☐   ☐

Comments:

Student signature _____   Date _____

Partner signature _____   Date _____

Instructor's signature _____   Date _____

PROCEDURE 17-9: Measuring Respirations

Equipment/Supplies: A watch with a sweeping second hand

Standards: Given the needed equipment and a place to work, the student will perform this skill with _____% accuracy in a total of _____ minutes. *(Your instructor will tell you what the percentage and time limits will be before you begin practicing.)*

Key: 4 = Satisfactory   0 = Unsatisfactory   NA = This step is not counted

Procedure Steps	Self	Partner	Instructor
1. Wash your hands.	☐	☐	☐
2. Greet and identify the patient and explain the procedure.	☐	☐	☐
3. Observe watch second hand and count a rise and fall of the chest as one respiration.	☐	☐	☐
4. For a regular breathing pattern count for 30 seconds and multiply by 2 (irregular for 60 seconds).	☐	☐	☐
5. Record the respiratory rate.	☐	☐	☐
6. Note the rhythm if irregular and any unusual or abnormal sounds such as wheezing.	☐	☐	☐

Calculation

Total Possible Points: _____

Total Points Earned: _____   Multiplied by 100 = _____   Divided by Total Possible Points = _____%

Pass   Fail

☐   ☐

Comments:

Student signature _____ Date _____

Partner signature _____ Date _____

Instructor's signature _____ Date _____

Name_____   Instructor _____

PROCEDURE 17-10: Measuring Blood Pressure

Equipment/Supplies: Sphygmomanometer, stethoscope

Standards: Given the needed equipment and a place to work, the student will perform this skill with _____% accuracy in a total of _____ minutes. (*Your instructor will tell you what the percentage and time limits will be before you begin practicing.*)

Key: 4 = Satisfactory   0 = Unsatisfactory   NA = This step is not counted

Procedure Steps

	Self	Partner	Instructor
1. Wash your hands and assemble your equipment.	☐	☐	☐
2. Greet and identify the patient and explain the procedure.	☐	☐	☐
3. Position the patient with upper arm supported and level with the patient's heart.	☐	☐	☐
4. Expose the patient's arm.	☐	☐	☐
5. Palpate the brachial pulse in the antecubital area.	☐	☐	☐
6. Center the deflated cuff directly over the brachial artery.	☐	☐	☐
7. Lower edge of the cuff should be 1 to 2 inches above the antecubital area.	☐	☐	☐
8. Wrap the cuff smoothly and snugly around the arm, secure with the Velcro edges.	☐	☐	☐
9. Turn the screw clockwise to tighten. Do not tighten it too tightly for easy release.	☐	☐	☐
10. Palpate the brachial pulse. Inflate the cuff.	☐	☐	☐
11. Note the point or number on the dial or mercury column at which the brachial pulse disappears.	☐	☐	☐
12. Deflate the cuff by turning the valve counterclockwise.	☐	☐	☐
13. Wait at least 30 seconds before reinflating the cuff.	☐	☐	☐
14. Place the stethoscope earpieces into your ear canals with the openings pointed slightly forward.	☐	☐	☐
15. Stand about 3 feet from the manometer with the gauge at eye level.	☐	☐	☐
16. Place the diaphragm of the stethoscope against the brachial artery and hold in place.	☐	☐	☐
17. Close the valve and inflate the cuff.	☐	☐	☐
18. Pump the valve bulb to about 30 mm Hg above the number noted during step 8.	☐	☐	☐
19. Once the cuff is inflated to proper level, release air at a rate of about 2–4 mm Hg per second.	☐	☐	☐
20. Note the point on the gauge at which you hear the first clear tapping sound.	☐	☐	☐

21. Maintaining control of the valve screw, continue to deflate the cuff. ❏ ❏ ❏

22. When you hear the last sound, note the reading and quickly deflate the cuff. ❏ ❏ ❏

23. Remove the cuff and press the air from the bladder of the cuff. ❏ ❏ ❏

24. If this is the first recording or the first time the patient has been into the office, the physician may also want a reading in the other arm or in a position other than sitting. ❏ ❏ ❏

25. Record the reading with the systolic over the diastolic pressure (note which arm was used or any position other than sitting). ❏ ❏ ❏

Calculation

Total Possible Points: _____

Total Points Earned: _____ Multiplied by 100 = _____ Divided by Total Possible Points = _____ %

Pass   Fail

❏   ❏

Comments:

Student signature _____ Date _____

Partner signature _____ Date _____

Instructor's signature _____ Date _____

Notes

Notes

Notes

Notes

Notes

Notes

Notes